# Programming Role Playing Games with DirectX®

PREMIER PRESS

GAME DEVELOPMENT

# Programming Role Playing Games with DirectX®

## Jim Adams

PREMIER PRESS

GAME DEVELOPMENT

Premier
Press

© 2002 by Premier Press, Inc. All rights reserved. No part of this book may be reproduced or transmitted in any form or by any means, electronic or mechanical, including photocopying, recording, or by any information storage or retrieval system without written permission from Premier Press, except for the inclusion of brief quotations in a review.

  The Premier Press logo, top edge printing, and related trade dress are trademarks of Premier Press, Inc., and may not be used without written permission. All other trademarks are the property of their respective owners.

**Publisher:** Stacy L. Hiquet

**Marketing Manager:** Heather Buzzingham

**Managing Editor:** Sandy Doell

**Acquisitions Editor:** Emi Smith

**Series Editor:** André LaMothe

**Project Editor:** Melba Hopper

**Editorial Assistant:** Margaret Bauer

**Technical Reviewer:** Ernest Pazera

**Interior Layout:** Shawn Morningstar

**Illustrator:** Susan Honeywell

**Cover Design:** Phil Velikan

**Indexer:** Katherine Stimson

**Proofreader:** Jenny Davidson

DirectX, DirectPlay, DirectSound, DirectMusic, DirectInput, Direct3D, DirectDraw, and Windows are registered trademarks of Microsoft. MilkShape 3-D is a registered trademark of chUmbaLum sOft. GoldWave is a registered trademark of GoldWave Inc. trueSpace is a registered trademark of Caligari Corporation. Poser is a registered trademark of Curious Labs, Inc. Paint Shop Pro is a trademark of Jasc Software, Inc.

*Important:* Premier Press cannot provide software support. Please contact the appropriate software manufacturer's technical support line or Web site for assistance.

Premier Press and the author have attempted throughout this book to distinguish proprietary trademarks from descriptive terms by following the capitalization style used by the manufacturer.

Information contained in this book has been obtained by Premier Press from sources believed to be reliable. However, because of the possibility of human or mechanical error by our sources, Premier Press, or others, the Publisher does not guarantee the accuracy, adequacy, or completeness of any information and is not responsible for any errors or omissions or the results obtained from use of such information. Readers should be particularly aware of the fact that the Internet is an ever-changing entity. Some facts may have changed since this book went to press.

ISBN: 1-931841-09-8

Library of Congress Catalog Card Number: 2001096217

Printed in the United States of America

02 03 04 05 06 RI 10 9 8 7 6 5 4 3 2

*To my wife 2E:*

*The love of my life and best friend till the end— you are my sunshine.*

# Acknowledgments

**P**ublishing a book takes considerable work and dedication on the part of everyone involved. First and foremost, I want to thank my family—my wife, 2E, for all her loving support; my mother, Pam, and my brother John for giving me moral support; the kids, Michael, John, and Jordan, for letting me play their video games and for giving me great ideas; and my sister, Jennifer, for irking me enough to show her that writing is a job worth pursuing.

I extend special thanks to the book's technical editor and fellow programmer-at-large, Ernest Pazera, for dropping my name into the mix and for ensuring that the technical material in this book is accurate. I'm particularly grateful to the book's acquisitions editor, Emi Smith, for her voice of calmness and for understanding that things sometimes become delayed. Thanks also to the project editor, Melba Hopper, undoubtedly the best editor with whom I've had the pleasure of working.

I offer sincere appreciation to Chris Taylor, president of Gas Powered Games, for writing the book's Foreword; to Wayne Peters (*aka* Scarecrow) for the great models in the book's demos; and to Andrew Russell for the cool music that fits the game demos perfectly.

I would be remiss not to also thank Susan Honeywell for her artistic renditions of my drawings, Shawn Morningstar for the excellent interior layout of the book, Katherine Stimson for the book's fine index, and the book's proofreader, Jenny Davidson, for her keen eyes.

Finally, I want to acknowledge friends and family members who were with me along the way, if only in spirit: To my brother Jeff—I wish you could have been here to see this; to Ian McArdle—as you can see, the motivation to write this book never wore out; to the rest of my friends and family—thanks for being there!

# About the Author

**Jim Adams'** current career, and his passion for programming, began at the age of nine when using an Atari computer and a few lines of code, he discovered that he could do just about anything his young mind imagined.

Over the years, with the help of increasingly advanced books on programming—and countless hours molding together small games—he moved from computer to computer until he finally discovered the world of IBM PCs. At the same time, he was progressing through the emerging programming languages—going from BASIC, to assembly, to PASCAL, to C, and finally to C++.

Thanks to Jim's knowledge and experience in programming games and business applications, he has led a satisfying career in game-making, writing, and consulting. He has written numerous articles and is coauthor of several books on consumer electronics and computer programming.

Jim is currently owner of The Collective Mind, a programming and consulting business. You can find Jim cruising the Internet and hanging out at various game-related Web sites.

# Contents at a Glance

## Part Four
## Role-Playing Game Programming . . . . . . . 465

## Part Five
## The Finishing Touches . . . . . . . . . . . . . . . . 907

## Part Six
## Appendixes . . . . . . . . . . . . . . . . . . . . . . 983

## Index . . . . . . . . . . . . . . . . . . . . . 1021

# Contents

# CHAPTER 3
# STORY-WRITING ESSENTIALS. . . . . . . 35

# Chapter 5
# Programming with Windows
# and Application Basics. . . . . . . . . 97

# CHAPTER 6
# DRAWING WITH DIRECTX GRAPHICS. . . 159

# Chapter 7
# Interacting with DirectInput . . . . . 261

# CHAPTER 9
# NETWORKING WITH DIRECTPLAY . . . . . 351

# Chapter 10
# Creating the Game Core. . . . . . . . 399

# CHAPTER 13
# MIXING 2-D AND
# 3-D GRAPHICS ENGINES . . . . . . . . 561

# CHAPTER 14
# IMPLEMENTING SCRIPTS . . . . . . . . 579

# CHAPTER 15
# DEFINING AND USING OBJECTS ...... 613

# Chapter 16
# Controlling Players
# and Characters • • • • • • • • • • • • 653

# CHAPTER 17
# WORKING WITH MAPS AND LEVELS . . . 761

# Chapter 18
# Creating Combat Sequences . . . . . 819

# Chapter 19
# Getting Online with
# Multiplayer Gaming. . . . . . . . . . . 843

# Part Five
# The Finishing Touches

## CHAPTER 20
## PUTTING TOGETHER A FULL GAME . . . 909

# APPENDIX B
# GETTING HELP ON THE WEB • • • • • • • 995

# APPENDIX C
# RECOMMENDED READING • • • • • • • • 999

# Foreword

**W**hen Jim asked me to write a foreword for this book, my first reaction was that he must be crazy to take on a task of this magnitude! After marveling over his ambition, however, I realized how fantastic a book like this would be for those who see their PC not only as a tool for doing e-mail, surfing the Internet or playing store bought games, but also as a device that allows them to create something fantastic—their *own* RPGs! This, of course, immediately had me reminiscing about the "good ole days." I remember when I hauled my first PC out of a box back in 1980. Actually, it was technically a PC, but nothing like the computers available today. It was a Radio Shack TRS-80 Model 1 level 2 personal computer with 16K of memory (yes, 16K, which is about 32,000 times less memory than I have on my current computer). Although that little state-of-the-art wonder had no real graphics to speak of, it was all I needed.

My imagination took flight. I was going to create video games like no one had ever seen. With really no idea about how or where to begin, I quickly discovered how thrilling, and how frustrating, this was going to be. I wanted to start creating worlds, but knew little more than how to switch the darn computer on!

I wanted to know what to do next, what to design, what to code, what sort of artwork to make. The reality was that I didn't have these answers, and nobody I knew could help me. Back at the store where I purchased my computer, I tracked down the salesman who, I thought, had the answers. He led me to a single book on programming the computer's central processing unit (CPU), the Z80 microprocessor. This technically complex book was not what I was looking for. It did not cover video games about monsters or missiles. It was just the details on how to program the machine in its native tongue, Z80 assembly language. Learning how to create games was going to take more than that, much more.

It was a long time before I managed to find what I was looking for, and much of my education on the subject of game creation came from hours of investigation and sweat over the computer, along with any and all information that I could scratch together on the topic. In fact, it was years before I truly started to understand the craft of making games.

Role-playing games (RPGs) are the mother of all video games because of the huge worlds and massive amounts of game content (artwork, sound, and animations). If you intend to make an RPG and you have never created a video game, be aware that this enormous task will be like battling a dragon with nothing more than an attitude and some cheap bathroom humor (which I can fix you up with if you need some). As you might guess, you'll need a little more in your back pocket than that.

I can only imagine how incredible it would have been to have found this book when I made that fateful trip to the computer store back in 1980. Consider yourself immediately ahead of the game!

Today, things have changed quite a bit. When you haul a new PC out of the box, you get a CPU that will execute billions of instructions per second. You get ultra powerful graphics cards that have dedicated microprocessors that draw amazing visuals and outrageous special effects on the screen. You get more system memory (at an affordable price) than I could ever have imagined for things like graphic textures, sound, and animation. And now you can communicate over the Internet to anywhere in the world! The list of features doesn't stop there. In many ways, all this power ought to make the task of creating an RPG a simple one; unfortunately, that's not the case. It's just as complex as it's ever been.

Besides what we can do technically with the powerful machines that are available today, let me add that RPGs are a very special form of entertainment. They not only provide the player with a fun and exciting gameplay experience, but also they allow the creators to do something very unique—create their very own world for people to explore and become completely immersed in. Being able to create a unique fantasy world is a very powerful form of art and entertainment, and for me, an RPG was one of the first things that I wanted to create when I got my first computer. Today I am finally fulfilling that dream. All of us have a different world inside of our heads that we want to bring to life on the computer, and it is up to each of us to find a way to bring that world to life!

Having said all that, creating a role-playing game is a crazy and outrageous amount of work. It requires a team of many dedicated and courageous individuals giving it all they've got. Our current endeavor at Gas Powered Games is called *Dungeon Siege*, a vast project that is packed with so many features that it boggles my mind.

First, we decided to make an RPG that exists completely in 3-D using a custom state-of-the-art engine. Achieving this goal would be a huge challenge, but we wanted many more features that would push the boundaries. We wanted to completely eliminate loading screens by creating something we call a "continuous world." Naturally, we wanted to include multiplayer gaming over the Internet and allow the player to create a party of up to eight characters. It became a huge game, with a ton of challenges. These challenges ultimately translated into a next-generation experience that provides both the single player and the multi-player game experience that players have not seen before. This is what makes the art and science of creating RPGs so fantastic. We are not only creating something new, but also we are doing it with tools and technology that were unavailable until now. Every day is a new and fantastic day for people who create RPGs.

I can say one thing for sure. Even though I often joke about getting into the "mess" of making an RPG, I'm glad that I did. Once past the technically challenging stuff, such as creating the core engine, setting up the combat systems, and ultimately putting all the different pieces together, we have a remaining and very different challenge—making the game fun to play! We do this by playing the game over and over again, watching people play, studying reports from the quality assurance labs and the play test experts. It's the home stretch in making an RPG!

Throughout this testing and tuning phase, the less exciting areas are trimmed back, new areas and ideas are added, while the game is continuously tested and balanced. So much goes into creating a game that the creation never really stops; even up to the release date, we will be adding or changing elements of the game with the latest information, the latest test data—all to make sure that the entire gaming experience is just right.

Now it's your turn to make that journey, the long and fantastic adventure to creating your own game. Don't be dismayed by the bumps and scrapes along the way. Once you get past the hard stuff, you'll have one of the greatest and most creatively challenging adventures of your life. You will find that this book will guide you, teach you, and answer many of the questions that you have about making an RPG. It will get you started planning, designing, and building. It will introduce you to the wonderful world of making your very own RPG.

I salute Jim for taking on this enormous task, and I thank him also for his desire to share what he knows, and to share so much.

Good luck! I can't wait to take a walk through your world!

— **Chris Taylor**

Chris Taylor, president of Gas Powered Games, is the lead designer of the upcoming and highly anticipated game *Dungeon Siege*. With past titles such as *Hardball 2*, *Triple Play Baseball*, and *Total Annihilation*, Chris continues to create games that shape the computer gaming world.

# Introduction

**W**ith fingers blistered and eyes bloodshot, all your hard work is about to pay off. After one hundred hours of playing the newest computer-based role-playing game, you've managed to reach the end. All that stands between you and victory is a very large, very angry dragon. Not to worry though—you have a couple of tricks up your sleeve to show this sucker who's boss. After a final climatic battle, your mission is over—the game is defeated.

Your quest was long and difficult, but when all is said and done, it was a very enjoyable quest. The story was compelling, the graphics eye-popping, the sound and music superb. Sitting back, you might be wondering how you could create such a masterpiece. Something with a snappy title, a great story, and that neat-o battle engine from that newest game with the kick-butt graphics engine. "Yes," you say, "I can do that!"

*Programming Role Playing Games with DirectX* is your ticket to bringing your ideas to life. Within these pages, I have crammed enough information about general programming and role-playing game topics to give you the help you need to create your own game. In this book, you find out how to create cool graphics and combat engines, handle players in your game, use scripts and items, and make your game multiplayer-capable.

> **NOTE**
> Before working with the code or examples in this book, you need to properly install DirectX 8.0 and set up your compiler accordingly. You can find the DirectX 8.0 installation program on this book's CD-ROM, or you can download the program from Microsoft's Web site at http://msdn.microsoft.com/directx/. Please turn to Appendix A, "Installing DirectX and Configuring the Compiler," for the details.

## What This Book Is About

This book is for programmers who want to go into the specialized field of programming role-playing games (RPGs). I think RPGs are some of the best games to play.

I also think that RPGs are the hardest to create. Information on RPG game programming is hard to come by, so to fill that need, I wrote this book.

In this book, I break a role-playing game into its essential components. I take those components one by one, giving you a detailed look at each and showing you how to use all of them in your game project. To see exactly what components I'm talking about, scan ahead to the section "How This Book Is Organized."

Within these pages and on the accompanying CD-ROM, you'll find example programs that were created using the information in each chapter. I constructed these example programs so that you can easily transfer the various general and RPG-specific game components into your projects. For the specifics on running the example programs, check out Appendix E, "What's on the CD." In fact, I recommend checking out the demo programs before reading the book. That way, you'll know what to expect in the book.

# Who Should Read This Book

If you want to put extra oomph in your game, this book is for you. You will find helpful hints and ideas and all the information you need to embark on your career as an RPG programmer.

I wrote this book for beginning- to intermediate-level RPG programmers. The information is clear and to the point, and regardless of your programming experience and skills, you will find that this book is a valuable tome.

I wrote this book on the assumption that you have a working knowledge of C. A good deal of the code is in C++, but I lead you through it in such a way that you will be able to fully comprehend the information.

So, if you're interested in programming a role-playing game or just want help on a specific gaming component, this is the book for you.

# How This Book Is Organized

The book is split into the following six parts, each one dealing with a different set of topics:

- **Part One**, "An Introduction to Role-Playing Games," describes role-playing games and their fundamental operation.

- **Part Two**, " Role-Playing Game Design," discusses game design topics and provides help for writing your game's story. This part begins with fundamental concepts and continues with RPG-specific design issues from a programmer's point of view.

- **Part Three**, "Programming Basics," is where things *really* heat up. This hefty part offers you the basics on using C++, getting a Windows application up and running, and utilizing DirectX in your game programming projects.

- **Part Four**, "Role-Playing Game Programming," contains all the RPG-specific gaming code that I could pack into those pages. Topics include creating 2-D and 3-D graphics engines, controlling your game's characters, using scripting and inventory, and multiplayer gaming.

- **Part Five**, "The Finishing Touches," helps you wrap up your project. In this part, you find out how I created a complete game using the information in this book. In addition, you learn how to promote, market, and publish your game.

- **Part Six**, "Appendixes," starts by showing you how to install DirectX and configure your compiler to use DirectX. You will find a list of recommended books and Web sites. Part Six ends with an appendix describing how to use this book's CD-ROM.

# What's on the CD

Appendix E, "What's on the CD," contains a list of the programs on this book's CD-ROM; however, I can't resist giving you a glimpse of what you'll find there. First and foremost are Microsoft's DirectX 8.0 software developer's kit and the complete source code to every demo program in this book.

DirectX is the leader among game development libraries, and it's the library I use in this book. Before reading this book, take a moment to install DirectX on your system. Appendix A tells you exactly how to install DirectX and prepare your compiler to use DirectX.

In addition to DirectX and the source code, the CD-ROM contains a plethora of useful programs. "Which programs," you ask? How about Calgiari's trueSpace4 trial edition and Curious Lab's Poser 4 demo! That's right; you get to test drive the newest, most powerful modeling programs out there! But there's more. The complete DirectX 8.0 SDK, chUmbaLum's MilkShape 3D, a Paint Shop Pro demo, and much more—all packed into that little round disc!

# Conventions Used in This Book

This book has the following special features, called icons, that point you to important or interesting information.

**NOTE**

Notes provide additional helpful or interesting information.

**CAUTION**

Cautions tell you how to avoid problems.

**TIP**

Tips often suggest techniques and shortcuts that make programming easier.

# What You Need to Begin

Before beginning, you need to install the Microsoft DirectX 8.0 Software Developer's Kit, which is on this book's CD-ROM (or you can download it from Microsoft at http://msdn.microsoft.com/directx). Appendix A provides the steps for installing DirectX.

You also need a C++ compiler; I recommend Microsoft's Visual C/C++ compiler. Even though you can compile the code and examples in this book with almost any C++ compiler, the DirectX-specific code was targeted for Visual C/C++ version 6.0 or higher.

Beyond those two items, you just need dedication and motivation! Although creating any game is a daunting task, with this book, you will have all the knowledge you need to do just that—and, remember, players are waiting for your masterpiece!

# Part One

# An Introduction to Role-Playing Games

# 1 A World of Role-Playing

# CHAPTER 1

# A WORLD OF
## OF
## ROLE-PLAYING

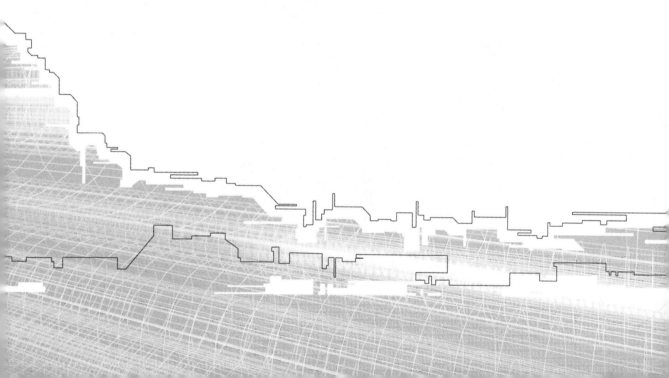

Playing games is a perfect way to escape the rigors of a long, hard day—board games, video games, card games, all of us have preferences. For me and millions of other players, role-playing games present the perfect medium for relaxation and fun.

My instinct is to begin this book by giving you the long and interesting history of role-playing games. However, that's not the purpose of this book, so I will move right along and share with you the concepts and information that you need to create your own role-playing games.

The chapter begins with a short, mood-setting story—just for ambience and maybe to tweak your appetite for writing stories—and continues with a brief excursion into the world of role-playing games and what they have to offer.

In this chapter, you encounter the following:

- A succinct, delightful narrative
- Role-playing concepts
- Role-playing games—past, present, and future

# A Story of Role-Playing

The night's heavy blanket had long since covered the dense jungle, extinguishing all light. Our trek through the jungle had become treacherous, with each step an adventure of its own. The mysterious loss of two more guides made all of us edgy, and we huddled together like scared children.

This is not how I envisioned a treasure hunt with a bunch of war-torn adventurers. And the inane chatter of cute little Deliah the elf was beginning to get on my last nerve. While admitting that we all probably needed something to keep calm, I wished Deliah had another means.

As the seemingly endless night dragged on, we stumbled upon our goal—the tomb of the ancient Myracs. Tales of untold wealth lying behind its grim, disfigured entryway had driven us here. We approached its massive doors, which were carved from some cursed quarry and erected as a warning to those foolish enough to enter.

Abruptly, our last guide fled, and we were left with the echo of his warning ringing in our ears. "What a bunch of superstitious fools," I thought. "That treasure is as good as ours; no curse is going to scare me away!"

I realized what a fool I was upon my first step into the tomb. An odor as nauseous as death filled my lungs, causing me to retch uncontrollably. Dark images began to race through my mind; sights of nameless demons ravaged my helpless body. Torturous devices held me down, tearing me limb from limb. My mind was slipping, and reality seemed beyond my grasp. I was now truly cursed. Blind greed had guided me here to my ultimate doom.

However, with each passing moment, my body adjusted to the sickly innards of this accursed place. Slowly, I came back to my senses—the initial onslaught of visions cleared. I was lucky to have survived nearly unscathed. Corpus, our half-orc strong arm, had collapsed, and no matter how hard we tried, we could not get him to budge. His mind was gone, most likely consumed by the same images that tore through my mind. With heavy hearts, those of us remaining struggled on.

As our party climbed its final set of gnarled stairs, I saw a pattern of countless faces etched into the walls—each face disfigured by a unique and personal agony. Nevertheless, the faces beckoned us forward, to enter this dark domain and join their countless ranks. Beyond the faces stood a single open door.

As the last one of us passed through the door, it slammed shut with a tremendous boom. The sound reverberated though my head, tearing the dark veil away from my stricken mind. At last, I was able to concentrate on my actions and gather enough power to cast a single spell.

With an effort, I flicked my withering hand, and a channel of power emanated from my body. I was able to touch the minds of my teammates, freeing them from the personal hells that had overtaken their pathetically weak minds.

My power also triggered something within this dark domain. The room suddenly flared into vision. Momentarily losing my ability to see, I staggered backwards and fell. My hands grasped at the ground, only to feel cold clanking metal. Focusing intently, however, I was able to see that I had landed on a large pile of gold coins!

Immediately, I realized that we had fallen upon the treasure trove of our wildest dreams. Gold, silver, platinum—all those colors gleaming off hordes of coins, the likes of which we had never beheld. Elegant armor, swords, and chests carved from gold lined every wall. I was truly in heaven.

With almost reckless lust, I scrambled toward the heart of the room. A rotting smell pressed forth, blasting me back. Again, I was overcome with nausea. From the opposite corner of the room, I beheld what I sensed—a pile of rotting, decomposed bodies of past adventurers, who weren't so lucky. With a scream, I rushed back to the door, but it was securely locked. We were trapped.

Suddenly, energy erupted from the pile of corpses. Our group spread out and prepared for the worst. From the pile of flesh arose five of the ugliest skeletons we had ever seen. Their scanty clothing was torn and tattered, and we had full view of the rotten flesh hanging from their bones. Death was the price they had paid for their attempt to rob this tomb. Now, because of the spell I had cast, they will live forever as walking tributes to the powers that resurrected them.

Their leader drew close to me, a cynical laugh emanating from his empty jaw. Leaping forward with weapon drawn, I swung. A miss! My companions yelled at me to watch out, but, alas, it was too late. The skeleton took advantage of my mistake and swung back.

A quick roll of the dice told me, unfortunately, that the skeleton's blow would strike me head on, killing me instantly. As my sight grew dim, I could just make out the silhouettes of my fellow adventurers fighting for their lives. Soon enough, our bodies would be raised from the dead to join these creatures in their timeless duty as protectors of the tomb's treasure trove.

All in all, it was a long adventure that ended badly, but it was all in good fun. The good thing, my friends, is that I can retry the tomb-raiding adventure again after a quick break.

# The Concepts of Role-Playing

A series of simple concepts lies at the root of every role-playing game. These concepts are strung together into a feasible set of rules that are used to conduct a game. In this section, I discuss those concepts and give you a brief glimpse at the history of role-playing games, from the pen-and-paper roots to the modern computerized versions.

## The Basic Concepts

Those of you who have already discovered the incredible world of *Dungeons & Dragons* and similar games might have realized that such games changed your life. In those games, you can drop your daily worries and assume an alter ego in a universe full of monsters and magic. You can embark on epic quests to save the world, or take it over if that's your fancy.

That's what makes role-playing so great—taking on the role of another person. Remember when you were a kid and pretended to be a mighty warrior, slaying hordes of evil creatures that held the beautiful princess captive? A role-playing game (RPG) is much like your imagination—you still assume the role of that big tough warrior. However, when you move into a RPG some rules apply, just as they might in real life. You have to be a little realistic; not everybody can be a superhuman at the start.

For that reason, games have specific rules, plus a referee or judge that enforces them. In *Dungeons & Dragons,* the referee is called a *Dungeon Master* (DM) or *Game Master* (GM). This person is the overseer of the world and controls everything the players can't, such as the monsters and other non-playable characters. The players control only their character(s). When needed, players inform the GM of their intentions—what actions their characters perform.

It's the GM's job to take these actions, apply the rules, and determine the outcome. Situations will occur that require a decision dependent on the abilities of the character. For example, in my earlier scenario, if I had swung at the skeletons, would my swing have hit them? If my swing did hit them, what kind of damage would I have done?

When situations such as combat occur, the GM and players roll dice to decide the outcome. Characters have a set of attributes that are used in conjunction with the dice rolls; these attributes include factors such as a character's strength, agility, intelligence, and so on. The higher the attributes, the more damage the character can cause, the faster the character can move, and the more spells he can learn.

As characters become more experienced, they begin to become more powerful. Their attributes increase, making them stronger, faster, and smarter. As characters grow in strength, they are able to get into bigger and tougher battles, gaining more experience and, in turn, becoming stronger, thus continuing the cycle. This aspect of increasing a character's abilities (and experiences) over time is called *character building*—it is the driving force of most RPGs.

By making their characters more powerful, players are able to enjoy more vigorous quests. With each new game bringing you spectacular weaponry with amazing capabilities, potent spells worthy of accolades, and story after story blending it all together, who wouldn't be hooked?

# Playing Traditional Pen-and-Paper Games

*Pen-and-paper* games are named as such because to play these games, you only need reference books, pens, and paper. Most traditional pen-and-paper games also make use of a set of dice, which works as a random number generator. (RPGs such as *Dungeons & Dragons* are traditional pen-and-paper games.)

You typically play a traditional pen-and-paper game something like this: The players enter a locality looking for an adventure. The GM has a previously laid-out path for the game and gradually manipulates everything so that the players become hopelessly involved in the adventure.

As the characters move along the path, they might come upon some planned or chance encounters that lead to combat. Entering combat slows everything down and game-play becomes turn-based, in which players take turns deciding what to do. Each turn of play represents a few seconds of game time. Players then must decide what actions to perform within a single turn. When they've decided, the GM takes these actions, applies the rules, rolls the dice, checks the players' abilities and determines the outcome. This usually results in players and monsters harming each other until some or all die.

Surviving players then collect their treasure and continue until the adventure is done. At this point, characters receive experience points that gauge how well they did. These experience points are later tallied—once a character's experience reaches a certain point, his abilities are increased slightly.

You can further enhance this gaming experience using miniaturized models of the land, characters, monsters, and many other things. Typical game sessions employing models involve a large table being pulled out and decorated with the scenario's landscape and small figurines that represent the characters being placed in their respective positions. Being able to see everything laid out on the table helps you get into the game.

> **TIP**
>
> Resources for such games are immense—the *Dungeons & Dragons* franchise has reached its third edition. There are even a few dedicated magazines for it: *Dragon Magazine* and *Dungeon Adventures*, as well as a full-length motion picture (with a few more in the works). Check out Appendix C, "Recommended Reading," for more references to books and magazines on the subject.

A plethora of traditional pen-and-paper games are out there, each centering on a different genre. Here's a short list of some of the most popular ones:

- **Dungeons & Dragons by Wizards of the Coast, Inc.** The granddaddy of fantasy pen-and-paper role-playing games. Embark on mythical quests full of magic and monsters to do whatever your little heart desires. Take the form of a human, elf, dwarf, or any of the other many races this game provides and stock up with magic, weapons, and armor. Originally developed by TSR, Inc., *Dungeons & Dragons* is now maintained by Wizards of the Coast, Inc.

- **Cyberpunk 2020 by R. Talsorian Games.** The future is a dark place, and this game does a brilliant job of immersing gamers into it. Imagine the world of Blade Runner, and you're halfway there. This game has so much going on, from massive weaponry, bionic implants, and chemical boosters, that you'll have your hands full taking it all in.

- **Traveller by Game Designers' Workshop.** Dating back to 1977, the *Traveller* RPG was quickly adapted as *the* sci-fi RPG that others modeled. Explore the galaxy, from the biggest spaceports to the lowliest outposts. Become raveled in an intriguing history that dates back thousands of years—all from the comfort of your own home!

- **Generic Universal Role-Playing System (GURPS) by Steven Jackson Games.** This role-playing system applies to pretty much any game you can think of. Shown in Figure 1.1, this gaming system comes with a single set of rules that you can apply to any setting. With so many resources out there, this one is quickly becoming a contender to the *Dungeons & Dragons* empire.

> **NOTE**
>
> A *gaming system* is the underlying set of rules and instructions used to play a game such as *GURPS* and *Dungeons & Dragons*.

**Figure 1.1**

*Currently in its third reprint, the GURPS Basic Set (by Steve Jackson Games) is your guidebook to the generic role-playing game rule set.*

# Going Live with Role-Playing Games

*LARP* (or Live-Action Role-Playing) games moved traditional RPGs up a notch. While maintaining their pen-and-paper roots, a *LARP* game has participants actually dressing for their parts and having parties in which they play their alter ego. (I'll admit that it does take a little bit—well, a lot—of imagination to get all dressed up and attend one of these parties.)

Even though RPG players have been dressing their alter-ego parts for as long as RPGs have existed, one game in recent history has really made LARP mainstream. That game, *Vampire: The Masquerade* (by White Wolf Publishing), takes players through a secret world full of blood-sucking demons bent on human conquest. This time, however, players assume the role of a "creature of the night." This game revolves around the wars among the brooding clans. With a political structure behind the game, there's bound to be dissension in the ranks and plenty of opportunities to make your clan come out ahead.

Players attack each other (proverbially speaking), using weapons just like in any other RPG. When the going gets tough, the tough pull out their special abilities (sort of like spells). Combat continues until one player becomes the victor by destroying his or her opponent, causing the opponent to surrender or making the opponent flee.

I'll admit, pretending to be a flying demon of the night, slashing and hacking at each other takes quite a bit of imagination. Players of *Vampire: The Masquerade* are comparable to Trekies, so some take their game-play quite seriously. Have a look-see on the Web (starting at White Wolf's Web site at http://www.white-wolf.com), and you're likely to find dedicated groups in every major city. Just remember that above all, the idea is to have fun!

# Role-Playing on the Computer

Breaking out of the pen-and-paper mold, computer RPGs first became mainstream back in 1980s. At that time, classic games such as *Ultima* and *Wizardry* burst onto the scene, bringing gamers a whole new type of gaming.

Gone were the hassles of getting a group of friends together to play. Also, the computer took the role of the GM, so players could jump in and start playing by themselves. Of course, the excitement of a group is sorely missed, but you have to make *some* sacrifices. It's still just as addictive to be crouched in front of your monitor, searching through ruins for a magic amulet, only to be surprised by a demon in hiding!

Now the computer takes care of everything for you. No need to write anything down; the game stores it all, and it can be saved for later play. You can view maps of any place you've visited, with each corner opening up new areas to explore.

Of course, the game-play is a bit more constrictive than the pen-and-paper type, where you have a human who can make some decisions better than the computer can, but with every new release of a computer RPG, the designers get a little bit closer.

The most impressive (and sometimes limiting) factor of these games are the stories. Again, with a game like *Ultima,* you have an entire history to learn as you play the game. You find out how the world was formed and what shaped it, and you take part in it all.

The only problem is that these games usually lead you through a planned route with very little variation, so there's really no need to play the game more than once. No matter how many times you play it, the story remains the same, events occur like last time, and very few surprises are left.

These are issues to consider, and over time, games continue to be more advanced, thus solving many of these issues. Here's a short list of games that have shaped the world of computer RPGs:

- **Ultima series by Origin Systems.** An entire history of a world (and other worlds in spin-off titles) spreads out before you to discover and participate in. Take the part of the Avatar, a visitor from another dimension where time goes at a slower pace (Earth), who must save a foreign land from the evil clutches of countless bad guys. The storyline has been refined and even has its own religious sects. The latest game of this series has become the model on which other online RPGs are created.

- **Wizardy series by Sir-Tech.** Another classic game series that helped revolutionize computer role-playing. Although the first game was constructed of simple line-drawn 3-D mazes, each subsequent game release has progressed into today's deeply intriguing games. The latest games in this series boast an artificial intelligence so advanced that other characters in the game can actually perform their own quests, interfering with yours!

- **Might and Magic by 3DO.** A true classic that spun off multiple game genres. The original RPGs series is actually the only that can boast features such as linking worlds together over multiple versions. That's right; if you own a certain version, you can install the next one in the series and play in both worlds in the same game!

- **Baldurs Gate by Interplay.** This gaming series is backed by the Advanced Dungeons & Dragons rules sets and gives the players a true-to-life vision of *Dungeons & Dragons* game-play at its best. Link up with other players or battle the evil minions by yourself. This game has all the ingredients of a RPG masterpiece.

- **EverQuest by Verant Interactive.** As the current reigning champion of online RPGs, this game is so vast that it would take a lifetime to conquer. With new add-ons coming out every few months, this game keeps it freshness for even long-time players. This game also has the distinction of being the first one in which players actually auction super weapons and artifacts on Web-based auction sites. A definite must for those seeking online gratification for their gaming addiction.

# The Evolution of Gaming

From its meager pen-and-paper roots, role-playing has progressed, or rather evolved, into the definitive gaming genre it is today. The floodgates have opened and the industry has surged forth—each new game title advancing the style and features of RPGs. In this section, you take a look back at the games that help to innovate the RPG world.

Again, take a look at a classic game such as *Ultima I*. With such simple graphics (see Figure 1.2) and controls, what power did it hold over players? An immense world for one; ability to play hero-to-the-world for another. This is one of the first games I've seen in which you're actually allowed to attack anybody, even innocent villagers (of course, the guards don't take a liking to that—but, hey, you pay a price for your evil deeds).

As the series matured, each release brought new features, including improved graphics, physics, and larger environments. The latest offers in the *Ultima* series, *Ultima Online* (Figure 1.3 shows a scene from the game) links thousands of players together to live out their digital lives in a world that doesn't revolve around them. You leave your game and then come back only to realize that the world has gone on without you.

Another such game in production is *Dungeon Siege*, by Gas Powered Games (see a scene from the game in Figure 1.4). *Dungeon Siege* allows players to join forces online, while at the same time, allowing game designers to alter the game in many ways. *Dungeon Siege*'s lead game designer, Chris Taylor, was kind enough to lend his services and write this book's Foreword.

**Figure 1.2**

*The first in the series of Origin's Ultima games, Ultima I blazed to the screen in 16-color glory.*

**Figure 1.3**

*Origin's Ultima Online still uses 2-D graphics, but the game-play makes up for the lack in graphics beauty.*

**Figure 1.4**

*Dungeon Siege (by Gas Powered Games) brings players together throughout the world for some hardcore action role-playing as never seen before.*

The ability to join forces over the Internet has to be the biggest improvement in RPGs in years because it brings back the glory days of having a group of people play together, not a couple of programmed artificial characters. Whole in-game societies (generally called *clans*) have been formed from players around the world.

Although not as subtle, over time, there has also been an increase in the games' features, making the games more realistic. Games like *Ultima Pagan* (my favorite) now apply physics to everything in the world. Throw an item like a ball, and it will arch (as it would in the real world), bounce a few feet, roll down a hill, and plop down into a pond.

Do RPGs really need this level of complexity? Physics in a game makes the experience truer-to-life, but at the cost of added complications. If you have to depend on challenges like rolling a ball into a hole, you need to keep them simple enough not to aggravate the player. Provide too little a challenge, and players get bored quickly. Provide too great a challenge, and you run the risk of aggravating your audience.

Only time will tell how much realism players will take before the point of gaming is lost. I mean, who wants to play a game in which you do everything you would in your daily life? With the release of home-gaming consoles such as the Nintendo Entertainment System (NES) in 1985, consumers of all ages were able to get into the digital age of RPGs. No need for an advanced computer hardware package here, just a TV set, a console, and a game.

Probably the most notable console gaming series to date is *Final Fantasy* by Squaresoft. From the simple graphics of the first version to the beautiful rendered graphics and 3-D characters of the ninth, this game remains a top contender in today's market.

Although I consider this game the best console series of all time, other games currently take the lead for playability and all out fun. The number one contender at this time has got to be Sega's *Phantasy Star Online* (*PSO*). (You can see a scene from the game in Figure 1.5.) Online interaction with real people and the host of secrets involved in playing the game make this game an instant classic.

Although I don't want to take a biased stand, some games just make the cut better than others do. Take a look at my pick of the best past and current console gaming legends:

- **Final Fantasy series by SquareSoft.** The definitive RPG series for consoles. *Final Fantasy* includes massive stories that have to be experienced by any die-hard role-playing gamer, memorable battles full of super weapons, powerful spells, and monsters so warped that you'll be wondering what kind of person could have dreamed them. Currently up to its ninth in the series, with the tenth one on the way, this game is bound to be better with each release.

**Figure 1.5**

*Sega's Phantasy Star Online offers gamers an action-packed experience while maintaining a role-playing feel.*

- **Phantasy Star series by Sega.** Another golden oldie that was way ahead of its time from the first game in the series. A truly massive story that revolves around the history and future of a dying race forced to leave its planet in search of another one. Things would go good for them if not for a ruthless demon that dogs them every thousand years. The latest, *Phantasy Star Online*, joins players from every nation, for the first time, on the Internet for some massive multiplayer mayhem.

- **Legend of Zelda by Nintendo.** Although not a true die-hard RPG, it does contain many RPG elements. It appears that the world is a treacherous place, and your hero (Link) must defend the world against the evil tyranny of one unusually relentless, bad dude named Ganondorf (*aka* Ganon). Definitely worth getting if you own any of the Nintendo gaming systems.

- **Breath of Fire series by Capcom.** Currently in its fourth release; this is another example of a series worth checking out. Although the graphics are a bit dated, being blocky and brightly colored (see a scene from the game in Figure 1.6), the game-play is top-notch. This is a classic game true to the old days of console RPGs.

**Figure 1.6**

*Breath of Fire by Capcom retains older 2-D graphics styles, but in such a way that it impresses even hardcore gamers.*

# Wrapping Up with a Look into the Future

What does the future hold for us gamers? It's hard to say, but Internet gaming is going to be a standard for all games to live up to. Some companies have a great head start, but that will soon change as others get into the groove.

Imagine being able to design a single online character that you can tailor to any online game. That's right! That grizzly, battle-scarred warrior from the fantasy-line games can be suited up with a mechanized combat suit. You will be able to maintain experience, weapons, spells, and all other character aspects that make character building worth it.

In addition, how about being able to stake out some prime new land in an online world as big as your own? Sounds cool, doesn't it? Form societies, define your laws (and enforce them), populate your land—the possibilities are endless!

Not only will game-play improve, but also as technology improves, the gaming platforms will be even better—with graphics cards pumping out millions of 3-D images per second, sound systems jamming out the beat, and enough game controllers out there to fill your every fantasy and need. There's so much waiting for us in the future of RPGs, but remember that the future is what we make it. Read on to learn how you can help mold these future adventures.

# Part Two

# Role-Playing Game Design

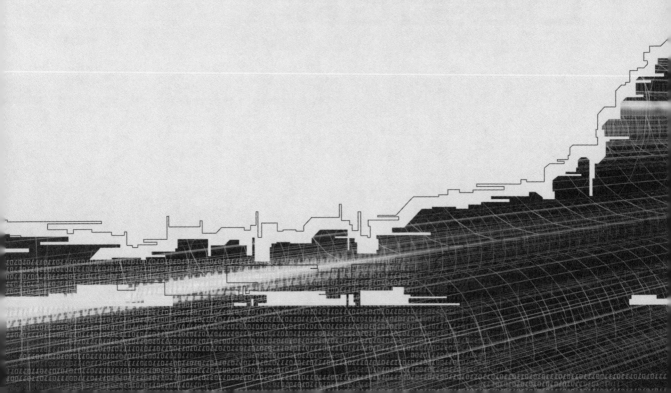

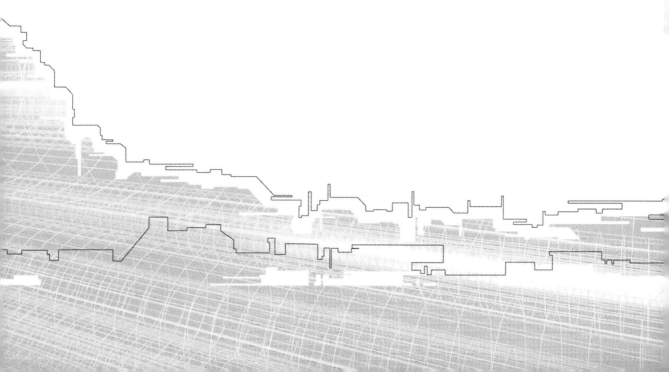

# CHAPTER 2

# Exploring RPG Design Elements

The crucial part of a movie is its script. The script contains every spoken word and special effect and all other details that describe the movie. It's then up to the director and actors to take the script and bring it to life in the best way that they can.

Just as a script is important to a movie, so is a design document important to a game. Any serious game project should have a design document, especially large projects such as a role-playing game (RPG). Beginning your project by planning and designing all aspects of the game will provide you with a guide to follow from the beginning to the end of the project. This planning will ensure that the information you need is readily available to you and others involved in the project. To that end, please consider this chapter a guide to creating your own design document.

In this chapter, you learn about the following:

- How to start your game design
- Creating a design document
- What information to include in the document

# General Game Design Issues

At the core of every game project lies a simple design that is blown to huge proportions. The best place to start your game project is with the general game design, and the best place to culminate your ideas is in a design document.

## The Importance of Design Documents

The *design document* is the instruction manual for your game. Within the document's pages are all aspects of the game: the story line, characters, dialogue, graphics style and engine, and all other details important to describing the game (as those you see in Figure 2.1).

All participants in the project should be able to refer to this document and proceed with their jobs based on the information they find there. For example, a programmer needing to know what type of combat engine will be used in a game might refer to the document and find that the game uses a 3-D engine that utilizes a moving camera, 3-D textured characters, and eye-pleasing graphics effects. Maybe he will even see a few concept pictures drawn by the designers.

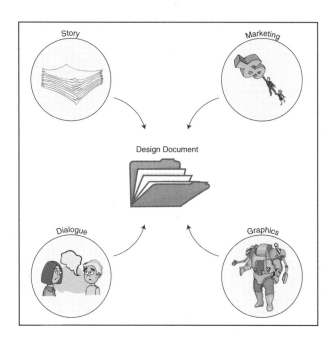

**Figure 2.1**

*The design document is packed with all the information you need to create your game.*

Not only does a design document contain information about a game's design, but also it should contain marketing information if you are planning on selling the game. This information includes product highlights, estimated completion dates, and other information pertinent to making your game available commercially.

Although the design document cannot possibly contain all the minute information about your game, a design document does help ease the process of the game's development. Just as producers and actors interpret their scripts in different ways, so do people creating a game interpret the design document differently—and remember that it's up to them to mold the game into a masterpiece.

# Creating Your Design Document

For large projects, such as RPGs, I find that using a multiple document format is essential. This means that each component of the design (art, design, music, and so on) is broken down by category and listed in separate documents that are referred to as *books* or *bibles*. I recommend using a total of six documents, as follows:

- Master bible
- Art bible

- Story bible
- Design bible
- Sound bible
- Tech bible

Each document contains only the information pertinent to its own topic; for example, all the artwork goes into the art bible, and all the design issues go into the design bible. Tables 2.1 through 2.6 list some major topics that each design bible might contain, as well as the type of information each section should contain.

## Table 2.1  Master Bible Contents

| Section | Description |
|---|---|
| Table of contents | Lists all sections contained within this document. |
| Proposal | The game submission proposal if you are trying to submit your game to a publishing company. Check out Chapter 21, "Marketing and Publishing Your Game," for more information about what information to include in the proposal. |
| Introduction | Introduction to the design document and what it contains. |
| Concept | Game concept and idea (using brief and concise text). This includes the game title and genre. |
| Story summary | Short summary of the game story highlighting key points. |
| Character introduction | At-a-glance list of the game's main characters. |
| Highlights | Key elements of your game, such as story plot points, licensed engines or technology, and graphics styles used to create the game. |
| Game description | Description of how the game looks and feels. |
| Game elements | Lists actual gaming elements divided into topics such as game-play, characters in the game, computer A.I., and so on. |
| Hardware specifications | Information such as system requirements (required CPU, graphics acceleration, and so on). |
| Schedule | Milestone and time-of-completion schedule for marketing purposes. |

## Table 2.1  Master Bible Contents *(continued)*

| Section | Description |
| --- | --- |
| Budget | Breakdown of the estimated cost of production. You see more about this in Chapter 21. |
| Team members | List of your team members or a list of people needed to work on the project (including required skills such as artist, C++ programmer, and so on). |
| Marketing | Marketing information such as competitive analysis, target audience, projected sales, and so on. Again, Chapter 21 contains more information about this. |

## Table 2.2  Art Bible Contents

| Section | Description |
| --- | --- |
| Table of contents | Lists all sections contained within this document. |
| Concept | Sketches and idea drawings that might or might not be included in the final game. |
| Storyboard | Story sequences are drawn out for the designers to follow. |
| Character | Pictures of the game characters. |
| Items | Pictures of the game items. |
| Levels and terrain | Pictures and suggested layouts of maps and terrain features (such as trees, buildings, and so on). |
| Magic effects | Drawings of the game's magic effects (usually in combat sequences). |
| Combat | Drawings of combat scenes (terrain, effects, and so on). |

## Table 2.3  Story Bible Contents

| Section | Description |
| --- | --- |
| Table of contents | Lists all sections contained within this document. |
| Idea | The "Plain-Jane" game idea, written in a couple paragraphs. |
| Summary | Summary of the entire game, highlighting key points such as combat features, game engines, look and feel of game, and so on. |
| Game story | Linear game story. |
| Plots | Lists plots and descriptions. |
| Dialogue | Full script of every spoken word. |
| Character history | Story behind each character. |
| Prelude (manual story) | The introductory story to your game that helps prepare the player for playing the game. This story is usually written for the game manual. |

## Table 2.4  Design Bible Contents

| Section | Description |
| --- | --- |
| Table of contents | Lists all sections contained within the document. |
| Ideas | All general ideas that designers might like to see in the game. |
| Game-play | Description of how the game is played. |
| General control | Control features such as moving your characters through the levels and issuing commands during combat. |
| Characters | Description of the players and their vital information, such as their HP, experience, allowable weapons, and so on. |
| Items | Lists all items in the game and the data related to them that are needed for the game (such as usage, description, and so on). |
| Magic spells | Lists all magic spells in the game and the information about them (magic points used, effects, and so on). |
| Levels | Level-by-level breakdown of the game, what it features, how the levels are laid out, what to place where, and so on. |

## Table 2.5  Sound Bible Contents

| Section | Description |
| --- | --- |
| Table of contents | Lists all sections contained within this document. |
| Sound effects | All sound effects other than voice. |
| Music | All musical compositions. |
| Voice overs | All voice recordings (such as spoken dialogue). |

## Table 2.6  Tech Bible Contents

| Section | Description |
| --- | --- |
| Table of contents | Lists all sections contained within the document. |
| System engine | Describes the basics of the entire system that runs the game. |
| Graphics engine | Describes the graphics engine(s). |
| Sound engine | Describes the sound engine. |
| Input engine | Describes the input engine. |
| Network engine | Describes the network engine. |
| General system | Shows all general system information not listed elsewhere. |
| GUI system | Shows the GUI (menu) system. |
| Game system | Shows the layout and flow of the game system. |
| Scripting engine | Describes the scripting system. |
| Character control engine | Shows how the characters control engine works. |
| AI engine | Talks about the AI system used in the game. |
| Combat system | A breakdown of the combat engine. |

At this point, you can decide to include all the design documents in one file or in multiple files. For large projects, it makes sense to divide the documents into multiple files. If you have many people working on a game, you can control which team members get which documents.

If you use a single document for your design, and thus a single file to save it, name the file by the tentative game name, appending _DesignDoc at the end. For example, if you name your game RolePlayingGame, the filename might be RolePlayingGame_DesignDoc.doc.

If you decide to split the document into multiple bibles, you need to create a file-naming convention for those documents. For example, you might want to append the bible name to the end of each document: RolePlayingGame_Art.doc, RolePlayingGame_Design.doc, RolePlayingGame_Master.doc, and so on.

## Starting with the Table of Contents

Regardless of the type of design document you use, the place to start is with the *table of contents* (*TOC* for short). Take your time to flesh out the TOC; it's a major part of your design document (see Figure 2.2). You might use the layouts that I showed you earlier in section "Creating Your Design Document" to get started.

People need to be able to quickly find exactly what they are looking for in the design document. For example, a marketing representative might want to see only projected sales figures. At a glance, he can see that this information is in the master bible, on page 5 (yes, you need to number the pages).

Starting with the TOC ensures that you have a firm grasp on how you want to lay out your project. In fact, the design document is one of the first things a publishing company wants to see. For that reason, create an easy-to-follow indexing system, with page numbers, appendixes, and so on.

## Adding the Topics

At this point, start asking yourself questions about the game. Answer every question that is conceivably related to the game and include the answers in the design document (see Figure 2.3). For example, what engine do you use for the combat? Put the answer in the document. What happens when you push the joystick to the right while playing the game? That answer goes in the document.

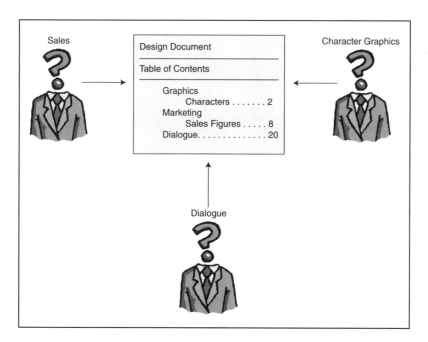

**Figure 2.2**

*A table of contents makes looking up specific information in your bibles easier.*

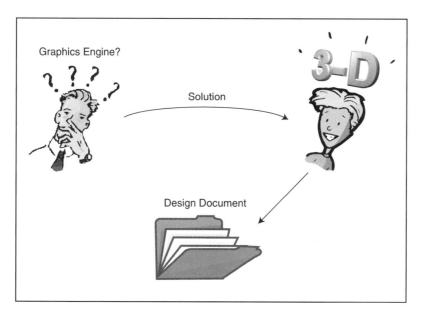

**Figure 2.3**

*If you have a question about your game, find an answer and insert it into your design document.*

Classify each question and answer (the design) by the various topics that you lay out in the TOC for each design bible. Art topics go in the art bible, design issues go in the design bible. Continue doing this until you have a fleshed-out series of documents. At this point, go through each document, adding more detail to each topic. You want your game's design document to be clear-cut and concise. Remember that you will be following this instruction manual when it comes time to create your game.

Notice I'm not going into a great deal of detail here. It's your game, and it is impossible for me to tell you how to design it. Instead, this chapter helps you create a shell, which you then fill with your own words. Upcoming chapters in this book cover the various topics that are included in a design document—topics such as the various engines, RPG elements, marketing information, and much more.

As you go through this book, keep tabs on your design document, adding the information you need as you come across it. By the end of this book, you should have enough information to complete your design document and program your game.

# The Perfect Design Document

Although I wish that I could give you the complete layout for a perfect design document, I just can't do so. The fact is that no one uses a standard design document; they're all different in one aspect or another. What works for some project teams doesn't work for others. As a result, you must go with your own flow and create a design document that fits your needs.

With that said, here's a little secret. You can find a plethora of information about design documents on the Internet. First, go to http://www.gamedev.net and check out the resources section (or go directly to the design documents section at http://www.gamedev.net/reference/list.asp?categoryid=23#Design Documents).

Next, go to http://www.gamasutra.com and search for "design document." You'll be surprised what turns up! A number of free design-document templates are out there, which you can download and tailor to your own needs.

Although this book is geared more toward the programming side of RPGs, I recommend that you check Appendix C, "Recommended Reading," for information on *Swords and Circuitry*, a book that examines the design side of RPGs in greater detail than I can do in this book. Before that, however, take a closer look at the design of RPGs, or at least the design issues you deal with in this book.

# RPG Design Aspects

RPGs are a funny lot. Ask ten different game companies what a RPG is, and you'll most likely get ten different answers. The simple fact is that the aspects that make an RPG what it is are really undefined. If you tell me that a RPG is all about character building, I can show you 100 different games that fit into that category and that are not called RPGs. The same goes for other supposedly RPG features—story telling, exploring, resource management, and so on.

The fact is that as the gaming industry evolves, so do the concepts of games. The characteristics of different styles of games become mixed. Take, for example, the popular game *Phantasy Star Online* by Sega, inc., a habit-forming action game with character-building aspects. Is it a RPG or not? You make the call.

The reality is that any one of the typical RPG features can be mixed into your game design, each useful in its own way. For that matter, what features are considered role-playing ones? Take a look:

- **Character building.** Your virtual alter ego, started from scratch, is usually the weakling in the bunch. With hard work, you build this character into a powerhouse that strikes fear into the hearts of his enemies. Character building is the term used to describe the character's upbringing.

- **Exploration.** What game doesn't include a bit of exploration? RPGs usually take this feature to the extreme with a large world to explore, dungeons to crawl through, and secrets to uncover.

- **Resource management.** Items, treasures, spells, and other gaming commodities abound in RPGs, and part of the fun comes from dealing with those commodities. Items have purposes, and it's the player's job to discover those purposes.

- **Problem-solving.** What better way to challenge your brain than with every mind-bending puzzle that you can design. RPGs generally send players on a wild chase to solve one puzzle or another as they save the world.

- **Story involvement.** The player, in all his trials and tribulations, typically takes center-stage during the game, with the entire story revolving around the player. With gripping plots and twists, the player needs to be driven on until the end.

- **Combat.** Though you probably already know this, every RPG devotes a major portion of time to combat. Weapons swinging, spells erupting, and creatures dying, all in the name of good as the player strives for justice in a world of evil. Combat is a major contributor to character building; the more creatures killed, the stronger the player character becomes.

The list could go on, but I've hit upon some of the most important aspects. From a designer's point of view, each of the preceding aspects deserves an entire chapter, but unfortunately, this book (and my publisher) does not allow for that kind of space. Besides, that is not the purpose of this book. My aim is to show you how the just-mentioned aspects fit into the programming side of role-playing games.

# Turning to the Technical Side

The design issues that I cover relate specifically to the technical side of RPGs, such as the graphics engine, item handling, and character control. Concentrating on this technical side of the design, note the following components that are needed for your game:

- **Core technical engines.** These engines are the guts to your game. They handle drawing graphics, playing sounds, and processing device input.
- **Graphics engines.** As the users' viewports into the world, the graphics engines are major workhorses that display what is happening in your game.
- **Scripting.** To expand the functionality of your game, you can use external scripts (external to the game's source code) to quickly change game-play without the hassles of dealing with a C/C++ compiler. Instead, you use a custom-built script editor that works hand-in-hand with the finished game engine.
- **Items and inventory control.** Game players need "stuff" to play with, so as the game's developer, you need to create these items and develop ways for players to manage them.
- **Character control.** What's a game without a hero? Controlling all characters in your game is issue *numero uno*.
- **Maps and levels.** What is a game world without places to explore? Your map and level engines maintain the world around your characters.
- **Multiplayer gaming.** Be sure to link players over the Internet for some major gaming action. The multiplayer component of your game is just what you need.

In case you didn't notice, the preceding list of components is almost dead-on with this book's table of contents; the major components of a RPG are all there, and you will need each of them at one point or another.

Within the pages of this book, you find every component you need to make your own RPG. Although basic in nature, the majority of the components are powerful enough to drive your largest project. It all starts with a little understanding.

# Knowing Your Role

When you begin creating your game, you must understand just what you're getting into. You need to be aware of the minimal system requirements, the current technological capabilities and trends, and the available resources.

Minimal system requirements aren't as big an issue as they used to be because computer systems are continually becoming more powerful. It's safe to say that you can create a game and rest assured that it will run decently on the majority of systems, assuming that you keep things compatible, which is where technical capabilities and trends come in.

If you lived in a strictly non-techie cave during the past five years, you probably missed the introduction of the DirectX gaming libraries by Microsoft. Merging all the functionality you'll ever need into a set of programming libraries, Microsoft managed to wipe clear all compatibility issues among varying hardware setups, thereby giving all programmers an equal opportunity to create great games (from a technical point of view, that is). Using DirectX, you can be further assured that your game will run on any computer that utilizes the DirectX libraries.

With DirectX, you have the following at your disposal:

- **3-D graphics.** Now you can wander around immense worlds from a 3-D perspective. Powerful new graphics hardware takes care of the hard work. You're left with the easy job of laying out your virtual world. Graphics, at a minimum, will use resolutions from 640 x 480 and up, harnessing 16-bit to 32-bit color resolutions.

- **A high-quality sound system.** Music and sound effects never sound so great, blasting the user with high quality playback. Use 16-bit, 22 KHz, stereo playback features to ensure that your game sounds are crisp and effective.

- **Access to virtually all input devices.** Using DirectX- and DirectInput-capable drivers, any input device is usable for your projects, from that old dusty analog joystick to the futuristic jumpsuit that's just around the corner.

- **Networking gaming at its finest.** No more dealing with overwhelming technical issues of networking; with DirectX on your side, network gaming becomes a reality for your game, via an easy-to-use set of libraries.

As for available resources, you're limited only by the tools that you have available for your game project. Need 3-D modeling programs to lay out your game characters and world? No problem, because each day brings more tools. No longer are you limited by the availability of high-quality, high-cost programs. Now you can get your hands on some great tools at a low cost. In fact, the CD-ROM that comes with this book is packed with useful programs (see Appendix E, "What's on the CD-ROM," for more information).

Now you can model in 3-D, construct music and sound effects, and dish out almost any materials you need to finish your game. With this book at your side, nothing will slow you down!

# Wrapping Up Design

As I noted earlier in this chapter, this book is geared more to the programming aspects of RPGs. If you're interested in the design side of gaming, check out Appendix C at the back of this book for the information about a book on that topic.

Throughout this book, I incorporate an overall design ideology—to keep things simple. The simpler you keep things, the faster things get done, and contrary to popular belief, those awesome features you see in games are not hard to duplicate; they just seem that way. At the same time, I discuss quite a few of the RPG design aspects, especially when it comes to the technical side of things. With that in mind, it's time to move on to a design aspect that is important to role-playing games—writing stories.

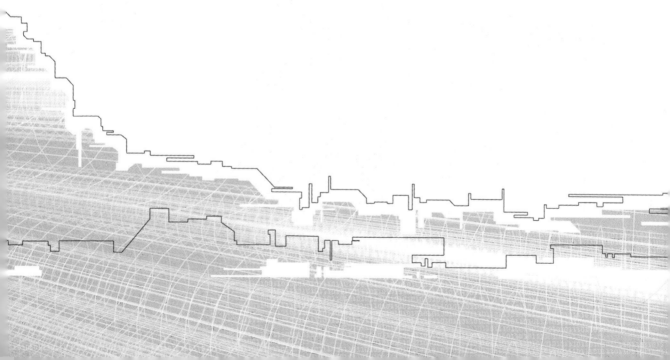

# CHAPTER 3

# STORY-WRITING ESSENTIALS

In order to produce a first-class role-playing game, you need a story that immerses the players in a world of danger and deception—a game that constantly challenges the protagonist (the hero who plays the role of the main character) in his quest to win the day.

Just as with a movie, the storyline is what makes a game memorable. What was the best thing about the movie *The Matrix*? I still remember the massive blow I received when Neo woke up inside his battery compartment in the far future. Or how about in *Final Destination* in which a group of high schools kids realize that their adversary is death itself? The players of your game can have similar experiences. You *can* create a storyline that will sweep players off their feet when they least expect it!

In this chapter, you find out how to create such a game by doing the following:

- Brushing up on story basics
- Understanding the writing process
- Improving your writing with some helpful tips
- Applying stories to games

# The Art of Telling Stories

The ancient art of storytelling is based on the ability to structure and communicate events that occur during the resolution of a situation. Put another way, a story reveals the details about what happened while someone endeavored to achieve a goal (essentially, who, what, why, where, when, and how).

The real art, however, is relating those events in an entertaining way. Some authors are adept at telling stories, relating them in a way that pulls you in and changes your perception in some way. These writers are the ones who keep you up late at night reading just one more page. Their stories exist in a world in which every detail and character is alive, a world that you feel privileged to experience.

You, of course, want to achieve the same reaction with your stories. However, the ability to write such stories doesn't come at the snap of a finger. You have to work your way up, first learning the basics, then coming up with ideas. You need to develop characters and the situations that drive them through the story. Before doing any of these things, however, you must understand how stories are structured so that you can later piece everything together in logical order.

## The Five Components of a Story

All stories follow a basic format (called the *story structure*) that can be broken into five components: the inciting incident, complications, plot points, climax, and denouement.

The *inciting incident* is the event that triggers a major event and drives the story. The incident forces the main characters' involvement and gives them a reason to resolve a situation. *Complications* are the obstacles that stand in the way of reaching a resolution.

Along the way, the story experiences *plot points,* which are major turning points in the story. These events affect the flow of the story. Plot points are also called *plot twists* because they can change the outlook of the story.

The *climax* is the point where excitement builds and everything is resolved in a blaze of glory. Last is the *denouement,* the point where everything winds down and the story concludes.

## The Story Ladder and the Three Acts

You can almost think of a storyline as a ladder, as illustrated in Figure 3.1. As you climb the ladder, you reach specific components of a story. At the bottom of the ladder is the inciting incident. Moving up, you have the complications mixed in with the plot points. At the top of the ladder, you reach the climax. Although the climax is at the top of the ladder, the climax is not the end of your climb. At this point, the point of denouement, you jump down and into the story's downfall; here the story "comes down" to its end.

Although the story ladder gives you a way to visualize the story's progress (the rise in action), you can think of the whole story as a play, complete with acts. Traditionally, a story is split into three acts, the beginning, the middle, and the end. Even if a book has 24 chapters, it still has a beginning, a middle, and an end.

Each act has a purpose: to introduce the characters, the conflict, the plot points, and finally the conclusion. Now, take a closer look at each act in detail and outline what occurs in each.

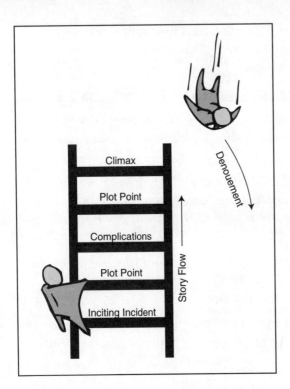

**Figure 3.1**

*The story ladder can be broken into components.*

# Act 1: The Beginning

The beginning represents approximately the first 25 percent of the story. Here, you introduce the important characters. You don't have to introduce all the characters here, but this part of the story should introduce the protagonist and other characters that help support the story. You need to start building a relationship between the reader and the protagonist of the story as soon as possible.

Along the way, you introduce the inciting incident, which presents the protagonist with a situation that needs to be resolved. This situation might play a minor role in the beginning. At any rate, the situation gives the protagonist a reason to be involved; that is, it presents him with something that must be resolved.

It's this situation (and the underlying inciting incident) that conveys the story's conflict. The conflict builds into a crisis that fully involves the protagonist over time. This crisis marks the first plot point (turning point) that leads into the second act.

## Act 2: The Middle

Here's where all the fun happens! The middle story represents about 50 percent of the story and is where most of the reader and character relationship building takes place. Here, the reader needs to fully understand the main character, including his personality, history, and purpose. The reader needs to "experience" everything the main character does, says, and feels.

In the second act, the main character attempts to resolve the crisis introduced in the first act. Because the story would not be intriguing if the protagonist solved the problems too easily, you present obstacles that stand in his way, including conflicts and plot twists that are eventually overcome. The action continues to build up as you near the end of the second act. You don't want the story to slow down in any way; you want to keep the reader excited.

The overall crisis still remains (seemingly a hopeless cause), and constant reminders of it should occur throughout the story. The protagonist must prevail, and soon it will be time. But first, another complication pokes it head up and the main character is rushed into the final act.

## Act 3: The End

Alas, all good stories must come to an end. The third act represents the final 25 percent of the story. Now is when the protagonist overcomes the crisis and prevails. This is the moment of truth. You can't dilly-dally—the readers are counting on you.

The climax continues to build until it's ready to pop. The excitement rises, the obstacles mount, all seems doomed. The goal is within reach, but it seems unobtainable. The protagonist seemingly reaches the point of no return, but finally, through thick and thin, blood and sweat, the hero makes a final push, and then. . . .

Sorry, but you wouldn't want me to give away the ending, would you? Just kidding. As you can guess, the hero destroys the bad guy, rescues the damsel, saves the world— that is, he achieves the desired goal. Notice that I said "desired goal." Even though the outlook of the story might be grim, the protagonist's personal goal is reached.

For example, consider the *Second Chronicles of Thomas Covenant* by Stephen R. Donaldson, which details the adventures of Thomas Covenant, the Unbeliever. In the third book of these chronicles (*White Gold Wielder*), the protagonist of the story, Thomas Covenent, reaches his goal of defeating the bad guy, but at the cost of his own life. The ending comes as a surprise and leaves you in awe. Even though Thomas's death is a shock, his original goal is achieved.

At the conclusion of the climax comes the denouement. Things wind down—because the day was won. The readers see the aftereffects of all that occurred. At this point, you want the reader to know that all the struggles were worth it and that everything is better, now that the crisis is over. Life goes on; all is well.

# Characters

The characters are the lifeblood of your story. For that reason, character creation is the single most important step in writing stories. Every story has two types of characters, major and minor. Just like in the movies, characters in your story can play a major role (such as the protagonist (hero) or a supporting character) or a minor role (extras and those guys who get killed within the first five minutes of every "Star Trek" episode).

## Know Your Roles

First and foremost is the lead character (or rather the character, or sometimes characters, that the story revolves around). This person is the *protagonist*. The protagonist is the most important character in your story, so you need to describe this person in as much detail as possible.

Opposing the protagonist is the *antagonist* (the bad character or factor), the second most important character in your story. The protagonist of your story has a vested interest in the antagonist, even if the antagonist is not a person. In reality, stories don't need an antagonist—the story is really about the protagonist.

What good is a world with only one or two people? For that reason, you create many character roles in your game's story. But be careful not to mix up your characters' roles—either they play a major part in your story or they don't. Minor characters require very little attention, except when they are needed to add some support. Characters who play a major role (the protagonist, antagonist, and supporting characters) in the story require the most detail, the most attention. Figure 3.2 illustrates the interaction of the three most important character roles.

Your protagonist tops the list of major roles and, as such, requires the most attention. That is not to say that the antagonist gets little attention, just not as much as the protagonist. You want the reader to form an emotional bond with the hero. In addition, you want believable characters to play your main roles. In order to create a believable character, you must make them three-dimensional characters.

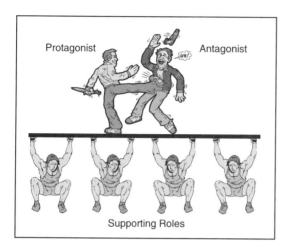

Protagonist Antagonist

Supporting Roles

**Figure 3.2**

*Supporting roles help the major characters move along in the story.*

# Building Three-Dimensional Characters

The three dimensions of a character, *physical, sociological,* and *psychological,* are described in the following list. These characteristics are the most common ones that you can use to describe a person, and in order to be complete, your story characters should have these traits.

- **Physical.** Traits that describe the physical nature of a character and his life, including body type, health, and appearance. Appearances include how they carry themselves, the manner in which they walk, how they dress, and so on.
- **Sociological.** A character's name, age, residence, job, and beliefs; his educational, intellectual, social, and economic status; and all other details regarding his social development and social life.
- **Psychological.** A character's personality, manner of speech, attitude, abilities, and emotions.

As an exercise in developing three-dimensional characters, prepare a comprehensive list of your own characteristics (at least those in the preceding list); then using this information, compose a few paragraphs that describe you—in terms of how you perceive yourself. Don't be afraid; you'll be doing a lot of this kind of work when you develop your story's characters.

Treat these three characteristics as a set of "rules" when it comes to describing characters. Try to assume the roles that you create, and check to see whether what is being said and what is occurring are consistent with the characters' traits.

## Dialogue

They walk, they talk, and they even have feelings! That's right, your characters are real—at least, they are in your mind. In order for your readers to believe in them, too, you have to write about your characters as though they are real people; give them feelings, purpose, and history.

What's the principal thing that you can write to help readers relate to a character? The dialogue, of course. What your characters say has a crucial effect, just as in real life. By listening to what people say, you can judge what type of people they are, what they believe in, like, or hate, and sometimes even what they ate for dinner last night.

In the best stories, characters speak clearly (or at least understandably). No jive talk, slang, or otherwise confusing lingo that's bound to get in the way of comprehension. This is important, because you want your readers to understand what is going on. Ideas are brought out in clear, concise words and get right to the point; there's no idle chitchat.

In addition to verbal dialogue, there's inner dialogue, which is a person's thoughts. Readers need insight into the minds of characters, including their fears, objectives, lusts, and other driving forces. Nothing is sacred in script.

Both verbal and inner dialogues are important to your story; they represent two-thirds of how people, including your characters, are perceived (the other one-third being visual perception or body language). Develop each character according to his beliefs and thoughts, and be sure that they all react to each other accordingly.

## Setting Mood and Atmosphere

It was a dark, stormy night. A flash of light and an ear-splitting boom rupture forth from the gloom, illuminating the fields in a slight hue of blue and white. With each flash of lightning, the sickly form of the approaching invader becomes more apparent. Its long face, sharp fangs, and slinky red body covered in matted, bloody hair dredge up thoughts of long forgotten nightmares. As it nears, you can feel its purpose burning down to your soul—it has come for you!

Eerily, the last paragraph describes a scene you might see only in your worst nightmares (or in your imagination). The setting is dark and foreboding, a perfect mood for nightmarish stories. The atmosphere is heavy, creating a feeling of fear. The poor hapless soul has bland, dark surroundings, the lightning providing brief glimpses of an approaching horror.

Those elements are very important ones in a story—mood and atmosphere. Although only a minute portion of what could be conceivably a love story (yeah, right), that short paragraph presents a grim mood setting and manages to set the atmosphere perfectly. Typically, a story will maintain the mood and atmosphere it sets early on, but those elements can change as the story progresses (from good to bad or vice versa!). Be sure to express the mood and atmosphere in a concise and exact way so that your readers can experience it themselves.

# The Point of View

All stories are related through a particular point of view (or perspective), and an author describes a given story's events from that story's particular point of view. A story can be told from the point of view of the protagonist. Say that the character is a woman who hears a knock on her front door; she answers it and sees a door-to-door salesman standing on her porch. Turning him away, she returns to her activities.

An outside source able to view the entire scene sees things from a broader perspective. The tired salesman has failed to make a successful pitch all day. He stumbles along from house to house, only to reach a pretty, small one-story abode. Inside, Mrs. Jones is relaxing after a hard day of work. The salesman approaches the door, rings, and soon comes Mrs. Jones to answer. As the salesman is turned away yet again (only to trot along to the next house), Mrs. Jones returns to her previous activities.

In this second example, you can see the perspective of both characters. The form in which you relay your story is the same; just be sure to select one point of view and stick with it.

Generally, stories are written either in *first person* (the "I" perspective) or *third person* (the he/she perspective). When writing in first person, you tell the story from a character's point of view or from the perspective of a narrator who is an eyewitness to the events of the story—note that this narrator is not the author and might or might not be reliable.

When writing in third person, you generally write from the point of view of the effaced narrator or the omniscient narrator. The *effaced narrator* can have a fixed point of view (focusing on the perspective of only one character) or a broad perspective. The *omniscient narrator* intrudes into the story with editorial comments, judgments, forecasts, and so on. The primary difference between the effaced narrator and the omniscient narrator is intrusion.

Be careful not to switch the point of view mid-story; doing so can cause confusion for the reader. Even though you should not switch the point of view, it is perfectly plausible to switch the focus from one character to another—but do so sparingly because that might also cause confusion.

## Your Narrative Voice

The language you use, the style you employ, and the details you describe are all a matter of choice. This is the power of prose, and the manner in which you relate your story is called your *narrative voice*. Authors with a strong narrative voice bring life to their imaginary worlds, describing the details in a special way, making you believe their stories are real. You, too, need to develop a strong narrative voice. Here are a few tips for doing so:

- **Choose descriptive words.** The reader wants to understand what is occurring, in the least number of words. Choose descriptive words and don't be redundant.

- **Use clear and concise language.** Don't fill the text with jargon and slang that only a limited number of people will understand. The members of your intended audience should all be able to understand and enjoy your story.

- **Balance the flow.** Action, adventure, love scenes, and dialogue—there's a place for all of these elements in your story, but space and balance them appropriately. Don't overload too many scenes with too much of one element, or too little of another.

- **Keep a good pace.** To keep your readers interest, try to maintain a pace that keeps them on the edge of their seats at all times.

- **Use emotion.** Just as in real life, emotions cannot be underestimated. Emotions cause wars and create peace. The bottom line—use emotions freely and portray them just as they happen in real life.

- **Maintain one point of view.** If you begin relaying a story from the main character's point of view, don't switch to another point of view (don't switch from a first-person perspective to a third-person perspective).

## Plots, Subplots, and Twists

The *plot* is your story's bread and butter. It carries the story from beginning to end. The plot is sometimes confused with the *premise,* which is a quick, simple description of the story—"The good guy gets mad at the bad guy and hunts him down."

The plot, on the other hand, consists of the major points of the story. Remember the story ladder I mentioned in the section "The Story Ladder and the Three Acts," earlier in this chapter? The inciting incident, obstacles, and climax are all part of the plot. As an example, try to describe your day. Although much of it might be dull and drab, the major experiences are what make it count and are what you want to concentrate on.

## Plot Twists

Along the way, a story presents the reader with the turn of events—the turning points. As I mentioned earlier, these are called plot twists and are essential to good storytelling. You don't want readers to be wondering what will happen next. You want that to come as a surprise. Change the way the story flows much as Figure 3.3 illustrates. When the "twist" of the story events finally hits them, everything they know and understand about the story changes.

You can pack your story with twists; however, don't use so many that readers wind up continually scratching their heads trying to figure out what is going on. The path from crisis to resolution is still there, but twists change things a bit, sometimes they even introduce the real crisis or resolution. Just don't let readers lose sight of the real goal once it is introduced.

## Subplots

Although not essential, a subplot is an "off-to-the-side" series of events that occur during the main plot. Think of the subplot as a story within a story, one that doesn't take away from the main plot. You can use subplots to build the reader's relationships with the characters or to reveal the characters' past.

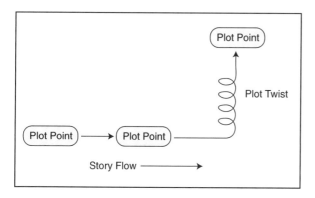

**Figure 3.3**

*Plot twists are great for shaking up a story or for turning a story in a different direction.*

# The Writing Process

While I'm in no way a literary prodigy, I found that by following some simple rules and guidelines, I'm able to better structure, develop, and finish writing my stories. Time-tested and proven, the following information is no secret—it's fairly standard in the writing industry. As you read the following guidelines, try to relate them to your story (whether that story is on paper or still in your mind).

# Eight Rules to Writing

In my experiences, there really are no ironclad rules to writing—the most creative stories come from unhindered thought. However, you can follow guidelines that will help make your stories more appealing. I find that by adhering to at least a few of the following guidelines, I'm better able to convey my story, make it more to the point (without losing clarity), and write so that the story appeals to a wider audience.

- **Don't overwrite.** The number one guideline is don't overwrite. At the beginning of the writing process, let your creative juices flow and write anything that comes to mind. As your story takes shape and nears its final draft, begin cutting out the "dead-weight," leaving only the content that actively conveys the story.

- **Don't explain too much.** The mind's world is a wondrous place; every little pebble has a story behind it. You're bursting at the seams to flood the reader with every minute detail about this fantasy world you've created, but wait! Too much of anything can diminish the experience. Even though details add to an experience, too many can hurt your story. You must decide which aspects of the story are important enough to require extra details—even then, try to keep the details to a minimum. The tension is always between what the readers need to know and what they don't need to know.

- **Be consistent.** You've already selected your narrative voice, character bios, story atmosphere, and all the other little facets that construct the base of your story. Here's a word of advice—stick to them! Nothing can ruin all your hard work more than straying from your intended path. Don't switch scenes at inopportune moments, don't present facts at improper times, don't change the characters' personalities, and don't change the narrative voice.

- **Use good language structure.** When writing your first draft, use shorthand, abbreviated words, symbols, and simple phrases to speed up your writing. When writing the second draft, however, be sure to replace those words and symbols, being sure to use proper spelling, grammar, and punctuation—unless you're striving for a particular effect.

- **Don't over or under spice.** Although spicing a story with elaborate words can sometimes give the story a certain creative flare, there is a fine line that you don't want to cross. If readers have to rely on their dictionaries more than once per page, they might put your story down and move on. If you are an aspiring writer, just remember that cooks spend a good deal of time testing spices in their recipes before achieving the perfect taste. You, too, will want to spend a bit of time achieving the perfect balance in your writing. Work with your text until you've added just the right amount of spice. The text should be neither bland nor overpowering; it should be just right.

- **Be clear, concise, and to the point.** This guideline comes into play after your first draft. Read your text and see if you can make your point in, say, half the number of words that are in your first draft. Cut out unnecessary words and make sure that the remaining text gets to the point.

- **Don't force your opinions or views.** Life is hard enough without someone constantly telling you what to do, say, think, or feel. Readers are intelligent and capable of choosing their own paths, so don't force your opinions or views on unsuspecting readers. Specifically, you don't want to feed readers your opinions on matters that do not directly relate to the story. Allow readers to develop their own opinions and points of view. In other words, write your story so that you stimulate readers to use their own opinions and views.

- **Have fun.** I can't say this enough. If you are not enjoying what you're writing, why are you writing it? Your attitude is reflected in your work, and if you are enjoying what you are writing, your words will reflect that pleasure. The journey you take as a writer is wrought with many perils, but the rewards are great. At the end, you will have a "masterpiece" to call your own!

# Six Steps to Writing

I have found that by following six easy steps, I'm able to maintain flow and order in the chaos called *creative writing*. While not comprehensive by any means, these six steps help form a base from which to work:

1. Begin with thought and planning. Think about what you want in the story; take notes, brainstorm, write down little blurbs that come to mind, and keep a running document of everything you can think of. It doesn't matter how big or small your ideas are, write them down!

2. Shape your thoughts. Using the information from the first step, begin to mold your ideas into a plausible structure. Introduce major topics before

talking about them, and introduce characters and give them purpose. Bring together everything that you intend to include in your story.

3. Write a draft. This is the first big step you're going to take in actually writing your story. Take the thoughts and ideas that you've begun to shape and write about them. Follow the standard flow for writing stories: introduce characters and provide back-story (the who, what, why, where, and how that got them to that point in the story), introduce the conflict, establish and lay out the plot and the plot twists, and finally lead up to the conclusion.

4. Revise your work. Writing a good story is an ongoing process of writing, updating and revising, writing some more, revising some more—you get the picture. There's never an end (especially for perfectionists like me!), but you will reach a point when you're happy with what you've molded. After one more draft, you'll reach a point where you want to remove the unnecessary parts and polish your text to perfection!

5. Edit your work. When you complete your story, edit it to make sure that you're using proper punctuation, look for misspelled words, check for proper grammar, and look for other kinds of errors.

6. Proofread your work. At last it is time to share your story with others! Give your story a complete reading, keeping in mind your intentions for the story. Imagine that you are reading it for the first time. Now, ask a friend to read it and to give you his reaction to the story. Don't feel badly about constructive criticism; it helps you gain a better perspective. If needed, rewrite portions of the story. Remember, you want a great story!

The preceding steps and their descriptions are meant strictly to serve as a quick reference. Now, I want to describe each step in greater detail.

## Thought and Planning

The first step is to pick a topic for your game's story. This topic is usually the basis of the game. Imagine that your "topic" is that an evil wizard is terrorizing a small town and the hero needs to destroy the wizard.

However, that topic is fairly broad, so you need to narrow it a bit. Why is the wizard doing this evil deed? What led to his actions, and how is the hero involved? There must be a purpose for everything that happens. Even though many games don't tell you why, a hero needs a reason to be there (even as generic as showing up and feeling justified in helping the needy).

You don't have to include the specifics for every detail yet; just keep writing all your thoughts. To expand on the wizard story, imagine that you've brainstormed and determined the hero was a child at the time the wizard was banished; it's the hero's village that is being tormented by the now vengeful sorcerer. Just write that down as a note and move on.

This stage in the writing process might take a while. It's time well spent, however, because it is where you'll have the most fun fleshing out what occurs throughout your story. Keep adding notes until you feel you have enough information to proceed to the next step.

## Shaping Your Thoughts

After you have a sufficient collection of ideas (all written down, of course!), you are ready to put them together. Your goal here is to clarify the generalized information contained in your notes. For example, characters in your story need a history and a reason for being involved (the back-story). What events led them to their present situations?

Situations such as the evil wizard terrorizing a town need a purpose as well. Most things don't just happen, they happen for a reason, and you need to reveal and "build up" those reasons. For example, why is the town being attacked? Why was the wizard banished in the first place? What in the child's past causes him to defend the village?

The bottom line is that you must make your story plausible; the reader must be able to believe that the story could happen in real life (if not in their lives, then in the life of the hero). Even if you base your story on fantasy, the world needs to seem plausible. Although you don't want to go into explicit detail about everything, remember that the little details are what make your story believable.

## Writing a Draft

This is your first chance to begin actually writing your story. Taking your notes and ideas from the previous two steps, begin writing your story. Start at the beginning and make it all flow together. It helps to create a timeline of major events that occur in your story, filling in the gaps between those events as you write.

Make sure that you lead up to major topics; you don't want to introduce them too quickly. For example, if you're writing a story about the evil wizard that takes over the village, be sure to describe his history and the events leading up to that point (even if that point is not at the beginning of the story). If you jump right into the attack on the village, you rob your readers of crucial background information that might help them actually care why the wizard is attacking the village or what is motivating the hero.

You need to describe important characters in great detail. Give them traits with which the reader is sure to associate, weave a history that brings the reader and characters closer together, and provide the characters with a personality that gives them a foundation from which you can build.

Continuing with the wizard story, say that the hero was an innocent child who fell victim to the wizard's previous misdeeds and that the wizard was banished from the village for his actions. These misdeeds could conceivably have been the invocation of an evil spell that led to the destruction of the hero's family, home, and farmland.

> **NOTE**
>
> Don't go overboard on developing the characters' personalities. Remember that players of games generally like to develop those personalities.

As you develop the history of the child (now alone in life since the loss of his family), readers should understand (and believe) that the child's upbringing molded him into a strong person-of-the-land with a snappy attitude. Although life was hard, the hero remains of good heart and doesn't want the home village to fall into the hands of the wizard, the very character who years ago harmed the hero.

## Revising the Story

Just because you've written the last page of your story doesn't mean that it's complete. Now it's time to go back and fix all the inconsistencies, all the drawn out sections, and the portions that have nothing to do with the situations at hand. Basically, you want all the pieces to fall into place, and you want your story to "sound" just right.

You can do many things to improve your story. Read and evaluate each sentence. Does it relate correctly to the story or does it need to be cut? Is it dull or boring? The best way to dress up a dull sentence is to give it a little spice! Add some colorful language that preserves the meaning of the sentence. One resource for such words is a thesaurus.

Once you've gone through the story and think that every sentence sounds just right, you are ready to edit your work.

## Editing

Here comes the dirty part! Now you get to have fun going over your work and making sure that you are using proper punctuation, spelling, and grammar. Basically, you get your story into a presentable form.

I hate to sound like your high school English teacher, but using proper sentence structure is essential. Use proper noun, verb, and adjective placement and agreement while writing in order to maintain clarity. Your best tools here are a dictionary and a thesaurus (which are usually built into word-processing programs, such as Microsoft Word).

You're close to being finished, so don't give up. You have only one more step to go!

## Proofreading

At this point, take a break for a day or two. Move on to some other portion of your project and get the story off your mind. The purpose here is come back with a fresh mind. Read the story slowly. Authors tend not to see their own mistakes, so scrutinize every word of every sentence. Again, does the story flow logically? Are major topics introduced too quickly or without a proper build up?

Let others read and judge your story as well. Have them tell you exactly what they think about the story. Is anything missing, confusing, or unneeded? Don't be offended by their criticism; every little bit helps. In the end, you'll thank your friends for helping you create your literary masterpiece!

# Writing the Three Drafts

No writer can sit down and write a story all in one round. Small inconsistencies emerge, dead-ends occur, and drab portions make the text sluggish. For those reasons, you should write a minimum of three drafts. As illustrated in Figure 3.4, those three drafts have a definite purpose of their own.

## The Rough Draft

You write the first draft just to get everything in there. This draft gives you a good understanding about how your story will unfold, bonds you with the characters, and pretty much ensures that you have a firm grip on the story. Don't worry too much about this draft; just write until you reach the end.

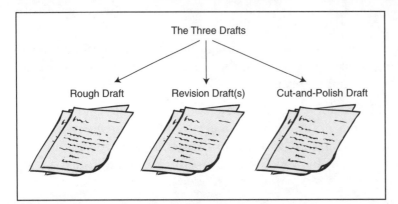

The Three Drafts

Rough Draft        Revision Draft(s)        Cut-and-Polish Draft

**Figure 3.4**

*The three drafts separate your writing process into three helpful steps.*

## The Revision Draft

Here's where you get to clean up the problems with the story. Now, you can edit and add better details, introduce topics at the appropriate times, remove inconsistencies, and basically brush up all that you're not happy with. By the end of this draft, everything is in order and no unanswerable questions regarding the story should come up.

The story is almost finished—don't undercut yourself here; think of this draft as your last opportunity to add or revise your text. Be sure that you're completely happy with the results before moving on.

## The Cut-and-Polish Draft

The final draft represents your story honed to perfection. Now you remove irrelevant portions, shorten long sections (while maintaining meaning), and polish the details. You basically are checking to see whether you can convey your story in fewer words, but with more flare, all the while maintaining its integrity. When you finish this draft, your story is complete. Congratulations!

# Tips for Better Stories

Stories are rarely clean-cut, beginning to end ordeals. Breaks in action occur, the focus of the story might shift from one character to another, and some out-of-the-way bits of information might need to be blended in to fully develop the story. How you deal with the details is entirely up to you, but by using techniques in the following sections, you can breathe new life into an otherwise drab story.

# Back-Stories

Have you ever noticed that owners of antique shops have a tendency to trap you for what seems like hours, telling you the story behind every piece of furniture in their shops, adding proof to the notion that there's a story behind everything. This should certainly be true for your story.

Your characters have a past—the reasons for the who, why, what, and where of their lives—that needs to be explored. Everyone (and everything) has a back-story. It's your job to explore and relate these back-stories in a structured and useful way.

# Flashbacks and Cut-Scenes

Anytime action is taking place outside the current point of view (in location or time), it's appropriate to cut to another scene, hence the name *cut-scenes*. A *flashback* is a cut-scene of a special type, usually in the form of a memory from a different point of view. For example, the character might remember something that happened in the past, something that is relevant to his quest. Think of a flashback as a momentary break in the action of the main story.

However, cut-scenes can break the flow of the story to a greater degree. Think of a cut-scene like this: While describing your day to a person, you stop midway and allow your buddy to tell you about his day up to the time that you two met. The story continues with the two of you together for the remainder of the day.

By taking two different points of view (yours and your friend's), you have most effectively used cut-scenes. By relating the stories of individual major characters, you can weave their individual stories together as the climax approaches and develop a strong relationship between the characters and reader.

# Foreshadowing

Remember back to when you were a child. Perhaps you were playing in a field and tripped over a small rock, only to come face to face with a huge, scary garden snake (remember, you were a kid then, so every creature was huge and scary). You were so frightened by the experience that you could never look at a snake again without fear. Now, you find yourself standing knee deep in a pit of snakes (garden snakes at that), paralyzed and praying for some higher power to save your life.

Another person might not understand your fear—they're just garden snakes. But they are witnessing the scene from their perspective; they did not have the horrible experience of your childhood. That's where foreshadowing comes in handy. You can use *foreshadowing* to reveal the reason behind something (in this case, you might show the person standing in the pit of snakes, remembering his childhood experience through the use of cut-scenes).

Here's another example of foreshadowing. Imagine that a story's main character is standing in front of a bomb, wire cutters in hand. Two wires stand between victory and death. Thinking back (foreshadowing), the hero remembers the bomb-diffusing class he took last year at the YMCA; thankfully, he chooses the correct wire (thanks, the reader assumes, to the class).

# Don't Say It—Experience It

You need to immerse readers in the details of a story. You want readers to see the whole scene; you want them to imagine that they are experiencing what they are reading.

Here is an example of what I'm talking about: Jane opens the front door. There is a light wind, and she can smell the flowers in her garden. She remembers planting those flowers many years ago. The sun begins to rise, and she shades her eyes as she looks across the street at something that is moving.

Now, read this next paragraph, which is a rewrite of the previous one: As Jane opens the door, a slight breeze caresses her, carrying with it the light scent of roses. The soft, sweet smell triggers long lost memories of when she and her young daughter worked together to plant those lovely flowers. Those days are long past; her daughter is grown and has moved on with a life of her own. The morning sun begins to peek over the horizon, casting a glorious shade of yellow over the street. Jane, lost in her memories, instinctively raises her hand to shield her eyes. From across the way, she catches a glimpse of a figure moving behind the bushes.

Although both paragraphs say basically the same thing, the second one provides more detail. As you can see, in a small space, you can convey numerous details about a character's past and bring the reader closer to "experiencing" the events (you can build the reader's relationship with the character as well).

# Harnessing Emotion

Emotion plays a major part in our daily lives, and in order to write a compelling story, you need to use emotions to their full potential. If you're having trouble doing so, just image yourself in the same situation that your story's character is in. Don't worry, no one will see you doing this, so just get out of that seat and into the role! If your character is angry, experience it yourself and then make that emotion obvious in the story (don't be afraid to do the same with a sad or gloomy emotion).

Anger and sorrow are two of the most powerful emotions you can harness, and learning to use them correctly is essential. To see what I mean, consider the movie *Titanic*. Now, truthfully, how many of you teared up when the hero, Jack, was finally released into his watery resting place?

Take the movie *The Fifth Element*. In that movie, the sly and villainous Zorg was so evil that you gritted your teeth every time you saw his ugly mug. If this guy were for real, you'd be jumping in line with everyone else to kick him in the rear! Now, imagine that same evil guy, only a little kinder—he doesn't provoke as much emotion, does he?

The major emotions you'll want to use in your story are as follows:

- Anger
- Sorrow
- Happiness
- Fear
- Excitement
- Humiliation
- Depression

# Studying the Greats

Before embarking on your story-writing journey, I first suggest you do a little research. The best way to learn how to write a good story is to read stories written by other people, stories by authors who understand how important it is to use emotion, concentrate on detail and realism, and who present it all to you in a manner that keeps you glued to a book until you read the last page.

Which authors, you ask? Since I am stuck on the fantasy theme, how about J.R.R. Tolkien and Thomas Donaldson. Their writing methods are so ingenious that they can make the tiniest details explode into life, filling your head with wondrous images of distant lands filled with magic and mayhem.

Each author has his own style. J.R.R. Tolkien effectively uses cutaways to slowly introduce you to the story's characters one by one and to lead them (and you) through their trials and tribulations all the way to a major event. At that point, he immediately switches to the next major character, leaving you wondering what happened to the first (in a cliffhanger sort of way). Once the characters are introduced and you're left wondering what happened to them all, he brings them together and explains what has occurred.

This method of writing keeps readers guessing all the time, plus it forces them to always be wondering what happened to the other characters. If you haven't had a chance to read any of Tolkien's works, do yourself a favor and find a copy of *The Hobbit* or *The Lord of the Rings* trilogy.

The next author, whom I highly recommended earlier, is Stephen R. Donaldson. His style of dressing up even the smallest details creates a story so intriguing that you can actually imagine you're there along with the hero, struggling with this character until the final moment of glory when the story comes to its ultimate conclusion. One of his greatest fantasy forays is the *Chronicles of Thomas Covenant* series, mentioned earlier in this chapter.

It's hard to relate these stories to games at times, and it goes without saying that some games have better stories than others do. Look at the *Final Fantasy* series created by Squaresoft; they all have huge and intriguing stories, plus the benefit of having the player act as the hero (or at times multiple heroes). Their method of cutaway storytelling is similar to Tolkien's: Introduce a character, then switch to the next, and later come back to end the story with all the characters together. You, too, can write amazing stories using cutaway techniques.

# Applying Stories to Games

While writing a story is one thing, applying it to your game is another. Game stories don't progress in the same way; instead, they progress section by section. The player of the game becomes the hero, and it becomes harder to create the story from an outside viewpoint.

For this reason, you need to write your stories based around the player (a first-person viewpoint). Keep in mind that if you write a story in a different point of view (which for all purposes is better for the story), you must decide later on how to change it to a first-person point of view.

Dialogue is also different. Whereas a story has a set dialogue, a game can have dialogue that changes, depending on the choices of the player. These choices might even change the outcome of your story, in either a minor or a major way.

The best way to convert your story (or even start the story) for game use is to take a small portion and experiment. First, break it into its major components: dialogue, plot, and flow. Remember, the flow of a story in a game is based on the actions the player takes, not on a flow developed by the author.

# Enveloping the Player

The biggest thing to remember is that the story must wrap around the player—that is, the player should be involved in all aspects of story. This means that you should write from a first-person point of view. Everything happens around the player, and you should never let the player experience anything beyond his own perceptions.

It does help, however, to relate those portions of the story outside the player's perceptions within a cut-scene. Although the player, in all reality, does not have a way of knowing what is happening across the world, a cut-scene might reveal the actions of another character (one who plays a major or supporting role).

Remember that the player's actions are the driving force behind the story's movement, so make sure that the player experiences all aspects of the story.

# Breaking Up the Plot

The plot represents the major events in a story. However, how different players move from plot point to plot point might differ. As illustrated in Figure 3.5, it doesn't matter what the player does, just as long as he reaches the plot points. If you properly convey the story's situations, players can experience the whole story just as though it was created at their own pace.

One way to accomplish this is to use *scenes,* which are a preset series of events. For example, after you open the locked chest hidden in the temple, a scene begins in which you must escape the now-crumbling temple. This scene covers an entire plot

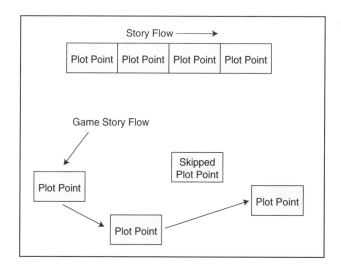

**Figure 3.5**

*Although the story plots are linear, the author can break them up and separate them as the game develops.*

point—the point at which you found the chest and must escape the device of the self-destructing template. Every player must go through the same sequence, as it is a major plot point.

Not to confuse you, but scenes can also be cinematic cut-scenes that reveal portions of the story. For example, if you open the hidden chest, the game-play stops, and the player is treated to a full-motion movie of his or her character narrowly escaping death from the collapsing temple.

# Linear and Nonlinear Story Lines

Games rarely have a clean-cut beginning-to-end story line. Although the main plot is always there, subplots are introduced that pepper up the experience, even though they might have nothing to do with the main plot. The player might not experience these subplots, but adding them gives your game the added replay value it needs to keep players coming back for more.

Also, stories can be *dynamic*. That is, the story can change as the game goes on, based on the player's actions. Heck, there can even be multiple endings to a story that always starts the same. How do you handle these multiple ends? By writing them, of course!

If you're writing a story from scratch, keep notes and mark positions in the story that represent a change in the plot. You then follow this branch, conveying the viewpoint created by the player's potential decisions. As you branch off, continue to write the story, keeping in mind that the player will alter something or other that will change the remainder of the story.

During the course of writing a nonlinear (or even a linear) storyline, you might find it helpful to track the branches, much like I did in Figure 3.6. At every plot point, I branch off to possible outcomes. This branching outline continues until all the plot points are outlined.

Of course, I'm assuming that the story is linear, flowing from beginning to end, and that it is pretty much laid out by the author. Nonlinear stories, on the other hand, don't depend on a beginning-to-end flow. In these stories, the end can always be within range, but not yet achievable (or it's too difficult to handle at this point). With nonlinear stories, the games twist in ways that don't provide a good story experience unless all aspects of the game are searched for and discovered.

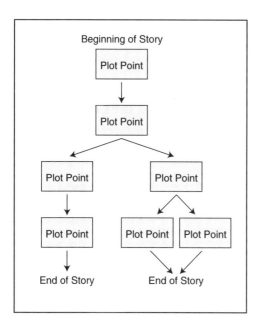

Beginning of Story

Plot Point

Plot Point

Plot Point

Plot Point

Plot Point

Plot Point

Plot Point

End of Story

End of Story

**Figure 3.6**

*It helps to track the plot points in your story, especially if they branch off.*

# Dialogue

Unlike in a book, dialogue in a game is usually verbal; there's very little (if any) inner dialogue. For that reason, a story that uses more verbal dialogue is essential. You can effectively convey feelings or thoughts to the player through the use of foreshadowing and flashbacks.

When it does come time for verbal dialogue, you need to separate it from the text of the main story. The purpose here is to form a movie-script–like breakdown of every possible conversation that can take place in your game. If you're creating a clear-cut game, where everything is the same every time the game is played, this separation of dialogue is a simple task—the dialogue remains the same no matter what happens.

But what about dynamic dialogue? The conversation changes based on the possible decisions made by the player. Just as your story can branch off, so can the dialogue. At every conversational point in the game, it pays to write the text based on the choices that were made earlier.

Imagine that in a game, you meet a conceited store clerk. You praise him about his charm, and you purchase a rare weapon at a good price. However, your language offends him, and rather than receive your praise and purchase, he prefers to teach you a few, new words in his native tongue. He becomes so offended by your further choice of words that he has you arrested! How will that change your story?

# Involving the Design Document

Don't forget about your design document! Remember those story-related sections you have to fill in? Now is the time to take the story, individual plot points, and dialogue, and put those into their appropriate positions within the design document.

Later on in the game's creation (specifically when it comes to map design, scripting, and characters conversing), you'll need to start referencing these story components from the design document. The locations in which the players can visit during their travels need to be related using graphics that help convey their respective descriptions in the story. Using a 3-D engine such as the one developed in Chapter 12, "Creating 3-D Graphics Engines," and Chapter 13, "Mixing 2-D and 3-D Graphics Engines," is perfect for your map needs.

As for scripting and characters' dialogue, using the methods developed in Chapter 14, "Implementing Scripts," and Chapter 16, "Controlling Players and Characters," is perfect for relaying the dialogue and controlling the flow of the story in the game.

# Wrapping Up Stories

Stories play a major part in role-playing games, and a good story is what makes certain games stand out more than others. Think back to the two best role-playing games you've played and compare the stories to the two worst games you've played. I'll bet many of the differences are related to the stories! You want your game to be one that players fondly remember.

In this chapter, you discovered the basic structure and guidelines for writing stories and how to convey those stories in your game. As I said earlier, a good story is what makes certain games, and using the information in this chapter, you can enhance your stories. In addition to using the information in this chapter, I suggest picking up a book on writing short stories. I find that short stories get right to the point of the story, thus holding my interest (refer to Appendix C, "Recommended Reading," for one such book).

# Part Three

# Programming Basics

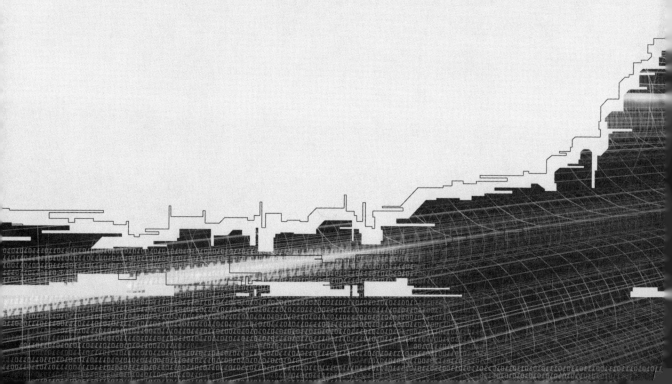

# CHAPTER 4

# STARTING WITH C++

You've been reading the newest books, browsing the latest magazines, and downloading all the code from the Internet that you can get your hands on. With so many resources out there, you've finally decided to take the plunge and learn C++. Let met tell you, it's going to be one heck of a ride, but it'll be worth every penny of it.

With C++, you're thrown into a whole new dimension of programming. Don't worry, you're still able to rely on the standard C code you've grown to know and love (C++ merely builds on C), but you now have at your fingertips the enhanced features that C++ provides.

Features like object-oriented programming enable you to create modular code you can use over and over in your different projects, all with little to no recoding. Other features include useful new keywords, enhanced function-calling capabilities, structure handling, and so many more additions that I could go on forever!

While most beginners look at the most advanced features of C++ first, the only real way to learn is to start at the bottom with what you already know in C. With the help of this chapter, you can use C++ in a step-by-step manner, getting the easiest stuff first and then moving on to the more advanced topics. Before you know it, you'll be a C++ expert!

In this chapter, you do the following:

- Learn about object-oriented programming
- Work with functions and variables
- Take advantage of new keywords and features
- Find out about constructing and using classes
- Use advanced structures

# Introducing C++

C++ is an object-oriented language, so you need to think in those terms. *Object-oriented programming*, or OOP for short, involves creating program code that enables you to group sets of instructions into packages known as *objects*. An object can represent anything: your player character, a weapon, or even the world. Although these

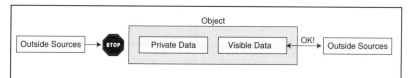

**Figure 4.1**

*An object contains internal information that outside sources can, or cannot, access.*

objects "know" only about themselves, they are constructed so that outside objects can work with them. That is, the data within these objects is self-contained and is shared only through exposure, which means that an object hides its data, except for the data that outside sources are allowed to access (as illustrated in Figure 4.1).

A world object, for example, takes care of only itself, but if I want to know the temperature at a specific point on the globe, I ask the world object for this information. A player character object, on the other hand, might be able to tell me its health or its position in the world.

Object-oriented programming introduces a whole new way of structuring your code, and learning how to cope with this change does take time. You're not only dealing with OOP, but also with C++ in general. With so much to take in, where can you start? How about with what you already know, C, and building up from that.

# Moving from C to C++

C++ is considered a superset of C, with C++ bringing you a bunch of new object-oriented features and enhancements to existing C coding methods. You don't have to use the new features, but it helps a lot to be familiar with them.

First, instead of using the .c extension, C++ source files use the .cpp extension (as do all the source files included with this book). All header files still use the .h extension. Most compilers will automatically compile the code as C++ because of the extension, but please make sure this is the case with your specific compiler.

Probably the most obvious place to start is with the new features that C++ gives you when working with functions.

> **NOTE**
>
> At this point, I'm assuming that you are familiar with the C programming language. Although you don't need to know all the idiosyncrasies of C, you should understand its basic program flow, structure usage, pointers, and other general information.

# Working with Functions

C++ brings a whole new world of defining and calling functions. The improvements are handy, but you're not required to use them all. Take your time and get familiar with these new features; they're powerful assets in your programming arsenal.

## Function Prototyping

The most important rule when working with functions in C++ is that you should provide a prototype for each one (for reasons that will soon become apparent). Appropriately, this method is called *function prototyping*.

Typically, function prototypes are placed in a header file (.h), with each source file including the header as needed. For example, say that you want a function that adds two numbers. It takes two numbers as arguments and returns a summed number, all using a long data type. Here's what your function prototype and code might look like:

> **NOTE**
>
> *Function prototyping* is the method of predefining a function-calling convention so that other program code calling on that function knows how to use it. This function prototype includes return data types and calling arguments.

```
// Function prototype - placed inside a header file (.h)
long AddNumbers(long Argument1, short Argument2);


// The actual function - placed inside a source file (.cpp)
long AddNumbers(long Argument1, short Argument2)
{
   return Argument1 + Argument2;
}
```

Instead of declaring variable names in the function prototypes, you can specify only their data types, leaving the variable naming to the actual function code, as in the following:

```
// Function prototype
long AddNum(long, long);


// Function code
long AddNum(long Num1, long Num2)
{
   return Num1 + Num2;
}
```

Previously with C, you didn't really have to prototype a function in order to call it. The compiler merely created the prototypes, figuring out the arguments and return types as best it could. Why then do you have to prototype all your functions? There are a few reasons why, the first being something called *default function argument values*.

# Default Function Argument Values

Function arguments can now have default values assigned to them, which saves you time and space because you don't have to type frequently used argument values. For example, say that you have a financial program that takes a loan amount and adds an interest percentage to it.

Suppose that the standard loan amount is $10,000 and the interest rate is normally set at eight percent. You'll want to prototype the function to use the default values for the arguments. Here's what the sample prototype looks like:

```
float AddInterest(float Amount=10000.0, float Interest=0.08);
```

You can see in the preceding function prototype that Amount has a default value of 10000.0 and Interest has its default value set at 0.08, both of which the compiler will substitute if the calling function does not include it.

> **TIP**
>
> Place default argument values only in the function prototype. You don't need to place them in the actual function.

Here's the function in use, along with the different methods of calling it:

```
// Function prototype
float AddInterest(float Amount=10000.0, float Interest=0.08);

// The actual function - no need to add default values to line
float AddInterest(float Amount, float Interest)
{
   return Amount * Interest;
}

main()
{
   float Amount;
   Amount = AddInterest(30000.0, 0.07); // Figure $30,000 at 7%
   Amount = AddInterest(20000.0);       // Figure $20,000 at 8%
   Amount = AddInterest();              // Figure $10,000 at 8%
}
```

**CAUTION**

If you omit a value, leaving the compiler to use the default, you have to omit the remaining values as well. In the AddInterest example, if you omit Amount, you must also omit Interest (and any other arguments that follow).

The only problem with this is that all following arguments must also have default values assigned, or the compiler will complain. Take the following function prototype, for example:

```
float AddInterest(float Amount = 10000.0f, float Interest);
```

Because no default value for Interest is provided, the compiler will again complain if you call AddInterest with less than two values:

```
AddInterest(10.0f);
```

## Function Overloading

While assigning default argument values is a good reason why you should prototype all functions, probably the biggest reason is the introduction of function overloading.

With function overloading, you can provide many functions that share the same name but differ in their arguments. In this way, you can construct two (or more) functions that share the same name but accept data provided in different ways.

**NOTE**

*Function overloading* is the method of providing multiple prototypes of the same function, each with a different set of calling arguments.

For example, you can construct one function that takes a few individual variables as arguments, or those variables can be wrapped in a structure and have a pointer to that structure passed to a second function of the same name.

Overloading ensures that the compiler knows what functions to call. In Figure 4.2, notice that the object in the middle (compiler) poses questions and the arrows show possible functions to call with the same name.

**NOTE**

Internally, compilers encode function names with a list of their argument types as a way to easily distinguish one function from another of the same name. This encoding is called *name decoration* or *name mangling*.

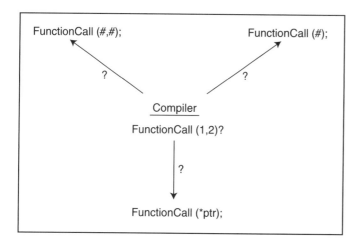

**Figure 4.2**

*Functions can have the same name but different argument lists. Prototyping functions ensures that the compiler doesn't get them mixed up.*

Look at the following bit of code, which prototypes and defines two functions that add numbers, both using the same function name (with different arguments):

```
// Function prototypes

// Add 2 numbers
long AddNumbers(long Num1, long Num2);

// Add an array of numbers
long AddNumbers(long *NumArray, long NumOfNums);

// Function code
long AddNumbers(long Num1, long Num2)
{
   return Num1 + Num2;
}


long AddNumbers(long *NumArray, long NumOfNums)
{
   long Result, i;

   Result = 0;
   while(NumOfNums--)
      Result += NumArray[i];

   return Result;
}
```

These two functions can coexist in a C++ program because of function overloading. The compiler will distinguish which function to call based on the arguments you pass to the function. So, the following two functions calls are valid:

```
Result = AddNumbers(10, 20);      // Result = 30
long Array[5] = { 10, 20, 30, 40, 50 };
Result = AddNumbers(Array, 5);    // Result = 150
```

## Inline Functions

Programmers are stuck with the old expression, to gain speed you must sacrifice space, and vice versa. You can give your code a slight increase in speed a couple of ways—but at the cost of a bigger executable. One of these ways is to signify functions as *inline*.

By preceding your function declarations with the keyword `inline`, the compiler will place an actual copy of the function code at the calling location rather than push everything on the stack and call the function (as in Figure 4.3). This means that if you call the function five times, the function code will be inserted into the executable five times at the calling locations.

Here's an example that uses an inline function to add two numbers:

```
inline long AddNumbers(long Num1, long Num2);

long AddNumbers(long Num1, long Num2)
{
   return Num1 + Num2;
}

main()
{
   long Result;
   Result = AddNumbers(10, 20); // Code to AddNums inserted here
   Result = AddNumbers(11,  6); // Code to AddNums inserted here
   Result = AddNumbers(1,  13); // Code to AddNums inserted here
}
```

Although this method increases the execution speed a little, sometimes it's just not worth implementing. Besides, some compilers will cut inline declarations out during the optimization process, so there's not much call for them.

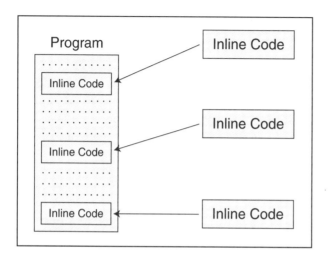

**Figure 4.3**

*Inline functions are inserted into the compiled code, thus increasing the speed of execution and the resulting file size.*

# Working with Variables

Along with adding new function-calling capabilities, variables were also given a leg-up in C++. Although not as handy as some of the previous features might seem to be, these enhancements to variables hold their own.

## Variable Declaration

The biggest improvement is that you can now declare a variable anywhere in your code rather than at the beginning of the code block. With this capability, you can also declare a variable data type while you are setting its value, as in the following example:

```
long SomeFunction(long Num1, long Num2)
{
  long Result;  // accessible to entire function

  if(Num1 < Num2) {
    long AddResult;  // accessible to next two lines
    AddResult = Num1 + Num2;
    Result = AddResult;
  } else {
    long SubResult = Num1 - Num2;  // accessible to next line
    Result = SubResult;
  }
```

```
SubResult = 0;   // ERROR - out of declaring code-block

return Result;
}
```

You can see that I declared AddResult in the conditional block right before using it, and I declared and set the SubResult variable as well. Both are valid methods and completely allowable, except for the one line I commented. You can see from my remark that there's an error, which I explain next.

## Scope and Precedence

The preceding example introduces *variable scope*. Variables declared are retained only inside the scope of their declaration. So a variable declared at the start of a function is accessible throughout it, while one declared inside a conditional block is invalid outside the block (as shown in Figure 4.4). A declaration must precede its usage and remain in scope.

In the preceding example, Result is declared at the top of the function, making Result accessible throughout the entire function. But AddResult and SubResult are not. Those variables are accessible only within the conditional blocks in which they are defined. Trying to access either of those values outside their scope will cause an error, as seen in the comment line in the preceding function.

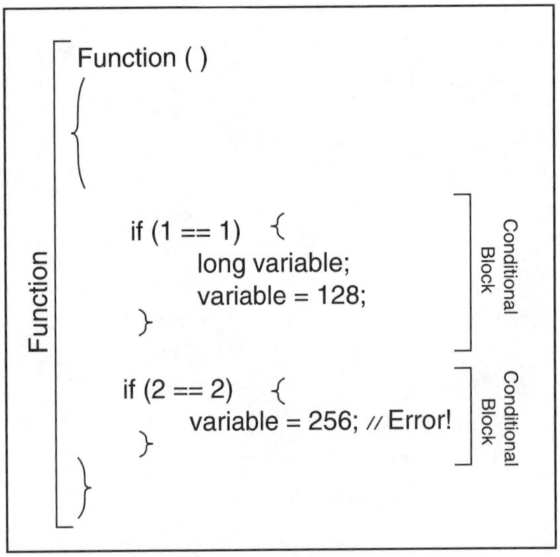

**Figure 4.4**

*The variable is valid only within its declaring conditional block. Trying to access it outside this block causes an error.*

Because of variable scope, at times you might have a global variable with the same name as a local variable. Just as in C, the local variable takes precedence. In C++, you can explicitly tell the compiler to use the global variable by using the scope resolution operator (defined as two consecutive colons) prefixed to the variable in question, as in the follow example:

```
long Result;        // Global variable

long SomeFunction(long Num1, long Num2)
{
  long Result;            // Local variable
  Result = Num1 + Num2;   // Local variable = Num1 + Num2
  // Note the two colons in the next line of code
  ::Result = Num1 + Num2; // Global variable = Num1 + Num2
  Result += ::Result;     // Local = Global

 return Result;
}
```

Precedence also works with functions, but it may not be readily apparent why at this point. Just keep the idea of precedence in mind until later in this chapter.

## Static Variables

Variables take space, and you want to preserve as much space as you can, but what about those times when you need to keep track of a variable over multiple function calls? Because of scope issues, a variable loses its value whenever its scope is lost. Take a look at this example:

```
long IncreasePeopleCount()
{
  long NumberOfPeople = 0;
  NumberOfPeople += 1;
  return NumberOfPeople;
}
```

**CAUTION**

The only drawback is that you can't have multiple variables with the same names in different scopes and use those variables together. For example, if you have a global variable called Result and you define Result at the top of a function and then again within a conditional block, only the conditional block and global Result are accessible.

For this, you might find it easier to prefix a global variable with g_ to indicate the variable as such. This is part of a coding standard called *Hungarian Notation*, which is the method of prefixing a variable name with specific letters to signify its data type and/or scope.

```
main()
{
  long Num;
  Num = IncreasePeopleCount();  // Num = 1;
  Num = IncreasePeopleCount();  // Num = 1;
}
```

This example has a function that tries to keep track of a number (some number of people to be exact). The only problem is that NumberOfPeople is always reset to 0 whenever the function is called. Of course, you could define that variable globally, but since you only want that variable associated with that specific function, you could instead declare the variable as static:

```
static long NumberOfPeople = 0;
```

By prefixing the variable declaration with the keyword static, you informed the compiler to maintain the variable's value, even after losing scope. The value you assigned the variable during the declaration is the starting value, and you are allowed to modify it in any way after that.

Now, each time you call IncreasePeopleCount (this time with a static variable), you get an incremental count, as in the following:

```
main()
{
  long Num;
  Num = IncreasePeopleCount();  // Num = 1;
  Num = IncreasePeopleCount();  // Num = 2;
  Num = IncreasePeopleCount();  // Num = 3;
}
```

## Protecting with Const

What about those unscrupulous functions that try their best to mess with your variables? For those guys, you have the power of const at your disposable. By declaring a variable (or even function!) with the const keyword, you tell the compiler that the variable is strictly read-only, as illustrated in Figure 4.5.

The only way to write a value to a variable protected by the const keyword is when you actually declare the variable, as in the following (notice the error trying to set the value afterwards):

```
const long ReadOnlyVariable = 10;  // Assign the value 10
ReadOnlyVariable = 20;  // Error! Read-only!
```

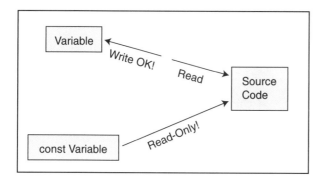

**Figure 4.5**

*Variables protected by* const *in their declaration can only be read, not written to.*

Using const also pertains to function arguments, so when you pass a non-const variable to a function, that function in return can classify the variable as const and thus protect it, but only within the function's code block. Here are a couple of examples to get you going:

```
main()
{
  const long Var = 10;
  long i;

  Var = 20;  // Error!  Is read-only
  SomeFunction(i);
}

void SomeFunction(const long Val)
{
  Val = 10;  // Error!  Is read-only
}
```

# New Keywords and Enhancements

Past frustrations with C features led to some great enhancements and additions that were included in C++. The biggest problems were allocating and deallocating memory, referencing enumerated lists, and depending on NULL being a consistent value among different compilers. The list goes on, but these are the major problems that I want to address.

Again, although you do not have to use these enhancements, they sure do make your coding easier. With the enhancements you're about to learn, you'll have no reasons to ever go back to the old methods!

> **NOTE**
>
> C++ isn't just some add-ons to an existing language; it's a complete standard adopted by every company that markets C++ compilers. Although you can still find a little discrepancy in some compilers, it's safe to assume that they all stick to the standard.

## Memory Allocation

The computer's memory is where everything is held, program code, graphics, sound effects, and what have you. Now, it's time for you to get a piece of the pie and grab hold of some memory for your own use.

Allocating memory is new in C++. You now have access to the super-intelligent new and delete operators. These two babies will allocate any type of memory, whether it's a single data type (such as char, long, or float), class, or structure—and all with the same call!

To allocate memory, use the new operator, which takes this form:

```
void *Ptr = new DataType;  // for a single element
void *Ptr = new DataType[NumElements];  // for multiple array
```

Ptr is the pointer to the memory you are allocating, while DataType is the type of data you are requesting (as well as an optional array size). The pointer can be cast into anything, usually the same as the data type you are requesting.

> **NOTE**
>
> If it was unable to allocate memory, new will return a NULL value. If non-NULL, new returns the pointer to the newly allocated memory, which is cast to the data type allocated.

For example, say that you want to allocate an array of 10 long values, 100 structures (called sMyStruct), a single float value, and an array of 20 pointers:

```
long *Ptr1 = new long[10];
sMyStruct *Ptr2 = new sMyStruct[100];
float *Ptr3 = new float;  // single float value
char *Ptr4 = new char*[20];
```

All memory you allocate using new needs to be released in order to free the system resources. You accomplish freeing this memory with the delete operator. Since C++ is doing the hard work for you, just call delete with the pointer to the allocated memory.

The only catch here is that, if the memory allocated was an array, you need to append a pair of open and close square brackets after the delete keyword. Take a look at the following code bit, which shows how to release the preceding allocated memory:

```
delete[] Ptr1;    // long[10]
delete[] Ptr2;    // sMyStruct[100]
delete Ptr3;      // float - no brackets
delete[] Ptr4;    // char*[20]
```

As an added bonus and to make your life a little easier, it becomes possible to call delete on a memory pointer that is set to NULL. Doing so saves you the trouble of having to check the pointer before freeing it. For example, the following code bit is valid:

> **TIP**
>
> **In order to allocate a multidimensional array, such as** long[5][10][20], **you must declare the pointer a little differently:**
>
> ```
> long (*Ptr)[10][20];
> Ptr = new long[5][10][20];    // allocate
> delete[] Ptr;    // free
> ```
>
> **If you're trying to allocate an array of pointers, then simply do this:**
>
> ```
> char **Pointers = NULL;
> Pointers = new char*[10];    // array of 10 char * pointers
> delete [] Pointers;    // make sure to delete it!
> ```

```
char *DataPtr = NULL;
delete DataPtr;
```

## NULL and Enum

While not readily apparent, some other smaller changes have occurred with existing C functions. Previously, NULL could have been any variable that the compiler's manufacturer picked, but with C++, NULL is always 0 (although it still helps to use the macro NULL).

Also, an enumerated list is even easier to work with because you don't have to prefix the usage with the enum keyword anymore. For example, you can do the following:

```
enum Numbers {
    First = 1,
```

```
    Second,
    Third,
    Tenth = 10
};
short Value = Second;   // equals 2
```

You can see that the last line does not cast to
the enumeration because the compiler figured
the enumeration part out for you. What a boon!

**NOTE**

As always, enum values are of
the int data type, so be sure
to cast to the appropriate
data type when storing one.

# Classes

Drum roll please . . . introducing the biggest feature in C++—*classes*! Being an
object-oriented language, C++ deals with classes as objects. These objects are self-
contained, each one having its own set of data and functions with which to work,
thus making these objects portable and highly reusable.

You can think of a class as being
a C structure on steroids. You
declare a class much like a structure, first with the keyword class
and then with the actual name
of the class you are defining.
The class data is then enclosed
within a pair of brackets. Here's
an example of an empty class
declaration:

**NOTE**

Notice that I prefix all class names with
the lowercase letter c. Notice too that
Hungarian Notation (and thus Microsoft)
uses an uppercase C instead. I find this style
confusing with certain class names, such as
CHitPoints, because the C blends in with the
first letter of the class name. The same goes
for my structure names; they are prefixed
with a lowercase letter s, as in sMyStructure.

```
class cClassName
{
};
```

One of the major differences between a class and a structure is that with a class,
you can protect the data within from being exposed (visible to outside code), as
Figure 4.6 shows.

For example, if I create the following, you can see that the three declared variables
are accessible from anywhere:

```
struct sMyStructure
{
```

```
    long Var1, Var2, Var3;
};

main()
{
    sMyStructure TestStruct;

    TestStruct.Var1 = 1;
    TestStruct.Var2 = 2;
    TestStruct.Var3 = 3;
}
```

Although doing this might seem desirable, what about those times when you have a crucial value stored in a variable that you don't want anything to mess with? With C++, you can tell exactly what data can be accessed from outside the class.

> **TIP**
>
> **I suggest that you always forward-reference classes (just as you would any variable) inside a header file (.h). Do this by inserting the keyword** class, **followed by the name of the class, as shown here:** class cClassName;.
>
> **In this manner, the compiler knows that a class by that name does exist and can be used before it is declared.**

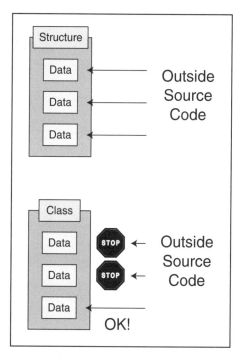

**Figure 4.6**

*Structures allow free access to internal data, while classes do not.*

# Class Visibility

You limit access to class contents *(class visibility)* by using three keywords: public, private, and protected. *Public* data is freely accessible from outside the class. *Private* data is restricted to the class itself; nothing outside can access it.

Last is *protected* data, which is almost the same as private—nothing outside the class can access the data, but classes derived from it can. Ooops! I'm getting ahead of myself again; I'll get to derived classes in a moment.

When referring to the data enclosed within a class, I'm referring to variables and functions. Yes, that's right—functions as well. Internal functions can be executed by outside program code or used internally only from within the class.

Look back at the empty class (cClass) I created; you can add the visibility keywords, plus start listing variables and functions under them:

```
class cClassName
{
  public:
    // Place public variables and functions here
    long m_PublicVar;
    long PublicFunction();

  private:
    // Place private variables and functions here
    long m_PrivateVar;
    long PrivateFunction();

  protected:
    // Place protected variables and functions here
    long m_ProtectedVar;
    long ProtectedFunction();
};
```

You can now instance this class just like a structure and begin accessing data within it, but remember that some of the data is protected. The following code bit shows you what can and can't be accessed:

```
cClassName MyClass;

MyClass.m_PublicVar = 10;      // OK!
MyClass.PublicFunction();      // OK!
MyClass.m_PrivateVar = 11;     // Not acceptable
```

```
MyClass.PrivateFunction();      // Not acceptable
MyClass.m_ProtectedVar = 12;    // Not acceptable
MyClass.ProtectedFunction();    // Not acceptable
```

How do you then access those protected functions and variables? Only code from within the same class can access those protected variables and functions (as shown in Figure 4.7). Some examples of this are coming up.

**TIP**

Just as you prefix global data with g_, you prefix class variables with m_ to signify that they belong to a class. Again, this is standard Hungarian Notation.

# Class Variables and Functions

There's not much to defining a variable or function inside a class, as you previously saw. For variables, just inserting the variable declaration under the appropriate access keyword handles it. In the preceding class declaration, you can see that I defined three variables.

Only the public data is accessible to outside code, such as the case with m_PublicVar and PublicFunction. Attempting to access anything else from outside will generate an error. The only way to access the other data is within the class, which is usually in the form of a function.

Just as you define the visibility of variables in the class, so do you with functions. Function declarations are identical to all other declarations; they just belong to the class only. From the prior example class, you can call only PublicFunction, but internally you have access to all three functions.

From here, the next step is to write the code to the functions themselves in the .cpp source file belonging to the class. Each function you write must have the class name prefixed by two colons, as shown here:

```
long cClassName::PublicFunction(void)
```

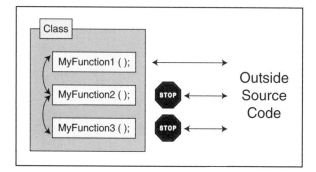

**Figure 4.7**

*A class can access its own functions, but can determine which functions can't be accessed from code outside the class.*

This addition of the colons informs the compiler that the upcoming function is part of that class. A source file might or might not contain functions contained within a class, so adding the two colons is the only way to link the functions to their respective classes (as illustrated in Figure 4.8).

The preceding function takes no arguments and returns a `long` value. Not too hard so far, so let's go on. Taking the sample class again, have each function return its respective variable, with the public function returning the sum of the three (by adding the public variable, private variable, and the return value of the protected function).

```
long cClassName::PublicFunction()
{
   return m_PublicVar + ProtectedFunction() + m_PrivateVar;
}


long cClassName::ProtectedFunction()
{
   return m_ProtectedVar;
}


long cClassName::PrivateFunction()
{
   return m_PrivateVar;
}
```

As you can see, the public function is freely accessing the other data and functions inside the class. In this way, you can alter the way a class accesses its internal data, but still present it in the same manner to outside code.

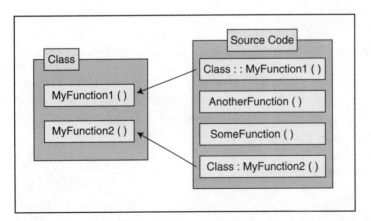

**Figure 4.8**

*Source files can contain many functions, but those functions related to classes need to be linked via colons.*

Another bonus to using functions in classes is that you can define the function inside the class declaration. Doing so is useful for smaller functions that you don't need to waste space with in the source file. The following example, which is based on the preceding code, shows what I mean:

```
class cClass
{
  public:
    long PublicFunction(void) { return m_PublicVar +          \
                       ProtectedFunction() + m_PrivateVar; }
  // rest of class declaration
};
```

# Using Static Variables and Functions

Normally, class instances have access to their own copy of internal data. If you instance a class, it has no knowledge of any other instances of it. In order to share data between classes, you must use a static variable or function, which makes it global to all instances of the class.

Start by prefixing the variable or function with the keyword static:

```
class cClassName
{
  public:
    static long m_Variable;
    static long Function();
};
```

A default value should be set for static variables in the class code portion (declared globally):

```
long cClassName::m_Variable = 100;
```

Now, just access the variable as you normally would inside an instance of that class. It will be the same value for all instances of the class, and any instance modifying it will change it for the rest (as shown in Figure 4.9).

**CAUTION**

Notice that static is used a little differently than it was previously. These differences can get confusing at times, so take care not to get the two mixed up.

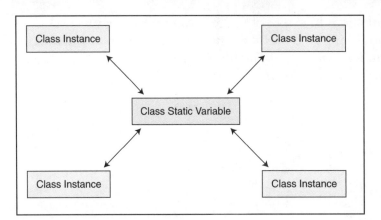

**Figure 4.9**

*A static class variable remains fixed, no matter how many class instances access the variable.*

As for functions, declaring one as static makes it accessible to all instances, but the function itself has no knowledge of the calling class instance. For this, you might want to provide the static function with a pointer to the calling class.

This example program declares both a static variable and function and then demonstrates their use.

```
class cClassName
{
  public:
    static long m_Var;
    static long Function();
};

// declare the default value of static variable
long cClassName.m_Var = 10;

long cClassName::Function()
{
  m_Var++;        // increase static value
  return m_Var;   // return it
}

main()
{
  cClassName Class1, Class2;
  printf("%lu\r\n", Class1.Function());  // prints 11
  printf("%lu\r\n", Class2.Function());  // prints 12
}
```

**CAUTION**

Remember that static functions have no knowledge of the class instances themselves. Keep that in mind while coding your classes. You can see how to use these methods effectively in later chapters.

# The Constructor and Destructor

Along with the functions you provide, every class contains two built-in functions called the *constructor* and *destructor,* which are called when an instance is created and destroyed, respectively. These declarations can be overloaded (remember function overloading!) for your use under public visibility, and they always have the same name as the class (with the deconstructor prefixed by a tilde character), as shown here:

```
class cClassName
{
  public:
    cClassName();                          // default constructor
    cClassName(long Var1, long Var2); // overloaded constructor
    cClassName(char *Data);                // overloaded constructor
    ~cClassName();                         // destructor
};

cClassName::cClassName()
{
  // do whatever class initialization here
}

cClassName::cClassName(long Var1, long Var2)
{
  // do whatever class initialization here with two variables
  // even call on the other constructor or other functions!
  cClassName();
}

cClassName::cClassName(char *Data)
{
  // And again - do whatever here
}

cClassName::~cClassName()
{
  // free whatever used data here
}
```

A constructor is called whenever the class is instanced or allocated (with new) and can be overloaded to provide multiple ways of setting up the internal data when instanced. A destructor does not take arguments and is called when out of scope or deleted. Neither of the two returns values. Here are some examples of using constructors and destructors:

```
cClassName MyClass;   // default constructor called when program
                      // is first started


main()
{
  cClassName SomeClass(10, 22);   // 1st overloaded constructor
                                  // called when main start
  cClassName My2ndClass("Hello"); // 2nd constructor called
                                  // when main starts
  cClassName *ClassPtr;           // not yet

  ClassPtr = new cClassName;      // now constructor called

  delete ClassPtr;                // destructor called now
  // My2ndClass destructor called when this function exits
}
// MyClass called now that program has terminated
```

## Operator Functions

Class functions can also take the form of operators. No, not those nice people you get when you press 0 on the phone, but operators such as add, subtract, multiply, and divide (along with others found in Table 4.1).

You need to know a few things in order to use operators. First, the return type must be the class name (using operators such as += or = that return a value to another class of the same type) or a standard data type (= for comparing a value). Second, you must use the operator keyword, followed by the operator to use. Last is the standard function argument list.

Here's a sample that uses two operators (= and +=) to manipulate an internal number:

```
class cClassName
{
  public:
    cClassName operator=(long Val);
```

```
    cClassName operator+ (long Val);
    long Value() { return m_Value; }  // return protected value

  protected:
    long m_Value;
};

// No need for return value
cClassName::operator=(long Val)
{
  m_Value = Val;
}

// returns value to another class of same type
cClassName cClassName::operator+=(long Val)
{
  m_Value += Val;
}

main()
{
  cClassName MyClass;
  MyClass = 10;
  MyClass += 20;
  printf("%lu\r\n", MyClass.Value());  // prints 30
}
```

## Table 4.1  Overloadable Operators

| + | - | * | / | % | ^ |
|---|---|---|---|---|---|
| += | -= | *= | /= | %= | ^= |
| ++ | -- | < | > | ! | = |
| & | \| | << | >> | != | == |
| &= | \|= | <= | >= | () | [] |
| && | \|\| | <<= | >>= | new | delete |

# Using the this Keyword

At times, a class needs to know a pointer to itself, and that's the purpose of the this keyword. The this keyword is a reserved pointer that every class has; as a matter of fact, it is inserted into every class function call (although invisible to you). To see what I mean, take this typical C++ class function:

```
long cClassName::SomeFunction(long Val)
{
   return Val + 10;
}
```

This function, when compiled and with the hidden argument added, looks like this:

```
long cClassName::SomeFunction(cClassName *this, long Val)
{
   return this->Val + 10;
}
```

The biggest use of this is with static functions or other functions that need a pointer to the calling class. Just pass the this pointer to a function, and use it as a reference, as shown here:

> **NOTE**
>
> You can use the this keyword in order to access internal data, but there's really no need to because the compiler does it for you. Static functions are the only functions inside a class that do not have the this keyword inserted into the argument list.

```
class cClassName
{
   public:
   cClassName() { SomeFunction(this); }
   long m_PublicVar;
};

void SomeFunction(cClassName *Ptr)
{
   Ptr->m_PublicVar = 10;
}

main()
{
   cClassName c1;  // c1.m_PublicVar now equals 10
}
```

# Class Friends

When declaring multiple classes, it sometimes becomes necessary to share information between them, but still limit their visibility to outside code. For example, if you have a protected variable in Class1 that Class2 needs access to, how do you go about using that variable without having to write a public function? And in that instance, how do you make sure that no outside code takes advantage of this newly created public function?

One simple way is by classifying variables, functions, or even entire classes as friends. You do this within the class from which you want to share data. However, this sharing of data is not mutual—a class can share data only with other functions and classes that it knows about.

For example, if the first class declares a second class as a friend, the second class has free access to the first. This does not give the first class access to the second, however, because the first class needs to be declared as a friend in the second class (as shown in Figure 4.10).

Code is worth a thousand words, so check this following bit to see what I mean:

```
class cClass1
{
    friend cClass2;     // cClass2 can access my data

    protected:
      long m_Value;

    public:
      // next line not acceptable as cClass2
      // has not declared me as a friend
      cClass1() { cClass2 MyClass;  MyClass.m_Value = 1; }
};

class cClass2
{
    // cClass1 cannot access me as it's not declared as a friend
    protected:
      long m_Value;
    public:
      // next line acceptable
      cClass2() { cClass1 MyClass; MyClass.m_Value = 2; }
};
```

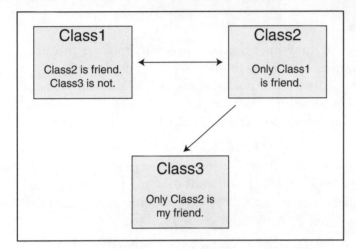

**Figure 4.10**

*Classes can allow free access to each other, but they need to be declared as friends first.*

You can see that cClass2 can access cClass1 because it is a friend, but it's not necessarily mutual. cClass1 has no access rights to cClass2 *unless* cClass2 defines cClass1 as a friend. You'll see many examples of using this "friendly" feature throughout the book.

# Derived Classes

When it comes time to add functionality to an existing class, you merely piggy-back onto it, borrowing its foundation of data and then adding your own or improving on existing functions and variables. This method of creating a new class based on an existing class's data is called *inheritance*.

With inheritance, you are actually deriving a new object from an existing one. The original class you use is called the *base class,* while the new class you are creating is called the *derived class,* as illustrated in Figure 4.11.

When you want to derive a class, define it in the following way:

```
class cDerivedClass : public cBaseClass
{
    // Derived Class Data goes here
    // This data is in addition to data already in cBaseClass
};
```

Because the original data already exists in cBaseClass, there's no need to duplicate it here; just add the new data. You can still access the base class's variables and functions, except for those in the base declared as private.

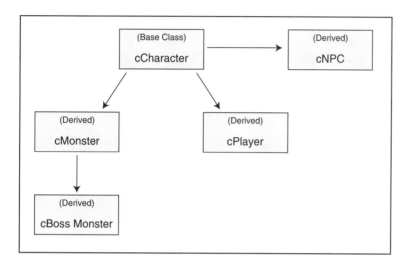

**Figure 4.11**

*Derived classes are constructed from a base class. You can also derive a class from a previously derived class.*

Here's an example of a derived class being created from a base class:

```
class cBaseClass
{
  public:
    long m_PublicVar;
};

class cDerivedClass : public cBaseClass
{
  public:
    long m_PublicVar2;
};

main()
{
  cBaseClass BClass;
  cDerivedClass CClass;
  BClass.m_PublicVar = 10;
  DClass.m_PublicVar2 = 100;
  DClass.m_PublicVar = 11;
}
```

**NOTE**

By prefixing the cBaseClass class name with the public keyword, I am telling the compiler that any further derived classes from cDeriveClass can freely access the base class's data. To protect the base class's data from further derived classes, I can use the private or protected keyword instead of public.

**CAUTION**

Private data in the base class does not become visible to a derived class, but it still exists. You accomplish this by using private visibility, and it is useful when there is a piece of crucial data that you absolutely do not want to get modified, not even by a derived class.

Functions that use a base class as an argument can use derived classes as well. Such functions simply treat the derived class as the base class and can access only the data defined in the base class, as shown here:

```
class cBase
{
  public:
    long m_Var;
};

class cDerived : public cBase
{
  public:
    cDerived(long Var) { m_Var = Var; }   // using m_Var from
                                          // inherited cBase
};

long AddValue(cBase *Base, long ToAdd)
{
  m_Var += ToAdd;   // Add the specified value to cBase m_Var
                    // even though passed class might be
                    // derived from it
}

main()
{
  cDerived MyClass(50);     // instance class, set m_Var to 50
  AddValue(&MyClass, 100); // MyClass.m_Var now equals 150
}
```

> **NOTE**
>
> This ability to call a base function from any derived (or base class) is called *polymorphism*. You'll see many examples of this throughout the book.

As I previously noted, a base class's data can be protected from further derived class access by specifying the private or protected keyword in the derived class declaration, as in the following:

> **TIP**
>
> From the last example, you can see the derived class has been passed by reference to a function, which is completely acceptable. But in order to protect data in the class from the calling function, you need to specify the class argument as a const variable in the calling function.

```
class cBaseClass { private: long Var; };
class cDerivedClass : private cBaseClass { private: long Var2; };
```

```
class cDerivedAgainClass : public cDerivedClass
{
  public:
    long GetValue() { return Var; }    // Error - can't access
};
```

In the preceding code, by declaring the cDerivedClass from cBaseClass (this time declaring the base class access as private), only instances of the cDerivedClass (and not cDerivedAgain) can access Var.

## Virtual Functions

With derived classes, there will be times when you will want to overwrite the functionality of a base class function using the derived class's function instead. For example, if you want a class to print a specific number, do the following:

```
class cBaseClass
{
  public:
    void PrintIt() { PrintNum(1); }
    void PrintNum(long Num) { printf("%lu", Num); }
};
```

When you call the cBaseClass's PrintIt function, it will print the number 1. To add better features to the base class, say print the number with a little text, you can derive a class and declare the new PrintNum function:

```
class cDerivedClass : public cBaseClass
{
  public:
    void PrintNum(long Num) { printf("The number is %lu",Num); }
};
```

If you were to instance cDerivedClass and call the PrintIt function (which in turn calls PrintNum), you might expect the output to be as follows:

```
The number is 1
```

However, instead of seeing the preceding line of text, you'll see only the number 1, which means that the base class's PrintNum function is being called instead of the derived class's PrintNum function. This is correct, because the compiler doesn't really know about the derived class's version of the PrintNum function—after all, the base class knows only about itself, not derived classes of it.

To remedy this problem, let me introduce you to virtual. By marking the function in the base class declaration as virtual, you inform the class that a derived class may or may not override the function. If the function is overridden, the class is to use the derived version.

Knowing this, you can rewrite the base class declaration as follows:

```
class cBaseClass
{
  public:
    void PrintIt() { PrintNum(1); }
    virtual void PrintNum(long Num) { printf("%lu", Num); }
};
```

Declaring your derived class (no need to declare anything as virtual) and calling PrintIt will now have the desired effect of printing the whole line of text shown previously. The compiler is merely seeing that the function has been overridden in the derived class and uses that version (as illustrated in Figure 4.12).

Later in the book, you see virtual functions put to some great use. By creating a skeleton class of sorts (one that contains the bare-bones code to define the class), you can derive the class and add better features to it.

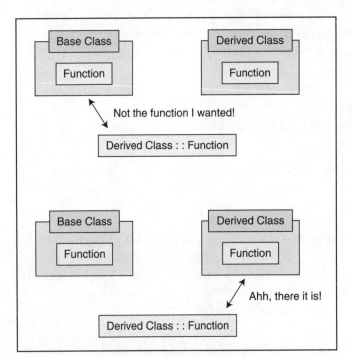

**Figure 4.12**

*Using* virtual, *the compiler can scan the functions in the base class and derived class looking for the proper one to call, which in this case, is the derived class's version.*

# Using Const with Classes

I've mentioned how the const keyword protects variables by declaring them as read-only, so now is the time to show you how you can use classes. The first way is by declaring the entire class as const, as follows:

```
const cClass MyClass(Var);
```

From now on, even the class itself can modify nothing in that class. On the other hand, if you want to declare a function as one that reads only class data, declare it as const by appending it to the function declaration:

```
long cClass::ReadValue() const
{
  return m_Value;  // Only returning the value
}
```

In fact, if you declare a class as const and then declare a function as const, the compiler will not complain as much. Doing this ensures that the compiler knows the function is not trying to modify any of the class data, thus allowing the function access to this data.

# Advanced Structures

It might seem as though structures were given the old boot with the invention of classes, but don't throw them out yet. Even structures can have functions embedded within them (including constructors and destructors), just like a class!

This point (of using embedded functions) becomes handy when you want to use a structure to contain information, but set the variables to a default value. For example, I can create the following structure that allocates its own memory and then deallocates it when destroyed:

```
typedef struct sMyStruct {
  char *Ptr;
  sMyStruct() {
    Ptr = new char[100];
  }
  ~sMyStruct {
    delete[] Ptr;
  }
} sMyStruct;
```

> **NOTE**
>
> In fact, structures are C++ classes. The only difference between a class and structure is that a structure specifies its data as public by default.

```
main()
{
    sMyStruct *MyStruct;

    MyStruct = new sMyStruct;
    MyStruct->Ptr[50] = 10;
    delete MyStruct;
}
```

Just follow the ways of the classes, and you should fully understand using advanced structures!

# Wrapping Up C++

Whew! There's a lot to C++, but at least now you have a fighting chance. As you go through the book, you'll see that I make heavy use of the techniques discussed in this chapter, so it pays to fully understand all the material. If you find yourself having trouble with code, you can always refer to this chapter.

# CHAPTER 5

# PROGRAMMING WITH WINDOWS AND APPLICATION BASICS

**M**any moons ago, developers had to rely on their DOS skills to milk their computer systems for every last drop of processing power in order to get their games to run smoothly. At that time, Windows was a business-oriented application platform, but not a viable platform for gaming.

As time went on, Windows 95 was released, and then with the release of DirectX (a product that aids programmers in the development of games), Windows blasted onto the scene of game development. With no reason to deal with the restrictions of DOS, programmers slowly worked their way to writing only Windows-supported games. So, my programming friend, you need to know the basics for programming Windows in order to survive as a programmer of games.

Tackling the subject of Windows programming is by no means an easy task, especially in this limited space. Entire volumes have been written on this topic (such as Charles Petzold's *Programming Windows, Fifth Edition,* by Microsoft Press), and I'll leave it to them to give you the level of detail that you need to fully understand the topic. In this chapter, you can find the basic information that you need to get a Windows program up and running.

In addition, because you need to start your projects on the "right foot," I cover the basics for structuring an application and tell you how to make your programming tasks a little easier.

In this chapter, you learn how to do the following:

- Think in Windows' terms
- Create your windows and deal with messages
- Use advanced Windows features
- Prepare yourself for using DirectX
- Organize the program flow of execution
- Do modular programming
- Use states and processes and handle application data
- Build an application framework and debug your programs

# Programming with Windows

You program Windows using the Win32 SDK (Windows 32-bit software development kit) and a compiler (typically C/C++). The development kit has been around as long as Windows, so the SDK is packed to the brim with functions that ease the development of both business and gaming applications.

Microsoft wanted to provide a stable development platform that everybody could understand. To that end, Microsoft created and maintains the Win32 SDK, which is a set of standards to which all its applications and development kits abide. One of the most notable things that Microsoft worked on was its *coding conventions.*

## Coding Conventions

Microsoft's coding conventions are vast (and esoteric at times), but the ones you're likely to notice are those that dictate the naming of variables and functions and that declare data types.

### Hungarian Notation

Microsoft's coding conventions include specifications on declaring variables, called *Hungarian Notation.* Named after its Hungarian creator, Charles Simonyi, this seemingly ingenious method involves prefixing variable names with specific characters that define what data type the variable is: a char, byte, long, const, class member, global variable, and so on. Table 5.1 shows several common Hungarian prefixes and an example of how to use them.

Although using Hungarian Notation might seem like a good idea, doing so makes the variable names appear unreadable at times. When dealing with Windows-related programming in this book, I tend to maintain this convention, but I don't stick to it consistently.

### Win32 Data Types

The Win32 SDK also uses predefined data types. These are just macros that you substitute for a standard data type when declaring variables, making your code smaller and at times more readable. Table 5.2 lists several of the common data type macros that you'll encounter during your programming endeavors.

## Table 5.1 Typical Hungarian Notation Prefixes

| Prefix | Data Type | Example |
|--------|-----------|---------|
| f | Boolean | `BOOL fFlag;` |
| b | Byte | `char bVariable;` |
| dw | Double word (long) | `long dwValue;` |
| h | 32-bit handle | `long hWindow;` |
| i | Integer | `int iNumber;` |
| p | Pointer | `void *pData;` |
| I | Interface | `IUnknown *IInterface;` |
| g_ | Global | `char g_GlobalVariable;` |
| m_ | Member | `short m_MemberData;` |

To use one of these data type macros, just replace the macro with your variable data type:

```
BOOL  bValue;   // Holds the value TRUE or FALSE
DWORD dwValue;  // an unsigned long value
```

## Function Naming

Typical function naming consists of words packed together, with no underscores or spaces between words, and each word is capitalized in order to separate it from other words, as in the following:

```
DWORD MyFunctionName();
```

> **NOTE**
>
> You will find the standard data types and these data macros throughout the book. Because they are interchangeable, you don't have to worry about your compiler complaining or the code breaking.

At times, however, you'll notice that this convention is broken by leaving the first letter of the function name in lowercase, as shown here:

```
DWORD myFunctionName();  // notice m in my is lowercase
```

## Table 5.2  Common Win32 Data Types

| Macro | Description |
| --- | --- |
| BOOL | A Boolean value (TRUE or FALSE) |
| BYTE | An 8-bit integer that is not signed (unsigned char) |
| DWORD | A 32-bit unsigned integer (unsigned long) |
| LONG | A 32-bit signed integer (signed long) |
| LPARAM | A 32-bit value passed as a parameter to a window procedure or callback function |
| LPCSTR | A 32-bit pointer to a constant character string |
| LPSTR | A 32-bit pointer to a character string |
| LPVOID | A 32-bit pointer to an unspecified type |
| LRESULT | A 32-bit value returned from a window procedure or callback function |
| UINT | A 32-bit unsigned integer on Win32 |
| WNDPROC | A 32-bit pointer to a window procedure |
| WORD | A 16-bit unsigned integer (unsigned short) |
| WPARAM | A value passed as a parameter to a window procedure or callback function |

I personally prefer (and use in this book) the method of every word beginning with an uppercase letter; doing so makes the code cleaner and easier to read. Another problem arises with function arguments (and sometimes data structures) in which the notation method is used in some variables and not in others, as shown here:

```
HRESULT MyFunction(
    DWORD Variable,       // where's dw?
    DWORD dwVariable2);   // here it is!
```

That's right, even Microsoft isn't able to stick to Hungarian Notation at times, which is readily apparent when you browse its SDK. You see this lapse of using the notation in Chapters 6 through 9 when you use DirectX; it's no big deal.

# Working Inside a Window

The majority of programs operate inside a *window*, the area onscreen in which text, pictures, animation, scroll bars, menus, and many other objects and information are displayed, as illustrated in Figure 5.1.

One great advantage to working with a window is that Windows does much of the lower-level processing. Most of the controls (such as buttons and edit boxes) update and draw themselves, so their content and the user's interaction with them are all that you have to worry about.

> **NOTE**
>
> A window can consume the entire screen, and this is the typical display used for games.

Generally, with little effort on your part, you can minimize or maximize windows (shrink them so that they appear as an icon on the Windows desktop or taskbar or enlarge them so that they fill up the entire screen); you can also drag them to different locations within the screen and resize them.

The whole idea of programming for Windows is to design the look of your program first (by laying out windows, buttons, edit controls, and so on) and then add the functionality. To start your own programming escapades, you'll need to first understand the basics of every Windows program—from what files need to be included with your project to what is expected of you as the programmer and from Windows' maintenance of the application.

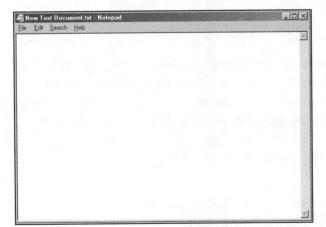

**Figure 5.1**

*A typical Windows application is contained within a window and has everything you need to interface with the application—from menus and icons to toolbars and scrollbars.*

## Including the Headers

When developing applications for Windows, you need to include header files to ensure that your compiler knows what is going on. Here is the most typical header file of the bunch (and the one you'll always use):

```
#include <windows.h>
```

It's rarely necessary to include additional library files because the default project space that Visual C/C++ creates at the start of every new application does a decent job of including the proper library files. Throughout the book, I let you know when it's time to link in additional library files or include additional header files.

## The WinMain Function

When working with a C program in DOS, the entry point of an application is the main function. This function begins executing the program. For Windows, this entry function is WinMain, which looks like this:

```
int WINAPI WinMain(
  HINSTANCE hInstance,        // Instance handle of application
  HINSTANCE hPrevInstance,    // Unused
  LPSTR lpCmdLine,            // Command line options (if any)
  int nCmdShow);              // Show window flag
```

Whenever your application is executed, it is assigned an instance handle (hInstance) that you can use to refer to the process running your program. The biggest reason for using and maintaining an instance handle is that you can have multiple instances of the application running at once, so at times, you must be able to refer to each one by its handle.

A Windows application can receive command-line options (as do DOS programs). Your application receives these command-line options in the form of a string pointer (lpCmdLine), which you can parse to your liking. You'll rarely deal with the command line when using Windows applications, however.

Last is nCmdShow, which tells you how the user configured the application to open when executed: minimized, maximized, normal size, and so on. These configurations are not mandatory; you can do what you like with the nCmdShow variable.

At this point, you can create an empty `WinMain` function as follows:

```
int WINAPI WinMain(HINSTANCE hInstance,                    \
     HINSTANCE hPrevInstance, LPSTR lpCmdLine, int nCmdShow)
{
  return 0;
}
```

From this point on, you have complete control of execution, and you're now about to start hacking away at that code and creating a Windows application. Before going any further, however, you need to understand how Windows communicates vital information to your application.

## Events and Messages

Old-school programmers probably remember the DOS days in which you had complete control of everything. Although good in some aspects, this usually meant that you spent a major chunk of your processing time scanning the input, sound, and graphics devices to see whether they needed updating.

On the flip side, Windows introduced the idea of letting the operating system inform the application when something comes up. Say that the user moves the mouse. This action creates an *event*, which Windows receives and processes. In turn, Windows sends this event to the application in the form of a *message*.

Windows has a *global queue* in which it stores all messages; Windows slowly weeds its way through them and sends them off to the applications that are running, stuffing the various messages into an *application message queue*. Inside your program is something called a *message pump* (or *message loop*) that continually scans the message queue looking for messages to process.

The message pump pulls out application messages and sends them to a function called the *window message procedure,* which is located within your program. This function processes individual messages. You don't have to deal with every message though. Some messages are discarded or passed back to Windows, where it handles the message with a default set of functions.

> **NOTE**
>
> All messages have an ID associated with them, such as WM_, which stands for window message (the majority of messages are prefixed with WM_). For example, when a user closes your application, your message procedure eventually receives a WM_DESTROY message.

Figure 5.2 demonstrates the path a message takes from the moment it is created as an event to the moment you process it via the event handler.

Once executed, your application starts receiving many messages, including just about every type that you can think of: device input, multimedia functions, Windows operations, menu navigation, buttons clicked—the list goes on. In the section "Common Messages," later in this chapter, you will learn about the messages you need to deal with at this point in your life as a programmer.

## Registering a Windows Class

Every Windows object (such as the window, button, text field, and so on) is organized and controlled by means of *classes*. Every class of objects has special properties and methods of processing, much like you see in Figure 5.3.

Many of these classes are already built into Windows, such as the push button class or edit box class. For your Windows application, you need to create a custom class structure that describes the application and basically how Windows should treat it.

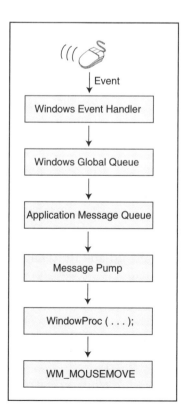

**Figure 5.2**

*A message has a long way to go from creation to completion.*

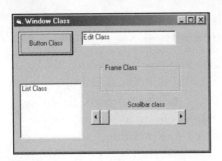

**Figure 5.3**

*Most Windows objects are classified by . . . classes! Each class is specific in its control of the object or objects it represents.*

Filling in a special structure called WNDCLASSEX with the information about your custom class and registering it with Windows does this:

```
typedef struct _WNDCLASSEX {
    UINT cbSize;              // Size of this structure
    UINT style;              // Style of window
    WNDPROC lpfnWndProc;     // Window message procedure
    int cbClsExtra;          // 0
    int cbWndExtra;          // 0
    HANDLE hInstance;        // Instance handle from WinMain
    HICON hIcon;             // Handle to application icon
    HCURSOR hCursor;         // Handle to application cursor
    HBRUSH hbrBackground;    // Handle to background brush
    LPCTSTR lpszMenuName;    // Handle to application menu
    LPCTSTR lpszClassName;   // Class name
    HICON hIconSm;           // Handle to small application icon
} WNDCLASSEX;
```

To simplify this process of creating your custom class, let me explain the basic way to use this structure. First and foremost is to set the style variable with the desired method of dealing with the application window. This field has a selection of about 11 flags that you can combine and use, but realistically you'll use only three.

These three flags are CS_CLASSDC, CS_HREDRAW, and CS_VREDRAW. The second and third flags tell Windows that you want the window redrawn anytime it's horizontal (CS_HREDRAW) or vertical (CS_VREDRAW) size changes. You commonly use CS_HREDRAW and CS_VREDRAW when creating a non-DirectX game.

CS_CLASSDC tells Windows to share the drawing resources with all windows that use the same class. This way, a single process finishes what it is drawing before the next process begins to draw. This is the flag you use when working with DirectX for graphics.

Next, you see the pointer to your message procedure (`lpfnWndProc`). This message procedure is a function you'll write later on, and one that you see in the later section "The Window Message Procedure." Moving on, you see that `hInstance` is the variable you set to the instance handle of your program (which you received from the `WinMain` function). Skipping ahead a bit, you see `lpszClassName`, which is a pointer to a string that holds the name of the class you are creating.

Throughout the `WNDCLASSEX` structure, you see several handles: the background brush, application icon, menu, and cursor. These are the default objects Windows uses to draw your application's window and associated controls. For example, if you assign an hourglass cursor in `hCursor`, your application will use the hourglass icon until the cursor is specifically changed.

Normally, the only handle that you provide is one to an application icon (you use a standard Windows object for the other handles). If you're not creating a game, the only other handle you have to worry about is the background brush, which will be the window's background color when it is redrawn.

Because you bought this book in order to learn how to create games—not learn the intricacies of Windows programming—here is the basic (and seemingly standard) setup that you use for the `WNDCLASSEX` structure. Actually, the following code shows two structures, one for games and the other for standard applications:

```
// for DirectX games, use:
WNDCLASSEX wcex = { sizeof(WNDCLASSEX), CS_CLASSDC,         \
        WindowProc, OL, OL, hInstance,                      \
        NULL, NULL, NULL, NULL,                             \
        "GameClass", NULL };

// for standard applications, use:
WNDCLASSEX wcex = { sizeof(WNDCLASSEX),                     \
        CS_HREDRAW | CS_VREDRAW,                            \
        WindowProc, OL, OL, hInstance,                      \
        LoadIcon(NULL, IDI_APPLICATION),                    \
        LoadCursor(NULL, IDC_ARROW),                        \
        (HBRUSH)GetStockObject(LTGRAY_BRUSH),               \
        NULL, "AppClass", NULL };
```

Registering your window's class is accomplished via the `RegisterClassEx` function, which takes a single parameter—the `WNDCLASSEX` structure that you've already created:

```
ATOM RegisterClassEx(CONST WNDCLASSEX *lpwcx);
```

When you finish with the application, you can (and should) unregister the class as follows:

```
BOOL UnregisterClass(
    LPCTSTR lpClassName,    // Class name to unregister
    HINSTANCE hInstance);   // Instance handle
```

Using the preceding information, you can rework your WinMain function to look something like this:

```
int WINAPI WinMain(HINSTANCE hInstance,                           \
    HINSTANCE hPrevInstance, LPSTR lpCmdLine, int nCmdShow)
{
  WNDCLASSEX wcex = { sizeof(WNDCLASSEX), CS_CLASSDC,             \
      WindowProc, 0L, 0L, hInstance,                             \
      NULL, NULL, NULL, NULL,                                    \
      "GameClass", NULL };

  // Register the class and exit on error
  if(!RegisterClassEx(&wcex))
    return FALSE;

  // Do other application stuff here

  // Unregister class
  UnregisterClass("GameClass", hInstance);

  // Exit application
  return 0;
}
```

NOTE

If it succeeds, the RegisterClassEx function returns a non-zero value; if it does not succeed, it returns 0. The ATOM return value is rarely needed.

## Creating a Window

Now that you've created and registered your class, it is time to create the actual window, which you do using the CreateWindow function:

```
HWND CreateWindow(
    LPCTSTR lpClassName,    // Class to use
    LPCTSTR lpWindowName,   // Window name (caption)
    DWORD dwStyle,          // Style of window
    int x,                  // x coordinate of window
    int y,                  // y coordinate of window
    int nWidth,             // width of window
```

```
    int nHeight,              // height of window
    HWND hWndParent,          // NULL
    HMENU hMenu,              // NULL (or menu handle)
    HANDLE hInstance,         // instance handle from WinMain
    LPVOID lpParam);          // NULL
```

This function returns a HWND variable, which is the handle to your newly created window, or NULL if there was an error. As for lpClassName, use the name of the class you've already registered and set lpWindowName with the string you want displayed as the window caption (the title of the application).

To size and position the window, fill in the nWidth, nHeight, x, and y fields; they are measured in pixels. For example, you can create a 640 x 480 window at x=0,y=0. Be sure to also set the hInstance field to the instance handle you received from WinMain.

I saved the best for last. The dwStyle field holds the settings that determine your window's appearance. The dwStyle variable can be a combination of the flags in Table 5.3.

If you want to create a window that is sizable (you can drag the edges to resize the window), use the WS_OVERLAPPEDWINDOW style. On the other hand, if you don't want the user to resize the window, use a WS_BORDER style.

> **NOTE**
>
> Typically, in games (and the majority of this book), you use WS_OVERLAPPEDWINDOW (DirectX Graphics resizes the view as it is displayed).

You can expand the previous WinMain function by adding the following:

```
// ... previous WinMain code

  // Register the class and exit on error
  if(!RegisterClassEx(&wcex))
    return FALSE;

  // Create the window (320x240 at 0,0 using overlapped style)
  HWND hWnd;  // our window's handle
  hWnd = CreateWindow("GameClass", "My Game Title",           \
      WS_OVERLAPPEDWINDOW, 320, 240, 0, 0,                    \
      NULL, NULL, hInstance, NULL);

  // Return on error creating the window
  if(hWnd == NULL)
    return FALSE;
```

## Table 5.3  CreateWindow's dwStyle flags

| Flag | Description |
| --- | --- |
| WS_BORDER | Creates a window with a thin border. |
| WS_DLGFRAME | Creates a window with a dialog box border. |
| WS_THICKFRAME | Creates a window with a thick sizable border. |
| WS_CAPTION | Creates a window with a caption (title). |
| WS_SYSMENU | A system menu is displayed at top of the window. |
| WS_MINIMIZEBOX | Window displays a minimize box. |
| WS_MAXIMIZEBOX | Window displays a maximize box. |
| WS_HSCROLL | Creates a horizontal scroll bar in the window. |
| WS_VSCROLL | Creates a vertical scroll bar in window. |
| WS_MINIMIZE | Window is minimized on creation. |
| WS_MAXIMIZE | Window is maximized on creation. |
| WS_OVERLAPPED | Creates an overlapped window. |
| WS_POPUP | Creates a pop-up window. |
| WS_OVERLAPPEDWINDOW | Same as using the WS_OVERLAPPED, WS_CAPTION, WS_SYSMENU, WS_THICKFRAME, WS_MINIMIZEBOX, and WS_MAXIMIZEBOX flags. |
| WS_POPUPWINDOW | Same as using the WS_BORDER, WS_POPUP, and WS_SYSMENU flags. |

```
// Show the window
ShowWindow(hWnd, SW_SHOWNORMAL);
UpdateWindow(hWnd);

// Do other application stuff here

// ... go on with WinMain
```

New in this code are the ShowWindow and UpdateWindow functions. These ensure that your window appears where you want it to be and that all visible objects within the window are drawn.

# The Message Pump

You're getting down to the nitty-gritty of a Windows application now—the *message pump.* Here's where your application is going to enter an endless loop, waiting for Windows to start throwing messages at you. As your application receives these messages from the message queue via a call to GetMessage or PeekMessage, you send them off to your message procedure to handle, much as shown in Figure 5.4.

The code to a standard message pump that you'll use in an application looks something like this:

```
// ... previous RegisterClass and CreateWindow function calls
MSG Msg;
while(GetMessage(&Msg, NULL, 0, 0)) {
  TranslateMessage(&Msg);
  DispatchMessage(&Msg);
}
```

First you see the MSG declaration, which is a structure that Windows uses to store message-related information. The GetMessage function fills the MSG structure with waiting messages (or waits until a message is available).

After the call to GetMessage, you give the message structure to the TranslateMessage function, which in turn translates key presses into message information. At long last is the call to the DispatchMessage function, which sends the message off to your application's message procedure. This loop continues until the GetMessage function receives a quit message (signified by a return value of 0), which will cause the loop to break.

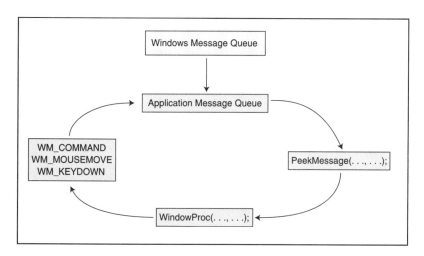

**Figure 5.4**

*The application message pump continuously asks Windows whether any messages are waiting to be processed. If so, the message makes its way to the window's message procedure to be processed.*

Here's the WinMain function in its entirety (it uses all that you've learned up to this point about creating the application window and filtering through the messages using a message pump):

```
int WINAPI WinMain(HINSTANCE hInstance,                         \
     HINSTANCE hPrevInstance, LPSTR lpCmdLine, int nCmdShow)
{
  WNDCLASSEX wcex = { sizeof(WNDCLASSEX), CS_CLASSDC,           \
       WindowProc, 0L, 0L, hInstance,                           \
       NULL, NULL, NULL, NULL,                                  \
       "GameClass", NULL };

  // Register the class and return on error
  if(!RegisterClassEx(&wcex))
    return FALSE;

  // Create the Window (320x240 at 0,0 using overlapped style)
  HWND hWnd;  // our window's handle
  hWnd = CreateWindow("GameClass", "My Game Title",            \
       WS_OVERLAPPEDWINDOW, 320, 240, 0, 0,                    \
       NULL, NULL, hInstance, NULL);
  // return on error creating the window
  if(hWnd == NULL)
    return FALSE;

  // Show the window
  ShowWindow(hWnd, SW_SHOWNORMAL);
  UpdateWindow(hWnd);

  // Enter the message pump
  MSG Msg;
  while(GetMessage(&Msg, NULL, 0, 0)) {
    TranslateMessage(&Msg);
    DispatchMessage(&Msg);
  }

  // Unregister class
  UnregisterClass("GameClass", hInstance);

  // Exit application
  return 0;
}
```

When creating games, your use of the message pump changes a bit. With the previous method, the application waited until a message came along and then handled it. For games, you can't just sit there and wait—input must be processed, graphics must be drawn, sound must be played, all in real time. You can change the way you deal with Window's messages by creating the following new-and-improved message pump:

```
MSG Msg;

// Clear out the message structure
ZeroMemory(&Msg, sizeof(MSG));

// Loop endlessly until you receive a quit message
while(Msg.message != WM_QUIT) {
  // Peek into the queue and see if there's a message waiting
  if(PeekMessage(&Msg, NULL, 0, 0, PM_REMOVE)) {
    // There's a message!  Handle it normally.
    TranslateMessage(&Msg);
    DispatchMessage(&Msg);
  } else {
    // No messages waiting. Go ahead and do time-crucial
    // stuff here, such as rendering the game's graphics.
  }
}
```

Wow! That's a lot bigger, but in essence it's simple. You start out with a zeroed out MSG structure, then enter a loop that scans for a specific message (WM_QUIT), which then breaks the loop. Instead of using GetMessage, you use PeekMessage, which looks in the message queue to see if a message is waiting.

If there is a message, PeekMessage pulls it out and handles it with TranslateMessage and DispatchMessage. If there are no messages waiting, then the flow is passed on to whatever time-crucial processing you need to perform, such as processing your per-frame game information.

## The Window Message Procedure

Because of the Windows "Don't call me, I'll call you" scheme, you are required to supply your application with a window message procedure (aka, the *window procedure*) that receives the incoming flow of messages. You declare the procedure as follows:

```
LRESULT CALLBACK WindowProc(HWND hWnd, UINT uMsg,                    \
                            WPARAM wParam, LPARAM lParam);
```

Not many parameters are being passed here, but you can do plenty with what you receive. The hWnd argument is the handle to the window to which the message belongs. The uMsg is the generated message that needs to be processed, whereas wParam and lParam contain information that is pertinent to the message (they could be values or pointers).

What you do inside this function is essential to your application. As the messages roll in, you must determine whether you want to process them. If a message is important to your application and you want to process it, do so and then allow Windows to resume its operations by returning a value of 0 (signifying that you have processed the message). If the message in question is not required by your application, let Windows deal with it, using the following line of code:

```
return DefWindowProc(hWnd, uMsg, wParam, lParam);
```

Let me show you a common window procedure that takes a message and uses a switch...case statement to determine what to do with the message—either handle it here by yourself or let Windows handle it:

```
LRESULT CALLBACK WindowProc(HWND hWnd, UINT uMsg,                    \
                            WPARAM wParam, LPARAM lParam)

  switch(uMsg) {
    case WM_DESTROY:
      PostQuitMessage(0);   // Tell Windows to close application
      break;

    // Pass remaining messages to the default message handler
    default: return DefWindowProc(hWnd, uMsg, wParam, lParam);
  }

  return 0;
}
```

The preceding is one of the most common window procedures you will use—it looks for a single message that tells you to shut down your application and passes all other messages to the *default window procedure* function for Windows to handle. As you can see, processing messages is a simple task; it just requires knowing which messages you need to process.

## Common Messages

I can't possibly deal with all the Windows messages in this book. Instead, I'll just go over the ones that you are most likely to encounter while programming your games (see Table 5.4 for this list of messages). Again, the majority of the messages that you must work with are assigned macros that begin with WM_.

When Windows sends you a message, you need to know the type of parameters and the extra information that Windows is sending with the message. This extra data is stored in the wParam and lParam arguments of the message procedure. For the specifics on each message (plus a list of all Windows messages), consult the Win32 SDK.

### Table 5.4  Standard Windows Messages

| Message | Description |
|---------|-------------|
| WM_CREATE | Sent whenever a window is created via CreateWindow or CreateWindowEx. |
| WM_DESTROY | Sent whenever a window is destroyed. |
| WM_RESIZE | Sent when the application window is resized. |
| WM_ACTIVATE | Sent when your window has been activated or deactivated. |
| WM_PAINT | Sent when a portion of the window needs to be redrawn. |
| WM_COMMAND | Sent when a user selects a command item (such as a menu item or when the user clicks a button). |
| WM_MOUSEMOVE | Periodically sent to inform the application that the mouse has been moved. |
| WM_LBUTTONDOWN | Sent when the left mouse is pressed. |
| WM_LBUTTONUP | Sent when the left mouse is released. |
| WM_RBUTTONDOWN | Sent when the right mouse is pressed. |
| WM_RBUTTONUP | Sent when the right mouse is released. |
| WM_KEYDOWN | Sent when a key is pressed. |
| WM_KEYUP | Sent when a key is released. |

As a quick example, examine the WM_MOUSEMOVE message. According the Win32 SDK, the low-word value (lowest 16-bits) of the lParam contains the X-coordinate of the mouse cursor, although the high-word value (highest 16-bits) of the lParam contains the Y-coordinate of the mouse cursor. To extract the low- and high-word values, use the LOWORD and HIWORD macros, as you see here:

```
int XCoordinate = LOWORD(lParam);
int YCoordinate = HIWORD(lParam);
```

In order to deal with the messages inside your message procedure, you can borrow from my previous example and use a switch...case statement:

```
LRESULT CALLBACK WindowProc(HWND hWnd, UINT uMsg,             \
                            WPARAM wParam, LPARAM lParam)
  switch(uMsg) {
    case WM_CREATE:
      // handle window creation information here
      break;

    case WM_DESTROY:
      PostQuitMessage(0);  // Tell Windows to close application
      break;

    case WM_COMMAND:
      // handle user-defined operation here
      break;

    default: return DefWindowProc(hWnd, uMsg, wParam, lParam);
  }

  return 0;
}
```

Throughout the book's demo programs, you will find many of the Windows messages that I present in this chapter, so I'll make sure to comment the code so you know how the window procedure's parameters are being used when processing the various messages.

## An Application Shell

The following code is the complete code for a *shell application,* an application that creates only a window (such as the one in Figure 5.5) and that enters the message pump (a game-style message pump, that is).

**Figure 5.5**

*A simple window shell, as shown here, will form the basis for all the demos and the game I create in this book.*

The only message that needs processing at this point is WM_DESTROY, which informs you that the application is being closed (quit).

```
#include <windows.h>

// Function prototypes
int WINAPI WinMain(HINSTANCE hInstance,                        \
     HINSTANCE hPrevInstance, LPSTR lpCmdLine, int nCmdShow);
LRESULT CALLBACK WindowProc(HWND hWnd, UINT uMsg,              \
                            WPARAM wParam, LPARAM lParam);

int WINAPI WinMain(HINSTANCE hInstance,                        \
     HINSTANCE hPrevInstance, LPSTR lpCmdLine, int nCmdShow)
{
  HWND hWnd;
  MSG Msg;
  WNDCLASSEX wcex = { sizeof(WNDCLASSEX), CS_CLASSDC,          \
       WindowProc, 0L, 0L, hInstance,                          \
       NULL, NULL, NULL, NULL,                                 \
       "GameClass", NULL };

  // Register the class and exit on error
  if(!RegisterClassEx(&wcex))
    return FALSE;
```

```
    // Create the window (400 x 400 at 0,0 using overlapped style)
    hWnd = CreateWindow("GameClass", "My Game Title",              \
          WS_OVERLAPPEDWINDOW, 0, 0, 400, 400,                     \
          NULL, NULL, hInstance, NULL);

    // return on error creating the window
    if(hWnd == NULL)
      return FALSE;

    // Show the window
    ShowWindow(hWnd, SW_SHOWNORMAL);
    UpdateWindow(hWnd);

    // Clear out the message structure
    ZeroMemory(&Msg, sizeof(MSG));

    // Loop endlessly until you receive a quit message
    while(Msg.message != WM_QUIT) {
      // Peek into queue and see if there's a message waiting
      if(PeekMessage(&Msg, NULL, 0, 0, PM_REMOVE)) {
        // There's a message!  Handle it normally.
        TranslateMessage(&Msg);
        DispatchMessage(&Msg);
      } else {
        // No messages waiting. Go ahead and do time-crucial
        // stuff here, such as a rendering graphics.
      }
    }

    // Unregister class
    UnregisterClass("GameClass", hInstance);

    // Exit application
    return 0;
}

// The message procedure
LRESULT CALLBACK WindowProc(HWND hWnd, UINT uMsg,                  \
                                WPARAM wParam, LPARAM lParam)
{
  switch(uMsg) {
```

```
    case WM_DESTROY:
      PostQuitMessage(0);  // Tell Windows to close application
      break;

    // Handle every other message
    default: return DefWindowProc(hWnd, uMsg, wParam, lParam);
  }

  return 0;
}
```

Although there's much more to Windows programming, you really don't need to go into much greater detail when using DirectX to create games. However, you do need to know about a few advanced features, which I introduce in the next section.

# Advanced Features

Although I couldn't possibly cover the vast range of advanced features here, let me show you a few that you're most likely to use in your game-programming endeavors —features such as using simplified windows to relay quick bits of information, attaching data to the application's executable file, and ways to execute multiple sections of code simultaneously.

## Using Message Boxes

Conveying information to the user is at times a difficult task. The text that you output must be in a window, and creating a window is somewhat involved. You must register a window class, create a window, and monitor the message queue; it's almost not worth it.

This is where a *message box* comes in handy. A message box is a window that contains a caption, a message, an optional icon, and up to three buttons (as illustrated in Figure 5.6). Once displayed, a message box simply waits for the user to click on a button, at which point, the message box closes and returns execution to the calling code.

The message box function is easy to use. Take a look at its prototype:

```
int MessageBox(
  HWND hWnd,          // Parent window or NULL for none
  LPCTSTR lpText,     // Message to display in box
  LPCTSTR lpCaption,  // Caption of window to use
  UINT uType);        // Buttons and icon settings
```

**Figure 5.6**

*A message box is the simplest window you can work with. It's useful for relaying small bits of information that might be crucial to the program's execution.*

uType is a combination of flags determining which buttons to display, as well as optional icons to display with the window's text. You can compose the uType variable from a combination of the flags shown in Table 5.5 (consult the Win32 SDK for a complete list of flags).

After selecting the type of buttons and icons (if any) to use, set the caption (1pCaption) and message (1pText). As one final step, pass the handle to the parent window that owns the message box, or use NULL to specify no owner.

## Table 5.5  MessageBox Display Flags

| Flag | Description |
|------|-------------|
| MB_OK | Displays an OK button. |
| MB_OKCANCEL | Displays OK and CANCEL buttons. |
| MB_RETRYCANCEL | Displays RETRY and CANCEL buttons. |
| MB_YESNO | Displays YES and NO buttons. |
| MB_YESNOCANCEL | Displays YES, NO, and CANCEL buttons. |
| MB_ABORTRETRYFAIL | Displays ABORT, RETRY, and FAIL buttons. |
| MB_ICONEXCLAMATION | An exclamation icon is displayed. |
| MB_ICONINFORMATION | An icon with an encircled lowercase *i* is displayed. |
| MB_ICONQUESTION | An question-mark icon is displayed. |
| MB_ICONSTOP | A stop-sign icon is displayed. |
| MB_DEFBUTTON1 | The first button is clicked when the user presses enter. |
| MB_DEFBUTTON2 | The second button is clicked when the user presses enter. |
| MB_DEFBUTTON3 | The third button is clicked when the user presses enter. |
| MB_DEFBUTTON4 | The fourth button is clicked when the user presses enter. |

## Table 5.6  Return Values from MessageBox

| Value | Reason |
|-------|--------|
| IDABORT | ABORT button was clicked. |
| IDCANCEL | CANCEL button was clicked. |
| IDIGNORE | IGNORE button was clicked. |
| IDNO | NO button was clicked. |
| IDOK | OK button was clicked. |
| IDRETRY | RETRY button was clicked. |
| IDYES | YES button was clicked. |

After a button is selected, the MessageBox function returns one of the values shown in Table 5.6.

Here's an example using the message box function that directs users to click on YES or NO when they are asked if they want to exit the program without saving. For added visual appeal, a question mark icon is displayed inside the message box:

```
int Result = MessageBox(
  NULL,
  "Exit program without saving changes?"
  "Exit Program",
  MB_YESNO | MB_ICONQUESTION);
```

If the user clicks the YES button, MessageBox returns IDYES. If the user clicks NO, a value of IDNO is returned.

## Dialog Boxes

Dialog boxes are another advanced feature of Windows. A *dialog box* is an application window created by using a template designed through utilizing a dialog box resource editor. The reasons for using a dialog box are many. First, layout of the controls is a breeze. You just point and click where you want a control to be placed in the application window.

Second, with a dialog box, you can quickly create an application window or multiple windows using the same template. These dialog box windows are identical to a regular window—they all use a window message procedure to process messages. With dialog boxes, however, some of the messages change. Instead of receiving a WM_CREATE message when the application window is created, a dialog box receives a WM_INITDIALOG message. These differences in messages from a regular application window and a dialog box window are shown in the Microsoft Win32 SDK help files.

As for this book, I tend to use dialog boxes to quickly construct application windows full of controls ranging from push buttons to text boxes. When you're browsing through the book's projects, you'll sometimes notice an attached dialog box resource. If this resource exists, that project creates the application window using the dialog box template.

To create an application window from a dialog box template, use the following function:

```
HWND CreateDialog(
   HINSTANCE hInstance,    // Handle to application instance
   LPCTSTR lpTemplate,     // Dialog box template name pointer
   HWND hWndParent,        // Handle to owner window
   DLGPROC lpDialogFunc);  // Dialog box's message procedure
```

Even though you haven't learned about them yet, a resource file contains the dialog box template. A unique identifier names each template. To create the window from a dialog box template, you need to pass this unique identifier along with the application's instance handle and message procedure function to the CreateDialog function. After calling CreateDialog, you receive a handle to the newly created application window.

You've already seen how a window processes messages using the message procedure in the section "Working Inside a Window," so let's move on and look at how to store a dialog box template using resources.

## Resources

*Resources* are data appended to the end of an application's executable file. These resources can range from program-specific data to icons, menu definitions, and even bitmap images (see Figure 5.7, which shows a breakdown of an application's executable file).

By packaging these resources together inside the file, you save space and ensure that the data exists when your program needs it. You can save any type of data in a

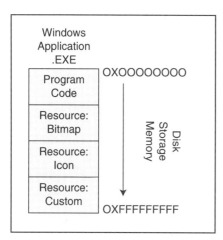

**Figure 5.7**

*Resources such as bitmaps and menus are appended to the program's executable file.*

resource—bitmaps, sound files, icons, and even game-related data such as dialogue. You just have to know how to insert that data as resources into your application.

## Attaching Resources to an Application

Visual C/C++ comes with a built-in resource manager that makes attaching resources to your program a breeze. To attach a resource file, open your project and choose Insert, Resource. A list of typical resource types, such as menus and dialog boxes, appears.

Windows comes with a set of default resources, such as bitmaps and icons, but aside from those, you must do a little work in order to use your custom resources (the resources you're interested in at this point):

1. To attach a custom resource, click IMPORT, select your file, and, if asked, give it a resource type name. (For example, if you were to attach a custom file named MYMAP.MAP, you might use the name GameMaps. From then on, anytime you attach a *.MAP file, it would be placed under the GameMaps listing of resources inside the project editor.)

2. Enter the resource list inside your project navigator. The resources are listed by their types, with each resource having a different name. These names might begin with IDC_ (for cursors), IDB_ (for bitmaps), or IDM_ (for menus). Use your prefix-naming convention here, with the default custom resource using IDR_.

**3.** To rename a resource, right-click it and choose Properities (or press Alt+Enter). Go ahead and change the name of the resource in the ID box as you see fit. Just remember this name, because you'll use it later to access the resource. (I'll name the map resource IDR_MAP1 and use that name in upcoming examples.)

## Retrieving Resource Data

After a custom resource is attached to an application, you can access the resource directly with a memory pointer that is obtained by using the three functions shown in Table 5.7.

The first function, FindResource, locates the resource attached to your application and returns a handle to it that is used during the LoadResource call. As you might guess, the LoadResource call loads the resource into memory and returns yet another handle used to access the resource with the LockResource function. At long last, you can lock the resource memory, thus retrieving a data pointer to it for your own use.

Here are the function prototypes for FindResource, LoadResource, and LoadResource:

```
HRSRC FindResource(
   HMODULE hModule,   // Module handle from WinMain
   LPCTSTR lpName,    // Resource name
   LPCTSTR lpType);   // Type of resource
```

Using the hModule field is easy—set it to the instance handle received from WinMain. lpName is the name of your resource (such as IDR_MAP1), and lpType is the name of your custom resource (GameMaps). Be sure to include the parentheses as I've done here (the compiler usually adds those for you in the resource type name).

### Table 5.7 aResource Handling Functions

| Function | Description |
| --- | --- |
| FindResource | Finds an attached resource and returns a handle to it. |
| LoadResource | Loads a resource into global memory and returns a handle to it. |
| LockResource | Locks the resource memory and returns a memory pointer to it. |

> **CAUTION**
>
> The MAKEINTRESOURCE macro converts the resource's name into a string pointer that is used by certain functions. For example, you obtain the IDR_MAP1 resource pointer with the following code:
>
> ```
> LPTSTR *ResourcePointer = MAKEINTRESOURCE(IDR_MAP1)
> ```

```
HGLOBAL LoadResource(
    HMODULE hModule,  // here's the module handle again!
    HRSRC hResInfo);  // handle from FindResource call
```

There's not too much to explain here; you can actually combine the LoadResource function with the FindResource function into one call:

```
HGLOBAL hResource = LoadResource(hInstance, FindResource(        \
            hInstance, MAKEINTRESOURCE(IDR_MAP1), "GameMaps"));
```

At long last is the LockResource function, which takes only one parameter; the handle received from the LoadResource function call (the return value from the LockResource value is a void pointer that you can cast to any data type you like):

```
LPVOID LockResource(HGLOBAL hResData);
```

As an example of loading your own resource, say that you attach a text file called readme.txt and give it a resource type of "TEXT". Say that you name the resource IDR_TEXT1. This short code will load the resource for you and display it within a message box:

```
HGLOBAL hResource = LoadResource(hInst, FindResource(hInst,    \
                        MAKEINTRESOURCE(IDR_TEXT1), "TEXT"));
if(hResource != NULL) {
  char *pText = (char*)LockResource(hResource);
  MessageBox(NULL, pText, "Text", MB_OK);
}
```

# Threads and Multithreading

Windows 95 introduced programmers to the idea of using a multitasking system (even though Windows really isn't a true multitasking system because it uses preemptive multitasking, which processes small bits of many programs, one at a time). The idea is that you can have multiple processes (applications) operating at the same time, each taking a portion of processing time (called a *time slice*).

Multitasking also enables each process to split into separate processes, called *threads.* Each thread has its own purpose, such as scanning for network data, handling user input, or playing sounds when required. Using more than one thread in an application is called *multithreading*.

Creating additional threads within your application really isn't difficult. To create a thread, you create a function (using a special function prototype) that contains the code you want to execute. The prototype to use for the thread function looks like this:

```
DWORD WINAPI ThreadProc(LPVOID lpParameter);
```

The lpParameter argument is a user-defined pointer that you provide when you create the thread, which you accomplish with a call to CreateThread:

```
HANDLE CreateThread(
   LPSECURITY_ATTRIBUTES lpThreadAbilities,  // NULL
   DWORD dwStackSize,                        // 0
   LPTHREAD_START_ROUTINE lpStartAddress,    // thread function
   LPVOID lpParameter,      // user supplied pointer- can be NULL
   DWORD dwCreationFlags,   // 0
   LPDWORD lpThreadId);     // receives thread identifier
```

This is a complex function, so I will not go into the details here, other than to give you an example to follow. Here's a simple thread function and the call to initialize it:

```
// The custom thread function
DWORD WINAPI MyThread(LPVOID lpParameter)
{
   BOOL *Active;

   Active = (BOOL*)lpParameter;
   *Active = TRUE;  // flag thread as active

   // Insert custom code here
```

> ### CAUTION
> The return value of this function is a handle, which must be closed when you're done, or the system resources will not be released. Release the resources used by the thread with a call to CloseHandle:
>
> ```
> CloseHandle(hThread);  // use handle received from CreateThread
> ```

```
  // Terminate the thread
  *Active = FALSE;  // flag thread as no longer active
  ExitThread(0);  // special call to close thread
}

void InitThread()
{
  HANDLE hThread;
  DWORD ThreadId;
  BOOL Active;

  // Create the thread, passing a user-defined variable that
  // is used to store the status of the thread.
  hThread = CreateThread(NULL, 0,                          \
          (LPTHREAD_START_ROUTINE)MyThread, (void*)&Active, \
          0, &ThreadId);

  // Wait for the thread to complete by continuously
  // checking the state of the flag.
  while(Active == TRUE);

  // Close the thread handle
  CloseHandle(hThread);
}
```

The preceding code creates a thread, which executes immediately when the CreateThread function completes. During the creation call, you supply a pointer to a BOOL variable that tracks the state of the thread; the flag signifies when the thread is active by storing a value of TRUE (the thread is active) or FALSE (the thread is not active).

When the thread's execution is complete, you flag the thread as being no longer active (by storing a value of FALSE in the previously mentioned BOOL variable) and terminate it with a call to ExitThread, which has a single parameter—the termination code of the thread, or rather the purpose for which the thread was closed. It's safe to just use a value of 0 in the call to ExitThread.

> **NOTE**
>
> ExitThread **is not the only way to stop a thread's execution. Any function outside the thread can call** TerminateThread, **which will immediately stop the thread's execution. This is really not desirable; it wastes system resources in most cases and can cause a system crash. Only use** TerminateThread **if you absolutely must. To call** TerminateThread, **provide two arguments—the first parameter being the thread handle and the second being the termination code to return):**
>
> TerminateThread(hThread, 0);

Basically, a thread is just a function that runs concurrently with your application. In Chapter 8, "Playing Sound with DirectX Audio," you find more about how to use threads.

## Critical Sections

Because Windows is a multitasking system, Windows applications can really get in the way of each other, especially applications using multiple threads. For example, what if one thread is filling a data structure with some crucial data when suddenly a second thread alters or accesses that very data?

There is a way to make sure that only one thread (called a *process*) has complete control when needed, and this is by using *critical sections*. When activated, a critical section will block all processes from trying to access shared memory (the application's memory that all threads utilize), thus allowing each process to individually alter the application data without having to worry about other processes interfering. To use a critical section, you must first declare and initialize one:

```
CRITICAL_SECTION CriticalSection;
InitializeCriticalSection(&CriticalSection);
```

At this point, you can enter a critical section, process your crucial data, and leave the critical section, as done in the following example:

```
EnterCriticalSection(&CriticalSection);
// Do crucial data processing here
LeaveCriticalSection(&CriticalSection);
```

When you finish with the critical section (such as when the application is closing), you release it with a call to

```
DeleteCriticalSection(&CriticalSection);
```

Although I'd like to go into more detail about the use of critical sections, there really isn't a need to. Using them is easy and a must for multithreaded applications. The only rule to remember is to make sure that the code contained within a critical section executes quickly; you're locking up the system's processes, and that could lead to a system crash if your program takes too long.

## Using COM

*COM*, or *Component Object Module*, is a programming technique adopted by Microsoft. With COM, you can create software components so that their functionality is compatible with all programs. Take Internet Explorer v4+, for example. I bet you didn't know that the toolbar and browser window are COM objects. What's more, you can use those objects in your applications!

Although that is a cool reason to start using COM, the biggest reason is DirectX; DirectX is composed entirely of COM-based components.

## Initializing COM

You'll have to initialize the COM system in order to use COM objects. To initialize COM, you use these two functions:

```
// For single-threaded applications
HRESULT CoInitialize(
  LPVOID pvReserved);   // NULL

// For multithreaded applications
HRESULT CoInitializeEx(
  void *pvReserved,     // NULL
  DWORD dwCoInit);      // concurrency model
```

Either of the two preceding functions will work, but when you're using multi-threaded applications, you must use the second function, CoInitializeEx because you must specify the COINIT_MULTITHREADED flag in dwCoInit in order for the COM system to work correctly.

When you finish with the COM system, you shut it down with a call to CoUninitialize, which takes no parameters:

```
void CoUninitialize();
```

You follow each call to CoInitialize and CoInitializeEx with an equal number of calls to CoUninitialize. If you call CoInitialize twice (which is allowed), you need to follow with two calls to CoUninitialize. You can see this in the following code:

```
// Initialize the COM system
CoInitialize(NULL);

// Initialize COM with a multithreaded concurrency
CoInitializeEx(NULL, COINIT_MULTITHREADED);

// Release the COM (twice)
CoUninitialize();
CoUninitialize();
```

## IUnknown

IUnknown is the base class for all COM interfaces. It contains only three functions: AddRef, Release, and QueryInterface. AddRef initializes whatever it needs and increases the reference count of the number of times this class has been instanced. You must match the number of reference counts with the same number of Releases, which frees all the data that the object instance is using.

You use the third function, QueryInterface, to obtain the interfaces to contained objects, including newer interfaces. Such is the case when objects can span through multiple versions, as in DirectX. You can still use an older interface, but to get a newer one, query for it. If a newer interface exists, the object pointer is passed; otherwise, QueryInterface returns NULL to represent no interface or an error.

In order to build on functions, an object will need to derive a class from the IUnknown object and insert the extra functions into the derived class declaration. It's interesting to note that the COM standard that Microsoft maintains states that objects cannot expose their variables—only functions.

Functions are required to return an HRESULT value that represents an error or success code. To retrieve any type of value from a COM object, you pass a pointer to a variable (which must be a word or double word—no bytes are allowed here) to a function used to retrieve the value contained within the object.

As an example, you can create a simple object (derived from IUnknown) that takes two numbers, adds them together, and returns the result in a third provided variable:

```
class IMyComObject : public IUnknown
{
  public:
    HRESULT Add(long *Num1, long *Num2, long *Result);
};

HRESULT IMyComObject::Add(long *Num1, long *Num2, long *Result)
{
  // Add the numbers and store in result
  *Result = *Num1 + *Num2;

  // return a success code
  return S_OK;
}
```

> **NOTE**
> Notice that all **COM** objects begin with an uppercase I rather than the letter **C**. This is to signify that the object is a **COM** interface.

## Initializing and Releasing Objects

To use a COM object, you must create it (and the code library loaded by Windows) using the `CoCreateInstance` function:

```
STDAPI CoCreateInstance(
    REFCLSID rclsid,      // Class identifier of object
    LPUNKNOWN pUnkOuter,  // NULL
    DWORD dwClsContext,   // CLSCTX_INPROC
    REFIID riid,          // Reference to interface identifier
    LPVOID *ppv);         // Pointer to received object
```

To make use of `CoCreateInstance`, you have to know the object's class and interface identifiers. The class identifier, prefixed with `CLSID_`, is the class of object that you are creating, and the reference, prefixed with `IID_`, is the exact interface for which you are looking.

Say that you have a class called `Math` that has a class identifier of `CLSID_MATH`. The `Math` class contains three objects: `IAdd` (reference identifier `IID_IAdd`), `ISubtract` (`IID_ISubtract`), and `IAdd2` (`IID_IAdd2`). To reference the `IAdd2` object, a call to `CoCreateInstance` looks like this:

```
IAdd2 *pAdd2;

if(FAILED(CoCreateInstance(CLSID_MATH, NULL, CLSCTX_INPROC,   \
        IID_IAdd2, (void**)&pAdd2))) {
  // Error occurred
}
```

All COM objects you create must eventually be released. This is the purpose of the `IUnknown::Release` function, which takes no parameters:

```
HRESULT IUnknown::Release();
```

After you finish with the `IAdd2` interface, you need to release it with the following:

```
IAdd2->Release();
```

## Querying Interfaces

One of the best things about COM is that it is backward-compatible. If you have a newer COM object (containing new interfaces), you still have full access to old interfaces through the object. This method of keeping old interfaces ensures that your code will not break if the end user has newer COM objects installed.

This also means that older interfaces will be able to query for newer interfaces.

This is done by using the `IUnknown::QueryInterface` method:

```
HRESULT IUnknown::QueryInterface(
  REFIID iid,            // Reference identifier of new interface
  void **ppvObject); // New object pointer
```

Because the original object calling the query function has already been created, there's no need to worry about class identifiers here, just the reference identifier of the new interface that you want. Going back to the `Math` class object, say that you want to obtain an `IAdd` interface and then query for the `IAdd2` interface:

```
IAdd *pAdd;
IAdd2 *pAdd2;

// Get the IAdd interface first
if(FAILED(CoCreateInstance(CLSID_MATH, NULL, CLSCTX_INPROC,   \
        IID_IAdd, (void**)&pAdd))) {
  // Error occurred
}

// Query for the IAdd2 interface
if(SUCCEEDED(pAdd->QueryInterface(IID_IAdd2, (void**)&pAdd2))) {
  // Interface obtained, release the first
  IAdd->Release();
}
```

Although there's much more information on COM, I've covered the information that you need to start using DirectX. Speaking of DirectX, now is the time to take a quick look at it.

# DirectX

According to the introduction in the DirectX Software Development Kit (DX SDK) documents:

> Microsoft® DirectX® is a set of low-level application programming interfaces (APIs) for creating games and other high-performance multimedia applications. It includes support for two-dimensional (2-D) and three-dimensional (3-D) graphics, sound effects and music, input devices, and support for networked applications such as multiplayer games.

As stated in the SDK, DirectX is a set of programming interfaces that will help you create high-performance games and applications. Now let me tell you what DirectX is not.

DirectX is not a game-creation package; it merely aids in the development of your applications through the use of APIs designed to interface directly with your computer's hardware. If the hardware is equipped with DirectX drivers, you have access to the accelerated functions that device provides. If no accelerated functions exist, DirectX will emulate them.

This means that you will have a consistent interface with which to work, and you will not have to worry about things such as hardware features. If a feature doesn't exist on the card, it's still likely that the feature will work through DirectX's emulation functions. No fuss, no muss; just program the game and rest assured that it will work on the majority of systems.

New versions of DirectX are frequently released, with each new version adding newer features and improving older ones. At the time of this writing, version 8 has been released and that is the version on which this book is based. The following major components are included in DirectX 8:

- **DirectX Graphics.** A complete 3-D graphics system
- **DirectX Audio.** Includes sound and music systems
- **DirectPlay.** Network (Internet) functionality at its simplest
- **DirectInput.** Easy access to keyboards, mice, and joysticks

Version 8 represents a major change for DirectX. Gone is DirectDraw, the 2-D graphics library. Instead, it has been merged with Direct3D to create a single, easier-to-use graphics interface called DirectX Graphics. The same goes for DirectSound and DirectMusic—these have been merged into DirectX Audio.

DirectX 8 gives you an interface that is streamlined for beginners, while still remaining powerful enough to give advanced users full control. You might compare its ease of use to that of OpenGL.

The DirectX SDK also comes with various helper classes and libraries, such as D3DX, which makes using DirectX easier by giving you some handy classes with which to work. D3DX is a great library, and I tend to use it as much as possible throughout this book.

I don't want to make DirectX out to be something that it is not. As I've mentioned, it is only a method of accessing low-level functions, not a game-creation package.

Also, it does lack some features as of version 8. DirectDraw is sorely missed, which means that if you want straight 2-D functionality, you'll have to use the version 7 interface of DirectDraw.

This means that you cannot mix DirectX 8's 3-D capabilities with DirectX 7's 2-D functions. Although this might seem like a major drawback, don't worry—I'll work around it. By using 3-D functions for emulating 2-D, you'll get the benefit of extra features, as you see in Chapter 11, "Using 2-D Graphics."

# Downloading and Installing DirectX

If you haven't already, go ahead and install DirectX 8.0 on your system. The SDK is on the CD-ROM at the back of this book. You can find the installation instructions for DirectX in Appendix A, "Installing DirectX and Configuring the Compiler." You can also download the DirectX SDK straight from Microsoft's Web site. Just point your browser to http://msdn.microsoft.com/directx and look for the download section.

# Including DirectX in Your Project

Including DirectX in your project takes a little set-up work. Again, refer to Appendix A for instructions on installing DirectX and configuring your compiler.

# Understanding the Program Flow

When immersing yourself in a major project, it becomes all too easy to be over-whelmed with house-keeping chores such as modifying the code to work with something that you've added, modified, or removed. These chores take precious time that could be better spent working on your game.

By starting with a solid understanding of what your needs are, you'll be able to structure your program's flow of operation (called the *program flow*) and ensure that you can make changes easily. Because you've already written a design document (you did, didn't you?), there is little left to do but build a structure of the processing flow.

A typical program begins by initializing all systems and data and then entering the main loop. The main loop is where the majority of things happen. Depending on the game state (title screen, menu screen, in-game-play, and so on) that is occur-ring, you'll need to process input and output differently.

Here are the steps that you follow in a standard game application:

1. Initialize the systems (Windows, graphics, input, sound, and so on).
2. Prepare data (load configuration files).
3. Configure the default state (typically the title screen).
4. Start with the main loop.
5. Determine state and process it by grabbing input, processing, and outputting.
6. Return to Step 5 until application terminates and then go to Step 7.
7. Clean up data (release memory resources, and so on).
8. Release the systems (windows, graphics, input, and so on).

Steps 1 through 3 are typical for every game: set up the entire system, load the necessary support files (graphics, sound, and so on), and prepare for the actual game play. Your application will spend the majority of time handling the in-game processing (Step 5), which can be broken into three parts: pre-frame processing, per-frame processing, and post-frame processing.

The pre-frame processing deals with small tasks, such as getting the current time (for timed events such as synching) and other details (such as updating the game elements). The per-frame processing deals with updating objects (if not already done in the pre-frame stage) and rendering the graphics. The post-frame processing deals with the remaining functions, such as synching by the time or even displaying the graphics already rendered.

Here's a kicker for you. In your game, you might have multiple per-frame states: one that handles the main menu, one that handles the in-game play, and so on. Maintaining multiple states like that can lead to some messy code, but employing something known as *state-processing* can help ease the burden a bit. You learn more about state processing in the section "Application States," later in this chapter.

Cleaning data and shutting down the system (Steps 7 and 8) release the system and resources that you allocated when you started up the game. Graphics need to be freed from memory, the application window destroyed, and so on. Skipping these steps is a definite no-no, as it would leave your system in a wacky state that could lead to a system crash!

Every step in the program flow is represented by an associated block of code, so the better the structure of that code, the easier your application will be to create. To aid in better structuring your program code, you can utilize a common programming technique known as *modular programming*.

# Modular Programming

Modular programming is the basis for many techniques used in programming today, including C++ and COM. Modular programming creates independent code modules that are fully self-sustaining; they need no external help and, in a lot of cases, can be used on a multitude of operating platforms. Imagine a true modular programming system in which a program you write will work on all existing computers! You may not have to wait long—such things are on their way (or are already here).

You can think of a modular program as a C++ class. It contains its own variables and functions. If the code is written properly, the class needs no outside assistance. Given your class, any application can utilize the features within the class only by knowing how to call the functions (through the use of function prototypes). Calling a class function is as simple as instancing a class and calling its functions:

```
cClass MyClass;        // Instance the class
MyClass.Function1();   // Call a class function
```

To obtain true modularity, your code must protect its data. Doing so is easy because using C++, you can classify variables as protected. To gain access to those class variables, you have to write public functions that outside code can use. This is actually the basis of COM.

Take a look at some code that demonstrates what I'm talking about. Here a class holds a counter. You can increment the counter, set it to a specific number, and retrieve the current counter value, all by using the following class:

```
class cCounter
{
  private:
    DWORD m_dwCount;

  public:
    cCounter()            { m_dwCount = 0; }
    BOOL Increment()      { m_dwCount++; return TRUE; }
    BOOL Get(DWORD *Var)  { *Var = m_dwCount; return TRUE; }
    BOOL Set(DWORD Var)   { m_dwCount = Var; return TRUE; }
};
```

The cCounter class sets the m_dwCount variable as private. In that way, even derived classes can't access it. The other functions are pretty much self-explanatory. The only notable function is Get, which takes a pointer to a DWORD variable. The function stores the current count value in that variable and returns TRUE (as all functions in the cCounter class).

That is a pretty basic example of modular programming. A more complex example is DirectX, which is completely modular. If you want to use only a single feature of DirectX, say DirectSound, then you need only include the proper DirectSound objects. DirectSound does not depend on other DirectX components in order to operate.

Throughout the book, I incorporate modular coding techniques, most notably to create a core of gaming libraries, each independent of one another. To use these libraries, just include them in your project and hack away!

# States and Processes

Trying to optimize the program flow should be one of your top priorities from the get-go. While small, your application's code is easy to manage. However, once that application grows in size, it becomes increasingly difficult to work with, requiring a major rewrite to change even the slightest bit.

Think of this—your game project is well under way, and you decide to add a new feature to the game that opens an inventory display screen whenever the user presses the I key. The inventory display screen can be displayed only while playing the game, not while viewing the main menu screen. This means that you must embed the code that detects when the I key is pressed, and when pressed, it must render the inventory display screen instead of the normal game-play screen.

If you've locked yourself into using a single function that renders each display screen out depending on what the user is doing in the game (such as viewing the main menu or playing the game), you're going to quickly come to the realization that the rendering function can become quite large and complicated, having to encompass all possible *states* in which the game can exist.

## Application States

Did I just mention states—what are those? A *state* is short for a *state of operation*, which is the current process your application is involved in executing. The main menu to your game is a state much like the in-game-play state is. The inventory display you want to add to the game is a state as well.

When you start adding the various states to your application, you'll also need to provide a way to determine how to process those states based on the current state of operation (which changes during project execution). Deciding which state your application needs to process each frame can result in something as horrible looking as this:

```
switch(CurrentState) {
  case STATE_TITLESCREEN:
    DoTitleScreen();
    break;
  case STATE_MAINMENU:
    DoMainMenu();
    break;
  case STATE_INGAME:
    DoGameFrame();
    break;
}
```

Ack! You can tell something like that won't do, especially when your game has a truckload of states to work with, and even worse, trying to process a state for each frame! Instead, you can use something I like to call *state-based programming,* or *SBP* for short. In essence, SBP branches (directs) execution based on a stack of states. Each state represents an object or set of functions. As you require functions, you can add them to the stack. When you're done with the functions, remove them from the stack. You can see this demonstrated in Figure 5.8.

You add, remove, and process states by using a state manager. When a state is added, it is pushed into the stack, thus having current control when the manager is processed. Once popped, the topmost state is discarded, leaving the next highest state to be processed next.

For the preceding reasons, you need to implement a state manager that accepts pointers to functions (which represent the states). Pushing a state adds the function pointer to the stack. It's your job to call the state manager, which will process the topmost state on the stack. The state manager is really easy to work with, so let me quickly show you the state manager object that does it all:

```
class cStateManager
{
  // A structure that stores a function pointer and linked list
  typedef struct sState {
    void  (*Function)();
```

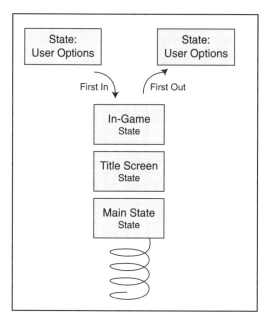

**Figure 5.8**

*A stack lets you push and pop states as needed.*

```
  sState *Next;
} sState;

protected:
  sState *m_StateParent; // The top state in the stack
                         // (the head of the stack)

public:
  cStateManager() { m_StateParent = NULL; }

  ~cStateManager()
  {
    sState *StatePtr;

    // Remove all states from the stack
    while((StatePtr = m_StateParent) != NULL) {
      m_StateParent = StatePtr->Next;
      delete StatePtr;
    }
  }
```

```
// Push a function on to the stack
void Push(void (*Function)())
{
  // Don't push a NULL value
  if(Function != NULL) {
    // Allocate a new state and push it on stack
    sState *StatePtr = new sState;
    StatePtr->Next = m_StateParent;
    m_StateParent = StatePtr;
    StatePtr->Function = Function;
  }
}


BOOL Pop()
{
  sState *StatePtr = m_StateParent;

  // Remove the head of stack (if any)
  if(StatePtr != NULL) {
    m_StateParent = StatePtr->Next;
    delete StatePtr;
  }

  // return TRUE if more states exist, FALSE otherwise
  if(m_StateParent == NULL)
    return FALSE;
  return TRUE;
}


BOOL Process()
{
  // return an error if no more states
  if(m_StateParent == NULL)
    return FALSE;
  // Process the top-most state (if any)
  m_StateParent->Function();
  return TRUE;
}
};
```

You can see that the class is tiny, but don't let it fool you. With the cStateManager object, you can continually add states as needed, and during the frame-rendering function, you can call only the Process, resting assured that the proper function will be called. Here's an example:

```
cStateManager SM;

// Macro to ease the use of MessageBox function
#define MB(s) MessageBox(NULL, s, s, MB_OK);

// State function prototypes - must follow this prototype!
void Func1() { MB("1"); SM.Pop(); }
void Func2() { MB("2"); SM.Pop(); }
void Func3() { MB("3"); SM.Pop(); }

int PASCAL WinMain(HINSTANCE hInst, HINSTANCE hPrev,            \
                   LPSTR szCmdLine, int nCmdShow)
{
  SM.Push(Func1);
  SM.Push(Func2);
  SM.Push(Func3);
  while(SM.Process() == TRUE);
}
```

With the preceding little program, you can track three states, each displaying a message box with a number. Each state pops itself from the stack and gives the next state in the stack a turn, until finally all the states are exhausted, and the program exits. Pretty neat, huh?

Think of the preceding more as being embedded in the per-frame message pump now. Say that you need to display a message to the user, but darn it, you're in the middle of the in-game screen routines. No problem, just push the message display function on the stack and call the process function next frame!

## Processes

Moving on, allow me to introduce you to another technique that simplifies the use of per-frame function calling. If you're using separate modules to handle the medial functions (called processes) such as input, network, and sound processing, instead of calling each individually, you can create an object that handles it all for you.

```
class cProcessManager
{
  // A structure that stores a function pointer and linked list
  typedef struct sProcess {
    void  (*Function)();
    sProcess *Next;
  } sProcess;

  protected:
    sProcess *m_ProcessParent; // The top state in the stack
                               // (the head of the stack)

  public:
    cProcessManager() { m_ProcessParent = NULL; }

    ~cProcessManager()
    {
      sProcess *ProcessPtr;

      // Remove all processes from the stack
      while((ProcessPtr = m_ProcessParent) != NULL) {
        m_ProcessParent = ProcessPtr->Next;
        delete ProcessPtr;
      }
    }

    // Add function on to the stack
    void Add(void (*Process)())
    {
      // Don't push a NULL value
      if(Process != NULL) {
        // Allocate a new process and push it on stack
        sProcess *ProcessPtr = new sProcess;
        ProcessPtr->Next = m_ProcessParent;
        m_ProcessParent = ProcessPtr;
        ProcessPtr->Function = Process;
      }
    }
```

```
    // Process all functions
    void Process()
    {
      sProcess *ProcessPtr = m_ProcessParent;

      while(ProcessPtr != NULL) {
        ProcessPtr->Function();
        ProcessPtr = ProcessPtr->Next;
      }
    }
};
```

Again, this is a simple object much like the cStateManager object, with one major difference. The cProcessManager object only adds processes; it does not remove them. Here's an example using cProcessManager:

```
cProcessManager PM;

// Macro to ease the use of MessageBox function
#define MB(s) MessageBox(NULL, s, s, MB_OK);

// Processfunction prototypes - must follow this prototype!
void Func1() { MB("1"); }
void Func2() { MB("2"); }
void Func3() { MB("3"); }

int PASCAL WinMain(HINSTANCE hInst, HINSTANCE hPrev,              \
                   LPSTR szCmdLine, int nCmdShow)
{
  PM.Add(Func1);
  PM.Add(Func2);
  PM.Add(Func3);
  PM.Process();
  PM.Process();
}
```

Note that every time Process is called, all processes on the stack are called (as demonstrated in Figure 5.9). This is very useful for calling frequent functions quickly. You can maintain a different process manager object for different situations—for example, one that handles input and network processing and one that handles input and sound.

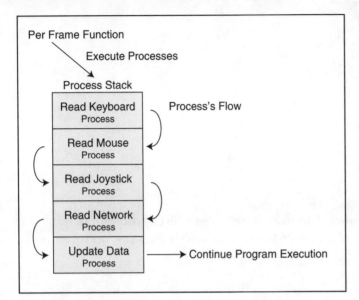

**Figure 5.9**

*A process stack is composed of frequently called functions. Every function added to the manager is subsequently executed when* cProcessManager::Process *is called.*

# Handling Application Data

All applications use data in some form or another, especially in games. You know that game character you've been playing in your favorite game for the last three weeks? Every little bit of information about that character is application data—his name, hit points, experience level, and armor and weapons the character is carrying. Every time you quit the game, your character's data is saved, only to be waiting for you to load later.

## Using Data Packaging

The easiest way to deal with application data is to create a data packaging system that handles saving and loading the data. By creating an object that contains a buffer of data, you can add a few functions that save and load it for you. To see what I mean first, take a look at this class:

```
class cDataPackage
{
  protected:
    // Data buffer and size
    void           *m_Buf;
    unsigned long  m_Size;
```

```
public:
  cDataPackage()  { m_Buf = NULL; m_Size = 0; }
  ~cDataPackage() { Free(); }

  void *Create(unsigned long Size)
  {
    // Free a previously created buffer
    Free();

    // Allocate some memory and return a pointer
    return (m_Buf = (void*)new char[(m_Size = Size)]);
  }

  // Free the allocated memory
  void Free() { delete m_Buf; m_Buf = NULL; m_Size = 0; }

  BOOL Save(char *Filename)
  {
    FILE *fp;

    // Make sure there's something to write
    if(m_Buf != NULL && m_Size) {
      // Open file, write size and data
      if((fp=fopen(Filename, "wb")) != NULL) {
        fwrite(&m_Size, 1, 4, fp);
        fwrite(m_Buf, 1, m_Size, fp);
        fclose(fp);
        return TRUE;
      }
    }

    return FALSE;
  }

  void *Load(char *Filename, unsigned long *Size)
  {
    FILE *fp;

    // Free a prior buffer
    Free();
```

```
        if((fp=fopen(Filename, "rb"))!=NULL) {
          // Read in size and data
          fread(&m_Size, 1, 4, fp);
          if((m_Buf = (void*)new char[m_Size]) != NULL)
            fread(m_Buf, 1, m_Size, fp);
          fclose(fp);

          // Store size to return
          if(Size != NULL)
            *Size = m_Size;

          // return pointer
          return m_Buf;
        }

        return NULL;
      }
};
```

The cDataPackage class contains only four functions that you can use (actually six including the constructor and destructor). The first function you'll want to call is Create, which allocates a block of memory according to the size you give it. The Free function frees this block of memory. As for Save and Load, they do just that—save the data block and load it from hard drive, using the filename you supplied.

Notice that the Create and Load functions each return a pointer. That pointer is to the data buffer, so you can use it to cast your own data pointer.

# Testing the Data Package System

Imagine that you want to create a data package that stores a list of names, and you want to use a custom structure to work with the names. By creating a data package and casting the return pointer to a structure, you can quickly work with the name, as in the following:

```
// A structure to contain a name
typedef struct {
  char Name[32];
} sName;
```

```
int PASCAL WinMain(HINSTANCE hInst, HINSTANCE hPrev,                \
                   LPSTR szCmdLine, int nCmdShow)
{
  cDataPackage DP;
  DWORD Size;

  // Create the data package (w/64 bytes) and get the
  // pointer, casting it to an sName structure type.
  sName *Names = (sName*)DP.Create(64);

  // Since there are 64 bytes total, and each name uses
  // 32 bytes, then I can have 2 names stored.
  strcpy(Names[0].Name, "Jim");
  strcpy(Names[1].Name, "Adams");

  // Save the names to disk and free the data buffer
  DP.Save("names.dat");
  DP.Free();

  // Load the names from disk.  Size will equal 64
  // when the load function returns.
  Names = (sName*)DP.Load("names.dat", &Size);

  // Display the names
  MessageBox(NULL, Names[0].Name, "1st Name", MB_OK);
  MessageBox(NULL, Names[1].Name, "2nd Name", MB_OK);

  // Free up the data package
  DP.Free();
}
```

Looking more closely at the data buffer in use, you see that out of the 64 bytes used, two blocks of 32 bytes each are used to store the names, as illustrated in Figure 5.10.

The possibilities for using data packing are enormous. By creating a few small data package objects, you can cast all the pointers you want, keeping all your application data in a single, contained object that can save and load itself.

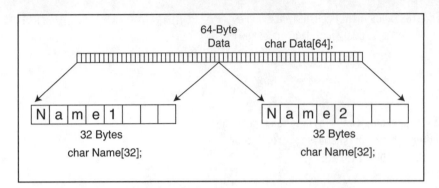

**Figure 5.10**

*The data buffer is large enough to store every instance of a person's name. In this case, two names are stored, each using 32 bytes, giving the total buffer a size of 64 bytes.*

# Building an Application Framework

I'm sure you'll agree that having to retype the same code again and again—the code to create a window, draw graphics, play sounds . . . you get the idea—every time you start a new project is bothersome. Why not just create a main library of those functions that you can plug into your new project, leaving you more time to program the actual application.

That's the idea behind an *application framework*. At the basic level, a framework should contain the code to initialize the application window, various engines (graphics, input, network, and sound), handle initialization, per-frame routines, and shutdown functions. Using modular-coding techniques also helps because the major components, such as the engines, can be contained in individual objects.

The goal at this point is to build a simple project that you can use as a base for your applications. Start with a new project and name it framework (or some other descriptive name). Within this project, you create a file, called WinMain.cpp. This file represents the entry point of your application.

> **NOTE**
>
> In the project settings, be sure to include the proper search paths for the various headers (such as DirectX) and to link in all the libraries you are likely to use, such as D3DX8.LIB (the DirectX helper library).

The WinMain.cpp source code will be very minimal, containing only the code needed to initialize the window. Take a look at the WinMain.cpp source file that I typically use for my base framework:

```cpp
// Include files
#include <windows.h>
#include <stdio.h>
#include <stdarg.h>


// Main application instances
HINSTANCE g_hInst;    // Global instance handle
HWND g_hWnd;          // Global window handle


// Application window dimensions, type, class and window name
#define WNDWIDTH   400
#define WNDHEIGHT  400
#define WNDTYPE    WS_OVERLAPPEDWINDOW
const char g_szClass[]   = "FrameClass";
const char g_szCaption[] = "FrameCaption";


// Main application prototypes

// Entry point
int PASCAL WinMain(HINSTANCE hInst, HINSTANCE hPrev,           \
                   LPSTR szCmdLine, int nCmdShow);
// Function to display an error message
void AppError(BOOL Fatal, char *Text, ...);

// Message procedure
long FAR PASCAL WindowProc(HWND hWnd, UINT uMsg,               \
                              WPARAM wParam, LPARAM lParam);


// Functions to register and unregister windows' classes
BOOL RegisterWindowClasses(HINSTANCE hInst);
BOOL UnregisterWindowClasses(HINSTANCE hInst);


// Function to create the application window
HWND CreateMainWindow(HINSTANCE hInst);


// Functions to init, shutdown, and handle per-frame functions
BOOL DoInit();
```

```
BOOL DoShutdown();
BOOL DoPreFrame();
BOOL DoFrame();
BOOL DoPostFrame();

int PASCAL WinMain(HINSTANCE hInst, HINSTANCE hPrev,                \
                   LPSTR szCmdLine, int nCmdShow)
{
  MSG Msg;

  // Save application instance
  g_hInst = hInst;

  // Register window classes - return on FALSE
  if(RegisterWindowClasses(hInst) == FALSE)
    return FALSE;

  // Create window - return on FALSE
  if((g_hWnd = CreateMainWindow(hInst)) == NULL)
    return FALSE;

  // Do application initialization - return on FALSE
  if(DoInit() == TRUE) {

    // Enter the message pump
    ZeroMemory(&Msg, sizeof(MSG));
    while(Msg.message != WM_QUIT) {

      // Handle Windows messages (if any)
      if(PeekMessage(&Msg, NULL, 0, 0, PM_REMOVE)) {
        TranslateMessage(&Msg);
        DispatchMessage(&Msg);
      } else {
        // Do pre-frame processing, break on FALSE return value
        if(DoPreFrame() == FALSE)
          break;

        // Do per-frame processing, break on FALSE return value
        if(DoFrame() == FALSE)
          break;
```

```
        // Do post-frame processing, break on FALSE return value
        if(DoPostFrame() == FALSE)
          break;
      }
    }
  }

  // Do shutdown functions
  DoShutdown();

  // Unregister window
  UnregisterWindowClasses(hInst);

  return TRUE;
}

BOOL RegisterWindowClasses(HINSTANCE hInst)
{
  WNDCLASSEX wcex;

  // Create the window class here and register it
  wcex.cbSize        = sizeof(wcex);
  wcex.style         = CS_CLASSDC;
  wcex.lpfnWndProc   = WindowProc;
  wcex.cbClsExtra    = 0;
  wcex.cbWndExtra    = 0;
  wcex.hInstance     = hInst;
  wcex.hIcon         = LoadIcon(NULL, IDI_APPLICATION);
  wcex.hCursor       = LoadCursor(NULL, IDC_ARROW);
  wcex.hbrBackground = NULL;
  wcex.lpszMenuName  = NULL;
  wcex.lpszClassName = g_szClass;
  wcex.hIconSm       = LoadIcon(NULL, IDI_APPLICATION);
  if(!RegisterClassEx(&wcex))
    return FALSE;

  return TRUE;
}

BOOL UnregisterWindowClasses(HINSTANCE hInst)
{
```

```
    // Unregister the window class
    UnregisterClass(g_szClass, hInst);

    return TRUE;
}


HWND CreateMainWindow(HINSTANCE hInst)
{
    HWND hWnd;

    // Create the Main Window
    hWnd = CreateWindow(g_szClass, g_szCaption,
           WNDTYPE, 0, 0, WNDWIDTH, WNDHEIGHT,
           NULL, NULL, hInst, NULL);
    if(!hWnd)
      return NULL;

    // Show and update the window
    ShowWindow(hWnd, SW_NORMAL);
    UpdateWindow(hWnd);

    // Return the window handle
    return hWnd;
}

void AppError(BOOL Fatal, char *Text, ...)
{
    char CaptionText[12];
    char ErrorText[2048];
    va_list valist;

    // Build the message box caption based on fatal flag
    if(Fatal == FALSE)
      strcpy(CaptionText, "Error");
    else
      strcpy(CaptionText, "Fatal Error");

    // Build variable text buffer
    va_start(valist, Text);
    vsprintf(ErrorText, Text, valist);
    va_end(valist);
```

```
  // Display the message box
  MessageBox(NULL, ErrorText, CaptionText,                         \
             MB_OK | MB_ICONEXCLAMATION);

  // Post a quit message if error was fatal
  if(Fatal == TRUE)
    PostQuitMessage(0);
}


// The message procedure - empty except for destroy message
long FAR PASCAL WindowProc(HWND hWnd, UINT uMsg,                  \
                           WPARAM wParam, LPARAM lParam)
{
  switch(uMsg) {
    case WM_DESTROY:
      PostQuitMessage(0);
      return 0;

  }

  return DefWindowProc(hWnd, uMsg, wParam, lParam);
}


BOOL DoInit()
{
  // Perform application initialization functions here
  // such as those that set up the graphics, sound, network, etc.
  // Return a value of TRUE for success, FALSE otherwise.

  return TRUE;
}


BOOL DoShutdown()
{
  // Perform application shutdown functions here
  // such as those that shut down the graphics, sound, etc.
  // Return a value of TRUE for success, FALSE otherwise

  return TRUE;
}
```

```
BOOL DoPreFrame()
{
  // Perform pre-frame processing, such as setting up a timer.
  // Return TRUE on success, FALSE otherwise.
  return TRUE;
}

BOOL DoFrame()
{
  // Perform per-frame processing, such as rendering.
  // Return TRUE on success, FALSE otherwise.
  return TRUE;
}

BOOL DoPostFrame()
{
  // Perform post-frame processing, such as time synching, etc.
  // Return TRUE on success, FALSE otherwise.
  return TRUE;
}
```

The preceding framework code will initialize a window and enter a message pump waiting for the destruction of the application. All the functions are in place to handle all aspects of setting up and shutting down the application. Note that the application window created has no background; it is suitable for using with DirectX Graphics, which you learn about in Chapter 6, "Drawing with DirectX Graphics."

To alter any of the window settings, such as the width, height, or type, you can change the definitions at the top of the code. The same goes for the window class and caption, which are defined in two const variables declared at the beginning of the code.

Notice that I added a function that doesn't appear to be called anywhere. That function is AppError, which I like to use to display error messages to the user. Passing a value of TRUE as the Fatal parameter forces Windows to close the application window, whereas a value of FALSE allows the program to continue.

In each function, you see the comments on what each function does—it's your job to insert the code that handles the initialization of objects, loading graphics, per-frame processing, and so on.

# Structuring a Project

At the start of each project, many options are available to you. All the various functions that compose your application can be combined into a single source file, or split into separate files by their individual functionality. For example, graphics functions go into a graphics source file, sound functions go into a sound source file, and so on. As long as you include those files in your project and provide a source header file for each, there's nothing to worry about.

I always start my programs with the `WinMain.cpp` file. This file contains the entry point for the application. It initializes the window and calls all the necessary setup, per-frame, and shutdown functions (which might be located in separate source files). In fact, I use that methodology throughout the book.

Chapter 10, "Creating the Game Core," introduces a series of class objects that I use to speed the development of my games. You can include these files, all separated by their functionality (graphics, sound, network, and so on), in your project (as well as their respective include files). All you have to do is create a class instance of the individual objects you want to use and hack away.

The bottom line is this: Arrange your entire project in easy-to-use modules that will not overwhelm you.

# Debugging Your Program

A perfect programmer is indeed rare, so you will spend part of your coding time tracking down those awful bugs that love to crash your programs. Getting to know your way around a debugging program helps in the long run, but don't spend too much time on it. Although the debugger can help a lot, there are those times when you can pull out your hair trying to figure out what is going wrong.

Typical bugs are misspelled variables, incorrect values, and use of uninitialized pointers. The first mistake you can make when programming is to give variables similar names, such as the following:

```
char *MyName;
char *MyNames;
```

The simple addition of the letter s creates the possibility of getting the two variables mixed up at an inopportune time. Be sure to avoid this mistake.

You can use the `assert` function to track incorrect values and uninitialized pointers.

The sole purpose of the assert function is to evaluate an expression. When the evaluation returns a value of FALSE, a debug message is displayed (much like the message seen in Figure 5.11), and the application aborts.

By placing assert function calls at strategic positions in your code, you can verify that a variable is set appropriately or that a pointer is initialized. If that is not the case, you'll be notified and can track down the nasty bugs. What's cool is that after you fix the bug, you can leave the assert function calls in place and have the compiler skip them just by defining a macro at the top of your code.

First, though, check out this code, which shows you how to work with assert:

```
// Include assert header - a must!
#include <assert.h>

// Instance a variable and pointer to work with
long dwValue = 10;
char *pPtr = NULL;

// check variable (looking for 20)
assert(dwValue == 20);

// check pointer (must not be NULL)
assert(pPtr != NULL);
```

Note that at each assert function call, an error message is displayed because neither expression is true. The dwValue is initialized with a value of 10, but the call to assert wants to make sure that a value of 20 is stored, which is not the case. The same goes for pPtr, which needs to be non-NULL. At each point, an error is displayed, and the program aborts.

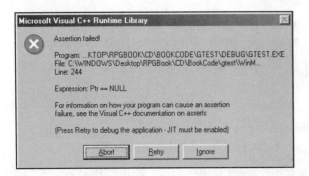

**Figure 5.11**

*The* assert *error message is useful for tracking down uninitialized or incorrectly set variables. As seen here,* assert *has informed me what the error is, which file the error is in, and the line number in which I can expect to see the problem.*

Now, assume that you've worked out the bugs and don't want assert to work its magic anymore. Going through your source code and clipping out all the assert statements that you've added is a lot of work. Not to worry; the addition of this single line of code at the beginning of your source code will cause the compiler to skip all assert calls:

```
#define NDEBUG
// Follow NDEBUG definition with include statements
// ...

// Include assert header - a must!
#include <assert.h>
```

Other than using your compiler's debugger features, that's it folks.

> **TIP**
>
> I like to track bugs by using assert and occasionally displaying the value of the variables and pointers using the MessageBox procedure. Find what works best for you, and for goodness sakes, don't pull out your hair!

# Wrapping Up Windows and Application Basics

Getting Windows to work in your game project is really a simple chore. By knowing only the basics to creating a window and processing the window's messages, you're able to begin concentrating on the real task at hand—creating your game.

Speaking of creating your game, using the information in this chapter, such as state-based processing and data packaging, you'll be able to manage any size project with minimal effort. Correctly structuring your project is your first and highest priority. Take advantage of the techniques in this chapter and see just how quickly you can get a game project up and running.

## Programs on the CD-ROM

Programs that demonstrate the code discussed in this chapter are located on the CD-ROM at the back of this book. You can find the following demo programs in the \BookCode\Chap05\ directory:

- ◆ **State.** Demonstrates using the state stack methods used in this chapter. Location: \BookCode\Chap05\State\.

- ◆ **Process.** Demonstrates using a process stack, as shown in this chapter. Location: \BookCode\Chap05\Process\.

- ◆ **Data.** A data packaging example application. Location: \BookCode\Chap05\Data\.

- ◆ **Shell.** A complete shell application used to create a window and call various functions in order to ease development time. Location: \BookCode\Chap05\Shell\.

# CHAPTER 6

# DRAWING WITH DIRECTX GRAPHICS

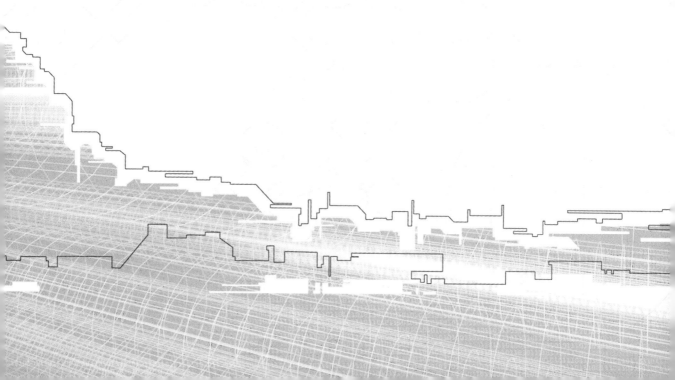

Recent games have dazzled us with their remarkable graphics and awesome effects. It's those graphical effects that catch most players' eyes, so graphics are a major component in your projects. Fortunately, most graphics engines and the concepts behind them are straightforward and easy to understand. By applying the basics of drawing graphics, you can re-create the awesome effects you see in games and also create some new effects of your own.

Now that it's time to create your own graphics engine, you can turn to DirectX Graphics, the graphical component of DirectX. In this chapter, I show you how to use DirectX Graphics, including basic drawing techniques and the DirectX Graphics advanced features such as texture-mapping and alpha blending. By the end of this chapter, you'll be a graphics-programming pro!

In this chapter, you learn about the following:

- DirectX graphics
- How to work in 3-D
- Matrix math
- Using the D3DX Library
- Drawing with vertices and polygons
- Working with texture maps
- Using alpha blending
- Billboarding and particles
- Working with meshes
- Using .X files
- Animating meshes

# The Heart of 3-D Graphics

Although jumping to a topic as advanced as 3-D at this point in the book might not seem logical, doing so is actually very logical. Specifically, the entire graphics system of DirectX is based on Microsoft's 3-D foray, which is Direct3D. For that reason, everything you do with DirectX Graphics is couched in 3-D terminology and usage.

Everything, and I mean everything, drawn with Direct3D is composed of polygons. A *polygon* is typically a triangular shape composed of three points, called *vertices*. A *vertex* is the smallest unit in 3-D; it is a single point (coordinate) located in 2-D or 3-D space. You create edges (lines) by joining two vertices together, with three edges forming a polygon.

> **NOTE**
>
> In this section, I want to introduce you to 3-D terminology and the theory of drawing with 3-D graphics. In the section "Getting Down to Drawing," later in this chapter, you apply theory to practice by beginning to draw using DirectX Graphics.

You can think of this relationship of vertices, edges, and polygons as a sort of connect-the-dots game. The dots are vertices, and the lines you draw are edges. The connected edges form a *polygon face*, and the whole picture is called a *mesh* (a mesh is the culmination of all basic drawing objects—vertices, edges, and polygons) or a *model*. You can see the relationship of vertices, edges, polygons, and meshes demonstrated in Figure 6.1.

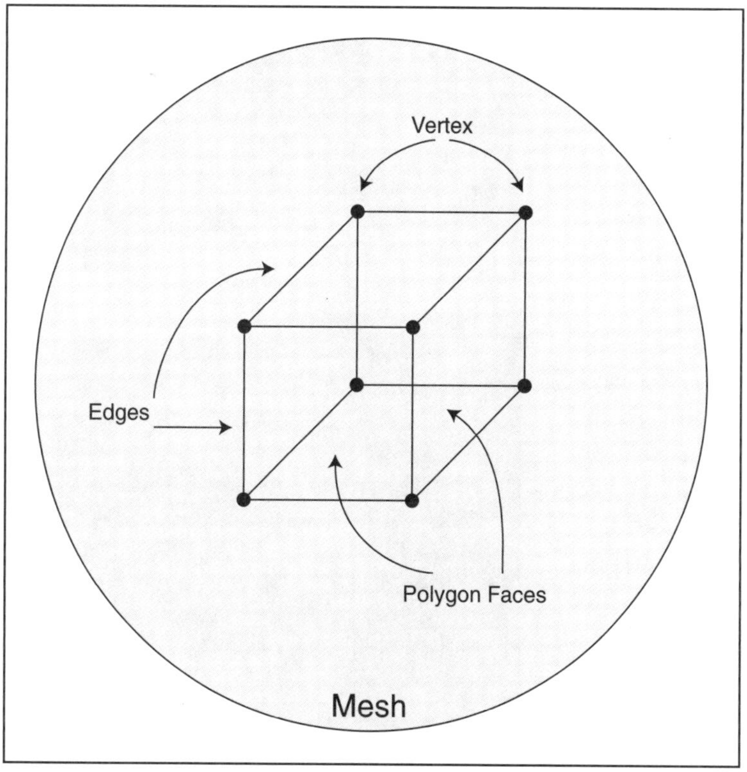

**Figure 6.1**

*Connect-the-dots to create a 3-D object.*

In order to present a more realistic looking 3-D object, Direct3D uses what is called *materials* to fill the empty polygons of a mesh with colors you designate. A material is represented by a combination of color components, as well as an optional bitmap image, known as a *texture*, that is stretched onto the surface of a polygon when the polygon is being rendered.

## Coordinate Systems

You might already be familiar with using 2-D coordinates when dealing with images; they have a width and height, measured in pixels. The horizontal span of the width is considered the *X-coordinate*, while the vertical span is the *Y-coordinate*. Each coordinate is measured from its offset from the upper-left corner of the image.

In Figure 6.2, you can see the coordinates in place. The X-coordinate runs left to right, with the origin (X-coordinate = 0) at the far left. The Y-coordinate runs top to bottom, with the origin (Y-coordinate = 0) at the very top. These coordinates extend in a positive direction to the other end of their respective spans. In Direct3D, 2-D coordinates are commonly referred to as *transformed coordinates* because they represent the final coordinates used to draw objects to the display.

In 3-D, an additional coordinate is added, the *Z-coordinate*. Typically, the Z-coordinate represents the depth of the image. More importantly, the Y-coordinate is flipped, running from bottom to top (the positive direction moving up). You can see this layout of the three coordinates in Figure 6.3.

You can use the Z-coordinate two ways: with the positive direction going from the origin forward (away from you) or backward (towards you). These two ways are commonly called *left-handed* and *right-handed* coordinate systems, respectively. In this book, I use the left-handed coordinate system.

> **NOTE**
>
> The left- and right-handed coordinate systems got their names from the fact that you can determine in which directions the three coordinates run by using your hands. Stick your left hand out with your palm facing upward. Point your thumb forward away from you (your fingers should be pointing right). Your thumb is pointing in the positive **Z** direction, and your fingers are pointing in the positive **X** direction. Now, point your fingers up (without moving your hand), and they'll be pointed in the positive **Y** direction. This is the left-handed coordinate system. Do the same with the right hand (with your fingers pointed right) to achieve the right-handed coordinate system layout.

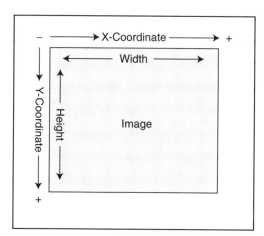

**Figure 6.2**

*You measure an image by the width and height in pixels. You reference coordinates in the image by using the appropriate X- and Y-coordinates.*

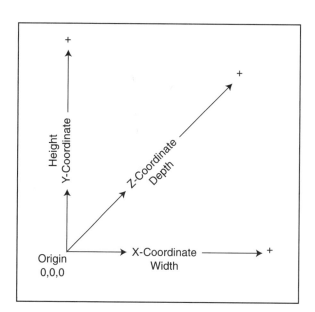

**Figure 6.3**

*The three dimension coordinates: X, Y, and Z. X and Y are analogous to the display, while the Z-coordinate represents the depth of the display, or rather the depth of a displayed image.*

Everything in the 3-D world is measured in those coordinate systems—2-D for images and video display and 3-D for everything else. So, if you were to define a point in space (using 3-D coordinates) that is in front of you (along the Z-axis), slightly to your right (along the X-axis), and at about eye-level (along the Y-axis), you would state those coordinates as X=100, Y=50, Z=200. Those coordinates would represent a coordinate that is 100 units to your right, 50 units above the ground, and 200 units in front of you, respectively.

As for 2-D coordinates, you would say that a picture on the wall is 200 units wide by 200 unit in height. The center of that picture would be at X=100, Y=100, and the upper-left corner of the picture would be at X=0, Y=0.

Those 3-D coordinates are referred to as *untransformed coordinates* because they do not represent the final coordinates that are used to render an object to the display. On the other hand, 2-D coordinates are referred to as *transformed coordinates*, as they map directly to the display's coordinates. Later in this chapter, in the section "The Math of 3-D," you find out how to convert an untransformed coordinate into a transformed coordinate, but for now let's focus on how to define objects using the coordinates you just read about.

## Constructing Objects

When constructing objects such as meshes and models (and even flat 2-D images), you begin at the vertex level. Each vertex has an X-, Y-, and Z-coordinate assigned to it. You can specify these coordinates in three ways: *screen space* (using transformed coordinates), *model space* (using untransformed coordinates), and *world space* (also using untransformed coordinates).

You use screen space to map vertices to the actual screen coordinates. Model space (also called *local space*) refers to coordinates you place around an arbitrary origin that represents the center of a model. The vertices in local space belong to a model, and you can move them with the object in order to draw it appropriately.

You convert the vertices contained in local space into world space before rendering the object. When rendering the object, you convert the world space coordinates into screen space coordinates.

Vertices placed in world space represent the final position used to render an object. World space is the actual position around a fixed point in the 3-D world. For example, consider yourself a mesh. Your joints are vertices that are defined in local space, because they can be defined with coordinates from the center of your chest.

As you move around your house (which is world space), the coordinates of your joints move around in the world but remain local to your body, as demonstrated in Figure 6.4.

After deciding on the type of coordinates to use to draw an object (in screen, local, or world space), you then place the vertices (numbering them by the order in which they are placed). You then join these vertices in groups of three to create triangular polygon faces. Figure 6.5 shows a couple of polygon faces being constructed by grouping vertices.

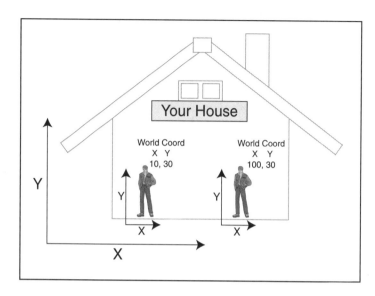

**Figure 6.4**

*Rarely do you refer to an object's vertex coordinates directly when moving the object around the world. Instead, you specify an object's placement by its world space coordinates and let Direct3D worry about the placement of the vertices.*

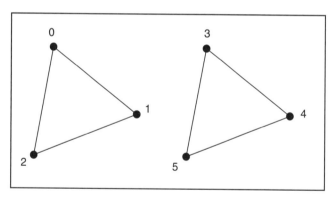

**Figure 6.5**

*You use six vertices to draw two polygons. Each polygon must be triangular, so each polygon uses only three vertices.*

# Lists, Strips, and Fans

Something you must consider when constructing the polygon faces is the sharing of vertices (that is, a polygon can use the same vertex, or vertices, as another polygon). A set of polygon faces can fall into three categories: triangle lists, triangle strips, and triangle fans.

A *triangle list* is a set of faces with no common vertices, so each polygon gets its own trio of vertices. A *triangle strip* is a set of faces with common vertices, so each polygon shares an edge with another polygon. A *triangle fan* occurs when a number of faces share a single vertex, almost like a fan does at its base. These three categories are shown in Figure 6.6.

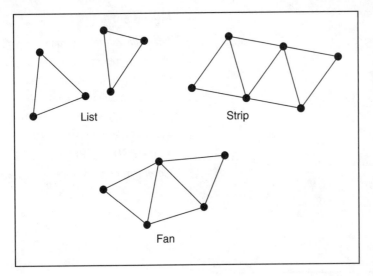

**Figure 6.6**

*Triangle lists don't allow vertices to be shared, unlike triangle strips and fans. Using strips and fans reduces the number of vertices, thus saving on memory and increasing rendering speeds.*

# Vertex Ordering

Later, when you get into rendering the polygons, the order of the vertices you use to define a face becomes important because you must determine which side of the face is the front and which is the back. For your current purposes, you want to order the vertices that define a face in a clockwise fashion (when viewed from the front side of the polygon), as shown in Figure 6.7. This way, you know you're looking at the front of the face if the vertices constructing the face are defined in a clockwise order.

Astute readers probably noticed that the triangle strip in Figure 6.7 has every other one of the face's vertex order reversed. This reversal of vertex ordering is a requirement for drawing triangle strips using Direct3D.

**NOTE**

Even lines and pixels can be drawn with Direct3D using vertices and polygons. Pixels are polygons that use one vertex, whereas lines are polygons that use two vertices. Both pixels and lines are created using triangle lists.

**NOTE**

In a 3-D engine, the backside of a face is normally not drawn, so it is skipped during the rendering process. This is known as *backface culling* and is a major optimization that should be performed. If you are using a right-handed coordinate system, this clockwise order is reversed and all polygon faces need to be ordered in a counter-clockwise manner.

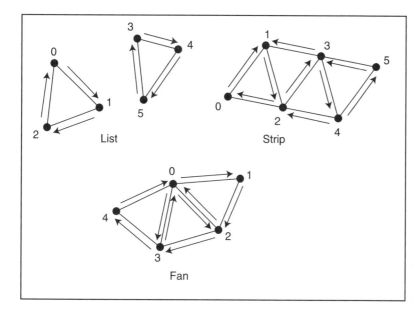

**Figure 6.7**

*Watch how you order the vertices, because you'll need to construct the triangle lists, strips, and fans using a specific order of those vertices.*

# Coloring Polygons

Once you define a group of polygons or a mesh, you are ready to color the polygon faces. Direct3D has two simple techniques that I discuss in this book. The first technique involves defining *materials*, which are basically single colors. Materials are defined by their diffuse, ambient, and specular color components. The *diffuse* and *ambient* colors are typically the same color—the color that represents the actual color of the object. *Specular* is the color of the highlight that appears when a nearby light brightens an object. (See the section "Materials and Colors," later in this chapter, for more on these color components.)

The second technique, called *texture-mapping*, involves painting the polygon with an image. Texture maps are images that are typically loaded from a bitmap file. These bitmap images are stretched or tiled (repeated) across the face of a polygon.

# Transformations

After you define a model (or even just a set of polygons), you are ready to place it into the world at the desired location. Figure 6.8 shows a couple of models that are placed inside the 3-D world. You can move, scale, and rotate any object as you see fit, so you can use the same model to draw a bunch of objects in different orientations.

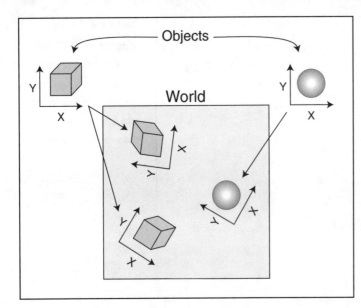

**Figure 6.8**

*Although you define 3-D objects in their own local space, you can position them within world space.*

You refer to these actions of moving (also called *translating*), rotating, and scaling as *transformations*. A number of transformations are required to take an object from its model space into a set of coordinates ready to view.

First, there is the *world transformation*, which is a transformation used to convert from the local coordinates to world coordinates. This includes scaling, rotation on the X-, Y-, and Z-axis, and translating (specifically in that order). The second transformation is the *view transformation*, which orients all objects around a viewing position within the 3-D world, thus converting world coordinates into view coordinates.

The last important transformation is the *projection transformation*, which is the transformation used to flatten the 3-D world into a 2-D image. It acts almost like a camera lens, with different zooms, short and wide-angles, and various other effects such as fisheye distortion.

# Getting Started with DirectX Graphics

Now that you're acquainted with the basics on drawing 3-D graphics, it is time to start applying that knowledge. Before you can move on, however, you need to understand how to prepare the graphical system for your use. In this section, I introduce you to the components of DirectX graphics that I use throughout this book and to how to get the graphics system running and ready for drawing. Prior to DirectX version 8, programmers were able to draw 2-D graphics using the DirectDraw component of DirectX. With the release of DirectX 8, however, DirectDraw was merged into Direct3D, resulting in DirectX Graphics.

Even DirectX veterans might need a bit of time getting accustomed to all the new and altered features in the latest version of DirectX. Don't let this fact daunt you, however, because Microsoft did simplify the use of the graphics system.

> **NOTE**
>
> Even though the new graphics component is called *DirectX Graphics*, I commonly refer to it as Direct3D, as all 3-D graphics objects utilize it.

To begin, always be sure to include D3D8.H in your source code and link in the D3D8.LIB library. (Appendix A, "Installing DirectX and Configuring the Compiler," has information on how to link in files. Consult that appendix to find out how to link in D3D8.LIB.) These are the essential files you need to start using Direct3D. You'll notice that your project begins adding many different external include files when using Direct3D; but you'll never have to worry about them— just let Direct3D do its thing to get you up and running.

## Direct3D Components

Direct3D separates the graphics functionality into a multitude of COM objects. Each object has its own purpose, such as an IDirect3D8 object used to control the overall graphics system, or an IDirect3DDevice8 object used to control how graphics are rendered to the display. In this book, I show you only those objects listed in Table 6.1; those are the objects that you're most likely to use in your game development project.

> **NOTE**
>
> Although there are a few more Direct3D components to deal with, they are beyond the scope (and usefulness) of this book. You can refer to the DirectX SDK documents for more information on those additional objects.

## Table 6.1 The Major Direct3D Components

| Component | Description |
|---|---|
| IDirect3D8 | Use this object to gather information about the graphics hardware and setup device interfaces. |
| IDirect3DDevice8 | Deals directly with the 3-D hardware. With it, you render graphics, handle image resources, create and set render states and shade filters, and so much more. |
| IDirect3DVertexBuffer8 | Contains an array of vertex information used to draw polygons. |
| IDirect3DTexture8 | Utilize this object to store all images used to paint the faces of 3-D (and 2-D) images. |

# Initializing the System

Starting to use the graphics system is an easy task, thanks to the simplification of Direct3D. Here are the four general steps for setting up and running the graphics system:

1. Obtain an interface to Direct3D.
2. Select a display mode.
3. Set the presentation method.
4. Create the device interface and initialize the display.

That's a pretty sparse list! I told you that getting the graphics system up and running is a simple task, so let's get a move on and find out how to handle each step.

## Obtaining the Direct3D Interface

The first step to using graphics is to initialize an IDirect3D8 object. Using the Direct3DCreate8 function does this for you:

```
IDirect3D8 *Direct3DCreate8(
  UINT SDKVersion);  // D3D_SDK_VERSION
```

The one and only argument to this function should be D3D_SDK_VERSION, which signifies the version of the SDK that you are using. The return variable is a pointer to the newly created IDirect3D8 object that you need, or the return variable is NULL if an error occurred during creation of the Direct3D interface.

**NOTE**

The majority of DirectX functions (as well as all COM objects) return an HRESULT value. Every now and then, you'll see functions (such as Direct3DCreate8) return a non-HRESULT value, so keep a close watch!

Using this function is as simple as instancing an IDirect3D8 object and calling the create function:

```
IDirect3D8 g_D3D;  // global IDirect3D8 object

if((g_D3D = Direct3DCreate8(D3D_SDK_VERSION)) == NULL) {
  // Error occurred
}
```

## Selecting a Display Mode

After the IDirect3D object is created, you can begin querying it for information about the graphics system, which includes the display modes that Direct3D can handle. In fact, you can also query the IDirect3D object for information about the current display mode if you want to use that format.

Display modes are categorized by their dimensions (width and height in pixels), color depth (number of displayable colors), and refresh rate. For example, you might want to use a 640 x 480 resolution with a 16-bit color depth display mode and the adapter default for the refresh rate.

This display mode information is stored in a D3DDISPLAYMODE structure:

```
typedef struct _D3DDISPLAYMODE {
  UINT Width;          // Screen width in pixels
  UINT Height;         // Screen height in pixels
  UINT RefreshRate;    // Refresh rate (0=default)
  D3DFORMAT Format;    // Color format
} D3DDISPLAYMODE;
```

You can see the width, height, and refresh rate, but what about the color format? In graphics, you usually have a choice of the number of bits to use per pixel (16, 24, or 32) to store color information. The more bits you use, the more colors you're able to display (and the more memory you use).

You commonly refer to color modes by the number of bits each color component (red, green, blue, and sometimes alpha) takes. For example, say that I want a 16-bit color mode—5 bits for red, 5 bits for green, 5 bits for blue, and 1 bit for an alpha value. With 5 bits of storage, each color component can use 32 shades. The alpha value has one bit, meaning that it's either off or on.

When you refer to a color mode, you don't say 16-bit, but the number of bits per color component, as in 1555 (1 alpha, 5 red, 5 green, and 5 blue). Standard colors modes are 555 (5 red, 5 green, 5 blue, no alpha), 565 (5 red, 6 green, 5 blue), and 888 (8 bits per color component). Notice that the alpha value isn't required at times.

Direct3D defines these color modes as enum values, which you can see in Table 6.2.

At this point, say that you want to start setting up a display mode that is 640 x 480 and uses the D3DFMT_R5G6B5 color format. Here's how you set up the D3DDISPLAYMODE structure:

```
D3DDISPLAYMODE d3ddm;
d3ddm.Width      = 640;
d3ddm.Height     = 480;
d3ddm.RefreshRate = 0; // use default
d3ddm.Format     = D3DFMT_R5G6B5;
```

### Table 6.2  Direct3D Color Mode Macros

| Value | Format Description |
|---|---|
| D3DFMT_R8G8B8 | (24-bit) 8 red, 8 green, 8 blue |
| D3DFMT_A8R8G8B8 | (32-bit) 8 alpha, 8 red, 8 green, 8 blue |
| D3DFMT_X8R8G8B8 | (32-bit) 8 unused, 8 red, 8 green, 8 blue |
| D3DFMT_R5G6B5 | (16-bit) 5 red, 6 green, 5 blue |
| D3DFMT_X1R5G5B5 | (16-bit) 1 unused, 5 red, 5 green, 5 blue |
| D3DFMT_A1R5G5B5 | (16-bit) 1 alpha, 5 red, 5 green, 5 blue |

To check whether the display adapter can handle the color format you want, fill the D3DDISPLAYFORMAT structure with the required information and give a call to

```
// g_pD3D = pre-initialized Direct3D object
// d3ddm = pre-initialized D3DDISPLAYMODE structure

// Check if display mode exists
if(FAILED(m_pD3D->CheckDeviceType(D3DADAPTER_DEFAULT,            \
            D3DDEVTYPE_HAL, &d3ddm, &d3ddm, FALSE))) {
  // Error occurred - color mode not supported
}
```

**NOTE**

As do all COM interfaces, Direct3D returns an HRESULT value. A value of D3D_OK means that the function call was successful; anything else is a failure. You can use the standard FAILED or SUCCEEDED macros to easily test the return codes.

**CAUTION**

Certain display adapters are unable to use specific display modes. It's your job to determine whether an adapter can or cannot support the various modes. If you are using windowed mode, this is not a big problem because Direct3D handles the color mode settings for you.

Setting the display mode information assumes that you are using a full screen. If, on the other hand, you want to support windowed mode (such as a standard Windows application), you have Direct3D fill in the display mode information for you. You accomplish this with the following call:

```
// g_pD3D = pre-initialized Direct3D object
D3DDISPLAYMODE d3ddm;
if(FAILED(g_pD3D->GetDisplayMode(                               \
                     D3DADAPTER_DEFAULT, &d3ddm))) {
  // Error occurred
}
```

Upon success, the preceding call to IDirect3D8::GetDisplayMode will return a valid D3DDISPLAYMODE structure.

## Setting the Presentation Method

The next step to setting up Direct3D is to decide how to present the graphics to the user. Do you want to do so within a window, a full screen, or a backbuffer (see the upcoming note for more on backbuffers)? What refresh rate will you use? All this information (and more as you'll see) is stored with a D3DPRESENT_PARAMETERS structure:

```
typedef struct _D3DPRESENT_PARAMETERS {
  UINT BackBufferWidth;              // Width of backbuffer
  UNIT BackBufferHeight;             // Height of backbuffer
  D3DFORMAT BackBufferFormat;   // Same as display mode format
  UINT BackBufferCount;              // 1
  D3DMULTISAMPLE_TYPE MultiSampleType;   // 0
  D3DSWAPEFFECT SwapEffect;     // how to display backbuffer
  HWND hDeviceWindow;                // NULL
  BOOL Windowed;                       // TRUE for windowed mode
                                       // FALSE for fullscreen mode

  BOOL EnableAutoDepthStencil;          // FALSE
  D3DFORMAT AutoDepthStencilFormat;     // 0
  DWORD Flags;                             // 0
  UINT FullScreen_RefreshRateInHz;     // 0
  UINT FullScreen_PresentationInterval;  // 0
} D3DPRESENT_PARAMETERS;
```

Although this operation might seem involved, you really don't have to deal with the majority of the fields in the D3DPRESENT_PARAMETERS structure; however, you do need to understand the fields related to the backbuffer.

> **NOTE**
>
> A *backbuffer* is an off-screen drawing surface (the same size as a window or video screen) that receives all drawing operations. In order to view the graphics drawn on a backbuffer, you use an operation known as a *flip*, which displays the contents of the backbuffer on the video screen or window. This operation displays smooth updates—the user never sees what is being drawn until you are ready to display it.
>
> You can see this concept demonstrated in Figure 6.9, which shows the front (display) and back (off-screen) screens. You draw on the back screen, and when you finish drawing, you flip the two screens to display the back one.

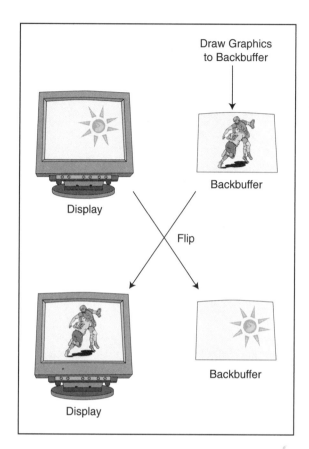

**Figure 6.9**

*Drawing on the backbuffer keeps things out of view until you flip the two screens.*

Here are two possible setups that you can use, depending on whether you are using a windowed or a full-screen graphics mode:

```
// d3ddm = pre-initialized D3DDISPLAYMODE structure
D3DPRESENT_PARAMETERS d3dpp;

// Clear out the structure
ZeroMemory(&d3dpp, sizeof(D3DPRESENT_PARAMETERS));

// For windowed mode, use:
d3dpp.Windowed = TRUE;
d3dpp.SwapEffect = D3DSWAPEFFECT_DISCARD;
d3dpp.BackBufferFormat = d3ddm.Format;  // use same color mode
```

```
// For fullscreen mode, use:
d3dpp.Windowed = FALSE;
d3dpp.SwapEffect = D3DSWAPEFFECT_FLIP;
d3dpp.FullScreen_RefreshRateInHz = D3DPRESENT_RATE_DEFAULT;
d3dpp.FullScreen_PresentationInterval =                        \
                              D3DPRESENT_INTERVAL_DEFAULT;
d3dpp.BackBufferFormat = d3ddm.Format; // use same color mode
```

## Creating the Device Interface and Initializing the Display

At last you're able to create the Direct3D device interface, which is the workhorse of the 3-D system. Using the D3DDISPLAYMODE and D3DPRESENT_PARAMETERS structures that you previously set up, call the IDirect3D8::CreateDevice function to create and initialize the display interface:

```
HRESULT IDirect3D8::CreateDevice(
   UINT Adapter,              // D3DADAPTER_DEFAULT
   D3DDEVTYPE DeviceType,  // D3DDEVTYPE_HAL
   HWND hFocusWindow,         // window handle to use for rendering
   DWORD BehaviorFlags,    // D3DCREATE_SOFTWARE_VERTEXPROCESSING
   D3DPRESENT_PARAMETERS *pPresentationParameters, // d3dpp
   IDirect3DDevice8 *ppReturnedDeviceInterface); // device object
```

In the CreateDevice function, you see where to pass the presentation structure that you created, plus the handle to the window that belongs to your application (and which Direct3D will use to display the rendered graphics). The rest of the arguments are pretty standard fare, and you rarely change them. The last argument is the pointer to the Direct3D device object that you are creating. A call to the IDirect3D8::CreateDevice might look something like this:

```
// g_pD3D = pre-initialized Direct3D object
// hWnd = window handle to use for rendering
// d3dpp = pre-initialized presentation structure
IDirect3DDevice8 *g_pD3DDevice;

if(FAILED(g_pD3D->CreateDevice(D3DADAPTER_DEFAULT,             \
    D3DDEVTYPE_HAL, hWnd, D3DCREATE_SOFTWARE_VERTEXPROCESSING,
    &d3dpp, &g_pD3DDevice))) {
  // Error occurred
}
```

## Losing the Device

Normally, the device interface operates as expected, and everything works great; graphics are drawn, and memory resources are maintained. Although it would be great to think that your device will stay in this operational state, there will be times when it just can't. Enter the world of lost devices.

A lost device is one that has lost control of the graphics resources for one reason or another. It could be that another application gained control of the graphics adapter and dumped all the memory that contained your application's graphics data. It could be that Windows powered down the system while entering sleep mode. Whatever the reason, your control of the graphics device is gone, and you need to get it back.

How do you know when control is lost? By examining the return calls to any device function that you call! For example, in the section "Presenting the Scene," later in this chapter, you see how to display graphics to the video display. During that call, if the device object returns a value of D3DERR_DEVICELOST, you'll know that the device is lost.

Regaining control of the device is a drastic step, in a manner of speaking. It's all done through the following function:

```
HRESULT IDirect3DDevice8::Reset(
  D3DPRESENT_PARAMETERS *pPresentationParameters);
```

The one and only parameter is the presentation structure that you used when you initialized the device:

```
// g_pD3DDevice = pre-initialized device object
// d3dpp = pre-setup presentation structure
g_pD3DDevice->Reset(&d3dpp);
```

I'd like to say that this is a magic function that handles everything for you when restoring a device, but I'm sorry to convey some bad news. Calling the reset function resets the device and wipes out all resources—which really isn't too bad, because there's a chance they've already been lost (because the device was lost).

The bottom line is that you'll need to reload all resources that have to do with the graphics (such as textures), and you'll need to restore the device states (the settings). Much of what is lost is data you haven't yet learned about, so now I'll bring you up to speed.

## Introducing D3DX

Dealing with Direct3D is at times a major task. Although Microsoft has simplified many of the interfaces, you still have a bit of work to do. To help speed up application development time, Microsoft created the D3DX library.

The D3DX library is packed to the brim with useful functions for dealing with graphics, such as meshes, textures, fonts, math, and so on. Throughout this book, you will see how to utilize the D3DX library in order to make your game-programming quest a little smoother.

To use the D3DX library in your project, you include only D3DX8.H and link in D3DX8.LIB. All D3DX functions start with the prefix D3DX (for example, D3DXCreateFont). Not only does the D3DX library contain functions, but it also contains COM objects, such as ID3DXBaseMesh.

# The Math of 3-D

As you can probably tell by now, using 3-D graphics involves considerable math, and dealing with so many numbers can bog things down quickly. Many years ago, real-time 3-D graphics were a dream rather than a reality. Computers just couldn't handle the computations fast enough.

Of course, things got better with time, and now we're able to achieve some awesome effects. Advancements in the math involved with 3-D graphics is one reason for this change.

## Matrix Math

No, this section is *not* about Keanu Reeves and his next movie in which he is stuck inside a calculator. Matrix math is a form of linear algebra that simplifies and reduces certain calculations. For your current purposes, the calculations are the 3-D transformations I just mentioned.

Because each 3-D object is composed of many vertices, Direct3D's job is to transform those vertices into coordinates that are ready to render the graphics to the display. You could transform thousands of vertices that construct a scene for each frame. That's some serious math—enough to choke any college math professor.

Direct3D deals with all the transformations by using matrices. A matrix is a grid of numbers, with each element in the grid having a specific meaning. For your current purposes, the numbers represent the transformations you want to apply to the vertices. By combining all the necessary calculations into a packed form, such as a matrix, the math is greatly simplified.

> **CAUTION**
>
> Note that matrix math is involved only when you work with 3-D coordinates. If you're using transformed coordinates (coordinates in screen space), you do not have to apply further transformations to them.

## Matrix Construction

A matrix comes in many sizes, but as far as you need to be concerned right now, its size is 4 x 4, which means that you have a grid with four rows and four columns. Direct3D stores a matrix as a D3DMATRIX structure:

```
typedef struct _D3DMATRIX {
    D3DVALUE _11, _12, _13, _14;
    D3DVALUE _21, _22, _23, _24;
    D3DVALUE _31, _32, _33, _34;
    D3DVALUE _41, _42, _43, _44;
} D3DMATRIX;
```

> **NOTE**
>
> D3DVALUE is a macro that expands to a float data type.

In order to fill a matrix with the transformation data you'll use, you can actually use the D3DX library. Instead of using the D3DMATRIX structure, make use of the D3DXMATRIX object, which contains the same variables as D3DMATRIX, along with a number of useful functions.

Each transformation you will use has its own matrix to start with, whereas the rotation takes three matrices (one for each axis). This means that you need five transformation matrices: X-rotation, Y-rotation, Z-rotation, translation, and scaling. The first set of functions is used to set up the rotation matrices:

```
D3DXMATRIX *D3DXMatrixRotationX(
    D3DXMATRIX *pOut,  // output matrix
    FLOAT Angle);      // X angle around center

D3DXMATRIX *D3DXMatrixRotationY(
    D3DXMATRIX *pOut,  // output matrix
    FLOAT Angle);      // Y angle around center

D3DXMATRIX *D3DXMatrixRotationZ(
    D3DXMATRIX *pOut,  // output matrix
    FLOAT Angle);      // Z angle around center
```

By passing each of the preceding functions with a matrix and providing a rotational value (in radians representing the angle along the axis origin), you obtain the values with which you need to work. The next function creates a translation matrix, which is used to move objects:

> **NOTE**
>
> Notice that all the matrix functions used by **D3DX** also return a `D3DXMATRIX` pointer. This is a pointer to the output matrix, and it enables you to use the matrix functions inline with another function, as shown here:
>
> `D3DXMATRIX matMatrix, matResult;`
>
> `matResult = D3DXMatrixRotationZ(&matMatrix, 1.57f);`

```
D3DXMATRIX *D3DXMatrixTranslation(
  D3DXMATRIX *pOut,  // output matrix
  FLOAT x,           // X coordinate offset
  FLOAT y,           // Y coordinate offset
  FLOAT z);          // Z coordinate offset
```

The coordinates are actually offsets based on the origin of the object. The translation values are used to convert an object from local space coordinates to world space coordinates. Next in line is the function that scales objects around their origin:

```
D3DXMATRIX *D3DXMatrixScaling(
  D3DXMATRIX *pOut,  // output matrix
  FLOAT sx,          // X scale
  FLOAT sy,          // Y scale
  FLOAT sz);         // Z scale
```

An object's scale is normally 1.0. To double the size of an object, specify a value of 2.0; to make the object half its size, use 0.5.

You'll also use a special type of matrix called an *identity matrix*. It has all but a few values set to zero; the others are set to one. When applied to another matrix, the identity matrix has no effect and leaves the resulting values the same as the original ones. Identity matrices are useful when you have to combine two matrices but don't want the original one altered.

In order to create an identity matrix, you can use the following function (which takes only the output matrix as a parameter):

```
D3DXMATRIX *D3DXMatrixIdentity(D3DXMATRIX *pOut);
```

Although the function prototypes are not much to look at, here are some examples:

```
D3DXMATRIX matXRot, matYRot, matZRot;
D3DXMATRIX matTrans, matScale;

// Setup the rotations at 45 degrees (.785 radians)
D3DXMatrixRotationX(&matXRot, 0.785f);
D3DXMatrixRotationY(&matYRot, 0.785f);
D3DXMatrixRotationZ(&matZRot, 0.785f);

// Setup the translation to move to 100,200,300
D3DXMatrixTranslation(&matTrans, 100.0f, 200.0f, 300.0f);

// Scale object to twice the size in all directions
D3DXMatrixScaling(&matScale, 2.0f, 2.0f, 2.0f);
```

## Combining Matrices

After filling the various matrices with the values used in transformations, you can apply them to each individual vertex. In fact, to make it even easier, you can combine the separate matrices that contain the values for translating, rotating, and scaling into a single matrix by multiplying them together. This procedure is known as *matrix concatenation*, and it is the heart of optimizing all matrix calculations.

By constructing a single matrix once per frame, you can then use this matrix for every vertex in the scene. When applied to a vertex, this single matrix has the same effect as applying the separate matrices in succession.

Matrices are not hard to use. They just take a little understanding. In fact, with the power of D3DX, you're able to combine the matrices effortlessly with the use of the D3DXMatrixMultiply function:

```
D3DXMATRIX *D3DXMatrixMultiply(
    D3DXMATRIX *pOut,        // output matrix
    CONST D3DXMATRIX *pM1,   // Source matrix 1
    CONST D3DXMATRIX *pM2);  // Source matrix 2
```

By passing two matrices as pM1 and pM2, you get a resulting matrix (pOut) calculated from multiplying the first two matrices. To expand on the example scaling, rotation, and translation matrices created in the previous section, combine them all into a single matrix that represents all the transformations:

```
D3DXMATRIX matResult;  // The resulting matrix
```

```
// Clear the resulting matrix to identity
D3DXMatrixIdentity(&matResult);

// Multiply in the scaling matrix
D3DXMatrixMultiply(&matResult, &matResult, &matScale);

// Multiply in rotation matrices
D3DXMatrixMultiply(&matResult, &matResult, &matXRot);
D3DXMatrixMultiply(&matResult, &matResult, &matYRot);
D3DXMatrixMultiply(&matResult, &matResult, &matZRot);

// Multiply in translation matrix
D3DXMatrixMultiply(&matResult, &matResult, &matTrans);
```

Notice that the order in which you combine the matrices is essential. In the preceding example, I combined them in this order: scale, X-rotation, Y-rotation, Z-rotation, and translation. If you were to combine the matrices in any other order, the resulting matrix would be different and would cause some future undesirable results.

## The Steps from Local to View Coordinates

In order for a vertex to be used to render a face, the vertex must be converted from its local coordinates (untransformed coordinates) to world coordinates. The world coordinates are then converted to view coordinates, and then finally projected into 2-D coordinates (transformed coordinates).

You convert local coordinates to world coordinates using a *world transformation matrix* (or *world matrix* for short). This matrix contains the transformations used to position the object in the 3-D world (local to world). The second transformation matrix, which is used to transform the object into viewing coordinates, is called the *viewing matrix*. Last is the *projection matrix*, which converts 3-D coordinates from the viewing coordinates into transformed vertices that are used to render graphics.

> **NOTE**
>
> When working with the view transformation, you must use the reverse values of the viewing position to orient objects into view. You do so because a viewing position actually stays locked at coordinates 0,0,0. When the view "moves," the world and all objects in it are actually moving around you. For example, if you want to walk forward 10 units, move the world's objects 10 units back toward you instead. Look left 10 degrees, and the world's objects rotate 10 degrees right around you.

When constructing the world matrix and the view matrix, you must pay close attention to the order in which you combine the individual matrices. For a world transformation, you combine the individual transformation matrices in this order:

$R = S * X * Y * Z * T$

R is the resulting matrix, S is the scale matrix, X is the X-axis rotation matrix, Y is the Y-axis rotation matrix, Z is the Z-axis rotation, and T is the translation matrix.

The view matrix must combine the individual transformation matrices in this order (using only translating and rotation):

$R = T * X * Y * Z$

The projection matrix is a special case and is a little harder to work with. You must take many things into consideration when building a projection matrix because it doesn't work with transformations such as translation, scaling, or rotation. I'll be using the D3DX library to help construct the projection matrix later on in the section "The Projection Transformation."

Figure 6.10 shows the path that a vertex takes through the various transformations to its final set of drawing coordinates.

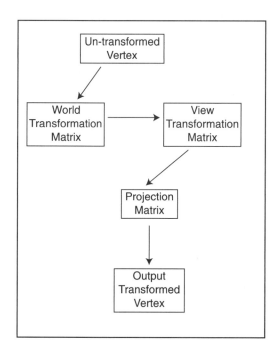

**Figure 6.10**

*An untransformed vertex passes through various transformation matrices in order to obtain its final rendering coordinates.*

# Getting Down to Drawing

Enough of the basics; it's time to check out how Direct3D actually draws graphics. In this section, I cover the basics on using vertices and polygons to draw graphics. You learn about the various ways Direct3D uses vertices to draw polygons, how to color those polygons, and finally how to present those graphics to the user.

It's the little things that make it count, so check out how to deal with vertices and move up from there.

## Using Vertices

Direct3D gives you the freedom to define a vertex in many different ways. For example, if you're using 2-D graphics, you can specify coordinates in 2-D screen coordinates (transformed coordinates).

On the other hand, if you're using local or world space coordinates, you can specify coordinates in 3-D (untransformed coordinates). How about using colors and textures? You can choose to include that information as well in your vertex definitions.

How do you keep track of all that information and make sure that Direct3D knows what you're doing? Behold the flexible vertex format.

### Flexible Vertex Format

The *flexible vertex format* (or *FVF* for short) is used to construct the custom vertex data for use in your applications. With FVF, you get to decide what information to use for your vertices; information such as the 3-D coordinates, 2-D coordinates, color, and so on.

You construct the FVF using a standard structure in which you add only the components you want. There are some restrictions of course, as you must list the components in a specific order, and certain components cannot conflict with others (such as using 2-D and 3-D coordinates at the same time). Once the structure is complete, you construct a *FVF descriptor*, which is a combination of flags that describe your vertex format.

The following code bit contains a vertex structure using the various variables allowed with FVF (or at least those I use in this book). The variables in the structure are listed in the exact order they should appear in your own structures; if you cut any variables, make sure you maintain the order as shown:

```
typedef struct {
  FLOAT x, y, z, rhw;    // 2-D coordinates
  FLOAT x, y, z;         // 3-D coordinates
  FLOAT nx, ny, nz;      // Normals
  D3DCOLOR diffuse;      // Diffuse color
  FLOAT u, v;            // Texture coordinates
} sVertex;
```

As you can see, the only conflicting variables are those for the coordinates, including the normals. Normals are coordinates that define a direction and can be used only in conjunction with 3-D coordinates. You need to pick which set of coordinates (either 2-D or 3-D) to keep and which to discard. If you are using the 2-D coordinates, you cannot include the 3-D coordinates, and vice versa.

The only real difference between the 2-D and 3-D coordinates is the addition of the rhw variable, which is the reciprocal of the homogeneous W. In English, this typically represents the distance from the viewpoint to the vertex along the Z-axis. You can safely set rhw to 1.0 in most cases.

Notice also that the sVertex structure uses the data type FLOAT (which is a floating-point value), but what about D3DCOLOR? D3DCOLOR is a DWORD value you use to store color values in Direct3D. To construct a color value to use for D3DCOLOR, you choose from two functions: D3DCOLOR_RGBA and D3DCOLOR_COLORVALUE:

```
D3DCOLOR D3DCOLOR_RGBA(Red, Green, Blue, Alpha);
D3DCOLOR D3DCOLOR_COLORVALUE(Red, Green, Blue, Alpha);
```

Each function (actually they are macros) takes four parameters, which are the amount of each color component to use, including an alpha value (transparency). These values can range from 0 to 255 for the D3DCOLOR_RGBA macro and 0.0 to 1.0 (fractional) for D3DCOLOR_COLORVALUE. If you are using solid colors (opaque), always specify 255 (or 1.0) for the alpha value.

As an example, say that you need to include only the 3-D coordinates and a diffuse color component in your own vertex structure:

```
typedef struct {
  FLOAT x, y, z;
  D3DCOLOR diffuse;
} sVertex;
```

The next step in constructing your FVF is to create the FVF descriptor using any combination of the flags listed in Table 6.3.

## Table 6.3  Flexible Vertex Format Descriptor Flags

| Flag | Description |
|------|-------------|
| D3DFVF_XYZ | 3-D coordinates are included. |
| D3DFVF_XYZRHW | 2-D coordinates are included. |
| D3DFVF_NORMAL | Includes normals (a vector). |
| D3DFVF_DIFFUSE | A diffuse color component is included. |
| D3DFVF_TEX1 | Texture coordinates are included. |

In order to describe a FVF descriptor, you combine all the appropriate flags into a definition (assuming that you're using the 3-D coordinates and diffuse color component):

```
#define VertexFVF (D3DFVF_XYZ | D3DFVF_DIFFUSE)
```

Just make sure that all the flags match the components that you added to your vertex structure, and everything will go smoothly.

## Using Vertex Buffers

After you construct your vertex structure and descriptor, you create an object that contains an array of vertices. Direct3D gives you two objects with which to work: IDirect3DVertexBuffer8 and IDirect3DIndexBuffer8. The object that I'll use for this book is IDirect3DVertexBuffer8, which stores the vertices used to draw triangle lists, triangle strips, and triangle fans.

Used with triangle lists, the IDirect3DVertexBuffer8 object stores at least three vertices for each polygon to be drawn (with the vertices arranged in a clockwise order). With triangle strips, the first polygon to be drawn uses three vertices, while each subsequently drawn polygon uses one additional vertex. As for triangle fans, there is one central vertex stored, while each polygon to be drawn has two additional vertices stored.

Figure 6.11 should help you better understand how you use stored vertices and in which order you arrange those vertices. In the figure, there is a square that can be defined in one of three ways. In the first way, using a triangle list, you need to use

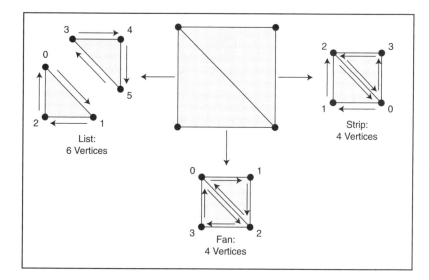

**Figure 6.11**

*You can store a simple polygon like this box (with four vertices and two polygons) a number of ways. Depending on the vertex storage, you can use up to six vertices to define the square.*

six vertices to define the square—three vertices for each of the two triangles.

The second way of ordering the square is to use a triangle strip. The triangle strip uses only four vertices, defined expressly as shown in the figure. The first three vertices construct the first face, and the last polygon defines the second face. As for the third method of ordering, the triangle fan, you again use only four vertices. With a fan, however, the first vertex you define becomes the base of the fan, while additional vertices define the faces.

> **NOTE**
>
> A polygon can use one, two, or three vertices, depending on what you're drawing. Pixels need only a single vertex, lines take two, and a triangle polygon takes three. Throughout this book, I mainly deal with and refer to triangular polygons.

## Creating a Vertex Buffer

You create a vertex buffer object by using the initialized IDirect3DDevice8 object:

```
HRESULT IDirect3DDevice8::CreateVertexBuffer(
  UINT Length,        // # of bytes to use
                      // in multiples of vertex structure size
  DWORD Usage,        // D3DCREATE_WRITEONLY or 0
  DWORD FVF,          // FVF descriptor
  D3DPOOL Pool,       // D3DPOOL_MANAGED
  IDirect3DVertexBuffer **ppVertexBuffer);  // the buffer
```

The only real parameter you want to change in the CreateVertexBuffer call is the Usage flag, which tells Direct3D how to treat the memory. You will rarely need to set Usage to a value other than D3DCREATE_WRITEONLY, but if you do, you can use D3DCREATE_SOFTWAREPROCESSING as an alternative. I explain those special cases as they arise in the book.

Here's a quick example (building on my earlier vertex format—in the section "Flexible Vertex Format"—that uses only the 3-D coordinates and diffuse color component) for constructing a vertex buffer containing four vertices:

```
// g_pD3DDevice = pre-initialized device object
// sVertex = pre-defined vertex structure
// VertexFVF = pre-defined Vertex FVF descriptor
IDirect3DVertexBuffer8 *pD3DVB = NULL;

// Create the vertex buffer
if(FAILED(g_pD3DDevice->CreateVertexBuffer(                    \
      sizeof(sVertex) * 4, D3DCREATE_WRITEONLY, VertexFVF,     \
      D3DPOOL_MANAGED, &pD3DVB))) {
  // Error occurred
}
```

## Locking the Vertex Buffer

Before you can add vertices to the vertex buffer object, you must lock the memory that the buffer uses. This ensures that the vertex storage memory is in an accessible memory area. You then use a memory pointer to access the vertex buffer memory. You lock the vertex buffer's memory and retrieve a memory pointer by calling the buffer object's Lock function:

> **NOTE**
>
> As always, be sure to release the vertex buffer COM objects when you are done with them by calling their Release function.

```
HRESULT IDirect3DVertexBuffer8::Lock(
  UINT OffsetToLock,   // offset to lock buffer, in bytes
  UINT SizeToLock,     // how many bytes to lock, 0=all
  BYTE** ppbData,      // pointer to a pointer (to access data)
  DWORD Flags          // 0
);
```

Here you have the offset into the buffer at the position you want to access (in bytes), as well as the number of bytes you want to access (0 for all). Then all that you need to do is give the function the pointer to the memory pointer that you're going to use to access the vertex buffer (cast to a BYTE data type). Here's a sample call that locks the entire vertex buffer:

```
// pD3DVB = pre-initialized vertex buffer object
BYTE *Ptr;

// Lock the vertex buffer memory and get a pointer to it
if(FAILED(pD3DVB->Lock(0, 0, (BYTE**)&Ptr, 0))) {
  // Error occurred
}
```

After you finish accessing the vertex buffer, always follow up every call to Lock with a call to IDirect3DVertexBuffer8::Unlock:

```
HRESULT IDirect3DVertexBuffer8::Unlock();
```

## Stuffing in Vertex Data

Now you have your vertex structure, description, and buffer, and you're locked and ready to store vertex data. Because you've already received the data pointer to the vertex buffer memory from the call to Lock, all you need to do is copy the appropriate number of vertices into the vertex buffer.

Continuing my example and using the vertex format I've defined (using 3-D coordinates and the diffuse color components), I create a local set of vertex data inside an array:

```
sVertex Verts[4] = {
  { -100.0f,  100.0f, 100.0f, D3DCOLOR_RGBA(255,255,255,255) },
  {  100.0f,  100.0f, 100.0f, D3DCOLOR_RGBA(255,  0,  0,255) },
  {  100.0f, -100.0f, 100.0f, D3DCOLOR_RGBA(  0,255,  0,255) },
  { -100.0f, -100.0f, 100.0f, D3DCOLOR_RGBA(  0,  0,255,255) }
};
```

Lock the vertex buffer, thus getting a pointer to the vertex buffer memory, and then copy over the local vertex data (and unlocking the vertex buffer when complete):

```
// pD3DVB = pre-initialized vertex buffer object
BYTE *Ptr;

// Lock the vertex buffer memory and get a pointer to it
if(SUCCEEDED(pD3DVB->Lock(0, 0, (BYTE**)&Ptr, 0))) {
```

```
// Copy local vertices into vertex buffer
memcpy(Ptr, Verts, sizeof(Verts));

// Unlock the vertex buffer
pD3DVB->Unlock();
}
```

That's all there is to constructing a vertex buffer and filling it with vertex data! Now you only have to assign a stream source and vertex shader in order to use the vertex information.

## Vertex Streams

Direct3D 8 enables you to feed the vertices to the renderer through a series of multiple streams called *vertex streams.* You can create very impressive results by merging multiple streams of vertex data into a single stream, but in this book, I use only a single stream because the complexity of using multiple streams is beyond this book's scope.

In order to assign your vertex data to a stream, you use the IDirect3DDevice8::SetStreamSource function:

```
HRESULT IDirect3DDevice8::SetStreamSource(
   UINT StreamNumber,                    // 0
   IDirect3DVertexBuffer8* pStreamData,  // Vertex buffer object
   UINT Stride);                         // Size of vertex structure
```

All you do now to set the vertex stream source is call this function with the pointer to the vertex buffer object and supply the number of bytes used to store the vertex structure (using sizeof). From my example of storing vertices in a vertex buffer in the previous section, you can use the following:

```
// g_pD3DDevice = pre-initialized device object
// pD3DVB = pre-initialized vertex buffer
if(FAILED(g_pD3DDevice->SetStreamSource(0,                        \
          pD3DVB, sizeof(sVertex)))) {
  // Error occurred
}
```

## Vertex Shaders

As a final step in using vertices to draw graphics, you need to understand the concept of vertex shaders. A *vertex shader* is a mechanism that handles the loading and processing of vertices; which includes modifying vertex coordinates, applying color and fogging, and numerous other vertex components.

A vertex shader can take two forms. It can be a *fixed* vertex shader (in which all the functionality needed for typical functions is already built in), or it can be a *programmable* vertex shader (in which you can customize routines to modify vertex information before rendering to the display).

Trying to explain programmable vertex shaders, which involves programming in a low-level assembly-like language, is beyond the scope of this book. Instead, I concentrate on using fixed vertex shaders because they contain all the functionality that you will ever need.

In order to use a fixed vertex shader on your vertices, you pass your custom vertex FVF descriptor to the `IDirect3DDevice8::SetVertexShader` function:

```
HRESULT IDirect3DDevice8::SetVertexShader(
  DWORD Handle);      // Custom vertex FVF
```

Using the preceding function is as easy as this:

```
// g_pD3DDevice = pre-initialized device object
// VertexFVF = pre-defined vertex FVF descriptor
if(FAILED(g_pD3DDevice->SetVertexShader(VertexFVF))) {
  // Error occurred
}
```

You've now set up the vertex information. The next step is to set up the various transformations needed to position the vertices (in local space) to their world space coordinates. Of course, that is the case only if you are using 3-D coordinates.

# Transformations

So far, you've learned how to initialize the graphics system and create vertices. If you're dealing with 3-D objects, such as polygons, the vertices are likely to be defined in local space. If so, you pass the vertices through a few transformations (the world, view, and projection) to make sure that they are positioned correctly when you render the objects.

Each transformation requires the construction of a special matrix that represents the appropriate orientation (or projection) values. The next few sections show you how to construct and use each of those three transformations, starting with the world transformation.

## The World Transformation

Vertices that are defined in local space need to be oriented into their respective coordinates within world space. For example, if you create a box from vertices (in local space) and you want it to appear at a specific location in the world, you apply a world transformation to it (as illustrated in Figure 6.12).

Use your old friend, the D3DX library, to help construct the world transformation matrix. In order to orient an object, you need to construct three rotation matrices (one for each axis), a translation matrix, and a scaling matrix:

```
D3DXMATRIX matWorld;
D3DXMATRIX matRotX, matRotY, matRotZ;
D3DXMATRIX matTrans;
D3DXMATRIX matScale;


// Create the rotation matrices
D3DXMatrixRotationX(&matRotX, XAngle);
D3DXMatrixRotationY(&matRotY, YAngle);
D3DXMatrixRotationZ(&matRotZ, ZAngle);


// Create the translation matrix
D3DXMatrixTranslation(&matTrans, XPos, YPos, ZPos);


// Create the scaling matrix
D3DXMatrixScaling(&matScale, XScale, YScale, ZScale);
```

Next, you combine all the matrices into the world transformation matrix. They must be combined in this order: scale, X-rotation, Y-rotation, Z-rotation, and then translation:

```
// Set matWorld to identity
D3DXMatrixIdentity(&matWorld);


// Combine all matrices into world transformation matrix
D3DXMatrixMultiply(&matWorld, &matWorld, &matScale);
D3DXMatrixMultiply(&matWorld, &matWorld, &matRotX);
D3DXMatrixMultiply(&matWorld, &matWorld, &matRotY);
D3DXMatrixMultiply(&matWorld, &matWorld, &matRotZ);
D3DXMatrixMultiply(&matWorld, &matWorld, &matTrans);
```

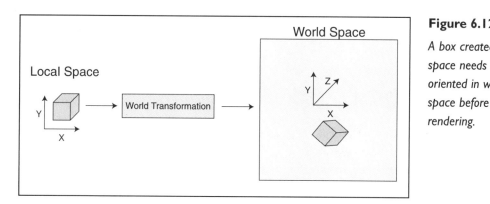

**Figure 6.12**

*A box created in local space needs to be oriented in world space before rendering.*

You're just about done. Now, you just tell Direct3D to use the world transformation matrix that was just created. You do this through the following function:

```
HRESULT IDirect3DDevice8::SetTransform(
  D3DTRANSFORMSTATETYPE State,   // D3DTS_WORLD
  CONST D3DMATRIX *pMatrix);     // World matrix to set
```

Notice that the second parameter is a pointer to a D3DMATRIX structure, but thankfully, you can use the D3DXMATRIX object that you constructed. Setting the first parameter as D3DTS_WORLD tells Direct3D that the matrix is used for the world transformation and that anything drawn afterward needs to be oriented by the supplied matrix.

If you have more than one object to orient in the world, simply construct a new world transformation matrix for each one (in their respective orientations) and then call SetTransform again, being sure to draw the object before going to the next world transformation.

## The View Transformation

In basic terms, the view transformation acts as a camera (called the *viewpoint*). By creating a matrix that contains the offsets in which you orient vertices in the world, you can align the entire scene around the viewpoint. All vertices must be oriented (using the view transformation) around the center of the world at the same relative position in which they are located around the viewpoint.

To create the view transformation, you build a matrix from the viewpoint position and rotation, this time going in this order: translation, Z-rotation, Y-rotation, and X-rotation. The trick, however, is that you use the opposite values for the position and rotation. For example, if the viewpoint is at X=10, Y=0, Z=-150, you use the values X=-10, Y=0, Z=150.

Here's the code that builds the view transformation matrix:

```
D3DXMATRIX matView;
D3DXMATRIX matRotX, matRotY, matRotZ;
D3DXMATRIX matTrans;

// Create the rotation matrices (opposite values)
D3DXMatrixRotationX(&matRotX, -XAngle);
D3DXMatrixRotationY(&matRotY, -YAngle);
D3DXMatrixRotationZ(&matRotZ, -ZAngle);

// Create the translation matrix (opposite values)
D3DXMatrixTranslation(&matTrans, -XPos, -YPos, -ZPos);

// Set matView to identity
D3DXMatrixIdentity(&matView);

// Combine all matrices into view transformation matrix
D3DXMatrixMultiply(&matView, & matView, &matTrans);
D3DXMatrixMultiply(&matView, & matView, &matRotZ);
D3DXMatrixMultiply(&matView, & matView, &matRotY);
D3DXMatrixMultiply(&matView, & matView, &matRotX);
```

To have Direct3D use the view transformation matrix you created, use the
IDirect3DDevice8::SetTransform function again, this time specifying D3DTS_VIEW for the
State parameter:

```
// g_pD3DDevice = pre-initialized device object
if(FAILED(g_pD3DDevice->SetTransformat(D3DTS_VIEW, &matView))) {
  // Error occurred
}
```

You can see that setting the view transformation is easy; it's constructing the view
matrix that is a problem. To make things easier, D3DX comes with a function that,
in a single call, sets up the view transformation matrix:

```
D3DXMATRIX* D3DXMatrixLookAtLH(
    D3DXMATRIX* pOut,          // output view transformation matrix
    CONST D3DXVECTOR3* pEye,   // coordinates of viewpoint
    CONST D3DXVECTOR3* pAt,    // coordinates at target
    CONST D3DXVECTOR3* pUp);   // up direction
```

At first glance, the D3DXMatrixLookatLH function doesn't make too much sense. You can see the typical output matrix pointer, but what are the three D3DXVECTOR3 objects? D3DXVECTOR3 is much like a D3DXMATRIX object, except that it contains only three values—in this case, three coordinates values. This D3DXVECTOR3 object is called a *vector object*.

pEye represents the coordinates of the viewpoint, and pAt represents the target coordinates at which the viewpoint is looking. pUp is the vector that represents the upward direction of the viewpoint. Normally, pUp can be set to 0,1,0 (meaning that up is in a positive direction along the Y-axis), but since the viewpoint can tilt (much like you tilt your head side to side), the upward direction can point in any direction and along any axis.

In order to use the D3DXMatrixLookAtLH function, you can use the following bit of code (assuming that viewpoint is at XPos, YPos, ZPos and that it's looking at the origin):

```
D3DXMATRIX matView;
D3DXVECTOR3 vecVP, vecTP, vecUp(0.0f, 1.0f, 0.0f);

vecVP.x = XPos;
vecVP.y = YPos;
vecVP.z = ZPos;
vecTP.x = vecTP.y = vecTP.z = 0.0f;
D3DXMatrixLookAtLH(&matView, &vecVP, &vecTP, &vecUp);
```

## The Projection Transformation

Last comes the projection transformation, which converts 3-D vertices (untransformed) into 2-D coordinates (transformed) that Direct3D uses to draw your graphics to the display. Think of the projection transformation as a way of squishing the 3-D graphics onto your display (as illustrated in Figure 6.13).

A number of aspects come into play when dealing with the projection transformation, such as the aspect ratio of the viewport, field of view, and the near and far clipping ranges.

The clipping what? When drawing 3-D graphics, sometimes objects are too near or too far from the viewpoint; you let Direct3D know when to clip out those sections (in order to speed things up). In order to construct the projection matrix and define the area in which objects are seen and not clipped out, you use the D3DXMatrixPerspectiveFovLH function:

```
D3DXMATRIX* D3DXMatrixPerspectiveFovLH(
  D3DXMATRIX* pOut,  // Output matrix
```

```
FLOAT fovy,        // Field of view, in radians
FLOAT Aspect,      // Aspect ratio
FLOAT zn,          // Z-value of near clipping plane
FLOAT zf);         // Z-value of far clipping plane
```

The fovy parameter indicates the width of the projected view, so the higher the number, the more you see. This is a double-edged sword, however, because the view becomes distorted if you use a value too small or too large. A typical value for fovy is D3DX_PI/4, which is one-fourth of pi.

The next important parameter is Aspect, which is the aspect ratio of the viewing area. If you have a window that is 400 x 400 pixels, the aspect ratio is 1:1, or 1.0 (because it is square). If you have a window that is 400 x 200 (twice as wide as it is high), the aspect ratio is 2:1, or 2.0. To calculate this value, divide the width of the window by the height of the window:

> **NOTE**
>
> The D3DXMatrixPerspectiveFovLH function builds a perspective transformation matrix using a left-handed coordinate system. If you are using right-handed coordinates, use the D3DXMatrixPerspectiveFovRH function instead (which uses the same argument as the left-handed version).

```
FLOAT Aspect = (FLOAT)WindowWidth / (FLOAT)WindowHeight;
```

The zn and zf parameters are the values for the near and far clipping plane and are measured in the same units that you used for defining the 3-D vertices. Typical values for the near and far clipping are 1.0 and 1000.0, respectively. These two values

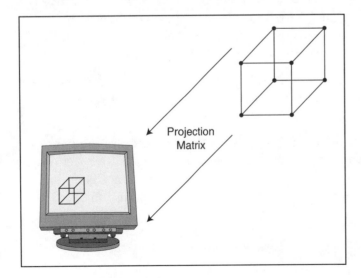

Projection
Matrix

**Figure 6.13**

*A projection transformation makes it possible to see objects defined by using 3-D coordinates on a flat, 2-D display.*

mean that polygons closer than 1.0 units (and 1000.0 units away) to the viewpoint are not drawn. You might want to set zf to a higher value in your own projects if you need to draw objects further than 1000.0 units away.

After you construct the projection matrix, you set the projection transformation matrix using the IDirect3DDevice8::SetTransform function, this time specifying D3DTS_PROJECTION as the State parameter:

```
// g_pD3DDevice = pre-initialized device object
D3DXMATRIX matProj;

// Create the projection transformation matrix
D3DXMatrixPerspectiveFovLH(&matProj, D3DX_PI/4,            \
          1.0f, 1.0f, 1000.0f))) {

// Set the projection matrix with Direct3D
if(FAILED(g_pD3DDevice->SetTransform(D3DTS_PROJECTION,     \
              &matProj))) {
  // Error occurred
}
```

## Materials and Colors

You've already seen how to declare colors in the vertex information, but when it comes to polygons, they too can have special color attributes assigned to them. Colors that you apply to a polygon face are called *materials*. Before drawing a polygon using Direct3D, you have the option of assigning a material to be used (if you choose not to use materials, you can use the vertex colors, if any exist).

Each material has a number of color values to describe it. With Direct3D, the color values that define a material are stored in a structure:

```
typedef struct _D3DMATERIAL8 {
  D3DCOLORVALUE Diffuse;   // Diffuse color component
  D3DCOLORVALUE Ambient;   // Ambient color component
  D3DCOLORVALUE Specular;  // Specular color component
  D3DCOLORVALUE Emissive;  // Emissive color component
  float         Power;     // Sharpness of specular highlights
} D3DMATERIAL8;
```

Realistically, you want to deal with only one color component: Diffuse. You can set the Ambient value to the same value as Diffuse, and you can set Specular to 0.0 or 1.0

(with Power set to 0.0). I suggest that you work with the values a bit, just to get an idea about the effect each component produces.

For current purposes, you apply the Diffuse color to a polygon face; the material's color can take the place of the vertex diffuse color component. If you were to apply a material's color to a polygon face that also uses colored vertices, you would cause a perceivable (and usually unwanted) change in the polygon's color. So, it's best to use either materials or vertex colors, not both.

When dealing with the material color components, you set the color component directly instead of using a macro such as D3DCOLOR_RGBA. Not to worry though—each color component is represented by its first letter (r for red, g for green, b for blue, and a for alpha) and by its range in value (from 0.0 to 1.0). If you were to create a material to use as the color yellow, you would set up the material structure as follows:

```
D3DMATERIAL8 d3dm;

// Clear out the material structure
ZeroMemory(&d3dm, sizeof(D3DMATERIAL8));

// Fill Diffuse and Ambient to Yellow color
d3dm.Diffuse.r = d3dm.Ambient.r = 1.0f;   // red
d3dm.Diffuse.g = d3dm.Ambient.g = 1.0f;   // green
d3dm.Diffuse.b = d3dm.Ambient.b = 0.0f;   // blue
d3dm.Diffuse.a = d3dm.Ambient.a = 1.0f;   // alpha
```

How you set up the material structure is your choice, but once that structure is set up, you need to tell Direct3D to use it before rendering a polygon. This is the job of the IDirect3DDevice8::SetMaterial function, which only takes a pointer to your material structure as a parameter:

```
IDirect3DDevice8::SetMaterial(CONST D3DMATERIAL8 *pMaterial);
```

Once called, all polygons rendered afterward will use the material settings. Here's an example that sets the previously defined yellow material:

```
g_pD3DDevice->SetMaterial(&d3dm);
```

## Clearing the Viewport

You need to wipe the backbuffer clean in order to prepare it for drawing, thus clearing graphics that might exist there. This is a simple chore using IDirect3DDevice8::Clear:

```
HRESULT IDirect3DDevice8::Clear(
    DWORD Count,              // 0
    CONST D3DRECT* pRects,    // NULL
    DWORD Flags,              // D3DCLEAR_TARGET
    D3DCOLOR Color,           // Color to clear to
    float Z,                  // 1.0f
    DWORD Stencil);           // 0
```

The only parameter to worry about at this time is `Color`, which is the color you want the backbuffer cleared to. The color value to use can be constructed using the typical `D3DCOLOR_RGBA` or `D3DCOLOR_COLORVALUE` macros that you've grown to love. Say that you want to clear the backbuffer to a light blue:

```
// g_pD3DDevice = pre-initialized device object
if(FAILED(g_pD3DDevice->Clear(0, NULL, D3DCLEAR_TARGET,        \
            D3DCOLOR_RGBA(0,0,192,255), 1.0f, 0))) {
    // Error occurred
}
```

# Beginning and Ending a Scene

Before you can render anything, you must tell Direct3D to prepare itself. This is the purpose of the `IDirect3DDevice8::BeginScene` function (which takes no parameters):

```
HRESULT IDirect3DDevice8::BeginScene();
```

When you finish rendering a scene, you need to inform Direct3D using the `EndScene` function:

```
HRESULT IDirect3DDevice8::EndScene();
```

You don't have to embed the `Clear` function call between `BeginScene` and `EndScene`; you can do so before you call the `BeginScene`. The only thing that must be sandwiched between the beginning and ending scene calls are the function calls that render the polygons.

# Rendering Polygons

At long last, you are ready to render the polygons! A typical frame of your game engine will clear the backbuffer, begin the scene, set the material to use, draw the polygons, and end the scene. You've seen how to do all of this, except for drawing the actual polygons.

You draw with an `IDirect3DVertexBuffer8` object using the following function (after the calls to set the vertex stream and shader, of course):

```
HRESULT IDirect3DDevice8::DrawPrimitive
    D3DPRIMITIVETYPE PrimitiveType,   // Primitives to draw
    UINT StartVertex,                 // Vertex to start with (0)
    UINT PrimitiveCount);             // # of primitives to draw
```

The first parameter, `PrimitiveType`, tells Direct3D what type of polygons to draw (which can be one of those listed in Table 6.4). The `StartVertex` enables you to decide from which vertex to start drawing (typically 0). You set `PrimitiveCount` to the total number of primitives (polygons) that you want to draw.

The primitive type you use depends on how you stuff the vertex data into the buffer. If you use three vertices per polygon, you use the `D3DPT_TRIANGLELIST` type. If you use a more efficient type, such as triangle strips, use the `D3DPT_TRIANGLESTRIP` type.

The only thing to remember at this point is that you must start a scene with `IDirect3DDevice8::BeginScene` before rendering polygons; otherwise, the `DrawPrimitive` function call will fail.

Say that you've created a vertex buffer that contains six vertices that construct two triangle polygons that form a square. Rendering them (with the addition of the

## Table 6.4  DrawPrimitive Primitive Types

| Type | Description |
|---|---|
| D3DPT_POINTLIST | Draws all vertices as pixels. |
| D3DPT_LINELIST | Draws a list of isolated lines using two vertices each. |
| D3DPT_LINESTRIP | Draws a list of lines connected to each other. |
| D3DPT_TRIANGLELIST | Draws polygons using three vertices per polygon face. |
| D3DPT_TRIANGLESTRIP | Draws a strip of polygons using the first three vertices for the first polygon and then an additional vertex for each subsequently drawn polygon. |
| D3DPT_TRIANGLEFAN | Draws polygons as a fan using the first vertex as the handle (all polygons are attached to it). |

BeginScene and EndScene functions as well as setting the vertex stream and shader) looks something like this:

```
// g_pD3DDevice = pre-initialized device object
// pD3DVB = pre-initialized vertex buffer
// sVertex = pre-constructed vertex structure
// VertexFVF = pre-constructed FVF descriptor


// Set the vertex stream and shader
g_pD3DDevice->SetStreamSource(0, pD3DVB, sizeof(sVertex));
g_pD3DDevice->SetVertexShader(VertexFVF);


if(SUCCEEDED(g_pD3DDevice->BeginScene())) {
  // Render the polygons
  if(FAILED(g_pD3DDevice->DrawPrimitive(D3DPT_TRIANGLELIST,    \
                                        0, 2))) {

    // Error occurred
  }

  // End the scene
  g_pD3DDevice->EndScene();
}
```

# Presenting the Scene

At long last, you're ready to flip the backbuffer to the viewport and show the user your graphics, which you do using the following function:

```
HRESULT IDirect3DDevice8::Present(
  CONST RECT* pSourceRect,
  CONST RECT* pDestRect,
  HWND hDestWindowOverride,
  CONST RGNDATA* pDirtyRegion);
```

You can safely set all arguments in the IDirect3DDevice8::Present function to NULL, which tells Direct3D to update the entire screen (because this function is capable of displaying small portions at a time), as in the following code:

```
// g_pD3DDevice = pre-initialized device object
if(FAILED(g_pD3DDevice->Present(NULL, NULL, NULL, NULL))) {
  // Error occurred
}
```

That's it! In order to create more realistic scenes, you use a multitude of different vertex buffers used to draw the various 3-D objects in your world. Another way to increase the realism of your graphics is to use texture-mapping.

# Using Texture Maps

Although you've learned to draw 3-D objects to the display, the plain colored polygons are rather bland. It's time to spice things up a bit and add a little detail. One of the easiest ways to increase the detail of 3-D objects is to use a technique known as texture-mapping. *Texture-mapping* is the technique you use to paint a polygon face with an image (as shown in Figure 6.14), thus increasing the visual appearance of rendered objects. Bitmaps are generally referred to as *textures*, so I use the two terms interchangeably when discussing 3-D rendering.

With texture-mapping, you assign each vertex in the polygon a pair of coordinates. These coordinates (called the *U,V coordinates*) define a point inside the texture image. The U,V coordinates are analogous to the texture image's X,Y coordinates, but instead of specifying the coordinates based on the texture image's width and height in pixels, you specify the coordinates in a range from 0.0 to 1.0.

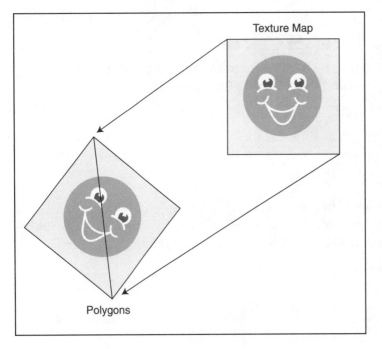

Texture Map

Polygons

**Figure 6.14**

*With texture-mapping, you can take plain polygons and paint pictures on their surfaces.*

Typically, the X- and Y-coordinates range from zero to the image's width and height, respectively, so if you have an image 640 x 480 in size, X will range from 0 to 639, and Y will range from 0 to 479. To access a pixel in the middle of the image, you specify X=319 and Y=239.

The U- and V-coordinates range in the value from 0 (the top or left edge of an image) to 1 (the right or bottom edge of an image), as shown in Figure 6.15. To access a pixel in the center of a 640 x 480 image, you use the coordinates X=0.5 and Y=0.5.

The U- and V-coordinate arrangement might seem a little strange at first. However, it works great because you can quickly swap out textures that are different sizes without having to worry about their dimensions.

Textures can be anything you want, although they are almost always bitmap images. Recent advances in video hardware have added bump-mapping technology, which takes a texture and treats it as a rough surface, making the rendered 3-D object appear as though it has bumps on it.

Using bump maps is a little too advanced for our current purposes, so to keep things simple, I'm only going to show you how to apply texture images to a polygon surface to enhance the visual appearance of your graphics system.

> **TIP**
>
> Here's a nifty trick. You can specify a U- or V-coordinate value over 1.0. This will cause the texture to wrap around as it's being rendered to the polygon. For example, if you use a U value of 2.0, the texture will be drawn twice (wrapped around once) horizontally. A U value of 3.0 means that the texture is wrapped around three times. The same goes for the V-coordinate.

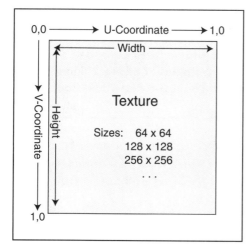

**Figure 6.15**

*The U- and V-coordinates of a texture image are constant, regardless of the size of the image.*

# Using Texture-Mapping with Direct3D

Textures are controlled with Direct3D via an `IDirect3DTexture8` object. This object holds the texture information and provides access to the texture information (including a pointer to the pixel data of the texture image).

When you first use textures, you begin to realize some of the restrictions placed on them by Direct3D and the various hardware manufacturers. First, a texture is limited in its dimensions, which must be a power of two (such as 8, 32, 128, and 256). Normally, you would use the same size for the texture's width and height, such as 128 x 128 or 256 x 256. Watch out, however, as there is a catch when using 3-D graphics: Quite a few video cards don't allow differing widths and heights of a texture (such as 128 x 64 or 32 x 256).

For those reasons, you should always try to use textures with the same width and height. In addition, you should ensure that your textures don't exceed 256 x 256 in size, which seems to be the maximum size that most video cards can handle (and you want to make sure that your game is as compatible as possible).

Finally, don't use too many textures. Although the process of rendering a texture-mapped polygon is easy for the graphics hardware to handle, preparing the texture for use is not easy. Every time the hardware needs a texture, Direct3D and your video card must do a little work to prepare themselves for the texture.

This work includes copying the texture into the appropriate memory (if it is not already there) and setting up the color format to match the display mode (as well as its internal color mode usage). This process is a time-consuming one, and the less you use it, the better.

> **TIP**
>
> To alleviate the setup time that a graphics card uses when preparing a texture, you can pack multiple images into a single-texture image. Doing so ensures that the texture needs to be set up only once; then all images can be pulled from the textures as needed. You see examples of this technique throughout the rest of this book.

# Loading a Texture

To obtain texture images, you generally load them from a disk or another resource. In fact, the D3DX library contains a number of functions to load and manage textures for you, making your job much easier. These D3DX texture-loading functions are shown in Table 6.5.

## Table 6.5  D3DX Texture-Loading Functions

| Function | Description |
| --- | --- |
| D3DXCreateTextureFromFile | Loads a texture image from a bitmap file. |
| D3DXCreateTextureFromFileEx | A more advanced version of the D3DXCreateTextureFromFile function. |
| D3DXCreateTextureFromFileInMemory | Loads a texture image from a file already loaded in memory. |
| D3DXCreateTextureFromFileInMemoryEx | An advanced version of the D3DXCreateTextureFromFileInMemory function. |
| D3DXCreateTextureFromResource | Loads a texture image from a resource. |
| D3DXCreateTextureFromResourceEx | An advanced version of the D3DXCreateTextureFromResource function. |

You can see from Table 6.5 that the texture-loading functions each have two versions, one is the quick-and-easy version of loading textures, whereas those ending with Ex are advanced versions that give greater control over the texture creation process.

To start your texture-mapping odyssey, check out D3DXCreateTextureFromFile, the first and easiest function to use:

```
HRESULT D3DXCreateTextureFromFile(
  IDirect3DDevice8 *pDevice,  // pre-initialized device object
  LPCSTR pSrcFile,            // filename of bitmap to load
  IDirect3DTexture8 **ppTexture);  // texture object to create
```

Again, this function is not difficult to deal with; just pass it the pre-initialized 3-D device object you created, the filename of the bitmap image you want to load, and the pointer to the IDirect3DTexture8 object you are creating. Here's an example using the D3DXCreateTextureFromFile function to load a bitmap titled texture.bmp into a texture object:

```
// g_pD3DDevice = pre-initialized 3-D device object
IDirect3DTexture8 *pD3DTexture;
```

```
if(FAILED(D3DXCreateTextureFromFile(g_pD3DDevice,              \
                "texture.bmp", (void**)&pD3DTexture))) {
  // Error occurred
}
```

The great thing about this function is that it handles all initialization for you and "sticks" the texture in the D3DPOOL_MANAGED memory class, which means that the texture remains in memory (lost textures were a major pain that pre-DX8 programmers had to deal with).

# Setting the Texture

As noted in the earlier section "Using Texturing-Mapping with Direct3D," a 3-D device needs to prepare itself to use a texture for rendering. This preparation must be done before a polygon is rendered using the texture. If you have 1,000 polygons with each polygon using a different texture, you loop through each polygon, set its texture, and render it.

You repeat this process until each polygon is rendered. If multiple polygons use the same texture, to be efficient, set the texture and then render all the polygons that use it, rather than use the set-then-render loop for each polygon.

To set a texture, use the IDirect3DDevice8::SetTexture function:

```
HRESULT IDirect3DDevice8::SetTexture(
  DWORD Stage,                        // Texture stage 0-7
  IDirect3DBaseTexture8 *pTexture);   // Texture object to set
```

You can see where to pass the texture object you created (as pTexture), but what is the Stage parameter? This is called *texture stages*, and it is one of the most exciting Direct3D texture-mapping techniques.

Texture-mapping with Direct3D is highly versatile. A texture does not have to come from a single source, but can be built from as many as eight different sources. These sources, called *texture stages,* are numbered from 0 to 7.

When rendering polygons, for each pixel to be drawn, Direct3D starts at stage 1 and queries for a texture pixel. From there, Direct3D moves to stage 2 and asks for another texture pixel or allows you to modify the previous texture pixel. This process continues until all 8 stages are processed.

Each stage can alter the texture pixel however it wants, including blending the pixel with a new texture pixel, increasing or decreasing the color or brightness, or even performing a special effect known as *alpha blending* (a technique that blends the colors of multiple pixels). You can see this process illustrated in Figure 6.16, in which an input pixel goes through each stage, starting with stage 0 in which the diffuse color component (the red, green, and blue color levels) of a pixel is pulled from the texture. From there, the pixel is alpha-blended and then darkened, leading to the final output pixel that is rendered to the display.

With texture stages, the possibilities are endless, and unfortunately I don't have the space to go into detail about them. In this book, I use only a single texture stage that will pull the pixel color from the texture, apply the polygon color information, and render the resulting colored pixel onto a polygon.

The following code bit selects a texture to use in stage 0 and tells the renderer to grab a texture pixel, apply the vertex color information to it, and disable alpha blending:

```
// g_pD3DDevice is a pre-initialized 3-D Device object
// pD3DTexture is a loaded texture object

// Set texture in stage 0
g_pD3DDevice->SetTexture(0, pTexture);

// Set stage parameters - only need to do this once in program
g_pD3DDevice->SetTextureStageState(0,                        \
                D3DTSS_COLOROP,   D3DTOP_MODULATE);
g_pD3DDevice->SetTextureStageState(0,                        \
                D3DTSS_COLORARG1, D3DTA_TEXTURE);
g_pD3DDevice->SetTextureStageState(0,                        \
                D3DTSS_COLORARG2, D3DTA_DIFFUSE);
g_pD3DDevice->SetTextureStageState(0,                        \
                D3DTSS_ALPHAOP,   D3DTOP_DISABLE);
```

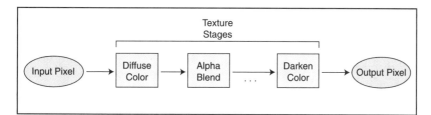

**Figure 6.16**

*Each texture stage modifies the final output pixel in a number of ways. Here an input pixel goes through a number of alterations to arrive at the final output pixel.*

This is the basic set of texture operations, so you're likely to see it quite a bit. Note that you set the stage state parameters only once and then just rely on the SetTexture call from then on. For more information on using stage state parameters, consult the DX SDK.

When you finish using a texture (after rendering the polygons), you call the SetTexture function once more, specifying NULL as the pTexture argument as follows:

```
g_pD3DDevice->SetTexture(0, NULL);
```

This releases the texture from memory and the hardware processor. Failing to do so can cause a memory leak and maybe even cause your game to crash.

# Using Texture Filters

Every now and then, you will see references to *texture filtering*. Texture filtering comes into play when rendering polygons with textures. Because the display has a finite resolution, images tend to have little visual anomalies, such as jagged edges when drawing diagonal lines or pixilated (oversized) samples of a texture image when it is scaled up.

For these reasons (plus many more), filters were created to smooth out these little imperfections. Direct3D uses a number of filters that seamlessly ensure that your graphics have a cleaner look. In order for Direct3D to use a filter, you must make use of the IDirect3DDevice8::SetTextureStageState function:

```
HRESULT IDirect3DDevice8::SetTextureStageState(
    DWORD Stage,                         // Texture State 0-7
    D3DTEXTURESTAGESTATETYPE Type,  // State to set
    DWORD Value);                        // Value to use
```

Again, you see the use of the texture stages, but the second and third arguments are of concern here. The Type argument is the state of the texture stage that you are modifying; in this case, it is either D3DTSS_MAGFILTER or D3DTSS_MINFILTER.

Both of these states determine how Direct3D blends surrounding pixels inside a texture before outputting a pixel to the display. You use the first state, D3DTSS_MAGFILTER, when magnifying a texture (enlarging it) on a polygon, whereas you use D3DTSS_MINFILTER when minimizing a texture (shrinking it).

The Value argument can be one of those listed in Table 6.6.

## Table 6.6  Direct3D Texture Stage State Filter Values

| Value | Description |
| --- | --- |
| D3DTEXF_NONE | Don't use a filter. |
| D3DTEXF_POINT | The fastest mode of filtering. Uses a single pixel color from the texture map. |
| D3DTEXF_LINEAR | Bilinear interpolation mode. This mode combines four pixels from the texture map to produce a blended output pixel. A fairly quick mode of texture-mapping that produces nice, smooth pixels. |
| D3DTEXF_ANISOTROPIC | Anisotropic filtering compensates for angular differences from the screen and the texture-mapped polygon. Nice but slow. |

Typically, you would use the D3DTEXF_POINT or D3DTEXF_LINEAR filter modes; they are quick, with the linear mode producing a smoother output. In order to use either filter mode, just use the following code:

```
// g_pD3DDevice = pre-initialized device object

// Set magnification filter
if(FAILED(g_pD3DDevice->SetTextureStageState(0,                    \
      D3DTSS_MAGFILTER, D3DTEXF_POINT))) {
  // Error occurred
}

// Set minification filter
if(FAILED(g_pD3DDevice->SetTextureStageState(0,                    \
      D3DTSS_MINFILTER, D3DTEXF_POINT))) {
  // Error occurred
}
```

# Rendering Textured Objects

Before an object (a polygon or series of polygons) can be drawn with a texture, you must ensure that the polygon vertices include a pair of U,V coordinates. A custom vertex structure that contains only a set of 3-D coordinates and texture coordinates is as follows:

```
typedef struct {
  D3DVECTOR3 Position;  // vertex position vector
  float       tu, tv;   // Adding texture coordinates here!
} sVertex;
```

At this point, you have to construct your flexible vertex format macro to inform Direct3D of the vertex components you are using, and in this case those components are the untransformed 3-D coordinates and a pair of texture coordinates. Using the D3DFVF_XYZ and D3DFVF_TEX1 values accomplishes this:

```
#define VERTEXFMT (D3DFVF_XYZ | D3DFVF_TEX1)
```

Now for the fun part—placing your graphics onscreen. With the addition of a few lines of code, you can expand a simple polygon drawing function to include your texture. Assuming that you've initialized the device, defined the vertex buffer with the texture information, and have the world, viewing, and projection matrices set, here's an example of loading a texture and using it to draw a triangle list of polygons:

```
// g_pD3DDevice = pre-initialized device object
// NumPolys = number of primitive polygons to draw
// g_pD3DVertexBuffer = pre-created vertex buffer w/polygon info
IDirect3DTexture8 *pD3DTexture;  // Texture object

// Load the texture
D3DXCreateTextureFromFile(g_pD3DDevice, "texture.bmp",         \
                          (void**)&pD3DTexture);

if(SUCCEEDED(g_pD3DDevice->BeginScene())) {
  // Set the texture
  g_pD3DDevice->SetTexture(0, pD3DTexture);

  // Set the stream source and vertex shader
  g_pD3DDevice->SetStreamSource(0, g_pD3DVertexBuffer,         \
                                   sizeof(sVertex));
  g_pD3DDevice->SetVertexShader(VERTEXFMT);

  // Draw triangle list
```

```
g_pD3DDevice->DrawPrimitive(D3DPT_TRIANGLELIST, 0, NumPolys);

// End the scene
g_pD3DDevice->EndScene();

// Free the texture resources
g_pD3DDevice->SetTexture(0, NULL);
}
```

# Alpha Blending

Imagine standing inside one of the world's tallest buildings, walking up to a window, and peering out over the vast city below. The slight blue hue of the colored window gives everything a peaceful shade similar to that of the morning sky.

Imagine the same scene, this time in the language of 3-D graphical. The entire world is constructed from polygons, which for all practical purposes are solid objects. You can't see through them. What if you want a see-through window in your game? What about the nice hue that the window gave everything?

Not only do you want cool effects like those just mentioned, but how about things such as *transparent blits* (that is, you want to draw a polygon with portions completely transparent). Think of drawing as a partially transparent object in terms of a wall with a hole in its center. The hole is completely transparent, even though the wall is solid; your view through the hole is unobstructed.

These effects are possible using a technique known as *alpha blending*. Using alpha blending, you can alter the transparency of a polygon so that you can see through it. If the polygon is colored, that color will blend with anything behind the polygon. What's better, you can even use a texture on the polygon to create some awesome effects!

An object's degree of transparency is known as an *alpha value*. As you might have already noticed, Direct3D uses an alpha value in a number of ways. Using textures, for example, you can specify a format that uses an alpha value. The alpha values are stored in what's called an *alpha channel*.

> **NOTE**
>
> An *alpha channel* is a value much like a color component (red, green, blue). It specifies the amount of transparency to apply, with each pixel of a surface having an alpha channel of its own.
>
> This alpha channel can range anywhere from 1 to 8 bits. If you have an 8-bit alpha channel, you can specify 256 alpha values (0–255). A 4-bit alpha channel uses 16 alpha values (0–15).

# Enabling Alpha Blending

Enabling the Direct3D alpha-blending functions is as easy as setting the proper render states using the IDirect3DDevice8::SetRenderState function. The first render state, which actually enables the alpha blending, is D3DRS_ALPHABLENDENABLE:

```
// g_pD3DDevice = pre-initialized 3-D device object

// To enable alpha-blending, use:
g_pD3DDevice->SetRenderState(D3DRS_ALPHABLENDENABLE, TRUE);

// Set the type of alpha blending
g_pD3DDevice->SetRenderState(D3DRS_SRCBLEND,                    \
                             D3DBLEND_SRCALPHA);
g_pD3DDevice->SetRenderState(D3DRS_DESTBLEND,                   \
                             D3DBLEND_INVSRCALPHA);

// To disable alpha-blending, use:
g_pD3DDevice->SetRenderState(D3DRS_ALPHABLENDENABLE, FALSE);
```

Note the two additional render states (D3DRS_SRCBLEND and D3DRS_DESTBLEND) in the preceding code. Those two tell Direct3D that you want to specify the alpha values to use when rendering. At times, you'll see that the D3DRS_DESTBLEND value is set to D3DBLEND_ONE rather than D3DBLEND_INVSRCALPHA. I'll point that out to you whenever it occurs.

# Drawing with Alpha Blending

The only other information you need in order to use alpha blending is how to add the alpha values to your custom vertex information. You accomplish this by adding the diffuse color component to the custom vertex structure and descriptor. When you define the diffuse color, you must then specify the alpha value.

The following example sets up a simple vertex structure that stores the 3-D coordinates, plus the diffuse color component (that now includes an alpha value):

```
// The custom vertex structure and descriptor
typedef struct {
  FLOAT x, y, z;
  D3DCOLOR diffuse;
} sVertex;
#define VertexFVF (D3DFVF_XYZ | D3DFVF_DIFFUSE)
```

```
// Define 3 vertices in a local array
sVertex Verts[3] = {
  {    0.0f,  100.0f, 0.0f, D3DCOLOR_RGBA(255,0,0,64) },
  {  100.0f, -100.0f, 0.0f, D3DCOLOR_RGBA(0,255,0,128) },
  { -100.0f, -100.0f, 0.0f, D3DCOLOR_RGBA(0,0,255,255) }
};
```

The first vertex is set to a red color and is ¼ translucent (¼ of the color will blend through). The second vertex is green, using ½ translucency (½ of the color will blend through). The third vertex is blue and fully opaque, meaning that no color will blend through.

If you add texture map coordinates and set a valid texture, you can set the diffuse color to full (255 for red, green, and blue) and then specify the alpha value to blend the texture.

# Transparent Blitting with Alpha Testing

*Alpha testing* is a technique of testing the alpha values of pixels before they are drawn to the display. Pixels that have alpha values that do not fall into a specified range are rejected and, therefore, do not reach the rendering stage. Similarly to the way you achieve semi-transparent effects in the preceding section, you can use alpha testing to render polygons that contain completely transparent sections.

Using the hole-in-the-wall example in the preceding section, imagine that the wall is a polygon and you want to draw a hole in its center. You want the polygon to be completely opaque (solid) except for the hole. You want the hole to be completely transparent. To accomplish that effect, you use a technique called *transparent blit*, which enables you to exclude portions of a texture while rendering, thereby allowing background graphics to peek through the blank spots.

The secret to transparent blitting is to set up your texture and assign a single color as the *color* key. The *color key* is the color that will *not* be drawn when the polygon is rendered. For example, if you have a texture that has a circle in the middle surrounded by black (as illustrated in Figure 6.17), you can set the color key to black. When the texture is applied to a polygon and that polygon is drawn, Direct3D will not draw those black pixels, thereby leaving only the circle in the middle to be rendered.

In actuality, it's not the color key that marks pixels as being transparent, but the pixels' alpha values. In order for a pixel to be completely transparent, its alpha value must be set to zero. In order for the pixel to be drawn, the alpha value must

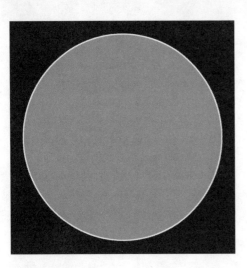

**Figure 6.17**

*A texture with a circle in the middle can use transparent blitting to exclude the dark surrounding area.*

be at its highest, which is typically 255. As you might guess, pixels that match the color key have an alpha value of 0; all others use a higher alpha value.

## Loading Textures with Color Keying

When using alpha testing in this manner, you don't have to specify the diffuse color component in your custom vertex structure or descriptor. The alpha values are stored directly in the texture pixel data. In order to set the alpha values in the texture pixel data, you load the texture using the expanded version of the D3DXCreateTextureFromFile function, which is as follows:

```
HRESULT D3DXCreateTextureFromFileEx(
    LPDIRECT3DDEVICE8 pDevice,      // device object to create with
    LPCSTR pSrcFile,                // filename of texture to load
    UINT Width,                     // D3DX_DEFAULT
    UINT Height,                    // D3DX_DEFAULT
    UINT MipLevels,                 // D3DX_DEFAULT
    DWORD Usage,                    // 0
    D3DFORMAT Format,               // color format to use
    D3DPOOL Pool,                   // D3DPOOL_MANAGED
    DWORD Filter,                   // D3DX_FILTER_TRIANGLE
    DWORD MipFilter,                // D3DX_FILTER_TRIANGLE
    D3DCOLOR ColorKey,              // Color key to use!
    D3DXIMAGE_INFO* pSrcInfo,       // NULL
    PALETTEENTRY* pPalette,         // NULL
    LPDIRECT3DTEXTURE8* ppTexture); // texture object to create
```

Most of the parameters use the default settings shown. The only things that you need to supply are the filename of the bitmap to load, which 3-D device object to use when creating the texture, which color format to use when loading the texture (D3DFMT_* type, which must use an alpha value such as D3DFMT_A8R8G8B8), and the color key (in a D3DCOLOR format).

When specifying the color key value, use the D3DCOLOR_RGBA or D3DCOLOR_COLORVALUE macros to specify the color you want. For example, if you want to exclude the color black from being drawn, load the texture using a color key value:

```
D3DCOLOR_RGBA(0,0,0,255);
```

Notice the value of 255 for alpha. This is very important! When loading bitmap files (.BMP), you must also specify a value of 255 for the alpha value. If you are dealing with non-bitmap files (such as .TGA) that already include alpha channel values, you must match the alpha value with the alpha values already stored in the image file. In this book, I use only bitmap files, so just remember to use an alpha value of 255.

After setting the alpha values for each pixel in the texture, it's a simple matter of using alpha testing to reject the pixels based on their alpha values.

## Enabling Alpha Testing

Once the texture is loaded (and the color key and alpha values are set), you can enable alpha testing by adding the following code during your initialization or rendering loop:

```
// g_pD3DDevice = pre-initialized device object
g_pD3DDevice->SetRenderState(D3DRS_ALPHATESTENABLE, TRUE);
g_pD3DDevice->SetRenderState(D3DRS_ALPHAREF, 0x08);
g_pD3DDevice->SetRenderState(D3DRS_ALPHAFUNC,                    \
                             D3DCMP_GREATEREQUAL);
```

The D3DRS_ALPHAREF state is the magic one because it tells Direct3D which alpha values to allow (ranging from a value of 0 to 255). After the three functions just shown are called, all pixels with an alpha value lower than 8 are rejected. If you set your color key up correctly, the three function calls will force all textures with an alpha value of zero to be excluded from the rendering stage, thereby making them transparent!

## A Transparent Blitting Example

Enough talk; it's time for some code! Here's a small example that loads a button image and displays it onscreen. The black pixels of the texture are excluded, allowing the background color to peek through.

```
// g_pD3DDevice = pre-initialized device object

// Custom vertex structure and descriptor
typedef struct {
  FLOAT x, y, z, rhw; // Screen coordinates
  FLOAT u, v;         // Texture coordinates
} sVertex;
#define VertexFVF (D3DFVF_XYZRHW | D3DFVF_TEX1)

// Vertex buffer and texture
IDirect3DVertexBuffer8 *g_pVB = NULL;
IDirect3DTexture8      *g_pTexture = NULL;

// Set up the vertex buffer and texture
// assuming a 400x400 window
BYTE *Ptr;
sVertex Verts[4] = {
    {   0.0f,   0.0f, 0.0f, 1.0f, 0.0f, 0.0f },
    { 399.0f,   0.0f, 0.0f, 1.0f, 1.0f, 0.0f },
    {   0.0f, 399.0f, 0.0f, 1.0f, 0.0f, 1.0f },
    { 399.0f, 399.0f, 0.0f, 1.0f, 1.0f, 1.0f }
  };

// Create vertex buffer and stuff in data
g_pD3DDevice->CreateVertexBuffer(sizeof(sVertex)*4, 0,          \
          VertexFVF, D3DPOOL_DEFAULT, &g_pVB))) {
g_pVB->Lock(0,0, (BYTE**)&Ptr, 0)))
memcpy(Ptr, Verts, sizeof(Verts));
g_pVB->Unlock();

// Get texture
D3DXCreateTextureFromFileEx(g_pD3DDevice, "button.bmp",        \
  D3DX_DEFAULT, D3DX_DEFAULT, D3DX_DEFAULT, 0,                  \
  D3DFMT_A8R8G8B8, D3DPOOL_MANAGED, D3DX_FILTER_TRIANGLE,       \
  D3DX_FILTER_TRIANGLE, D3DCOLOR_RGBA(0,0,0,255), NULL,         \
  NULL, &g_pTexture);

// Set alpha testing
g_pD3DDevice->SetRenderState(D3DRS_ALPHATESTENABLE, TRUE);
g_pD3DDevice->SetRenderState(D3DRS_ALPHAREF, 0x01);
g_pD3DDevice->SetRenderState(D3DRS_ALPHAFUNC,                   \
```

```
                               D3DCMP_GREATEREQUAL);

// Clear device backbuffer
g_pD3DDevice->Clear(0, NULL, D3DCLEAR_TARGET,                    \
                    D3DCOLOR_RGBA(0,128,128,255), 1.0f, 0);

if(SUCCEEDED(g_pD3DDevice->BeginScene())) {
  // Set stream source to particle vertex buffer
  g_pD3DDevice->SetStreamSource(0, g_pVB, sizeof(sVertex));

  // Set vertex shader to particle type
  g_pD3DDevice->SetVertexShader(VertexFVF);

  // Set texture
  g_pD3DDevice->SetTexture(0, g_pTexture);

  // Draw vertex buffer
  g_pD3DDevice->DrawPrimitive(D3DPT_TRIANGLESTRIP, 0, 2);

  g_pD3DDevice->EndScene();

  // Clear texture
  g_pD3DDevice->SetTexture(0, NULL);

  // Turn off alpha testing
  g_pD3DDevice->SetRenderState(D3DRS_ALPHATESTENABLE, FALSE);
}

// Flip surfaces to display work
g_pD3DDevice->Present(NULL, NULL, NULL, NULL);
```

# Lighting

Next on the list of advanced graphics techniques is the use of lighting. Unlike in real-life, most games fully illuminate the scene, which does make graphics look sharp, albeit unrealistic. To get a more true-to-life scene, and to give your graphics those subtle lighting effects that players will go ga-ga over, you need to utilize Direct3D's lighting capabilities. You can use four types of light in Direct3D: ambient, point, spot, and directional.

*Ambient light* is a constant source of light that illuminates everything in the scene with the same level of light. Because it is part of the device component, ambient light is the only lighting component handled separately from the lighting engine.

The other three lights (illustrated in Figure 6.18) have unique properties. A *point light* illuminates everything around it (like a light bulb does). *Spotlights* point in a specific direction and emit a cone-shaped light. Everything inside the cone is illuminated, whereas objects outside the cone are not illuminated. A *directional light* (a simplified spotlight), merely casts light in a specific direction.

Lights are placed in a scene just as other 3-D objects are—by using X-, Y-, and Z-coordinates. Some lights, such as spotlights, also have a direction vector that determines which way they point. Each light has an intensity level, a range, attenuation factors, and color. That's right, even colored lights are possible with Direct3D!

With the exception of the ambient light, each light uses a D3DLIGHT8 data structure to store its unique information. This structure is defined as follows:

```
typedef struct _D3DLIGHT8 {
    D3DLIGHTTYPE Type;        // Type of light
    D3DCOLORVALUE Diffuse;    // Diffuse color
    D3DCOLORVALUE Specular;   // Specular color
    D3DCOLORVALUE Ambient;    // Ambient color
    D3DVECTOR Position;       // Position of light
    D3DVECTOR Direction;      // Direction light is pointing
    float Range;              // Range of light
    float Falloff;            // Falloff of spotlight
    float Attenuation0;       // Light attenuation 0
    float Attenuation1;       // Light attenuation 1
    float Attenuation2;       // Light attenuation 2
    float Theta;              // Angle of inner cone
    float Phi;                // Angle of outer cone
} D3DLIGHT8;
```

Wow! That's a big puppy, but it contains all the information you need in order to describe a light. Although the lights don't necessarily use every variable in the D3DLIGHT8 structure, all the lights share a few common fields.

The first variable you set is Type, which is the type of light you are using. This can be D3DLIGHT_POINT for a point light, D3DLIGHT_SPOT for a spotlight, or D3DLIGHT_DIRECTIONAL for a directional light.

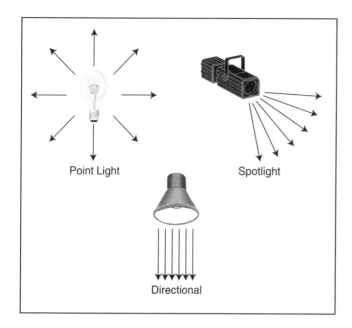

Next in line is the color of the light. You'll use the Diffuse field most often; it determines the color of the light emitted. Notice that the color fields are in the form D3DCOLORVALUE, which is a structure that looks like this:

```
typedef struct _D3DCOLORVALUE {
    float r;   // Red value   (0.0 to 1.0)
    float g;   // Green value (0.0 to 1.0)
    float b;   // Blue value  (0.0 to 1.0)
    float a;   // Alpha value (Unused)
} D3DCOLORVALUE;
```

You can set each color component in the structure in the range of 0.0 (off) to 1.0 (full). A red light will be r=1.0, g=0.0, b=0.0, and a white light will be r=1.0, g=1.0, b=1.0. Because you're dealing with lights, the alpha value is not used here.

**TIP**

In addition to using the color levels of a light to illuminate an object, you also can use them to darken the object. Instead of using positive color values, use negative values and watch the results!

The Specular and Ambient light fields in the D3DLIGHT8 structure determine the highlight color and ambient color, respectively. You can safely set both fields for each color component to 1.0 (except for Specular, which you can set to 0.0 values if you don't want to use highlights).

As I mentioned previously, each light can be positioned in the 3-D scene using an XYZ-coordinate (the world coordinates), which is stored in the vector Position. The Direction is also a vector, but is used to point the light in a specific direction. You can find more on using the direction vector in the section "Using Spotlights."

The Range variable determines how far the light can travel before falling off (falloff is the value used to determine how quickly a light fades from the inner to outer cone). Typically, a falloff value of 1.0 creates a smooth transition.) No objects beyond this distance are illuminated by the light. The trio of attenuation fields determines how fast the light falls off over distance—those three attenuation fields are typically all set at zero. Whether you use the rest of the variables depends on the type of light you are using.

## Using Point Lights

Point lights are the easiest lights with which to work; you just set their positions, color components, and ranges. To set up a point light, instance the D3DLIGHT8 structure and fill it with the required information:

```
D3DLIGHT8 PointLight;

// Clear out the light data
ZeroMemory(&PointLight, sizeof(D3DLIGHT8));

// Position the light at 0.0, 100.0, 200.0
PointLight.Position = D3DVECTOR3(0.0f, 100.0f, 200.0f);

// Set the diffuse and ambient colors to white
PointLight.Diffuse.r = PointLight.Ambient.r = 1.0f;
PointLight.Diffuse.g = PointLight.Ambient.g = 1.0f;
PointLight.Diffuse.b = PointLight.Ambient.b = 1.0f;

// Set the range to 1000 units
PointLight.Range = 1000.0f;
```

## Using Spotlights

Spotlights work a little differently than the other lights do because spotlights cast light in a cone shape away from the source. The light is brightest in the center, dimming as it reaches the outer portion of the cone. Nothing outside the cone is illuminated.

You define a spotlight by its position, direction, color components, range, falloff, attenuation, and the radius of the inner and outer cone. You don't have to worry about falloff and attenuation, but you do need to think about both radiuses of the cone.

**CAUTION**

Spotlights are the most computational light source you can use, so it's a good idea not to have too many of them in the scene.

The Phi variable in the D3DLIGHT8 structure determines the size of the outer cone. Phi, as well as Theta, are represented as angles (in radians). The farther the light travels from the spotlight source, the wider the projected radius becomes. Programmers determine which values to use, and you'll just have to play around until you find the values you like.

The following creates a spotlight that sets up the position, color, range, falloff, and cone radiuses:

```
D3DLIGHT8 Spotlight;

// Clear out the light data
ZeroMemory(&SpotLight, sizeof(D3DLIGHT8));

// Position the light at 0.0, 100.0, 200.0
SpotLight.Position = D3DVECTOR3(0.0f, 100.0f, 200.0f);

// Set the diffuse and ambient colors to white
SpotLight.Diffuse.r = SpotLight.Ambient.r = 1.0f;
SpotLight.Diffuse.g = SpotLight.Ambient.g = 1.0f;
SpotLight.Diffuse.b = SpotLight.Ambient.b = 1.0f;

// Set the range
SpotLight.Range = 1000.0f;

// Set the falloff
SpotLight.Falloff = 1.0f;

// Set the cone radiuses
Spotlight.Phi   = 0.3488; // outer 20 degrees
Spotlight.Theta = 0.1744; // inner 10 degrees
```

Now, you point the spotlight in a specific direction. D3DX comes to the rescue again with a duo of functions that help you point the spotlight (and any light for that matter). One function is the D3DXVECTOR3 object's overloaded constructor that lets you specify the three coordinates.

For these three coordinates, you use world space coordinates to define the distance from the origin. If you have a spotlight anywhere in the scene and you want it to point upward at a target 500 units above the light, you set the vector object's values to X=0, Y=500, Z=0 (notice that these three coordinates are relative to the light's position). For example, the following code sets the vectors values:

```
D3DXVECTOR3 Direction = D3DXVECTOR3(0.0f, 500.0f, 0.0f);
```

The only problem with the preceding Direction vector declaration is that Direct3D likes the vectors to be normalized, which means that the coordinates need to be in the range 0 to 1. No problem, because the second D3DX function, D3DXVec3Normalize, handles this for you:

> **CAUTION**
>
> A light's directional vector must contain at least one value that is not 0. In other words, you cannot specify a direction of X=0, Y=0, Z=0.

```
D3DXVECTOR3 *D3DXVec3Normalize(
    D3DXVECTOR3 *pOut,        // normalized vector
    CONST D3DXVECTOR3 *pV);   // source vector
```

When you pass the original vector (for example, the preceding one that contains the coordinates X=0, Y=500, Z=0) and the pointer to a new vector, the D3DXVecNormalize function converts the coordinates into values that range between 0 and 1. The new vector now contains the directional values you can use for light direction field in the D3DLIGHT8 structure.

Continuing with the previous example, set up the direction of the spotlight by pointing it up and normalizing the vector and storing it in the D3DLIGHT8 structure:

```
D3DXVECTOR3 Dir = D3DXVECTOR3(0.0f, 500.0f, 0.0f);
D3DXVec3Normalize((D3DXVECTOR3*)&Spotlight.Direction, &Dir);
```

# Using Directional Lights

In terms of processing, directional lights are the fastest type of light that you can use. They illuminate every polygon that faces them. To ready a directional light for use, you just set the direction and color component fields in the D3DLIGHT8 structure.

If you're wondering why a position vector isn't used, the answer is logical. Think of a directional light as an infinitely large river flowing in one direction. Regardless of the position of objects in the river, the flow of the water remains the same; it's the *direction* of the flow that makes a difference. Using this analogy with lighting, the water represents the light's rays, and the direction that the water flows represents the angle of the light. Any object in the world, regardless of its position, receives light.

Recalling the techniques for the previous two types of light, take a look at this example, which sets up a yellowish light that is cast down on your scene:

```
D3DLIGHT8 DirLight;

// Clear out the light data
ZeroMemory(&DirLight, sizeof(D3DLIGHT8));

// Set the diffuse and ambient colors to yellow
DirLight.Diffuse.r = DirLight.Ambient.r = 1.0f;
DirLight.Diffuse.g = DirLight.Ambient.g = 1.0f;
DirLight.Diffuse.b = DirLight.Ambient.b = 0.0f;

D3DXVECTOR3 Dir = D3DXVECTOR3(0.0f, 500.0f, 0.0f);
D3DXVec3Normalize((D3DXVECTOR3*)&Dirlight.Direction, &Dir);
```

# Ambient Light

Ambient lighting is the only type of light that Direct3D handles differently. Direct3D applies the ambient light to all polygons without regard to their angles or to their light sources, so no shading occurs. Ambient light is a constant level of light, and like the other types of light (point, spot, and directional), you can color it as you like.

You set the ambient light level by setting the render state `D3DRS_AMBIENT` and passing the `D3DCOLOR` (using the `D3DCOLOR_COLORVALUE` macro, specifying the red, green, and blue levels to use in a range from 0.0 to 1.0) value that you want to use:

```
g_pD3DDevice->SetRenderState(D3DRS_AMBIENT,                        \
              D3DCOLOR_COLORVALUE(0.0f, Red, Green, Blue));
```

# Setting the Light

After you set up the `D3DLIGHT8` structure, you pass it to Direct3D using the `IDirect3DDevice8::SetLight` function:

```
HRESULT IDirect3DDevice8::SetLight(
```

```
DWORD Index,              // Index of light to set
CONST D3DLIGHT8 *pLight);  // D3DLIGHT8 structure to use
```

You can see that pLight passes the D3DLIGHT8 structure, but the Index field is something different. Direct3D allows you to set multiple lights in a scene, so Index is the zero-based index of the light you want to set. For example, if you are using four lights in a scene, index 0 is the first light, index 1 is the second, index 2 is the third, and index 3 is the fourth and last.

There doesn't seem to be a limit to the number of lights that you can use in a scene with Direct3D 8, but I recommend keeping the number of lights to four or less. Each light that you add to the scene increases the complexity and the time required for rendering.

## Using Normals

In order for Direct3D to properly illuminate polygon faces from the lights that you provide, you must first provide each vertex in the polygon with a normal. A *normal* is a 3-D vector that defines the direction in which an object (such as a vertex or polygon) that a vector is attached to is facing. You generally use normals in a complex calculation that determines how much illumination the object receives from any given light.

If you take a close look at a polygon face (similar to the one in Figure 6.19), you'll see that the three vertices have a direction, which is the normal. When light hits these vertices, it bounces off at an angle based on the normals. Using normals ensures that all polygon faces are illuminated correctly and shaded according to their angle relative to the viewer and the lights.

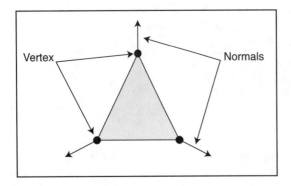

**Figure 6.19**

*Each vertex has a normal that points in a particular direction. You use the angle of the normal to determine how light bounces off the polygon's face and how to perform shading calculations.*

Adding a normal to your custom vertex information is as easy as providing texture information. You just insert the normal as a D3DVECTOR3 type and redefine the custom flexible vertex format (including D3DFVF_NORMAL), as shown here:

```
typedef struct {
  D3DVECTOR3 Position;   // Vector coordinates
  D3DVECTOR3 Normal;     // Normal
  D3DCOLOR   Color;      // Color
} sVertex;
#define VERTEXFMT (D3DFVF_XYZ | D3DFVF_DIFFUSE | D3DFVF_NORMAL)
```

You calculate a normal the same way that you created a directional vector when working with lights, in the earlier section "Using Spotlights." When you begin to deal with 3-D models, the task of calculating normals is taken off your hands—because the 3-D modeling programs used to generate the models typically calculate the normals.

The following function (borrowed from the DirectX SDK examples) generates a cylinder and gives each vertex a normal that points away from the middle of the cylinder (see also Figure 6.20):

```
// g_pD3DDevice = pre-initialized 3-D device object
IDirect3DVertexBuffer8 *GenerateCylinder()
{
  IDirect3DVertexBuffer8 *pD3DVertexBuffer;
  sVertex *pVertex;
  DWORD i;
  FLOAT theta;

  // Create the vertex buffer
  if(SUCCEEDED(g_pD3DDevice->CreateVertexBuffer(            \
              50 * 2 * sizeof(sVertex), 0, VERTEXFMT,       \
              D3DPOOL_DEFAULT, &pD3DVertexBuffer))) {

    // Fill the vertex buffer with the cylinder information
    if(SUCCEEDED(pD3DVertexBuffer->Lock(0, 0,               \
                (BYTE**)&pVertex, 0))) {
      for(i=0; i<50; i++) {
        theta = (2 * D3DX_PI * i) / (50 - 1);
        pVertex[2*i+0].Position = D3DXVECTOR3(sinf(theta),  \
                                            -1.0f, cosf(theta));
```

```
            pVertex[2*i+0].Normal   = D3DXVECTOR3(sinf(theta),    \
                                                  0.0f, cosf(theta));
            pVertex[2*i+1].Position = D3DXVECTOR3(sinf(theta),    \
                                                  1.0f, cosf(theta));
            pVertex[2*i+1].Normal   = D3DXVECTOR3(sinf(theta),    \
                                                  0.0f, cosf(theta));
        }
        pD3DVertexBuffer->Unlock();

        // Return a pointer to new vertex buffer
        return pD3DVertexBuffer;
    }
}

// Return NULL on error
return NULL;
}
```

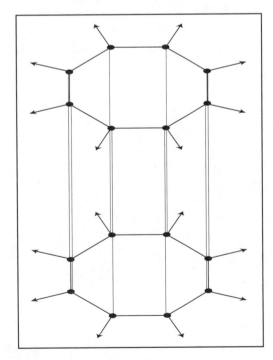

**Figure 6.20**

*The* GenerateCylinder *function creates a cylinder object with normals that point away from the center.*

# Let There Be Light!

Now that you've decided on the type of light to use and have set up its respective structure, it is time to activate the lighting pipeline and turn on the light(s). To activate the lighting pipeline, you set a single rendering state, D3DRS_LIGHTING to TRUE:

```
// g_pD3DDevice = pre-initializing device object
_pD3DDevice->SetRenderState(D3DRS_LIGHTING, TRUE);
```

To deactivate the lighting pipeline, use the following code:

```
// g_pD3DDevice = pre-initializing device object
g_pD3DDevice->SetRenderState(D3DRS_LIGHTING, FALSE);
```

After activating the lighting pipeline, you turn the individual lights on and off using the IDirect3DDevice8::LightEnable function. Here's the prototype for LightEnable:

```
IDirect3DDevice8::LightEnable(
  DWORD LightIndex,  // Light index, 0 - max # lights
  BOOL bEnable);     // TRUE to turn on, FALSE to turn off
```

If you've already set up a point light as LightIndex 0, you can turn it on and off with the following code:

```
// g_pD3DDevice = pre-initializing device object

// Turn light on
g_pD3DDevice->LightEnable(0, TRUE);

// Turn light off
g_pD3DDevice->LightEnable(0, FALSE);
```

That's it for using Direct3D's lighting system! One last word of warning before moving on: Direct3D does a decent job of using lights in the graphics system, but if a user's video card does not support lighting, Direct3D has to emulate the lighting effects. While not a bad thing, emulation can slow down rendering if lighting is used. Don't let the threat of light emulation stop you, however, as using light effects in your game enhances your graphics tremendously.

# Using Fonts

One drawback to DirectX 8 is its lack of font support. Older versions of DirectX are able to harness Window's font-drawing functions. With version 8, you must manually draw a font onto a texture surface and draw each font letter as a small texture-mapped polygon.

Managing a texture that contains a font is a bit much to do just to draw text, but thanks to D3DX, you have access to a special object, ID3DXFont, that handles those texture map fonts for you. The ID3DXFont object contains only one useable function, ID3DXFont::DrawText, which you use to draw the fonts. Before you go any further, however, take a look at how to create a font.

## Creating the Font

In order to use the ID3DXFont object, you must first initialize it with the D3DXCreateFontIndirect function:

```
HRESULT D3DXCreateFontIndirect(
    IDirect3DDevice8 *pDevice,    // Device to associate font to
    CONST LOGFONT* pLogFont,      // Structure defining font
    ID3DXFont **ppFont);          // Pointer to created font object
```

You supply this function with the pre-initialized device object and pointer to the ID3DXFont object that you are initializing, but what do you do with the pLogFont parameter? As you can see, the pLogFont points to a LOGFONT (which stands for *logical font*) structure, which looks like this:

```
typedef struct tagLOGFONT {
    LONG lfHeight;
    LONG lfWidth;
    LONG lfEscapement;
    LONG lfOrientation;
    LONG lfWeight;
    BYTE lfItalic;
    BYTE lfUnderline;
    BYTE lfStrikeOut;
    BYTE lfCharSet;
    BYTE lfOutPrecision;
    BYTE lfClipPrecision;
    BYTE lfQuality;
    BYTE lfPitchAndFamily;
    TCHAR lfFaceName[LF_FACESIZE];
} LOGFONT;
```

Wow, that's a lot of information! You can safely skip setting most of the fields in the LOGFONT structure shown and stick with the default values that I've shown. The only ones that you're bound to work with are lfHeight, lfWeight, lfItalic, lfUnderline, and lfFaceName.

Starting with the easiest ones, you can set lfItalic and lfUnderline to 0 or 1 to set or clear the use of italics and underlines, respectively. With lfWeight, you can set the level of boldness to use when drawing; you can set it to 0 for normal or 700 for bold. lfHeight represents the point size of the font. The lfHeight value is a bit tricky because it doesn't take a direct size per se. Instead, you must give it a negative value that represents the approximate height in pixels. For example, for a font that is 16 pixels in height, you use a value of -16.

Last is lfFaceName, which is the name of the font that you want to use. It might be Times New Roman, Courier New, or any other font installed on your system. You just copy the name into the lfFaceName field.

Here's an example that uses the Times New Roman font with a point size of 16:

```
// g_pD3DDevice = pre-initialized device object
// hWnd = handle to parent window
ID3DXFont *pD3DFont;
LOGFONT lf;

// Clear out the font structure
ZeroMemory(&lf, sizeof(LOGFONT));

// Set the font name and height
strcpy(lf.lfFaceName, "Times New Roman");
lfHeight = -16;

// Create the font object
if(FAILED(D3DXCreateFontIndirect(g_pD3DDevice,            \
                              &lf, &pD3DFont))) {
  // Error occurred
}
```

**CAUTION**

Because ID3DXFont is a COM object, always be sure to release it when you are done with it.

# Drawing with Fonts

Once your ID3DXFont object is initialized, you can begin drawing text using the ID3DXFont::DrawText function:HRESULT ID3DXFont::DrawText(

```
   LPCSTR pString,     // String to print
   INT Count,          // -1
   LPRECT pRect,       // Area to draw text in
   DWORD Format,       // 0
   D3DCOLOR Color);    // Color to use to draw with
```

The only thing to watch out for when using the DrawText function is the pRect parameter, which is a pointer to a RECT structure that contains the area in which to draw the text. You can set this area to the size of the screen, or if you want to contain the text within a specific area, use those screen coordinates. The RECT structure looks like this:

```
typedef struct tagRECT {
   LONG left;          // Left coordinate
   LONG top;           // Top coordinate
   LONG right;         // Right coordinate
   LONG bottom;        // Bottom coordinate
} RECT;
```

Last in the DrawText function is the Color parameter, which determines the color to use for drawing the text. Use the handy D3DCOLOR_RGBA or D3DCOLOR_COLORVALUE macro to define the color for drawing the text.

The following example assumes that you've initialized the font object and are ready to draw text:

```
// g_pD3DDevice = pre-initialized device object
// pD3DXFont = pre-initialized font object

// Setup the RECT structure with drawable area
RECT rect = { 0, 0, 200, 100 };

// Begin the drawing code block
if(SUCCEEDED(g_pD3DDevice->BeginScene())) {

   // Draw some text
   pD3DXFont->DrawText("I can draw with text!", -1,                 \
               &rect, 0, D3DCOLOR_RGBA(255,255,255,255));

   // End the scene
   g_pD3DDevice->EndScene();
}
```

# Billboards

*Billboarding* is a cool technique that allows 2-D objects to appear in three dimensions. For example, a complex object such as a tree can be rendered from a side view in a modeling program and then drawn as a texture on a rectangular polygon. This rectangular polygon always faces the viewpoint, so regardless of the angle from which the polygon is viewed, it will appear as though the tree texture is viewed from the side at which it was rendered (as illustrated in Figure 6.21).

Many programmers use billboarding for creating games because they can easily implement it. A perfect example of billboarding use can be seen in Paper Mario for the N64. All the characters are drawn in 2-D and then texture-mapped onto polygons. The game adds a twist by allowing you to see the billboard polygons as they turn around, thereby giving the graphics a rather comical style.

Billboarding works by using a world matrix that aligns the polygons with the view. Because you already know the angle of the view (or can obtain a view transformation matrix), you only need to construct a matrix using the opposite view angles. You don't have to alter the position of the polygon because only the angle concerns you.

The first way to construct the billboard world matrix (which you can apply to a mesh or polygons) is to use the opposite values of the view angles that you already know. For example, assume that a vertex buffer is already set up with the vertices.

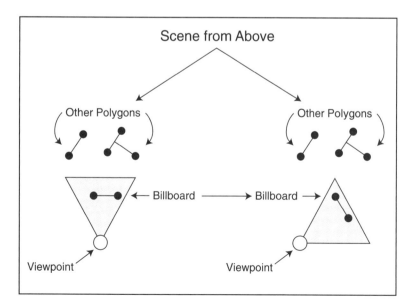

**Figure 6.21**

*Billboarding ensures that polygons face the viewpoint regardless of the position or angle from which the polygon is viewed.*

The viewpoint angles are stored as XRot, YRot, and ZRot, and the billboard object's coordinates are XCoord, YCoord, ZCoord. Here's how to set up the matrix to use for rendering the billboard vertex buffer:

```
// g_pD3DDevice = pre-initialized device object
D3DXMATRIX matBillboard;
D3DXMATRIX matBBXRot, matBBYRot, matBBZRot;
D3DXMATRIX matBBTrans;

// Construct the billboard matrix

// Use the opposite angles of the viewpoint to align to view
D3DXMatrixRotationX(&matBBXRot, -XRot);
D3DXMatrixRotationY(&matBBYRot, -YRot);
D3DXMatrixRotationZ(&matBBZRot, -ZRot);

// Use the billboard object coordinates to position
D3DXMatrixTranslation(&matBBTrans, XCoord, YCoord, ZCoord);

// Combine the matrices
D3DXMatrixIdentity(&matBillboard);
D3DXMatrixMultiply(&matBillboard, &matBillboard, &matBBTrans);
D3DXMatrixMultiply(&matBillboard, &matBillboard, &matBBZRot);
D3DXMatrixMultiply(&matBillboard, &matBillboard, &matBBYRot);
D3DXMatrixMultiply(&matBillboard, &matBillboard, &matBBXRot);

// Set the matrix
g_pD3DDevice->SetTransform(D3DTS_WORLD);

// Continue to draw the vertex buffer, which is aligned
// to face the viewport, but at the proper coordinates.
```

After the last line of code, the world transformation matrix is set up and ready to be used to render the billboard object.

The second way to create a billboard world matrix is to grab the current view matrix from Direct3D and transpose it (inverse it). This transposed matrix will align everything properly to face the view. You just apply the mesh's translation matrix to position the mesh properly in your world. Here's how to construct the billboard matrix from the view matrix and use it to draw the billboard object:

```
// g_pD3DDevice = pre-initialized device object
```

```
D3DXMATRIX matTrans, matWorld, matTransposed;

// Get the current Direct3D view matrix
g_pD3DDevice->GetTransform(D3DTS_VIEW, &matTranspose);

// Create the mesh's translation matrix
D3DXMatrixTranslation(&matTrans, XCoord, YCoord, ZCoord);

// Multiply them together to form world transformation matrix
D3DXMatrixMultiply(&matWorld, &matTranspose, &matTrans);

// Set the world transformation matrix
g_pD3DDevice->SetTransform(D3DTS_WORLD, &matWorld);

// Continue to draw the vertex buffer, which is aligned
// to face the viewport, but at the proper coordinates.
```

Billboarding is a powerful technique that is actually the basis to some other special effects, such as particles.

# Particles

Huge explosions, smoke trails, and even those tiny sparkles of light that trail off the tail of a hurdling magic missile are all the work of a special effect known as *particles*. Particles follow the same principles as billboarding and are just as easy to use.

With particles, you set up polygons that are texture-mapped with smoke, fire, sparks, or whatever graphics you want to use. At the appropriate time, you enable alpha blending (optional) and draw the particles so that they face the viewpoint (using billboarding). The result is a collage of blended objects that you can use for some awesome effects.

The cool thing about particles is that they can be virtually any size, because you can create a scaling matrix to combine with the world transformation matrix of the particle polygon. This means that you need to use only a single polygon to draw all your particles, except when the particle texture varies, in which case the number of polygons should match the number of textures.

It's time to create a particle image. You might start with a circle shape that is solid (opaque) in the center and that gradually becomes transparent on the way to the outside edge (as illustrated in Figure 6.22).

**Figure 6.22**

*You generally draw a particle using a circular image, as shown here. When you use materials, the image is colored when drawn.*

Now, set up four vertices that use two polygons (using a triangle strip for optimization). The vertex's coordinates represent the default size of a particle that you'll scale to size later on. Each particle can have unique properties, including its own color (by using materials).

You then use this structure, combined with a single vertex buffer containing two polygons (creating a square), to render the polygons to the 3-D device. Before being drawn, each particle is oriented by its own world matrix (using billboarding, of course). You combine the world transformation matrix with each particle's scale matrix transformation. Then you set a material (using the IDirect3DDevice8::SetMaterial function) to change the color of the particle, and finally you draw the particle.

Here's an example that creates a particle vertex buffer and draws it to a device:

```
// g_pD3DDevice = pre-initialized device object

// define a custom vertex structure and descriptor
typedef struct {
  FLOAT x, y, z;    // Local 3-D coordinates
  FLOAT u, v;        // Texture coordinates
} sVertex;
#define VertexFVF (D3DFVF_XYZ | D3DFVF_TEX1)

// Particle vertex buffer and texture
IDirect3DVertexBuffer8 *g_pParticleVB = NULL;
IDirect3DTexture8       *g_pParticleTexture = NULL;
```

```
BOOL SetupParticle()
{
  BYTE *Ptr;
  sVertex Verts[4] = {
    { -1.0f,  1.0f, 0.0f, 0.0f, 0.0f },
    {  1.0f,  1.0f, 0.0f, 1.0f, 0.0f },
    { -1.0f, -1.0f, 0.0f, 0.0f, 1.0f },
    {  1.0f, -1.0f, 0.0f, 1.0f, 1.0f }
  };

  // Create particle vertex buffer and stuff in data
  if(FAILED(g_pD3DDevice->CreateVertexBuffer(                    \
          sizeof(sVertex)*4, 0, VertexFVF,                       \
          D3DPOOL_DEFAULT, &g_pParticleVB)))
    return FALSE;
  if(FAILED(g_pParticleVB->Lock(0,0, (BYTE**)&Ptr, 0)))
    return FALSE;
  memcpy(Ptr, Verts, sizeof(Verts));
  g_pParticleVB->Unlock();

  // Get particle texture
  D3DXCreateTextureFromFile(g_pD3DDevice, "particle.bmp",        \
                            &g_pParticleTexture);

  return TRUE;
}

BOOL DrawParticle(float x, float y, float z, float scale)
{
  D3DXMATRIX matWorld, matView, matTransposed;
  D3DXMATRIX matTrans, matScale;
  D3DMATERIAL8 d3dm;

  // Set render states (alpha blending and attributes)
  g_pD3DDevice->SetRenderState(D3DRS_ALPHABLENDENABLE, TRUE);
  g_pD3DDevice->SetRenderState(D3DRS_SRCBLEND, D3DBLEND_SRCALPHA);
  g_pD3DDevice->SetRenderState(D3DRS_DESTBLEND, D3DBLEND_ONE);

  // Turn on ambient lighting
  g_pD3DDevice->SetRenderState(D3DRS_AMBIENT, 0xffffffff);

  // Set stream source to particle vertex buffer
```

```
        g_pD3DDevice->SetStreamSource(0, g_pParticleVB, sizeof(sVertex));

        // Set vertex shader to particle type
        g_pD3DDevice->SetVertexShader(VertexFVF);

        // Set texture
        g_pD3DDevice->SetTexture(0, g_pParticleTexture);

        // Set the particle color
        ZeroMemory(&d3dm, sizeof(D3DMATERIAL8));
        d3dm.Diffuse.r = d3dm.Ambient.r = 1.0f;
        d3dm.Diffuse.g = d3dm.Ambient.g = 1.0f;
        d3dm.Diffuse.b = d3dm.Ambient.b = 0.0f;
        d3dm.Diffuse.a = d3dm.Ambient.a = 1.0f;
        g_pD3DDevice->SetMaterial(&d3dm);

        // Build scaling matrix
        D3DXMatrixScaling(&matScale, scale, scale, scale);

        // Build translation matrix
        D3DXMatrixTranslation(&matTrans, x, y, z);

        // Build the billboard matrix
        g_pD3DDevice->GetTransform(D3DTS_VIEW, &matView);
        D3DXMatrixTranspose(&matTransposed, &matView);

        // Combine matrices to form world translation matrix
        D3DXMatrixMultiply(&matWorld, &matScale, &matTransposed);
        D3DXMatrixMultiply(&matWorld, &matWorld, &matTrans);

        // Set world transformation
        g_pD3DDevice->SetTransform(D3DTS_WORLD, &matWorld);

        // Draw particle
        g_pD3DDevice->DrawPrimitive(D3DPT_TRIANGLESTRIP, 0, 2);

        // Turn off alpha blending
        g_pD3DDevice->SetRenderState(D3DRS_ALPHABLENDENABLE, FALSE);

        return TRUE;
    }
```

These two functions demonstrate setting up a vertex buffer and texture to use for the particle and drawing the actual particle. The code for a full particle example is fairly lengthy. I just wanted to give you a glimpse at how to handle a single particle. For a complete example application that demonstrates using particles to a higher degree, check out the Particle project on this book's CD-ROM (look for \BookCode\Chap06\Particle).

# Depth Sorting and Z-Buffering

It quickly becomes apparent that while you are rendering polygon mesh objects to the scene, the objects farther from the viewer need to be obscured by those objects that are closer. This is call *depth sorting*, of which there are two common methods.

The first method is called the *painter's algorithm*. This method breaks objects apart by their polygons and sorts these polygons from back to front, thus drawing them in that order (as illustrated in Figure 6.23). Drawing in this manner ensures that a polygon is always drawn in front of a polygon behind it.

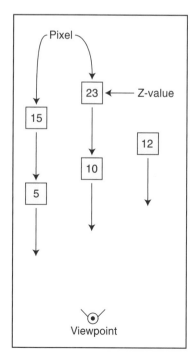

**Figure 6.23**

*When one pixel overlaps another, only the pixel with a lower Z-value is drawn. Here, only three pixels are drawn, because the two farthest pixels are overdrawn with the closer pixels.*

The second way of depth sorting, and one that graphics hardware devices use the most, is called the *Z-Buffer method*. This method works on a per-pixel basis, with each pixel having a Z value (the distance from the viewer).

As each pixel is being written, the renderer first checks to see whether a pixel with a smaller Z-value is already there. If not, the pixel is drawn; if so, the pixel is skipped. You can see this concept illustrated in Figure 6.23.

Most accelerated 3-D graphics cards have a built-in Z-Buffer, so that is the depth-sorting method of choice. The easiest way to use a Z-Buffer in your application is to initialize it while you are creating the device object and setting the presentation methods.

You do this by first selecting the precision of the buffer (16, 24, or 32 bits) using the appropriate D3DFORMAT setting. You will find quite a few settings to use for the Z-buffer, but I'll concentrate on using D3DFMT_D16 (16 bits) and D3DFMT_D32 (32 bits).

You use the different precisions for two reasons—for storage and for quality. In terms of storage, a 32-bit Z-Buffer takes up considerably more space than a 16-bit Z-Buffer, so try to stick with a 16-bit Z-Buffer if possible.

In terms of quality, using a 16-bit Z-Buffer with objects that are very close together sometimes causes the wrong pixel to be drawn, because there is less precision. Going for a 32-bit Z-Buffer solves the precision issues, but at the cost of the Z-Buffer using twice the memory. You don't need to worry though; in the fast-action gaming world, speed and optimization are more important, so stay with a 16-bit Z-Buffer.

Going back to the presentation setup, you can add the following two lines to enable Z-Buffering in your application:

```
d3dp.EnableAutoDepthStencil = TRUE;
d3dp.AutoDepthStencilFormat = D3DFMT_D16; // or D3DFMT_D32
```

Now you can proceed with your initialization routines. When you're ready to render using the Z-Buffer (it doesn't kick on automatically), you have to set the appropriate render state:

```
// g_pD3DDevice = pre-initialized device object

// To turn on Z-Buffer, use:
g_pD3DDevice->SetRenderState(D3DRS_ZENABLE, D3DZB_TRUE);

// To turn off Z-Buffer, use:
g_pD3DDevice->SetRenderState(D3DRS_ZENABLE, D3DZB_FALSE);
```

If you have already tired the new Z-Buffer capabilities, you might have noticed that something is awry. For example, the screen is not updated after a few frames, or objects too far away are clipped. That's because you must clear the Z-Buffer before every frame and you need to read-just your projection matrix to allow for distance settings.

> **NOTE**
>
> Although it might seem logical to leave the Z-Buffer on at all times, you can gain some speed by shutting it off when it's not needed. When you draw images such as a menu onscreen, you'll need total control of what is drawn where, so feel free to turn the Z-Buffer on and off as you see fit.

To clear the Z-Buffer before each frame, change your `IDirect3DDevce8::Clear` call as follows:

```
g_pD3DDevice->Clear(0, NULL,                                    \
    D3DCLEAR_TARGET | D3DCLEAR_ZBUFFER,                         \
    D3DCOLOR_RGBA(0.0f, 0.0f, 0.0f, 0.0f) 1.0f, 0);
```

Notice the addition of the `D3DCLEAR_ZBUFFER` flag in the preceding code. This flag tells the clear function that it has to clear the Z-Buffer to the supplied value (the fifth argument, which is `1.0f`). This value ranges from `0.0` (minimum Z-Buffer depth) to `1.0` (maximum Z-Buffer depth).

Using the value of `1.0` tells the clear function to set all depth values to their maximum. If you want to clear the Z-Buffer to half the maximum range, use `0.5`. The only remaining question is what is the maximum range?

The Z-Buffer measures distance from the viewpoint, so as the rendering takes place, objects farther than the maximum viewing distance (and those objects that are too close) are not drawn. During your call to set up the projection matrix (using D3DX), set the minimum and maximum viewing ranges, such as in the following code bit:

```
// Set a min distance of 1.0 and a max of 1000.0
D3DXMatrixPerspectiveFovLH(&MatrixProj, D3DX_PI/4, 1.0f, 1.0f, 1000.0f );
```

The last two values are the ones that you want to adjust—the minimum range and the maximum range, respectively. Experiment with the values to see which values work best for you; just remember that the greater the distance between the minimum and maximum ranges, the poorer the quality of the Z-Buffer. Typical values for the distances are `1.0` for the minimum range and `1000.0`, `2000.0`, or `5000.0` for the maximum range.

# Working with Viewports

At times, you'll want to render to smaller portions of the display, somewhat like rendering to a smaller window with the main application window. The main viewport typically covers the entire display, but when you need to, you can change the size of the viewport to cover small areas of the screen.

To set a viewport, you first fill in a D3DVIEWPORT8 structure with the coordinates and dimensions of the new viewport you want to use:

```
typedef struct _D3DVIEWPORT8 {
    DWORD       X;        // left X coordinate of viewport
    DWORD       Y;        // top Y coordinate of viewport
    DWORD       Width;    // Width of viewport
    DWORD       Height;   // Height of viewport
    float       MinZ;     // 0.0
    float       MaxZ;     // 1.0
} D3DVIEWPORT8;
```

After you set the structure with the appropriate data, you tell Direct3D to use it with a call to ID3DDevice8::SetViewport, as in the following code bit:

```
// pD3DDevice = pre-initialized 3-D device

// Create a viewport
D3DVIEWPORT8 d3dvp = { 0,0, 100, 100, 0.0f, 1.0f };

// Set the new viewport
pD3DDevice->SetViewport(&d3dvp);
```

From this point on (after calling SetViewport), all graphics are rendered within the viewport window you defined. After you finish with the new viewport, you restore the old viewport. To grab the old viewport settings and later restore them, you call ID3DDevice8::GetViewport, as in the following code:

```
// pD3DDevice = pre-initialized 3-D device
D3DVIEWPORT8 OldViewport;

// Get old viewport settings
pD3DDevice->GetDevice(&OldViewport); // get old viewport

// .. change viewport settings as needed

// Restore old viewport
pD3DDevice->SetDevice(&OldViewport);
```

# Working with Meshes

At its lowest level, Direct3D doesn't work with meshes, only with polygons. D3DX adds to the functionality of the Direct3D system by giving you a series of objects that handle the containment and rendering of such meshes.

At the lowest level, meshes are constructed from possibly thousands of vertices and polygons, all requiring complex manipulation. Fortunately, Direct3D comes complete with a native 3-D file format used to store the information that describes a 3-D model, including (but not limited to) vertex, face, normal, and texture data. This file format is referred to as .X.

## The .X Files

An .X file is Microsoft's proprietary 3-D model storage format (sorry, we're not going to be visited by Mulder and Scully). It is template-driven and completely expandable, which means that you can use it for all your 3-D file storage.

Although I could go on about the intricacies of the .X file format at this point, it would overload this chapter with information that only the most hard-core programmers and graphics artists would ever use. Let's face it—trying to manually edit a mesh constructed from thousands of vertices is ludicrous. Why would you want that daunting task when you could easily use a program like trueSpace or MilkShape 3-D to design your meshes in a user-friendly environment? That's what I thought!

Instead, let me give you a quick overview of the way .X files are formatted; then you can move on to the good stuff—using models in your games!

## The .X File Format

An .X file, identified by its .X file extension, is highly versatile. It can be text-based in order to make editing easier or binary-based in order to make the file smaller and easier to protect from prying eyes. The entire format of .X is based on templates, which are similar to C structures.

### Templates Galore

You use templates to contain an array of data. Generally, the templates in an .X file are used to store information about a mesh (or a number of meshes). For example, there are templates that define mesh vertices, polygons, texture maps, and normals. Most of these templates are wrapped up in other meshes, forming a *template hierarchy*.

For example, a template that defines vertex normals can be embedded with a mesh definition template. In turn, that mesh definition template can be embedded within a frame of reference template (a special template that you'll read more about in a moment).

You can instance templates in much the same way that you instance a structure in C/C++. Known as *template referencing*, this capability enables you to define a template in an .X file and reuse that template data as many times as you want without having to redefine the template. Imagine that you define a single mesh that you want to use multiple times in the same .X file. Rather than define the mesh again and again (wasting considerable memory), you can define the mesh once and use template referencing to refer back to the template whenever the mesh data is needed.

Most templates are transparent; you'll never have to deal with them directly when loading an .X file. The only exceptions are those of mesh templates and frame templates.

## Using a Frame Hierarchy

You use a *frame template,* also known as a *frame of reference* template, to group one or more templates (usually mesh templates) together for easier handling. You can also create a single mesh and use multiple frames to contain mesh references, which enables you to use a single mesh multiple times.

For example, say that you have a mesh of a billiard ball. Because there are 15 balls to a set, you create 15 frames, each containing a reference to the original ball mesh. From then on, you can orient each frame (using a frame transformation matrix template) around the pool table, causing each mesh instance to move with the frame. In essence, you have created 15 billiard ball mesh instances from a single mesh.

In addition to using frames to create multiple instances of a single mesh, you can also use them to create a frame hierarchy. A *frame hierarchy* defines the structure of a scene or grouping of meshes. Whenever a frame moves, all frames embedded within it move as well.

For example, think of a human skeleton as a set of frames (as illustrated in Figure 6.24). At the top of the hierarchy is the chest. From the chest down, you can attach each bone in line with the previous bone—that is, chest to hip, hip to leg, and leg to foot. Going in reverse (up), you have chest to arm and arm to hand. This ordering goes on until all the bones are attached in one way or another leading back to the chest.

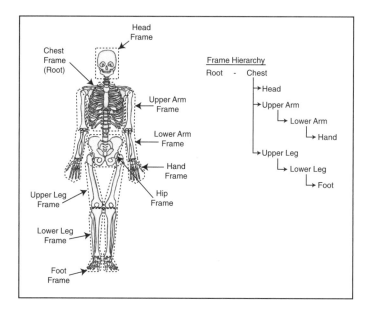

**Figure 6.24**

*Your skeleton is the perfect example of a frame hierarchy. Each bone in the hierarchy leads back to the chest.*

At this point, you have a *root frame,* which is the chest. The root has no parent frames, meaning that it is at the top of the hierarchy and does not belong to another frame. Frames that are connected to other frames are called *child frames* (also referred to as *nodes*). For example, the upper arm is the parent of the lower arm and the hand is the child of the lower arm. Going up the hierarchy, the hand, lower arm, and upper arm are all children of the chest.

When a frame moves, all of its child frames move as well. If you move your upper arm, your lower arm and hand will move as well. On the other hand (no pun intended), if you move your hand, metaphorically speaking, only your hand will change position, because it has no child frames (the lower arm is the hand's parent frame).

Each frame has its own orientation, which in .X file terms is a *frame transformation.* You apply this transformation on top of the transformation that is applied to the higher-level template in the hierarchy. Each transformation is translated down, from the top of the hierarchy all the way to each child frame. For example, if your upper arm rotates, that rotation transformation works its way down to the lower arm and hand (with each of the frames combining with their own transformations).

The frame hierarchy is essential to using advanced mesh and animation techniques. In fact, they are required in order to use such things as skinned meshes (see the section "Meshes with D3DX," later in this chapter, for more on skinned meshes).

Another reason for using a frame hierarchy is to isolate portions of a scene. That way, you can modify a small section of a scene by moving specific frames, leaving the remainder of the scene alone. For example, if you have a frame that represents your house and another one that represents a door, you can alter the door's frame without disturbing the house's frame.

## Creating .X Meshes

You can create your own .X files a number of ways. Microsoft has written a few exporters that you can use with modeling programs such as 3D Studio Max or Maya. If you can't afford those awesome modeling programs, you can create models by hand (by manually entering each of the vertices' and polygons' data into a text .X file) or use a low-cost alternative program, such as MilkShape 3-D, which is a low-polygon modeler developed by Mete Ciragan.

MilkShape 3-D started as a modeling program for creating models for the game *Half-Life*, but it grew into something much larger. MilkShape 3-D now supports multiple model formats (mainly for games), but it still remains a useful program. You know this is getting somewhere, so I'll go ahead and let the cat out of the bag—MilkShape 3-D has an .X file exporter, written by your favorite author (that's right, me!) that you can use. Check out Appendix E, "What's on the CD," for details on installing the exporter, or go to the official MilkShape 3-D Web site (at http://www.swissquake.ch/chumbalum-soft) to download it.

Except for using third-party programs to create an .X file for you, your only option is to do so by hand. However, because creating models yourself is not an optimal solution, I don't cover that topic in this book.

## Parsing .X Files

Later in this chapter and throughout this book, it will become necessary to parse an .X file manually in order to pull out vital mesh information. To parse an .X file, you use the IDirectXFile family of objects, which has the job of opening an .X file and enumerating through the file's templates, thereby giving them to you in an easy-to-access manner.

Parsing an .X file is really not as hard as it might seem at first. The trick is to scan the entire template hierarchy, looking for the templates that you want to use—typically, templates for meshes and frames. The hardest part is remembering that templates can be embedded within other templates, so instead of templates, you might encounter template references (which need to be resolved in order to access the original template data). Figure 6.25 illustrates this organization of templates.

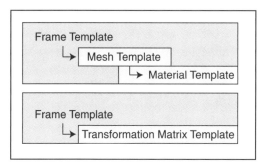

**Figure 6.25**

*An .X file enables you to embed templates within other templates, thus creating a template hierarchy.*

The following code opens and parses the templates contained within an .X file. Remember that these functions are essential for later use in this chapter (and the rest of the book), so don't worry too much about using them at this point.

```
BOOL ParseXFile(char *Filename)
{
  IDirectXFile          *pDXFile = NULL;
  IDirectXFileEnumObject *pDXEnum = NULL;
  IDirectXFileData       *pDXData = NULL;

  // Create the .X file object
  if(FAILED(DirectXFileCreate(&pDXFile)))
    return FALSE;

  // Register the templates in use
  // Use the standard retained mode templates from Direct3D
  if(FAILED(pDXFile->RegisterTemplates((LPVOID)              \
            D3DRM_XTEMPLATES, D3DRM_XTEMPLATE_BYTES))) {
    pDXFile->Release();
    return FALSE;
  }

  // Create an enumeration object
  if(FAILED(pDXFile->CreateEnumObject((LPVOID)Filename,       \
            DXFILELOAD_FROMFILE, &pDXEnum))) {
    pDXFile->Release();
    return FALSE;
  }

  // Enumerate all top-level templates
```

> **NOTE**
>
> To use the `IDirectXFile` components, you have to include `dxfile.h`, `rmxfguid.h`, and `rmxftmpl.h`. Also, you must link the `dxguid.lib` and `d3dxof.lib` libraries to your project.

```
    while(SUCCEEDED(pDXEnum->GetNextDataObject(&pDXData))) {
      ParseXFileData(pDXData);
      ReleaseCOM(pDXData);
    }

    // Release objects
    ReleaseCOM(pDXEnum);
    ReleaseCOM(pDXFile);

    // Return a success
    return TRUE;
  }

  void ParseXFileData(IDirectXFileData *pData)
  {
    IDirectXFileObject *pSubObj  = NULL;
    IDirectXFileData    *pSubData = NULL;
    IDirectXFileDataReference *pDataRef = NULL;
    const GUID *pType = NULL;
    char        *pName = NULL;
    DWORD       dwSize;
    char        *pBuffer;

    // Get the template type
    if(FAILED(pData->GetType(&pType)))
      return;

    // Get the template name (if any)
    if(FAILED(pData->GetName(NULL, &dwSize)))
      return;
    if(dwSize) {
      if((pName = new char[dwSize]) != NULL)
        pData->GetName(pName, &dwSize);
    }

    // Give template a default name if none found
    if(pName == NULL) {
      if((pName = new char[9]) == NULL)
        return;
      strcpy(pName, "Template");
    }
```

```
    // See what the template was and deal with it
    // This is where you'll jump in with your own code

    // Scan for embedded templates
    while(SUCCEEDED(pData->GetNextObject(&pSubObj))) {

      // Process embedded references
      if(SUCCEEDED(pSubObj->QueryInterface(                    \
          IID_IDirectXFileDataReference, (void**)&pDataRef))) {
        if(SUCCEEDED(pDataRef->Resolve(&pSubData))) {
          ParseXFileData(pSubData);
          ReleaseCOM(pSubData);
        }
        ReleaseCOM(pDataRef);
      }

      // Process non-referenced embedded templates
      if(SUCCEEDED(pSubObj->QueryInterface(                    \
                   IID_IDirectXFileData, (void**)&pSubData))) {
        ParseXFileData(pSubData);
        ReleaseCOM(pSubData);
      }
      ReleaseCOM(pSubObj);
    }

    // Release name buffer
    delete[] pName;
}
```

ParseXFile and ParseXFileData work together to parse every single template within an .X file. The ParseXFile function opens the .X file and enumerates through it, looking for the topmost templates in the hierarchy. As each template is found, it is passed to the ParseXFileData.

The ParseXFileData function processes the template data. It starts by getting the template type and the template instance name (if any). From there, you can process the template data, and then let the function enumerate all child templates using recursion. This process continues until all templates are processed.

You just call ParseXFile with the name of the .X file that you want processed, and the two functions take care of the rest. You learn how to put these functions to good use in section "Skinned Meshes," later in this chapter.

# Meshes with D3DX

You, essentially, will deal with two types of meshes in Direct3D: the *standard mesh* and the *skinned mesh*. The standard mesh is just that—standard. It has no bells or whistles, except that it can use texture-mapping to enhance its appearance.

Skinned meshes are unique because they are *deformable*. That is, the mesh can dynamically alter its shape during run-time. To prepare the mesh for deformation, you must attach the vertices of the mesh to an imaginary set of bones inside your 3-D modeling program. Anytime the bones move, the vertices attached to them move as well.

Before going into more detail about standard and skinned meshes, take a look at a special object used by both meshes to store data—the ID3DXBuffer object.

## The ID3DXBuffer Object

You use the ID3DXBuffer object to store and retrieve data buffers. D3DX uses the ID3DXBuffer object to store information about meshes, such as material and texture-map lists. You learn more about this data buffer object in action in the later section "Standard Meshes."

The ID3DXBuffer has only two functions. The first function is ID3DXBuffer::GetBufferPointer, which you use to get a pointer to the data contained within the object's buffer. A call to the GetBufferPointer function returns a void pointer that you can cast to any data type:

```
void *ID3DXBuffer::GetBufferPointer();
```

The second function is ID3DXBuffer::GetBufferSize, which returns the number of bytes used to store the data:

```
DWORD ID3DXBuffer:GetBufferSize();
```

You create an ID3DXBuffer object for your own use with the D3DXCreateBuffer function:

```
HRESULT D3DXCreateBuffer(
    DWORD NumBytes,              // Size of buffer to create
    ID3DXBuffer **ppvBuffer);   // Buffer object to create
```

What good is a function prototype without an example to show it off—so here it is (creating a buffer object 1,024 bytes in size and filling it with zeros):

```
ID3DXBuffer *pBuffer;

// Create the buffer
if(SUCCEEDED(D3DXCreateBuffer(1024, &pBuffer))) {
```

```
   // Get the buffer pointer
   char *pPtr = pBuffer->GetBufferPoint();

   // Set the buffer to all 0's
   memset(pPtr, 0, pBuffer->GetBufferSize());

   // Release the buffer
   pBuffer->Release();
}
```

## Standard Meshes

A standard mesh is a simple beast; it contains a single mesh definition. It is the easiest mesh to work with, and so is a great place to start. Using D3DX makes dealing with standard meshes even easier, because D3DX requires only a short series of code to load and display a standard mesh. The standard mesh I work with in the book is represented by an ID3DXMesh object, which has the responsibility of storing and drawing a single mesh.

After instancing an ID3DXMesh object, use the following function to load the object with a mesh from an .X file:

```
HRESULT D3DXLoadMeshFromX(
   LPSTR pFilename,             // Filename of .X file to load
   DWORD Options,              // D3DXMESH_SYSTEMMEM
   IDirect3DDevice8 *pDevice, // initialized device object to use
   ID3DXBuffer **ppAdjacency, // NULL
   ID3DXBuffer **pMaterials,   // Buffer containing material info
   DWORD pNumMaterials,        // # of materials in mesh
   ID3DXMesh **ppMesh);        // D3DX Mesh object to create
```

Most of the arguments in the D3DXLoadMeshFromX function are filled in by D3DX during the execution of the D3DXLoadMeshFromX function. You supply the filename of the .X file to load, an uninitialized ID3DXBuffer and ID3DXMesh object, and a DWORD variable to store the number of materials used in the mesh.

If you attempt to load an .X file consisting of multiple meshes, the D3DXLoadMeshFromX function will collapse them all into a single mesh. That's perfectly okay for your current purposes. Take a look at some working code that loads a single mesh:

```
// g_pD3DDevice = pre-initialized Direct3D device object
ID3DXBuffer *pD3DXMaterials;
DWORD         g_dwNumMaterials;
ID3DXMesh    *g_pD3DXMesh;
```

```
if(FAILED(D3DXLoadMeshFromX("mesh.x", D3DXMESH_SYSTEMMEM,        \
   g_pD3DDevice, NULL, &pD3DXMaterials, &g_dwNumMaterials,
  &g_pD3DXMesh))) {
  // Error occurred
}
```

Following a successful load of your mesh, you query for the material and texture map information using the following bit of code:

```
D3DXMATERIAL        *pMaterials = NULL;
D3DMATERIAL8        *g_pMaterialList = NULL;
IDirect3DTexture8 **g_pTextureList;

// Get the pointer to the material list
pMaterials = (D3DXMATERIAL*)pD3DXMaterials->GetBufferPointer();
if(pMaterials != NULL) {
  // Allocate some material structure to copy data into
  g_pMaterialList = new D3DMATERIAL8[dwNumMaterials];

  // Allocate an array of texture object pointers
  g_pTextureList = new IDirect3DTexture8[dwNumMaterials];

  // Copy over the materials
  for(DWORD i=0;i<dwNumMaterials;i++) {
    g_pMaterialList[i] = pMaterials[i].MatD3D;

    // Set the ambient color to the same as diffuse
    g_pMaterialList[i].Ambient = g_pMaterialList[i].Diffuse;

    // Create and load the texture (if any)
    if(FAILED(D3DXCreateTextureFromFileA(g_pD3DDevice,           \
        g_pMaterials[i]->pTextureFilename, &g_pTextureList[i])))
      g_pTextureList[i] = NULL;
  }
  // Release material buffer used for loading
  pD3DXMaterials->Release();
} else {
  // Create a default material if no materials were loaded
  g_dwNumMaterials = 1;

  // Create a white material
  g_pMaterialList = new D3DMATERIAL8[1];
```

```
    g_pMaterialList[i].Diffuse.r = 1.0f;
    g_pMaterialList[i].Diffuse.g = 1.0f;
    g_pMaterialList[i].Diffuse.b = 1.0f;
    g_pMaterialList[i].Diffuse.a = 1.0f;
    g_pMaterialList[i].Ambient = g_pMaterialList[i].Diffuse;

    // Create an empty texture reference
    g_pTextureList = new IDirect3DTexture8[1];
    g_pTextureList[0] = NULL;
}
```

When the preceding code bit is complete, you have a spanking new list of materials and textures all set up and ready to use in your scene. The only remaining task is to render your mesh.

## Rendering Meshes

At the heart of the ID3DXMesh object is a single rendering function named DrawSubset, which has the job of rendering a subset of the mesh. A *subset* is a portion of a mesh that is separated because of a changing rendering condition, such as a change in the material or texture from the last subset. You can split a mesh into many subsets (for example, as illustrated in Figure 6.26). Your job is to understand what each subset represents and to render it.

After you load an .X file, you are left with a mesh object, as well as the materials. The subsets of a mesh correlate to those materials, so if you have five materials in a mesh, the mesh contains five subsets to draw.

This arrangement of subsets enables you to easily render a mesh; simply scan through each material, set it, then render the subset. Repeat these steps until the entire mesh is drawn. To position the mesh in the world, set the world transformation matrix before drawing it. Here's an example, using a previous loaded mesh:

```
// g_pD3DDevice = pre-initialized device object
// pD3DXMesh = an ID3DXMesh object, already loaded
// matWorld = mesh world transformation matrix

// Begin the scene
if(SUCCEEDED(g_pD3DDevice->BeginScene())) {

  // Set the meshes world transformation matrix
  g_pD3DDevice->SetTransform(D3DTS_WORLD, &matWorld);
```

```
// Loop for each material in a mesh
for(DWORD i=0;i<g_dwNumMaterials;i++) {

  // Set the material and texture
  g_pD3DDevice->SetMaterial(&g_pMaterialList[i]);
  g_pD3DDevice->SetTexture(0, g_pTextureList[i]);

  // Draw the mesh subset
  pD3DXMesh->DrawSubset(i);
}

// End the scene
g_pD3DDevice->EndScene();
}
```

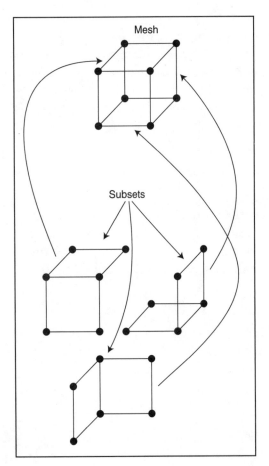

**Figure 6.26**

*You use subsets to separate various portions of the mesh.*

Remember that before you can render a mesh, you set its world transformation matrix in order to position it anywhere and at any angle within your 3-D world. If you load multiple meshes, you can connect them to form an animated object by altering the individual orientations of each mesh. This is the basis of 3-D animation (for more on this topic, see "Using 3-D Animation .X Style," later in this chapter).

## Skinned Meshes

One of the most exciting features of Direct3D is skinned meshes. As I've mentioned, a skinned mesh can be deformed dynamically. You accomplish this by joining the individual vertices that construct a mesh to a structure of underlying "bones," or frame hierarchy. A skinned mesh uses the bones to define its shape; as the bones move, the mesh deforms to match.

The bones are represented as a frame hierarchy inside an .X file. When modeling your meshes, you connect the frame in a parent-child manner. When a parent frame is reoriented, all child frames attached to it inherit the parent's transformation and combine their own transformations. This makes achieving animation easier—you move a single frame and all attached frames will move as well.

To load and use a skinned mesh, you deal directly with the .X file templates, just as you did in the earlier section "Parsing .X Files" (I told you that code would come in handy). As you parse the templates, you need to maintain a list of frames (and their hierarchy).

### Loading Skinned Meshes

As you're enumerating the mesh templates contained within an .X file, you need to call on the various D3DX mesh-loading functions to handle the template data. The one function that's of interest to you when loading skinned meshes is D3DXLoadSkinMeshFromXof. This function has the job of reading in the mesh template from the .X file and creating an ID3DXSkinMesh that contains the skinned mesh object.

Because the code for parsing the frame hierarchy and loading the meshes is a bit complex, you will find it on the CD-ROM at the back of this book (look for \BookCode\Chap06\XFile). I can just hear you sighing, but don't worry; the code is very well commented, and I'll take a moment right now to explain it. First, you find a couple of structures that contain the frame hierarchy (complete with frame transformation matrices) and meshes.

The LoadMesh function uses a slightly modified version of the parsing function shown earlier in this chapter (in the section "Parsing .X Files"). Frame templates, as they are enumerated in the LoadFile function, are added to a frame hierarchy. Other templates within the Frame template are then enumerated, providing the hierarchy with a series of child templates.

If a Mesh template is found during the enumeration of the .X file's templates, the LoadFile function will load the mesh using the D3DXLoadSkinMeshFromXof file. The loaded mesh object is then added to a linked list of loaded mesh. The frames contain pointers back to the meshes, so you can use a single mesh multiple times (using referencing).

After a mesh is loaded, the loading function matches the mesh's bones to their appropriate frames, and the mesh's materials are loaded. If a mesh does not contain bones, the load function converts the mesh into a standard mesh.

To load a skinned mesh or series of meshes, call the LoadFile function using the name of the .X file. In turn, LoadFile will call the ParseXFile function. Then, in return of the LoadFile function, you will receive a pointer to a frame that is the root of all other frames. In order to render a skinned mesh, you must first update the mesh. Updating a mesh retrieves a pointer to a standard mesh object, which you use to render the mesh.

## Updating and Rendering a Skinned Mesh

Before you can render a skinned mesh, you must update it. A skinned mesh really doesn't know how to draw itself. That's because you must first apply all the transformations to each bone in the mesh and then by calling the ID3DXSkinMesh:: UpdateSkinnedMesh function (which you'll see in just a moment), retrieve a pointer to an ID3DXMesh that represents the final deformed appearance of the mesh.

To alter a frame transformation, you modify the frame's rotation transformation matrix (which makes perfect sense because, except for the root object, objects can't be translated). Your first objective is to find the frame that you want to modify. To do so, just scan through the frame list. Using standard D3DXMatrix* functions, go ahead and alter the rotation of a frame now.

Once you complete rotating each frame into the orientations you want, you are ready to update all the transformations in the frame hierarchy. You start at the root, which has been oriented in the world where you want the mesh to be rendered. Then you pass the transformation matrix to the next child frame, which is combined with its own transformation matrix. Continue this process down the hierarchy until all transformation matrices are updated.

Here's an example function that processes the entire frame hierarchy for you (assuming that you are using the sFrame structure from the code examples on the CD-ROM):

```
// Call the following function with your root frame
// and a matrix that is the orientation of the
// mesh in the world.
void UpdateFrameMatrix(sFrame *Frame, D3DXMATRIX *pMatrix)
{
  // Multiply the matrices
  D3DXMatrixMultiply(&Frame->matWorld, &Frame->matRotation,    \
                     pMatrix);

  // update child frames
  if(Frame->Child != NULL)
    UpdateFrameMatrix(Frame->Child, &Frame->matWorld);

  // update sibling frames
  if(Frame->Sibling != NULL)
    UpdateFrameMatrix(Frame->Sibling, pMatrix);
}
```

Once all frames are oriented, you update the skinned mesh and generate an ID3DXMesh which is used to render the final orientation of the mesh:

```
HRESULT ID3DXSkinMesh::UpdateSkinnedMesh(
  CONST D3DXMATRIX* pBoneTransforms,  // Frame matrices
  ID3DXMesh *pMesh);                  // Output mesh
```

The first parameter, pBoneTransforms, is the pointer to the array of matrices used to store the bone transformations. The second parameter, pMesh, is the pointer to the updated output mesh that you use to render (using the DrawSubset function). Just refer back to the previous section on rendering meshes to see how to process from here.

# Using 3-D Animation .X Style

Animation in 3-D is a whole new deal than animation in 2-D. No longer can you afford the luxury of drawing images and then displaying them in sequence to create animation. With 3-D, an object can be viewed from virtually any orientation.

The basis for 3-D animation is to alter the frame transformation matrices used to orient your meshes during run-time, thereby causing the various meshes located within the frames to move. This movement of the meshes is animation. You can translate, rotate, and even scale the meshes almost any way you want.

When dealing with skinned meshes, using frame transformations is the only way to animate the mesh. Because a skinned mesh is a single mesh (not composed of multiple meshes), you need to alter the frames in order for the vertices to deform.

The easiest way to modify the frame transformation matrices is through a technique called *key framing*.

## Key Frame Techniques

In computer animation, *key framing* describes the technique for taking two complete, separate orientations (key frames) and interpolating between them based on a factor such as time. In other words, by taking the orientation of two different frames (with each orientation called a *key*), you can calculate their orientation anywhere and any time between those keys (as illustrated in Figure 6.27).

Key framing is memory efficient and ensures that the animation will run at the same speed on all systems. Slower computers drop frames (at the cost of choppy animation), whereas faster computers generate more frames, providing smoother animation.

As you now know, a hierarchy of frames is constructed in which all frames are attached in one way or another. You also know how to animate the frames of a mesh using the .X file animation templates. Now, you just need to plug in the calculations to interpolate between those frames in order to create smooth animation.

> **NOTE**
>
> *Interpolating* is a way of calculating the transitional values between two numbers over a set amount of time. For example, if your house is two miles from your workplace and it takes you 30 minutes to get to work, you can determine your distance to work at any specific time by using interpolation with the following calculation:
>
> ```
> Distance = (DistanceToWork /
> TravelTime) * CurrentTime;
> ```
>
> As you can see, after 26 minutes, you have traveled (Distance = (2 / 30) * 26) 1.73 miles.

The form of key framing that I prefer, and the one that I show in this book, is *matrix key framing*. Because you're already using the D3DX matrix object, using this form of key framing is easy. Say that you have two matrices: Mat1 and Mat2, representing the starting and ending matrices, respectively. The distance in time between

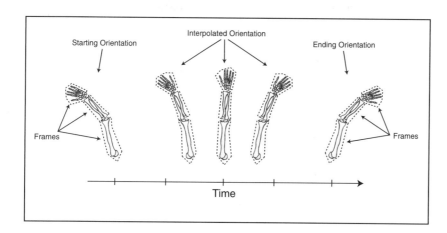

**Figure 6.27**

*The orientations of the frames are interpolated over time from starting to ending orientations.*

them is represented as Length, and the current time is represented as Time (which ranges from 0 to Length). You calculate the interpolated matrix as follows:

```
// D3DXMATRIX Mat1, Mat2;
// DWORD Length, Time;
D3DXMATRIX MatInt;  // Resulting interpolated matrix

// Calculate the interpolated matrix
MatInt = (Mat2 - Mat1) / Length;

// Multiply by time
MatInt *= Time;

// Add back to Mat1 and that's the result!
MatInt += Mat1;
```

The final calculation is complete, and you're left with a matrix that holds the orientation somewhere between the matrices that you used.

## Animation in .X

Microsoft has provided animation data in .X files. This animation data is within a set of special templates, and you can load the data from those animation templates using the same techniques you use to load a skinned mesh.

Loading animations from an .X file is messy; there are entire animations, each with an animation template, an animation set template, time templates, key-frame templates—way too much to deal with!

Rather than wade through the creation of an entire animation package here, check out the code on this book's CD-ROM (look for \BookCode \Chap06\XFile). You can also refer to Chapter 10, "Creating the Game Core," to check out an entire animation package developed for this book. For now, though, continue reading this section to find out how animation works in .X.

Special templates contain the various keys that are used in key framing techniques. Each key represents a single transformation: rotation, scaling, and translation. To make it easier, you can specify matrix keys that combine all the transformations at once (which is the type of key that I use in this book).

Each key has an associated time at which it is active. In other words, a rotation key at time=0 means that when time is 0, the rotation value in the key is used. A second rotation key becomes active at time=200. As time goes on, an interpolated rotational value is calculated somewhere between the first and second rotation keys. As time hits 200, the rotational value equals that of the second rotation key. This form of interpolation to the values applies to all key types.

Animations come in sets, and each set is assigned to a specific frame. You can have multiple keys assigned to the same set so that more than one animation key affects the frame. For example, a frame can be modified by a set of rotation-keys and a set of translation-keys at the same time in order to rotate and translate the frame at once.

Again, with the help of modeling programs such as 3D Studio Max and MilkShape 3-D, you'll never have to deal directly with an .X file's animation data. In addition, by using the code provided in this book, you can have fully animated meshes up and running in your games in no time flat! Refer to Chapter 10 for information on loading and using animation

**NOTE**

When discussing time, realize that it has no real measurement. You must decide how to measure it. For example, time can be the number of seconds passed from a certain point, or time can be the number of frames that have elapsed. To make it easy, time should be based on the computer system's time, which makes it possible to time animations down to the exact second (that is, you want an animation to complete in two seconds).

# Wrapping Up Graphics

Congratulations! This chapter finishes the whirlwind tour on DirectX Graphics! With so much to see and learn, you might want to take a little time to be sure that you fully understand the basics—vertices, polygons, textures, and materials. Understanding these basics is your only ticket to the big-time effects shown earlier in this chapter and later in the book.

## Programs on the CD-ROM

Programs that demonstrate the code discussed in this chapter are on the CD-ROM at the back of this book. You can find the following programs in the \BookCode\Chap06\ directory:

- **Enum.** A program that enumerates all display adapters and shows their mode information. Location: \BookCode\Chap06\Enum\.

- **Draw2D.** This program shows how to draw polygons (plain and textured) using 2-D coordinates. Location: \BookCode\Chap06\Draw2D\.

- **Draw3D.** This program shows how to draw polygons (plain and textured) using 3-D coordinates and 3-D transformations. Location: \BookCode\Chap06\Draw3D\.

- **Alpha.** This program demonstrates using alpha blending and transparent blitting. Location: \BookCode\Chap06\Alpha\.

- **Lights.** With this program, you can see the effects that each type of light has on objects. Location: \BookCode\Chap06\Lights\.

- **ZBuffer.** This program demonstrates the use of a Z-buffered to depth sort. Location: \BookCode\Chap06\ZBuffer\.

- **Font.** This program shows how to use the font features illustrated in this chapter. Location: \BookCode\Chap06\Font\.

- **Particle.** This program draws a collage of moving particles, using billboarding techniques. Location: \BookCode\Chap06\Particle\.

- **XFile.** This program demonstrates the use of the D3DX library mesh functions. Location: \BookCode\Chap06\XFile\.

# CHAPTER 7

# INTERACTING WITH DIRECTINPUT

One thing definitely holds true for most applications—they need user input. Whether you are using a joystick to guide your on-screen hero, clicking your mouse on a Web page link, or just typing a letter using your keyboard, the results are all considered to be *input*. Wouldn't it be great to use all three input devices in your own game engine? With so many devices out there, how could you handle them all?

Don't worry; Microsoft has come to the rescue with DirectInput! No longer do you have to worry about the minute details of every input device, because DirectInput gives you a simple, generalized method of accessing them.

This chapter begins with a brief discussion on how input devices work and then moves on to using them with DirectInput. Specifically, in this chapter, you learn how to do the following:

- Use input devices
- Work with DirectInput
- Initialize DirectInput
- Use DirectInput devices
- Read and use device data

# Introducing Input Devices

Computers use three common input devices: keyboards, mice, and joysticks. All are invaluable, and each has its own pros and cons. Keyboards, while good for typing things, are no replacement for a mouse, and they are too bulky to use as joysticks.

As for the mouse, it's great for pointing and movement, but lacks the simplicity of joystick control. As for joysticks, they're great for simple movements—up, down, left, and right—but almost useless for anything else. It's like the old phrase, "Can't live with 'em, can't live without 'em."

Each input device interfaces with the computer in its own special way—some through the use of device drivers (small programs that have the sole purpose of dealing with the input device), while others deal directly with the computer's memory. It's your job to query the device drivers or operating system for any information the input device may be relaying, and then handle that information as you see fit.

# Interacting via the Keyboard

Press a key on the keyboard and the corresponding letter, number, or symbol seems to magically appear on the screen. However, the interaction between a keyboard and a computer is quite involved, and as a game programmer, this interaction is something you must understand.

Basically, a keyboard is an array of keys arranged in a logical pattern. With just a few differences, most keyboards have a standard layout. Each key on a keyboard is essentially a switch that is triggered when you press or release the key.

Pressing or releasing a key sends a signal to the keyboard's microprocessor, which in turn generates what is called an *interrupt* on the computer system. In turn, the system retrieves the data from the keyboard's microprocessor, thereby ascertaining what was pressed or released. This data is called a *scan code*.

> **NOTE**
>
> An *interrupt* is a signal of sorts that informs the system that a device or program needs processing as soon as possible. Using interrupts ensures the system knows that a device's state has been changed.
>
> *Scan codes* are values that determine which key on the keyboard was pressed or released. These codes are a single byte (although the operating system can present them to you in a number of ways), with a portion of the byte telling you which key is involved, and a single bit telling you whether the key was pressed or released.

Because keyboards can have different layouts, scan codes might change from keyboard to keyboard. This, however, is not too great a problem, because most keyboards follow the standard 101–102 key layout. For the uninitiated, every keyboard has a layout referred to by the number of keys on the keyboard, and in most cases, this number of keys is 101 or 102.

Figure 7.1 shows you a portion of a typical 101–102 key scan code arrangement. Notice that the scan codes are arranged according to the arrangement of the keys on the keyboard; in rows of keys, a key to the right of another key is usually a single scan code higher.

> **NOTE**
>
> Because a scan code recognizes only single key presses, it can't distinguish between uppercase and lowercase letters. So the scan code for uppercase *A* and for lowercase *a* are the same. The operating system automatically detects and distinguishes between uppercase and lowercase letters by tracking whether the shift key is being held.

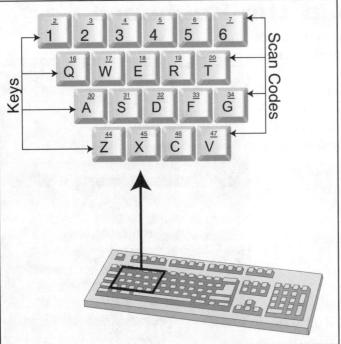

**Figure 7.1**

*A closer look at the keyboard shows a few keys with their respective scan codes. Scan codes are bit-encoded numbers.*

The lowest 7 bits (bits 0–6) of the scan code represent the key value (which key was pressed or released), while the highest bit of the scan code (bit 7) signifies if that key was pressed (bit set) or released (bit clear). The highest number a byte can represent is 255, and the highest bit is reserved, which gives us room for 128 keys.

## Dealing with the Keyboard in Windows

Windows is able to handle the mundane task of retrieving keyboard input for you. To make the job easier, Windows converts incoming scan codes from the keyboard (which, based on the keyboard, could be anything) to standardized values called *Virtual Key Codes* and *ASCII* codes. Windows reports these values in a number of ways to the programmer, usually through the message procedure, which is shown in Chapter 5, "Programming with Windows and Application Basics."

What you do with these newly received Virtual Key Codes or ASCII codes is now up to you and your application. For word processors, you may insert the corresponding key's letter in the body of text. For games, you can process the key presses and move the player's character around the screen.

**NOTE**

A Virtual Key Code is the Windows version of a scan code. Instead of using the scan code of 30 for the letter A (and hoping it is correct), you instead use the Virtual Key Code macro of the letter A, VK_A, and rest assured that it will always be the letter A, regardless of the keyboard in use (and the scan codes the keyboard reports).

*ASCII (American Standard Code for Information Interchange)* is the standard that dictates what values can be mapped to what characters. With ASCII, you can tell the difference between an uppercase *A* and a lowercase *a* because they have different values. ASCII can map values for up to 128 different characters, which range from numbers, alphabet, common symbols, and control codes.

Windows actually uses *Extended ASCII* codes and *Unicode* characters (or *wide characters*). Extended ASCII adds an extra bit of information to regular ASCII, thus boosting the maximum number of characters to 256. The downside is that the extended characters could be anything—there is no real standard for them. Also, some other languages need more characters, so *Unicode* was invented, which brought the maximum amount of characters to 16 bits, enough for 65,536 characters.

Did I just say use the keyboard for games? Yes, that's right—you can use the keyboard quite efficiently for playing games. The only problem is that Windows just can't keep up with the mad key-pressing actions of some games. What's the solution then? You find out in just a bit in the section "Using DirectInput."

# Playing with the Mouse

If the plural of goose is geese, is more than one mouse called meese? Well, I'll leave that for others to argue; for me, mice are sufficient. Unlike their furry counterparts, computer mice help us immensely.

A mouse consists of very few components. It usually has two or three buttons and a ball underneath that tracks the movement of the mouse. The buttons are easy to understand—press one, and it sends a signal to the computer; release it and it again sends a signal to the computer. Some other mouse devices use optics to track the movement so that there is no need for a ball, but these devices do the same thing as others.

There's really nothing difficult to understand under the little rodent's hard cover. At the lowest level, the mouse is informing the system that it just moved in a certain direction, one little tick at a time. The driver reading this data converts the ticks into relative movement values.

In a typical application, Windows takes these movements and reports them as messages to the user through the message procedure, as shown in Chapter 5. Remember that working with the message procedure is quite slow at times— each message passed to the message procedure is inserted into a queue that only processes the messages in the order they are added.

To speed up the process of receiving and processing mouse input, you interface direction with the mouse driver, leaving the Windows message procedure out of the loop.

Regardless of the way you receive the mouse movements, you start tracking the coordinates of the mouse on the screen. You have the option of tracking absolute or relative mouse coordinates. *Absolute* means the current position of the mouse based on a fixed point (usually the upper-left corner of the screen as seen in Figure 7.2). *Relative* refers to the amount of movement from the last known position, either left, right, down, or up. Both are easy to implement, as you'll soon see.

Mouse buttons can flag only whether a button is currently pressed, much in the same way the keyboard is able to report that a key is pressed.

> **NOTE**
>
> A *relative* movement is the amount of movement from the last recorded position. For instance, if you were to stand up and walk five steps forward, then your relative position from where you last were is five steps back.
>
> The small amount of movement that a mouse signals is called a *Mickey*. (I'm sure that old Walt would have gotten a kick out of that!) The mouse driver has the responsibility of converting these Mickeys into values that the driver is able to pass on to the system.

## Jammin' with the Joystick

Ahhh, the feel of a new joystick. The molded plastic pieces, rubber grips, and shiny buttons all seem to fit your hand perfectly. Thoughts of conquering fill your head. Memories of past victories, and losses, flood through you. It's almost like you were born to play games.

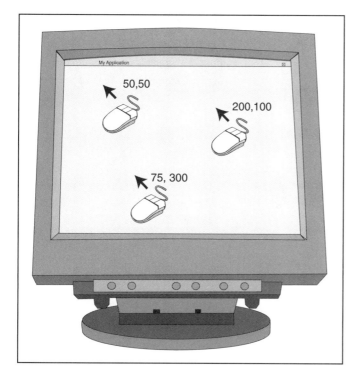

**Figure 7.2**

*You measure the mouse's absolute coordinates by the number of pixels that the mouse is away from the upper-left corner of the screen.*

Joysticks are the bread and butter of game controls. While not the only input device used for games, it seems to be the most intuitive. Push left on the stick, and your character walks left. Push a button, and your hero swings his sword. What could by easier?

Joysticks come in a myriad of shapes and sizes. That steering wheel controller you see on the store shelf—that's a joystick. If you've ever been to an arcade, you've probably played games that allow (or require) you to stand on huge snowboards or to sit on small motorcycles while controlling your onscreen persona. While amazingly deceitful, even those snowboards and motorcycles are considered joysticks!

Joysticks are devices that are axis-controlled and have a few buttons. The steering wheel has a single axis control for steering left and right. Maybe it has two more axis controls for brake and gas pedals. Even your basic two-button joystick has two axis controls, one for up and down and the other for left and right. Figure 7.3 shows you a few of these.

An *axis control* is just a potentiometer (variable resister), which regulates the level of voltage passing through the circuit. The least amount of voltage passing through

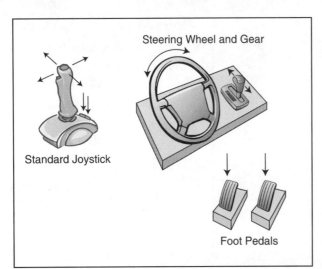

Standard Joystick

Steering Wheel and Gear

Foot Pedals

**Figure 7.3**

*Directional, rotational, and push-style input are all common traits among joysticks, regardless of their appearance.*

represents one extent (the furthest point a joystick can be pushed) of the axis, while the most voltage represents the other extent. All levels in between represent the axis somewhere between the extents.

This voltage level makes its way to the system which is thankfully handled by Windows (or DirectInput) and then given to you for your use. The joystick's buttons operate almost the same way, but have voltage either applied or not, signaling that a button is pressed or released, respectively.

Joystick data is read in by absolute values, which are relative to the center of the joystick. Push left or up, and you receive negative values representing the distance away from the center. Press down or right, and you get positive values. Buttons are single flags that state whether a button is up.

**NOTE**

The only big differences that you might notice in joysticks are those with digital axis controls that work like a bunch of buttons. Pushing left on the joystick is just like pushing a button that signifies left. Whenever the programmer queries the joystick for the axis reading, the joystick will return the lowest or highest possible value along the axis.

# Using DirectInput

You'll most likely use the keyboard and the mouse, and it will be handy to have access to a joystick as well. However, so many different types of these devices are available that your head will spin trying to support them all.

Also, as mentioned in Chapter 5, dealing with the window's message procedure to obtain input is just plain slow and certainly not suited for the fast action needs of gaming. Why wait for crucial key press data or mouse movement information to pass through the message queue when you need it now? Behold DirectInput—the solution to your need. With it, you have a method to quickly retrieve data when you need it, and not have to wait for Windows to give it to you.

As it turns out, DirectInput is hands down the easiest component of DirectX to work with. With DirectInput, your programs can easily use any keyboard, mouse, or joystick connected to the user's system (as well as any other input device compatible with DirectInput). And if you want to go barebones working with code, you might be able to do so in less than a few dozen lines!

# Presenting DirectInput Basics

DirectInput is a collection of COM objects (like all DirectX components) that represents the input system as well as the individual input devices (as shown in Table 7.1). The main object, IDirectInput8, is used to initialize the system and create the input device interfaces.

Each input device (such as the keyboard, mouse, and joystick) uses a common interface object to work with, which is IDirectInputDevice8. Certain devices, such as joysticks and mice, are able to query their respective IDirectInputDevice8 objects for an additional interface, IDirectInputEffect, which is used to control the force feedback effects of the device. This relationship among the IDirectInput8, IDirectInputDevice8, and IDirectInputEffect interfaces is shown in Figure 7.4.

## Table 7.1  DirectInput COM Objects

| Object | Description |
|---|---|
| IDirectInput8 | The main DirectInput 8 COM interface. All other interfaces are queried from this. |
| IDirectInputDevice8 | COM interface for input devices. Each device has a separate interface of its own to use. |
| IDirectInputEffect | The COM interface for force-feedback effects, such as those on joysticks and some mice. |

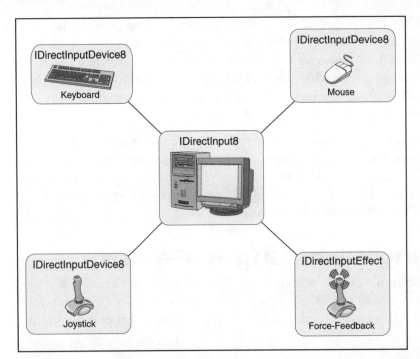

IDirectInputDevice8
Keyboard

IDirectInputDevice8
Mouse

IDirectInput8

IDirectInputDevice8
Joystick

IDirectInputEffect
Force-Feedback

**Figure 7.4**

*The head of the show is* IDirectInput8, *which creates the various* IDirectInputDevice8 *objects. In turn, the* IDirectInputDevice8 *objects can be used to create their own* IDirectInputEffect *objects.*

The IDirectInput8 component object contains a number of functions used to initialize the input system and obtain device interfaces (where the real work takes place). Of these functions, you'll typically need only two, IDirectInput8::EnumDevices and IDirectInput8::CreateDevice. You learn more about these when it comes time to deal with input devices, starting in the section "Employing DirectInput Devices."

**NOTE**

For the purposes of this book, I use only the first two COM objects, thus excluding IDirectInputEffect.

# Initializing DirectInput

To start using DirectInput, be sure to include DInput.h and link DInput8.lib with your project. An IDirectInput8 object represents the main DirectInput object, so go ahead and declare it globally:

```
IDirectInput8 g_pDI;  // global DirectInput object
```

**NOTE**

As with all COM objects, be sure to call Release() on them when you are finished:

```
g_pDI->Release();
```

DirectInput supplies the helper function `DirectInput8Create` to initialize this interface for you. Here's its prototype:

```
HRESULT WINAPI DirectInput8Create(
    HINSTANCE hInstance,      // instance handle of your program
    DWORD dwVersion,          // DIRECTINPUT_VERSION
    REFIID riidltf,           // IID_IDirectInput8
    LPVOID *ppvOut,           // pointer to your new object
    LPUNKNOWN pUnkOuter);     // set to NULL
```

The arguments are easily understood; you only need to supply the pointer to the object you want to create and set the rest as specified in the comments. The following code bit shows how you can create the DirectInput interface:

```
IDirectInput8 *g_pDI;  // global DirectInput object

int PASCAL WinMain(HINSTANCE hInst, HINSTANCE hPrev,          \
                   LPSTR szCmdLine, int nCmdShow)
{
  HRESULT hr;

  hr = DirectInput8Create(hInst, DIRECTINPUT_VERSION,         \
                  IID_IDirectInput8, (void**)&g_pDI, NULL);

  // return failure if an error occurred
  if(FAILED(hr))
    return FALSE;

  // Go on with program here
```

> **NOTE**
>
> As do all COM interfaces, the `DirectInput8Create` function returns an `HRESULT` value. DirectInput will return a value of `DI_OK` if the function completed successfully, or another value if it did not. Refer to the DirectX Software Developer's Kit for specifics on Error Codes. When you test a return code, use the `FAILED` or `SUCCEEDED` macro to test it. Functions can still succeed but return an error code, so the macros will detect this for you.

That's about all there is to setting up DirectInput! Next, you learn how to set up the device objects to work with the actual hardware (keyboard, mouse, and joystick).

# Employing DirectInput Devices

Microsoft went to great lengths to simplify dealing with input devices. It's so simple, in fact, that you can use the same COM interface (`IDirectInputDevice8`) to deal with just about every input device you can think of (and probably a few that you can't!)

The steps for creating and using an input device are similar for each one, so let me jump ahead a bit and show you how to do that. Table 7.2 shows the steps in general and in their correct order along with the DirectInput interface and function that handles the step.

Before moving on, be sure to declare a DirectInput device object (`IDirectInputDevice8`):

```
IDirectInputDevice8 *pDIDevice;
```

# Obtaining a Device GUID

Every device installed has a *GUID* (*Global Unique IDentification*) number assigned to it. In order to use a device, you need to know its GUID first. For the system keyboard and mouse, this is easy. DirectInput defines these as `GUID_SysKeyboard` and `GUID_SysMouse`, respectively. For all other devices, you must enumerate to find the ones you want.

Enumerating devices is the job of the `IDirectInput8::EnumDevices` function:

```
HRESULT IDirectInput8::EnumDevices(
    DWORD dwDevType,                    // device type to look for
    LPDIENUMCALLBACK lpCallback,  // enum callback function
    LPVOID pvRef,                      // user-set data pointer
    DWORD dwFlags);                    // enumeration flags
```

## Table 7.2  Steps to Creating and Using a Device

| Step | Interface/Function |
| --- | --- |
| Obtain a device GUID | `IDirectInput8::EnumDevices` |
| Create the device COM object | `IDirectInput8::CreateDevice` |
| Set the data format | `IDirectInputDevice8::SetDataFormat` |
| Set the cooperative level | `IDirectInputDevice8::SetCooperativeLevel` |
| Set any special properties | `IDirectInputDevice8::SetProperty` |
| Acquire the device | `IDirectInputDevice8::Acquire` |
| Poll the device | `IDirectInputDevice8::Poll` |
| Read in data | `IDirectInputDevice8::GetDeviceState` |

dwDevType is a bit field describing which types of devices to enumerate. This could range from general device types, such as joysticks and mice, to something more specific, such as trackballs or yokes. Consult the DX SDK for a full list or Table 7.3 for a few common ones.

> **NOTE**
>
> To use GUID_SysKeyboard or GUID_SysMouse, you must define INITGUID before all other preprocessor directives or link DXGuid.lib to your project:
>
> #define INITGUID
>
> You only need to define INITGUID once in your project (inside a single source code file); doing so more than once causes compiler errors.

The lpCallback variable is the pointer to an enumeration function that is called every time a matching device is found on the system. I get to this in a bit. As for pvRef, you can set this to anything, typically having it point to a structure in which you want to store information. When the enumeration function is called, it supplies this data pointer to the structure (or other data) you provided, giving you the chance to retrieve or set data.

## Table 7.3  DirectInput Device Enumeration Types

| Value | Description |
| --- | --- |
| DI8DEVCLASS_ALL | All devices. |
| DI8DEVCLASS_GAMECTRL | All game controllers (joysticks). |
| DI8DEVCLASS_KEYBOARD | All keyboard devices. |
| DI8DEVCLASS_POINTER | All pointer devices (mouse). |
| DI8DEVCLASS_DEVICE | All devices that don't fit into the previous three types. |
| DI8DEVTYPE_MOUSE | Mouse or mouse-like device, such as a trackball. |
| DI8DEVTYPE_KEYBOARD | Keyboard or keyboard-like device. |
| DI8DEVTYPE_JOYSTICK | Joystick or similar device, such as a steering wheel. |
| DI8DEVTYPE_DEVICE | Device that doesn't fit into the three previous types. |
| DI8DEVTYPEMOUSE_TOUCHPAD | Device is a touchpad (sub-type). |
| DI8DEVTYPEMOUSE_TRACKBALL | Device is a trackball (sub-type). |

Last is dwFlags, which tells DirectInput how to enumerate devices. You can set the dwFlags argument to any value listed in Table 7.4.

The previously mentioned lpCallback function pointer needs to point to a DIEnumDeviceProc defined enumeration function, which uses the following prototype:

```
BOOL CALLBACK DIEnumDevicesProc(
  LPDIDEVICEINSTANCE lpddi,    // device structure
  LPVOID pvRef);               // the user-specified pointer
```

lpddi is a pointer to a DIDEVICEINSTANCE structure, which contains information on the currently enumerated device during this call. Here's the structure:

```
typedef struct {
  DWORD dwSize;        // Size of this structure
  GUID  guidInstance;  // device GUID
  GUID  guidProduct;   // OEM supplied GUID of device
  DWORD dwDevType;   // Device type
  TCHAR tszInstanceName[MAX_PATH];  //Name of device
  TCHAR tszProductName[MAX_PATH];   //Name of product
  GUID  guidFFDriver;  // GUID of force-feedback driver
  WORD  wUsagePage;    // Usage page if an HID device
  WORD  wUsage;        // Usage code if an HID device
} DIDEVICEINSTANCE;
```

Let me take a moment now and build a couple of functions that initialize DirectInput and enumerate all devices, displaying the name of each one found, one at a time, in a message box. At each one, you get to select whether you want to stop enumeration or continue by clicking either the Cancel button or the OK button, respectively.

## Table 7.4  Enumeration Flags

| Value | Description |
| --- | --- |
| DIEDFL_ALLDEVICES | Enumerates all installed devices (default). |
| DIEDFL_ATTACHEDONLY | Enumerates only devices that are attached. |
| DIEDFL_FORCEFEEDBACK | Enumerates only devices that have force-feedback. |
| DIEDFL_INCLUDEALIASES | Includes devices that are aliases for other devices. |
| DIEDFL_INCLUDEPHANTOMS | Includes phantom (placeholder) devices. |

> **NOTE**
>
> The only fields you need to work with in the DIDEVICEINSTANCE structure
> are guidInstance, dwDevType, and tszInstanceName. guidInstance is the **GUID**
> needed to initialize the device (which is what you are looking for).
> dwDevType is the type of device that is currently being enumerated.
>
> Lastly, tszInstanceName is a text buffer that contains a description name of
> the device (such as "JoyStick 1") that you can use, possibly to enable the
> user to select the device from a list.

> **NOTE**
>
> A quick note on enumeration: During the enumeration function, you
> must determine whether you need to continue enumerating devices
> or stop, which you do by returning the values DIENUM_CONTINUE or
> DIENUM_STOP, respectively.

```
// Global DirectInput COM object
IDirectInput8 *g_pDI;

// Function prototypes
BOOL InitDIAndEnumAllDevices(HWND hWnd, HINSTANCE hInst);
BOOL CALLBACK EnumDevices(LPCDIDEVICEINSTANCE pdInst,              \
                          LPVOID pvRef);

BOOL InitDIAndEnumAllDevices(HWND hWnd, HINSTANCE hInst)
{
  if(FAILED(DirectInput8Create(hInst, DIRECTINPUT_VERSION,        \
               IID_IDirectInput8, (void**)&g_pDI, NULL)))
    return FALSE;

  g_pDI->EnumDevices(DI8DEVCLASS_ALL, EnumDevices,                \
                     (LPVOID)hWnd, DIEDFL_ALLDEVICES);
  return TRUE;
}
BOOL CALLBACK EnumDevices(LPCDIDEVICEINSTANCE pdInst,             \
                          LPVOID pvRef)
{
  int Result;
```

```
// Display a message box with name of device found
Result = MessageBox((HWND)pvRef, pdInst->tszInstanceName,   \
                    "Device Found", MB_OKCANCEL);
// Tell it to continue enumeration if OK pressed
if(Result == IDOK)
  return DIENUM_CONTINUE;
// Stop enumeration
return DIENUM_STOP;
}
```

Just insert the preceding code into your own program and call `InitDIAndEnumAllDevices()`.

> **NOTE**
>
> Say that of all the devices you want to enumerate only the joysticks that are attached. Just replace the g_pDI->EnumDevices line with the following:
>
> g_pDI->EnumDevices(DI8DEVTYPE_JOYSTICK,
> EnumDevices, (LPVOID)hWnd, DIEDFL_ATTACHEDONLY);

# Creating the Device COM Object

Now that you have the device GUID, you can create the actual `IDirectInputDevice8` COM object. This is the work of the `IDirectInput8::CreateDevice` function:

```
HRESULT IDirectInput8::CreateDevice(
  REFGUID rguid,            // GUID of device to create
                            // predefined or from enumeration
  LPDIRECTINPUTDEVICE *lplpDirectInputDevice,  // pointer to
                                    // the object you're creating
  LPUNKNOWN pUnkOuter);  // NULL - not used
```

Here's an example of using `IDirectInput8::CreateDevice`:

```
IDirectInputDevice8 *pDIDevice;
HRESULT hr = g_pDI->CreateDevice(DeviceGUID, &pDIDevice, NULL);
```

Or, as an example, to create an object using the system keyboard with predefining GUID, use the following:

```
IDirectInputDevice8 *pDIDevice;
HRESULT hr = pDI->CreateDevice(GUID_SysKeyboard,             \
                               &pDIDevice, NULL);
```

> **NOTE**
>
> You can embed this function call within an enumeration function, when you discover the section, "Using DirectInput with Joysticks," later in this chapter.

# Setting the Data Format

Each device has a specific data format used to read in data. There are numerous things to consider: keys, buttons, axes, and so on. You have to tell DirectInput this format in order for your program to begin reading data from the device.

You do this via the `IDirectInputDevice8::SetDataFormat` function:

```
HRESULT IDirectInputDevice8::SetDataFormat(
  LPCDIDATAFORMAT lpdf);
```

The `SetDataFormat` function has only one argument, which is a pointer to a `DIDATAFORMAT` structure:

```
typedef struct {
    DWORD dwSize;       // Size of this structure
    DWORD dwObjSize;    // Size of DIOBJECTDATAFORMAT structure
    DWORD dwFlags;      // Flags determining if device works in
                        //   absolute mode (DIDF_ABSAXIS)
                        //   or relative (DIDF_RELAXIS)
    DWORD dwDataSize;   // Size of data packets received
                        //   from device (in multiples of 4)
    DWORD dwNumObjs;    // Number of objects in the rgodf array
    LPDIOBJECTDATAFORMAT rgodf;  // Address to an array of
                                 //   DIOBJECTDATAFORMAT structures.
} DIDATAFORMAT, *LPDIDATAFORMAT;
```

Most objects do not have to deal with setting up this structure because DirectInput comes with a few predefined ones that you can use, as shown in Table 7.5.

I will not go into the specifics on how to create your own formats because the three device data structures shown in Table 7.5 are all that you need for this book. Consult the DirectX SDK for information on creating your own device data format structures.

# Setting the Cooperative Level

Let's face it—every program will use only so many input devices. Nearly every program uses a keyboard and a mouse, while some also use the joystick. When it comes down to it, you must share access to those devices with other applications that may be running—or you can be a bully and hog all access to the devices for your own application, thus not allowing other applications to take control of those devices until you're finished with them.

## Table 7.5 Preset DirectInput Device Data Structures

| Device | Data Structure | Example |
|--------|----------------|---------|
| Keyboard | c_dfDIKeyboard | pDIDevice->SetDataFormat(&c_dfDIKeyboard); |
| Mouse | c_dfDIMouse | pDIDevice->SetDataFormat(&c_dfDIMouse); |
| Joystick | c_dfJoystick | pDIDevice->SetDataFormat(&c_dfDIJoystick); |

The next step in using a device is setting the cooperative level, which you handle using the following function:

```
HRESULT IDirectInputDevice8::SetCooperativeLevel(
   HWND hWnd,           // handle to the parent window
   DWORD dwFlags);  // flags determining how to share access
```

Set the hWnd argument of the SetCooperativeLevel function to your application's window handle. In order to share the device access with other applications, set the dwFlags argument to one of the values in Table 7.6, which describes how to share device access.

When you set your cooperative level, it must be either DISCL_EXCLUSIVE or DISCL_NONEXCLUSIVE, and it must be combined with DISCL_FOREGROUND or DISCL_BACKGROUND. I recommend that you use the DISCL_FOREGROUND and DISCL_NONEXCLUSIVE for the three devices:

> **NOTE**
>
> Use of DISCL_NOWINKEY is optional, but I recommend doing so for full-screen applications so that the user doesn't inadvertently break out of the program.

```
pDIDevice->SetCooperativeLevel(hWnd, DISCL_FOREGROUND |         \
                              DISCL_NONEXCLUSIVE);
```

# Setting Special Properties

This is where you can set any special properties for the device, such as axis mode, buffering, and minimum or maximum ranges. For axis mode, you have two choices—relative and absolute. Absolute mode reports coordinates based on a central coordinate. Values to the left or above that point are reported as negatives, while values to the right or below are positive.

## Table 7.6 IDirectInputDevice8 Cooperative Levels

| Level | Description |
|---|---|
| DISCL_NONEXCLUSIVE | Using this setting allows the input device to share its access with others and does not interfere with other programs using it. |
| DISCL_EXCLUSIVE | This setting makes your program the bully. When acquired, you have sole access to the device, even if others have set exclusive use of it. |
| DISCL_FOREGROUND | The application requires foreground access. This means that your program must be active to use the device. If your program is set inactive, the device will be automatically unacquired, and you will have to restore it when your program gets focus. |
| DISCL_BACKGROUND | Your program requires background access, which means your device can be accessed even if your program is not currently active. |
| DISCL_NOWINKEY | This disables the Windows logo key. |

Relative coordinates are reported by the difference in movement from the last position. For example, if the mouse were at coordinates 100,40 and then moved right 5 units, then DirectInput would report the value 5, not 105. It's your job to use these relative movement values as you see fit.

As for buffering, you can set the amount of data to buffer in (if any) to a data buffer that you provide. This allows you to read the device's data at your own pace without having to worry about skipped data. While handy, using buffered data is not what you'll need for gaming. It's preferable to know the exact state of the device when you need it, so I skip using buffering.

The last interesting properties are the minimum and maximum range settings for the device. For example, pressing the joystick to the far left produces the minimum value reported, while pushing to the far right reports the maximum value. What these two values are depends on you. Setting these applies only to joysticks, so I use that for an example.

Setting the special properties is the job of `IDirectInputDevice8::SetProperty`:

```
HRESULT IDirectInputDevice8::SetProperty(
    REFGUID rguidProp,        // GUID of property
    LPCDIPROPHEADER pdiph);   // DIPROPHEADER containing data
                              // about the property being set
```

The GUID of property is set. Refer to Table 7.7 for a list of Property GUIDs.

The `DIPROPRHEADER` just used is defined as follows:

```
typedef struct {
    DWORD dwSize;        // Size of the enclosing structure
    DWORD dwHeaderSize;  // Size of this structure
    DWORD dwObj;         // What value we're setting
    DWORD dwHow;         // How you're setting the value
} DIPROPHEADER, *LPDIPROPHEADER;
```

`dwSize` and `dwHeaderSize` are set to the sizes of the structures in bytes as described in the comments. As for `dwObj`, this can vary depending on what property you are setting. For your use later on, it is either `DIJOFS_X` or `DIJOFS_Y`, which represents the X- or Y-axis.

Last, you set `dwHow` to `DIPH_BYOFFSET`. The DirectX SDK defines this as the offset into the current data format of the object whose property is being accessed. This means that `DIJOFS_X` and `DIHOFS_Y` are offsets into the current data format you are setting.

> **NOTE**
>
> Only one property can be set at a time. Use multiple calls to set the other properties that you need.

Later in this chapter, I show you how to set the properties of the joystick.

## Acquiring the Device

Before any device can be used, it must be *acquired*. Acquiring a device ensures that your program has access to it, whether that access is shared with other programs or your program has complete control of the device. Be careful though, other programs might be fighting for the same rights and can snatch control away from you. To remedy this, you have to reacquire the device for your use.

## Table 7.7 Property GUIDs

| REFGUID | Description |
| --- | --- |
| DIPROP_AUTOCENTER | Specifies if the device is self-centering. |
| DIPROP_AXISMODE | Sets the axis mode as discussed previously. |
| DIPROP_BUFFERSIZE | The input buffer size. |
| DIPROP_CALIBRATIONMODE | Specifies if DirectInput needs to retrieve calibrated data from the device. By default, all data is calibrated. |
| DIPROP_DEADZONE | This is the deadzone value that is allowed to register a change. This ranges from 0 (none) to 10,000 (100 percent). |
| DIPROP_RANGE | Sets the minimum and maximum range values. |
| DIPROP_SATURATION | This is the value that marks the extreme range on a device. It ranges from 0 to 10,000. For example, a value of 9,500 means once a device has passed 95 percent of its movement, such as a joystick being pushed 95 percent of its range, it is considered pressed all the way. |

How do you know when you have to acquire the device? The first time is always when you create the interface—you must acquire it before using it. The only other time is when another program snatches control and DirectInput informs your program.

Acquiring a device is accomplished with a call to IDirectInputDevice8::Acquire:

HRESULT IDirectInputDevice8::Acquire();

You can also unacquire a device when you're done with it. This is the job of IDirectInputDevice8::Unacquire:

HRESULT IDirectInputDevice8::Unacquire();

### NOTE

Referring to the DX SDK, you can see that a standard error code returned from IDirectInputDevice8 calls is DIERR_INPUTLOST, which means the device needs to be acquired, because access to it has been lost.

# Polling the Device

Polling readies the device and in certain cases reads the device's data for you, since it might be time-critical. Such is the case with joysticks; the computer needs to send a burst of power to the device in order to read from it. While this is essential to joystick input, it is not required for a keyboard or a mouse.

**CAUTION**

Make sure to call Unacquire on a device when you're done with it. Failing to do so can result in a system hang.

This is not going to stop us from using it though, as the code we're writing in the core is generic and will run the same for each device. Don't worry—polling a device that doesn't require it has no effect. In the end, the code will be much cleaner.

Polling a device is done via IDirectInputDevice8::Poll:

```
HRESULT IDirectInputDevice8::Poll();
```

# Reading In Data

At last! You've reached the goal of finally reading in device data, which is handled by IDirectInputDevice8::GetDeviceState. You must pass a data buffer to this function so that it can store the device's information for your program's use. For each device, this data is different, as you soon see.

Here's the function prototype:

```
HRESULT IDirectInputDevice8::GetDeviceState(
  DWORD cbData,      // size of buffer to store device data
  LPVOID lpvData);   // buffer to hold device data
```

Regardless of the device, you can read in the data with the following code bit. It takes into account that you can lose focus of the device and reacquire it as needed. You must pass a pointer to a buffer that is large enough to hold the device information, as well as the amount of data to read in. In upcoming sections ("Using DirectInput with the Keyboard," "Using DirectInput with the Mouse," and "Using DirectInput with Joysticks"), I show you how to utilize the following function in each device's data:

```
BOOL ReadDevice(IDirectInputDevice8 *pDIDevice,                 \
                void *DataBuffer, long BufferSize)
{
  HRESULT hr;
```

```
while(1) {

    // Poll device
    g_pDIDevice->Poll();

    // Read in state
    if(SUCCEEDED(hr = g_pDIDevice->GetDeviceState(BufferSize,(LPVOID)DataBuffer)))
      break;

    // Return on an unknown error
    if(hr != DIERR_INPUTLOST && hr != DIERR_NOTACQUIRED)
      return FALSE;

    // Reacquire and try again
    if(FAILED(g_pDIDevice->Acquire()))
      return FALSE;

  }

  // Return a success
  return TRUE;
}
```

# Using DirectInput with the Keyboard

Here it is—how to set up and use the keyboard. The following initialization function returns the pointer to a newly created IDirectInputDevice8 object, or NULL if the function failed. Just pass the handle to the parent window and the preinitialized DirectInput object.

```
IDirectInputDevice8*InitKeyboard(HWND hWnd, IDirectInput8 *pDI)
{
  IDirectInputDevice8 *pDIDevice;

  // Create the device object
  if(FAILED(pDI->CreateDevice(GUID_SysKeyboard,                    \
                              &pDIDevice, NULL)))
    return NULL;
```

```
// Set the data format
if(FAILED(pDIDevice->SetDataFormat(&c_dfDIKeyboard))) {
  pDIDevice->Release();
  return NULL;
}

// Set the cooperative mode
if(FAILED(pDIDevice->SetCooperativeLevel(hWnd,                       \
           DISCL_FOREGROUND | DISCL_NONEXCLUSIVE)))
  pDIDevice->Release();
  return NULL;
}

// Acquire the device for use
if(FAILED(pDIDevice->Acquire()))
  pDIDevice->Release();
  return NULL;
}

// Everything was a success, return the pointer
return pDIDevice;
}
```

The InitKeyboard function pretty much follows what I've already talked about in this chapter. Later in the section "Using DirectInput with the Mouse," you see that the mouse init code is very similar, so I eventually wrap all this up into a single function in order to handle both in the core. To read in data from the keyboard, you can now make use of the ReadData function.

First, you need to understand how the keyboard stores data. You must give it an array that is 256 bytes in size, with each byte storing the status of a single key. That gives you room for 256 keys. Each byte stores information about the current state of the key—whether or not it is being pressed. To find the status of a key, check the high bit (bit 7). If set, that key is pressed. If clear, the key is not pressed.

> **NOTE**
>
> Each key has a macro, prefixed with DIK_, assigned to it in DirectInput. The A key is defined as DIK_A, the Esc key is DIK_ESCAPE, and so on. Consult the DX SDK or DInput.h for the other macros.

Here's an example of creating and reading the keyboard:

```
// make sure to preinitialized a global DirectInput
// object and parent window handle
// g_pDI and g_hWnd
IDirectInputDevice8 *pDIDKeyboard;

// The data buffer to store the key states
char KeyStateBuffer[256];
if((pDIDKeyboard = InitKeyboard(g_hWnd, g_pDI)) != NULL) {
  // read in the data
  ReadData(pDIDKeyboard, (void*)KeyStateBuffer, 256);
}
```

You can create a macro to easily check the status of a key, whether it is pressed or released. This macro gives you a value of TRUE if the key is pressed or FALSE if not.

```
#define KeyState(x) ((KeyStateBuffer[x] & 0x80) ? TRUE : FALSE)
```

Here is an example of using the macro:

```
if(KeyState(VK_LEFT) == TRUE) {
  // Left arrow is being pressed
}
```

# Using DirectInput with the Mouse

Next in line is the mouse. Initializing the mouse is almost identical to initializing the keyboard, except that you specify the mouse identifier and mouse data format:

```
IDirecInputDevice8* InitMouse(HWND hWnd, IDirectInput8* pDI)
{
  IDirectInputDevice8 *pDIDevice;

  // Create the device object
  if(FAILED(pDI->CreateDevice(GUID_SysMouse,&pDIDevice, NULL)))
    return NULL;

  // Set the data format
  if(FAILED(pDIDevice->SetDataFormat(&c_dfDIMouse))) {
```

```
    lpDIDevice->Release();
    return NULL;
  }


  // Set the cooperative mode
  if(FAILED(pDIDevice->SetCooperativeLevel(hWnd,                    \
          DISCL_FOREGROUND | DISCL_NONEXCLUSIVE))) {
    lpDIDevice->Release();
    return NULL;
  }


  // Acquire the device for use
  if(FAILED(lpDIDevice->Acquire())) {
    lpDIDevice->Release();
    return NULL;
  }


  // Everything was a success, return the pointer
  return lpDIDevice;
}
```

A call to DirectInputDevice8::GetDeviceState fills a DIMOUSESTATE structure up with information about the mouse such as relative movement and the state of the buttons. You define the DIMOUSESTATE structure as follows:

```
typedef struct {
  LONG lX;                 // Relative change in X coordinate
  LONG lY;                 // Relative change in Y coordinate
  LONG lZ;                 // Relative change in Z coordinate
  BYTE rgbButtons[4];  // Button pressed flags
} DIMOUSESTATE, *LPDIMOUSESTATE;
```

Because the coordinate values reported from the DIMOUSESTATE structure are relative, you need to track the absolute values. You do so by creating a couple of global variables that represent the absolute mouse coordinates, called g_MouseXPos and g_MouseYPos, respectively.

Here's how to create the object and then read in and process mouse information:

```
// make sure to preinitialize a global DirectInput
// object and parent window handle
// g_pDI and g_hWnd
IDirectInputDevice8 *pDIDMouse;
```

```
// The mouse coordinates
long g_MouseXPos = 0, g_MouseYPos = 0;

// The data buffer to store the mouse state
DIMOUSESTATE MouseState;

if((pDIDMouse = InitMouse(g_hWnd, g_pDI)) != NULL) {
  // read in the data
  ReadData(pDIDMouse, (void*)MouseState, sizeof(DIMOUSESTATE));
  // update the absolute coordinates
  g_MouseXPos += MouseState.lX;
  g_MouseYPos += MouseState.lY;
}
```

Just as you can use a macro to check the state of a key, you can do the same for the mouse buttons:

```
#define MouseButtonState(x) ((MouseState.rgbButtons[x] &       \
                                  0x80) ? TRUE : FALSE)
```

To use it, just give it the mouse button you are checking:

```
if(MouseButtonState(0) == TRUE) {
  // button 0 pressed
}
```

# Using DirectInput with Joysticks

In a way, this is the hardest device with which to work. The hardest part is setting it up. You must enumerate to find the joystick devices that are hooked up to the system. During the enumeration, you have to decide which joystick to use and then create the COM object for it. For this book, you look only for the first joystick on the system.

```
// make sure to preinitialize a global DirectInput
// object and parent window handle
// g_pDI and g_hWnd
IDirectInputDevice8 *g_pDIDJoystick = NULL;

BOOL CALLBACK EnumJoysticks(LPCDIDEVICEINSTANCE pdInst,        \
                                  LPVOID pvRef)
{
```

```
HRESULT hr;

g_pDIDJoystick = NULL;
```

The start of the enumeration is pretty basic. You create a global IDirectInputDevice8 object to use for the joystick. When the enumeration starts, it clears the interface pointer to NULL, meaning that nothing is found. After enumeration, you can check whether it's still set to NULL, meaning that no joysticks were initialized.

As for the enumeration function arguments, pdInst is a pointer to a DIDEVICEINSTANCE structure that contains information about the currently enumerated device. You can now obtain the crucial device GUID from the guidInstance field in this structure, which you use to create the device interface.

The user-provided pointer, pvRef, is really not needed at this point because the parent window handle is a global variable. You could pass a pointer to a data structure that contains such information as this, but I find it easier to use the global method at this point.

The next code bit follows the same pattern of creating a device interface as the others, except that it returns the value DIENUM_CONTINUE to force the enumeration to continue if there was an error. Because more than one joystick might be on the system, you deal here with only the first one possible:

```
// Create the device object using global DirectInput object
if(FAILED(g_pDI->CreateDevice(pdInst->guidInstance,            \
        &g_pDIDJoystick, NULL)))
  return DIENUM_CONTINUE;


// Set the data format
if(FAILED(g_pDIDJoystick->SetDataFormat(&c_dfDIJoystick))) {
  g_pDIDJoystick->Release();
  g_pDIDJoystick = NULL;
  return DIENUM_CONTINUE;
}


// Set the cooperative mode
if(FAILED(g_pDIDJoystick->SetCooperativeLevel(hWnd,            \
        DISCL_FOREGROUND | DISCL_NONEXCLUSIVE))) {
  g_pDIDJoystick->Release();
  g_pDIDJoystick = NULL;
  return DIENUM_CONTINUE;
}
```

You need to set the device properties now. These include the range of the joystick axis values, as well as the dead zone. Filling a `DIPROPRANGE` structure with the required values and using that structure in a call to `DirectInputDevice8::SetProperty` sets the ranges. You define a `DIPROPRANGE` structure as follows:

```
typedef struct {
  DIPROPHEADER diph;   // DIPROPHEADER as seen previously
  LONG lMin;           // minimum value of range (X or Y axis)
  LONG lMax;           // maximum value of range (X or Y axis)
} DIPROPRANGE, *LPDIPROPRANGE;
```

First, initialize the structure:

```
DIPROPRANGE dipr;
// Clear out the structure first
ZeroMemory(&dipr, sizeof(DIPROPRANGE));
dipr.diph.dwSize = sizeof(dipr);
dipr.diph.dwHeaderSize = sizeof(dipr);
```

At this point, you set `dipr.diph.dwObj` to what you are setting, either the X- or Y-coordinate. You can start with X and later switch to Y.

```
dipr.diph.dwObj = DIJOFS_X;
dipr.diph.dwHow = DIPH_BYOFFSET;   // offset into data format
```

The first property you set is the X-axis range. Set the minimum and maximum values to range from -1024 (far left) to +1024 (far right):

```
dipr.lMin = -1024;
dipr.lMax = 1024;
```

Now call `IDirectInputDevice8::SetProperty` to set the X-axis range:

```
  if(FAILED(g_pDIDJoystick->SetProperty(DIPROP_RANGE,          \
                                        &dipr.diph))) {
  g_pDIDJoystick->Release();
  g_pDIDJoystick = NULL;
  return DIENUM_CONTINUE;
}
```

Now you can set the Y-axis range. Just change the `dwObj` value and then set the property again:

```
dipr.diph.dwObj = DIJOFS_Y;
if(gFAILED(g_pDIDJoystick->SetProperty(DIPROP_RANGE,          \
                                       &dipr.diph))) {
```

```
   g_pDIDJoystick->Release();
   g_pDIDJoystick = NULL;
   return DIENUM_CONTINUE;
 }
```

That's it! All you need to do now is set the deadzone range so that the joystick doesn't jitter when it's moved slightly. You can safely set this to about 12 percent of the range.

```
dipdw.diph.dwObj = DIJOFS_X;
dipdw.dwData = 128;
if(FAILED(g_pDIDJoystick->SetProperty(DIPROP_DEADZONE,          \
                                      &dipdw.diph))) {

  g_pDIDJoystick->Release();
  g_pDIDJoystick = NULL;
  return DIENUM_CONTINUE;
}


dipdw.diph.dwObj = DIJOFS_Y;
if(FAILED(g_pDIDJoystick->SetProperty(DIPROP_DEADZONE,          \
                                      &dipdw.diph))) {

  g_pDIDJoystick->Release();
  g_pDIDJoystick = NULL;
  return DIENUM_CONTINUE;
}
```

At last the device is initialized, and it is time to acquire the device and stop the enumeration:

```
// Acquire the device for use
if(FAILED(g_pDIDJoystick->Acquire())) {
  g_pDIDJoystick->Release();
  g_pDIDJoystick = NULL;
  return DIENUM_CONTINUE;
}
// Stop enumeration
return DIENUM_STOP;
}
```

g_pDIDJoystick will now be the pointer to the new object, or it will equal NULL if no joystick was initialized. Once the device object is initialized, you can read in information just as you did before with the keyboard and mouse, but use a DIJOYSTATE structure with the ReadData function. Here's a look at the DIJOYSTATE structure:

```
typedef struct DIJOYSTATE {
  LONG  lX;                  // Absolute value for X coordinate
  LONG  lY;                  // Absolute value for Y coordinate
  LONG  lZ;                  // Absolute value for Z coordinate
  LONG  lRx;                 // X rotation value
  LONG  lRy;                 // Y rotation value
  LONG  lRz;                 // Z rotation value
  LONG  rglSlider[2];        // Slider values
  DWORD rgdwPOV[4];          // POV values
  BYTE  rgbButtons[32];      // Button flags (for 32 buttons)
} DIJOYSTATE, *LPDIJOYSTATE;
```

Now that you have the enumeration function down, you can set up the joystick with the following:

```
g_pDI->EnumDevices(DIDEVTYPE_JOYSTICK, EnumJoysticks,          \
                   NULL, DIEDFL_ATTACHEDONLY);
if(g_pDIDJoystick == NULL) {
  // no joystick initialized
}
```

To read in data from the joysticks, call ReadData with a DIJOYSTATE structure:

```
DIJOYSTATE JoystickState;
ReadData(g_pDIDJoystick, (void*)JoystickState,                \
         sizeof(DIJOYSTATE));
```

You can retrieve the axis values directly from the JoystickState structure, as the coordinates are absolute. There's no need to track the relative movements here:

```
JoystickX = JoystickState.lX;
JoystickY = JoystickState.lY;
```

Also, the same macro for reading the button states still applies here:

```
#define JoystickButtonState(x) ((JoystickState.rgbButtons[x]  \
                                 & 0x80) ? TRUE : FALSE)
```

# Wrapping Up Input

The information in this chapter, which focuses on the three most common input devices—the keyboard, mouse, and joystick, should prepare you for the current world of input devices. With technology constantly moving forward, however, new input devices are sure to come along that you'll want to incorporate into your game projects.

Think of the possibilities—virtual reality headgear, full-body biofeedback suits, and even brainwave scanners—all fully DirectInput-compatible! In such a world, you will be able to use sundry devices effortlessly, following the techniques you learned in this chapter.

## Programs on the CD-ROM

Programs that demonstrate the code discussed in this chapter are on the CD-ROM at the back of this book. You can find the following programs in the \BookCode\Chap7\ directory:

♦ **Shell.** A shell application that initializes DirectInput and devices for you. Location: \BookCode\Chap7\shell\.

♦ **Enum.** A program that uses the enumeration example from this chapter to display all input devices connected to the system. Location: \BookCode\Chap7\Enum\.

♦ **Keyboard.** A program that creates a keyboard interface and reads data from it. Location: \BookCode\Chap7\Keyboard\.

♦ **Mouse.** A program that creates a mouse interface and reads data from it. Location: \BookCode\Chap7\Mouse\.

♦ **Joystick.** A program that creates a joystick interface and reads data from it. Location: \BookCode\Chap7\Joystick\.

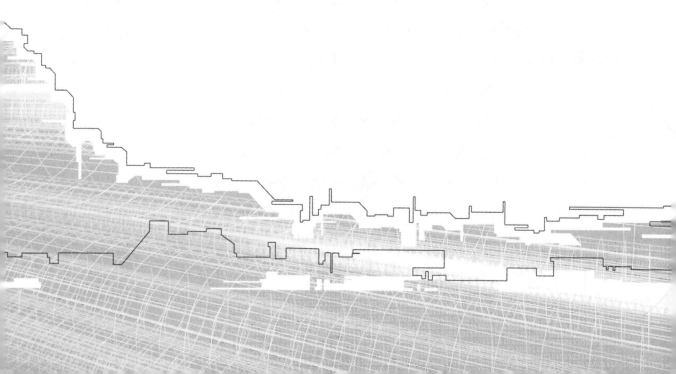

# CHAPTER 8

# PLAYING SOUND WITH DIRECTX AUDIO

**M**usic soothed the savage beast, and it will be a combination of sound and music that will soothe us. Anyway, what fun would a game be without sound? It would be like watching a killer movie such as *The Matrix* as a silent film! No loud explosions, kicking sound track, or actors talking to make the movie what it is—a total multimedia experience.

Your game deserves the same level of experience that you have watching a movie, including music and sound effects. You can do all this with DirectX Audio, Microsoft's latest addition to DirectX. DirectX Audio is the combination of DirectSound and DirectMusic from previous versions, and although the two still remain as separate components, they are more intertwined in this release.

In this chapter, you learn about the following:

- The basic properties of sound
- Digital audio and music formats
- How to use DirectX Audio in your own project
- How to work with DirectSound
- How to make DirectMusic sing

## Sound Basics

If a tree falls in the forest and nobody is around to hear it, does it make a sound? Although this is often considered a peculiar question, it does make sense. Sounds are simply waves traveling through a medium, such as air. For all practical purposes, these waves are "nothing" until they enter an ear canal and stimulate the eardrum, thus replicating the sound.

Most natural sounds have a "clean" wave in which you can visually see the clarity of its pattern. A *sine wave* is the perfect example of a clean wave—the sine wave rises and falls in a consistent pattern. Other waves, such as those from a human voice, are very complex, as they rise and drop in level very quickly and without a consistent pattern. Figure 8.1 shows two different sound waves.

Every sound has unique properties, such as amplitude (volume level) and frequency. Over a period of time, you can record the properties of sounds in order to digitally record them and play them back.

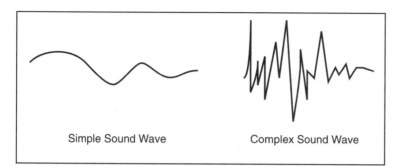

**Figure 8.1**

*Sound waves can have a simple, clean shape or can be very complex.*

In addition, you can use these sounds with music—for example, to play a composition on your computer. By recording sounds, such as a piano or a violin, you could almost realistically duplicate a real-world song. Imagine playing a Mozart piece and not knowing whether it's a real symphony playing or replicated!

# Recording Digital Sounds

The basis of recording and using digital sounds isn't too hard to comprehend. In general, you take a sound, say two seconds in length, and examine the sound wave from start to finish at a specific time rate (*sampling rate*), which is measured in hertz (Hz).

Say that you want to record a two-second sound at 11,025 Hz, which means the sound is split into 22,050 sections (with 11,025 sections per second). Those sections are called *samples*. For each sample, you examine the amplitude of the sound wave at each sample's position within the wave, which measures the wave's volume level at that period of time. You record this value and move on to the next sample. When you have completed reading the volume level of each sample in the wave, you will have a digital representation of the sound.

Figure 8.2 shows a sound wave split into a couple of samples. When digitized, the sound loses its "wave" shape. The digitized wave does not maintain the shape of the original wave because there are not enough samples to model the original wave correctly.

As you might be able to surmise, the higher the sampling rate used to capture the sound wave, the better you're able to replicate the original sound. "What sampling rate is the best," you ask? I don't have a set answer for you, but depending on the level of quality you want, use one of the following: 8000 Hz, 11,025 Hz, 22,050 Hz, or 44,100 Hz. The last level is the level that audio CDs use.

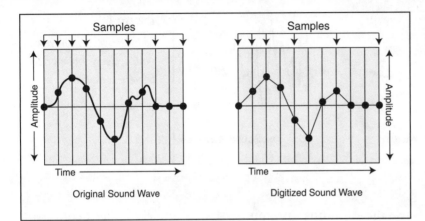

**Figure 8.2**

*The original wave on the left has been split over time into multiple samples. You can use those samples to create a digital representation of the sound as shown on the right.*

The next thing you need to understand is *storage*. When you grab a sample from the wave, you have a level value representing the amplitude. You have the choice of storing this value as either 8 bits or 16 bits. This means that you can have 256 levels using an 8-bit sampling or 65,536 levels using a 16-bit sampling.

Choose the higher value in order to have more levels to replicate. The 8-bit samplings are muffled and should be used only for low-quality sounds. Try to always use 16-bit sound, even though it's double the size—it's worth it.

Last, you decide how many channels to use. *Stereo* sounds (those that are different on the left and right sides) have two channels. *Mono* sounds have only one channel; thus, both sides sound the same.

You can store digital sounds in a number of ways, and you can use different encryption and compression methods for them. I always store them in the uncompressed Windows *wave file format* (.WAV) because it is the most popular (and therefore supported) way to store sound.

A bare-bones wave file contains a single sound, which is preceded with a header of data that describes it. Windows has a lot of wave functions in the Win32 SDK, so consult the documents there for more information on dealing with those wave functions.

# Musical Madness

Music takes many forms, and you can record and play it back many ways. Technological breakthroughs give us the ability to enjoy music that utilizes digital sounds, thus increasing our listening experience.

Music is nothing more than a series of notes, played and stopped at various amplitudes and times. Many instruments can be used to play a single song, but they all operate the same—by means of using notes. When you write a song on a computer, you store the notes and play them back using sound hardware.

## Midi

The *Midi* format (identified by the .MID extension) is a standard for storing musical scores. Midi files contain the messages, or directions, needed for playing a song. These directions tell the sound hardware what to do and when to do it, including when and how to play and release a note, change the tempo, play a different instrument, and so on.

Midi uses up to 128 standardized instruments, enabling you, for example, to compose a song using instrument 0 (which represents a piano). When others listen to the song, their playback device ensures that the instrument specified is the one that is played.

Songs are separated into tracks with each track containing the notes to be played by a single instrument. You can have approximately 128 tracks in a single file, and the length is not restricted. That means some major music madness!

Your computer is not the only one that can play Midi songs; so can Midi-enabled musical devices such as a synthesizer. That's right. You can hook up your computer system to an actual musical device and have the device play that instrument data for you.

## DirectMusic

The DirectMusic format is similar to the Midi format; however, the DirectMusic format adds more functionality, such as the ability to create dynamic musical sequences that consistently provide unique musical experiences. You can alter chords, tempo, and instruments during playback, thereby creating a powerful system.

DirectMusic musical *segments* (the actual song file) use the .SGT file extension. Other related files include *bands* (.BND) that contain instrument information, *chordmaps* (.CDM) that contain chords to alter playback, *styles* (.STY) for creating playback style, and *templates* (*.TPL) for constructing musical segments.

When you construct a DirectMusic song, all the necessary files are handled automatically by DirectMusic (so from now on, I refer to a DirectMusic song as being in *native* format). All this means is that you must deal with only segment files.

# Understanding DirectX Audio

DirectX Audio is composed of the two DirectX components, DirectSound and DirectMusic. Of the two components, DirectMusic is the most improved (DirectSound remains almost the same as it was in the prior version).

DirectSound is the main component used for digital sound playback. DirectMusic handles all song formats—including Midi, DirectMusic native format, and wave files—and sends them to DirectSound for digital reproduction (as you can see in Figure 8.3). This means that, with Midi, you can use digitally-recorded instruments during playback.

Now that you have a little background, you are ready to learn how to use DirectSound and DirectMusic, which I explain in the remaining sections of this chapter.

# Using DirectSound

Although DirectSound might seem complicated at first, it really is not difficult to understand and use. You create a COM object that interfaces with the sound hardware. With this COM object, you're then able to create individual sound buffers (called *secondary sound buffers*) that store sound data.

The data in these sound buffers are mixed together into a main mixing buffer (called the *primary sound buffer*) and played back in any sound format you specify. These playback formats can range in frequency, number of channels, and bits per sampling. Viable frequencies are 8000 Hz, 11,025 Hz, 22,050 Hz, and 44,100 Hz (CD audio quality).

You have two choices for the number of channels: one channel for monaural (mono) sound or two channels for stereo sound. The number of bits is also limited to two settings: 8 bits for lower-quality sound reproduction and 16 bits for high-quality sound reproduction. DirectSound has a default setting of 22,025 Hz, 8-bit samplings, stereo, if you don't manually adjust it.

You can modify the sound channels to play at different frequencies (thus changing the pitch), alter the volume and panning during playback, and even loop the sound. Not only that, but sounds can also be played in a virtualized 3D environment, simulating real sounds as they move around you.

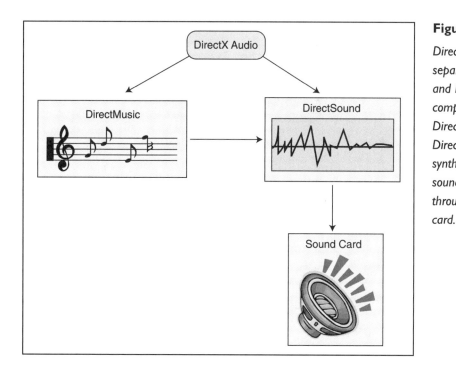

**Figure 8.3**

*DirectX Audio uses separate DirectMusic and DirectSound components, but allows DirectMusic to use DirectSound to synthesize instrument sounds and play them through your sound card.*

It's your job to take sounds and stuff them into these sound buffers. For sounds that are very large, you create a streaming playback method that loads small chunks of sound data, and once that has played, you stuff the next chunk of data in the sound buffer. This process continues until the sound is fully played.

You accomplish streaming by setting positions within the sound buffer that, when reached, signal the application that it's time to update the sound data. This process of signaling an update is called *notification*. You aren't limited to how many buffers can be playing at one time, but you should keep the buffers low because each buffer adds to the processing and memory overhead.

It really isn't hard to work with DirectSound. In fact, in this book, you work with only the three interfaces shown in Table 8.1.

Figure 8.4 shows the relationship each object has to each other. IDirectSound8 is the main interface, from which you create sound buffers (IDirectSoundBuffer8). A sound buffer then can create its own notification interface (IDirectSoundNotify8) that you use for marking positions with the sound buffer that notifies you when reached. This notification interface is useful for streaming sounds.

## Table 8.1  DirectSound COM Interfaces

| Interface | Description |
| --- | --- |
| IDirectSound8 | The main DirectSound interface object. |
| IDirectSoundBuffer8 | Primary and secondary sound buffer object. Stores data and controls playback. |
| IDirectSoundNotify8 | Notification object. Notifies the application when specific positions are reached within a sound buffer. |

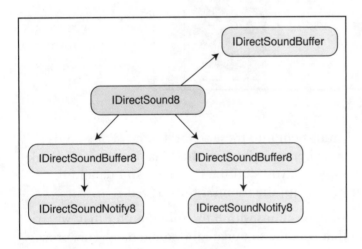

**Figure 8.4**

*You obtain sound buffers from the* IDirectSound8 *object.* IDirectSoundNotify8 *objects are created from their parent* IDirectSoundBuffer8 *objects.*

# Initializing DirectSound

Before anything else, you need to include DSound.h and link in DSound.lib. Other than that, the first step to using DirectSound is the creation of the IDirectSound8 object, which is the main interface representing the sound hardware. You accomplish this with the help of the DirectSoundCreate8 function:

```
HRESULT WINAPI DirectSoundCreate8(
  LPCGUID lpcGuidDevice,    // set to NULL (default sound device)
  LPDIRECTSOUND8 *ppDS8,    // object you are creating
  LPUNKNOWN pUnkOuter);     // NULL - not used
```

Using the `DirectSoundCreate8` function and a global `IDirectSound8` object instance, you can initialize the sound system object as follows:

```
IDirectSound8 *g_pDS;   // global IDirectSound8
object
if(FAILED(DirectSoundCreate8(NULL, &g_pDS, NULL))) {
  // Error occurred
}
```

> **NOTE**
> This function, like all DirectSound functions, returns `DS_OK` if the call was successful, or another error value if not. To make error checking easier, you can make use of the `FAILED` and `SUCCEEDED` macros to test return values.

# Setting the Cooperative Level

The next step in initialization is to set the *cooperative level* of the `IDirectSound8` object. You use the cooperative level to determine how to share the sound card resources with other applications. Do you want the card all to yourself, not letting others play with it; or do you want to share access? Or do you need a special playback format that doesn't jive with the default one?

Setting the cooperative level is the job of `IDirectSound8::SetCooperativeLevel`. There are four cooperative levels to work with, as shown in Table 8.2. Each one has its own macro to specify in DirectSound.

Here's the prototype of the `IDirectSound8::SetCooperativeLevel` function:

```
IDirectSound8::SetCooperativeLevel(
    HWND hwnd,         // handle to parent window
    DWORD dwLevel);    // cooperative level from Table 8.2
```

What cooperative level should you use? That really depends on the type of application you're creating. For full-screen applications, use exclusive. Otherwise, I recommend priority level. The only caveat when using a level other than the normal level is that you need to specify a playback format. I show you how to do that in the upcoming section, "Setting the Playback Format."

> **TIP**
> I highly recommend using the *priority* cooperative level because you have control of the primary buffer, even if you don't want to change the playback format. This way, you can easily alter the main volume as well as control panning changes during playback.

## Table 8.2 DirectSound Cooperative Levels

| Level | Macro | Description |
| --- | --- | --- |
| Normal | DSSCL_NORMAL | The normal level; lets all programs access the sound card at once using a default playback format of 8-bit, 11025 Hz, 1 channel (mono). This format cannot be changed. |
| Priority | DSSCL_PRIORITY | Same as normal, but lets you change the playback format. |
| Exclusive | DSSCL_EXCLUSIVE | Exclusive use of the sound card; no other application gets to use the sound device while your application is active (in the foreground). You specify the playback format. |
| WritePrimary | DSSCL_WRITEPRIMARY | An advanced level that gives you complete control of the system. You gain access only to the primary sound buffer (no secondary buffers allowed). This is for programmers who want to code their own mixer, so I won't go any further on this one. |

For now, here is an example of setting the cooperative level to priority using a pre-initialized IDirectSound8 object:

```
// g_pDS = pre-initialized IDirectSound8 object
// hWnd = pre-initialized handle to the parent window
if(FAILED(g_pDS->SetCooperativeLevel(hWnd, DSSCL_PRIORITY))) {
  // Error occurred
}
```

# Setting the Playback Format

The last step to initializing DirectSound is grabbing control of the primary sound buffer and setting the playback format of the system, but only if you are using a cooperative level other than normal. This is a two-step process: first using the IDirectSound8 object to create the buffer interface and second using the interface to modify the format.

# Creating the Primary Sound Buffer Object

An IDirectSoundBuffer object represents the primary sound buffer. No need for a version 8 interface here, as there was no change in the mixing system of this DX release. The function that creates a sound buffer (either primary or secondary) is IDirectSound8::CreateSoundBuffer, and it looks like this:

```
HRESULT IDirectSound8::CreateSoundBuffer(
   LPCDSBUFFERDESC pcDSBufferDesc,    // description of buffer
   LPDIRECTSOUNDBUFFER *ppDSBuffer,   // buffer object to create
   LPUNKNOWN pUnkOuter);              // NULL - not used
```

pcDSBufferDesc is a pointer to a DSBUFFERDESC structure, which holds a variety of information about the buffer you are creating. For the primary buffer, you're not going to use all the features the sound object provides, but here is the entire structure:

```
typedef struct {
   DWORD dwSize;            // Size of this structure
   DWORD dwFlags;           // Flags describing abilities of buffer
   DWORD dwBufferBytes;     // Size of sound buffer
   DWORD dwReserved;        // Not used - set to 0
   LPWAVEFORMATEX lpwfxFormat;  // playback format
   GUID guid3DAlgorithm;    // GUID_NULL (3D playback algorithm)
} DSBUFFERDESC, *LPDSBUFFERDESC;
```

The fields are pretty much self-explanatory, except for lpwfxFormat. This points to a structure describing the playback format of the buffer being created. Because you're not dealing with that one for now, skip it until later. As for dwSize, the primary sound buffer already exists, so set dwSize to 0.

The only thing you need to work with right now is dwFlags, which is a set of flags determining the capabilities of the buffer you are creating. Table 8.3 shows all the possible flags you can use.

> **NOTE**
>
> DirectSound automatically sets up a data buffer used for the primary sound buffer because there's no telling whether the buffer is located in system or hardware memory. Also, setting the playback format of the primary sound buffer is accomplished a little differently, so you need to set the lpwfxFormat pointer to NULL.

## Table 8.3  Flags for Sound Buffer Creation

| Flag | Description |
| --- | --- |
| DSBCAPS_CTRL3D | Buffer has 3D capabilities. |
| DSBCAPS_CTRLFREQUENCY | Allows on-the-fly frequency changes during playback of buffer. |
| DSBCAPS_CTRLFX | Buffer allows effects processing. |
| DSBCAPS_CTRLPAN | Buffer has panning capabilities. |
| DSBCAPS_CTRLPOSITIONNOTIFY | Buffer has notification capabilities. |
| DSBCAPS_CTRLVOLUME | Allows on-the-fly volume adjusting to buffer. |
| DSBCAPS_GETCURRENTPOSITION2 | This flag lets you ask a buffer exactly where its playing position is. |
| DSBCAPS_GLOBALFOCUS | Makes this a global sound buffer, which means it's audible even when another program is active. |
| DSBCAPS_LOCDEFER | Allows this buffer to use hardware and software resources. |
| DSBCAPS_LOCHARDWARE | Forces hardware resources, such as mixing and hardware memory storage. |
| DSBCAPS_LOCSOFTWARE | Forces software resources, such as mixing and system memory storage. |
| DSBCAPS_MUTE3DATMAXDISTANCE | This forces 3D sounds to stop playing when they reach the maximum distance from the listener. |
| DSBCAPS_PRIMARYBUFFER | Makes this buffer the primary sound buffer. Only use this once, and only when using a cooperative level other than normal. |
| DSBCAPS_STATIC | Places this buffer in hardware memory if available. Use only for small sounds. |
| DSBCAPS_STICKYFOCUS | Forces a buffer to continue playing when user switches to other applications that do not use DirectSound. Buffers are muted when this occurs, unless this flag is specified. |

The only flags of use to you now are DSBCAPS_PRIMARYBUFFER and DSBCAPS_CTRLVOLUME. Those flags are telling DirectSound that you want to create an interface to the primary sound buffer and to make sure that you have a master volume control. Later on, I talk about the rest of these flags.

> **CAUTION**
>
> Certain flags are not allowed with the primary buffer, such as frequency control flags. Including such flags will cause the creation of the primary sound buffer object to fail.

Here you jump ahead and grab the primary sound buffer interface:

```
IDirectSoundBuffer g_pDSPrimary;              // global access
DSBUFFERDESC dsbd;                              // buffer description
ZeroMemory(&dsbd, sizeof(DSBUFFERDESC));  // zero out structure
dsbd.dwSize = sizeof(DSBUFFERDESC);         // set structure size
dsbd.dwFlags = DSBCAPS_PRIMARYBUFFER | DSBCAPS_CTRLVOLUME;
dsbd.dwBufferBytes = 0;                         // no buffer size
dsbd.lpwfxFormat = NULL;                        // no format yet
if(FAILED(g_pDS->CreateSoundBuffer(&dsbd, &g_pDSPrimary,       \
                                   NULL))) {
  // Error occurred
}
```

## Setting the Format

Now that you have control of the primary sound buffer, it is time to set the playback format of the system. You have a number of choices, but I recommend using a sensible setting, such as 11,025 Hz, 16-bit samples, mono or 22,050 Hz, 16-bit samples, mono.

When picking the format, try not to use stereo. Using stereo is a waste of processing time, as true stereo sound effects are hard to record. Also, always try to use 16-bits per sample because the quality is much better than 8-bit. Never settle for less! As for the frequency, the higher the better, but don't go over 22,050 Hz. Even CD-quality audio can be played nicely at 22,050 Hz without much loss.

That being said, let's move on. You set the playback format via a call to IDirectSoundBuffer::SetFormat:

```
HRESULT IDirectSoundBuffer::SetFormat(
  LPCWAVEFORMATEX pcfxFormat);
```

The one and only argument is a pointer to a WAVEFORMATEX structure, which holds the format information you want to set:

```
typedef struct {
  WORD wFormatTag;          // set to WAVE_FORMAT_PCM
  WORD nChannels;           // 1 for mono, 2 for stereo
  DWORD nSamplesPerSec;     // sampling rate
  DWORD nAvgBytesPerSec;    // # bytes per second of format
  WORD nBlockAlign;         // alignment of sample data
  WORD wBitsPerSample;      // 8 or 16
  WORD cbSize;              // not used
} WAVEFORMATEX;
```

> **CAUTION**
>
> This function can only be called on a primary sound buffer object, and it must not be a version 8 interface.

You should be able to follow it easily, except for two fields, nBlockAlign and nAvgBytesPerSec. nBlockAlign is the number of bytes used for each sampling in the sound. Set this to

```
nBlockAlign = (nBitsPerSample / 8) * nChannels;
```

nAvgBytesPerSec is the number of bytes per second of sound. This takes into account the sampling rate and block alignment and can be calculated as

```
nAvgBytesPerSec = nSamplesPerSec * nBlockAlign;
```

Now that you have this information, it's time to try it out! I'm going to set the format to 22,050 Hz, 16-bit, mono:

```
// g_pDSPrimary = pre-initialized global primary sound buffer
WAVEFORMATEX wfex;
ZeroMemory(wfex, sizeof(WAVEFORMATEX));
wfex.wFormatTag = WAVE_FORMAT_PCM;
wfex.nChannels = 1;              // mono
wfex.nSamplesPerSec = 22050;  // 22050hz
wfex.wBitsPerSample = 16;     // 16-bit
wfex.nBlockAlign = (wfex.wBitsPerSample / 8) * wfex.nChannels;
wfex.nAvgBytesPerSec = wfex.nSamplesPerSec * wfex.nBlockAlign;
if(FAILED(g_pDSPrimary->SetFormat(&wfex))) {
  // Error occurred
}
```

# Jump-Starting the Primary Sound Buffer

You finally have control of the sound system and are ready to rock! You only need to get the primary buffer to start playing. Even though there are no sounds, it's best to start the buffer now and to keep it going until you're finished with the whole sound system. Starting the buffer playing at the start of your application saves processing time when starting and stopping.

Before showing you how to start the buffer playing, I want to describe the primary sound buffer. Because memory resources can be limited, especially in hardware, the data buffer you use can be any size (even a few thousand bytes). For this reason, the primary sound buffer and the secondary sound buffers use circular buffers.

> **NOTE**
>
> A *circular buffer* is a term used to describe a data buffer that wraps around to the beginning when the end has been reached, thus forming an endless loop, or circle.

You can see a visual example of a circular buffer in Figure 8.5. Even though the data buffer is a one-dimensional array of data, it wraps back to the beginning. This is a powerful technique that is capable of saving large amounts of memory.

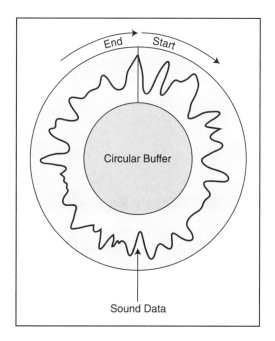

**Figure 8.5**

*Circular buffers always wrap around, connecting the start and end of the buffer so that sounds can continuously wrap around for seamless playback.*

Sounds, as they are played, get mixed into the primary sound buffer's circular data buffer. Once the end of the sound buffer is reached, the sound loops back to the beginning of the buffer and continues to play the sound seamlessly. In order to use a buffer's looping feature, you must specifically enable looping playback; otherwise, the buffer's playback stops when the end of the buffer is reached.

In order to play a sound buffer (with the option to loop playback), you must call the sound buffer's Play function, which looks like this:

```
HRESULT IDirectSoundBuffer8::Play(
  DWORD Reserved1,  // must be 0
  DWORD Priority,   // mixing priority - use 0
  DWORD dwFlags);   // playback flags
```

The only argument you need to be interested in here is dwFlags, which has two settings: 0, which forces the sound buffer to play once and stop when the end is reached, and DSBPLAY_LOOPING, which tells the sound to wrap around to the beginning in an endless loop when the end is reached.

For the primary sound buffer, this is exactly what you want, and here is how you do it:

```
g_pDSPrimary->Play(0, 0, DSBPLAY_LOOPING))) {
  // Error occurred
}
```

When you're done with the primary sound buffer (and the sound system in general), you need to stop it with a call to IDirectSoundBuffer::Stop, which takes no arguments:

> **CAUTION**
>
> The primary sound buffer will not stop playing unless all secondary sound buffers are first stopped. Anytime a secondary sound buffer is played, it automatically starts the primary.

```
if(FAILED(g_pDSPrimary->Stop())) {
  // Error occurred
}
```

# Using Secondary Sound Buffers

Next in line is the creation of secondary sound buffers that will hold the actual sound data you want to play. There's no limit to the number of secondary sound buffers you can have at once, and with the capabilities of DirectSound, you're able to play them all at once if you want!

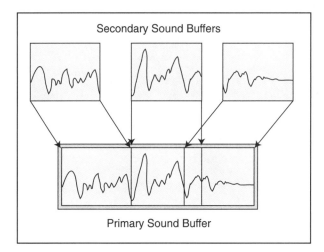

Secondary Sound Buffers

Primary Sound Buffer

**Figure 8.6**

*Secondary sound buffers mix together inside the primary sound buffer before being played.*

You accomplish this by stuffing the primary sound buffer with the sound data contained in the secondary sound buffers (similar to the process illustrated in Figure 8.6). This data is mixed as it goes along, so writing one sound and then another at the same location in the primary sound buffer will play the two sounds at the same time.

Secondary sound buffers use the IDirectSoundBuffer8 object, which is very similar to the IDirectSoundBuffer object. In fact, to create the version 8 interface, you must first create an IDirectSoundBuffer object and query for the newer one.

The only difference here in creating a secondary sound buffer is that you must set the playback format while initializing it. This means that the buffer will have only one format to use. If you need to change the format, you have to release the buffer and create another one.

Again, you're going to use the WAVEFORMATEX structure to store the format and the DSBUFFERDESC to describe the capabilities of the buffer. However, this time, you specify a pointer to the WAVEFORMATEX structure inside the DSBUFFERDESC structure.

Here's an example of creating a secondary sound buffer using a 22,050 Hz, 16-bit, mono format. I give the buffer two seconds worth of storage (because, at this point, I have no real sound to put in there) along with volume, panning, and frequency control.

```
// g_pDS = pre-initialized IDirectSound8 object
IDirectSoundBuffer8 *g_pDSBuffer;  // v8 global object we want
IDirectSoundBuffer *pDSB;          // local sound buffer
```

```
// Set up the WAVEFORMATEX structure
WAVEFORMATEX wfex;
ZeroMemory(wfex, sizeof(WAVEFORMATEX));
wfex.wFormatTag = WAVE_FORMAT_PCM;
wfex.nChannels = 1;              // mono
wfex.nSamplesPerSec = 22050;    // 22050hz
wfex.wBitsPerSample = 16;       // 16-bit
wfex.nBlockAlign = (wfex.wBitsPerSample / 8) * wfex.nChannels;
wfex.nAvgBytesPerSec = wfex.nSamplesPerSec * wfex.nBlockAlign;

// Set up the DSBUFFERDESC structure
DSBUFFERDESC dsbd;
ZeroMemory(&dsbd, sizeof(DSBUFFERDESC));  // zero out structure
dsbd.dwSize = sizeof(DSBUFFERDESC);        // need to zero-out
dsbd.dwFlags = DSBCAPS_CTRLFREQUENCY | DSBCAPS_CTRLVOLUME |   \
               DSBCAPS_CTRLPAN;
dsbd.dwBufferBytes = wfex.nAvgBytesPerSec * 2;  // 2 seconds
dsbd.lpwfxFormat = &wfex;

// Create the first version object
if(FAILED(g_pDS->CreateSoundBuffer(&dsbd, &pDSB, NULL))) {
  // Error occurred
} else {
  // Get the version 8 interface
  if(FAILED(pDSB->QueryInterface(IID_IDirectSoundBuffer8,     \
                   (void**)&g_pDSBuffer))) {
    // Error occurred - free first interface first
    // and then do something
    pDSB->Release();
  } else {
    // release the original interface - all a success!
    pDSB->Release();
  }
}
```

# Lock and Load—Loading Sound Data into the Buffer

Great! The sound buffer is created, and now you're ready to play sounds! The only problem now is getting the sound data into the buffers. Sound buffers have a pair of functions at their disposal: IDirectSoundBuffer8::Lock, which deals with locking the sound data buffer and retrieving pointers to the data buffer, and IDirectSoundBuffer8::Unlock, which releases the resources used during a lock operation.

When you *lock* a buffer, you are preparing it for write access. You tell the buffer the offset (in bytes) from which you want to start reading and the number of bytes you're going to access. In return, you receive two pointers to the data and two variables telling you how much data to access.

Why do you get two pointers and two sizes? Because the sound buffers are circular, you might have to wrap around to the start of the buffer to lock the requested number of bytes. The first pointer is the position you request, and the first size is clipped to the end of the buffer. The second pointer is usually the start of the buffer, and the second size is the remaining number of locked bytes that extend past the end of the sound buffer. Figure 8.7 shows an example of a data buffer with two pointers and sizes.

The lock function prototype looks like this:

```
HRESULT IDirectSoundBuffer8::Lock(
    DWORD dwOffset,            // offset in buffer where to lock
    DWORD dwBytes,            // # of bytes to lock
    LPVOID *ppvAudioPtr1    ,  // pointer to 1st data pointer
    LPDWORD *ppwAudioBytes1,  // pointer to 1st size
    LPVOID *ppvAudioPtr2,     // pointer to 2nd data pointer
    LPDWORD *ppwAudioBytes2,  // pointer to 2nd size
    DWORD dwFlags);           // locking flags
```

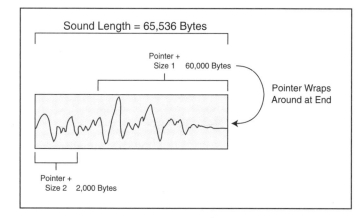

**Figure 8.7**

*Here, a data buffer 65,536 bytes in size has been locked in order to access 62,000 bytes. The first data pointer accesses 60,000 bytes, while the second data pointer accesses the remaining 2,000 bytes.*

Notice a couple things here. First, you need to pass the pointers to the pointers and sizes you are requesting. Second, you see dwFlags, which has three options: 0 to lock the section you are asking for, DSBLOCK_FROMWRITE-CURSOR to lock at the current write position, and DSBLOCK_ENTIREBUFFER to lock the entire buffer and skip the requested offset and size.

**CAUTION**

When you lock the sound buffer, make sure that you unlock it as quickly as possible. Taking too long during a lock can cause undesirable effects. Also, don't try to lock a portion of data that is currently being played.

Now, you can go ahead and lock the whole data buffer and throw in some random data:

**TIP**

It's best to set dwFlags to 0 — this ensures that you get exactly the position and the amount of bytes you are requesting. Also, if you don't want a second data pointer or size, set those appropriate variables to NULL and 0, respectively.

```
// g_pDSBuffer = pre-initialized secondary sound buffer
char *Ptr;
DWORD Size;
if(SUCCEEDED(g_pDSBuffer->Lock(0,0,(void**)&Ptr,                \
                (DWORD*)&Size,NULL,0,DSBLOCK_ENTIREBUFFER))) {
  for(long i=0;i<Size;i++)
    Ptr[i] = rand() % 65536;
```

At this point, you're through with the buffer and ready to unlock it, thus releasing the resources used in the process. You do this with IDirectSoundBuffer8::Unlock:

```
HRESULT IDirectSoundBuffer8::Unlock(
    LPVOID pvAudioPtr1,    // the 1st data pointer
    DWORD dwAudioBytes1,   // the 1st size
    LPVOID pvAudioPtr2,    // the 2nd data pointer
    DWORD dwAutioBytes2);  // the 2nd size
```

You need to pass only the values (not the pointers to them) received from locking the buffer:

```
if(FAILED(g_pDSBuffer->Unlock((void*)Ptr, Size, NULL, 0))) {
  // Error occurred
  }
}
```

# Playing the Sound Buffer

Now that the sound buffer is locked and the data is loaded, it is time to play the sound. The function call for playing a secondary sound buffer is identical to the primary sound buffer, described earlier in the chapter. This time, however, you don't want the sound to loop, so you exclude the DSBPLAY_LOOPING flag.

The only noteworthy difference at this point is that you need to tell the sound buffer where to start playing from within the buffer. Normally, the first time you play the sound, you play it from the start. However, stopping a sound doesn't reset the playing position because you can pause a sound just by stopping it, and then call the play function again to pick up from where it was last stopped. Setting the play position is easy with the following function:

```
HRESULT IDirectSoundBuffer8::SetCurrentPosition(
  DWORD dwNewPosition);
```

This function has only one argument—the offset in which you want the sound to start playing. You must align this to the sampling block size, as defined when you created the buffer. If you want to start the sound buffer playing at the beginning each time you play it, try the following code:

```
// g_pDSBuffer = initialized sound buffer pre-loaded with data
if(SUCEEDED(g_pDSBuffer->SetCurrentPosition(0))) {
  if(FAILED(g_pDSBuffer->Play(0,0,0))) {
    // Error occurred
  }
}
```

In order to stop playback, just use the IDirectSoundBuffer8::Stop function:

```
if(FAILED(g_pDSBuffer->Stop())) {
  // Error occurred
}
```

# Altering Volume, Panning, and Frequency Settings

When the correct flags are used to create the sound buffer, you can alter the volume, panning, and frequency of the sound buffer, even while it's playing! This means adding some great functions to your sound system, but don't go crazy—these capabilities strain the system a bit. Exclude the flags of unused features while creating the buffers.

## Volume Control

Volume is a bit strange to deal with at first. DirectSound plays sounds at full volume as they are sampled. It will not amplify sounds to make them louder, because that's the purpose of the actual sound hardware.

DirectSound only makes sounds quieter. It does this by attenuating the sound level, which is measured in hundredths of decibels ranging from 0 (full volume) to -10,000 (silence). The problem is that the sound can drop to silence anywhere in between depending on the user's sound system.

> **NOTE**
> You must create the sound buffer using the DSBCAPS_CTRLVOLUME flag in order to alter the volume.

> **NOTE**
> DirectSound defines two macros to represent full volume and silence; they are DSBVOLUME_MAX and DSBVOLUME_MIN, respectively.

To alter the volume, you need to call only this function:

```
HRESULT IDirectSoundBuffer8::SetVolume(LONG lVolume);
```

The only argument is the volume level in hundredths of decibels, as I just mentioned. As an example of altering the volume, check out the following code that will attenuate the volume level by 25 decibels:

```
// g_pDSBuffer = pre-initialized sound buffer
if(FAILED(g_pDSBuffer->SetVolume(-2500))) {
  // Error occurred
}
```

## Panning

Next in line is *panning*, which is the ability to shift the sound's playback between the left and right speakers (as depicted in Figure 8.8). Think of panning as a balance control on your typical stereo. Panning is measured by an amount that represents how far left or right to pan the sound. The far-left level (left speaker only) is -10,000, whereas the far-right level (right speaker only) is 10,000. Anywhere in between is balanced between the two speakers.

> **NOTE**
> DirectSound defines two macros to represent the far-left and far-right levels; they are DSBPAN_LEFT and DSBPAN_RIGHT, respectively.

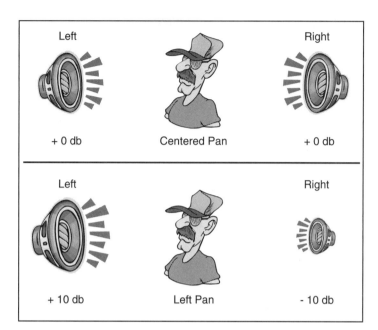

**Figure 8.8**

*The speakers normally play a sound at identical volume levels (measured in decibels, or db for short). Panning lowers the volume in one speaker and raises it in the opposite to give a pseudo 3-D effect.*

Here's the magic function:

```
HRESULT IDirectSoundBuffer8::SetPan(LONG lPan);
```

Just set the lPan argument to the panning level you want. Try it out on an example buffer by setting the panning value to -5,000, which decreases the right speaker's volume level by 50db:

```
// g_pDSBuffer = pre-initialized sound buffer
if(FAILED(g_pDSBuffer->SetPan(-5000))) {
  // Error occurred
}
```

> **NOTE**
> You need to create the sound buffer using the DSBCAPS_CTRLPAN flag in order to play with panning controls.

## Frequency Changes

Altering the frequency at which the sound buffer plays back effectively changes the pitch of the sound. Imagine changing your hero's voice into a chipmunk's by raising the frequency a bit! You could even use the same sampling of a man to simulate a female's voice by raising the frequency a bit. Do you believe me? Try it and find out.

> **CAUTION**
> Make sure that the primary buffer supports a 16-bit playback format, or the pan effect might not sound quite right.

You set the frequency with the following function:

```
HRESULT IDirectSoundBuffer8::SetFrequency(DWORD dwFrequency);
```

```
You only need to set the dwFrequency argument to the
level you want--for example:// g_pDSBuffer =
pre-initialized sound buffer
if(FAILED(g_pDSBuffer->SetFrequency(22050))) {
   // Error occurred
}
```

> **NOTE**
>
> Include the DSBCAPS_CTRLFREQUENCY flag when you create the sound buffer to use this feature.

Astute readers will notice that altering the playback frequency has the effect of squashing the sound wave, thus making it play in a shorter amount of time, as illustrated in Figure 8.9.

## Losing Focus

At times, other applications just have to grab resources away from you, leaving you with a device that's been altered. This usually happens to sound buffers, so you need to restore those lost resources with a call to `IDirectSoundBuffer8::Restore` (which takes no parameters). For example, if you have a buffer that's been lost, you can restore it (and all memory associated with the buffer) using the following code:

```
// g_pDSBuffer = pre-initialized sound buffer that's been lost
if(FAILED(g_pDSBuffer->Restore())) {
   // Error occurred
}
```

The unfortunate side effect of losing a buffer's resources is that the sound data is lost for good and must be reloaded.

> **TIP**
>
> When creating the sound buffer, use `DSBCAPS_LOCSOFTWARE` to tell DirectSound to use system memory resources, which are rarely lost. This way, you'll never have to worry about lost resources.

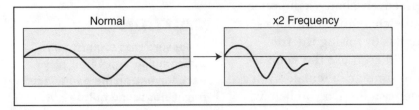

**Figure 8.9**

*Doubling the frequency of a sound makes it play twice as fast, and thus at a higher pitch.*

# Using Notifications

As you previously read, notifications are markers within a sound buffer that, when reached, signal an event you create. By working with notifications, you gain the ability to know when a sound has completed or stopped. You use those notifications to stream large sounds.

> **NOTE**
>
> Worried about a speed hit without hardware processing? The system is perfectly capable of dealing with a few sound buffers without any problems. Just try to make it easier on the system by making sure that all buffers (primary and secondary) use the same playback format.

Notifications use an object called IDirectSoundNotify8. Its only purpose is to mark positions within a sound buffer and trigger an event to your application, which you can process in the message loop or in a separate thread.

These positions are marked by their offset in the buffer (as shown in Figure 8.10), or by a macro signifying when the sound is stopped or complete. This macro is defined in DirectSound as DSBPN_OFFSETSTOP.

> **CAUTION**
>
> You can't just mark any offset within the buffer; it has to be aligned to the block size of a sample. Also, the notifications must be in order, from lowest offset to highest, and can never share an offset with another offset. If you use the DSBPN_OFFSETSTOP macro, it must be set last.
>
> For example, using a block alignment of 2 (mono with 16-bit) and trying to set offsets 4 and 5 will fail because offsets 4 and 5 share the same sample.

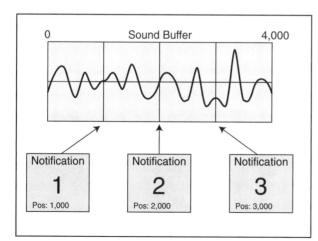

**Figure 8.10**

*Notifications can be placed (by an offset amount) anywhere inside the sound buffer.*

To obtain an `IDirectSoundNotify8` object, you have to query it from an `IDirectSoundBuffer8` object:

```
// g_pDSBuffer = pre-initialized secondary sound buffer
IDirectSoundNotify8 *g_pDSNotify;
if(FAILED(g_pDSBuffer->QueryInterface(IID_IDirectSoundNotify8, \
                      (void**)&g_pDSNotify))) {
  // Error occurred
}
```

Notification interfaces have only one function:

> **NOTE**
> In order to use notifications, you must create a sound buffer with the `DSBCAPS_CTRLPOSITIONNOTIFY` flag. If you create a buffer with this flag, you must create and use a notification object.

```
HRESULT IDirectSoundNotify8::SetNotificationPositions(
  DWORD dwPositionNotifies,                    // # notifications
  LPCDSBPOSITIONNOTIFY pcPositionNotifies); // array of offsets
```

`pcPositionNotifies` is actually a pointer to an array of `DSBPOSITIONOTIFY` structures. Here's a look at that structure and what it contains:

> **CAUTION**
> You cannot call `SetNotificationPositions` on a buffer that is currently playing. If you have to change notification positions, be sure to stop the buffer first. Use this function only on secondary sound buffers.

```
typedef struct {
  DWORD dwOffset;        // offset or DSBPN_OFFSET macro
  HANDLE hEventNotify;  // handle of event to signal
} DSBPOSITIONOTIFY, *LPCDSBPOSITIONNOTIFY;
```

The kicker here is the use of event handles. Events have two states—signaled (set) or non-signaled (clear). In order to create an event, you declare a handle variable and assign it as follows:

```
HANDLE hEvent;
hEvent =
CreateEvent(NULL,FALSE,FALSE,NULL);
```

> **NOTE**
> When you're done with an event, you must free it with a call to `CloseHandle(hEvent);`

You can create as many events as you want; you'll be able to distinguish among them later on. Typically, you create one event per sound channel, but that's not a rule. It's all up to you, and it's up to you to distinguish what each event means.

I want to pause here and show you how to set up the events and notification offsets. I'll use a sound buffer that's 65,536 bytes in size and create two events that represent the middle of the buffer and the end, respectively:

> **TIP**
>
> Try to keep all events in an array; later it becomes important to have them organized in this way.

```
// g_pDSBNotify = pre-initialize notification object
HANDLE g_hEvents[2];         // global handles
DSBPOSITIONNOTIFY dspn[2];   // 2 offsets to set - local

g_hEvents[0] = CreateEvent(NULL,FALSE,FALSE,NULL);
g_hEvents[1] = CreateEvent(NULL,FALSE,FALSE,NULL);
dspn[0].dwOffset = 32768;   // halfway marker
dspn[0].hEventNotify = hEvents[0];
dspn[1].dwOffset = DSBPN_OFFSETSTOP;  // end of sound marker
dspn[1].hEventNotify = g_hEvents[1];
if(FAILED(g_pDSBNotify->SetNotificationPositions(2, dspn))) {
  // Error occurred
}
```

At this point, the buffer is ready, so go ahead and start the sound buffer playing and let the events roll in. At this point, you only have to scan for the events, waiting for them to signal. Waiting for events is the purpose of the `WaitForMultipleObjects` function:

```
DWORD WaitForMultipleObjects(
   DWORD nCount,              // # of events to watch for <= 64
   CONST HANDLE *lpHandles,  // array of event handles to watch
   BOOL fWaitAll,            // FALSE (don't wait for all)
   DWORD dwMilliseconds);    // INFINITE (wait forever on events)
```

The only arguments you need to be interested in here are `nCount`, which holds the number of events to scan for, and `lpHandles`, which is an array of event handles that the function scans. In return from this function, you get the event number in the array that was signaled.

In actuality, you get a return value that has to be manipulated to retrieve the event number. This is as easy as subtracting the value WAIT_OBJECT_0 from the function's return value, which will give you a value of 0 to the number of events -1.

Now you see why you need to put the events in an array. From this, you can quickly determine which event was the trigger, so here is a function that plays a sound buffer, waiting for the end of the sound event that was already set up:

> **CAUTION**
>
> WaitForMultipleObjects can scan for only 64 objects at one time, so make sure that you don't exceed that limit.
>
> This function can also return a value of WAIT_FAILED to indicate there was an error while waiting for an event. Simply restart the wait, and everything should be all right.

```
// Pass a pre-initialized sound buffer w/notifications set up
// g_Events is an array of pre-initialized events 2 elements
// in size:
//    HANDLE g_Events[2];
void PlayItAndWait(IDirectSoundBuffer8 *pDSB)
{
  DWORD RetVal, EventNum;

  // Start sound playing from beginning of buffer
  pDSBuffer->SetCurrentPosition(0);
  pDSBuffer->Play(0,0,0);

  while(1) {
    while((RetVal = WaitForMultipleObjects(2, g_Events,        \
                    FALSE, INFINITE) ) != WAIT_FAILED) {
      EventNum = RetVal - WAIT_OBJECT_0;
      // check for end of sound event and break
      if(EventNum == 1)
        break;
    }
  }
  // Stop sound
  pDSBuffer->Stop();
}
```

The only problem with the preceding sound playing example is that the code should be placed within the main message loop of your program, and, as such, needs to scan for standard Windows messages. This is entirely possibly, and it seems that Microsoft prefers this method in the DirectX SDK examples.

The problem with constantly checking the status of a sound buffer as just shown is that it takes away from modular programming techniques that I prefer to use. In order to make this system work better, you have to create a separate thread and let that take care of the preceding event-scanning loop.

# Using Threads for Events

I think I just heard a sigh. Don't worry, using threads to work with the events is not that hard. If you read Chapter 5, "Programming with Windows and Application Basics," you already are aware that setting up a thread is easy. It's how you deal with this kind of setup that's difficult.

In Chapter 5, I wrote that in order for a thread to close, it has to call the ExitThread function from within itself. But how can the thread know when it's done if it's just endlessly scanning for events in a list? The solution—add an extra event used to trigger the closure of the thread!

In order to manually trigger an event, you use the following call with the event handle:

```
SetEvent(hEvent);
```

To reset an event, you can use the following function call:

```
ResetEvent(hEvent);
```

Take a look at the event-scanning loop again, this time adding functions to play a sound buffer, to stop the sound, and to add thread-processing:

```
HANDLE g_Events[2];  // global events
IDirectSoundNotify8 *g_pDSBNotify;  // global notification object

HANDLE g_hThread;         // thread handle
BOOL g_Active = FALSE;    // thread active flag
BOOL g_Playing = FALSE;   // flag is sound playing

// Pass a pre-initialized sound buffer w/notification abilities
// this function will set up the notifications for you.
void PlaySound(IDirectSoundBufffer8 *pDSBuffer)
{
  DSBPOSITIONNOTIFY dspn[1];
```

```
        DWORD ThreadId;

        // stop a sound already playing
        if(g_Playing == TRUE)
          StopSound(pDSBuffer);

        // get the notification object
        pDSBuffer->QueryInterface(IID_IDirectSoundNotify8,            \
                          (void**)&g_pDSBNotify);

        // create events and thread
        g_hEvents[0] = CreateEvent(NULL, FALSE, FALSE, NULL);
        g_hEvents[1] = CreateEvent(NULL, FALSE, FALSE, NULL);
        g_hThread = CreateThread(NULL, 0,                            \
              (LPTHREAD_START_ROUTINE)MyThread, NULL, 0, &ThreadId);

        // set the notification positions
        dspn[0].dwOffset = DSBPN_OFFSETSTOP;
        dspn[0].hEventNotify = g_hEvents[0];
        g_pDSBNotify->SetNotificationPositions(1, dspn);

        // play the sound and flag as so
        pDSBuffer->SetCurrentPosition(0);
        pDSBuffer->Play(0,0,0);
        g_Playing = TRUE;
      }

      void StopSound(IDirectSoundBuffer8 *pDSBuffer)
      {
        pDSBuffer->Stop();
        g_Playing = FALSE;

        // clear sound buffer events and signal thread closure
        while(g_Active == TRUE) {
          ResetEvent(g_Events[0]);
          SetEvent(g_Events[1]);
        }

        // Release all resources
        g_pDSBNotify->Release();
        CloseHandle(g_hEvents[0]);
```

```
    CloseHandle(g_hEvents[1]);
    CloseHandle(g_hThread);
}

DWORD WINAPI MyThread(void *lpParameter)
{
    DWORD RetVal, EventNum;

    g_Active = TRUE;

    while(1) {
        while((RetVal = WaitForMultipleObjects(2, g_Events,          \
                            FALSE, INFINITE) != WAIT_FAILED) {
            EventNum = RetVal - WAIT_OBJECT_0;

            // Check if the thread needs to close
            if(EventNum == 1)
                ExitThread(0);

            // the sound stopped - just flag for now
            if(EventNum == 1) {
                g_Playing = FALSE;
            }
        }
    }
}
```

That's about it. All you have to do is call PlaySound with a sound buffer that is already created and has sound in it; then you wait for the sound to end or call StopSound to forcibly stop it. Even if the sound is no longer playing, you have to free the resources and close the thread by calling StopSound.

# Loading Sounds into the Buffers

Now that you can access the sound buffer, where do you get the sound data? The easiest way is to use Microsoft's widely used digital sound files, called *wave files,* which use the .WAV file extension.

A wave file begins with a small header followed by the raw sound data, which can be compressed (hard to work with) or uncompressed (easy to deal with). In this section, you learn how to read in and parse the file header, how to read the uncompressed sound data, and how to place it in a sound buffer.

Following is a structure I created that will store the wave file header for your use:

```
typedef struct sWaveHeader {
{
  char   RiffSig[4];           // 'RIFF'
  long   WaveformChunkSize;    // 8
  char   WaveSig[4];           // 'WAVE'
  char   FormatSig[4];         // 'fmt ' (notice space after)
  long   FormatChunkSize;      // 16
  short  FormatTag;            // WAVE_FORMAT_PCM
  short  Channels;             // # of channels
  long   SampleRate;           // sampling rate
  long   BytesPerSec;          // bytes per second
  short  BlockAlign;           // sample block alignment
  short  BitsPerSample;        // bits per second
  char   DataSig[4];           // 'data'
  long   DataSize;             // size of waveform data
} sWaveHeader;
```

The only step required to handling the header is to open a wave file and immediately read it in. The structure will then contain all the information needed to determine the format of the sound, as well as the size of the sound data to read in.

At this point, you could create a sound buffer based on the data read in and then go about your business with it. However, I want to write a couple of functions that will load a wave file into a newly created secondary sound buffer for you. The first function reads and parses the wave file header, creating a sound buffer along the way; the second one reads sound data into the sound buffer.

> **CAUTION**
>
> Most wave files are saved using the header shown depicted by the sWaveHeader structure, but at times extra chunks are inserted, throwing everything into a spin. For example, a comment chunk might be inserted before the wave data chunk. Try to read only wave files that contain a single digital sound, and you should be fine.

> **NOTE**
>
> You can tell whether the sound header is to an actual wave file by checking the various signature (*Sig) fields in the sWaveHeader structure. See the comments for what each one should contain and make sure that they match when you load the header. If one is wrong, you have an indication that you might not be able to load the sound correctly.

The first function, CreateBufferFromWAV, takes a pointer to an open wave file as well as an sWaveHeader structure that is filled with the wave file header data from the file. Upon the return of the CreateBufferFromWAV file, you will receive a pointer to a newly created IDirectSoundBuffer8 object that is ready to accept the sound data received from calling the LoadSoundData function. Take a look at the code for the two functions:

```
// g_pDS = pre-initialized IDirectSound8 object
IDirectSounndBuffer8 *CreateBufferFromWAV(FILE *fp,               \
                                            sWaveHeader *Hdr)
{
  IDirectSoundBuffer *pDSB;
  IDirectSoundBuffer8 *pDSBuffer;
  DSBUFFERDESC dsbd;
  WAVEFORMATEX wfex;

  // read in the header from beginning of file
  fseek(fp, 0, SEEK_SET);
  fread(Hdr, 1, sizeof(sWaveHeader), fp);

  // check the sig fields, returning if an error
   if(memcmp(Hdr->RiffSig, "RIFF", 4) ||                          \
     memcmp(Hdr->WaveSig, "WAVE", 4) ||                           \
     memcmp(Hdr->FormatSig, "fmt ", 4) ||                         \
     memcmp(Hdr->DataSig, "data",4))
  return NULL;

  // set up the playback format
  ZeroMemory(&wfex, sizeof(WAVEFORMATEX));
  wfex.wFormatTag = WAVE_FORMAT_PCM;
  wfex.nChannels = Hdr->Channels;
  wfex.nSamplesPerSec = Hdr->SampleRate;
  wfex.wBitsPerSample = Hdr->BitsPerSample;
  wfex.nBlockAlign = wfex.wBitsPerSample / 8 * wfex.nChannels;
  wfex.nAvgBytesPerSec = wfex.nSamplesPerSec * wfex.nBlockAlign;

  // create the sound buffer using the header data
  ZeroMemory(&dsbd, sizeof(DSBUFFERDESC));
  dsbd.dwSize = sizeof(DSBUFFERDESC);
  dsbd.Flags = DSBCAPS_CTRLVOLUME | DSBCAPS_CTRLPAN |             \
               DSBCAPS_CTRLFREQUENCY;
  dsbd.dwBufferBytes = Hdr->DataSize;
```

```
        dsbd.lpwfxFormat = &wfex;
        if(FAILED(g_pDS->CreateSoundBuffer(&dsbd, &pDSB,NULL)))
          return NULL;

        // get newer interface
        if(FAILED(pDSB->QueryInterface(IID_IDirectSoundBuffer8,        \
                        (void**)&pDSBuffer))) {
          pDSB->Release();
          return NULL;
        }

        // return the interface
        return p-DSBuffer;
      }

      BOOL LoadSoundData(IDirectSoundBuffer8 *pDSBuffer,              \
                        long LockPos, FILE *fp, long Size)
      {
        BYTE *Ptr1, *Ptr2;
        DWORD Size1, Size2;

        if(!Size)
          return FALSE;

        // lock the sound buffer at position specified
        if(FAILED(pDSBuffer->Lock(LockPos, Size,                     \
                    (void**)&Ptr1, &Size1,                          \
                    (void**)&Ptr2, &Size2, 0)))
          return FALSE;

        // read in the data
        fread(Ptr1, 1, Size1, fp);
        if(Ptr2 != NULL)
          fread(Ptr2, 1, Size2, fp);

        // unlock it
        pDSBuffer->Unlock(Ptr1, Size1, Ptr2, Size2);

        // return a success
        return TRUE;
      }
```

Here's a sample function that will use the `CreateBufferFromWAV` and `LoadSoundData` functions to load in a wave file. Upon return of the following `LoadWAV` file, you will receive a sound buffer that's ready to be worked with:

```
IDirectSoundBuffer8 *LoadWAV(char *Filename)
{
  IDirectSoundBuffer8 *pDSBuffer;
  sWaveHeader Hdr;
  FILE *fp;

  // open the source file
  if((fp=fopen(Filename, "rb"))==NULL)
    return NULL;

  // create the sound buffer
  if((pDSBuffer = CreateBufferFromWAV(fp, &Hdr)) == NULL) {
    fclose(fp);
    return NULL;
  }

  // read in the data
  fseek(fp, sizeof(sWaveHeader), SEEK_SET);
  LoadSoundData(pDSBuffer, 0, fp, Hdr.DataSize);

  // close the source file
  fclose(fp);

  // return the new sound buffer fully loaded with sound
  return p-DSBuffer;
}
```

# Streaming Sound

I'm going to let you in on a little secret—streaming sound is an easy process. The secret to handling streaming playback is to use looping playback to ensure seamless and constant playback of the sound buffer, while continuously loading in new sound data to replace the sound data that has already been played.

The trick is to set a couple of markers in the sound buffer. When the sound being played passes one of these markers, you have an indication that it's time to load more sound data into the portion just played. In this way, you ensure that playback wraps around to the start of the buffer and finds new sound data. Figure 8.11 shows a sound buffer with four stream markers that signify when new sound data must be loaded.

To play a streaming sound, you first load the entire buffer with sound data (as much data as will fit in the buffer). Start playing the sound and wait until the first marker is hit. At this point, the next small chunk of sound data is inserted into the section just played. Playing continues until marker two is hit, at which point more data is loaded into the chunk just played.

This process continues until the entire sound is loaded and played, at which point a marker triggers the sound to stop. If the sound is to be looped, playback continues by restarting the entire playback sequence you just read about.

In the previous section, "Loading Sounds into the Buffers," I wrote a function called LoadSoundData that will load sound data into a buffer that you specify. Inside the thread that handles the notification events, you use the loading function to stream in data as it is finished, thus keeping the buffer full of sound information. The Sound Core does this to every sound channel, thus putting an awesome tool at your disposal.

Here's how it's all done:

1. Create a sound buffer, say 65,536 bytes in size.
2. Set four notification positions (one for each ¼ of the sound buffer).
3. Load the entire buffer with as much data as possible.
4. Start playing the sound buffer using the DSBPLAY_LOOP flag.
5. As each notification event is triggered, load the previously played section with new data. Continue until you reach a notification and there's no more sound left to buffer in; then play the last of the sound.

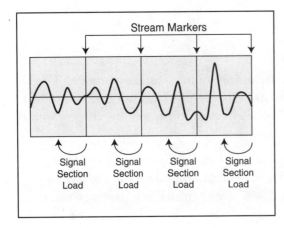

**Figure 8.11**

*The sound buffer has four stream markers. When playback reaches each marker, the sound buffer signals you to load new sound data into the section just played.*

6. To determine which event marks the end of the sound, determine the modulus from the sound size according to the buffer size (the remainder after dividing the sound size by the buffer size). Divide the modulus value by four (the number of notifications) to determine which of the events is used to signify the end of the sound position.

The Stream demo parses the wave header, creating a sound buffer, setting up four notifications and events, and then playing the sound, buffering in data as the events roll in. This process continues until the end of sound is reached, at which point playback ends.

You can find the actual code to the Stream demo in Chapter 10, "Creating the Game Core." There you'll find a working set of functions that you can use in your projects to stream sound.

> **NOTE**
>
> The entire streaming code example (called *Stream*) is on the **CD-ROM** that comes with this book (look for BookCode\Chap08\Stream). Because of its length, I can't provide the code list here, but it follows the techniques presented in this section. To play a streamed sound, call the PlayStreamedSound function with the filename of the sound to play, and the function will take care of the rest.

# Working with DirectMusic

Whereas DirectSound handles digital sound, DirectMusic handles music playback from Midi files (files ending with the .MID extension), DirectMusic native files (*.SGT files), and digitally recorded songs stored in a wave format (.WAV files). Which of these formats is best for you is a question you'll have to answer.

Each has its advantages and disadvantages. The real magic of DirectMusic is when you use the native format. A DirectMusic native song can consist of small musical patterns that can be randomly played one after another in various chords. Randomly picking patterns and chords means that the music will never be the same—it's always changing. Add tempo changes, and you have a kick-butt music system.

> **NOTE**
>
> Another feature is the use of *motif*'s, which are sounds you overlay on musical segments as they are playing. These can serve as cues that blend into the song. For example, if the player achieves a goal, a short bleat of horns can play to signify it.

The benefit of using Midi files is that they are highly supported. You can find literally hundreds of thousands of songs with this format on the Internet, and there are more Midi music authoring software packages than you can count. The great thing is that you can now use digitally sampled sounds as instruments.

Get this—instead of typical instruments, you can use other digitally sampled sounds, such as guns, monkey screeches, or whatever catches your fancy. You can finally set down that funky fresh tune you've been dreaming of using in your own game and use a music format such as Midi to do so!

> **NOTE**
>
> The problem with the native format is that it takes a bit of time to get used to writing the musical patterns and chords. There's no way I could begin to show you how to do so in this limited space, but I will refer you to the DirectMusic Producer, which is Microsoft's music editor package. You can find it on this book's CD-ROM, or you can download it at http://www.microsoft.com.

Using digital instruments also ensures that your song will sound the same on all computers. You accomplish this by using DirectSound to synthesize sound effects. DirectMusic has the option to create its own DirectSound interface or to use one you've already created.

Using Midi or DirectMusic native songs allows one common advantage (the ability to alter the tempo of playback) that adds a cool feature—the ability to slow down or speed up the music to match the on-screen action. When the gaming action gets intense, increase the music tempo to match, and then slow it down to signify that the action is over.

> **NOTE**
>
> The path musical data takes to the synthesizer (DirectSound) is called an *audio path*, which you can grab hold of and play with just as you can with a standard DirectSound sound buffer. Now imagine this—grabbing an audio path and creating a 3D sound buffer from it! This is all possible, and it is what makes DirectMusic 8 exciting.

Digitally recorded music creates an ultimate system . . . sort of. While the quality is superb, the song cannot be altered to match the action. The song sounds just as it is recorded, nothing more or nothing less.

## Starting with DirectMusic

Now I know you're excited, so let's get moving. The first step to using DirectMusic is to create a main object, called the *performance* object, that represents the music system. Second, create an object, called the *loader* object, that loads all essential music files. These two objects interact with each other as shown in Figure 8.12.

Last, you have to load the actual musical segments into *segment* objects. Multiple segments can be loaded and played after each other in order to create longer or more dynamic songs. In this chapter, I deal only with a single segment (which can represent an entire song).

DirectMusic doesn't have a function to help you create or initialize the main DirectMusic interface, so you need to initialize the COM system yourself. I cover this in Chapter 5, but will go over it quickly here. To initialize COM, call the following function:

> **NOTE**
>
> Before using DirectMusic, you need to include **DMusici.h** and link **DSound.lib** to your project. Also, you'll be using the **COM** system in the Win32 SDK, so include **ObjBase.h**.

```
CoInitialize(NULL);
```

Do this only once when you start using DirectMusic, because it keeps an internal count of the number of times it was initialized. You need to match every call to this function with a call to close down COM:

```
CoUninitialize();
```

This decreases the reference count of COM usage, and when it finally reaches 0, it will release the COM system from memory. This is memory efficient, and all COM objects follow this procedure. In order to create the objects, you use the `CoCreateInstance` function, which is also shown in Chapter 5. The following two sections show you how to create the respective performance and loader objects.

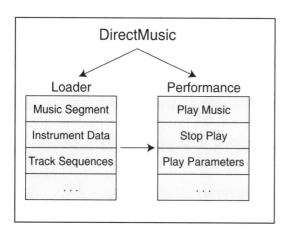

**Figure 8.12**

*The loader objects fetch the data that the performance object needs in order to play.*

# Creating the Performance Object

The performance object is the big daddy here and, as such, is the main object you'll be working with. You can have multiple performance objects, but I recommend using only one. In order to create the performance object, first declare an `IDirectMusicPerformance8` object and call `CoCreateInstance` as follows:

```
// global performance object
IDirectMusicPerformance8 *g_pDMPerformance;

CoCreateInstance(CLSID_DirectMusicPerformance, NULL,          \
                 CLSCTX_INPROC, IID_IDirectMusicPerformance8, \
                 (void**)&g_pDMPerformance);
```

The performance object needs to be initialized. This creates a DirectMusic and DirectSound object, and it creates sound buffers and sets the playback capabilities as well. It also sets up a default audio path on which music is played. A typical setup will use 128 channels (instruments) and have stereo and reverb (reflections of sounds off objects) effects. Here's the function call that does it all:

> **NOTE**
>
> In Chapter 5, I write that `CoCreateInstance` returns the value S_OK if the call is a success, or another value if the call is not a success.

```
HRESULT IDirectMusicPerformance8::InitAudio(
   IDirectMusic **ppDirectMusic,  // NULL
   IDirectSound **ppDirectSound,  // NULL
   HWND hWnd,                        // parent window handle
   DWORD dwDefaultPathType,       // type of default audio path
                     // use DMUS_APATH_SHARED_STEREOPLUSREVERB
   DWORD dwPChannelCount,         // # channels - use 128
   DWORD dwFlags,                 // DMUS_AUDIOF_ALL
                                  // (enable all music features)
   DMUS_AUDIOPARAMS *pParams);    // NULL (parameters structure)
```

There's a lot here, but the comments pretty much say it all. You don't need a pointer to the internal DirectMusic or DirectSound objects, so skip those. You have to give this function the handle to the parent window—this is a must. You can keep the other parameters as commented in the function `InitAudio` prototype.

Here is how to give this function a call:

```
// g_pDMPerformance = pre-initialized performance object
if(FAILED(g_pDMPerformance->InitAudio(NULL, NULL, hWnd,        \
```

```
                  DMUS_APATH_SHARED_STEREOPLUSREVERB, 128,      \
                  DMUS_AUDIOF_ALL, NULL))) {
   // Error occurred
}
```

# Creating the Loader Object

Creating the loader object is the next step to using DirectMusic. This object is basically a caching system that speeds up data loading and that loads support files for songs that need them (such as the digital samples used for instruments).

The `IDirectMusicLoader8` object represents the loader. You can create it with the following code:

```
IDirectMusicLoader8 *g_pDMLoader;  // global loader object
CoCreateInstance(CLSID_DirectMusicLoader, NULL,              \
                 CLSCTX_INPROC, IID_IDirectMusicLoader8,     \
                 (void**)&g_pDMLoader);
```

The next step to using the loader is telling it in which directory to search for files. This directory is referred to as the *default search directory*. Normally, when loading a single music file, such as a Midi file, setting the default directory isn't really needed as long as you give the loader the complete path. But for DirectMusic native files, the loader object must know where to find the support files.

> **CAUTION**
>
> Make sure that you create only one `IDirectMusicLoader8` object in your application. It helps to cache and control the frequently-used data and resources required for using DirectMusic.

Setting the default search directory is the job of the `IDirectMusicLoader8::SetSearchDirectory` function:

```
HRESULT IDirectMusicLoader8::SetSearchDirectory(
   REFGUID rguidClass,   // class (GUID_DirectMusicallTypes)
   WCHAR *pwszPath,      // directory path (in wide characters)
   BOOL fClear);         // FALSE - clear load cache info
```

The preceding call really needs only one parameter—the search directory path you are setting. Be careful; it's a wide character string, so convert it if needed or use the `WCHAR` data type.

To make it simple, I normally set the search directory to the current directory. That way you can reference song files from your own subdirectories (such as .\Songs\—notice the period to denote current directory).

> **NOTE**
>
> **To declare a wide character string, use the following line of code:**
>
> `WCHAR *Text = L"Testing";`
>
> **To copy a regular character string into a wide character string, use the** `mbstowcs` **function as shown here:**
>
> `char Text[] = "Roleplaying is fun!';  // source text buffer`
>
> `WCHAR WText[256];  // dest text buffer`
>
> `// convert at least 256 characters from source to dest`
>
> `mbstowcs(WText, Text, 256);`

Here's an example of setting the current directory as the default search directory:

```
// g_pDMLoader = pre-initialized loader object
CHAR strPath[MAX_PATH];     // current path
WCHAR wstrPath[MAX_PATH];   // wide character buffer

GetCurrentDirectory(MAX_PATH, strPath);
mbstowcs(wstrPath, strPath, MAX_PATH);
if(FAILED(g_pDMLoader->SetSearchDirectory(                     \
        GUID_DirectMusicAllTypes, wstrPath, FALSE))) {
  // Error occurred
}
```

# Working with Music Segments

Now that the system is initialized and the loader is ready, it is time to start loading in the songs and letting them play. This is the purpose of the `IDirectMusicSegment8` object. The DirectMusic loader object (as illustrated in Figure 8.13) has the job of loading the music and instrument data and creating the `IDirectMusicSegment8` object for you. Consider the loading process in two steps—first loading the music segment that contains the notes to play.

## Loading Music Segments

The first step is to set up an object description structure called `DMUS_OBJECTDESC` with the information on what you are loading (a song). Here's the structure:

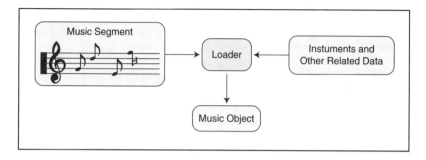

**Figure 8.13**

*The loader object is responsible for retrieving the data, such as the musical score and instrument data, needed to create a music object.*

```
typedef struct {
  DWORD dwSize;                // size of this structure
  DWORD dwValidData;           // flags determining valid fields
  GUID guidObject;             // unique GUID of object
  GUID guidClass;              // CLSID_DirectMusicSegement
  FILETIME ftDate;             // Date when object last edited
  DMUS_VERSION vVersion;       // structure containing
                               // version information
  WCHAR wszName[DMUS_MAX_NAME];  // name of object
  WCHAR wszCategory[DMUS_MAX_CATEGORY];  // category of object
  WCHAR wszFileName[DMUS_MAX_FILENAME];  // filename to load
  LONGLONG llMemLength;        // size of data in memory
  LPBYTE pbMemData;            // pointer to data in memory
  IStream *pStream;            // stream interface for loading
} DMUS_OBJECTDESC;
```

Fortunately, you can ignore most of the fields in DMUS_OBJECTDESC. The first thing you should pay attention to is the dwValidData variable. This stores a combination of flags telling the loader which fields in the structure to use. For example, if you want to use the wszFilename and guidClass objects, you set the appropriate flags. These flags are shown in Table 8.4.

The DMUS_OBJECTDESC structure is passed to the IDirectMusicLoader8::GetObject function, which ensures that all related data files are loaded and placed in the segment object. Here's the function prototype:

```
HRESULT IDirectMusicLoader8::GetObject(
  LPDMUS_OBJECTDESC pDesc,   // pointer to a
                             // DMUS_OJBECTDESC structure
  REFIID riid,               // IID_IDirectMusicSegment8
  LPVOID FAR * ppv);         // pointer to newly loaded object
```

## Table 8.4 dwValidData Flags

| Flag | Description |
| --- | --- |
| DMUS_OBJ_CATEGORY | wszCategory is valid. |
| DMUS_OBJ_CLASS | guidClass is valid. |
| DMUS_OBJ_DATE | ftDate is valid. |
| DMUS_OBJ_FILENAME | wszFileName is valid. |
| DMUS_OBJ_FULLPATH | wszFileName contains full path to object. |
| DMUS_OBJ_LOADED | Object is already loaded. |
| DMUS_OBJ_MEMORY | Object is in memory. llMemLength and pbMemData are valid. |
| DMUS_OBJ_NAME | wszName is valid. |
| DMUS_OBJ_OBJECT | guidObject is valid. |
| DMUS_OBJ_STREAM | pStream is valid. |
| DMUS_OBJ_URL | wszFileName represents a URL. DirectMusic does not yet support this flag. |
| DMUS_OBJ_VERSION | vVersion is valid. |

You are telling the GetObject function to use the structure you've already set up and to load the data into an IDirectMusicSegment8 object. Of course, you need to declare the segment object first, so here is a function that handles loading the music segment and returns the segment object (or NULL if an error occurs):

```
// g_pDMLoader = pre-initialized object w/search directory set

IDirectMusicSegment8 *LoadSong(char *Filename)
{
  DMUS_OBJECTDESC dmod;
  IDirectMusicSegment8 *pDMSegment;

  ZeroMemory(&dmod, sizeof(DMUS_OBJECTDESC));
  dmod.dwSize = sizeof(DMUS_OBJECTDESC);
  dmod.guidClass = CLSID_DirectMusicSegment;
```

```
dmod.dwValidData = DMUS_OBJ_CLASS | DMUS_OBJ_FILENAME |        \
                    DMUS_OBJ_FULLPATH;
mbstowcs(dmod.wszFileName, Filename, MAX_PATH);
if(FAILED(g_pDMLoader->GetObject(&dmod,                         \
        IID_IDirectMusicSegment8, (LPVOID)&pDMSegment)))
   return NULL;


// loading completed
return p_DMSegment;
}
```

## Loading Instruments

The DirectMusic loader will set up the default instrument data when you are using native or Midi songs, but what about those times when you want to switch between native and Midi instrument settings? In those cases, you need our friend DirectMusic, which allows you to use your own custom instrument data.

Instruments are referred to as *patches,* and a collection of patches is referred to as *DLS instrument data* (Downloadable Sounds), which is contained in *instrument collections.* Patches are numbered by a series of three values: *most-significant byte* (MSB), *least-significant byte* (LSB), and *patch number.*

General Midi patches are also standardized, so a patch number 1 (a piano) will always be a piano patch. If you want to use a new piano patch, you can just load it up from a DLS collection. DirectMusic comes with a General Midi instrument collection, called the *GM/GS set,* made by Roland.

If you're making new instruments to replace General Midi patches, make sure that they have a MSB and LSB of 0. Otherwise, try to use a different value for both to ensure that you're not intruding in the space of one or the other. Consult the DirectMusic Producer help files if you need help.

If you want to use only a couple of new instruments, by all means just save them to a DLS. When you load a new DLS, you overwrite the instruments in memory that are already loaded (as illustrated in Figure 8.14). After the DLS collection is ready to use, you tell DirectMusic to use the collection with your music segment.

> **NOTE**
>
> **To make your own DLS, install the DirectMusic Producer included on the CD-ROM. Just select File, New and create a DLS Collection. Begin adding wave files to the list and then add instruments, making sure to assign the appropriate wave data to them.**

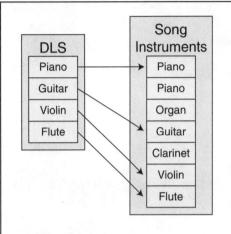

**Figure 8.14**

*When you load DLS instruments, you either overwrite existing instrument data or insert the new instrument data where no current instrument exists.*

To load a DLS collection, you need to obtain an IDirectMusicCollection8 object from the loader object. Again, you utilize the IDirectMusicLoad8::GetObject function, but this time, you specify the collection object and filename. Here's a function that will load a DLS collection for you, returning a pointer to the loaded collection object with which you work:

```
IDirectMusicCollection8 *LoadDLSCollection(char *Filename)
{
  DMUS_OBJECTDESC dmod;
  IDirectMusicCollection8 *pDMCollection;

  ZeroMemory(&dmod, sizeof(DMUS_OBJECTDESC));
  dmod.dwSize = sizeof(DMUS_OBJECTDESC);
  dmod.guidClass = CLSID_DirectMusicCollection;
  dmod.dwValidData = DMUS_OBJ_CLASS | DMUS_OBJ_FILENAME |     \
                     DMUS_OBJ_FULLPATH;
  mbstowcs(dmod.wszFileName, Filename, MAX_PATH);
  if(FAILED(g_pDMLoader->GetObject(&dmod,                     \
       IID_IDirectMusicCollection8, (void**)pDMCollection)))
    return NULL;

  // return the pointer to the collection object
  return IDirectMusicCollection8;
}
```

At this point, the collection is loaded, but you need to assign it to the segment. Do this by setting a specific segment track parameter using IDirectMusicSegment8::SetParam:

```
HRESULT IDirectMusicSegment8::SetParam(
   REFGUID rguidType,    // GUID of param to set
   DWORD dwGroupBits,    // which tracks to effect (0xFFFFFFFF)
   DWORD dwIndex,        // 0
   MUSIC_TIME mtTime,    // when to apply setting - use 0
   void* pParam);        // new parameter or NULL if none required
```

Specifically, you want to set the DLS collection type parameter, which has a GUID value of GUID_ConnectToDLSCollection. You want to affect every track and make sure the change of instruments takes effect immediately. Do this with the following code bit (which loads a DLS and sets it to a preloaded segment):

```
IDirectMusicCollection8 *pDMCollection;
if((pDMCollection = LoadDLSCollection("MyDLS.dls")) != NULL)
  pDMSegment->SetParam(GUID_ConnectToDLSCollection,            \
          0xFFFFFFFF, 0, 0, (void*)pDMCollection);
```

At times, you'll need to use the default collection, which you can do with a call to GetObject using the GUID value of GUID_DefaultGMCollection under the object class field:

```
IDirectMusicCollection8 *GetDefaultCollection()
{
  DMUS_OBJECTDESC mod;
  IDirectMusicCollection8 *pDMCollection;

  ZeroMemory(&dmod, sizeof(DMUS_OBJECTDESC));
  dmod.dwSize = sizeof(DMUS_OBJECTDESC);
  dmod.guidObject = GUID_DefaultDMCollection;
  dmod.dwValidData = DMUS_OBJ_OBJECT;
  if(FAILED(g_pDMLoader->GetObject(&dmod,                       \
        IID_IDirectMusicCollection8, (void**)pDMCollection)))
    return NULL;
  return pDMCollection;
}
```

Calling the preceding GetDefaultCollection function creates an instrument collection object that contains the default DLS instrument data that you can use.

# Configuring for Midi

A complete song in memory (with instruments) is almost ready to use. There are only a few problems to tackle. First, because the system must prepare itself by conforming to General Midi settings, you need to tell the system whether the load file is a Midi file.

To tell DirectMusic that the segment is a Midi file, you, again, set a segment track parameter using `IDirectMusicSegment8::SetParam`. This time, you use the GUID value of `GUID_StandardMidiFile`:

```
pDMSegment->SetParam(GUID_StandardMidiFile,                    \
                    0xFFFFFFFF, 0, 0, NULL);
```

You can insert the `SetParam` function, as just seen, in the `LoadSongFile` function (after the song is completely loaded):

> **CAUTION**
>
> Perform this call only on files that are Midi files, because it changes the way music information is perceived. If you play around with it, you will see that certain data tracks are changed or dropped.

```
if(FAILED(g_pDMLoader->GetObject(&dmod,                    \
            IID_IDirectMusicSegment8, (LPVOID)&pDMSegment)))
  return NULL;
// loading completed
// set as Midi file
if(strstr(Filename, ".mid") != NULL)
  pDMSegment->SetParam(GUID_StandardMidiFile,               \
                        0xFFFFFFFF, 0, 0, NULL);
return p_DMSegment;
}
```

# Setting Up the Instruments

The next step to preparing a segment to play is to set up the instrument data by downloading it to the performance object. You accomplish this with a call to `IDirectMusicSegment8::Download`:

```
HRESULT IDirectMusicSegment8::Download(IUnknown *pAudioPath);
```

This function's only parameter is the audio path to which you download the instrument data. In this case, it is the performance object, so the following code will work:

```
if(FAILED(g_pDMSegment->Download(g_pDMPerformance))) {
  // Error occurred
}
```

When you're done with a musical segment, you must follow up with a call to IDirectMusicSegment8::Unload, which frees the instrument data. Do this after you stop playback of a segment and are done with it or when you switch instrument collections. This call is identical to IDirectMusicSegment8::Download, so I'll skip the prototype and show you an actual call:

```
if(FAILED(g_pDMSegment->Unload(g_pDMPerformance))) {
  // Error occurred
}
```

## Using Loops and Repeats

The last step before playing a song is to set up repeat points and the number of times to repeat a loop. For example, if you have a kicking tune and want to repeat a small portion of it a couple of times, you can set the starting and ending loop points (as illustrated in Figure 8.15) and then set the number of times to repeat the loop.

> **TIP**
>
> To change instruments (such as assigning a DLS to a segment), you first unload the instrument data. After the instruments are unloaded, you can load the new instrument data and let the song continue playing.

Setting loop points is the purpose of the IDirectMusicSegment8::SetLoopPoints function:

```
HRESULT IDirectMusicSegment8::SetLoopPoints(
  MUSIC_TIME mtStart,
  MUSIC_TIME mtEnd);
```

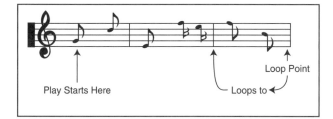

**Figure 8.15**

*You have to set starting and ending loop points within a song in order to use the loop and repeat features of DirectMusic.*

Normally, you want the entire song to repeat playback upon completion, so there's really no reason to mess with the SetLoopPoints function. If you do, be sure to measure the time based on the tempo (refer to the DX SDK documents for more on this topic).

After setting the loop points (or even if you haven't), you are ready to set the number of times

> **CAUTION**
>
> Notice the use of MUSIC_TIME, which is a time measurement used in DirectMusic. This time measurement is based on the tempo of the song, not the timing, so it is sometimes difficult to work with. Timing is another issue altogether, and one best left to the DirectX SDK documents. For your current purposes, you want all changes to take effect immediately, so specifying a value of 0 for the time will do fine.

the song repeats. If you want the song to play only once and then stop, you have it repeat zero times. If you want the song to play twice, you have it repeat one time.

You set the number of repeats with IDirectMusicSegment8::SetRepeats, which takes only one parameter—the number of times to repeat the song loop (or the macro DMUS_SEG_REPEAT_INFINITE, which causes the song to play forever):

```
pDMSegment->SetRepeats(0);  // play song once (no loops)
```

## Playing and Stopping the Segment

Now, at last it comes time to play your song. Yes, the road was long and hard, but it has all led to this point. The performance object plays segments through the use of the IDirectMusicPerformance8::PlaySegmentEx function:

```
HRESULT IDirectMusicPerformance8::PlaySegmentEx(
   IUnknown *pSource,       // segment to play
   WCHAR *pwzSegmentName,   // NULL - not used
   IUknown *pTransition,    // transition segment - use NULL
   DWORD dwFlags,           // flags to modify behavior
   __int64 i64Starttime,    // when to start playing
                            // use 0 for immediately
   IDirectMusicSegmentState **ppSegmentState, // pointer to
                    // object to receive a segment state object
   IUnknown *pFrom,         // NULL
   IUnknown *pAudioPath);   // audio path to use, or
                            // NULL for default one
```

Wow! That's a lot to take in; luckily, you really don't have to use all these arguments.

You can see that the segment pointer is the first argument, but what's a *segment state*? This is an object that tracks the status of the segment. You don't need this segment state object, so just set it to NULL.

The behavior flags allow you to alter the starting time of the segment, whether it starts on a beat measure, is aligned to prior tempos, or what have you. Because you're now interested only with playing the song, just skip the flags and tell the PlaySegmentEx function to play immediately.

You can kick-start your segment playing by calling the following code bit:

```
if(FAILED(g_pDMPerformance->PlaySegmentEx(g_pDMSegment,           \
                NULL, NULL, 0, 0, NULL, NULL, NULL))) {
  // Error occurred
}
```

To stop the segment from playing, use a call to IDirectMusicPerformance8::Stop:

```
HRESULT IDirectMusicPerformance8::Stop(
  IDirectMusicSegment *pSegment,              // segment to stop
  IDirectMusicSegmentState *pSegmentState,  // segstate to stop
  MUSIC_TIME mtTime,            // time to stop (0 for immediate)
  DWORD dwFlags);              // stop timing behaviors
```

Again, this call takes the segment as an argument as well as the time you want it to stop. All that information isn't required; you just provide the pointer to the segment object and the time to stop playing, as in the following:

```
if(FAILED(g_pDMPerformance::Stop(g_pDMSegment, NULL, 0, 0))) {
  // Error occurred
}
```

## Unloading Segment Data

After you've stopped a segment and are done with it, be sure to unload the instrument data:

```
pDMSegment->Unload(g_pDMPerformance);
```

You also need to have the loader to release the cached data using a call to IDirectMusicLoader8::ReleaseObjectByUnknown:

```
HRESULT IDirectMusicLoader8::ReleaseObjectByUnknown(
  IUnknown *pObject);
```

ReleaseObjectByUnknown takes one parameter—the pointer to the segment object you are unloading. Once the segment object is unloaded, you can release the segment COM object. Here's how to perform these two calls:

```
g_pDMLoader->ReleaseObjectByUnknown(pDMSegment);
pDMSegment->Release();
```

Also, if you've loaded an instrument collection, now is the time to unload it from the loader object as well, just as you did when releasing the music segment. To make clearing the cache easier, there is a single call that you can use to force the entire cache to clear. You don't need to call it before releasing the loader, as it does it automatically.

> **NOTE**
>
> You must unload the cache data only when you're sure that a new segment you're loading doesn't need the cached information. If you are loading a separate song, unloading is safe practice.

Clear the cache like this:

```
g_pDMLoader->ClearCache(GUID_DirectMusicAllTypes);
```

# Altering Music

You can do a number of things to music, including altering volume levels, changing the tempo, and applying special effects by using a DirectSound sound buffer object. Take a look at each method.

## Volume Settings

You can alter two volume settings—the volume of the entire performance object (and music system in general) and an individual segment's playback volume. As illustrated in Figure 8.16, each segment undergoes a volume change when passed to the performance object. The performance object is then affected by the global volume.

The performance volume (master volume) is represented as a global parameter and, as such, uses a call to IDirectMusicPerformance8::SetGlobalParam to set it:

```
HRESULT IDirectMusicPerformance8::SetGlobalParam(
   REFGUID rguidType,   // global param to set
   void *pParam,        // new param value
   DWORD dwSize);       // size of param data
```

The rguidType parameter is a GUID to the global parameter you need to set, which, in this case, is GUID_PerfMasterVolume. You can change many global parameters, so be sure to check out the DX SDK documents for more information.

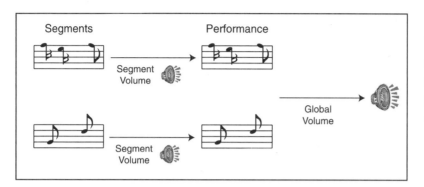

**Figure 8.16**

*Whereas each segment alters only its volume level, the global volume affects all segments.*

The pParam parameter is the volume level you need to set. The dwSize value is the size of a long value, which is the size of a variable you're using to store the volume level. DirectMusic uses two macros, called DMUS_VOLUME_MIN (-200 decibels) and DMUS_VOLUME_MAX (+20 decibels), to define the minimum and maximum volume settings. By using a value between these two macro values, you can specify the amount of attenuation in decibels.

You can simplify the volume level by creating a quick formula that uses percentages rather than levels to measure the volume. The percentages range from 0 to 100, with 0 representing no sound and 100 representing a slightly amplified volume level. That's right—the highest volume level amplifies the sound (and sometimes distorts it!), so be sure to set the appropriate level.

Here's a little function you can use to set the master volume level by specifying a percentage value from 0 to 100:

```
BOOL SetMasterVolume(long Level)
{
  long Volume, Range;

  // Get range of volume levels and calculate new volume level
  Range = labs(DMUS_VOLUME_MAX - DMUS_VOLUME_MIN);  // 220
  Volume = DMUS_VOLUME_MIN + Range / 100 * Level;

  // set the new volume level
  if(FAILED(g_pDMPerformance->SetParam(GUID_PerfMasterVolume, \
          &Volume, sizeof(long))))
    return FALSE;
  return TRUE;
}
```

You set the music segment volume by grabbing the audio path interface and then using it to set the new volume level. Because you've already created a default audio path, retrieving the pointer to it is easy using the following function:

```
HRESULT IDirectMusicPerformance8::GetDefaultAudioPath(
  IDirectMusicAudioPath8 **ppAudioPath);
```

This function takes only one parameter—the pointer to the IDirectMusicAudioPath8 object that you are using. Once you get the audio path pointer, you can use the IDirectMusicAudioPath8::SetVolume function:

```
HRESULT IDirectMusicAudioPath8::SetVolume(
  long lVolume,          // volume level to set
  DWORD dwDuration);  // time (milliseconds) taken for change
```

The volume level is ranged from -600 (silence) to 0 (full volume). There is no amplification here. The duration should be 0 to ease the strain on the processor. Setting the dwDuration to 0 also tells the music system to change the volume immediately.

Instead of having to specify volume levels in the range of -600 to 0, why not just specify the values as a percentage? You can create a simple function, much as the one I'm about to show you, that calculates the volume level. Using this volume level, you can obtain the audio path object and alter the volume, as shown here:

```
BOOL SetSegmentVolume(IDirectMusicSegment8 *pDSSegment,        \
                       long Level)
{
  long Volume;
  IDirectMusicAudioPath8 *pDMAudioPath;

  // Get the audio path object to work with
  if(FAILED(g_pDMPerformance->GetDefaultAudioPath(              \
           &pDMAudioPath)))
    return FALSE;

  // Calculate a volume setting then set it using the
  // audio path object
  Volume = -96 * (100-Level);
  if(FAILED(pDMAudioPath->SetVolume(Volume, 0))) {
    pDMAudioPath->Release();
    return FALSE;
  }
```

```
// release the audio path object and return a success
pDMAudioPath->Release();
return TRUE;
}
```

## Tempo Changes

Imagine being able to change the tempo of your music slightly, altering the game-play in such a way that the user knows something is going on. For example, when your player nears a monster that wants to fight, the tempo picks up, and you know there's trouble.

The tempo is measured in *beats per minute* (BPM), with a typical BPM being 120. In DirectMusic, you can change the tempo a number of ways. The easiest way is to adjust the *performance master tempo* by a scaling factor. For example, setting a scale of 0.5 cuts the tempo in half, whereas a scale of 2.0 doubles the tempo.

You accomplish this by setting a global parameter, which you've already done. This time, however, you alter the `GUID_PerfMasterTempo` setting using a scaling factor of the data type float. Here's a quick function for doing so. I've changed it so that you specify a percentage value instead of a scaling factor, which makes setting the tempo a little easier:

```
BOOL SetTempo(long Percent)
{
  float Tempo;

  Tempo = (float)Percent / 100.0f;
  if(FAILED(g_pDMPerformance->SetGlobalParam(              \
      GUID_PerfMasterTempo, (void*)&Tempo, sizeof(float)))
    return FALSE;
  return TRUE;
}
```

The only catch here is that it may take a couple seconds for the tempo change to take effect because of the beat timing. Also, remember that `SetTempo` affects the global tempo, so all segments played are scaled. You should reset the tempo to normal (1.0, or 100%) whenever you're done with a song.

## Grabbing an Audio Channel

Last in this long list of music features is the ability you have to grab a DirectSound sound buffer object that is used to synthesize the instruments and music. You can do this by retrieving an audio path object and then using it to snatch a sound buffer interface.

In Figure 8.17, you can see the default flow of data from the performance object through the audio path to the synthesizer. You want to intercept that flow and alter it in any way that you desire.

This is the purpose of the `IDirectMusicAudioPath8::GetObjectInPath` function:

```
HRESULT IDirectMusicAudioPath8::GetObjectInPath(
    DWORD dwPChannel,        // DMUS_PCHANNEL_ALL (search channel)
    DWORD dwStage,           // DMUS_PATH_BUFFER (stage in path)
    DWORD dwBuffer,          // 0 (index in buffer chain)
    REFGUID guidObject,      // GUID_NULL (class of object)
    DWORD dwIndex,           // 0 (index of object in buffer)
    REFGUID iidInterface,    // GUID of desired object
    void ** ppObject);       // pointer to object to create
```

To grab a sound object, you just specify its GUID and give it a pointer to set. The following function will get the default audio path from a performance object and get you an `IDirectSoundBuffer8` object with which to play:

```
IDirectSoundBuffer8 *GetSoundBuffer()
{
    IDirectMusicAudioPath8 *pDMAudioPath;
    IDirectSoundBuffer *pDMB;
    IDirectSoundBuffer8 *pDSBuffer;

    // get the default audio path
    if(FAILED(g_pDMPerformance->GetDefaultAudioPath(              \
              &pDMAudioPath)))
        return NULL;
```

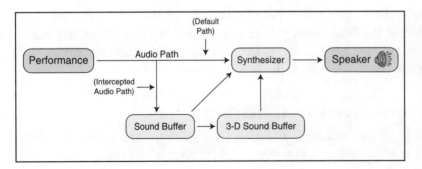

**Figure 8.17**

*Hijacking an audio path makes it possible to use DirectSound buffers (normal and 3-D) to create some awesome effects.*

```
  // create an IDirectSoundBuffer object then release
  // audio path object
  if(FAILED(pDMAudioPath->GetObjectInPath(DMUS_PCHANNEL_ALL, \
            DMUS_PATH_BUFFER, 0, GUID_NULL, 0,                \
            IID_IDirectSoundBuffer, (LPVOID*)*pDSB))) {
    pDMAudioPath->Release();
    return FALSE;
  }
  pDMAudioPath->Release();

  // query for newer sound buffer object and return it
  if(FAILED(pDSB->QueryInterface(IID_IDirectSoundBuffer8,    \
            (void**)&pDSBuffer))) {
    pDSB->Release();
    return FALSE;
  }
  pDSB->Release();

  return pDSBuffer;
}
```

You can alter the preceding function to query for a 3D buffer interface just by changing the interface ID to IID_IDirectSound3DBuffer8. However, be sure to release the new object when you're done with it.

# Finishing Up Sound

DirectX Audio is one tough customer. With two complex components (DirectSound and DirectMusic) to deal with, you have your hands full trying to figure out all the intricate details of each one. You create sound buffers and load them with sound data, weed through instrument data, and load and play musical segments.

Fortunately, you have this chapter at your disposal! With the information in this chapter, you'll be able to use streaming playback techniques, custom DLS instruments, and special playback effects such as altering volume, panning, and frequency settings.

This chapter covers a good deal of information that you will find highly useful in your programming endeavors. In addition, Chapter 10 tells you exactly how to use these techniques to create a library of handy sound and music functions.

## Programs on the CD-ROM

Programs that demonstrate the code discussed in this chapter are on the CD-ROM at the back of this book. You can find the following programs in the \BookCode\Chap8\ directory:

- ◆ **Shell.** A shell application that initializes DirectSound and DirectMusic. Location: \BookCode\Chap08\Shell\.

- ◆ **LockLoad.** A program that creates, locks, and loads sound buffers with random noise. Location: \BookCode\Chap08\LockLoad\.

- ◆ **WavPlay.** A program that loads small wave files (.WAV) and plays them back. Location: \BookCode\Chap08\WavPlay\.

- ◆ **Stream.** A program that loads a single wave file (.WAV) and uses streaming techniques to play. Location: \BookCode\Chap08\Stream\.

- ◆ **MidiPlay.** A program that loads a .MID file and plays it. Location: \BookCode\Chap08\MidiPlay\.

# CHAPTER 9

# NETWORKING WITH DIRECTPLAY

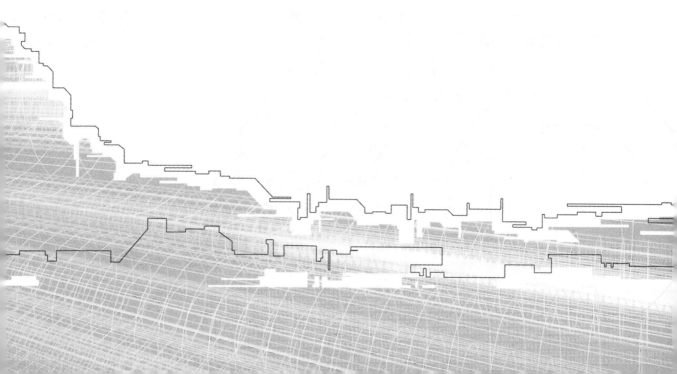

I still remember the late nights that I spent slumped over my computer hacking away at hordes of monsters, looking for treasure, and just having a good-old time with a couple of my Internet buddies. Heck, what am I talking about; I'm still that way!

Internet (and intranet) gaming has changed the world of gaming and made multi-player-gaming features a standard. No longer are gamers content with beating the tar out of the computer; they now want to test their skills on each other. In order for your game to stand a chance in today's demanding market, you'll need to give your players this ability. You, too, can add networking to your growing list of game features with the aid of Microsoft's DirectPlay.

In this chapter, you learn how to do the following:

- Understand networking
- Work with DirectPlay's interfaces
- Handle network messages
- Work with servers and clients

# Understanding Networking

A *network* is a system of computers connected to each other for data transfer and communications. In addition to two or more computers, a network requires net-working software (or *network operating system*), network adapters, and cables. Network adapters come in many shapes and sizes, but generally a network adapter takes the form of a modem. That's right; your modem is a network adapter that is capable of connecting you to millions of other computers over the world's largest network—the Internet.

In this chapter, I focus on networking from the perspective of programming and playing games. At first glance, networking might seem a little intimidating. With so many computers passing an endless stream of data, how and what can you possibly do to understand it all? As with all things, you need to start at the beginning and learn the concepts behind a network; then you can build your knowledge based on actual (and simple) examples.

# Network Models

There are three basic types of networking models: *server, client,* and *peer-to-peer.* Each model connects computers together in order to share information in one form or another. Which model you use is really up to you, but depending on your needs, each application has its pros and cons.

You use the server to create a centralized networking system. Other computers using the client model connect to the server and begin sending and receiving information from it.

Clients have no knowledge or direct link to other clients; they only know about the server. The server knows about all clients and routes information among them as it sees fit. Figure 9.1 shows the relationship between the server and client models.

> **NOTE**
>
> The server and client pair is usually described as one, the *server/client mode,* but when using DirectPlay, the separation is necessary because the server and client are composed of two separate components.

The third type of networking model is peer-to-peer, in which the computers connect to each other directly, as opposed to the server or client model. A new link is established for each new computer joining a network session, so each computer knows about the other computers. As illustrated in Figure 9.2, a network with four computers has 12 connections (remember that each computer has a connection for each of the other three computers).

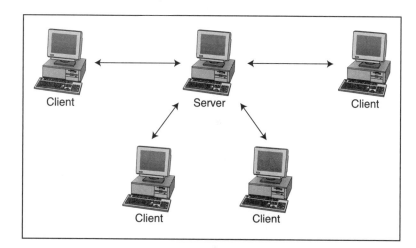

**Figure 9.1**

*Clients can connect to the server, but clients have no knowledge of each other.*

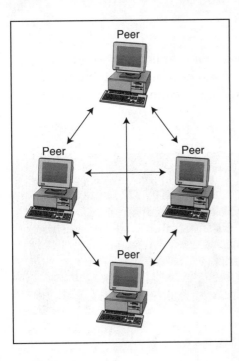

**Figure 9.2**

*Computers using the peer-to-peer network model create a link to every computer on the network.*

The type of network model that is best for you depends on the application that you're using. Client/server models are best suited for networks that have more than four users, whereas peer-to-peer models are best suited for direct connections or small-scale networks.

A major problem when dealing with a large number of networked computers is trying to locate other players. Although you might normally play with certain friends (and definitely know where to find them), what if that is not the case or you want to find somebody new with whom to play? In that case, network games typically use a lobby server.

**NOTE**

The time in which you're connected to a network is called a *session*. A session can have properties associated with it, such as a password, the maximum number of connections, and so on. In Chapter 19, "Getting Online with Multiplayer Gaming," you learn how this information relates to gaming.

**NOTE**

Some games use a peer-to-peer model because they generally only allow four to eight players. For example, *Diablo* (by Blizzard Entertainment) allows four players to connect. On the other hand, a game like *Ultima Online* (by Origin Systems) can handle thousands of players using the client/server model.

# Lobbies

You can think of a *lobby server* as a meeting hall for online gamers. A lobby enables all players to log in, communicate, and join in a round of their favorite game. Once the lobby server connects the players, the lobby is cut out of the loop (to save network bandwidth).

You can find a great lobby server at Microsoft's Gaming Zone Web site (at http://zone.msn.com). This lobby enables thousands of players to link to each other and then connects them directly for a go at their favorite network-enabled games. The Gaming Zone supports many games, and if you program your game right, it might even support yours!

> **NOTE**
> Network *bandwidth* refers to the amount of data that a network connection can handle with ease. For example, a high-bandwidth connection can handle large amounts of network data faster than a low-bandwidth connection can.

Although lobbies are helpful to multiplayer games, a discussion on using lobby servers is beyond the scope of this book. The DirectX SDK help files contain a great deal of information on using lobby servers, and included with the SDK are a number of lobby server-enabled applications in which you can browse. Consult the DX SDK for more information on those applications (you can find the DX SDK on this book's CD-ROM).

# Latency and Lag

Bandwidth brings up two new terms: latency and lag. *Latency* is the amount of time it takes for an operation to complete (the lower, the better). *Lag* is the word used to describe the delay in networking communications—the time from which the data is sent to the time it is received.

A low-lag means that network data is received quickly. High-lag (an undesirable thing) means that network data is delayed or not delivered at all. Lag is a major problem, especially when dealing with the Internet, and it's up to you to deal with it.

# Communication Protocols

Networks can communicate with each other in a variety of ways, but in order to understand one another, two systems must use the same protocol. Currently, the most popular protocol is TCP/IP *(Transfer Control Protocol/Internet Protocol),* the one used over the Internet, and the only one that I deal with in this book.

The TCP/IP protocol is a method of packaging data and sending it over the network. It does this by splitting the data into small packets, adding the sender and receiver addresses as well as the packet number used to reassemble it (as illustrated in Figure 9.3). These packets are whisked off into the great unknown, hopefully to make their way to a destination system.

> **NOTE**
>
> Communication protocols are also referred to as *service providers*. Think of a service provider as your interface to a network, whether it's a protocol such as IPX, TCP/IP, or a device such as a modem or serial cable.

TCP/IP enables a network to resend packets, just in case information is lost during the transfer (something that happens frequently). When lag becomes an issue, these packets can even be received in the wrong order, with older packets arriving after newer ones. Don't worry though; TCP/IP takes care of resending lost packets and rearranging out-of-order packets.

## Addressing

With so many computer systems on the Internet, how does the data know where to go? Just as envelopes are addressed before being mailed, with the TCP/IP protocol, a system is assigned a network address (an *IP address*) that consists of four numbers (ranging from 0 to 255), and each number is separated by a period. An IP address might look like this:

64.120.53.2

Although gibberish to us, the networks are able to successfully route data based on each value. If you do the math, you'll also see that those four numbers combined

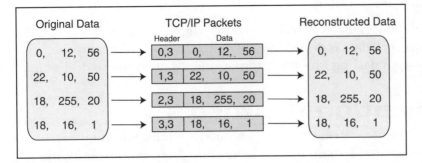

**Figure 9.3**

*TCP/IP splits data into packets and appends its own header information to them. The header contains the packet number, sender's address and the intended target's address.*

give you a total of 4,294,967,296 possible addresses. To increase the number of addresses, networks use additional address values, called *ports,* to which data is delivered.

Think of an IP address as a mailroom. This mailroom (IP address) represents a single computer system hooked to the network; that computer system is assigned only one IP address. Inside this mailroom are many bins (or ports) into which the mail is sorted. Each bin (port) belongs to a particular office (a particular application).

Some applications have multiple ports. Data is received only by a system that knows which IP address and which port to look in. A device called a *data router* directs incoming network data to a system that the router knows, or it passes the network data on to another network connection (called a *pass-along network*). Figure 9.4 illustrates the route that network data can flow via a data router.

# Introducing DirectPlay

DirectPlay is Microsoft's solution to the networking confusion. Although DirectPlay has undergone some major changes over the last few versions, it appears as though Microsoft has finally developed an easy-to-use system in version 8. So easy, in fact, that you'll be up and networking before you know it!

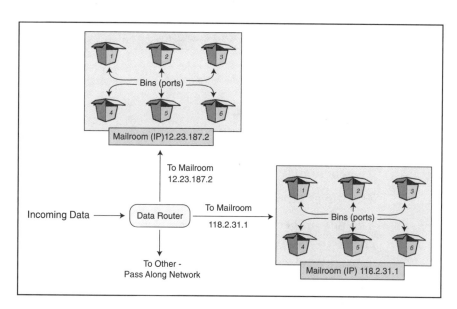

**Figure 9.4**

*A mailroom (IP address) has multiple bins (ports) to sort the incoming data. Multiple mailrooms can be connected to a data router.*

# The Network Objects

Using DirectPlay, you have access to the three network models that I mentioned earlier: client, server, and peer-to-peer. Each has its own interface object (as described in Table 9.1), all sharing similar functions.

To connect to a remote network system (or to host a *session*), you construct a network address using `IDirectPlay8Address` (shown in Table 9.1). Its sole purpose is to construct and contain a single network address.

> **NOTE**
>
> Large-scale role-playing games usually require a client/server setup to run efficiently, so I'll forgo the peer-to-peer network models in this book. Check out the DirectX SDK for examples on using it or take a look at Appendix C, "Recommended Reading," for some resources. For information on using peer-to-peer networking models for gaming, I suggest *Multiplayer Game Programming*, by Todd Barron.

> **NOTE**
>
> As I mentioned earlier, a *session* refers to the time you are hosting or are joined to a networked system. When you terminate that connection, the session is over. Each session has unique properties, such as name, password (if any), maximum number of users allowed, and so on. You learn more about sessions in the section "Configuring Session Information," later in this chapter.

## Table 9.1  DirectPlay COM Objects

| Object | Description |
| --- | --- |
| `IDirectPlay8Client` | The client network object. Connects to a server. |
| `IDirectPlay8Server` | The server network object. Connects to clients. |
| `IDirectPlay8Peer` | The peer-to-peer network object. Connects clients to other clients. |
| `IDirectPlay8Address` | An object that contains (and constructs) network addresses. |

After you create the network object and assign it an address, you are ready to host a game session or to connect to a remote system. To host a game, you simply wait for other systems (that is the people using the systems) to connect to you, at which point your system and the remote system begin transferring game-related network messages to each other. DirectPlay refers to those remote systems (as well as your computer), as *players.*

## Working with Players

In DirectPlay terms, a *player* is a single connection (usually a game player) that connects to another computer over the network. A single computer can have several players, but generally only one. In fact, a server is assigned as a player in order to identify it.

Each player receives an identification number *(Player ID)* that the system uses to direct messages to the individual players. These numbers are the only trusted method of tracking players, so you need to set up your program to keep track of them.

For large-scale games, you could have thousands of connected players. In order to improve handling of all the players in the game, some (or all) of the players can be assigned to *groups.* Using groups eases programming chores a little bit, primarily because you can group a series of players who are in a single game area (such as a map or level) and send network data to the entire group at once, rather than to each player individually. (There are a number of other reasons to use groups, but this is the most significant one.)

This relationship among players and groups is illustrated in Figure 9.5. There are no restrictions on the number of players in a group and no restrictions on the number of groups that you can create. As you can also see in Figure 9.5, groups (denoted by an enclosed box) can also belong to other groups (Groups 1 and 2 belong to Group 3 in the figure). Notice that Players 7 and 8 are isolated from the groups; it doesn't matter to DirectPlay whether a player belongs to a group or not.

Regardless of the way you group (or don't group) the game's players, once a connection is in place, the systems can begin communicating with each other via messages.

## Networking with Messages

A *message* is a categorized packet of data, wrapped inside a simple structure. Each message has a specific meaning, is assigned a macro (as shown in Table 9.2), and is dependent on the network model that you are using. For example, a client object will never receive a message intended for peer objects.

**Figure 9.5**

*Eight players are connected to a game session. Six of the players belong to a group (or two groups), while two players remain separate from all groups.*

In order to receive messages, your network object must have assigned itself a callback function that is called every time a message comes in. To ensure a smooth flow of data, this function parses the data based on its type and returns as quickly as possible.

To send messages, you use each network object's send function (of which there are two). These functions are easy to use, and they provide you with many delivery options, including guaranteed delivery, secure encryption, and asynchronous or synchronous delivery.

## Asynchronous and Synchronous

The first delivery option that DirectPlay provides you is the ability to send messages *asynchronously* or *synchronously*. This means that the system returns control to you after you give it the command to send data (asynchronous) or that it will wait until all the data is successfully sent (synchronous).

> **NOTE**
>
> Although some of the messages might not make sense at this moment, the descriptions give you the low-down. There are surprisingly few messages with which to work, but this is a case of when less is more.

> **NOTE**
>
> DirectPlay's network messages and their related information can be found in the DirectX SDK documents. I recommend that you keep that document open while creating your masterpiece.

## Table 9.2  Standard DirectPlay Messages

| Message Macro | Description |
| --- | --- |
| DPN_MSGID_ADD_PLAYER_TO_GROUP | A player was added to an existing group. |
| DPN_MSGID_APPLICATION_DESC | Application data was requested. |
| DPN_MSGID_ASYNC_OP_COMPLETE | An asynchronous send-data operation has completed. |
| DPN_MSGID_CLIENT_INFO | Client data was requested. |
| DPN_MSGID_CONNECT_COMPLETE | A network connection was completed. |
| DPN_MSGID_CREATE_GROUP | A group was created. |
| DPN_MSGID_CREATE_PLAYER | A player was created. |
| DPN_MSGID_DESTROY_GROUP | A group was destroyed (removed). |
| DPN_MSGID_DESTROY_PLAYER | A player was destroyed (removed). |
| DPN_MSGID_ENUM_HOSTS_QUERY | Signifies that another network application is looking for others with which to connect. |
| DPN_MSGID_ENUM_HOSTS_RESPONSE | A message to allow you to respond to a host query. |
| DPN_MSGID_GROUP_INFO | Group data was requested. |
| DPN_MSGID_HOST_MIGRATE | A host has moved its data to another system because of loss of connection. |
| DPN_MSGID_INDICATE_CONNECT | Signifies that a remote system is trying to connect. |
| DPN_MSGID_INDICATED_CONNECT_ABORTED | Informs you that the remote connecting system aborted its connection attempt. |
| DPN_MSGID_PEER_INFO | Peer-to-peer data was requested. |
| DPN_MSGID_RECEIVE | Data was received. |
| DPN_MSGID_REMOVE_PLAYER_FROM_GROUP | A player was removed from a group. |
| DPN_MSGID_RETURN_BUFFER | Lets you know that DirectPlay is done with a buffer that you previously gave it. |
| DPN_MSGID_SEND_COMPLETE | Data was sent successfully. |
| DPN_MSGID_SERVER_INFO | Server data was requested. |
| DPN_MSGID_TERMINATE_SESSION | A network session has terminated. |

Which is the best option? The asynchronous (async) method is most likely the one you'll want to use; it doesn't hold up the system as the synchronous (sync) method does. For example, if you're sending a large amount of data and trying to play a game at the same time, you don't want a break in the action while the network tries to send all the data. Just tell it to send, let DirectPlay handle it, and let the player go on as though nothing happened.

## Security

It's scary to know that at any given time someone might be intercepting and recording your network data. For this reason, you have the option to encrypt message data in a secure manner, making it much harder for those unscrupulous hackers to read your precious information.

The downside is that using secure network delivery will slow the system a bit because it must encrypt the message before it is sent and then decrypt the message after it is received. If you're sending crucial information, time really isn't the issue (but it is an issue for games).

DirectPlay has built-in support for secure messages. Fortunately, using it is as easy as specifying a single flag during a send operation. Now that's a big burden off your shoulders.

## Guaranteed Delivery

Just as some parcel delivery companies guarantee the arrival of a package, so can DirectPlay guarantee the arrival of messages. You can signify a message as guaranteed and rest assured that DirectPlay will get it to its destination (short of being disconnected) by continually performing the send operation until successful. Using guaranteed delivery is accomplished through a specific flag unique to the calling function, as you will see in the section "Sending Server Messages," later in this chapter.

The downside to guaranteed delivery is speed. Guaranteed delivery is much too slow to use in a real gaming situation. Games use a UDP *(User Datagram Protocol)* delivery method—which doesn't care whether data is received. You might think that's crazy, but when you come down to it, games send updated information so often that it's acceptable to lose a little data every now and then.

## Throttling

At times, your system can become overloaded trying to handle the flow of messages. However, DirectPlay has a built-in message-throttle system that discards low-priority messages from the send queue.

Perhaps Figure 9.6 can help you visualize the concept of using a throttling mechanism. As you look at the figure, imagine a line of people waiting in front of the hottest nightclub in town. Each patron represents a *message,* and the bouncers *(throttling mechanisms)* must weed those of lesser importance from the line when things get too busy.

> **NOTE**
> DirectPlay handles throttling excellently, so you typically don't have to mess around with its default settings.

# From Small Bytes to Big Words

The world is a big place and because we're all different, there are times when a happy medium is needed. Actually, what I'm talking about are language barriers, specifically the computer language barrier.

DirectPlay introduces you to the world of Unicode (if you're not already familiar with it). *Unicode* is a universal standard that enables different programs and computers to share information. Because a network can communicate with another network anywhere in the world, your game players might live in different countries and speak different languages.

Because Windows operates a little differently in each country, the users' systems might be configured to use Unicode characters (refer to Chapter 5, "Programming with Windows and Application Basics," for a description of Unicode).

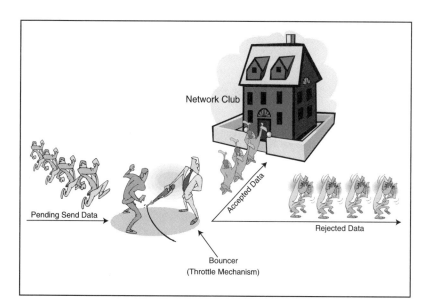

**Figure 9.6**

*A throttling mechanism (the bouncer) allows or rejects messages (patrons) based on their importance.*

As a result, the entire DirectPlay system is built around using Unicode characters (a single character uses 16 bits instead of 8 bits to store data), accommodating languages that use more than 256 characters. I can hear you groaning, so let me just say that Windows has all the functions you need to convert between the two character formats; there's nothing to worry about.

# Identifying Applications with GUIDs

Because there are so many network applications, how do you keep yours apart from others? Assign your application a unique number and allow only applications using the same number to connect with each other. This special number is, of course, the GUID *(Global Unique Identification)* familiar to Windows programmers.

When you create your application, take a few moments to give it a unique GUID and make sure that all applications needing to interface over the network with it use the same GUID.

That's really about all there is to sending data. The flow from creating a DirectPlay network object to sending and receiving data is strikingly similar for each object, so I'll be interweaving some of the information as I go along.

> **NOTE**
> The only way to generate a **GUID** is by using Microsoft's guidgen.exe program (usually located in the \common\tools subdirectory of the Visual C/C++ installation directory). To generate a **GUID**, locate and run the guidgen.exe file. Select option #4, "Registry Format," and click Copy (to copy the **GUID** onto the Clipboard). Open a source code file into which you can paste the **GUID**. Paste the **GUID** into your code by selecting Edit, Paste or by pressing Ctrl+V.

# Initializing a Network Object

The first step in using DirectPlay is to create a network object, whether it's a server, client, or peer.

To initialize each one of the network model interfaces, DirectPlay gives you a single helper function that handles all of them:

> **NOTE**
> To use DirectPlay in your projects, you need to include a dplay8.h and dpaddr.h header file, plus link in dplay.lib, dpnet.lib, and dpnaddr.lib.

```
HRESULT DirectPlay8Create(
  GUID *pcIID,           // GUID pointer to type of interface:
```

```
                         // &IID_IDirectPlay8Server
                         // &IID_IDirectPlay8Client
                         // &IID_IDirectPlay8Peer
void **ppvInterface,    // Pointer to receive interface object
IUnknown *pUnknown);    // NULL
```

> **CAUTION**
>
> To be on the safe side, always initialize the COM system before call-
> ing any DirectPlay functions. DirectPlay is supposed to initialize the
> COM system, but sometimes that just doesn't happen as planned,
> in which case your application might crash.
>
> For applications that do not use multiple threads (single-threaded),
> add the following line before any other DirectX calls:
>
> `CoInitialize(NULL);`
>
> On the other hand, if you are using multi-threading, use the following
> function call:
>
> `CoInitializeEx(NULL, COINIT_MULTITHREADED);`
>
> When your application is done, always be sure to call `CoUninitialize`,
> as follows:
>
> `CoUninitialize();`

The comments pretty much say it all, but you begin to notice one thing from here
on—DirectPlay uses pointers to the pointers of variables (unlike other DX objects).
So, to initialize a server network object, do the following:

```
IDirectPlay8Server *pDPServer;

if(FAILED(DirectPlay8Create(&IID_IDirectPlay8Server,            \
                            (void**)&pDPServer, NULL)) {
  // Error occurred
}
```

> **TIP**
>
> In the call to `DirectPlay8Create`,
> to use a different network model,
> you just change the object
> instance and **GUID** to the net-
> work object type you are creating.

To use any of the network model interfaces, the only other step is to assign the network object a callback function, which is called any time that a network message is received. This function takes the following prototype:

```
typedef HRESULT (WINAPI *PFNDPNMESSAGEHANDLER)(
    PVOID pvUserContext,    // An application specified pointer
    DWORD dwMessageType,    // The type of message received
    PVOID pMessage);        // Buffer with message-specific data
```

The pvUserContext is a pointer to anything you want to associate with the player; you set the pointer during the creation of a player. pvUserContext could be the pointer to a structure holding the game state or whatever you wish. The dwMessageType and pMessage arguments relate to messages, which you learn about in the section "Receiving Data," later in this chapter.

For now, you can skip the actual callback function and continue with the initialization of the network object. To complete the initialization, you call the following function:

```
HRESULT IDirectPlay8Server::Initialize(
    PVOID const pvUserContext,      // User specified data pointer
    const PFDNPMESSAGEHANDLER pfn,  // Message callback function
    const DWORD dwFlags);           // 0
```

Here's an example of creating your own callback function (just the prototype for now) and initializing the server network object just created:

> **NOTE**
>
> This function also works for each model (using the same argument lists):
>
> ```
> HRESULT IDirectPlay8Client::Initialize(...);
> HRESULT IDirectPlay8Peer::Initialize(...);
> ```

```
// Callback function prototype
HRESULT WINAPI MessageHandler(PVOID pvUserContext,              \
          DWORD dwMessageId, PVOID pMsgBuffer);

// Initialize the pre-created pDPServer object
if(FAILED(pDPServer->Initialize(NULL, MessageHandler, 0))) {
    // Error occurred
}
```

That's all there is to creating and initializing the network objects. The next step is creating an address object.

# Using Addresses

As you previously read, a network uses an IP address and port to deliver its data. In DirectPlay, you construct this address in its own special object, IDirectPlay8Address. The address object has a number of functions for you to use, but you work with only three in this book (as shown in Table 9.3).

## Initializing the Address Object

Before you can use the address object, you need to create it using the DirectPlay8AddressCreate helper function:

```
HRESULT DirectPlay8AddressCreate(
  GUID *pcIID,            // &IID_IDirectPlay8Address
  void ** ppvInterface,  // pointer to interface object
  IUnknown *pUnknown);   // NULL
```

Not much is going on here; you just specify that you are creating an address object and give it the pointer to the object you are creating:

```
IDirectPlay8Address pDPAddress;  // no need for global instance

if(FAILED(DirectPlay8AddressCreate(&IID_IDirectPlay8Address, \
                          (void**)&pDPAddress, NULL))) {
  // Error occurred
}
```

### Table 9.3  IDirectPlay8Address Functions

| Function | Description |
| --- | --- |
| IDirectPlay8Address::Clear | Clears all address data. |
| IDirectPlay8Address::SetSP | Sets the service provider. |
| IDirectPlay8Address::AddComponent | Adds an address component. |

# Adding Components

An address object is simply one that contains a string of Unicode text. This text string contains the service provider, port number, and other optional information. Its only purpose is to build this string for other objects to use.

In order to add a component to the address object, use the IDirectPlay8Address::AddComponent function:

```
HRESULT IDirectPlay8Address::AddComponent(
    const WCHAR *const pwszName,   // Name of component to set.
    const void *const lpvData,     // Buffer containing component
                                   // information you are setting.
    const DWORD dwDataSize,        // Size of above data buffer.
    const DWORD dwDataType);       // Type of data being sent.
```

This little function requires a good deal of description, so let's take it slow. The first argument, pwszName, is a pointer to a Unicode string containing the component to be added. DirectPlay has macros that define these components, as shown in Table 9.4.

The buffer you send to the AddComponent function via lpvData depends on the type of component you are sending, but it always takes the form of a string (Unicode or

## Table 9.4  Component Name Macros

| Component | Macro |
| --- | --- |
| Provider | DPNA_KEY_PROVIDER |
| Network device | DPNA_KEY_DEVICE |
| Port number | DPNA_KEY_PORT |
| Host name/address | DPNA_KEY_HOSTNAME |
| Phone number | DPNA_KEY_PHONENUMBER |
| Baud rate | DPNA_KEY_BAUD |
| Flow control | DPNA_KEY_FLOWCONTROL |
| Parity | DPNA_KEY_PARITY |
| Stop bits | DPNA_KEY_STOPBITS |

ANSI), double word (DWORD), GUID, or binary. This is the purpose of the dwDataType argument, which can be any of the macros shown in Table 9.5.

Last is the dwDataSize argument, which is the size of the data you are sending (DWORD, string length, GUID size, and so on). It's hard to imagine using this method for setting data, but doing so will make sense when you see the examples I provide in the section "Selecting a Port," later in this chapter. For now, take a look at Figure 9.7, which shows the components that you can add to the address object and each component's data type.

## Table 9.5  Component Data Types

| Type | Macro |
| --- | --- |
| String (Unicode) | DPNA_DATATYPE_STRING |
| String (ANSI) | DPNA_DATATYPE_STRING_ANSI |
| DWORD | DPNA_DATATYPE_DWORD |
| GUID | DPNA_DATATYPE_GUID |
| Binary | DPNA_DATATYPE_BINARY |

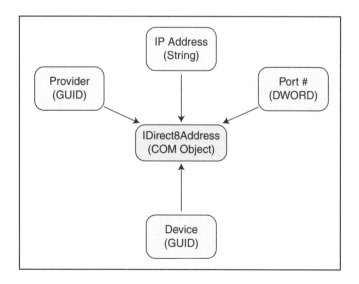

**Figure 9.7**

*The address object can hold various kinds of component information. Each component has its respective data type.*

# Setting the Service Provider

After you create the address object and understand the concept of components, the next thing to do is to select a service provider. This is the only setting that does not require the use of the AddComponent function. Instead, you use the IDirectPlay8Address::SetSP function:

```
HRESULT IDirectPlay8Address::SetSP(
  const GUID *const pguidSP);  // GUID of service provider
```

The GUID for each type of service provider is shown in Table 9.6. The choice is yours, but for this book, I use the TCP/IP service provider (CLSID_DP8SP_TCPIP).

To set the service provider utilizing what you've just read, you can use the following:

```
// Set the TCP/IP service provider
if(FAILED(pDPAddress->SetSP(&CLSID_DP8SP_TCPIP))) {
  // Error occurred
}
```

### Table 9.6  DirectPlay Service Providers

| Type | GUID |
| --- | --- |
| TCP/IP | CLSID_DP8SP_TCPIP |
| IPX | CLSID_DP8SP_IPX |
| Modem | CLSID_DP8SP_MODEM |
| Serial | CLSID_DP8SP_SERIAL |

# Selecting a Port

Next in line is to select a port, either to host a session (as a server or peer) or to connect to a remote system when using the client network model. If you are connecting to a remote system, you must know the port that an application is using in order to connect and send data to the remote system.

You set the port using the IDirectPlay8Address:AddComponent function. Although this is a confusing function, as you've already seen, you'll quickly see how easy it is to use.

**NOTE**

The port number you use is a matter of choice, but don't use a reserved one (1 to 1,024). Pick anything above those numbers, and you should be safe.

You can have DirectPlay pick a port for you by specifying 0 as the port number, but the downside is that the port could be anything, and you need to query for it. The preferred method is for you to select one.

Here's the call used to set a port using the AddComponent function:

```
// dwPort is a DWORD value representing the port # to use
if(FAILED(pDPAddress->AddComponent(DPNA_KEY_PORT, &dwPort,    \
         sizeof(DWORD), DPNA_DATATYPE_DWORD))) {
  // Error occurred
}
```

You can see that it's not hard to add components because DirectPlay makes it as easy as possible! At this point, you're pretty much finished with the address setup. What's left you ask?

# Assigning a Device

Even though you have selected a service provider, more than one device on your system might use it. Such is the case when you have a network adapter and a modem connected to the Internet—both use TCP/IP. In such cases, you must enumerate the devices and select.

Figure 9.8 illustrates an array of service providers. The enumerator grabs all the usable service providers and puts them together for you in a usable fashion. Enumeration with DirectPlay is a little different than the typical Windows method of enumeration; you do not use a callback function that is called every time an instance of the object in question is found. Instead, you ask for a buffer that contains every service provider in the form of an array of structures.

**TIP**

You can skip this step if there's only one adapter because DirectPlay will use the first occurrence of it.

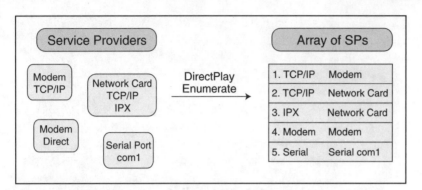

**Figure 9.8**

*Enumeration creates a list of every service provider on the system and places them all into an easily accessible array of providers.*

You handle enumeration using the following function (this also applies to the client and peer network objects):

```
HRESULT IDirectPlay8Server::EnumServiceProviders(
   const GUID *const pguidServiceProvider,  // GUID of the SP
   const GUID *const pguidApplication,      // NULL
   const DPN_SERVICE_PROVIDER_INFO *const pSPInfoBuffer,
   DWORD *const pcbEnumData,    // Pointer to DWORD holding size
                                // of data buffer.
   DWORD *const pcReturned,     // Pointer to DWORD holding #
                                // enumerated items in buffer.
   const DWORD dwFlags);        // 0
```

With this function, you pass the service provider GUID as the first argument (or NULL to specify all service providers). The pSPInfoBuffer is a pointer to an array of DPN_SERVICE_PROVIDER_INFO structures that this function will fill with the enumerated information. That structure is defined as follows:

```
typedef struct _DPN_SERVICE_PROVIDER {
   DWORD dwFlags;      // 0
   GUID  guid;         // Guid of device
   WCHAR *pwszName;    // Name of device
   PVOID pvReserved;   // 0
   DWORD dwReserved;   // 0
} DPN_SERVICE_PROVIDER;
```

When you call this function, give it a DWORD variable (such as pcdEnumData) that is filled with the total size of the data returned. This is here for one reason—to query the enumeration beforehand and ask for the size of the buffer in order to allocate the memory in which to store the enumeration data.

Here is an example that enumerates all TCP/IP service providers. This following example provides a list of devices in return that have access to this service provider, from which you can pick a device and use in the address object.

```
DPN_SERVICE_PROVIDER_INFO *pSP = NULL;
DPN_SERVICE_PROVIDER_INFO *pSPPtr;
DWORD dwSize = 0;
DWORD dwNumSP = 0;
DWORD i;


// Query the required size of the data buffer
hr = pDPServer->EnumServiceProviders(&CLSID_DP8SP_TCPIP,         \
            NULL, pSP, &dwSize, &dwNumSP, 0);
// return error code should be buffer too small if all OK
if(hr != DPNERR_BUFFERTOOSMALL) {
  // An unknown error occurred
} else {
  // Allocate a buffer and enumerate again
  pSP = (DPN_SERVICE_PROVIDER_INFO*)new BYTE[dwSize];
  if(SUCCEEDED(pDPServer->EnumServiceProviders(                  \
            &CLSID_DP8SP_TCPIP, NULL, pSP,                       \
            &dwSize, &dwNumSP, 0))) {

    // Enumeration is complete, scan through entries
    pSPPtr = pSP;
    for(i=0; i < dwNumSP; i++) {
      // pSPPtr->pwszName contains Unicode string of provider
      // pSPPtr->guid contains the GUID of the service provider

      pSPPtr++;  // go to next service provider in buffer
    }
  }

  // Delete data buffer memory
  delete[] pSP;
}
```

**TIP**

If you want to enumerate all service providers on the system rather than only TCP/IP, just substitute CLSID_DP8SP_TCPIP with NULL.

You'll most likely need to display the names of the service providers to the users in order for them to pick which one to use. The DirectX SDK comes with an example program called AddressOverride that shows you exactly how to do so.

When you have the service provider GUID, you can use it to complete the address. Do this with a call to IDirectPlay8Address::AddComponent function again, this time passing the GUID:

```
// guidSP is the GUID of the service provider
if(FAILED(pDPAddress->AddComponent(DPNA_KEY_PROVIDER,          \
        &guidSP, sizeof(GUID), DPNA_DATATYPE_GUID))) {
  // Error occurred
}
```

You now have a complete address component ready and waiting for use.

# Using Message Handlers

Before going much further, you must construct a message handler callback function. This function is really straightforward. It only needs to distinguish what kind of message was retrieved and handle it as quickly as possible. You can think of this message handler as a funnel, as illustrated in Figure 9.9.

You've seen the prototype already, so take a look at a sample function:

```
// Callback function prototype
HRESULT WINAPI MessageHandler(PVOID pvUserContext,          \
        DWORD dwMessageId, PVOID pMsgBuffer)
{
  switch(dwMessageId) {
    case DPN_MSGID_CREATE_PLAYER:
      // handle creation of player
      return S_OK;

    case DPN_MSGID_DESTROY_PLAYER:
      // handle removal of player
      return S_OK;
  }

  return E_FAIL;
}
```

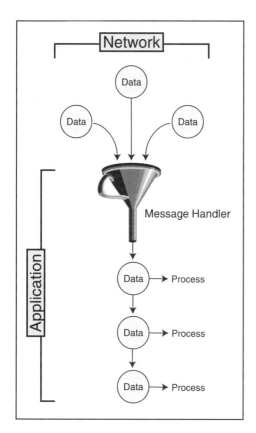

**Figure 9.9**

*The network object receives network messages and lets the message handler deal with those messages one-by-one.*

By creating a switch...case system, you can quickly scan for the messages you want, passing up the rest. Returning a value of S_OK signifies that you processed the message successfully. A return value of E_FAIL means that you did not.

Each message carries with it a data buffer, which is cast into the appropriate structure. These structures share almost the same naming scheme as the message macros, except that they start with DPNMSG_ rather than DPN_MSGID_, as in the following:

> **NOTE**
>
> DPNSUCCESS_PENDING **is a third return value that you see when learning how to deal with the server in the section "Receiving Data." Check out that section for information on this value.**

```
DPNMSG_CREATE_PLAYER  *pCreate;   // DPN_MSGID_CREATE_PLAYER
DPNMSG_DESTROY_PLAYER *pDestroy;  // DPN_MSGID_DESTROY_PLAYER
pCreate = (DPNMSG_CREATE_PLAYER*)pMsgBuffer;
pDestroy = (DPNMSG_DESTROY_PLAYER*)pMsgBuffer;
```

Of course, the contents of these messages are useful only to the specific network object, so there's no reason to use all of them. In the sections "Working with Servers," and "Working with Clients," later in this chapter, you see each one used in its respective object.

# Configuring Session Information

Each network object needs to know a little bit about the session it's hosting or about to join. This information is contained within a single structure:

```
typedef struct _DPN_APPLICATION_DESC {
    DWORD dwSize;               // size of this structure
    DWORD dwFlags;              // session flags
    GUID guidInstance;          // NULL
    GUID guidApplication;       // set to application GUID
    DWORD dwMaxPlayers;         // set to maximum # players allowed
    DWORD dwCurrentPlayers;     // current number of players
    WCHAR *pwszSessionName;     // name of session
    WCHAR *pwszPassword;        // session password (if any)
    PVOID pvReservedData;                   // unused
    DWORD dwReservedDataSize;               // unused
    PVOID pvApplicationReservedData;        // NULL
    DWORD dwApplicationReservedDataSize;    // 0
} DPN_APPLICATION_DESC;
```

As I've said, you don't need all the information in the DPN_APPLICATION_DESC structure, so here's a breakdown of what you need for each network model.

## Server Session Data

A server needs to configure the maximum number of players allowed (if you want to set a limit), the name of the session and password used to log in, session flags, and the application GUID.

To do this, you first clear the structure (to 0s), set the dwSize variable, and fill in the required fields. As for the dwFlags variable, you have the choice of the flags shown in Table 9.7

## Table 9.7  Session Flags

| Flag Macro | Description |
|---|---|
| DPNSESSION_CLIENT_SERVER | This session is a client/server model. |
| DPNSESSION_MIGRATE_HOST | Used in peer models, the inclusion of this flag causes DirectPlay to transfer host information to another system if the current host is lost. |
| DPNSESSION_NODPNSVR | Tells DirectPlay not to allow enumerations of your application from a remote system. |
| DPNSESSION_REQUIREPASSWORD | The remote user must give the correct password to log in. |

Here's an example of setting up the session information:

```
// This application's GUID
GUID AppGUID = { 0xede9493e, 0x6ac8, 0x4f15,                    \
        { 0x8d, 0x1, 0x8b, 0x16, 0x32, 0x0, 0xb9, 0x66 } };

// Zero out the session information structure and set its size
DPN_APPLICATION_DESC dpad;
ZeroMemory(&dpad, sizeof(DPN_APPLICATION_DESC));
dpad.dwSize = sizeof(DPN_APPLICATION_DESC);

// Set the session name and password
dpad.pwszSessioName = L"MySession";
dpad.pwszPassword = L"MyPassword";

// Set maximum # of players to 4
dpad.dwMaximumPlayers = 4;

// Set the application GUID
dpad.guidApplication = AppGUID;

// Set flags to client/server and use password
dpad.dwFlags = DPNSESSION_CLIENT_SERVER |                    \
            DPNSESSION_REQUIREPASSWORD;
```

**NOTE**

If you don't want to set a maximum number of players, leave that field as 0. Do the same with the password; just don't use the flag and leave the password field alone.

## Client Session Data

The information you need to set for the client structure includes the name and password of the session you want to join, the client/server session flag, and the application GUID. Be sure to use the same application GUID as the server application so that they can find each other on the network. Here's an example:

```
// The server application GUID
GUID AppGUID = { 0xede9493e, 0x6ac8, 0x4f15,                      \
        { 0x8d, 0x1, 0x8b, 0x16, 0x32, 0x0, 0xb9, 0x66 } };

// Zero out the session information structure and set its size
DPN_APPLICATION_DESC dpad;
ZeroMemory(&dpad, sizeof(DPN_APPLICATION_DESC));
dpad.dwSize = sizeof(DPN_APPLICATION_DESC);

// Set the session name and password to join in
dpad.pwszSessioName = L"MySession";
dpad.pwszPassword = L"MyPassword";

// Set the application GUID
dpad.guidApplication = AppGUID;

// Set flags to client/server and use password
dpad.dwFlags = DPNSESSION_CLIENT_SERVER |                         \
                DPNSESSION_REQUIREPASSWORD;
```

# Working with Servers

At last, the real fun begins! The first step to getting a real network going is to create a server. The server will act as the central processing unit for your networked game. All players will connect to a server via a client application and begin transmitting data back and forth.

The server keeps the game data synchronized and informs the players of the current state of the game. Although this might not be the fastest method for smaller network games, it is the best method for larger ones, so I use it in Chapter 19.

Here's a complete function that creates the server object and initializes it with a message handler function (just a pretty bare one for now), that creates the address component and session structure, and that makes a special call to start the hosting.

As a result of calling the function, you receive a pointer to the server network object.

```
// Server GUID
GUID AppGUID = { 0xede9493e, 0x6ac8, 0x4f15,                  \
        { 0x8d, 0x1, 0x8b, 0x16, 0x32, 0x0, 0xb9, 0x66 } };

// Message handler prototype
HRESULT WINAPI ServerMsgHandler(PVOID pvUserContext,          \
          DWORD dwMessageId, PVOID pMsgBuffer);

IDirectPlay8Server *StartNetworkServer(
      char *szSessionName,  // Session name (in ANSI)
      char *szPassword,     // Password to use (NULL if none)
      DWORD dwPort,         // Which port to use
      DWORD dwMaxPlayers,   // Maximum # of players
{
  IDirectPlay8Server  *pDPServer;
  IDirectPlay8Address *pDPAddress;
  DPN_APPLICATION_DESC dpad;
  WCHAR wszSessionName[256];
  WCHAR wszPassword[256];

  // Create and initialize the server object
  if(FAILED(DirectPlay8Create(&IID_IDirectPlay8Server,        \
          (void**)&pDPServer, NULL)))
    return NULL;
  if(FAILED(pDPServer->Initialize(pDPServer,                  \
          ServerMsgHandler, 0))) {
    pDPServer->Release();
    return NULL;
  }

  // Create the address object, set the SP & port
  if(FAILED(DirectPlay8AddressCreate(                         \
      &IID_IDirectPlay8Address, (void**)&pDPAddress, NULL))) {
    pDPServer->Release();
    return NULL;
  }
  pDPAddress->SetSP(&CLDID_DP8SP_TCPIP);
  pDPAddress->AddComponent(DPNA_KEY_PORT, &dwPort,            \
      sizeof(DWORD), DPNA_DATATYPE_DWORD);
```

```
// Set up the session information
ZeroMemory(&dpad, sizeof(DPNA_APPLICATION_DESC));
dpad.dwSize = sizeof(DPNA_APPLICATION_DESC);
dpad.dwFlags = DPNSESSION_CLIENT_SERVER;

// Set session name by converting ANSI to Unicode
mbstowcs(wszSessionName, szSessionName,                       \
          strlen(szSessionName)+1);
dpad.pwszSessionName = wszSessionName;

// Set password information (if any)
if(szPassword != NULL) {
  mbstowcs(wszPassword, szPassword, strlen(szPassword)+1);
  dpad.pwszPassword = wszPassword;
  dpad.dwFlags |= DPNSESSION_REQUIREPASSWORD;
}
dpad.dwMaxPlayers = dwMaxPlayers;
```

I'll stop here for a second and introduce the special host function that starts the
server object's networking session:

```
HRESULT IDirectPlay8Server::Host(
  const DPN_APPLICATION_DESC *const pdnAppDesc, // session info
  IDirectPlay8Address **const prgpDeviceInfo, // Address object
  const DWORD cDeviceInfo,       // 1
  const DPN_SECURITY_DESC *const pdpSecurity,           // NULL
  const DPN_SECURITY_CREDENTIALS *const pdpCredentials, // NULL
  VOID *const dwPlayerContext,  // NULL
  const DWORD dwFlags);          // 0
```

Thankfully, you're all prepared for this monster function. You've already created
the address object and set up the session description, so the rest is child's play.
Here's the rest of the preceding function:

```
if(FAILED(pDPServer->Host(&dpad, &pDPAddress, 1,          \
                          NULL, NULL, NULL, 0))) {
  pDPAddress->Release();
  pDPServer->Release();
  return NULL;
}

// Release the address object - no longer required
pDPAddress->Release();
```

```
    // Return the server object
    return pDPServer;
}


// The server network message handler function with
// useable message switch...case statements in place.
HRESULT WINAPI ServerMsgHandler(PVOID pvUserContext,                \
          DWORD dwMessageId, PVOID pMsgBuffer)
{
    // Define DPNMSG_* message structures here

    // Pointer to calling server object
    // retrieved through user-specified pointer during
    // call to Initialize.
    IDirectPlay8Server *pDPServer;
    pDPServer = (IDirectPlay8Server*)pvUserContext;

    switch(dwMessageId) {
        // do case statements here based on message type
        // for instance:
        // case DPN_MSGID_CREATE_PLAYER:
        //     DPNMSG_CREATE_PLAYER dpcp;
        //     dpcp = (DPNMSG_CREATE_PLAYER*)pMsgBuffer;
        // do whatever you want with this data and
        // return success when done.
        //     return S_OK;
    }

    return E_FAIL;
}
```

As you can see, I again inserted only a skeleton message handler function. Before you can start working with the messages, you need to understand the theory behind them. The following sections begin with player-related messages, which are the messages you are most likely to use.

# Handling Players

When the server starts up, one of the first messages you receive is the message for creating a player. The first player created is always the host player. Then other players begin to come and go, but the host player remains throughout the session.

# Dealing with Create-Player Messages

The create-player message is defined as DPN_MSGID_CREATE_PLAYER, and the message buffer is cast into a DPNMSG_CREATE_PLAYER structure, which is declared as follows:

```
typedef struct _DPNMSG_CREATE_PLAYER {
  DWORD dwSize;                // Size of this structure
  DWORD dpnidPlayer;           // Player ID #
  PVOID pvPlayerContext;  // Pointer to player context data
} DPNMSG_CREATE_PLAYER;
```

This ingeniously simple structure contains only two useful bits of information: the assigned player ID # that you use to reference the player from now on and the player context data pointer.

As you can see, the DPNMSG_CREATE_PLAYER structure apparently has a lot of missing data, especially the player's name. This is actually the job of a separate function, as you see in the next section, "Retrieving a Player's Name." At this point, you set the player context, which is as easy as casting the pointer to it:

> **NOTE**
>
> A *player context* data pointer is the information you use to define a player in your application. This data pointer can point to a structure, class, or data buffer that contains the player's name, health, age, current weapon and armor, and so on.
>
> By giving DirectPlay a pointer to this player context, DirectPlay can refer you back to it for faster access. This beats having to go through a list of logged-in players searching for a matching player ID when the time comes!

```
DPNMSG_CREATE_PLAYER pCreatePlayer;
pCreatePlayer->pvPlayerContext = (PVOID)ContextDataPtr;
```

Of course, the ContextDataPtr is the pointer to whatever you are using to store the player data. To associate a single structure from an array of structures that contains in-game player information, pass a pointer to the structure as the context, as shown here:

```
typedef struct {
  char szPlayerName[32];       // Name of player
  DWORD dwXPos, dwYPos;        // Coordinates of player
} sPlayerInfo;
sPlayerInfo Players[100];   // room for 100 players

// inside message switch...case statement on create player:
pCreatePlayer->pvPlayerContext = (PVOID)&sPlayerInfo[1];
```

## Retrieving a Player's Name

A player has a name associated with it, and you should be able to retrieve that information to use in the game (who wants to be referred to by a number?). This is the job of IDirectPlay8Server::GetClientInfo:

```
HRESULT IDirectPlay8Server::GetClientInfo(
   const DPNID dpnid,          // the players ID #
   DPN_PLAYER_INFO *const pdpnPlayerInfo, // a player info struct
   DWORD *const pdwSize,       // size of above structure
   const DWORD dFlags);        // 0
```

Again, you're dealing with a data structure that can be any size, so you need to first query for the correct size, allocate a buffer, and then retrieve the structure. This data buffer is in the form of a DPN_PLAYER_INFO structure, as shown here:

```
typedef struct _DPN_PLAYER_INFO {
   DWORD dwSize;           // Size of this structure
   DWORD dwInfoFlags;      // DPNINFO_NAME | DPNINFO_DATA
   PWSTR pwszName;         // Name of player (in Unicode)
   PVOID pvData;           // Pointer to player data
   DWORD dwDataSize;       // Size of player data
   DWORD dwPlayerFlags;    // DPNPLAYER_LOCAL if a local player
                           // or DPNPLAYER_HOST if a host player
} DPN_PLAYER_INFO;
```

You can see the magic parameter, so jump ahead and find out how to process a create-player message and retrieve the associated players name:

```
HRESULT WINAPI ServerMsgHandler(PVOID pvUserContext,          \
           DWORD dwMessageId, PVOID pMsgBuffer)
{
   IDirectPlay8Server *pDPServer;
   HRESULT hr;
   DPNMSG_CREATE_PLAYER  *pCreatePlayer;
   DPN_PLAYER_INFO *dppi;
   DWORD dwSize;

   if((pDPServer = (IDirectPlay8Server*)pvUserContext)) == NULL)
     return E_FAIL;

   switch(dwMessageId) {
     case DPN_MSGID_CREATE_PLAYER:
       pCreatePlayer = (DPNMSG_CREATE_PLAYER*)pMsgBuffer;
```

```
      dwSize = 0;
      dppi = NULL;

      // Query for data buffer size
      hr = pDPServer->GetClientInfo(                          \
              pCreatePlayer->dpnidPlayer, dppi, &dwSize, 0);
      // Check for an error - if it's an invalid player, then
      // the player being added is the host player (skip it).
      if(FAILED(hr) && hr != DPNERR_BUFFERTOOSMALL) {
        if(hr == DPNERR_INVALIDPLAYER)
          break;
      }

      // Allocate a data buffer and get the information
      dppi = (DPN_PLAYER_INFO*)new BYTE[dwSize];
      ZeroMemory(dppi, sizeof(DPN_PLAYER_INFO));
      dppi.dwSize = sizeof(DPN_PLAYER_INFO);
      if(FAILED(pDPServer->GetClientInfo(                     \
            pCreatePlayer->dpnidPlayer, dppi, &dwSize, 0))) {
        delete[] dppi;
        break;
      }

      // At this point, we have the player information
      // inside the dppi structure.  To get the player
      // name in ANSI characters, just call wcstombs.
      // For now we'll just display it in a message box.
      char szName[32];
      wcstombs(szName, dppi->pwszName, 32);
      MessageBox(NULL, szName, "Player Joined", MB_OK);

      // get rid of player data buffer
      delete[] dppi;

      return S_OK;
    }

  return E_FAIL;
}
```

**CAUTION**

Notice that the call to get client information fails, which is not your fault. A client does not have to set its client information structure, which means that the server cannot retrieve it.

## Destroying Players

No, you're not killing them off in the game, but when players are disconnected, you receive a message saying so. Creating this message is just as easy as creating the create-player message. Cast the message buffer to a DPNMSG_DESTROY_PLAYER structure, as follows:

```
typedef struct _DPNMSG_DESTROY_PLAYER {
  DWORD dwSize;              // Size of this structure
  DPNID dpnidPlayer;        // ID # of player being removed
  PVOID pvPlayerContext;    // The player context pointer
  DWORD dwReason;           // Reason for leaving
} DPNMSG_DESTROY_PLAYER;
```

You again use the players' ID numbers and their context pointers, which you set earlier. The only questionable field is the last one, dwReason. Why did the player leave? Was he deleted for normal reasons, was the connection lost, did the session terminate, or was the player forcibly removed? Each reason has a unique macro assigned, as shown in Table 9.8. It's up to you to use the value in the dwReason field as you see fit.

To forcibly disconnect a player, you use the IDirectPlay8Server::DestroyClient:

```
HRESULT IDirectPlay8Server::DestroyClient(
  const DPNID pdnidClient,        // Player ID #
  const void *const pDestroyInfo,  // NULL
  const DWORD dwDestroyInfoSize,   // 0
  const DWORD dwFlags);            // 0
```

### Table 9.8  Reasons for Disconnection

| Macro | Description |
| --- | --- |
| DPNDESTROYPLAYERREASON_NORMAL | The player is removed for normal reasons. |
| DPNDESTROYPLAYERREASON_CONNECTIONLOST | The player is removed because the connection is lost. |
| DPNDESTROYPLAYERREASON_SESSIONTERMINATED | The player is removed because the session is terminated. |
| DPNDESTROYPLAYERREASON_HOSTDESTROYPLAYER | The player is forcibly removed by the server. |

There's not much new here—just the player ID number. Here's how to do disconnect a player:

```
pDPServer->DestroyClient(dpnidPlayerID, NULL, 0, 0);
```

The only other way to disconnect a player is to end the networking session, which you see in the section "Ending the Host Session," later in this chapter.

## Receiving Data

The actual game data will take the form of application-specific messages, but will always come wrapped inside a DPN_MSGID_RECEIVE message type, using the DPNMSG_RECEIVE data structure:

```
typedef struct _DPNMSG_RECEIVE
  DWORD dwSize;                // Size of this structure
  DPNID dpnidSender;           // Player ID # of sender
  PVOID pvPlayerContext;       // Player context pointer
  PBYTE pReceiveData;          // Received data buffer
  DWORD dwReceivedDataSize;    // Size of received data
  DPNHANDLE hBufferHandle;     // A buffer handle for data
} DPNMSG_RECEIVE;
```

To process this data, start accessing the pointer pReceiveData, using the Windows memory handle hBufferHandle if need be. This might not make sense at first, but it's actually in place to ensure that the message is held in memory until you're ready to work with the data.

As an example, say that the data received is 16 bytes in size. That data represents a player's state in the game. To access the data, cast it into a data structure pointer and retrieve the data, such as in the following example:

```
#define MSG_PLAYERSTATE   0x101
typedef struct {
  DWORD dwType;
  DWORD dwXPos, dwYPos, dwHealth;
} sPlayerState;

// And the message handler dealing with it:
HRESULT WINAPI ServerMsgHandler(PVOID pvUserContext,            \
          DWORD dwMessageId, PVOID pMsgBuffer)
{
```

```
IDirectPlay8Server *pDPServer;
HRESULT hr;
DPNMSG_RECEIVE *pReceive;
sPlayerState *pState;

if((pDPServer = (IDirectPlay8Server*)pvUserContext)) == NULL)
  return E_FAIL;

switch(dwMessageId) {
  case DPN_MSGID_RECEIVE:
    pReceive = (DPNMSG_RECEIVE*)pMsgBuffer;

    // Cast the data buffer into our message type
    pState = (sPlayerState*)pReceive->pReceivedData;
    if(pState->dwType == MSG_PLAYERSTATE) {
      // Do whatever you need with this structure data
    }
    return S_OK;
}

return E_FAIL;
}
```

Sometimes so many messages might be coming in that you cannot process them when received. In these cases, you can stuff them in a queue. When you're done with the memory, you need to pass this handle to the IDirectPlay8Server::ReturnBuffer function:

```
HRESULT IDirectPlay8Server::ReturnBuffer(
  const DPNHANDLE hBufferHandle,  // Handle of buffer
  const DWORD dwFlags);           // 0
```

In order for DirectPlay to know not to release this memory, you return a value of DPNSUCCESS_PENDING, rather than S_OK or E_FAIL, when you're done with the message.

# Sending Server Messages

What good is a network that doesn't transfer data? In order to have the server object send data to a connected client, you need to use the SendTo function, which sends the data to a single player, to all players at once, or to all players who belong to a specific group. Take a look at the SendTo function:

```
HRESULT IDirectPlay8Server::SendTo(
    const DPNID dpnid,  // player or group ID # to send to
                        // use DPNID_ALL_PLAYERS_GROUP to send
                        // the message to all players.
    const DPN_BUFFER_DESC *const pBufferDesc,  // see text
    const DWORD cBufferDesc,  // 1
    const DWORD dwTimeOut,    // Time-out (in milliseconds) to
                              // wait for message to send -
                              // 0 to not use time-out.
    void *const pvAsyncContext,      // a user supplied context
    DPNHANDLE *const phAsyncHandle,  // NULL for sync operations
    const DWORD dwFlags);     // see text
```

The SendTo function can definitely be a bit overwhelming. You need to consider security, delivery method, and throttling. You can see the player ID number to which you want the message sent as well as the DPN_BUFFER_DESC structure pointer.

This simple structure is defined as follows:

```
typedef struct _DPN_BUFFER_DESC {
    DWORD dwBufferSize;  // Size of data to send
    BYTE *pBufferData;   // Pointer to data to send
} DPN_BUFFER_DESC;
```

Here you have the size and the pointer to the data that you want to send. Next to the SendTo function is cBufferDesc, which you set to 1. Then you set the dwTimeOut value to the length of time (in milliseconds) this function waits before returning an error (from the time that you sent the data). Or you can set the value to 0 if you don't want to use the time-out feature.

pvAsyncContext is a user-specified context that you use to point to information you want when the send operation is complete. This is similar to the player context because it makes accessing information easier.

To use asynchronous sending, you supply phAsyncHandle with a handle that you can later use to cancel the send operation. There's a lot to dwFlags. See Table 9.9 for a list and description of macros that you can use to construct this value.

A typical combination of flags is DPNSEND_NOLOOPBACK and DPNSEND_NOCOPY, which gives you optimal performance without involving the server player in messages sent to groups.

Going back to the receive message example, you can turn around and resend this information to the same player, maybe with a slight change in the data.

## Table 9.9 SendTo Behavior Flags

| Macro | Description |
|---|---|
| DPNSEND_SYNC | Sends data synchronously. Does not return until data is sent. |
| DPNSEND_NOCOPY | Forces DirectPlay not to make an internal copy of the data being sent. This is the most efficient method of sending data; however, the pending data can be modified before DirectPlay has a chance to send it. |
| DPNSEND_NOCOMPLETE | Tells DirectPlay not to notify the server when a send operation is complete. |
| DPSEND_COMPLETEONPROCESS | Makes DirectPlay send the DPN_MSGID_SEND_COMPLETE message when the data is sent and verified by the destination system. This slows down the works, but makes sure that the data arrives. You must specify the DPSEND_GUARANTEED flags as well with this one. |
| DPSEND_GUARANTEED | Uses guaranteed delivery. |
| DPNSEND_PRIORITY_HIGH | Specifies the message as high priority. Use this to mark significant messages that must get through the throttler. |
| DPNSEND_PRIORITY_LOW | Specifies the message as low priority. Use this to mark less important data that the throttler might discard. |
| DPNSEND_NOLOOPBACK | Suppresses the DPN_MSGID_RECEIVE on the server if you are sending data to a group that includes the server player. |
| DPNSEND_NONSEQUENCIAL | Forces messages on the destination system to be received in the order they are sent (as opposed to being mixed up because of slowdowns in network transmissions). Using nonsequential messaging can slow down the network on the remote end—because the remote system tracks and reorders network messages (if they are received out of sequence). |

Here's the switch...case statement again, this time with send information:

```
DPNHANDLE g_hSendTo;  // an async handle for data

switch(dwMessageId) {
    case DPN_MSGID_RECEIVE:
        pReceive = (DPNMSG_RECEIVE*)pMsgBuffer;

        // Cast the data buffer into our message type
        pState = (sPlayerState*)pReceive->pReceivedData;
        if(pState->dwType == MSG_PLAYERSTATE) {
            // Modify the data
            pState->dwHealth += 10; // increase health

            // Cast the data to send
            DPN_BUFFER_DESC dpbd;
            dpbd.dwSize = sizeof(sPlayerState);
            dpbd.pBufferData = pState;

            // Send it using internal copy method and no
            // send notification.  Retrieves an async
            // handle for stopping send operation.
            pDPServer->SendTo(pReceive->dpnidSender, &dpbd,        \
                    1, 0, NULL, &g_hSendTo, DPNSEND_NOCOMPLETE);
        }
        return S_OK;
    }
```

To cancel this information before it is sent (while it's waiting in the send queue), use the globally-declared handle in the following manner:

```
// to cancel a single sendto operation use:
pDPServer->CancelAsyncOperation(g_hSendTo, 0);

// to cancel all pending operations use:
pDPServer->CancelAsyncOperation(NULL, DPNCANCEL_ALL_OPERATIONS);
```

# Ending the Host Session

Once the server finishes its job, it is time to stop the session, which stops all transmissions and destroys all players. You do so with the following function:

```
HRESULT IDirectPlay8Server::Close(
```

```
   const DWORD dwFlags);   // 0
```

Because this function works synchronously, it will not return until all transmissions are complete and all connections are closed. This ensures that the application can be shut down with no worries.

**TIP**

This handy function works with every network model object, so you're not limited to only servers.

Last, release all COM objects in use, which at this point should be only the server object:

```
pDPServer->Release();
```

# Working with Clients

Clients, on the other hand, aren't as complex as the servers. They typically use only two messages, the receive-data and session-terminated messages, and need to connect and keep track of a single connection (the server).

One major addition is that the client application must specify its player settings so that the host can retrieve them. Setting the player information is accomplished by first filling in a DPN_PLAYER_INFO structure with the relevant data and calling IDirectPlay8Client::SetClientInfo.

You have to be concerned about only a few fields in the DPN_PLAYER_INFO structure—particularly pwszName, which contains the Unicode string of the player name you want to use. You need to clear the structure, set its dwSize value, set the dwInfoFlags variable to DPNINFO_NAME | DPNINFO_DATA, and set the player name.

**NOTE**

As previously mentioned, you use the same application GUID for the server and the client so that they can recognize each other. Not doing so is one of the main reasons network applications won't connect, so make sure that those application GUIDs are the same.

Here's the prototype for IDirectPlay8Client::SetClientInfo:

```
HRESULT IDirectPlay8Client::SetClientInfo(
   const DPN_PLAYER_INFO *const pdpnPlayerInfo,   // player info
   PVOID const pvAsyncContext,           // NULL
   DPNHANLDE *const phAsyncHandle,       // NULL
   const DWORD dwFlags);                 // DPNSETCLIENTINFO_SYNC
```

Here you again see the pointer to the player information structure. Here's an entire function that you can use to create the client object, initialize it with a message handler, create an address object, set the session and client information, and connect to the server. You don't need the message handler function; it's the same thing as the server.

```
// Server/Client GUID
GUID AppGUID = { 0xede9493e, 0x6ac8, 0x4f15,                    \
        { 0x8d, 0x1, 0x8b, 0x16, 0x32, 0x0, 0xb9, 0x66 } };


// Message handler prototype
HRESULT WINAPI ClientMsgHandler(PVOID pvUserContext,           \
          DWORD dwMessageId, PVOID pMsgBuffer);


IDirectPlay8Client *StartClientServer(
      char *szPlayerName,    // Player's name
      char *szSessionName,   // Session name to join (in ANSI)
      char *szPassword,      // Password to use (NULL if none)
      char *szIPAddress,     // Text string of IP address
                             // in form: ###.###.###.###
      DWORD dwPort           // Which port to use
{
  IDirectPlay8Client  *pDPClient;
  IDirectPlay8Address *pDPAddress;
  DPN_APPLICATION_DESC dpad;
  DPN_PLAYER_INFO        dppi;
  WCHAR wszSessionName[256];
  WCHAR wszPassword[256];
  WCHAR wszIPAddress[256];
  WHCAR wszPlayerName[256];

  // Create and initialize the client object
  if(FAILED(DirectPlay8Create(&IID_IDirectPlay8Client,         \
        (void**)&pDPClient, NULL)))
    return NULL;
  if(FAILED(pDPServer->Initialize(pDPClient,                   \
        ClientMsgHandler, 0))) {
    pDPClient->Release();
    return NULL;
  }
}
```

```
// Create the address object and set the SP
if(FAILED(DirectPlay8AddressCreate(                         \
     &IID_IDirectPlay8Address, (void**)&pDPAddress, NULL))) {
  pDPClient->Release();
  return NULL;
}
pDPAddress->SetSP(&CLDID_DP8SP_TCPIP);

// convert IP address to Unicode and add component
mbstowcs(wszIPAddress, szIPAddress, strlen(szIPAddress)+1);
pDPAddress->AddComponent(DPNA_KEY_HOSTNAME, wszIPAddress,   \
     (wcslen(PlayerInfo->pwszName)+1)*sizeof(WCHAR),        \
     DPNA_DATATYPE_STRING);

// Add port component
pDPAddress->AddComponent(DPNA_KEY_PORT, &dwPort,            \
     sizeof(DWORD), DPNA_DATATYPE_DWORD);

// Set up the player information
ZeroMemory(&dppi, sizeof(DPN_PLAYER_INFO));
dppi.dwSize = sizeof(DPN_PLAYER_INFO);
dppi.dwInfoFlags = DPNINFO_NAME | DPNINFO_DATA;
mbstowcs(wszPlayerName, szPlayerName,                       \
         strlen(szPlayerName)+1);
dppi.pwszName = wszPlayerName;
pDPClient->SetClientInfo(&dppi, NULL, NULL,                 \
                         DPNSETCLIENTINFO_SYNC);

// Set up the session information
ZeroMemory(&dpad, sizeof(DPNA_APPLICATION_DESC));
dpad.dwSize = sizeof(DPNA_APPLICATION_DESC);
dpad.dwFlags = DPNSESSION_CLIENT_SERVER;

// Set session name by converting ANSI to Unicode
mbstowcs(wszSessionName, szSessionName,                     \
         strlen(szSessionName)+1);
dpad.pwszSessionName = wszSessionName;

// Set password information (if any)
if(szPassword != NULL) {
  mbstowcs(wszPassword, szPassword, strlen(szPassword)+1);
```

```
   dpad.pwszPassword = wszPassword;
   dpad.dwFlags |= DPNSESSION_REQUIREPASSWORD;
}
```

At this point, the client is ready to connect, but this time things are a little different. The function in use now is IDirectPlay8Client::Connect, and its prototype is another big one:

```
HRESULT IDirectPlay8Client::Connect(
  const DPN_APPLICATION_DESC *const pdnAppDesc,  // session info
  IDirectPlay8Address *const pHostAddr,    // server address
  IDirectPlay8Address *const pDeviceInfo, // local device to use
  const DPN_SECURITY_DESC *const pdnSecurity,             // NULL
  const DPN_SECURITY_CREDENTIALS *const pdnCredentials,  // NULL
  const void *const pvUserConnectData,  // data to send w/connect
  const DWORD dwUserConnectDataSize,     // size of data to send
  void *const pvAsyncContext,          // async op. context
  DPNHANDLE *const phAsyncHandle,      // async handle
  const DWORD dwFlags);  // 0 or DPNCONNECT_SYNC
```

I told you that the Connect function was a whopper, but most of the arguments are covered in the earlier section "Working with Servers." The most glaring difference is the addition of pDeviceInfo, which is an IDirectPlay8Address object that contains the local device to use for the connection.

You learned how to obtain the IDirectPlay8Address object in the section "Using Addresses." So, last is dwFlags, which tells DirectPlay to connect asynchronously (0) or synchronously (DPNCONNECT_SYNC).

Using async connection types returns control immediately, so you need to wait for a DPN_MSGID_CONNECT_COMPLETE message to signify a successful connection to the server. With sync connections, this function returns only on an error or successful connection.

Now, take the first TCP/IP device on the system and pass it to this function, using a sync connection method:

```
IDirectPlay8Address *pDPDevice = NULL;
DPN_SERVICE_PROVIDER_INFO *pSP = NULL;
DPN_SERVICE_PROVIDER_INFO *pSPPtr;
DWORD dwSize = 0;
DWORD dwNumSP = 0;
DWORD i;
```

```
   // Query the required size of the data buffer
   if(SUCCEEDED(pDPClient->EnumServiceProviders(              \
               &CLSID_DP8SP_TCPIP, NULL, pSP,                 \
               &dwSize, &dwNumSP, 0))) {
     // Allocate a buffer and enumerate again
     pSP = new BYTE[dwSize];
     if(SUCCEEDED(pDPClient->EnumServiceProviders(            \
               &CLSID_DP8SP_TCPIP, NULL, pSP,                 \
               &dwSize, &dwNumSP, 0))) {
       // Enumeration is complete, use first instance of TCP/IP
       pSPPtr = pSP;
       if(FAILED(DirectPlay8AddressCreate(                    \
        &IID_IDirectPlay8Address, (void**)&pDPDevice, NULL))) {
         pDPClient->Release();
         pDPAddress->Release();
         return NULL;
       }
       pDPDevice->AddComponent(DPNA_KEY_DEVICE, pSPPtr->guid, \
           sizeof(GUID), DPNA_DATATYPE_GUID);
     }

     // Delete data buffer memory
     delete[] pSP;
   }

   // Perform connection
   if(FAILED(pDPClient->Connect(&dpad, &pDPAddress,           \
             &pDPDevice, NULL, NULL, NULL, 0, NULL, NULL,     \
             DPNCONNECT_SYNC))) {
     pDPAddress->Release();
     pDPDevice->Release();
     pDPClient->Release();
     return NULL;
   }

   // Release the address objects - no longer required
   pDPAddress->Release();
   pDPDevice->Release();

   // Return the client object
   return pDPClient;
}
```

# Sending and Receiving Messages

Receiving messages with the client is identical to receiving them from the server, so you can take care of this inside the message handler function. As for sending, this is the job of IDirectPlay8Client::Send:

```
HRESULT IDirectPlay8Client::Send(
   const DPN_BUFFER_DESC *const pBufferDesc,  // data to send
   const DWORD cBufferDesc,  // 1
   const DWORD dwTimeOut,     // timeout value (in milliseconds)
   void *const pvAsyncContext,      // async context pointer
   DPNHANDLE *const phAsyncHandle,  // async op. handle
   const DWORD dwFlags);     // same flags as server SendTo
```

You used these arguments in the section "Sending Server Messages," so I will not describe them again. Instead, here is an example that constructs a packet of game-related data that is sent to a server via the client object's Send function:

```
#define MSG_PLAYERSTATE  0x101
typedef struct {
  DWORD dwType;
  DWORD dwXPos, dwYPos, dwHealth;
} sPlayerInfo;
sPlayerInfo PlayerData;

// later in program to send it
DPN_BUFFER_DESC dpbd;

dpbd.dwBufferSize = sizeof(sPlayerInfo);
dpbd.pBufferData = &PlayerData;
PlayerData.dwType = MSG_PLAYERSTATE;
pDPClient->Send(&dpbd, 1, 0, NULL, NULL, DPNSEND_NOCOPY);
```

# Terminating the Client Session

When it comes time to disconnect the client from the session, you should explicitly convey this to DirectPlay so that the proper steps can be taken to shut down the connection. You handle disconnecting the client from a session using the IDirectPlay8Client::Close function:

```
pDPClient->Close(0);  // always use 0 as argument
```

# Wrapping Up Networking

If you haven't noticed by now, using DirectPlay is very easy—something you wouldn't expect with such a complex topic as networking and with such a powerful tool. Microsoft really nailed the interface down and gave it to you in the best way possible.

The only way to go from here is up. With the information in this chapter under your belt, you will be able to give your project the special features that gamers are craving. Be sure to check out Appendix C for references to other books and for Web sites with information on networking—and, as always, refer to the DirectX SDK help files for more information and samples.

---

### Programs on the CD-ROM

Programs that demonstrate the code discussed in this chapter are on the CD-ROM at the back of this book. You can find the following programs in the \BookCode\Chap09\ directory:

- **Enum.** A program that enumerates all specific server provider devices on the system. Location: \BookCode\Chap09\Enum\.

- **Server.** A demonstration of a server application. Works in conjunction with the client demo. Creates a chat-server to relay messages to all connected clients. Location: \BookCode\Chap09\Server\.

- **Client.** A demonstration of a client application. Works in conjunction with the server demo. Connect to a server and start chatting away. Location: \BookCode\Chap09\Client\.

---

# CHAPTER 10

# CREATING
# THE GAME
# CORE

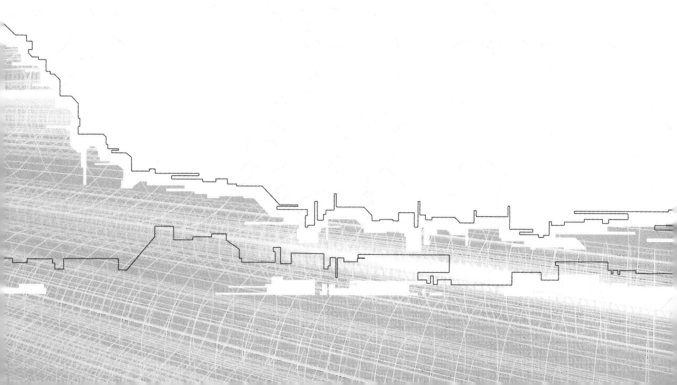

If you started at the beginning of this book, you've weeded through the basics. By now, you know that working with the coding techniques of DirectX and Windows can be a challenge. When working with these two programs, the trick to dealing with the repetitive (and mundane) code is to construct a core library of useful functions that handles the repetitive code for you. This library of functions helps you construct your game projects quickly, without having to write the same DirectX or Windows code again and again. In this chapter, I show you one library that I created to aid in the creation of the demonstration progams in this book, as well as to aid you in your own game projects.

In this chapter, you learn about the following:

- Getting the core concept
- Creating the core libraries

# Understanding the Core Concept

The Game Core is a collection of libraries that I created to simplify DirectX and Windows programming. Just about every function you'll want to use in your gaming project is represented in the Game Core, including functions for drawing graphics, playing sounds, processing user input, and dealing with application processing. This means that you will not have to deal with the low-level DirectX or Windows code every time you start a new project!

Instead, as you need them, just add the various core components to your game project. Here are the five cores that I developed for this book (each core is named based on its functionality):

- **System Core.** Handles Windows processing, including registering the window class, creating the application window, and dealing with processes, states, and data packages.
- **Graphics Core.** Draws graphics like the pros. Use 2-D methods to draw images quickly or blast into the scene using 3-D methods such as animated meshes.
- **Input Core.** Processes user input from keyboard, mouse, and joystick devices.

- **Sound Core.** Blasts the user with multiple channels of sound and music. Changes the instrument sounds and creates unique musical experiences.
- **Network Core.** Connects you to the Internet and some massive on-line gaming. Now you can join the networking bandwagon with this core.

You can use each core separately; there's no need to include all of them in your project. If you want only sound features, include only the Sound Core. Do you want the added benefit of state processing from the System Core? Go for it. The choices are yours.

Each core contains a collection of class components from which you must instance or derive your own objects. Each class has a unique purpose. For example, you use the cInputDevice class of the Input Core to control a single input device.

Nearly every core class has an initialization function and a shutdown function. These are typically called Init and Shutdown, respectively, but at times the two functions will take the names Create and Free. Most functions that you call in the cores return a BOOL value—TRUE if the function succeeded or FALSE if it did not.

You must initialize most class instances in order to use them, and you must shutdown those class instances in order to free system resources. Once initialized, the class object is ready to go.

The cores are very large, however, so I can't possibly list the complete code for each core in this chapter. Instead, I will provide you with an overview of each component class declaration, plus a small example of code that shows you how to use each class. You might want to skip to the section "Programs on the CD-ROM," at the end of this chapter, for information about the Game Core source code; it might help to browse those sources as you read this chapter.

> **NOTE**
> The Game Core is based solely on information you read in Chapters 4 through 9, covering C++, Windows, and DirectX programming.

# The System Core

The System Core handles the initialization and program flow of typical Windows gaming applications, as well as processes, states, and data packaging. This is the first place to start with your new gaming projects.

# Using the cApplication Core Object

The most useful core object in the System Core is cApplication, which creates your application's window and controls the program flow. This object registers the window class, creates the application window, and enters a message pump that processes application-window messages for you and calls the internal class functions as needed.

To process an application, the cApplication class calls on three overloaded functions that you provide (through a derived class declaration): Init, Shutdown, and Frame. Each of these functions has a specific purpose, as you'll see later in this section. When processing Windows messages, you also need to provide a message handler. Again, I cover this later in this section.

For now, go ahead and check out the following code listing, which contains the cApplication class declaration:

```
class cApplication
{
  private:
    HINSTANCE      m_hInst;       // Instance handle
    HWND           m_hWnd;        // Window handle

  protected:
    char           m_Class[MAX_PATH];     // Class name
    char           m_Caption[MAX_PATH];   // Window caption

    WNDCLASSEX     m_wcex;        // Windows class structure

    DWORD          m_Style;       // Window style
    DWORD          m_XPos;        // X coordinate of window
    DWORD          m_YPos;        // Y coordinate of window
    DWORD          m_Width;       // Default width of window
    DWORD          m_Height;      // Default height of window

  public:
    cApplication();              // Constructor

    HWND       GethWnd();        // Returns window handle
    HINSTANCE  GethInst();       // Returns instance handle

    BOOL Run();                  // Executes class code
    BOOL Error(BOOL Fatal, char *Text, ...);  // Prints error
```

```
    BOOL Move(long XPos, long YPos);        // Move window
    BOOL Resize(long Width, long Height); // Resize client area

    BOOL ShowMouse(BOOL Show = TRUE);   // Show or hide cursor

    // Default message handler
    virtual FAR PASCAL MsgProc(HWND hWnd, UINT uMsg,            \
        WPARAM wParam, LPARAM lParam) {                         \
           return DefWindowProc(hWnd, uMsg, wParam, lParam);   \
        }

    // Custom functions that will hold your game code
    virtual BOOL Init()        { return TRUE; }
    virtual BOOL Shutdown()    { return TRUE; }
    virtual BOOL Frame()       { return TRUE; }
};
```

The number of functions you call in the cApplication class is minimal because the cApplication class is designed to run almost by itself—you just plug in your game code.

To use the cApplication class, you must first create a derived class using cApplication as the base class. In that way, you can overload specific functions to do your own bidding. Those functions that you'll be overloading, as mentioned previously, are Init, Shutdown, and Frame.

In the cApplication::Init function, you place all class initialization code, such as loading data, preparing processing states, and so on. The opposite of Init is cApplication::Shutdown, which frees all previously allocated resources. The Shutdown function is the last function called, whereas Init is the first one called.

Last comes cApplication::Frame, which is called with every iteration of the message pump (in which a Windows message is not processed).
As you might guess, the Frame function processes a single frame of your game, which might include processing user input, checking network data, and drawing graphics.

You have little reason to overload the message handler function, unless you want to process Windows messages on your own. To process the messages, you overload the cApplication::MsgProc, which I will show you how to do in a moment.

> **NOTE**
>
> Each of the functions mentioned (Init, Shutdown, and Frame) return a BOOL value, which asks the cApplication class whether it should exit the program. If one of these three functions returns a FALSE value, execution of the application is terminated.

As for now, take a moment to work with the cApplication class by creating a quick application. Be sure to include the Core_System.h include file, add the Core_System.cpp file to your project, and derive your own application class to work with, as shown here:

```
#include "Core_System.h"
class cApp : public cApplication
{
  private:
    char *m_Name;

  public:
    cApp();                 // Constructor

    BOOL Init();       // Overloaded Init function
    BOOL Shutdown();   // Overloaded Shutdown function
    BOOL Frame();      // Overloaded Frame function
};
```

This example code initializes your application by registering the window class, creating a window, and entering the message pump, thus continuously calling the Frame function. The purpose of this example is to create a buffer and store a name in it (my name, in this case) and to display that name each frame. When you finish with the application, you free the name buffer and exit the application.

```
cApp::cApp()
{
  // Initialize instance data to default values
  m_Name = NULL;

  // Set up the window style, position, width, and height
  m_Style = WS_OVERLAPPEDWINDOW;    // Window style
  m_XPos = 100;     // X coordinate of window
  m_YPos = 20;      // Y coordinate of window
  m_Width = 400;    // Width of client area
  m_Height = 400;   // Height of client area

  // Assign a class name and window caption
  strcpy(m_Class, "NameClass");
  strcpy(m_Caption, "My Name Example");
}
```

```
BOOL cApp::Init()
{
  // Allocate room for my name
  if((m_Name = new char[10]) == NULL)
    strcpy(m_Name, "Jim Adams");
  else return FALSE;
  return TRUE;
}

BOOL cApp::Shutdown()
{
  // Free the name buffer
  delete m_Name;
  m_Name = NULL;   // reset buffer to NULL
}

BOOL cApp::Frame()
{
  // Display my name and wait for user to click
  // OK or CANCEL, exiting program on CANCEL
  if(MessageBox(GethWnd(), m_Name, "My name is",                \
                MB_OKCANCEL) == IDCANCEL)
    return FALSE;
  return TRUE;
}
```

Well, that's it! All you have to do now is instance your new class and run it using the
WinMain function:

```
int PASCAL WinMain(HINSTANCE hInst, HINSTANCE hPrev,           \
                   LPSTR szCmdLine, int nCmdShow)
{
  cApp App;
  return App.Run();
}
```

# State Processing
# with cStateManager

Chapter 5, "Programming with Windows and Application Basics," introduces the
use of a state-based-processing class. In this section, I build on that information and

show you a vamped-up version of the cStateManager developed in Chapter 5. When creating your game, you will find this version of cStateManager works better with a game's program flow.

The new state manager introduces a couple concepts: calling purposes and adding a user-defined data pointer to the functions in cStateManager.

Here's the code listing for the cStateManager class declaration:

```
class cStateManager
{
  // State function pointers (linked list)
  typedef struct sState {
    void (*Function)(void *Ptr, long Purpose);
    sState *Next;

    // Structure constructor that clears pointers
    sState() {
      Function = NULL;
      Next = NULL;
    }

    // Structure destructor to delete linked list
    ~sState() {  delete Next;  }
  } sState;

protected:
  sState *m_StateParent;    // State stack link list parent

public:
  cStateManager();      // Constructor
  ~cStateManager();     // Destructor

  // Pushes a state on the stack, along with a
  // user-defined pointer. The push function will call
  // the state function with an init purpose.
  void Push(void (*Function)(void *Ptr, long Purpose),      \
            void *DataPtr = NULL);

  // Pop top-most state off stack, calling it with a
  // shutdown purpose.
  BOOL Pop(void *DataPtr = NULL);
```

> **NOTE**
>
> A *calling purpose* is, just as it sounds, the reason that a state is called. The "purpose" can be INITPURPOSE (to signal that the function needs to prepare itself for use), FRAMEPURPOSE (to process a single frame), or SHUTDOWNPURPOSE (to release all resources when the processing is complete).

```
    // Pop all states, calling SHUTDOWN purpose for each.
    void PopAll(void *DataPtr = NULL);

    // Process the top-most state with a frame purpose.
    BOOL Process(void *DataPtr = NULL);
};
```

Working with the cStateManager class might seem strange at first (specifically with regard to the purposes), but don't worry, that's what examples are for! Check out this example, which is based on the previous cApplication example:

```
class cApp : public cApplication
{
  private:
    cStateManager m_StateManager;

    // State function prototypes
    static void Function1(void *, long);
    static void Function2(void *, long);

  public:
    BOOL Init() { m_StateManager.Push(Function1, this); }
}


void cApp::Function1(void *DataPtr, long Purpose)
{
  // Get a pointer to the calling class, as this function is
  // static, meaning it's not assigned a class instance.
  cApp *cc = (cApp*)DataPtr;

  // Display a message on INIT and push a 2nd state
  if(Purpose == INITPURPOSE) {
    MessageBox(cc->GethWnd(), "State 1", "Message", MB_OK);
    cc->m_StateManager.Push(Function2, cc);
    return;
  }

  // Force program to exit
  if(Purpose == FRAMEPURPOSE)
    cc->m_StateManager.Pop(cc);
}
```

```
void cApp::Function2(void *DataPtr, long Purpose)
{
  cApp *cc = (cApp*)DataPtr;

  // Display a message and pop itself
  if(Purpose == FRAMEPURPOSE) {
    MessageBox(cc->GethWnd(), "State 2", "Message", MB_OK);
    cc->m_StateManager.Pop(cc);
    return;
  }
}
```

Once executed, the cApp class pushes a state function (Function1) on the stack. Once pushed on the stack, the Function1 state function is called (by the cApp class) using an initialize purpose,

> **NOTE**
>
> Notice that all state functions follow the same function prototype. Be sure to duplicate the prototype in your programs:
>
> ```
> void StateFunction(void *DataPtr, long Purpose);
> ```

which in turn triggers Function1 to push a second state function (Function2) on the stack. Once the Function2 function has been called using a frame purpose, a message is displayed, the states are popped, and execution ends.

Notice that the addition of the user-defined variable has a purpose. Because you must declare state functions as static inside the class (or the code will not compile), you need to pass a pointer to the state functions. Because the state function is still part of the class, the state functions can use the pointers freely to access the class data (even private data).

# Processes and cProcessManager

cProcessManager is much like cStateManager, with one minor exception: Every function on the stack is called every frame. Not to be left behind from its earlier creation in Chapter 5, the new sProcessManager also takes a calling purpose and a user-defined pointer, just like cStateManager.

The class declaration for cProcessManager is identical to the class declaration of cStateManager. Rather than present that declaration again, you can skip right to an example of using the cProcessManager that, every frame, calls two functions that have been pushed onto the process stack:

```
class cApp : public cApplication
```

```
{
  private:
    cProcessManager m_ProcessManager;

    // Process function prototypes
    static void Function1(void *, long);
    static void Function2(void *, long);

  public:
    BOOL Init() {
      m_ProcessManager.Push(Function1, this);
      m_ProcessManager.Push(Function2, this);
    }
}

void cApp::Function1(void *DataPtr, long Purpose)
{
  // Get a pointer to the calling class, as this function is
  // static, meaning it's not assigned a class instance.
  cApp *cc = (cApp*)DataPtr;

  // Display a message
  if(Purpose == FRAMEPURPOSE) {
    MessageBox(cc->GethWnd(), "Process 1", "Message", MB_OK);
    return;
  }
}

void cApp::Function2(void *DataPtr, long Purpose)
{
  cApp *cc = (cApp*)DataPtr;

  // Display a message
  if(Purpose == FRAMEPURPOSE) {
    MessageBox(cc->GethWnd(), "Process 2", "Message", MB_OK);
    return;
  }
}
```

# Managing Data with cDataPackage

In Chapter 5, you learn how to use a data package manager. Now, you alter the data package manager that you created by adding two functions that return the size of the data buffer and the pointer to the data buffer. Here's the class declaration:

```
class cDataPackage
{
  protected:
    void              *m_Buf;     // Data buffer
    unsigned long  m_Size;    // Size of data buffer

  public:
    cDataPackage();    // Constructor
    ~cDataPackage();   // Destructor

    void *Create(unsigned long Size);  // Create a buffer
    void Free();                            // Free buffer

    BOOL Save(char *Filename);              // Save buffer to file
    void *Load(char *Filename, unsigned long *Size);  // Load

    void              *GetPtr();   // Get pointer to data buffer
    unsigned long  GetSize(); // Get data size
};
```

As you can see, the cDataPackage class remains the same (for help on using the cDataPackage class, please refer to Chapter 5).

# The Graphics Core

Now you're getting to the good stuff! The Graphics Core represents a major portion of the Game Core and is the largest and most complicated core object you'll see here. The Graphics Core features the classes shown in Table 10.1.

Most of the classes in the Graphics Core are easy to use, so you can just skim their features. The class declarations of each Game Core object are self-explanatory, so be sure to read the declarations carefully. You might as well start with cGraphics, the granddaddy of all Graphics Core objects.

## Table 10.1 Graphics Core Components

| Class | Description |
|---|---|
| cGraphics | Handles the initialization of Direct3D and enables rendering of states and setting up textures, materials, and lights. |
| cTexture | Holds a single texture and a function to draw 2-D portions of the texture to the display. |
| cMaterial | Holds a single material definition. |
| cLight | Contains a single light definition. |
| cFont | This class encloses the ID3DXFont object you see in Chapter 6, "Drawing with DirectX Graphics." |
| cVertexBuffer | A class that makes dealing with vertex buffers much easier. |
| cWorldPosition | Manages a world transformation matrix, enabling you to quickly position, scale, and rotate objects. |
| cCamera | Contains a view transformation matrix that you can modify using the object's interface. |
| cMesh | Contains a list of meshes loaded from an .X file and their materials. Use this class with the cObject class. |
| cObject | This class object represents a single object in the 3-D world. It controls the object's orientation, mesh, and animation status. |
| cAnimation | Contains a list of animations loaded from an .X file. Use this with the cObject class. |

# The Graphics System with cGraphics

You use cGraphics to set display modes, render states, clear the device, and much more. Once the cGraphics object is initialized, you use it in conjunction with just about every Graphics Core class component. Take a look at the cGraphics declaration:

```
class cGraphics
{
  protected:
```

```
     HWND                 m_hWnd;          // Parent window handle
     IDirect3D8        *m_pD3D;            // Direct3D object
     IDirect3DDevice8 *m_pD3DDevice;    // Device object
     ID3DXSprite       *m_pSprite;        // 2-D sprite object

     D3DDISPLAYMODE     m_d3ddm;     // Display mode properties

     BOOL                 m_Windowed;// Flag if using windowed mode
     BOOL                 m_ZBuffer; // Flag if using zbuffer
     BOOL                 m_HAL;       // Flag if hardware accelerated

     long                 m_Width;  // Width of display mode
     long                 m_Height; // Height of display mode
     char                 m_BPP;     // Bits-per-pixel of display

     char                 m_AmbientRed;   // Ambient light red
     char                 m_AmbientGreen; // Ambient light green
     char                 m_AmbientBlue;  // Ambient light blue

public:
  cGraphics();  // Construct
  ~cGraphics(); // Destructor

  // Functions to retrieve COM interfaces
  IDirect3D8        *GetDirect3DCOM();
  IDirect3DDevice8 *GetDeviceCOM();
  ID3DXSprite       *GetSpriteCOM();

  BOOL Init();      // Init graphics object
  BOOL Shutdown(); // Shutdown graphics object

  // Initialize a display mode using specified attributes
  BOOL SetMode(HWND hWnd, BOOL Windowed = TRUE,             \
                      BOOL UseZBuffer = FALSE,              \
                      long Width = 0, long Height = 0,  \
                      char BPP = 0);

  // Functions to get # of display modes and retrieve info
  long GetNumDisplayModes();
  BOOL GetDisplayModeInfo(long Num, D3DDISPLAYMODE *Mode);
```

```
// Return BPP for a specified display format
char GetFormatBPP(D3DFORMAT Format);


// See if specified display mode exists.
// Set Format and Windowed, then HAL to TRUE to test for
// hardware acceleration or FALSE to test for emulation.
BOOL CheckFormat(D3DFORMAT Format, BOOL Windowed, BOOL HAL);


BOOL Display();    // Display backbuffer (perform a flip)

BOOL BeginScene();    // Call before rendering anything
BOOL EndScene();      // Call after rendering everything


BOOL BeginSprite();   // Call to allow sprite drawing
BOOL EndSprite();     // Call to finish sprite drawing


// Functions to clear the display and/or zbuffer
BOOL Clear(long Color = 0, float ZBuffer = 1.0f);
BOOL ClearDisplay(long Color = 0);
BOOL ClearZBuffer(float ZBuffer = 1.0f);


// Functions to retrieve dimensions or bits-per-pixel
long GetWidth();
long GetHeight();
char GetBPP();


// Functions to see if hardware acceleration and
// ZBuffer features are used once display mode is set.
BOOL GetHAL();
BOOL GetZBuffer();


// Set a new perspective transformation
BOOL SetPerspective(float FOV=D3DX_PI/4,                    \
                    float Aspect=1.3333f,                  \
                    float Near=1.0f, float Far=10000.0f);


// Functions to set world and view transformations
BOOL SetWorldPosition(cWorldPosition *WorldPos);
BOOL SetCamera(cCamera *Camera);


// Functions to set the current light, material, and texture
```

```
BOOL SetLight(long Num, cLight *Light);
BOOL SetMaterial(cMaterial *Material);
BOOL SetTexture(short Num, cTexture *Texture);

// Set or get the ambient color level w/D3DCOLOR structure
BOOL SetAmbientLight(char Red, char Green, char Blue);
BOOL GetAmbientLight(char *Red, char *Green, char *Blue);

// Enable or disable a specific light (0-n)
BOOL EnableLight(long Num, BOOL Enable = TRUE);

// Enable or disable lighting, zbuffering, alphablending
// and alphatesting. Blending has optional blend values.
BOOL EnableLighting(BOOL Enable = TRUE);
BOOL EnableZBuffer(BOOL Enable = TRUE);
BOOL EnableAlphaBlending(BOOL Enable = TRUE,                \
                         DWORD Src = D3DBLEND_SRCALPHA,     \
                         DWORD Dest = D3DBLEND_INVSRCALPHA);
BOOL EnableAlphaTesting(BOOL Enable = TRUE);
};
```

You can do a great deal with cGraphics, and it all starts with a call to cGraphics::Init. From there, you can enumerate the various display modes or jump right in and call cGraphics::SetMode to get the ball rolling. At the minimum, SetMode requires only a handle to a parent window. By default, the display mode is set to use a window (as opposed to fullscreen) for output with no zbuffer.

If you want to use the full screen, you must set Windowed to FALSE and specify valid Width, Height, and bits-per-pixel (BPP) values. If you leave any of these three values at 0, SetMode will use the current desktop settings. If you are using Windowed mode and you specify a different Width or Height, the parent window will be resized to match those Width and Height values.

> **NOTE**
>
> The cGraphics::SetMode function is a talented one. It determines whether hardware acceleration and Z-Buffer support (if opted) exist. If neither of these properties exist, the SetMode function will have Direct3D emulate the 3-D functions and cut out the Z-Buffer to ensure that the mode is set.

From there, you might be wondering what to do next. Before rendering anything, you must call cGraphics::BeginScene. After rendering is complete, call cGraphics::EndScene. Then call on cGraphics::Display to display your graphics.

Want to clear the screen before rendering? Go right ahead with the trio of clear functions.

Now, you can begin turning on lights, materials, and textures (as shown throughout this section). cGraphics works just as I describe in Chapter 6, so nothing sneaky is going on here.

To set and enable the lighting, you call EnableLighting. Alpha blending works great, and you have the ability to specify the exact

> **CAUTION**
>
> If you're not using a Z-buffer, don't call Clear—because it takes a zbuffer value. Use ClearDisplay instead.

blending values (for source and destination blending). Alpha testing helps you draw those pesky transparent textures (as shown in Chapter 6).

# Images with cTexture

Textures are what make 3-D graphics worth their weight in gold. Plain polygons come to life, using full-color imagery. Trying to maintain a list of textures, however, can be a little painstaking, but with the help of cTexture, you can make your life easier:

```
class cTexture
{
  protected:
    cGraphics          *m_Graphics;          // Parent cGraphics
    IDirect3DTexture8 *m_Texture;            // Texture COM
    unsigned long      m_Width, m_Height;    // Dimensions of
                                             // texture image.

  public:
    cTexture();    // Constructor
    ~cTexture();   // Destructor

    IDirect3DTexture8 *GetTextureCOM();  // Return texture COM

    // Load a texture from file
    BOOL Load(cGraphics *Graphics, char *Filename,              \
              DWORD Transparent = 0,                            \
              D3DFORMAT Format = D3DFMT_UNKNOWN);
```

```
// Configure a cTexture class from an existing
// IDirect3DTexture8 object instance.
BOOL Create(cGraphics *Graphics, IDirect3DTexture8 *Texture);

BOOL Free();  // Free texture object

BOOL        IsLoaded();  // Returns TRUE if texture is loaded

long        GetWidth();   // Return width (pitch) of texture
long        GetHeight();  // Return height of texture
D3DFORMAT GetFormat();  // Return texture storage format

// Draw a 2-D portion of texture to device
BOOL Blit(long DestX, long DestY,                          \
          long SrcX = 0, long SrcY = 0,                    \
          long Width = 0, long Height = 0,                 \
          float XScale = 1.0f, float YScale = 1.0f,        \
          D3DCOLOR Color = 0xFFFFFFFF);
};
```

A cTexture class can be loaded with a texture from two sources: from an image file on a disk or from an existing IDirect3DTexture8 object. If you're loading an image from a disk, call cTexture::Load; it requires a few parameters in order to work: first, the pre-initialized cGraphics object and, second, the filename of the image to load.

The following two optional arguments are the transparent color key (if you're using textures with transparent pixels) and the storage format. The default value of 0 for Transparent tells the Load function not to use transparent pixels. Providing a value with D3DCOLOR_RGBA can remedy that problem (make sure you specify a value of 255 for the alpha parameter).

When using Format, use a Direct3D texture storage format such as D3DFMT_A1R5G5B5. Remember that textures with transparent pixels must use an alpha channel, so be sure to use a format such as D3DFMT_A1R5G5B5 or D3DFMT_A8R8G8B8.

From there, you'll most likely use the cTexture class in conjunction with the cGraphics::SetTexture function in order to draw texture-mapped polygons. On the other hand, if you are using a texture object's bitmap image to draw directly to the display, you can then use the cTexture::Blit function, which uses a special object called ID3DXSprite. You haven't learned about ID3DXSprite just yet—you'll get to see it in Chapter 11, "Using 2-D Graphics."

For now, I'll explain how to use the Blit function. You need to specify the destination coordinates for drawing a portion of the texture to the display, as well as the upper-left source coordinates, width, height, scaling factor, and color modulation values that you want to use. In Chapter 12, you see the Blit function used in more detail, but for now, here's a quick example that loads a texture (called texture.bmp) and draws it to the display:

```
// Assuming g_Graphics = pre-initialized cGraphics object
cTexture Texture;
Texture.Load(&g_Graphics, "texture.bmp");

// Draw texture to screen at 0,0 (using 2-D method)
Texture.Blit(0,0);

Texture.Free();  // Free texture from memory
```

# Colors and cMaterial

Chapter 6 discusses the importance of using materials that change the visual appearance of rendered objects by altering the color values of drawn faces. To make altering material color values easier, you use the cMaterial class:

```
class cMaterial
{
  protected:
    D3DMATERIAL8  m_Material;      // Material structure

  public:
    cMaterial();   // Constructor

    D3DMATERIAL8 *GetMaterial();  // Return D3DMATERIAL8 object

    // Set and get diffuse color components
    BOOL SetDiffuseColor(char Red, char Green, char Blue);
    BOOL GetDiffuseColor(char *Red, char *Green, char *Blue);

    // Set and get ambient color components
    BOOL SetAmbientColor(char Red, char Green, char Blue);
    BOOL GetAmbientColor(char *Red, char *Green, char *Blue);

    // Set and get specular color components
```

```
      BOOL SetSpecularColor(char Red, char Green, char Blue);
      BOOL GetSpecularColor(char *Red, char *Green, char *Blue);

      // Set and get emissive color components
      BOOL SetEmissiveColor(char Red, char Green, char Blue);
      BOOL GetEmissiveColor(char *Red, char *Green, char *Blue);

      // Set and get power value
      BOOL  SetPower(float Power);
      float GetPower(float Power);
};
```

As you can see, the cMaterial class holds a single D3DMATERIAL structure and gives you the functions to set and retrieve the various color components. To set a color component, specify an amount from 0 to 255. To retrieve a color component, supply the appropriate function with a pointer to a char type pointer.

Here's a quick example of using cMaterial to set a yellow material:

```
// Assuming g_Graphics is pre-initialized cGraphics object
cMaterial YellowMaterial;

YellowMaterial.SetDiffuseColor(255,255,0);
YellowMaterial.SetAmbientColor(255,255,0);

g_Graphics.SetMaterial(&YellowMaterial);  // Set material
```

You use the cMaterial class object in conjunction with cGraphics::SetMaterial to set the current rendering material.

> **NOTE**
>
> When you instance the cMaterial class, the m_Material member is cleared to an all-white material by default.

## Light It Up with cLight

Lights are simple beasts, just as materials are. You can do only so much with a light and in only so many ways, which is why I'm wrapping everything about lights (or at least everything you'll read about lights in Chapter 6 into a class called cLight:

```
class cLight
{
  protected:
    D3DLIGHT8 m_Light;   // Light structure

  public:
```

```
cLight();  // Constructor

D3DLIGHT8 *GetLight();  // Return light structure

BOOL SetType(D3DLIGHTTYPE Type);  // Set type of light:
                                  // D3DLIGHT_POINT
                                  // D3DLIGHT_SPOT
                                  // D3DLIGHT_DIRECTIONAL

// Move light to absolute position or relative from current
BOOL Move(float XPos, float YPos, float ZPos);
BOOL MoveRel(float XPos, float YPos, float ZPos);

// Get current position into provided variables
BOOL GetPos(float *XPos, float *YPos, float *ZPos);

// Set direction to absolute or relative from current
BOOL Point(float XPos, float YPos, float ZPos);
BOOL PointRel(float XPos, float YPos, float ZPos);

// Get current direction into provided variables
BOOL GetDirection(float *XPos, float *YPos, float *ZPos);

// Set and get the various color components
BOOL SetDiffuseColor(char Red, char Green, char Blue);
BOOL GetDiffuseColor(char *Red, char *Green, char *Blue);
BOOL SetSpecularColor(char Red, char Green, char Blue);
BOOL GetSpecularColor(char *Red, char *Green, char *Blue);
BOOL SetAmbientColor(char Red, char Green, char Blue);
BOOL GetAmbientColor(char *Red, char *Green, char *Blue);

// Set and get the range
BOOL SetRange(float Range);
float GetRange();

// Set and get the falloff value
BOOL SetFalloff(float Falloff);
float GetFalloff();

// Set and get the various attenuation values
BOOL SetAttenuation0(float Attenuation);
```

```
    float GetAttenuation0();
    BOOL SetAttenuation1(float Attenuation);
    float GetAttenuation1();
    BOOL SetAttenuation2(float Attenuation);
    float GetAttenuation2();

    // Set and get the Theta value
    BOOL SetTheta(float Theta);
    float GetTheta();

    // Set and get the Phi value
    BOOL SetPhi(float Phi);
    float GetPhi();
};
```

To use lights in your own project, you only need to instance the cLight class, pick a type of light to use (using standard Direct3D light types, as shown in the comments), set the light's color, and position (and point if necessary) the light anywhere you wish. To set the light, use the cGraphics::SetLight function as shown previously in the section "The Graphics System with cGraphics."

> **NOTE**
>
> When instanced, the cLight class is configured with a white point-light (see Chapter 6) located at 0,0,0. Also, directions are normalized (changed to a value of 1.0 or less, as you saw in Chapter 6) when you call Point or PointRel.

Here's a quick example of creating a white-colored directional light:

```
// Assuming g_Graphics = pre-initialized cGraphics object
cLight DirLight;

DirLight.SetType(D3DLIGHT_DIRECTIONAL);
DirLight.Move(0.0, 10.0f, 0.0f); // Place 10 units above origin
DirLight.Point(0.0, -1.0, 0.0f); // Point down

g_Graphics.SetLight(0, &DirLight); // Set as light 0
g_Graphics.EnableLight(0, TRUE);   // Turn on light
```

# Text and Fonts Using cFont

Although the ID3DXFont object is easy to deal with, it can be a pain setting up a font. However, you can use the cFont class to quickly and easily get fonts into your project:

```
class cFont
{
  private:
```

```
    ID3DXFont *m_Font;    // Font COM object

public:
  cFont();    // Constructor
  ~cFont();   // Destructor

  ID3DXFont *GetFontCOM(); // Return font COM object

  // Create and free a font
  BOOL Create(cGraphics *Graphics, char *Name,           \
              long Size = 16, BOOL Bold = FALSE,          \
              BOOL Italic = FALSE, BOOL Underline = FALSE, \
              BOOL Strikeout = FALSE);
  BOOL Free();

  // Begin and end font drawing sequence
  BOOL Begin();
  BOOL End();

   // Print specified text
  BOOL Print(char *Text, long XPos, long YPos,           \
             long Width = 0, long Height = 0,            \
             D3DCOLOR Color = 0xFFFFFFFF, DWORD Format = 0);
};
```

To begin using a font, you must create it with the cFont::Create function. You must pass it a pre-initialized cGraphics object, supply it with a font face name (such as Arial or Times New Roman), and specify the size in pixel height (more or less). You then have the option to use bold, italics, underline, and strikeout.

Notice the cFont::Begin and cFont::End pair which tells Direct3D that you're preparing to draw a font and that you're done printing with the font, respectively. You do not have to explicitly call these functions, because the Print function will call them for you (if you haven't already done so). Not calling Begin and End, however, can slow down printing, as the Print function will repeatedly call Begin and End for you every time you print a line of text.

When printing a line of text, you provide the cFont::Print function with a pointer to the text you want to print, the coordinates at which to start printing, the bounding box dimensions into which to clip the text (Width and Height defaults to 0, which means the full screen), the text color (defaults to white—use D3DCOLOR_RGBA macros to define color), and the text formatting (a combination of flags as shown in Table 10.2).

## Table 10.2 cFont::Print Format Flags

| Flag | Description |
|------|-------------|
| DT_BOTTOM | Justifies text to bottom of bounding rectangle. |
| DT_CENTER. | Centers text horizontally in bounding rectangle. |
| DT_LEFT | Left-justifies text to left edge of bounding rectangle. |
| DT_NOCLIP | Draws text without clipping to bounding rectangle. Provides faster printing. |
| DT_RIGHT | Right-justifies text (to right edge of bounding rectangle). |
| DT_TOP | Justifies text to top of bounding rectangle. |
| DT_WORDBREAK | Breaks words when right edge of bounding rectangle is reached. |

Here's a quick example of creating and using an instance of the cFont class:

```
// Assuming g_Graphics = pre-initialized cGraphics object
cFont ArialFont;

ArialFont.Create(&g_Graphics, "Arial"); // Arial font at size=16
ArialFont.Print("I can print fonts!", 0,0);  // Print at 0,0
```

# Vertices and cVertexBuffer

Vertices can be a burden, but unfortunately you can't do much about it at times. The cVertexBuffer class eases the burden a little by providing a quick way to create, set, and render sets of vertices, as illustrated here:

```
class cVertexBuffer
{
  private:
    cGraphics                *m_Graphics;  // Parent cGraphics
    IDirect3DVertexBuffer8 *m_pVB;         // Vertex buffer COM

    DWORD                    m_NumVertices;  // # vertices
    DWORD                    m_VertexSize;   // Size of vertex
    DWORD                    m_FVF;          // FVF descriptor
```

```
      BOOL                    m_Locked;  // Flag if buffer locked
      char                    *m_Ptr;    // Pointer to buffer

  public:
    cVertexBuffer();   // Constructor
    ~cVertexBuffer();  // Destructor

    // Functions to retrieve COM, Size, FVF, and # vertices
    IDirect3DVertexBuffer8 *GetVertexBufferCOM();
    unsigned long           GetVertexSize();
    unsigned long           GetVertexFVF();
    unsigned long           GetNumVertices();

    // Create and free a vertex buffer
    BOOL Create(cGraphics *Graphics,                        \
                unsigned long NumVertices, DWORD Descriptor, \
                long VertexSize);
    BOOL Free();

    BOOL IsLoaded();  // Return TRUE if buffer is allocated.

    // Copy a series of vertices into vertex buffer.
    BOOL Set(unsigned long FirstVertex,                     \
             unsigned long NumVertices, void *VertexList);

    // Render vertex buffer to device
    BOOL Render(unsigned long FirstVertex,                  \
                unsigned long NumPrimitives, DWORD Type);

    // Lock and unlock a vertex buffer for access
    BOOL  Lock(unsigned long FirstVertex = 0,              \
               unsigned long NumVertices = 0);
    BOOL  Unlock();

    void *GetPtr();  // Return pointer to locked vertex buffer
};
```

You must create a vertex buffer with cVertexBuffer::Create, which takes a parent cGraphics object, the number of vertices for which to allocate room, a flexible vertex format (FVF) descriptor, and the size (in bytes) of a single vertex. That's right, you still have to construct a vertex structure to work with this class, but don't worry; it's not hard to do, as you'll soon see.

When you're done with your class instance, be sure to free it with a call to cVertexBuffer::Free. Before that, however, fill the buffer with the vertex information you'll be using with a call to cVertexBuffer::Set. Call cVertexBuffer::Set using the index of the first vertex you'll be setting, the number of vertices to set, and a pointer to an array of vertex structures that you defined.

You are now ready to render polygons using cVertexBuffer:Render. Notice that you can specify the first vertex with which to start drawing and the total number of primitives (polygon faces) to draw. Use the Type parameter just as you did in Chapter 6 (and as described in Table 10.3).

Say that you want to create a simple vertex buffer, one that uses 2-D transformed vertices (vertices defined in screen coordinates) and a diffuse color component. To make things easier, create a square polygon using two triangles (using a triangle strip):

```
// assuming g_Graphics = pre-initialize cGraphics object

// define a vertex structure and FVF descriptor
typedef struct sVertex {
    float    x, y, z, rhw;
    D3DCOLOR Diffuse;
} sVertex;
#define VERTEXFVF (D3DFVF_XYZRHW | D3DFVF_DIFFUSE)

cVertexBuffer g_VB;
g_VB.Create(&g_Graphics, 4, VERTEXFVF, sizeof(sVertex));

// Triangle strip vertices in clockwise ordering
sVertex Verts[4] = {
    {   0.0f,   0.0f, 0.0f,1.0f, D3DCOLOR_RGBA(255,0,0,255) },
    { 200.0f,   0.0f, 0.0f,1.0f, D3DCOLOR_RGBA(0,255,0,255) },
    {   0.0f, 200.0f, 0.0f,1.0f, D3DCOLOR_RGBA(0,0,255,255) },
    { 200.0f, 200.0f, 0.0f,1.0f, D3DCOLOR_RGBA(255,255,255,255) },
};
g_VB.Set(0, 4, (void*)&Verts);

// Render the triangle strip
g_VB.Render(0, 2, D3DPT_TRIANGLESTRIP);

// Free vertex buffer
g_VB.Free();
```

### Table 10.3 cVertexBuffer::Render Type Flags

| Flags | Description |
|---|---|
| D3DPT_POINTLIST | A series of vertices to draw as pixels. |
| D3DPT_LINELIST | A set of isolated (unconnected) lines. |
| D3DPT_LINESTRIP | A series of connected lines. Each line is drawn from the previous vertex to the current vertex, much like connecting dots. |
| D3DPT_TRIANGLELIST | A list of triangles with three vertices per triangle. |
| D3DPT_TRIANGLESTRIP | A triangle strip. Each vertex uses the previous two vertices to create a face. |
| D3DPT_TRIANGLEFAN | A triangle fan. Each vertex attaches to a center vertex and the next vertex to create a face. |

# World Transformations with cWorldPosition

Although working with a world transformation matrix is not difficult, wouldn't it be nice to have a class handle all the details—details such as world coordinates, rotation values, and scaling factors? How about throwing billboards into the mix, just for the right flavor?

It's all here in cWorldPosition:

```
class cWorldPosition
{
  protected:
    BOOL  m_Billboard;    // Flag if billboard being used

    // Current position, rotation, and scale
    float m_XPos,       m_YPos,      m_ZPos;
    float m_XRotation, m_YRotation, m_ZRotation;
    float m_XScale,     m_YScale,    m_ZScale;

    D3DXMATRIX m_matWorld;            // World transformation matrix
```

```
        D3DXMATRIX m_matScale;          // Scale matrix
        D3DXMATRIX m_matRotation;       // Rotation matrix
        D3DXMATRIX m_matTranslation;    // Translation matrix
        D3DXMATRIX *m_matCombine1;      // Combined matrix 1
        D3DXMATRIX *m_matCombine2;      // Combined matrix 2

    public:
        cWorldPosition();  // Constructor

        // Return world transformation matrix
        D3DXMATRIX *GetMatrix(cGraphics *Graphics = NULL);

        // Set outside matrices to combine with world matrix
        BOOL SetCombineMatrix1(D3DXMATRIX *Matrix = NULL);
        BOOL SetCombineMatrix2(D3DXMATRIX *Matrix = NULL);

        BOOL Copy(cWorldPosition *DestPos);  // Copy to other class

        // Move to world coordinates (and relative from current)
        BOOL Move(float XPos, float YPos, float ZPos);
        BOOL MoveRel(float XAdd, float YAdd, float ZAdd);

        // Set rotation values (and relative from current)
        BOOL Rotate(float XRot, float YRot, float ZRot);
        BOOL RotateRel(float XAdd, float YAdd, float ZAdd);

        // Set scaling factors (and relative from current)
        BOOL Scale(float XScale, float YScale, float ZScale);
        BOOL ScaleRel(float XAdd, float YAdd, float ZAdd);

        // Update matrix and provide cGraphics object for billboard
        BOOL Update(cGraphics *Graphics = NULL);

        // Enabled or disable use of billboarding
        BOOL EnableBillboard(BOOL Enable = TRUE);

        // Retrieve current position, rotation, and scale
        float GetXPos();
        float GetYPos();
        float GetZPos();
        float GetXRotation();
```

```
      float GetYRotation();
      float GetZRotation();
      float GetXScale();
      float GetYScale();
      float GetZScale();
};
```

Most of the functions are fairly self-evident; the only questionable ones are `Update`, `GetMatrix`, `SetCombineMatrix1`, and `SetCombineMatrix2`. The `Update` function rebuilds the world transformation matrix using the contained orientation, taking a billboard matrix and two outside matrices (which I call *combine matrices*) into account. To set the two combined matrix sources, use the `SetCombineMatrix1` and `SetCombineMatrix2` functions.

The `GetMatrix` function returns the current world transformation matrix. Be sure to pass the `GetMatrix` function the current `cGraphics` object that you're using in order to calculate the billboard matrix (it's calculated from the transposed view matrix).

Here's an example that orients two objects inside the 3-D world (with one attached to the other):

```
cWorldPosition ObjectPos, ObjectPos2;

ObjectPos.Move(10.0f, 100.0f, -56.0f);
ObjectPos.Rotate(1.57f, 0.0f, 0.785f);
ObjectPos.Update();  // Calculate updated matrix

// Combine the 2nd object with the 1st (inherits orientation)
ObjectPos2.SetCombineMatrix1(ObjectPos.GetMatrix());
ObjectPos2.Rotate(0.0f, 0.0f, 3.14f);
ObjectPos2.Update();  // Calculate update matrix using combined
```

> **NOTE**
>
> **Combined matrices (or *attached matrices*) represent the transformations required to attach one object to another, such as to attach a weapon to a mesh's hand. The two matrices represent the local orientation of the attached mesh frame and the world orientation of the attached mesh, respectively.**

# View Transformations and cCamera

Much like `cWorldPosition`, the `cCamera` class deals with view transformation matrices:

```
class cCamera
{
  protected:
```

```
       float m_XPos, m_YPos, m_ZPos;   // Position coordinates
       float m_XRot, m_YRot, m_ZRot;   // Rotation values

       // Camera tracking orientations
       float m_StartXPos, m_StartYPos, m_StartZPos;
       float m_StartXRot, m_StartYRot, m_StartZRot;
       float m_EndXPos, m_EndYPos, m_EndZPos;
       float m_EndXRot, m_EndYRot, m_EndZRot;

       D3DXMATRIX m_matWorld;        // World transformation matrix
       D3DXMATRIX m_matTranslation;  // Translation matrix
       D3DXMATRIX m_matRotation;     // Rotation matrix

   public:
     cCamera();   // Constructor

       D3DXMATRIX *GetMatrix(); // Get view transformation matrix
       BOOL Update();            // Update transformation matrix

       // Move and rotate camera (view)
       BOOL Move(float XPos, float YPos, float ZPos);
       BOOL MoveRel(float XAdd, float YAdd, float ZAdd);
       BOOL Rotate(float XRot, float YRot, float ZRot);
       BOOL RotateRel(float XAdd, float YAdd, float ZAdd);

       // Point a camera from Eye position to At position
       BOOL Point(float XEye, float YEye, float ZEye,                \
                  float XAt, float YAt, float ZAt);

       // Set starting and ending track orientations
       BOOL SetStartTrack();
       BOOL SetEndTrack();

       // Interpolate camera orientation along track
       // using Time (0.0 - 1.0) and total Length.
       BOOL Track(float Time, float Length);

       // Retrieve translation and rotation values
       float GetXPos();
       float GetYPos();
```

```
      float GetZPos();
      float GetXRotation();
      float GetYRotation();
      float GetZRotation();
};
```

The cCamera class works much like the cWorldPosition class, so I will forgo the introductions. The only difference is the addition of the Point, SetStartTrack, SetEndTrack, and Track functions. You use the Point function to orient the viewpoint and point it in a specific direction all at once.

The trio of track-related functions track the path of a moving camera over time. To use the camera tracking orientations, position the camera in its desired starting location and call cCamera::SetStartTrack. Then move the camera to the desired ending orientation and call cCamera::SetEndTrack.

From there, it's a matter of calling cCamera::Track (before the call to cCamera::Update) to orient the camera along the track you created. The Time parameter of Track ranges from 0.0 (starting orientation) to 1.0 (ending orientation) and any value in between moves the camera along the track. Length can be any arbitrary value that you work with (milliseconds, for example).

Camera tracking creates some awesome effects, so jump right into this example:

```
cCamera Cam;

// Position at 0.0f, 100.0f, -100.0f and look at origin
Cam.Point(0.0f, 100.0f, -100.0f, 0.0f, 0.0f, 0.0f);
Cam.SetStartTrack();

// Move to ending orientation
Cam.Point(-100.0f, 0.0f, 0.0f, 0.0f, 100.0f, 0.0f);
Cam.SetEndTrack();

// Position camera to halfway mark over 10000 milliseconds
Cam.Track(0.5f, 10000);
Cam.Update();
```

To set a camera as the current view transformation matrix, use the cGraphics::SetCamera function:

```
g_Graphics.SetCamera(&Cam);  // Don't call Update beforehand
```

# Loadable Meshes using cMesh

Now, you can't say that dealing with meshes isn't difficult, can you? Of course, I'm talking about skinned meshes as well as the standard meshes you've been using from Chapter 6. The purpose of cMesh is to help you load those little demons into a series of easy-to-use classes and then use them with other objects that render the meshes to the display.

```cpp
class cMesh
{
  private:
    cGraphics *m_Graphics;    // Parent cGraphics object

    long       m_NumMeshes;   // # meshes in class
    sMesh     *m_Meshes;      // Mesh list

    long       m_NumFrames;   // # of frames in class
    sFrame    *m_Frames;      // Frame list

    D3DXVECTOR3   m_Min, m_Max; // Bounding box coordinates
    float         m_Radius;     // Bounding sphere radius

    // Function that parses a single .X file template
    void ParseXFileData(IDirectXFileData *pData,                 \
                        sFrame *ParentFrame, char *TexturePath);

    // Match bone and frame transformation matrices
    void MapFramesToBones(sFrame *Frame);

  public:
    cMesh();    // Constructor
    ~cMesh();   // Destructor

    BOOL    IsLoaded();   // Return TRUE if meshes are loaded

    long     GetNumFrames();        // Return # of frames in list
    sFrame *GetParentFrame();       // Get top-most frame in list
    sFrame *GetFrame(char *Name);   // Find frame in list

    long     GetNumMeshes();        // Return # of meshes in list
    sMesh   *GetParentMesh();       // Get top-most mesh in list
```

```
    sMesh   *GetMesh(char *Name);  // Find mesh in list

    // Get bounding box coordinates and bounding sphere radius
    BOOL GetBounds(float *MinX, float *MinY, float *MinZ,       \
                   float *MaxX, float *MaxY, float *MaxZ,       \
                   float *Radius);

    // Load and free an .X file
    // (specifying optional path of texture maps).
    BOOL    Load(cGraphics *Graphics, char *Filename,          \
                 char *TexturePath = ".\\");
    BOOL    Free();
};
```

While this class also looks small, I'm not showing you the sMesh and sFrame structures
that the cMesh class uses. Those two structures form a linked list of mesh objects and
frame definitions. They also hold the various orientations of the frames and lists of
materials and textures. Go ahead and load up the Graphics Core source and take a
look at them; they're highly commented and should be easy to follow.

The only thing you'll do with cMesh is use it to load meshes from .X files, such as in
the following:

```
// Assuming g_Graphics = pre-initialized cGraphics object
cMesh Mesh;
Mesh.Load(&g_Graphics, "Mesh.x");
Mesh.Free(); // Free mesh when done
```

# Drawing Objects Using cObject

When it comes time to draw meshes, you must create a bridge from the mesh definitions to the display. "Why not handle rendering by using the cMesh object," you
ask? The answer is *memory usage*. What if you want to use the same mesh again and
again? The solution is to use cObject:

```
class cObject
{
  protected:
    cGraphics       *m_Graphics;       // Parent cGraphics object
    cMesh           *m_Mesh;           // Meshes to draw
    sAnimationSet   *m_AnimationSet;   // Animation set
    cWorldPosition  m_Pos;             // World orientation
```

```
    BOOL            m_Billboard;        // Billboard object flag

    unsigned long  m_StartTime;      // Starting animation time

    // Functions to update frame orientations and draw meshes
    void UpdateFrame(sFrame *Frame, D3DXMATRIX *Matrix);
    void DrawFrame(sFrame *Frame);
    void DrawMesh(sMesh *Mesh);

public:
    cObject();     // Constructor
    ~cObject();    // Destructor

    // Create and free an object (setting optional mesh)
    BOOL Create(cGraphics *Graphics, cMesh *Mesh = NULL);
    BOOL Free();

    // Enable or disable billboarding
    BOOL EnableBillboard(BOOL Enable = TRUE);

    // Attach object to another object's frame
    // (this combines the matrices when update is called).
    // Defaults to first frame found in mesh.
    BOOL AttachToObject(cObject *Object,                      \
                        char *FrameName = NULL);

    // Orient object
    BOOL Move(float XPos, float YPos, float ZPos);
    BOOL MoveRel(float XAdd, float YAdd, float ZAdd);
    BOOL Rotate(float XRot, float YRot, float ZRot);
    BOOL RotateRel(float XAdd, float YAdd, float ZAdd);
    BOOL Scale(float XScale, float YScale, float ZScale);
    BOOL ScaleRel(float XAdd, float YAdd, float ZAdd);

    D3DXMATRIX *GetMatrix();  // Retrieve object's matrix

    // Retrieve object orientations
    float GetXPos();
    float GetYPos();
    float GetZPos();
```

```
        float GetXRotation();
        float GetYRotation();
        float GetZRotation();
        float GetXScale();
        float GetYScale();
        float GetZScale();

        // Get scaled bounding box and radius
        BOOL GetBounds(float *MinX, float *MinY, float *MinZ,        \
                       float *MaxX, float *MaxY, float *MaxZ,        \
                       float *Radius);

        // Set mesh that this class draws
        BOOL SetMesh(cMesh *Mesh);

        // Set new animation (w/name and start reference time)
        BOOL SetAnimation(cAnimation *Animation,                    \
                          char *Name = NULL,                        \
                          unsigned long StartTime = 0);

        char *GetAnimation(); // Get pointer to animation name

        // Reset animation playback with new start reference time
        BOOL ResetAnimation(unsigned long StartTime = 0);

        // Update animation based on time and
        // using smooth interpolation.
        BOOL UpdateAnimation(unsigned long Time, BOOL Smooth = TRUE);

        // Returns TRUE if animation is complete at Time
        BOOL AnimationComplete(unsigned long Time);

        BOOL Update();  // Update object transformation matrix
        BOOL Render();  // Draw object using world transformation
};
```

The cObject class has just about everything you need to work with 3-D objects in
your world. You can orient the object, set new meshes, align the object with the
view (billboard), set and update animations, attach to other objects, and retrieve
the bounding box and radius of the bounding sphere.

> **NOTE**
>
> A *bounding box* is a set of coordinates that represents the farthest extremes of the vertices within a mesh. For example, a mesh in which the highest vertex is at y=100.0 means that the box will have an extreme top value of 100.0. The same goes for the left, right, bottom, front, and back of the mesh. The *bounding radius* is almost the same, but rather than use a box, you use a sphere to enclose the mesh.
>
> Bounding boxes and spheres are very useful when it comes to collision detection, in which you check to see whether two objects have collided with one another.

To work with cObject, just instance it and attach a previously loaded mesh object. Then you can orient the object in any way and render it to the display, as in the following example:

```
// g_Graphics = pre-initialized cGraphics object
// g_Mesh = pre-loaded mesh object
cObject g_Object;

g_Object.Create(&g_Graphics, &g_Mesh);
g_Object.Move(100.0f, 50.0f, 100.0f);
g_Object.Render();
```

# Making Meshes Move with cAnimation

Rounding up the end of the Graphics Core is cAnimation, the mesh animation component. With cAnimation, you can load a series of animation sets from .X files and use them in conjunction with cObject to animate meshes.

The cAnimation class is small. Much like cMesh, cAnimation has a few structures that hold a list of animation data. Have a look at the class declaration:

```
class cAnimation
{
  protected:
    long              m_NumAnimations;  // # animations in class
    sAnimationSet *m_AnimationSet;    // Animations list
```

```
    // Parse a single .X file template
    void ParseXFileData(IDirectXFileData *DataObj,                 \
                        sAnimationSet *ParentAnim,                 \
                        sAnimation *CurrentAnim);

  public:
    cAnimation();  // Constructor
    ~cAnimation(); // Destructor

    BOOL    IsLoaded();  // Return TRUE if animations are loaded

    // Retrieve # of animations in list, topmost animation,
    // and length of a given animation.
    long            GetNumAnimations();
    sAnimationSet *GetAnimationSet(char *Name = NULL);
    unsigned long  GetLength(char *Name = NULL);

  // Load an free an animation (with optional mesh to map)
    BOOL Load(char *Filename, cMesh *MapMesh = NULL);
    BOOL Free();

    BOOL MapToMesh(cMesh *Mesh);   // Map animation to mesh

    // Set an animation to loop or not to loop.
    BOOL SetLoop(BOOL ToLoop, char *Name = NULL);
};
```

With the cAnimation class, you call only four common functions: Load, Free, MapToMesh, and SetLoop. Mapping an animation to a mesh is necessary in order to assure that the animation class can find the mesh's matrices that need to be altered. As for SetLoop, notice the Name parameter; Name refers to the name of the animation to set a repetitive loop for.

Animations (like frames and meshes) can be named inside the .X file (as they should be). In that way, you can pack multiple animations into an .X file and reference them by name. For example, if your .X file contains an animation set called Walk, you can pass the string "Walk" as Name. Using NULL as Name specifies the topmost animation in the list.

The other thing you're bound to notice is the StartTime parameter in the cObject class. The StartTime parameter provides a starting reference value that the animation uses to time the animation. In this way, if you base your animations on time (using a function such as timeGetTime), you set StartTime to the time that you started playing the animation.

Then subsequent calls to cObject::UpdateAnimation will use the difference between the time you provide and the StartTime reference, giving you a clean-cut timing mechanism (in other words, the exact timing based on a starting play time of 0 seconds, rather than on an arbitrary time value).

At long last, using the final Graphics Core example, here's how to load an animation, set its loop, and apply the animation object to a previously created 3-D object:

```
// g_Graphics = pre-initialized cGraphics object
// g_Mesh = pre-loaded cMesh object
// g_Object = pre-loaded cObject object
cAnimation Anim;

// Load animation and loop walk animation
Anim.Load("Mesh.x", &g_Mesh);
Anim.SetLoop(TRUE, "Walk");

// Apply walk animation to object
g_Object.SetAnimation(&Anim, "Walk", timeGetTime());

// Enter loop to render object, updating animation each frame
g_Object.UpdateAnimation(timeGetTime(), TRUE);
g_Object.Render();

// When done, free animation
Anim.Free();
```

# The Input Core

Whew! The Graphics Core is massive, and it may take a while to fully understand it. For now, let's slow it down a bit and take a look at the Input Core, which you use to provide a means to communicate players' actions to your games via the keyboard, mouse, and joystick.

> **NOTE**
> When playing animations, time is arbitrary; it can mean time in seconds, milliseconds, frames, and so on. You must decide, and maintain, the measurement of time that you want to use.

Device input takes place with two simple classes: cInput and cInputDevice. You use the cInput class to initialize DirectInput, and you use the cInputDevice class to contain a single DirectInput device interface object. If you use multiple devices, use separate cInputDevice objects for each one.

## Using DirectInput with cInput

The first step to using the input system is to initialize DirectInput, which is the purpose of the cInput class. Extremely compact, the cInput class delcaration is as follows:

```
class cInput
{
  protected:
      HWND            m_hWnd;      // Handle of owner window
      IDirectInput8 *m_pDI;        // DirectInput interface

  public:
    cInput();      // Constructor
    ~cInput();     // Destructor

    IDirectInput8 *GetDirectInputCOM(); // returns DI COM object
    HWND           GethWnd();           // returns window handle

    BOOL Init(HWND hWnd, HINSTANCE hInst);  // Initialize class
    BOOL Shutdown();                        // Shutdown class
};
```

This cInput class is fairly lightweight, with only two functions that you'll be calling (Init and Shutdown). The real magic comes in when using the cInputDevice class.

## Input Devices with cInputDevice

The cInputDevice class is where the real action is. The cInputDevice class is used to initialize a specific input device (the keyboard, mouse, or joystick) and give you the means to retrieve that device's information for use in your game. Whereas the cInput class was simple, the cInputDevice class makes up the rest of the input functionality with the following declaration:

```
class cInputDevice
{
  public:
```

```
    cInput              *m_Input;    // Parent cInput class

    short               m_Type;      // Type of device
                                     // MOUSE, KEYBOARD,
                                     // or JOYSTICK
    IDirectInputDevice8 *m_pDIDevice; // COM device

    BOOL                m_Windowed;  // TRUE if using Windows
                                     // mouse reading method
                                     // or FALSE if using
                                     // DirectInput method.

    char                m_State[256]; // States of all keys
                                      // and buttons
    DIMOUSESTATE        *m_MouseState;    // Mouse state
    DIJOYSTATE          *m_JoystickState; // Joystick state
    BOOL                m_Locks[256];    // Flags if keys or
                                         // buttons locked.

    // Mouse/joystick coordinates
    long                m_XPos, m_YPos;

    // Internal enumeration function
    static BOOL FAR PASCAL EnumJoysticks(                      \
            LPCDIDEVICEINSTANCE pdInst, LPVOID pvRef);

public:
    cInputDevice();    // Constructor
    ~cInputDevice();   // Destructor

    IDirectInputDevice8 *DeviceCOM();   // Return COM object

    // Functions to create a device interface and to free it
    BOOL Create(cInput *Input, short Type,                     \
            BOOL Windowed = TRUE);
    BOOL Free();

    BOOL Clear();   // Clear device data
    BOOL Read();    // Read in device data
    BOOL Acquire(BOOL Active = TRUE);   // Acquire or unacquire
                                        // device.
```

```
      BOOL GetLock(char Num);          // Get locked key/button state
      BOOL SetLock(char Num, BOOL State = TRUE); // Set lock state

      long GetXPos();                  // Get x position of mouse/joystick
      BOOL SetXPos(long XPos); // Set x position
      long GetYPos();                  // Get y position of mouse/joystick
      BOOL SetYPos(long YPos); // Set y position
      long GetXDelta();                // Get x delta (relative movement)
      long GetYDelta();                // Get y delta (relative movement)

      // Keyboard specific functions
      BOOL  GetKeyState(char Num); // Get key state . Returns:
                                   // TRUE=Pressed or FALSE=Released
                                   // Use Num = KEY_* or DIK_*
      BOOL  SetKeyState(char Num, BOOL State); // Set key state
      BOOL  GetPureKeyState(char Num);  // Get key state w/o locks
      short GetKeypress(long TimeOut = 0);     // Wait for keypress
                                               // and return ASCII value
      long  GetNumKeyPresses();     // Get # keys currently pressed
      long  GetNumPureKeyPresses();// Get # keys pressed w/o locks

      // Mouse/Joystick specific functions
      BOOL  GetButtonState(char Num);  // Get button state
                           // Num=LBUTTON, RBUTTON, MBUTTON
      BOOL  SetButtonState(char Num, BOOL State); // Set state
      BOOL  GetPureButtonState(char Num); // Get state w/o locks
      long  GetNumButtonPresses();        // Get # buttons pressed
      long  GetNumPureButtonPresses();  // Get # pressed w/o locks
};
```

The cInputDevice class has it all! It encompasses all devices: keyboards, mice, and joysticks, in one neat package. The class object works by calling cInputDevice::Create and passing along a pre-initialized cInput class object. You also need to tell the class which device to use by setting Type to the approiate value (KEYBOARD, MOUSE, or JOYSTICK). Lastly, you need to inform the class whether or not to use DirectInput's device-reading functions or Windows' device-reading functions. Setting Windowed to TRUE will force the class object to use Windows' device-reading functions, while a value of FALSE will force DirectInput's. If you're planing on using a windowed application (or want the Windows cursor visible), be sure to specify a value of TRUE for Windowed.

Moving on in the class's function list, you call cInputDevice::Read to read the current state of the device in question. Then you can check the state of each individual key or button using cInputDevice::GetKeyState, cInputDevice::GetButtonState, cInputDevice::GetPureKeyState, and cInputDevice::GetPureButtonState.

The reason for the two separate pure functions is that keys and buttons can be locked. A locked key or button cannot be triggered until it is released. Reading pure values ignores the state of the locks.

A call to GetKeyState or GetButtonState returns TRUE if the key is being pressed or FALSE if not. The Num parameter of these state-checking functions represents the key or button to check. Keys are referenced by name, prefixed with KEY_— for example, KEY_ESC or KEY_A. Check the Core_Input.h file for a full listing of KEY_ values (or use constants such as DIK_A and DIK_ESCAPE, which are supplied by DirectInput).

Buttons are referenced by mouse: MOUSE_LBUTTON (left button), MOUSE_RBUTTON (right button), and MOUSE_MBUTTON (middle button). For joysticks, use JOYSTICK_BUTTON0, JOYSTICK_BUTTON1, JOYSTICK_BUTTON2, JOYSTICK_BUTTON3, JOYSTICK_BUTTON4, and JOYSTICK_BUTTON5.

## Using the Input Core

Using the Input Core is easy; just instance a cInput class object and as many cInputDevice objects as you need, being sure to initialize each as you go. For example, say that you want to use two devices, the keyboard and mouse:

```
cInput          g_Input;          // Global declarations
cInputDevice g_Keyboard;
cInputDevice g_Mouse;

// Initialize the input system (required)
// Assumes hWnd and hInst are already initialized
// hWnd = window handle, hInst = instance handle
g_Input.Init(hWnd, hInst);

// Create keyboard and mouse devices
// Use DirectInput method of reading mouse
g_Keyboard.Create(&g_Input, KEYBOARD);
g_Mouse.Create(&g_Input, MOUSE, FALSE);

// Read in current state of devices
g_Keyboard.Read();
g_Mouse.Read();
```

```
// If ESC pressed, display a message
if(g_Keyboard.GetKeyState(KEY_ESC) == TRUE) {
  // Load the ESC key so user must release it before
  // it can be read again.
  g_Keyboard.SetLock(KEY_ESC, TRUE);
  MessageBox(hWnd, "ESCAPE", "Key Pressed!", MB_OK);
}

// If left mouse button pressed, display coordinates
if(g_Mouse.GetPureButtonState(MOUSE_LBUTTON) == TRUE) {
  char b[200];
  sprintf(b, "%ld, %ld", g_Mouse.GetXPos(), g_Mouse.GetYPos());
  MessageBox(hWnd, b, "Mouse Coordinates", MB_OK);
}

// Release everything
g_Mouse.Free();
g_Keyboard.Free();
g_Input.Shutdown();
```

# The Sound Core

What's a game without music and sound? The Sound Core is your solution to getting sound and music into your game quickly and easily. Five class components are contained within the Sound Core (see Table 10.4).

Let's go ahead and start at the top of the list by first looking at the cSound object.

## Using DirectX Audio Control with cSound

The cSound object controls the DirectSound and DirectMusic objects and sets the global volume for playback. It also controls the notification thread used to stream sounds. Take a look at the class declaration:

```
class cSound
{
  protected:
    HWND                        m_hWnd;  // Parent window handle

    long                        m_Volume;  // Global volume
```

```
// Events for each sound channel
// extra event used to shutdown thread
HANDLE                  m_Events[33];
cSoundChannel           *m_EventChannel[32];

// Streaming thread data
HANDLE                  m_hThread;       // thread handle
DWORD                   m_ThreadID;      // thread ID
BOOL                    m_ThreadActive;  // active thread
static DWORD            HandleNotifications(LPVOID lpvoid);

// DirectSound COM objects
IDirectSound8           *m_pDS;
IDirectSoundBuffer      *m_pDSBPrimary;

// Cooperative level, frequency, # channels, and BPS
long                    m_CooperativeLevel;
long                    m_Frequency;
short                   m_Channels;
short                   m_BitsPerSample;
```

## Table 10.4 The Sound Core Classes

| Class | Description |
|-------|-------------|
| cSound | Contains the DirectSound and DirectMusic objects, and controls sound streaming. |
| cSoundData | A class that contains wave data used to play with cSoundChannel. |
| cSoundChannel | The class used to play a single sound. You can have as many as 32 of these classes in use at once (meaning that you can play 32 simultaneous sounds)! |
| cMusicChannel | You can use this class to play a single song file, whether it's a MIDI file or a DirectMusic native song. You can use only one of these classes at a time. |
| cDLS | The DownLoadable Sound class object. This class allows you to load different instruments into the cMusicChannel object. |

```
    // DirectMusic COM objects
    IDirectMusicPerformance8 *m_pDMPerformance;
    IDirectMusicLoader8      *m_pDMLoader;

  public:
    cSound();    // Constructor
    ~cSound();   // Destructor

    // Assign and release events used in streaming
    BOOL AssignEvent(cSoundChannel *Channel,                     \
                     short *EventNum, HANDLE *EventHandle);
    BOOL ReleaseEvent(cSoundChannel *Channel, short *EventNum);

    // Functions to retrieve COM interfaces
    IDirectSound8            *GetDirectSoundCOM();
    IDirectSoundBuffer       *GetPrimaryBufferCOM();
    IDirectMusicPerformance8 *GetPerformanceCOM();
    IDirectMusicLoader8      *GetLoaderCOM();

    // Init and shutdown functions
    BOOL Init(HWND hWnd, long Frequency = 22050,                 \
              short Channels = 1, short BitsPerSample = 16,      \
              long CooperativeLevel = DSSCL_PRIORITY);
    BOOL Shutdown();

    // Get or set the global volume level
    long GetVolume();
    BOOL SetVolume(long Percent);

    // Restore system to known state
    BOOL Restore();
};
```

The primary functions to deal with in the cSound class are Init, Shutdown, and SetVolume. As I've mentioned, each class object needs to be initialized before using, and the cSound class is not an exception.

To use Init, you must pass it to the parent window handle, as well as the optional mixer settings (the system defaults to 22,050 Hz, mono, 16-bit samplings with a DSSCL_PRIORITY cooperative level). Refer to Chapter 8, "Playing Sound with DirectX Audio," for information on the various playback formats and cooperatives levels that you can use. Always follow up a call to Init with a call to Shutdown when you're done with the sound system.

To change the volume setting call cSound::SetVolume with Percent set to a value from 0 (silence) to 100 (full volume).

# Using Wave Data and cSoundData

You use the cSoundData class object to describe and contain a single sound (waveform). The sound frequency, bits-per-sample, number of channels, size, and source are all wrapped into this declaration:

```
class cSoundData
{
  friend class cSoundChannel;  // Let the sound channel have
                               // access to my class.

  protected:
    long  m_Frequency;      // Sound frequency.
    short m_Channels;       // # of channels in sound.
    short m_BitsPerSample;  // Bits-per-sample in sound.

    FILE *m_fp;     // Source sound file pointer.
    char *m_Ptr;    // Source sound memory pointer.
    char *m_Buf;    // Source sound memory buffer.

    long  m_Size;   // Size of sound (in bytes).
    long  m_Left;   // Data left to stream.

    long  m_StartPos;  // Starting position of sound in source.
    long  m_Pos;       // Current position of sound in source.

  public:
    cSoundData();   // Constructor
    ~cSoundData();  // Destructor

    char *GetPtr();   // Get the sound memory buffer pointer.
    long GetSize();   // Get the size of the sound.

    BOOL Create();            // Create sound using loaded size.
    BOOL Create(long Size);   // Create a sound using size.
    BOOL Free();              // Free sound buffer
```

```
    // Set playback format of loaded sound.
    BOOL SetFormat(long Frequency, short Channels, short BitsPerSample);

    // Set source from file or memory pointer, using specified
    // offset position from start, and total size of sound.
    BOOL SetSource(FILE *fp, long Pos = -1, long Size = -1);
    BOOL SetSource(void *Ptr, long Pos = -1, long Size = -1);

    // Load a .wav file into memory and configure for playback.
    BOOL LoadWAV(char *Filename, FILE *fp = NULL);

    // Load only the wav file header and configure format.
    BOOL LoadWAVHeader(char *Filename, FILE *fp = NULL);

    // Copy internal data to another cSoundData object
    BOOL Copy(cSoundData *Source);
};
```

The upcoming cSoundChannel structure uses the cSoundData class to play sounds. Before you can play sound, however, you must use a cSoundData class object to store the playback format and the sound's data source. Sounds can come from two sources: a file or a memory buffer. In addition, sounds too big to fit into memory can be configured to stream from their source.

The quickest way to load a single .WAV file is to use the cSoundData::LoadWAV function. The LoadWAV function takes two parameters: a filename to load and a source file pointer. Only one of these parameters can be used, with the other one being set to NULL. The source file pointer enables you to pack multiple .WAV files into a single file but still be able to load them separately.

To load a single .WAV file, try this:

```
cSoundData Data;

// Load a sound from a file
Data.LoadWAV("sound.wav");

// Load a sound from file pointer
FILE *fp = fopen("sound.wav", "rb");
Data.LoadWAV(NULL, fp);
fclose(fp);
```

Aside from loading a single .WAV file, you have the option to set up your own sound's data source. This is helpful if your sounds are too large for the sound buffer (greater than 64K). Your choices now are to stream the sound from a file or a memory buffer. That's the purpose of the SoundData::SetSource function, which has two versions you can use:

```
BOOL cSoundData::SetSource(FILE *fp, long Pos = -1,          \
                           long Size = -1);
BOOL cSoundData::SetSource(void *Ptr, long Pos = -1,         \
                           long Size = -1);
```

As you can see, you can pick a source file pointer or a memory pointer. The Pos parameter conveys the starting position (the offset) of the sound data to the class. The Size parameter sets the total number of bytes to stream (the size of the sound).

Note that the default value for both Pos and Size is -1, which enables the class to set the positions. For that to happen, you must first set up the playback format using SetFormat, which is self-explanatory. Then you must parse a wave file header using LoadWAVHeader, which works similarly to LoadWAV with respect to the parameters.

Finally, if the sound is to be stored and streamed from memory, you must create the buffer to use with the cSoundData::Create function. You can specify the buffer size yourself, or you can let the function use the buffer size parsed from the LoadWAVHeader function. Calling cSoundData::GetPtr retrieves the pointer to the memory buffer that you can safely use to store the sound.

> **CAUTION**
>
> **Anytime that you use a memory buffer, you should always free it with a call to cSoundData::Free. Also note that if you're streaming sounds from a file, you're responsible for closing the file yourself.**

For the sake of example, assume that you want to play a large .WAV file named BigSound.wav. You can use the following code to set up the cSoundData class:

```
cSoundData Data;
FILE *fp = fopen("BigSound.wav", "rb");
Data.LoadWAVHeader(NULL, fp);  // Get the playback specs
Data.SetSource(fp);            // Set source to file

// Play sound here and when done, close source file
fclose(fp);
```

# Blasting Sounds with cSoundChannel

At this point, you can initialize the sound system and load the sound data. Naturally, the next step is to play the sounds. That's the purpose of the cSoundChannel class, which looks like this:

```
// These are the fixed sizes for sound channel buffers
const long g_SoundBufferSize  = 65536;
const long g_SoundBufferChunk = g_SoundBufferSize / 4;
```

Before moving on, I want to explain the two global const variables. The first one shown, g_SoundBufferSize, represents the number of bytes allocated to each DirectSound buffer used to play the sound. I used 65,536 bytes, which is enough to hold a few seconds worth of data at high performance playback formats.

The second variable shown, g_SoundBufferChunk, is the size of a single chunk, of which there are four. Each chunk stores a small sampling of streamed sound. When a chunk finishes playing, the next chunk in line begins to play while the previously played chunk is loaded with new sound data.

You don't have to alter these two values unless you want to conserve memory, in which case, you just change the g_SoundBufferSize variable to a smaller amount. With that said, let's get back on track with the cSoundChannel class declaration:

```
class cSoundChannel
{
  friend class cSound;     // Let cSound has access to my class

  protected:
    cSound                 *m_Sound;       // parent cSound class
    IDirectSoundBuffer8 *m_pDSBuffer;  // DS sound buffer
    IDirectSoundNotify8 *m_pDSNotify;  // notification object
    short                  m_Event;       // Event # for notify

    long                   m_Volume;      // Current volume 0-100%
    signed long            m_Pan;         // Pan level -100 to +100
    BOOL                   m_Playing;     // Flag if channel playing
    long                   m_Loop;        // # loops to play sound

    long                   m_Frequency;    // Playback format
    short                  m_BitsPerSample; // as the channel
    short                  m_Channels;     // was initialized.
```

```
            cSoundData              m_Desc;     // Source sound description

         // Variables for streaming
         short                   m_LoadSection;  // next chunk to load
         short                   m_StopSection;  // which chunk stops
         short                   m_NextNotify;   // which chunk is next

         BOOL BufferData();  // Buffer streaming data in
         BOOL Update();          // Update playback of channel

      public:
         cSoundChannel();   // Constructor
         ~cSoundChannel();  // Destructor

         // Functions to retrieve COM objects
         IDirectSoundBuffer8 *GetSoundBufferCOM();
         IDirectSoundNotify8 *GetNotifyCOM();

         // Create and free sound channel
         BOOL Create(cSound *Sound, long Frequency = 22050,        \
                     short Channels = 1, short BitsPerSample = 16);
         BOOL Create(cSound *Sound, cSoundData *SoundDesc);
         BOOL Free();

         // Play and stop channel
         BOOL Play(cSoundData *Desc, long VolumePercent = 100,     \
                   long Loop = 1);
         BOOL Stop();

         // Get and set volume level (0-100%)
         long GetVolume();
         BOOL SetVolume(long Percent);

         // Get and set panning (-100 left to +100 right)
         signed long GetPan();
         BOOL SetPan(signed long Level);

         // Get and set new playback frequency
         long GetFrequency();
         BOOL SetFrequency(long Level);

         BOOL IsPlaying();              // Return TRUE if sound playing
      };
```

Compared to the simple cSoundData class, the cSoundChannel class is a piece of cake. You can instance this class up to 32 times, meaning that you can have up to 32 channels playing at once. You initialize each sound channel with a call to cSoundChannel::Create.

You provide the Create call with the pre-initialized cSound class and with the playback format. To make things a little easier, you can even create the sound channel using the playback format stored within a cSoundData class. When you are finished with the cSoundChannel class, you free it with a call to cSoundChannel::Free.

The most you'll probably do with cSoundChannel is to play and stop sounds, and possibly alter their volume. To play a sound, pass cSoundChannel a cSoundData class that holds the sound data to play, plus a volume level and the number of times to play the sound in succession. To play the sound in an endless loop, use a value of 0 for the Loop parameter.

The rest of the functions are self-explanatory. All levels for volume and panning use percentage levels, ranging from -100% (silence or full left pan) to +100% (full volume or full right pan). Calling cSoundChannel::IsPlaying returns TRUE if the sound is still playing or FALSE if not.

Here's an example that loads a single sound and streams a larger sound by using two sound channels:

```
// Global declarations
cSound        g_Sound;
cSoundData    g_Data[2];
cSoundChannel g_Channel[2];

// Initialize sound system
// Assuming hWnd is already a handle to initialized window
g_Sound.Init(hWnd);

// Load sounds
g_Data[0].LoadWAV("SmallSound.wav");
FILE *fp = fopen("BigSound.wav", "rb");
g_Data[0].LoadWAVHeader(NULL, fp);
g_Data[0].SetSource(fp);

// Create sound channels
g_Channels[0].Create(&g_Sound, &g_Data[0]);
g_Channels[1].Create(&g_Sound, &g_Data[1]);
```

```
// Begin playback
g_Channels[0].Play(&g_Data[0]);          // Play 1st sound once
g_Channels[1].Play(&g_Data[1], 100, 0);  // Play 2nd endlessly

// Once you're ready, stop everything and shutdown
g_Channels[0].Stop();
g_Channels[0].Free();
g_Channels[1].Stop();
g_Channels[1].Free();

g_Data[0].Free();
g_Data[1].Free();
fclose(fp);

g_Sound.Shutdown();
```

# Listening to Music with cMusicChannel

Again, what fun is a game without music? Now it's time to kick up the beat using the cMusicChannel class, which plays .MID and DirectMusic native songs (*.SGT):

```
class cMusicChannel
{
  friend class cSound;  // Let cSound class access my data.

  protected:
    cSound                *m_Sound;      // Parent cSound class
    IDirectMusicSegment8  *m_pDMSegment; // DM segment object
    long                  m_Volume;      // Volume level 0-100%

  public:
    cMusicChannel();  // Constructor
    ~cMusicChannel(); // Destructor

    IDirectMusicSegment8 *GetSegmentCOM();  // Get segment COM

    BOOL Create(cSound *Sound);    // Initialize the class

    BOOL Load(char *Filename);     // Load a music file
    BOOL Free();                   // Free a music file
```

```
    BOOL SetDLS(cDLS *DLS);   // Set a new DLS

    // Play and stop music
    BOOL Play(long VolumePercent = 100, long Loop = 1);
    BOOL Stop();

    // Get and set new volume level (0-100%)
    long GetVolume();
    BOOL SetVolume(long Percent = 100);

    BOOL SetTempo(long Percent = 100);   // Set new tempo 1%+

    BOOL IsPlaying();     // TRUE if playing, FALSE otherwise
};
```

Don't let the size of the cMusicChannel class fool you—it gets the job done. The difference between cMusicChannel and other classes is that you must initialize it only once with a call to cMusicChannel::Create.

The cMusicChannel::Free function frees songs from memory, leaving room for another song to be loaded. When loading a song, you provide it with the filename, which must be a .MID or DirectMusic native song file (.SGT). Midi files must end with .MID or the cMusicChannel function will not configure DirectMusic for proper playback. If you use only Midi song files, you might want to alter this function by forcing DirectMusic always to configure the song segment object for Midi playback (as you saw in Chapter 8).

Once a song is loaded, you can begin playback using cMusicChannel::Play, which works just like cSoundChannel::Play in regard to the Volume and Loop parameters. The rest of the functions are easy to understand—except for cMusicChannel::SetDLS, which alters the instruments used for music playback.

I get to the DLS stuff in the next section ("Mixing Up the Instruments with cDLS"), but now take a look at the cMusicChannel class in action:

```
// Global declarations
cSound          g_Sound;
cMusicChannel g_Music;

// Initialize sound system
// Assuming hWnd is already a handle to initialized window
g_Sound.Init(hWnd);
```

```
// Initialize the music channel
g_Music.Create(&g_Sound);

// Load and play a song (endless looping)
g_Music.Load("song.mid");
g_Music.Play(100,0);

// When you're done with playback, stop and free song
g_Music.Stop(;
g_Music.Free();

// Shutdown sound system
g_Sound.Shutdown();
```

# Mixing Up the Instruments with cDLS

At long last, you're reaching the end of the information on using the Sound Core. To enhance the music playback features of the cMusicChannel class, shown in the preceding section, you can use cDLS, as illustrated here (consult Chapter 8 for the benefits on using Downloadable Sounds, referred to as DLS):

```
// Macros to help deal with patches
#define PATCH(m,l,p) ((m << 16) | (l << 8) | p)
#define PATCHMSB(x)  ((x >> 16) & 255)
#define PATCHLSB(x)  ((x >>  8) & 255)
#define PATCHNUM(x)  (x & 255)

class cDLS
{
  protected:
    cSound                   *m_Sound;  // Parent cSound object

    // DM DLS collection object
    IDirectMusicCollection *m_pDMCollection;

  public:
    cDLS();  // Constructor
    ~cDLS();  // Destructor
```

```
      // Return the collection COM
      IDirectMusicCollection8 *GetCollectionCOM();

      BOOL Create(cSound *Sound);    // Initialize class

      // Load and free a DLS (NULL = load default set)
      BOOL Load(char *Filename = NULL);
      BOOL Free();

      long GetNumPatches();         // Return # of patchs in set
      long GetPatch(long Index);    // Get patch # in set
      BOOL Exists(long Patch);      // See if a patch # exists
};
```

As you can see, the only purpose of the cDLS class is to contain a single DLS set. As with cMusicChannel, you call cDLS::Create only once because cDLS::Free frees only a loaded set. Notice the default value of NULL for the Filename parameter in cDLS::Load, which specifies the default DLS set. Loading the default DLS set comes in handy for restoring instruments to their original sounds.

The last three functions show the instruments that a DLS set contains. This is also the purpose of the four PATCH macros at the top of the class declaration. To see how many instruments are contained in a class, call cDLS::GetNumPatches.

Now, you can iterate each instrument for its patch number using the cDLS::GetPatch function, or using cDLS::Exists, you can check to see whether a specific patch exists in the set. A return value of TRUE means that a patch exists; FALSE means that it doesn't.

To use cDLS with cMusicChannel, you load the specific DLS and use cMusicChannel::SetDLS to utilize the instrument set:

```
// Assuming previously loaded c_Music object
// and pre-initialized g_Sound object.
cDLS g_DLS;

g_DLS.Create(&g_Sound);
g_DLS.Load("custom.dls");
g_Music.SetDLS(&g_DLS);

// Once done with DLS, just free it
g_DLS.Free();
```

# The Network Core

In the earlier sections, you saw how easy it is to play DirectPlay. Now, you will learn how to work with DirectPlay by using the Network Core. The Network Core contains three classes: cNetworkAdapter, cNetworkServer, and cNetworkClient.

## Querying for Adapters with cNetworkAdapter

You use cNetworkAdapter to enumerate the installed TCP/IP devices on your system. In order to connect through a client connection, you must know the device's GUID, which is the purpose of cNetworkAdapter. Here is the class declaration for cNetworkAdapter:

```
class cNetworkAdapter
{
  protected:
    DPN_SERVICE_PROVIDER_INFO *m_AdapterList;  // Adapter list
    unsigned long m_NumAdapters;                // # adapters

    // Empty network message handler - required
    static HRESULT WINAPI NetMsgHandler(                    \
            PVOID pvUserContext, DWORD dwMessageId,         \
            PVOID pMsgBuffer) { return S_OK; }

  public:
    cNetworkAdapter();   // Constructor
    ~cNetworkAdapter();  // Destructor

    BOOL  Init();             // Initialize class object
    BOOL  Shutdown();         // Shut down object (free memory)
    long  GetNumAdapters();   // Get # of installed adapters

    // Store name of adapter in buffer (Num = 0 to # adapters-1)
    BOOL  GetName(unsigned long Num, char *Buf);

    // Return pointer to adapter GUID (Num = 0 to # adapters-1)
    GUID *GetGUID(unsigned long Num);
};
```

The cNetworkAdapter class is easy to use, just call the Init function, query for the number of installed adapters and begin pulling out the adapter names and GUIDs. When you're done with the object, call Shutdown to free the class's internal resources.

I'll get back to using the cNetworkAdapter class later in the next two sections. For now, you can move on to the cNetworkServer class.

## Servers with cNetworkServer

On the server side of networking, you deal with the cNetworkServer class, which allows you to initialize a DirectPlay server object, host a game session, and handle incoming and outgoing network messages. In this section, you see how I wrapped the server side of networking into the following cNetworkServer class:

```
class cNetworkServer
{
  protected:
    IDirectPlay8Server *m_pDPServer;  // Server Object
    BOOL                m_Connected;  // Flag is host started

    // Session name and password (stored as ASCII characters)
    char                m_SessionName[MAX_PATH];
    char                m_SessionPassword[MAX_PATH];

    long                m_Port;       // Port used
    long                m_MaxPlayers; // Max players allowed
    long                m_NumPlayers; // # current players

    // Network message handler
    static HRESULT WINAPI NetworkMessageHandler(          \
           PVOID pvUserContext, DWORD dwMessageId,         \
           PVOID pMsgBuffer);

    // Overloaded functions for various network message
    virtual BOOL AddPlayerToGroup(                         \
            DPNMSG_ADD_PLAYER_TO_GROUP *Msg) { return TRUE; }
    virtual BOOL AsyncOpComplete(                          \
             DPNMSG_ASYNC_OP_COMPLETE *Msg) { return TRUE; }
    virtual BOOL ClientInfo(                               \
                 DPNMSG_CLIENT_INFO *Msg) { return TRUE; }
```

```
        virtual BOOL ConnectComplete(                              \
                DPNMSG_CONNECT_COMPLETE *Msg) { return TRUE; }
        virtual BOOL CreateGroup(                                  \
                    DPNMSG_CREATE_GROUP *Msg) { return TRUE; }
        virtual BOOL CreatePlayer(                                 \
                    DPNMSG_CREATE_PLAYER *Msg) { return TRUE; }
        virtual BOOL DestroyGroup(                                 \
                    DPNMSG_DESTROY_GROUP *Msg) { return TRUE; }
        virtual BOOL DestroyPlayer(                                \
                    DPNMSG_DESTROY_PLAYER *Msg) { return TRUE; }
        virtual BOOL EnumHostsQuery(                               \
                DPNMSG_ENUM_HOSTS_QUERY *Msg) { return TRUE; }
        virtual BOOL EnumHostsResponse(                            \
            DPNMSG_ENUM_HOSTS_RESPONSE *Msg) { return TRUE; }
        virtual BOOL GroupInfo(                                    \
                      DPNMSG_GROUP_INFO *Msg) { return TRUE; }
        virtual BOOL HostMigrate(                                  \
                    DPNMSG_HOST_MIGRATE *Msg) { return TRUE; }
        virtual BOOL IndicateConnect(                              \
                DPNMSG_INDICATE_CONNECT *Msg) { return TRUE; }
        virtual BOOL IndicatedConnectAborted(                      \
        DPNMSG_INDICATED_CONNECT_ABORTED *Msg) { return TRUE; }
        virtual BOOL PeerInfo(                                     \
                       DPNMSG_PEER_INFO *Msg) { return TRUE; }
        virtual BOOL Receive(                                      \
                         DPNMSG_RECEIVE *Msg) { return TRUE; }
        virtual BOOL RemovePlayerFromGroup(                        \
            DPNMSG_REMOVE_PLAYER_FROM_GROUP *Msg) { return TRUE; }
        virtual BOOL ReturnBuffer(                                 \
                    DPNMSG_RETURN_BUFFER *Msg) { return TRUE; }
        virtual BOOL SendComplete(                                 \
                    DPNMSG_SEND_COMPLETE *Msg) { return TRUE; }
        virtual BOOL ServerInfo(                                   \
                     DPNMSG_SERVER_INFO *Msg) { return TRUE; }
        virtual BOOL TerminateSession(                             \
                DPNMSG_TERMINATE_SESSION *Msg) { return TRUE; }

    public:
      cNetworkServer();    // Constructor
      ~cNetworkServer();   // Destructor
```

```
    IDirectPlay8Server *GetServerCOM();  // Return server object

    BOOL Init();        // Initialize network server
    BOOL Shutdown();    // Shut down network server

    // Begin a hosting session
    BOOL Host(GUID *guidAdapter, long Port,                      \
            char *SessionName, char *Password = NULL,            \
            long MaxPlayers = 0);
    BOOL Disconnect();   // Disconnect a hosting session
    BOOL IsConnected();  // Checks if host started

    // Send raw data or a text string
    BOOL Send(DPNID dpnidPlayer, void *Data,                     \
            unsigned long Size, unsigned long Flags=0);
    BOOL SendText(DPNID dpnidPlayer, char *Text,                 \
            unsigned long Flags=0);

    // Forcibly disconnect a player
    BOOL DisconnectPlayer(long PlayerId);

    // Get IP address of host or player in supplied buffer
    BOOL GetIP(char *IPAddress, unsigned long PlayerId = 0);
    // Get name of player
    BOOL GetName(char *Name, unsigned long PlayerId);

    // Get port used to host
    long GetPort();

    // Get session name and password
    BOOL GetSessionName(char *Buf);
    BOOL GetSessionPassword(char *Buf);

    // Get max # players allowed and current # of players
    long GetMaxPlayers();
    long GetNumPlayers();
};
```

In order to use the cNetworkServer class (as well as cNetworkClient, as you'll soon see in
the following section, "Working with Clients and cNetworkClient"), you derive your
own class using cNetworkServer as the base class. You do so because you have to

overload the network handling functions with functions of your own construct. Each network message is represented in the cNetworkServer class, so there's no way for your derived class to miss the important messages.

To host a session, you need an adapter GUID, session name, optional password, and the maximum number of players allowed (with 0 meaning no limit). When cNetworkServer::Host is called, DirectPlay initializes the connection and returns control to you. At this point, you can expect messages to start coming in. It's your job to siphon through the incoming messages and deal with them as you see fit. Each message handler you create returns TRUE to signify the message was handled or FALSE to signify an error.

As a quick example, here's an instance of the cNetworkServer class that displays incoming text messages and sends the same message back to the originator (using guaranteed delivery):

```
// Create a derived class
class cServer : public cNetworkServer
{
  private:
    BOOL Receive(DPNMSG_RECEIVE *Msg);
}


BOOL cServer::Receive(DPNMSG_RECEIVE *Msg)
{
  // Display the message
  MessageBox(NULL, Msg->pReceivedData,                         \
             "Incoming Message", MB_OK);

  // Send it back
  Send(Msg->dpnidSender, Msg->pReceiveData,                    \
       Msg->dwReceivedDataSize, DPNSEND_GUARANTEED);

  return TRUE;
}


int PASCAL WinMain(HINSTANCE hInst, HINSTANCE hPrev,           \
                   LPSTR szCmdLine, int nCmdShow)
{
  cServer Server;
  cNetworkAdapter Adapter;
  GUID *guidAdapter;
```

```
    // Pick the first network adapter
    Adapter.Init();
    guidAdapter = Adapter.GetGUID(0);   // 0 = 1st adapter

    Server.Init();
    Server.Host(guidAdapter, 12345, "TextSession");

    // Wait until ESC pressed
    while(!(GetAsyncKeyState(VK_ESC) & 0x80));
    Server.Disconnect();
    Server.Shutdown();

    // Free the adapter list
    Adapter.Shutdown();

    return TRUE;
}
```

Don't worry if the preceding example doesn't show you much; you'll get to deal with the network components in more detail in Chapter 19, "Getting Online with Multiplayer Gaming."

# Working with Clients and cNetworkClient

At this point, take a look at the remaining network class object, cNetworkClient, which deals with the client end of networking:

```
class cNetworkClient
{
  protected:
    IDirectPlay8Client *m_pDPClient;    // DP client object

    BOOL               m_Connected;     // Flag if connected

    char               m_IPAddress[MAX_PATH]; // IP address
    long               m_Port;                    // connected port

    char               m_Name[MAX_PATH];  // Client name

    // Session name and password (as sent to host)
```

```
    char                    m_SessionName[MAX_PATH];
    char                    m_SessionPassword[MAX_PATH];


    // Network message handler function
    static HRESULT WINAPI NetworkMessageHandler(                \
                PVOID pvUserContext, DWORD dwMessageId,      \
                PVOID pMsgBuffer);

// Overloaded network message handlers (identical to
// cNetworkServer's) go here. They have been removed for
// sake of saving space.
public:
  cNetworkClient();    // Constructor
  ~cNetworkClient();   // Destructor


  // Return DirectPlay client object
  IDirectPlay8Client *GetClientCOM();


  BOOL Init();       // Init client network system
  BOOL Shutdown();   // Shutdown client system


  // Connect to remote host using specified adapter, IP,
  // port, player name, session name, and optional
  // password.
  BOOL Connect(GUID *guidAdapter, char *IP, long Port,      \
                char *PlayerName, char *SessionName,        \
                char *SessionPassword = NULL);              \
  BOOL Disconnect();     // Disconnect a session
  BOOL IsConnected();    // Returns TRUE if connected


  // Send raw data and text functions
  BOOL Send(void *Data, unsigned long Size,                 \
            unsigned long Flags=0);
  BOOL SendText(char *Text, unsigned long Flags=0);


  BOOL GetIP(char *IPAddress);      // Get IP address in buffer
  long GetPort();                   // Return connected port #
  BOOL GetName(char *Name);         // Return name
  BOOL GetSessionName(char *Buf);      // Return session name
  BOOL GetSessionPassword(char *Buf);  // Return password
};
```

Working with the cNetworkClient object is similar to using cNetworkServer, with the exception of connecting to a network. To connect using cNetworkClient::Connect, you must first pick a network adapter using the cNetworkAdapter class object, as illustrated in the following example:

```
// Create a derived class
class cClient : public cNetworkClient
{
  private:
    BOOL Receive(DPNMSG_RECEIVE *Msg);
}


BOOL cClient::Receive(DPNMSG_RECEIVE *Msg)
{
  MessageBox(NULL, Msg->pReceiveData,                     \
             "Incoming Message", MB_OK);
  return TRUE;
}


int PASCAL WinMain(HINSTANCE hInst, HINSTANCE hPrev,      \
                   LPSTR szCmdLine, int nCmdShow)
{
  cClient Client;
  cNetworkAdapter Adapter;
  GUID *guidAdapter;

  // Pick the first network adapter
  Adapter.Init();
  guidAdapter = Adapter.GetGUID(0);   // 0 = 1st adapter

  // Initialize client and connect to IP=123.123.123.123
  // using port 12345, session = TextSession and no password.
  Client.Init();
  Client.Connect(guidAdapter, "123.123.123.123",          \
                 12345, "MyName", "TextSession");

  // Wait until connection complete or until user
  // presses ESC.
  while(Client.IsConnected() == FALSE) {
    if(GetAsyncKeyState(VK_ESC) & 0x80) {
      Client.Disconnect();
```

```
        Client.Shutdown();
        return TRUE;
    }
}
// Now connected, proceed with application

// Send a text message
Client.SendText("Hello there!");

// Wait until ESC pressed
while(!(GetAsyncKeyState(VK_ESC) & 0x80));

// Disconnect and shutdown
Client.Disconnect();
Client.Shutdown();

// Free adapter list
Adapter.Shutdown();

    return TRUE;
}
```

Again, the samples here are minimal; you see the entire Network Core in action in Chapter 19. For now, you might want to look through the class declarations and the code on the CD-ROM at the back of this book.

# Wrapping Up the Game Core

Creating a core of reusable objects, such as those shown in this chapter, is one of the best things you can do to get started in programming games. Not only do you learn the intricate details of every object and component you are representing with the core classes, but you also form a solid framework with which to get your games developed at a much quicker pace.

In this chapter, I introduced you to the Game Core, a collection of classes I developed for use in my projects and for use in this book. I pass the core on to you in hopes you will find it useful in your projects. By following the examples in this chapter, and throughout the remainder of this book, you should be able to get a firm grasp on just what the core is capable of doing, and how you can use the core classes.

## Programs on the CD-ROM

A number of programs that demonstrate the code discussed in this chapter are located on the CD-ROM at the back of this book. You can find the following programs in the BookCode\Chap10\ directory:

+ **GameCore.** This is not a real application project because it contains the complete code for only the Game Core. Use this collection of classes as a starting point for your projects. Location: \BookCode\Chap10\GameCore\.

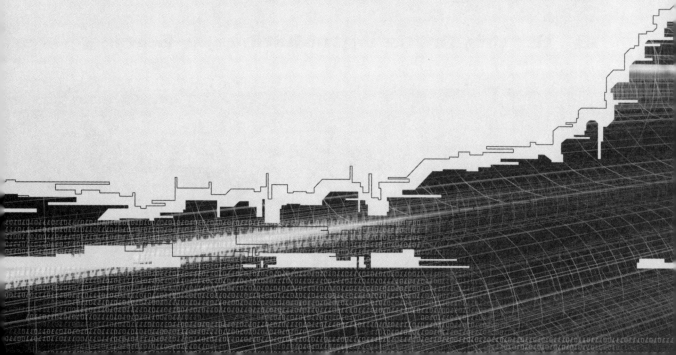

# Part Four

# Role-Playing Game Programming

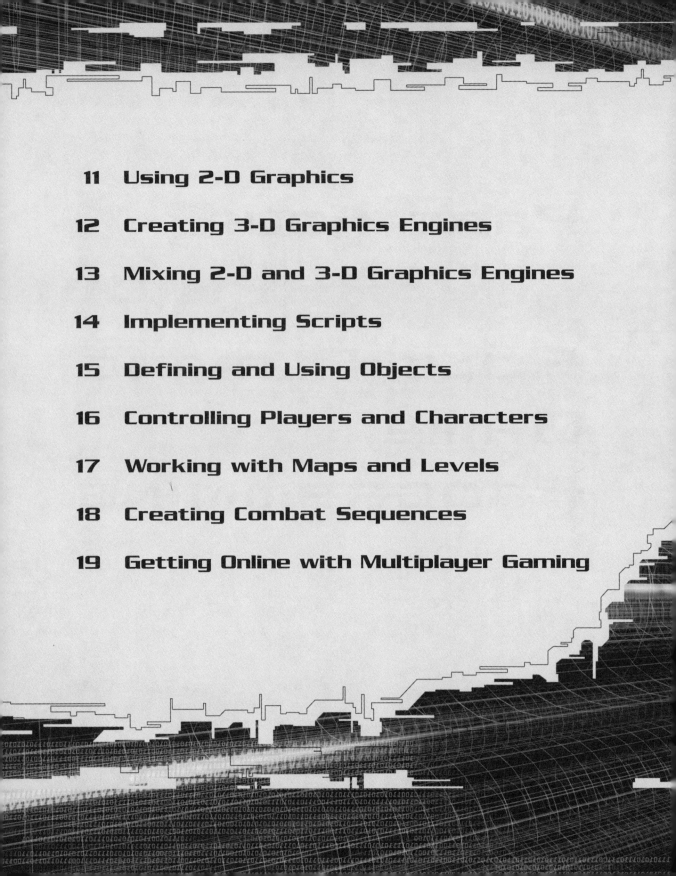

# CHAPTER 11

# USING 2-D GRAPHICS

You're finally getting past the basics of programming and on to the good stuff. Because this book is about programming role-playing games, let's start with one of the first things that a gamer notices—the graphics! Starting with the "yesterday" of gaming, you'll see that games evolved from a simple 2-D graphics style that still prevails in today's market with games such as *Final Fantasy, Baldur's Gate,* and the various *Ultima* games. Now, it's time for you to harness 2-D graphics in your own games.

In this chapter, you learn about the following:

- Using tiles and maps
- Building basic and angled 2-D tile engines
- Big bitmap engines

# Understanding Tiles and Maps

The heart of the 2-D games mentioned in the introduction to this chapter is a technique for drawing graphics known as *tiling*. When tiling, you use small rectangular groups of pixels (small bitmaps called *tiles*) to construct a large scene. The arrangement in which these tiles are drawn is called a *map*. (See Figure 11.1.)

In Figure 11.1, four small numbered images are on the left; these are the tiles. In the middle, you see a grid of numbers. This grid represents the layout in which you draw the tiles (in a sort of paint-by-numbers manner). For each grid element, you draw the respective tile that is represented by the number and continue until the entire scene is drawn. This grid is the map. When the grid is complete, you have the image shown on the right.

The benefits of using tiles and maps are clear; tiles and maps require very little memory for storage. By using the paint-by-numbers format for the map, you are able to construct huge (and I mean *huge*) scenes, using very little memory.

Consider this example, which uses tiles that are $16 \times 16$ pixels. Assuming that you use 8-bit colors, a set of 256 tiles will use 65,536 bytes of memory. In addition, you have the map, which is an array of bytes (each byte representing the tile number to draw) that is $1024 \times 1024$ (1,048,576 bytes). That's a total of 1,114,112 bytes to store the tiles and map.

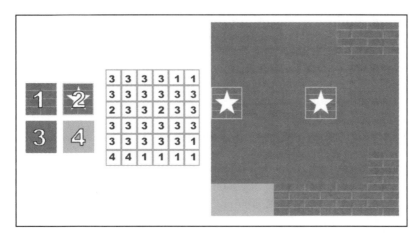

**Figure 11.1**

*Tiles and maps go hand in hand when drawing large scenes in 2-D graphics. You use the tiles on the left to render the map on the right.*

Because each tile is 16 pixels in size either way and the map is 1,024 units in size, a rendered map will generate an image 16,384 × 16,384 pixels in size, which takes a whopping 268,435,456 bytes to store. You can see that the savings in memory is between almost 300MB and a little more than 1MB.

# Tile Graphics

So far, you have a basic overview of tiles and maps. What you might not realize is how far you can take the concept of using tiles. Even though the tiles you are drawing are rectangular, the graphics used for the tiles do not have to be rectangular, nor do they have to be drawn to the screen in a rectangular grid-like pattern.

## Angled Tiles

In a typical 2-D game, the scene is usually from an above or side viewpoint. Whatever the case, in those typical games, you draw all the tiles to conform nicely to a rectangular shape.

*The Black Gate* (the seventh game in the *Ultima* sequel), on the other hand, changes the viewpoint. When viewing it from above and slightly rotated, you're able to see more than one side of all objects. The graphics, like the characters in the game, extend upward at an angle, and you can see their backs and sides at the same time! What's going on here? Angled tiles! That's what.

The game is still using rectangular tiles, but they are drawn with angled graphics. You might not be able to distinguish the rectangular shape of the tiles right away because a large chunk of each tile is transparent (not drawn). Take a look at Figure 11.2 to see what I mean.

You now have the basics on working with the various types of tiles used in games today. Next, you find out how to use tiles in your own project by means of DirectX.

# Using Tiles with DirectX

As you've already seen in previous chapters, it's not too difficult to render small rectangular texture-mapped polygons, which are perfect for representing your tiles. You can accomplish this with a special D3DX object called ID3DXSprite. In Chapter 10, "Creating the Gaming Core," I mention the ID3DXSprite interface when discussing the Game Core; now is your chance to take a look at that interface.

The ID3DXSprite object has the sole job of drawing rectangular polygons to the screen, using the specific texture you assign. Of course, the texture you give it will be packed with tiles.

To start using tiles in Direct3D, instance an ID3DXSprite object and use the D3DXCreateSprite function to initialize it:

```
// g_pD3DDevice = pre-initialized device object
ID3DXSprite *pSprite = NULL;

if(FAILED(D3DXCreateSprite(g_pD3DDevice, &pSprite))) {
  // Error occurred
}
```

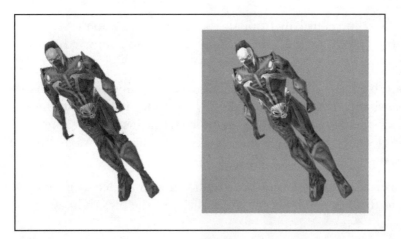

**Figure 11.2**

*Here is a typical character drawn in an angled tile (the left with transparency and the right without transparency of the tile shown).*

**TIP**

**For efficiency, pack a texture used for tiles with as many tiles as you can fit and lay them out in rows and columns. For example, if you have 64 tiles that are 32 × 32 pixels in size, create a bitmap that can store 8 rows and 8 columns of tiles, which gives you a texture that is 256 × 256 pixels in size. Figure 11.3 demonstrates one such arrangement of tiles.**

**The tiles are numbered and referenced starting at the upper-left corner. The upper-left tile is considered tile 0. The next tile to the right is tile 1, and so on, until the next row, in which the tile numbers continue all the way to 63 (the lower-right tile). From now on, you reference a tile by its number and let the tile-drawing routines figure out the coordinates in the texture.**

You can see that the D3DXCreateSprite function takes two parameters—one pointer to your pre-initialized 3-D device object and another to the ID3DXSprite object you are creating. After this function call, you're ready to roll. All that you need to do is load a texture that represents the tile (or tiles) you want to draw and use the ID3DXSprite::Draw function to draw the tile:

```
HRESULT ID3DXSprite::Draw(
    IDirect3DTexture8 *pSrcTexture,    // Texture to use
    CONST RECT *pSrcRect,              // Source rectangle
    CONST D3DXVECTOR2* pScaling,       // Scaling vector
    CONST D3DXVECTOR2* pRotationCenter, // Rotation center
    FLOAT Rotation,                    // Rotation angle
    CONST D3DVECTOR2* pTranslation,    // Translation vector
    D3DCOLOR Color);                   // Modulation color
```

The trick to using the Draw function is to construct a source rectangle RECT structure with the coordinates inside the texture that you want to use as the tile. For example, say that you have a texture 256 × 256 pixels in size that contains 64 tiles (32 × 32 pixels in size each) packed in 8 rows by 8 columns (as shown in Figure 11.3).

If you draw the second tile from the left, third from the top, your source rectangle will be from 64,96 to 96,128. Because all your tiles are 32 × 32, you need to know only the upper-left coordinates of the tile in the texture; then you just add 32 for the bottom and right coordinates of the tile. Use those values to configure the RECT structure:

```
RECT SrcRect;
SrcRect.left = 64;   // left coordinate of tile
SrcRect.top = 96;    // top coordinate of tile
SrcRect.right = SrcRect.left + 32;   // add tile width
SrcRect.bottom = SrcRect.top + 32;   // add tile height
```

Note that setting pSrcRect to NULL tells the draw function to use the entire texture as a tile. pScaling is a vector that specifies the size that you want to scale the tile. If you're not going to scale the tiles, set pScaling to NULL; otherwise, you'll need to construct a vector containing the scaling values.

Scaling is about as far as I'm going to go for special features using tiles. So, you can set pRotationCenter to NULL and Rotation to 0.0.

### TIP

The ability to scale tiles with Direct3D makes for some awesome possibilities. By using smaller tile images, say 16 × 16 pixels in size, you can then draw them at a much larger size, say 64 × 64. As the tile is drawn, the texture is stretched to fit the scaled-up tile. When these scaled tiles are applied with maps, you can greatly expand the size of the map while conserving memory for tile textures. I'll show you more of this technique in the section "Big Bitmap Engines," later in this chapter.

**Figure 11.3**

*Here you see 64 tiles arranged in an 8 × 8 pattern.*

The only parameter you need to be concerned about is pTransform, which is a vector that tells the sprite object the coordinates at which to draw the tile, in screen space ranging from 0 to the width and height of the window. Note that you draw all tiles down and right from the coordinates you specify, meaning that the upper-left corner of the tile is considered the origin.

The last argument of the Draw function is Color, which is a D3DCOLOR value used to modulate the output texture. Normally, you'd set this to a value of 0xFFFFFFFF in order to draw the tiles just as they appear in the texture, but by using a macro such as D3DCOLOR_RGBA, you can modify the colors or alpha values of the tiles as they are drawn.

For example, to draw a tile with half the alpha value, use the following:

```
D3DCOLOR_RGBA(255,255,255,127);   // 127 = half of full
```

You can see that the values range from 0 (no color or alpha) to 255 (full color or alpha). In the same way you altered the alpha values, you can cut the red component out completely by using the following:

```
D3DCLOR_RGBA(0,255,255,255);   // 0=no color
```

This creates some splendid possibilities, such as creating day and night scenes or tiles that show through to underlying graphics (such as windows).

Getting back to the subject at hand, you can now use the Draw function to draw tiles. Here's a sample function that takes a texture, source coordinates, and destination coordinates in order to draw a tile (notice that the coordinates are still float, but they are defined in screen space—that is, in the dimensions of the display):

```
// Before calling this function, make sure you have called
// IDirect3DDevice::BeginScene and have already loaded
// the texture you are using to store the tiles.

// pSprite = pre-initialized ID3DXSprite object
void DrawTile(float SrcX, float SrcY,                       \
              float DestX, float DestY,                      \
              float TileWidth, float TileHeight              \
              float ScaleX, float ScaleY,                    \
              IDirect3DTexture8 *pTileTexture,               \
              D3DCOLOR Color)
{
  RECT SrcRect;          // source rectangle
```

```
// Set up the source rectangle
SrcRect.left   = SrcX;
SrcRect.top    = SrcY;
SrcRect.right  = SrcRect.left + TileWidth;
SrcRect.bottom = SrcRect.top + TileHeight;

// Draw the tile using specified coordinates, color,
// and scale. If you want the tile to be drawn at the
// normal scale, specify a value of 1.0 for ScaleX and ScaleY
pSprite->Draw(pTileTexture, &SrcRect,                          \
              &D3DXVECTOR2(ScaleX, ScaleY), NULL, 0.0f,        \
              &D3DXVECTOR2(DestX, DestY), Color);
}
```

Although using the ID3DXSprite object to draw tiles might seem a little odd at first (and a little unoptimized), I assure you that it does the job very well. The only way to go from here is to build a special class that handles tiles for you, including loading and drawing them.

> **NOTE**
>
> As you can see in the DrawTile function, I added the ability to draw scaled tiles. This is a power technique that I'll be using later in this chapter in the section, "Big Bitmap Engines."

## Building a Tile-Handler Class

Because you've learned how to draw tiles, now is a good time to construct a class that handles tiles for you. This class should be minimal, only loading the tile textures and drawing them to the specified device. Here's a look at a simple tile class that I created. To make things easier to deal with, I integrated the Graphics Core into the following tile class:

```
class cTiles
{
  private:
    cGraphics *m_Graphics;      // Parent cGraphics object

    long       m_NumTextures;   // # of textures
    cTexture  *m_Textures;      // cTexture array
    short     *m_Widths;        // Tile widths array
    short     *m_Heights;       // Tile heights array
    short     *m_Columns;       // # columns in texture
```

```
public:
    cTiles();
    ~cTiles();

    // Functions to create and free the tile interface
    BOOL Create(cGraphics *Graphics, long NumTextures);
    BOOL Free();

    // Functions to load and free a single texture
    BOOL Load(long TextureNum, char *Filename,                    \
              short TileWidth = 0, short TileHeight = 0,          \
              D3DCOLOR Transparent = 0,                          \
              D3DFORMAT Format = D3DFMT_A1R5G5B5);
    BOOL Free(long TextureNum=-1);

    // Functions to retrieve tile dimensions and
    // # of tiles in a texture.
    long GetWidth(long TextureNum);
    long GetHeight(long TextureNum);
    long GetNum(long TextureNum);

    // Enable or disable transparent blitting
    BOOL SetTransparent(BOOL Enabled = TRUE);

    // Draw a single tile to location
    BOOL Draw(long TextureNum, long TileNum,                      \
              long ScreenX, long ScreenY,                        \
              D3DCOLOR Color = 0xFFFFFFFF,                       \
              float XScale = 1.0f, float YScale = 1.0f);
};
```

The cTiles class presented here works
by allocating an array of cTexture objects
in which to store the tile graphics. The
actual code for the cTiles class is contained within the Chapter 11 source code
directory on this book's CD-ROM (look
for \BookCode\Chap11\). The following
sections provide a breakdown of the
public functions and what they do
(as well as how to call them).

> **NOTE**
> All public functions in the cTiles
> class return a BOOL value; TRUE
> represents a successful call, and
> FALSE means there was an
> unspecified error.

## cTiles::Create

```
BOOL cTiles::Create(
  cGraphics *Graphics,        // Pre-initialized cGraphics object
  long        NumTextures);   // # texture objects to create
```

The first function called, cTiles::Create, allocates the array of cTexture objects in which to store the tile graphics. Be sure to pass this Create function a pre-initialized cGraphics object and a sufficient number of textures in which to store tiles.

```
BOOL cTiles::Create(cGraphics *Graphics, long NumTextures)
{
  Free(); // Free in case of existing data

  // Error checking
  if((m_Graphics = Graphics) == NULL)
    return FALSE;
  if((m_NumTextures = NumTextures) == NULL)
    return FALSE;

  // Allocate texture objects
  if((m_Textures = new cTexture[m_NumTextures]) == NULL)
    return FALSE;

  // Allocate width, height, and column count arrays
  m_Widths  = new long[m_NumTextures];
  m_Heights = new long[m_NumTextures];
  m_Columns = new long[m_NumTextures];

  return TRUE;  // Return success!
}
```

## cTiles::Free

```
BOOL cTiles::Free();
```

This function takes no parameters because it frees all resources and class objects. No further calls to Load, Draw, or Free will work until the cTiles class instance is reinitialized with a call to cTiles::Create.

```
BOOL cTiles::Free()
{
  m_Graphics = NULL;
```

```
// Free all textures
if(m_NumTextures) {
  for(short i=0;i<m_NumTextures;i++)
    m_Textures[i].Free();
}
delete [] m_Textures;
m_Textures = NULL;

// Free width, height, and column arrays
delete [] m_Widths;
delete [] m_Heights;
delete [] m_Columns;
m_Widths = m_Heights = m_Columns = NULL;
m_NumTextures = 0;

return TRUE;
}
```

## cTiles::Load

```
BOOL cTilesLoad(
  long TextureNum,       // Texture # to load graphics into
  char *Filename,        // Filename of image to load (*.bmp)
  short TileWidth,       // Width of tiles in image
  short TileHeight,      // Height of tiles in image
  D3DCOLOR Transparent,  // Transparent color (use alpha=255)
  D3DFORMAT Format);     // Storage format
```

The cTiles::Load function handles loading a texture into a specific texture array element. For example, if you create the cTiles object to use five textures, you can specify any element from 0 to 4 in which to load a texture. All textures are referenced by their index in the texture array.

When loading a texture file, you must specify the size of the tiles stored on the texture (using pixels as measurement). Those tiles must be packed on the texture, running left to right, top to bottom, with the first tile starting at the upper-left pixel of the texture. For example, you could have a texture containing 64 tiles, with each tile being $32 \times 32$ pixels in size. That means that the texture will have 8 columns and 8 rows of tiles, much like the set shown in Figure 11.3.

The last two parameters are useful only if you are using transparent blitting. Set the Transparent parameter to a valid D3DCOLOR value (using D3DCOLOR_RGBA or the like, being

sure to use an alpha value of 255) and either leave Format as its default setting of
D3DFMT_A1R5G5B5 or specify your own from the list of possible formats provided by
Direct3D.

Here's the Load function code:

```
BOOL cTiles::Load(long TextureNum, char *Filename,
          short TileWidth, short TileHeight,
          D3DCOLOR Transparent, D3DFORMAT Format)
{
  // Error checking
  if(TextureNum >= m_NumTextures || m_Textures == NULL)
    return FALSE;

  Free(TextureNum);

  // Load the texture
  if(m_Textures[TextureNum].Load(m_Graphics, Filename,            \
                                 Transparent, Format) == FALSE)
    return FALSE;

  // Store height value (get width of texture if
  // no TileWidth was specified).
  if(!TileWidth)
    m_Widths[TextureNum] = m_Textures[TextureNum].GetWidth();
  else
    m_Widths[TextureNum] = TileWidth;

  // Store height value (get height of texture if
  // no TileHeight was specified).
  if(!TileHeight)
    m_Heights[TextureNum] = m_Textures[TextureNum].GetHeight();
  else
    m_Heights[TextureNum] = TileHeight;

  // Calculate how many columns of tiles there are
  // in the texture. This is used to speed up calculations
  // when drawing tiles.
  m_Columns[TextureNum] = m_Textures[TextureNum].GetWidth()     \
                          / m_Widths[TextureNum];

  return TRUE;
}
```

## cTiles::Free

```
BOOL cTiles::Free(long TextureNum);  // Texture # to free
```

This function frees a single texture from the array, but still allows you to reuse the texture object via a call to cTiles::Load. Just by specifying the texture number to free in the TextureNum argument, you can use this function to free older textures and make room for newer textures.

```
BOOL cTiles::Free(long TextureNum)
{
  // Error checking
  if(TextureNum >= m_NumTextures || m_Textures == NULL)
    return FALSE;

  // Free a single texture resource
  m_Textures[TextureNum].Free();

  return TRUE;
}
```

## cTiles::GetWidth, cTiles::GetHeight, and cTiles::GetNum

```
long cTiles::GetWidth(long TextureNum);   // Read from texture #
long cTiles::GetHeight(long TextureNum);
long cTiles::GetNum(long TextureNum);
```

You use these three functions to retrieve the width, height, and number of tiles per texture, respectively. You will rarely use these functions directly, but it helps to have them in the tile class:

```
long cTiles::GetWidth(long TextureNum)
{
  // Error checking
  if(TextureNum >= m_NumTextures || m_Widths == NULL)
   return 0;

  return m_Widths[TextureNum];
}

long cTiles::GetHeight(long TextureNum)
{
```

```
  // Error checking
  if(TextureNum >= m_NumTextures || m_Heights == NULL)
   return 0;

  return m_Heights[TextureNum];
}

long cTiles::GetNum(long TextureNum)
{
  // Error checking
  if(TextureNum >= m_NumTextures || m_Textures == NULL ||      \
    m_Columns == NULL || m_Widths == NULL || m_Heights == NULL)
   return 0;

  return m_Columns[TextureNum] +                               \
         m_Textures[TextureNum].GetHeight() /                  \
         m_Heights[TextureNum];
}
```

## cTiles::SetTransparent

```
BOOL cTiles::SetTransparent(BOOL Enabled); // Enable/disable
```

The cTiles::SetTransparent function enables or disables alpha testing, which means that textures loaded with an appropriate transparent color and color format will use transparent blitting when enabled. As a default value, Enabled is set to TRUE. Here's a look at the code for the SetTransparent function:

```
BOOL cTiles::SetTransparent(BOOL Enabled)
{
  // Error checking
  if(m_Graphics == NULL)
    return FALSE;
  return m_Graphics->EnableAlphaTesting(Enabled);
}
```

## cTiles::Draw

```
BOOL cTiles::Draw(
  long TextureNum,    // Texture # to draw from
  long TileNum,       // Tile # to draw
```

```
   long ScreenX,        // X-coordinate
   long ScreenY,        // Y-coordinate
   D3DCOLOR Color,      // Modulation color/alpha value
   float XScale,        // x-scale factor
   float YScale);       // y-scale factor
```

This is the function to use to draw your tiles. Once a texture is loaded into the array, you can draw the individual tiles contained within the texture. All tiles are numbered starting with 0 at the upper-left, increasing from left to right, top to bottom. For example, a texture with 64 tiles (in an $8 \times 8$ pattern) will be numbered from 0 to 63. Tile 0 is the upper-left tile, tile 8 is the next tile down, and tile 1 is the one to the right of tile 0.

When drawing, you need to specify the screen coordinates in long values (which are later converted to float values), as well as a scaling factor (to increase or decrease the size of the tiles from their previously defined size). As mentioned previously in this chapter, the modulation value is utilized to decrease the color or alpha values using the ID3DXSprite interface.

```
BOOL cTiles::Draw(long TextureNum, long TileNum,            \
          long ScreenX, long ScreenY,                        \
          D3DCOLOR Color, float XScale, float YScale)
{
  long SrcX, SrcY;

  // Error checking
  if(m_Graphics == NULL)
    return FALSE;
  if(TextureNum >= m_NumTextures || m_Textures == NULL)
    return FALSE;

  // Calculate the source tile coordinates from texture
  SrcX=(TileNum % m_Columns[TextureNum])*m_Widths[TextureNum];
  SrcY=(TileNum / m_Columns[TextureNum])*m_Heights[TextureNum];

  return m_Textures[TextureNum].Blit(ScreenX, ScreenY,       \
                SrcX, SrcY,                                   \
                m_Widths[TextureNum], m_Heights[TextureNum], \
                XScale, YScale);
}
```

## Using the Tile Class

Here's a quick example that loads two textures for tiles. The first texture contains 64 tiles, each 32 × 32 pixels in size. The second texture contains 16 tiles, with each tile being 64 × 64 pixels in size.

```
// Graphics = pre-initialized cGraphics object
cTiles Tile;

// Create the tile class with room for 2 textures
Tile.Create(Graphics, 2);

// Load both textures using transparent value of black
Tile.Load(0, "Tiles1.bmp", 32, 32,                          \
          D3DCOLOR_RGBA(0,0,0,255), D3DFMT_A1R5G5B5);
Tile.Load(1, "Tiles2.bmp", 64, 64,                          \
          D3DCOLOR_RGBA(0,0,0,255), D3DFMT_A8R8G8B8);

// Draw a couple of tiles from the first texture
// with no transparency
Tile.SetTransparent(FALSE);
// Tiles 0 (at 128,128) and 3 (at 0,0)
Tile.Draw(0, 0, 128,128);
Tile.Draw(0, 3, 0,0);

// Draw a couple of tiles from second texture
// with transparency
Tile.SetTransparent(TRUE);
// Tiles 1 (at 28,18) and 16 (at 100,90)
Tile.Draw(1, 1, 28,18);
Tile.Draw(1, 16, 100,90);

// Free the tile class and free textures
Tile.Free();
```

That's about it. The tile class is very compact and is the perfect addition to your 2-D graphics engine because the class is able to handle all tile drawing-related functions for you. All you have to do is give the class the tile graphics you want to use and you're ready to go.

# A Basic Tile Engine

The time has come. You're ready to create an actual tile engine (not a tile-drawing engine). Although almost as old as computer gaming itself, this first method of creating a tile engine remains the most highly used 2-D graphics technique. In fact, every game made for the Gameboy Advance hand-held gaming system uses the following tile engine technique. That game system exclusively uses tile graphics in one form or another to bring you its portable gaming graphics goodness (did I just write that?).

Now is your chance to brush up on some old techniques that just might help you in your next project.

## Drawing Basic Maps

Drawing the basic tile map is a quick and painless process; you need to loop through only so many columns and rows, drawing the tiles as you go along. The total number of tiles you draw is based on the size of the tiles and the display resolution. For example, for a display that's $384 \times 384$ pixels in size, using tiles that are $64 \times 64$ means that you can fit 6 columns of tiles with 6 rows in the display, for a grand total of 36 tiles.

At this point, refer to Figure 11.1, which shows four tiles, a map, and the final rendering of the map. To represent that map array utilizing the tile numbers used to draw the map, you can do the following:

```
char Map[6][6] = {   // Map[y][x]
  { 3, 3, 3, 3, 1, 1 },
  { 3, 3, 3, 3, 3, 3 },
  { 2, 3, 3, 2, 3, 3 },
  { 3, 3, 3, 3, 3, 3 },
  { 3, 3, 3, 3, 3, 1 },
  { 4, 4, 1, 1, 1, 1 }
};
```

In order to draw the preceding map, you scan through each element in the array and draw the associated tile:

```
// Tile = pre-initialized and loaded cTiles object
for(short row=0; row<6; row++) {
  for(short column=0; column<6; column++) {
    // Get the tile number to draw
    char TileNum = Map[row][column];
```

```
        // Draw the tile (64x64 in size) associated with TileNum
        // from the first texture loaded.
        Tile.Draw(0, TileNum, column*64, row*64);
    }
}
```

Assuming that you have a set of three tiles and the preceding map (and drawing function), you wind up with a rendered map on the display as shown earlier in Figure 11.1.

# Using Multiple Layers

Moving up a step, you can add a lot of power to your tiled map engine with little effort. Most tile-based games use multiple layers (scenes stacked upon each other as illustrated in Figure 11.4) to create some cool effects. For example, by first drawing the ground, drawing the characters on the ground, and then drawing a layer of other overlapping objects, you can simulate a 3-D scene.

In order to use multiple layers, you just declare another map array (a map array for each layer) and fill it with its own tile information. Starting at the first layer, draw each tile contained with the layer. After you draw the last tile of the layer, move on to the next layer and draw its tiles. Continue until you draw all layers.

Consider, for example, an engine that uses four layers. You have a base layer that represents the ground and objects that the characters can't walk behind, a layer in

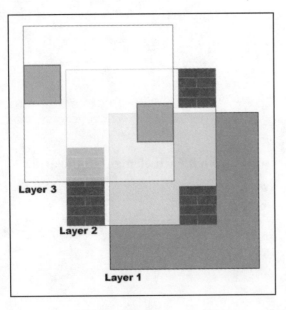

**Figure 11.4**

*To create a simulated 3-D environment, you can stack layers of maps on top of one another.*

which all characters are drawn, a layer for objects that characters can walk behind, and a layer that can cover everything (such as clouds floating overhead).

At this point, you create five map arrays and fill each array element with the tile information to draw. Entering the map rendering function, you then step through each map-layer array and draw it to the screen. Continue until all layers are drawn. The code for drawing multiple map layers is as follows:

```
// Tile = pre-initialized and loaded cTiles object

char Map[5][10][10];  // Map data, assuming already loaded

// Loop through each layer
for(short Layer=0;Layer<5;Layer++) {
  // Loop through each row and column
  for(short row=0; row<10; row++) {
    for(short column=0; column<10; column++) {
      // Get the tile number to draw
      char TileNum = Map[Layer][row][column];

      // Draw the tile (32x32 in size) associated with TileNum
      // from the first texture loaded.
      Tile.Draw(0, TileNum, column*32, row*32);
    }
  }
}
```

# Adding Objects

Earlier in the chapter, I mentioned drawing characters as map layers; however, that statement is not entirely accurate because characters can move freely around the world and don't conform to the whole map array theory. Instead, characters and other moving objects only need to be drawn as free-floating tiles; there is no need to use a map array for them. More exactly, you track all characters and objects according to their respective coordinates in the world; then you convert those objects' coordinates into coordinates that are ready to draw to the screen when they appear in the view.

To keep things simple at this point, just set up a structure to store the object coordinates and a single tile that is drawn (which represents the object):

```
typedef struct sObject {
  long XPos, YPos;  // object coordinates
```

```
  char Tile;          // tile to draw
} sObject;
```

From now on, notice that I'll consider everything that can freely move as an object, including the player characters. As you keep track of those characters, be sure to add them to a list of objects to be drawn. That list of objects can be a simple array declared as follows:

```
#define MAX_OBJECTS            1024
sObject Objects[MAX_OBJECTS];   Allow 1024 objects in list
```

For each frame, track the number of objects to be drawn using a variable:

```
long NumObjectsToDraw = 0;
```

For each frame of your game, NumObjectsToDraw is reset to 0, and as objects are added to the list, the count increases. For example, to add an object, you can use the following function:

```
void AddObject(long XPos, long YPos, char Tile)
{
  if(NumObjectsToDraw < MAX_OBJECTS) {
    Objects[NumObjectsToDraw].XPos = XPos;
    Objects[NumObjectsToDraw].YPos = XPos;
    Objects[NumObjectsToDraw].Tile = Tile;
    NumObjectsToDraw++;
  }
}
```

When it comes time to render those objects, you can just scan through the number of used objects in the list and render the tile. Notice that the map coordinates that are used to render the map to the display must offset each object:

```
// Tiles = pre-initialized and loaded cTiles object
// MapXPos, MapYPos = map coordinates
for(i=0;i<NumObjectsToDraw;i++)
  Tiles.Draw(0, Objects[i].Tile,
             Objects[i].XPos - MapXPos,
             Objects[i].YPos - MapYPos);
```

# Smooth Scrolling

When you play with the tile engine a bit, you'll notice that larger maps need to scroll around in order for the players to see the entire map. At its current incarnation, the tile engine produces a jerky movement whenever you try to alter the coordinates at which the map is drawn. To improve the visual quality of the engine, you need to smooth out the movement using a technique known as *smooth scrolling*.

To visualize smooth scrolling, imagine a tile-drawn map as a large bitmap. Each pixel in the bitmap has its own pair of coordinates, known as the map's *fine coordinates.* Each grouping of pixels that represents a tile is given its own set of map coordinates. For example, if the tiles are $16 \times 16$ pixels in size, and the map array is $10 \times 10$, when fully rendered, the map image will be $160 \times 160$ pixels in size (meaning that the map has a fine coordinate resolution of $160 \times 160$ pixels). You can see a similar example of this in Figure 11.5.

If the display is only $100 \times 100$ pixels, only that number of pixels is drawn from the map. Of course, those pixels belong to tiles, which must be drawn in the properly aligned positions on the display. In order to do that, you must now specify the map coordinates on a pixel level (using the fine map coordinates) and be able to draw only smaller portions of the tiles.

I don't want to overcomplicate the matter at hand; using smooth scrolling is as simple as adding a couple of extra lines of the code. The fact is that when you are drawing the map tiles, you only need to offset them a little bit to align them to the fine map coordinates.

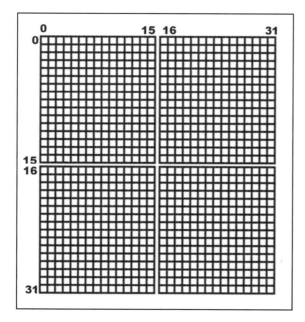

**Figure 11.5**

A $2 \times 2$ map that uses tiles $16 \times 16$ pixels in size has a fine map coordinate resolution of $32 \times 32$ pixels. Notice that each pixel has its own pair of coordinates.

To calculate this offset when drawing the tiles, you just take the fine coordinates at which you want the map drawn (with the fine map coordinates representing the first pixel to be drawn at the upper-left corner of the display) and calculate a few variables, as in the following:

```
// Assuming FineX and FineY are the fine map coordinate to use
// TileWidth and TileHeight are the dimensions of a tile

// Calculate the actual map array coordinates to use
long MapX, MapY;  // The map array coordinates
MapX = FineX / TileWidth;  // Get map x coordinate
MapY = FineY / TileHeight; // Get map Y coordinate

// Calculate the amount of pixels to offset the tiles
long XOff, YOff;  // Pixel offset amounts
XOff = FineX % TileWidth;   // x offset
YOff = FineY % TileHeight;  // Y offset
```

Notice that I calculated four variables. You use the first pair of coordinates, MapX and MapY, when accessing the map array. For example, if you specify fine map coordinates of 8,8 (and the tiles are $16 \times 16$), the actual map array coordinates are 0,0 (because the pixel at $8 \times 8$ lies within the upper-left map tile).

The second pair of coordinates, XOff and YOff, offsets the tiles as they are drawn. To calculate XOff and YOff, you take the modulus (the remainder) of the fine coordinate divided by the tile dimensions. From now on, whenever you want to draw a map tile (or any tile that uses fine map coordinates), subtract the XOff value from the X-coordinate of the tile and the YOff value from the Y-coordinate of the tile.

Here's how the smooth-scrolling offsets work into the rendering loop:

```
// Tile = pre-initialized and loaded cTiles object
for(short row=0; row<11; row++) {
  for(short column=0; column<11; column++) {
    // Get the tile number to draw
    char TileNum = Map[row][column];

    // Draw the tile (32x32 in size) associated with TileNum
    // from the first texture loaded.
    Tile.Draw(0, TileNum, column*32-XOff, row*32-YOff);
  }
}
```

# The Map and the Mouse

Even if you haven't been playing games for very long, you have probably noticed that most of the games for computers take full advantage of the mouse. Point-and-click control is definitely intuitive. Game players just click at a particular place on the screen, and their personas walk to that location; or they might click an item in order to pick it up. What if you want to use that point-and-click functionality in your own game—how do you determine where a player has clicked?

With rectangular maps, you have two options for determining where players click. The first, and simplest, method is to divide the mouse's coordinates by the size of the tiles. This gives you the coordinates within the map array. If you're using smooth scrolling, the offsets used to draw the tiles must also be taken into account.

For example, assume that you are using a smooth-scrolling map that uses tiles that are $32 \times 32$ pixels in size. The map coordinates (in fine coordinates) are at 48,102, and the mouse coordinates are at 45,80. First, calculate the offset amounts for the smooth scrolling:

```
XOff = 48 % 32;    // FineX / TileWidth
YOff = 102 % 32;   // FineY / TileHeight
```

Next, subtract the offset values from the mouse coordinates and add the fine map coordinates where the map is to be drawn:

```
// assuming MouseX, MouseY are the mouse coordinates
long MouseFineX, MouseFineY; // fine coordinates where clicked
MouseFineX = MouseX - XOff + 48;
MouseFineY = MouseY - YOff + 102;
```

You now have the exact fine map coordinates where the user clicked. You can then divide `MouseFineX` and `MouseFineY` by the tile dimensions to get the map array coordinates:

```
long MouseMapX, MouseMapY; // map coordinates where clicked
MouseMapX = MouseFineX / 32;
MouseMapY = MouseFineY / 32;
```

Although the preceding bits of code are all you'll need in most cases, you will find at times that it will not suffice when working with free-floating objects such as game characters. Say that the player clicks a character who is walking around the screen. Because the character doesn't belong to the map array data, you use a method that scans tiles as they are drawn and that compares their coordinates to the coordinates of the mouse pointer. This is a simple matter of *bounds checking*.

Now, assume that a tile $64 \times 64$ pixels in size is about to be drawn at display coordinates 48,100. If the mouse pointer is located at display coordinates 60,102, it will be considered to be touching the tile because the tile covers the area from 48,100 to 112,164. You can write a short function that takes the coordinates of a tile (in screen space), the tile's dimensions, and the coordinates of the mouse and have the function return TRUE if the mouse is touching the tile or FALSE if it is not touching the tile.

```
BOOL IsMouseTouchingTile(
   long TileX, long TileY,           // tile coordinates
   long TileWidth, long TileHeight, // tile dimensions
   long MouseX, long MouseY)          // mouse coordinates
{
   // check if mouse too far left from tile
   if(MouseX < TileX) return FALSE;
   // check if mouse too far right from tile
   if(MouseX >= TileX + TileWidth) return FALSE;
   // check if mouse too far above tile
   if(MouseY < TileY) return FALSE;
   // check if mouse too far below tile
   if(MouseY >= TileY + TileHeight) return FALSE;

   // mouse must be touching tile
   return TRUE;   // return success
}
```

Going back to the example of seeing which tile was clicked, you can call the preceding defined function to determine whether the mouse is touching the tile:

```
if(IsMouseTouchingTile(48,100,64,64,60,102) == TRUE)
   // Mouse was touching tile!
else
   // Mouse not touching tile
```

## Creating a Map Class

Because you've gone to all the trouble of learning how to use tiles, multiple layers, smooth scrolling, and object rendering, let's wrap it all together into a small class (and supporting structure).

To keep your game running smoothly, you first limit the number of free-floating tiles (sprites) that can be drawn for each frame. Defining a macro does a fine job of informing the map class how many sprites can be drawn each frame:

```
#define MAX_OBJECTS   1024
```

Next comes the sprite tile structure that tracks the coordinates and tile number of the sprite object to draw during the next frame render function call:

```
typedef struct {
  long XPos, YPos;
  char Tile;
} sObject;
```

The map class declaration is next. It contains an array of sObject structures and an array of map layers. You store the map's dimensions within two variables, m_Width and m_Height, that are set when you initialize the map class with a call to Create.

Each map class instance can store a huge number of layers (well over one million). You store each layer's tile data within a single array, m_Map. Because the map is fixed in size once it is created, you can access each layer's tile data by calculating the current offset into the m_Map array and, using a pointer, read and write from that layer. The class's SetMapData and Render functions demonstrate accessing the layer data.

As for the graphics tiles to use, the map class is limited to one set of tiles (using only one texture to store the tiles). You inform the map class which tile class object to use for drawing the map's tiles by calling the UseTiles function you see in the map class declaration.

Speaking of the map class declaration, have a look:

```
class cMap
{
  private:
    long    m_Width, m_Height;  // Width and height of map
    long    m_NumLayers;        // # of layers
    char    *m_Map;             // array for tile information
    cTiles  *m_Tiles;          // cTile class to use for tiles

    long    m_NumObjectsToDraw; // # objects to draw
    sObject m_Objects[MAX_OBJECTS];  // Object list

  public:
    cMap();   // Constructor
    ~cMap();  // Destructor

    // Function to create and free a map class
    BOOL Create(long NumLayers, long Width, long Height);
```

```
      BOOL Free();

      // Function to set a map's layer data
      BOOL SetMapData(long Layer, char *Data);

      // Function to clear and add an object to list
      void ClearObjectList();
      BOOL AddObject(long XPos, long YPos, char Tile);

      char *GetPtr(long Layer); // Get pointer to map array
      long GetWidth();   // Get width of map
      long GetHeight();  // Get height of map

      // Assign cTile class object to use for drawing map tiles
      BOOL UseTiles(cTiles *Tiles);

      // Render map using specified top-left map coordinates, as
      // well as # of columns and rows to draw, plus layer used
      // to draw objects.
      BOOL Render(long XPos, long YPos,                       \
                  long NumRows, long NumColumns,              \
                  long ObjectLayer);
};
```

Most of the functions are commented and pretty much self-explanatory, so go
ahead and take a look at the full cMap class code. The code starts with the constructor and destructor functions, which ensure that the class's data is reset to a known
state and that all resources are freed when the class object is destroyed:

```
cMap::cMap()
{
  m_Map   = NULL;
  m_Tiles = NULL;
  m_NumObjectsToDraw = 0;
  m_Width = m_Height = 0;
}


cMap::~cMap()
{
  Free();
}
```

In order to use the map class, you first must instance the class and call the Create function. The Create function takes the number of layers to use for the map, as well as the width and height of the map to use:

```
BOOL cMap::Create(long NumLayers, long Width, long Height)
{
  // Free a prior map
  Free();

  // Save # layers, width, and height
  m_NumLayers = NumLayers;
  m_Width     = Width;
  m_Height    = Height;

  // Allocate map data memory
  if((m_Map = new char[m_NumLayers*m_Width*m_Height]) == NULL)
    return FALSE;

  // Clear it out
  ZeroMemory(m_Map, m_NumLayers*m_Width*m_Height);

  // Reset # objects to draw
  m_NumObjectsToDraw = 0;

  return TRUE;
}
```

Short and to the point, the Create function allocates an array of char values to hold the tile information. The array's size is determined by the width, height, and number of layers to use; multiply those three values to come up with the final array size.

To ensure that the map layer array is released when you're done with the map class, you call on the Free function:

```
BOOL cMap::Free()
{
  // Free map array
  delete [] m_Map;
  m_Map = NULL;
  m_Width = m_Height = 0;
  m_NumLayers = 0;

  return TRUE;
}
```

In order to fill the map layer array with useful tile information, you first construct an array of char values that represents a layer as shown earlier in the section "Drawing Basic Maps." Using that array as an argument, call the SetMapData function along with the layer number in the map to which you want the array of data copied:

```
BOOL cMap::SetMapData(long Layer, char *Data)
{
  // Error checking
  if(Layer >= m_NumLayers)
    return FALSE;

  // Copy over data
  memcpy(&m_Map[Layer*m_Width*m_Height],Data,m_Width*m_Height);

  return TRUE;
}
```

For each frame that you want to render the map, you construct a list of sprite objects that might need to be drawn. By first calling ClearObjectList, you prepare the map class to begin receiving the sprite information used during the render:

```
void cMap::ClearObjectList()
{
  m_NumObjectsToDraw = 0;
}
```

To add a sprite to the list to be drawn for each frame, call on AddObject, providing the screen coordinates where the specified tile is to be drawn:

```
BOOL cMap::AddObject(long XPos, long YPos, char Tile)
{
  if(m_NumObjectsToDraw < MAX_OBJECTS) {
    m_Objects[m_NumObjectsToDraw].XPos = XPos;
    m_Objects[m_NumObjectsToDraw].YPos = XPos;
    m_Objects[m_NumObjectsToDraw].Tile = Tile;
    m_NumObjectsToDraw++;

    return TRUE;
  }

  return FALSE;
}
```

In case you want to directly alter the map's layer data, you can call on the GetPtr, GetWidth, and GetHeight functions of the map class to respectively retrieve the pointer to the layers' data array, the width of the map, and the height of the map:

```
char *cMap::GetPtr(long Layer)
{
  if(Layer >= m_NumLayers)
    return NULL;

  return &m_Map[Layer*m_Width*m_Height];
}

long cMap::GetWidth()
{
  return m_Width;
}

long cMap::GetHeight()
{
  return m_Height;
}
```

Earlier I said you can use only one set of tiles to draw the map. In order to tell the map class which tile class object to use, pass the pointer to the class instance to the map class's UseTiles function:

```
BOOL cMap::UseTiles(cTiles *Tiles)
{
  if((m_Tiles = Tiles) == NULL)
    return FALSE;

  return TRUE;
}
```

At long last, you come to the Render function, which renders the map to the display using the specified fine map coordinates you provide, as well as the number of rows and columns of tiles to draw. If you're using sprites, you must also specify after which layer to draw those sprites by setting the ObjectLayer argument:

```
BOOL cMap::Render(long XPos, long YPos,
                  long NumRows, long NumColumns,
                  long ObjectLayer)
{
```

```
        long MapX, MapY;
        long XOff, YOff;
        long Layer, Row, Column, i;
        char TileNum;
        char *MapPtr;

        // Error checking
        if(m_Map == NULL || m_Tiles == NULL)
          return FALSE;

        // Calculate smooth scrolling variables
        MapX = XPos / m_Tiles->GetWidth(0);
        MapY = YPos / m_Tiles->GetHeight(0);
        XOff = XPos % m_Tiles->GetWidth(0);
        YOff = YPos % m_Tiles->GetHeight(0);

        // Loop through each layer
        for(Layer=0;Layer<m_NumLayers;Layer++) {
          MapPtr = &m_Map[Layer*m_Width*m_Height];

          // Loop for each row and column
          for(Row=0;Row<NumRows;Row++) {
            for(Column=0;Column<NumColumns;Column++) {
              TileNum = MapPtr[(Column + YPos)*m_Width+Row+XPos];
              m_Tiles->Draw(0, TileNum,                          \
                            Column * m_Tiles->GetWidth(0) - XOff, \
                            Row    * m_Tiles->GetHeight(0) - YOff);
            }
          }

          // Draw objects if on object layer
          if(Layer == ObjectLayer) {
            for(i=0;i<m_NumObjectsToDraw;i++)
              m_Tiles->Draw(0, m_Objects[i].Tile,               \
                            m_Objects[i].XPos - XOff,            \
                            m_Objects[i].YPos - YOff);
          }
        }

        return TRUE;
      }
```

Each function in cMap is straightforward and to the point and basically a repetition of the information in the earlier section "A Basic Tile Engine." I'll leave it up to you to check out the sample programs from this chapter to see the cMap class in action. You will find these on the CD-ROM at the back of this book (look for BookCode\Chap11\).

# Angled Tile Engine

With no changes whatsoever to your basic tile engine, you can begin using angled tiles to start giving your graphics that extra visual dimension. Now your graphics can illustrate width, height, and depth. The only changes are the tile graphics.

Going back to my previous tile example, let's swap out a few tiles and see what you can come up with. Take a look at Figure 11.6 to see the new set of tiles you'll be using.

Now, using the same map from previous examples, run through the map-drawing function again (only this time with the new tiles). As a result, you get something like the scene shown in Figure 11.7.

The same techniques that are used for regular tile engines apply to other angled-tile topics such as map-mouse clicking, with no changes except to account for the new tile sizes.

**NOTE**

If you want to check out the full source code for the angled tiles example, go to the \BookCode\Chap11\Tile directory on the CD-ROM at the back of this book.

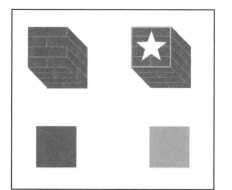

**Figure 11.6**

*A group of angled tiles gives bland, flat maps an extra dimension. Angled tiles show width, depth, and height.*

**Figure 11.7**

*Using the angled tiles and a map, you get fantastic results!*

# Big Bitmap Engines

The last type of 2-D graphics engine that I'd like to show you is commonly called the *big bitmap engine*. Made popular by games such as *Baldur's Gate*, the big bitmap engine takes a new look at using 2-D graphics. The name says it all—big bitmap. The big bitmap engine uses a huge bitmap as the level, which means that the visual quality of the map is much better than it would be if you were using small tiles.

For texture memory reasons, the bitmaps used to store the levels are split into multiple image files. For example, a level might be $1024 \times 1024$ pixels in size. Because you want to constrain to the texture limits of Direct3D, you can split that level into 16 textures that are $256 \times 256$ pixels in size (arranged in a $4 \times 4$ grid). Basically, you're splitting the level into 16 tiles.

Because you're using tiles to render the level, you have at your disposal some powerful options. For example, you can reuse the tiles in the level, saving on textures. Take grass, for example; it's a common image that can be tiled repeatedly, and in the big picture, the grass will blend in perfectly.

Not only can you reuse tiles, but also you can scale them in order to create much larger levels. For example, by scaling the tiles up to twice their size, you can effectively double the size of your level. How about tripling or quadrupling the size of your level? It's all possible, and by using multiple layers of tiles, you can construct extremely large (and beautiful) levels.

> **NOTE**
>
> Each map layer in your engine can have its own set of tiles that can be scaled to any size. For example, the bottommost layer can use huge 256 × 256 tiles, scaled to twice their size. The second layer up can then use 64 × 64 sized tiles with no scaling. Each layer has its own map array with which to work, so the hardest part is making sure that they all line up with each other.

## Creating Big Tiles

The only problem when dealing with big bitmaps is that you have to split them into multiple textures. Say that all your levels are 1024 × 1024 pixels in size; that means you must split the level images into 16 textures, each 256 × 256 pixels in size. Because Direct3D has no way of doing this, you must turn to another program for help.

After you save your big bitmap tiles to the various files, it's time to load them up. You can use the ever-so-useful cTiles class object developed earlier in this chapter in the section "Building a Tile-Handler Class" to load those bitmap images from the disk and draw them to the display. That's right—no need for more special programming; it's already done!

Because you're at the point now where you can load your big bitmap tiles, and you can use the earlier developed cMap class to store your map information, you can move on to drawing some big bitmap levels.

> **NOTE**
>
> A demo version of Paint Shop Pro (PSP), an awesome digital image editor program, is located in the \Utils\Paint Shop Pro 7\ directory of this book's CD-ROM. Using PSP, you can split bitmaps into smaller, usable images.
>
> You might want to divide your favorite large image and use it as an example in the next section, or you can open the example provided on the CD-ROM (look for \BookCode\Chap11\Bitmap\).

## A Big Example

Now that you have a series of big tiles and a set of smaller ones, it's your time to shine. In fact, the big bitmap engine I described and developed for this book doesn't differ a bit from the previous tile engine I showed you earlier in this chapter (see the section "A Basic Tile Engine"). For that reason, there's really no need to reinvent the wheel and show you the same code again. Instead, check out the big bitmap demo program on the CD-ROM for an example. The only difference you'll notice is that certain layers use big tiles.

# Wrapping Up 2-D Graphics

At this point, you've learned how to utilize Direct3D's 2-D drawing capabilities. This includes using memory-conserving graphics tiles to construct huge levels. With very little extra work, you can turn the basic engines found in this chapter into full-fledged game engines, ready to be used in your next project.

If you're feeling adventurous, why don't you try to spruce up the map engines a bit to include features such as tile animation? Tile animation is easy; by altering the tile number values in the map array, you can dynamically change which tiles are drawn at specific locations in the map. By creating a sequence of animated tiles, you can then continuously alter the tile values in the map array to use those sequences of tile numbers.

Beginning with Chapter 12, "Creating 3-D Graphics Engines," and in several subsequent chapters, I concentrate mainly on using 3-D graphics engines.

## Programs on the CD-ROM

Three programs discussed in this chapter that demonstrate the 2-D engine are located on the CD-ROM at the back of this book. You can find the following programs in the \BookCode\Chap11\ directory:

- **Tile.** An example of the basic tile engine that demonstrates using tiles, maps, and smooth-scrolling techniques. Location: \BookCode\Chap11\Tile\.

- **Angled.** An example much like Tile, except using angled tiles. Location: \BookCode\Chap11\Angled\.

- **Bitmap.** Demonstrates the use of a big bitmap engine. Location: \BookCode\Chap11\Bitmap\.

# CHAPTER 12

# CREATING 3-D GRAPHICS ENGINES

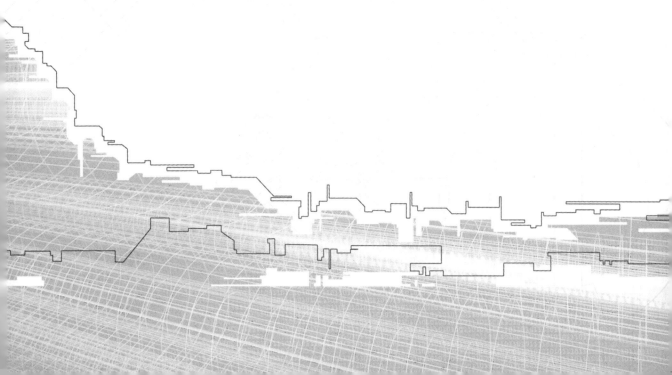

In Chapter 6, "Drawing with DirectX Graphics," you learn how to render 3-D graphics, but only when working with small meshes. What you need now is the ability to render large maps and levels for your gaming denizens to navigate. You've already seen how to work with 2-D worlds—now is the time to move up to the world of 3-D!

In this chapter, you learn how to do the following:

- Use meshes as levels
- Use a viewing frustum
- Render levels with nodes and trees
- Integrate 3-D objects
- Use collision detection
- Use sky boxes

## Meshes as Levels

You might think I'm crazy, but nothing is as simple as using a mesh for a level. In this way, you can easily use the Graphics Core at *the* basic level. The flip side to using single meshes, however, is that you're rendering the entire level at once, meaning that even those sections that are not seen are passed through the rendering pipeline to be clipped out. In English, this means that you're wasting time.

Don't let that daunt you, though, because there are some great ways to use a single mesh for rendering levels. Say that your game world consists solely of dungeons. Each dungeon consists of various rooms, all linked together by corridors. See what I'm getting at? Each room and corridor is a single mesh—all you have to do is load and free the meshes that represent the dungeon rooms as the game-play progresses.

To see what I'm talking about, load up the MeshLvl example program located on this book's CD-ROM (look for BookCode\Chap12\MeshLvl\). MeshLvl demonstrates a way to load a few meshes and then draw them together to form a larger level. In Figure 12.1, you see a screenshot from the MeshLvl demo.

Here's how the MeshLvl demo works: The main function (stripped down here) loads two meshes: a corridor and a room. Each room in the game uses a cObject object from the Graphics Core, which in turn is associated with the meshes. For

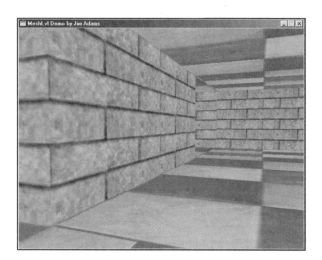

**Figure 12.1**

*The MeshLvl demo in action. Notice that only two meshes are used to draw the various rooms.*

each frame of animation, the rooms are rendered according to the viewer's position. In the demo, you can use the arrow keys to move within the corridors and rooms, using the mouse to rotate the view.

# Loading Levels

As I mentioned in the previous section, levels are constructed using various meshes that you must load. For our purposes, those meshes are loaded into a series of Graphics Core mesh (cMesh) and 3-D object (cObject) class instances. To load those meshes used by the MeshLvl demo, as well as assigning the meshes to the 3-D objects, the MeshLvl uses the following code:

```
// Declarations in class
cMesh   m_LevelMeshes[2];
cObject m_LevelObjects[8];

// ... later on in init code
// Load the room meshes
m_RoomMeshes[0].Load(&m_Graphics,                         \
            "..\\LevelData\\Corridor.x", "..\\LevelData\\");
m_RoomMeshes[1].Load(&m_Graphics, "..\\LevelData\\Room.x",  \
            "..\\LevelData\\");

// Set up the room objects
m_RoomObjects[0].Create(&m_Graphics, &m_RoomMeshes[1]);
```

```
m_RoomObjects[1].Create(&m_Graphics, &m_RoomMeshes[0]);
m_RoomObjects[2].Create(&m_Graphics, &m_RoomMeshes[1]);
m_RoomObjects[3].Create(&m_Graphics, &m_RoomMeshes[0]);
m_RoomObjects[4].Create(&m_Graphics, &m_RoomMeshes[0]);
m_RoomObjects[5].Create(&m_Graphics, &m_RoomMeshes[1]);
m_RoomObjects[6].Create(&m_Graphics, &m_RoomMeshes[0]);
m_RoomObjects[7].Create(&m_Graphics, &m_RoomMeshes[1]);
```

The preceding code shows two meshes being loaded: Corridor.x and Room.x. Then eight objects are created, each representing a room. At this point, the rooms need to be oriented:

```
m_RoomObjects[0].Move(-2000.0f, 0.0f,  2000.0f);
m_RoomObjects[1].Move(    0.0f, 0.0f,  2000.0f);
m_RoomObjects[2].Move( 2000.0f, 0.0f,  2000.0f);
m_RoomObjects[3].Move(-2000.0f, 0.0f,     0.0f);
m_RoomObjects[4].Move( 2000.0f, 0.0f,     0.0f);
m_RoomObjects[5].Move(-2000.0f, 0.0f, -2000.0f);
m_RoomObjects[6].Move(    0.0f, 0.0f, -2000.0f);
m_RoomObjects[7].Move( 2000.0f, 0.0f, -2000.0f);

m_RoomObjects[1].Rotate(0.0f,  1.57f, 0.0f);
m_RoomObjects[2].Rotate(0.0f,  1.57f, 0.0f);
m_RoomObjects[5].Rotate(0.0f, -1.57f, 0.0f);
m_RoomObjects[6].Rotate(0.0f, -1.57f, 0.0f);
m_RoomObjects[7].Rotate(0.0f,  3.14f, 0.0f);
```

That's it! Now, you are ready to draw the rooms.

## Drawing the Rooms

Once the meshes are loaded, it now comes time to render them to the display. With each frame, the MeshLvl demo determines where the user is located within the series of rooms that construct the level. Once the user's location is determined, the demo then orients and renders each mesh that represents a room. There are a total of four rooms and four corridors that connect the rooms. With two meshes in use, that means each mesh is drawn four times.

The code that renders the view is therefore very simple. By looping through an array that stores the orientation of each of the rooms, the demo can render each mesh using a short series of commands. In the following code, you see the short loop that is in place to orient and draw each room. Also notice that I added some code that reads the user's input and appropriately moves the viewpoint (using a cCamera object). Using the arrow keys moves the viewpoint, whereas moving the mouse rotates the view.

Take a look at the function that handles the rendering and input:

```
BOOL cApp::Frame()
{
  static DWORD  Timer = timeGetTime();
  unsigned long Elapsed;
  float         XMove, ZMove;
  short         i;

  // Calculate elapsed time (plus speed boost)
  Elapsed = (timeGetTime() - Timer) * 2;
  Timer = timeGetTime();

  // Get input
  m_Keyboard.Read();
  m_Mouse.Read();

  // Process input and update everything.
  // ESC quits program
  if(m_Keyboard.GetKeyState(KEY_ESC) == TRUE)
    return FALSE;

  // Process movement
  XMove = ZMove = 0.0f;

  // Process keyboard input to move view
  if(m_Keyboard.GetKeyState(KEY_UP) == TRUE) {
    XMove = (float)sin(m_Camera.GetYRotation()) * Elapsed;
    ZMove = (float)cos(m_Camera.GetYRotation()) * Elapsed;
  }
  if(m_Keyboard.GetKeyState(KEY_DOWN) == TRUE) {
    XMove = -(float)sin(m_Camera.GetYRotation()) * Elapsed;
    ZMove = -(float)cos(m_Camera.GetYRotation()) * Elapsed;
  }
  if(m_Keyboard.GetKeyState(KEY_LEFT) == TRUE) {
    XMove = (float)sin(m_Camera.GetYRotation() - 1.57f) * Elapsed;
    ZMove = (float)cos(m_Camera.GetYRotation() - 1.57f) * Elapsed;
```

```
        }
        if(m_Keyboard.GetKeyState(KEY_RIGHT) == TRUE) {
            XMove = (float)sin(m_Camera.GetYRotation() + 1.57f) * Elapsed;
            ZMove = (float)cos(m_Camera.GetYRotation() + 1.57f) * Elapsed;
        }

        // Update view coordinates
        m_XPos += XMove;
        m_ZPos += ZMove;

        // Position camera and rotate based on mouse movement
        m_Camera.Move(m_XPos + XMove, 400.0f, m_ZPos + ZMove);
        m_Camera.RotateRel((float)m_Mouse.GetYDelta() / 200.0f,
                           (float)m_Mouse.GetXDelta() / 200.0f,
                           0.0f);

        // Set camera
        m_Graphics.SetCamera(&m_Camera);

        // Render everything
        m_Graphics.Clear(D3DCOLOR_RGBA(0,64,128,255));
        if(m_Graphics.BeginScene() == TRUE) {
            // Render each room
            for(i=0;i<8;i++)
                m_RoomObjects[i].Render();
            m_Graphics.EndScene();
        }
        m_Graphics.Display();

        return TRUE;
}
```

# Improving on Basic Techniques

Although drawing 3-D worlds is not difficult, one problem creeps in. Although you can draw as many meshes as you like (characters, objects, and levels), you begin to notice that your 3-D engine slows down each time you draw a new object.

Each polygon that you add to the pipeline slows down the whole works as the data is processed. That holds true for all the polygons in each mesh, including the meshes that aren't visible (that are behind your view).

Ideally, you want to discard the meshes that are out of view so that Direct3D is free to deal with only those meshes (and polygons) that are in the view—and thereby speed things up a bit. But how can you possibly know when something is in the view before processing it? That's where the viewing frustum comes into play.

# Introducing the Viewing Frustum

The *viewing frustum* is a collection of six planes that extend outward from the view-point that determines which polygons are, and are not, seen by the viewer. The viewing frustum is very helpful in optimizing graphics processing, so I'd like to acquaint you with the intricate details regarding the viewing frustum.

First, you can think of a frustum as a pyramid that extends away from you (as illustrated in Figure 12.2). This pyramid represents your *field of view* (FOV). Everything you see is within this pyramid, and everything outside the pyramid is out of your view.

If you're wondering how a viewing frustum can help you in your 3-D engine, consider this: Everything in your 3-D graphics engine consists of 3-D points (called *vertices*). The viewing frustum has six sides (front, back, left, right, top, and bottom). Using some mathematical calculations, you can determine which vertices are within the frustum and which vertices are outside. The vertices inside the frustum are rendered,

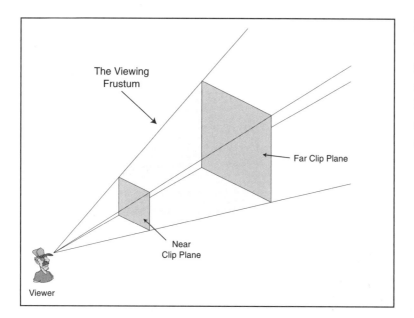

**Figure 12.2**

*The viewing frustum typically takes the shape of a pyramid. Everything inside the frustum is considered within the viewer's field of view.*

and the vertices outside the frustum are not rendered. The same is true when rendering polygons—only those with vertices within the frustum are rendered.

## Planes and Clipping

The six sides of the viewing frustum are called the *clipping planes*. To make things easy, think of a plane as an infinitely long piece of paper (with a front and back side). A plane is defined by four numbers, typically referred to as A, B, C, and D. Those four numbers define the plane's orientation in 3-D.

In Chapter 6, I mention normals—those numbers that define the direction in which an object points. Although typically used for lighting, a normal can be used to define the direction of anything, and in this case, it's the direction a plane's face is pointing. You define a plane by pointing it in a specific direction and moving it into position away from the origin. (A plane is actually defined just like a normal, but with the addition of the distance of the plane away from the origin.) Take a look at Figure 12.3, which demonstrates a plane oriented in 3-D space.

> **NOTE**
>
> Direct3D, or rather **D3DX**, uses a special object named D3DXPLANE to contain plane data. D3DXPLANE contains four variables: a, b, c, and d— all of which are float data types.

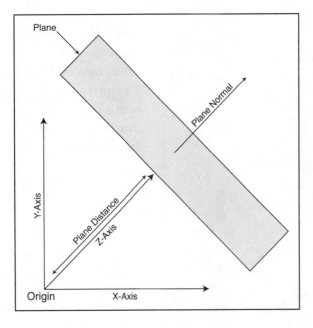

**Figure 12.3**

*A plane's definition includes the direction its face is pointing, as well as the distance from the origin. Here, a plane has been oriented after pointing it away from the origin.*

Rather than specifying the plane's normal values as X,Y,Z, you use the variables A, B, and C. An additional value is required to determine the plane's distance from the origin. This distance is represented as D. In order to define a plane, you set the A, B, and C values to the normal values and set D to the distance of the plane from the origin. Once the normal and distance values are set up, you can use a plane to check whether a specific point is located in front of or behind the plane.

To calculate the six planes of the viewing frustum, you combine the current viewing transformation matrix and the projection matrix. Then you deal directly with the combined matrix to calculate the A, B, C, and D values for each plane.

Here's how to combine the two required matrices and calculate the plane's values from those matrices (placing the plane values into the appropriate D3DXPLANE objects):

```
// Graphics = pre-initialized cGraphics object
D3DXPLANE Planes[6]; // six planes to the viewing frustum
D3DXMATRIX Matrix, matView, matProj; // Matrices to work with

// Get the view and projections matrices, then combine them
Graphics.GetDeviceCOM()->GetTransform(D3DTS_PROJECTION,        \
                                      &matProj);
Graphics.GetDeviceCOM()->GetTransform(D3DTS_VIEW, &matView);
D3DXMatrixMultiply(&Matrix, &matView, &matProj);

// Calculate the planes
Planes[0].a = Matrix._14 + Matrix._13; // Near plane
Planes[0].b = Matrix._24 + Matrix._23;
Planes[0].c = Matrix._34 + Matrix._33;
Planes[0].d = Matrix._44 + Matrix._43;
D3DXPlaneNormalize(&Planes[0], &Planes[0]);

Planes[1].a = Matrix._14 - Matrix._13; // Far plane
Planes[1].b = Matrix._24 - Matrix._23;
Planes[1].c = Matrix._34 - Matrix._33;
Planes[1].d = Matrix._44 - Matrix._43;
D3DXPlaneNormalize(&Planes[1], &Planes[1]);

Planes[2].a = Matrix._14 + Matrix._11; // Left plane
Planes[2].b = Matrix._24 + Matrix._21;
Planes[2].c = Matrix._34 + Matrix._31;
Planes[2].d = Matrix._44 + Matrix._41;
D3DXPlaneNormalize(&Planes[2], &Planes[2]);
```

```
Planes[3].a = Matrix._14 - Matrix._11; // Right plane
Planes[3].b = Matrix._24 - Matrix._21;
Planes[3].c = Matrix._34 - Matrix._31;
Planes[3].d = Matrix._44 - Matrix._41;
D3DXPlaneNormalize(&Planes[3], &Planes[3]);

Planes[4].a = Matrix._14 - Matrix._12; // Top plane
Planes[4].b = Matrix._24 - Matrix._22;
Planes[4].c = Matrix._34 - Matrix._32;
Planes[4].d = Matrix._44 - Matrix._42;
D3DXPlaneNormalize(&Planes[4], &Planes[4]);

Planes[5].a = Matrix._14 + Matrix._12; // Bottom plane
Planes[5].b = Matrix._24 + Matrix._22;
Planes[5].c = Matrix._34 + Matrix._32;
Planes[5].d = Matrix._44 + Matrix._42;
D3DXPlaneNormalize(&Planes[5], &Planes[5]);
```

> **NOTE**
>
> Notice that each plane has to be normalized to ensure that the A, B, and C values are <= 1.0f and that D contains the distance of the plane from the origin.

## Checking for Visibility with the Plane

At this point, you have a plane (or a set of planes) that points in a specific direction. To check whether a point lies in front of or behind the plane, you compute the *dot product*. The *dot product* is a special vector (coordinate) typically used to calculate the angle between two vectors. When checking points against planes, the dot product tells you the distance from a point to the plane. If the value is positive, the point is in front of the plane. If the value is negative, the point is behind the plane.

To calculate the dot product, you use the D3DXPlaneDotCoord function:

```
FLOAT D3DXPlaneDotCoord(
  CONST D3DXPLANE* pP,      // D3DXPLANE to check
  CONST D3DXVECTOR3* pV);   // Point to check
```

With the D3DXPlaneDotCoord function you supply the plane structure (that contains the plane's values) as well as the point (a vector contained inside a D3DXVECTOR3 object). You are checking to determine which side that point is on the plane, either the front or the back. Upon return of D3DXPlaneDotCoord, you will receive the distance of the vector from the plane. This return value can be 0, a negative value, or a positive value.

If the return value is 0, the point you're checking lies on the plane; if it's negative, the point is behind the plane; if it's positive, the point lies in front of the plane you're checking, as demonstrated here:

```
// Plane = pre-configured D3DXPLANE object
// XPos, YPos, ZPos = point to check
float Dist = D3DXPlaneDotCoord(&Plane,                        \
                               &D3DXVECTOR3(XPos, YPos, ZPos));
// If dist > 0 then point is in front of plane
// If dist < 0 then point is in back of plane
// If dist = 0 then point is on plane
```

## Checking the Entire Frustum

Although checking a single point is useful, you can expand on it a bit by checking if entire objects are contained within the frustum. These objects to test are cubes, rectangles, and spheres. For cubes and rectangles, you check all the corners, making sure that at least one or all are contained within each frustum plane. As for spheres, as long as the distance from each plane is equal to or more than the sphere's radius, the sphere is visible.

To check any number of points, you check each one individually, making sure that at least one falls in front of all the planes. In the next section, you learn how to create a class that constructs the viewing frustum as well as checks the visibility of objects with the frustum.

# The cFrustum Class

Up to this point you've seen the math behind using the viewing frustum, and although this math is relatively easy to handle, you'll want to use the frustum without constantly retyping the same code. Because the math is the same every time you use the frustum, it makes sense to create a class that handles the math for you, including calculating the frustum using the frustum to check whether an object is visible. The class I'm speaking of is cFrustum:

```
class cFrustum
{
  private:
    D3DXPLANE m_Planes[6]; // The frustum planes

  public:
    // Construct the six planes from current view and
    // projection. Can override the default depth value.
    BOOL Construct(cGraphics *Graphics, float ZDistance = 0.0f);
```

```
    // The following functions check a single point, cube,
    // rectangle, and sphere if contained in the frustum.
    // A return value of TRUE means visible, FALSE not visible.
    BOOL CheckPoint(float XPos, float YPos, float ZPos);
    BOOL CheckCube(float XCenter, float YCenter,              \
                      float ZCenter, float Size);
    BOOL CheckRectangle(float XCenter, float YCenter,            \
                          float ZCenter, float XSize,
                          float YSize, float ZSize);
    BOOL CheckSphere(float XCenter, float YCenter,             \
                      float ZCenter, float Radius);
};
```

## cFrustum::Construct

You use this function, which must be called every time the viewing or projection matrix is changed, to construct the six testing planes:

```
BOOL cFrustum::Construct(cGraphics *Graphics, float ZDistance)
{
  D3DXMATRIX Matrix, matView, matProj;
  float      ZMin, Q;

  // Error checking
  if(Graphics == NULL || Graphics->GetDeviceCOM() == NULL)
    return FALSE;

  // Calculate FOV data
  Graphics->GetDeviceCOM()->GetTransform(D3DTS_PROJECTION,     \
                                           &matProj);

  if(ZDistance != 0.0f) {
    // Calculate new projection matrix based on
    // distance provided.
    ZMin = -matProj._43 / matProj._33;
    Q = ZDistance / (ZDistance - ZMin);
    matProj._33 = Q;
    matProj._43 = -Q * ZMin;
  }
  Graphics->GetDeviceCOM()->GetTransform(D3DTS_VIEW, &matView);
  D3DXMatrixMultiply(&Matrix, &matView, &matProj);
```

```
        // Calculate the planes
        m_Planes[0].a = Matrix._14 + Matrix._13; // Near plane
        m_Planes[0].b = Matrix._24 + Matrix._23;
        m_Planes[0].c = Matrix._34 + Matrix._33;
        m_Planes[0].d = Matrix._44 + Matrix._43;
        D3DXPlaneNormalize(&m_Planes[0], &m_Planes[0]);


        m_Planes[1].a = Matrix._14 - Matrix._13; // Far plane
        m_Planes[1].b = Matrix._24 - Matrix._23;
        m_Planes[1].c = Matrix._34 - Matrix._33;
        m_Planes[1].d = Matrix._44 - Matrix._43;
        D3DXPlaneNormalize(&m_Planes[1], &m_Planes[1]);


        m_Planes[2].a = Matrix._14 + Matrix._11; // Left plane
        m_Planes[2].b = Matrix._24 + Matrix._21;
        m_Planes[2].c = Matrix._34 + Matrix._31;
        m_Planes[2].d = Matrix._44 + Matrix._41;
        D3DXPlaneNormalize(&m_Planes[2], &m_Planes[2]);


        m_Planes[3].a = Matrix._14 - Matrix._11; // Right plane
        m_Planes[3].b = Matrix._24 - Matrix._21;
        m_Planes[3].c = Matrix._34 - Matrix._31;
        m_Planes[3].d = Matrix._44 - Matrix._41;
        D3DXPlaneNormalize(&m_Planes[3], &m_Planes[3]);


        m_Planes[4].a = Matrix._14 - Matrix._12; // Top plane
        m_Planes[4].b = Matrix._24 - Matrix._22;
        m_Planes[4].c = Matrix._34 - Matrix._32;
        m_Planes[4].d = Matrix._44 - Matrix._42;
        D3DXPlaneNormalize(&m_Planes[4], &m_Planes[4]);


        m_Planes[5].a = Matrix._14 + Matrix._12; // Bottom plane
        m_Planes[5].b = Matrix._24 + Matrix._22;
        m_Planes[5].c = Matrix._34 + Matrix._32;
        m_Planes[5].d = Matrix._44 + Matrix._42;
        D3DXPlaneNormalize(&m_Planes[5], &m_Planes[5]);

        return TRUE;
}
```

You saw most of the preceding code earlier in this chapter in the section "Introducing the Viewing Frustum," but the one thing added is the ability to override the distance to the far clipping plane when computing the frustum. If you want only the closer objects to be seen, you can specify a new distance value to the far clipping plane. To calculate the new far plane, you must recalculate the matrix values for the minimum and maximum planes, as shown in the preceding code.

## cFrustum::CheckPoint, CheckCube, CheckRectangle, and CheckSphere

You use these four functions to find out whether anything is visible within the viewing frustum. These functions are fairly self-explanatory, as you can see here:

```
BOOL cFrustum::CheckPoint(float XPos, float YPos, float ZPos)
{
  // Make sure point is in frustum
  for(short i=0;i<6;i++) {
    if(D3DXPlaneDotCoord(&m_Planes[i],                            \
                    &D3DXVECTOR3(XPos, YPos, ZPos)) < 0.0f)
      return FALSE;
  }
  return TRUE;
}
```

In the preceding CheckPoint function, the point in question is checked to make sure it is in front of all six of the clipping planes. Remember that the point is in front of a plane if the dot product is positive. If the dot product is negative for any plane, the function reports FALSE, meaning that the point is behind the plane, and thus out of view.

```
BOOL cFrustum::CheckCube(float XCenter, float YCenter,           \
                         float ZCenter, float Size)
{
  // Make sure at least one point is completely in frustum
  for(short i=0;i<6;i++) {
    if(D3DXPlaneDotCoord(&m_Planes[i],                           \
        &D3DXVECTOR3(XCenter-Size, YCenter-Size,                 \
                    ZCenter-Size)) >= 0.0f)
      continue;
    if(D3DXPlaneDotCoord(&m_Planes[i],                           \
        &D3DXVECTOR3(XCenter+Size, YCenter-Size,                 \
                    ZCenter-Size)) >= 0.0f)
```

```
        continue;
    if(D3DXPlaneDotCoord(&m_Planes[i],                          \
        &D3DXVECTOR3(XCenter-Size, YCenter+Size,                \
                    ZCenter-Size)) >= 0.0f)
        continue;
    if(D3DXPlaneDotCoord(&m_Planes[i],                          \
        &D3DXVECTOR3(XCenter+Size, YCenter+Size,                \
                    ZCenter-Size)) >= 0.0f)
        continue;
    if(D3DXPlaneDotCoord(&m_Planes[i],                          \
        &D3DXVECTOR3(XCenter-Size, YCenter-Size,                \
                    ZCenter+Size)) >= 0.0f)
        continue;
    if(D3DXPlaneDotCoord(&m_Planes[i],                          \
        &D3DXVECTOR3(XCenter+Size, YCenter-Size,                \
                    ZCenter+Size)) >= 0.0f)
        continue;
    if(D3DXPlaneDotCoord(&m_Planes[i],                          \
        &D3DXVECTOR3(XCenter-Size, YCenter+Size,                \
                    ZCenter+Size)) >= 0.0f)
        continue;
    if(D3DXPlaneDotCoord(&m_Planes[i],                          \
        &D3DXVECTOR3(XCenter+Size, YCenter+Size,                \
                    ZCenter+Size)) >= 0.0f)
        continue;

    return FALSE;
  }

  return TRUE;
}
```

In the same way that the CheckPoint function checks a single point's position relative to all six frustum planes, the CheckCube function checks the eight points of a cube. Because a cube is symmetrical, you just specify the center coordinates and the width from the center to one edge (much as you specify a cube's radius).

```
BOOL cFrustum::CheckRectangle(float XCenter, float YCenter,   \
                              float ZCenter, float XSize,      \
                              float YSize, float ZSize)
{
```

```
// Make sure at least one point is in frustum
for(short i=0;i<6;i++) {
  if(D3DXPlaneDotCoord(&m_Planes[i],                     \
      &D3DXVECTOR3(XCenter-XSize, YCenter-YSize,          \
                   ZCenter-ZSize)) >= 0.0f)
    continue;
  if(D3DXPlaneDotCoord(&m_Planes[i],                     \
      &D3DXVECTOR3(XCenter+XSize, YCenter-YSize,          \
                   ZCenter-ZSize)) >= 0.0f)
    continue;
  if(D3DXPlaneDotCoord(&m_Planes[i],                     \
      &D3DXVECTOR3(XCenter-XSize, YCenter+YSize,          \
                   ZCenter-ZSize)) >= 0.0f)
    continue;
  if(D3DXPlaneDotCoord(&m_Planes[i],                     \
      &D3DXVECTOR3(XCenter+XSize, YCenter+YSize,          \
                   ZCenter-ZSize)) >= 0.0f)
    continue;
  if(D3DXPlaneDotCoord(&m_Planes[i],                     \
      &D3DXVECTOR3(XCenter-XSize, YCenter-YSize,          \
                   ZCenter+ZSize)) >= 0.0f)
    continue;
  if(D3DXPlaneDotCoord(&m_Planes[i],                     \
      &D3DXVECTOR3(XCenter+XSize, YCenter-YSize,          \
                   ZCenter+ZSize)) >= 0.0f)
    continue;
  if(D3DXPlaneDotCoord(&m_Planes[i],                     \
      &D3DXVECTOR3(XCenter-XSize, YCenter+YSize,          \
                   ZCenter+ZSize)) >= 0.0f)
    continue;
  if(D3DXPlaneDotCoord(&m_Planes[i],                     \
      &D3DXVECTOR3(XCenter+XSize, YCenter+YSize,          \
                   ZCenter+ZSize)) >= 0.0f)
    continue;

  return FALSE;
}

return TRUE;
}
```

The CheckRectangle function is identical to the CheckCube function, except that you can specify the width, height, and depth of the rectangle independently. Remember that the sizes depict half the actual size of the rectangle in the width, height, and depth. For example, a rectangle 30 x 20 x 10 is specified as 15 x 10 x 5 to the CheckRectangle function.

Moving on to the next, and last, object to determine visibility is the sphere. The CheckSphere function is somewhat different from the others—it only takes the position and radius of the sphere:

```
BOOL cFrustum::CheckSphere(float XCenter, float YCenter,       \
                           float ZCenter, float Radius)
{
  short i;

  // Make sure radius is in frustum
  for(i=0;i<6;i++) {
    if(D3DXPlaneDotCoord(&m_Planes[i], &D3DXVECTOR3(XCenter, YCenter, ZCenter)) < -Radius)
      return FALSE;
  }
  return TRUE;
}
```

The preceding CheckSphere function is probably one of the easiest functions to deal with when checking viewing frustums. If a sphere is in front of (or touching) a viewing plane, the distance is more than the negative radius. If the distance is less than the negative sphere radius, the sphere is out of view.

As you can see, the cFrustum class has many uses, including developing an advanced 3-D engine that you can use to draw levels, which brings us to the next topic.

# Developing an Advanced 3-D Engine

Rendering levels as single meshes is fairly easy, albeit a little inefficient at times. What about those times when a level needs a little more detail—buildings, trees, caverns, and other gaming graphics necessities? Also, how about making levels a little easier to design? Wouldn't it be cool to draw a level in a 3-D model editor such as 3D Studio Max or MilkShape 3-D and then drop it into your game?

The problems with large, detailed levels arise because of the number of polygons you must deal with. Drawing all those polygons each frame is inefficient. To speed things up a bit, you might render only the polygons that are in the view, and to make the process even faster, avoid scanning through each polygon in the scene to determine which polygons are visible.

How can you possibly know which polygons are in the view without scanning through all of them every frame? The solution is to divide a 3-D model (that represents the level) into small chunks (called *nodes*) that contain fewer polygons. Then you arrange the nodes in a special structure (a *tree*) that you can quickly scan to determine which nodes are visible. You then render the visible nodes.

You find out which nodes are visible by using the viewing frustum. Now, instead of scanning through thousands of polygons, you can scan a small set of nodes to decide what to draw. See how easy this improved drawing process is becoming?

Now I know you're getting anxious to know how you can perform such a stunning feat. So let me introduce you to the *NodeTree* engine. Created specially for this book, the NodeTree engine is capable of taking any mesh and splitting it up into nodes that are used to quickly render meshes (such as those meshes used for your game's levels).

## Introducing the NodeTree Engine

The NodeTree engine is very versatile because it can operate in two different modes (in regard to node splitting): the *quadtree* mode and the *octree* mode. The *quadtree* mode splits the world (and subsequent nodes) into four nodes at a time.

This mode is best suited for level meshes in which the Y-axis doesn't vary much (the viewpoint height doesn't change much). The octree mode splits the world (and subsequent nodes) into eight nodes at a time. Use this mode for large 3-D meshes in which the viewpoint can move anywhere in the world. To understand the quadtree/octree splitting process, take a look at Figure 12.4.

**NOTE**

Deciding which splitting mode to use is up to you. Consider your meshes—do you have a castle to comb through, caverns to delve, or landscape to wander through? If the mesh doesn't vary much in height (for example, the landscape), a quadtree mode is best. On the other hand, if each axis in the mesh is really spread out (for example, a castle with many levels), use the octree mode.

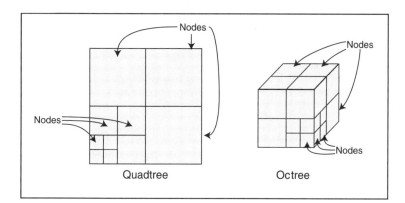

**Figure 12.4**

*A quadtree mode splits the world (and subsequent nodes) four nodes at a time, and an octree mode splits the world (and subsequent nodes) eight nodes at a time.*

The world (which can be represented by a cube that encases every polygon used to define the world) can be split continuously into smaller nodes of equal size. A quadtree splits the nodes in 2-D space (using the X- and Z-axes), and an octree splits nodes in 3-D space (using all axes).

I'll get back to splitting in a moment, but before going on, I want to clear up a few points. A node represents a group of polygons, while at the same time representing an area of 3-D space. Each node can belong to another node, in a parent-child type of relationship. This means that a node can contain other nodes with each subsequent node being a fraction smaller than the parent node. In general, the 3-D world is considered the *root node* (the topmost node to which all other nodes belong).

Here's the trick to the nodes and tree: By determining which polygons are contained within a node's 3-D space, you can group them; then starting at the root node, you can traverse each node in the tree quickly.

## Creating Nodes and Trees

To begin creating the nodes and building the tree structure, you examine every polygon in the mesh. Don't worry; you do this only once, so the overall affect on speed isn't a factor. Your goal is to decide how to arrange the nodes in the tree.

> **NOTE**
>
> To better understand nodes, think of a Rubik's Cube in this way: The whole cube is the root node, and each colored piece of the cube is a child node. Each child node is assigned a few colors, or polygons. These polygons (colors) belong to nodes (pieces), which in turn belong to higher-level nodes (the whole cube).

Each polygon in the mesh is enclosed within a box (called a bounding box, as illustrated in Figure 12.5). This box represents the extent of the polygon in any direction. As long as the polygon's bounding box is enclosed within a node's 3-D space (either completely or partially), then that polygon belongs to the node. A polygon can belong to multiple nodes because the extents of the polygon can pass through many nodes.

As you're going along grouping polygons to nodes, notice whether the space between the polygons are very large or whether you have too many polygons in a large space. If so, you need to split the nodes into more nodes and then scan the polygon list again, taking the new nodes into account. Continue this process until all the polygons are in groups that are sufficiently small and until each node containing polygons is small enough.

**TIP**

To optimize the tree structure, discard all nodes that do not contain polygons. Discarding empty nodes saves memory and enables you to quickly traverse the tree. And you know that saving memory and time is the key.

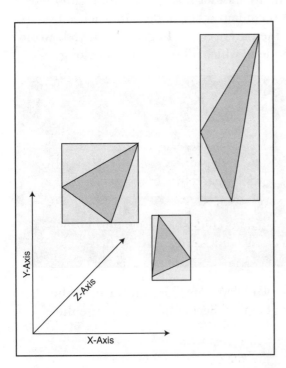

**Figure 12.5**

*Polygons have an imaginary (bounding) box that surrounds them. This bounding box is useful for quickly determining a polygon's location in 3-D space.*

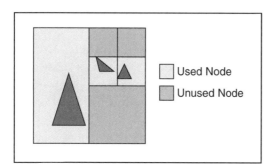

**Figure 12.6**

*Here is an example world with a few polygons that can be grouped into nodes.*

In Figure 12.6, which shows a few polygons, the world (root node) is surrounded by a square. It's the square that is split up into smaller nodes that, in turn, are split up into further nodes. Each node is considered to be used (the node contains a polygon or polygons) or unused (the node contains no polygons).

Because the polygons in Figure 12.6 are far apart, you can split the root node into four smaller nodes (making it a quadtree mode). Then check each node and continue to split the larger ones. You can skip the empty nodes to speed up the process. In the end, you'll have a perfect tree structure ready for scanning.

## Scanning and Drawing the Tree

Once you build the tree structure, you are ready to render it. Starting at the root node, you need to perform a viewing frustum check on the node. A node is considered in view if any one of the eight points (think of each corner of a cube) that forms its 3-D space is within the frustum.

After you decide that a node is visible, perform the same check on its child nodes (if any). If a node doesn't contain child nodes, check whether the current node contains polygons that haven't been drawn (child nodes can draw the same polygon during the scan). After polygons are drawn in a node, they are marked as drawn and scanning returns to the parent node (and any other remaining nodes to be scanned).

You can see the magic in this process: Higher-level nodes are discarded, along with their child nodes. In this way, you might remove thousands of polygons from the rendering process and save time.

When working with Direct3D and the tree structure, you might find that a mesh contains multiple textures. Remember that switching textures is an expensive operation, so you want to tread carefully here. How can you draw all visible polygons without switching the textures again and again (even back to textures already used)? This is where texture groups come into play.

# Working with Texture Groups

*Texture groups* are sets of polygons that are grouped together based on their assigned textures. Because a mesh can contain multiple textures, it makes sense to render only those groups of polygons that belong to a given texture at a given time. In that way, you set each texture only once, render the polygons that use the texture, and go on to the next texture.

Although the use of texture groups sounds logical, grouping the polygons together by their texture makes it hard to deal with the NodeTree structure. You can't know which polygons will be drawn without scanning the tree structure. You must scan the tree structure and build lists of polygons that need to be rendered. When you complete your scanning, just check the lists of polygons that belong to each texture and work with them.

Texture grouping doesn't really affect only the order in which visible polygons are drawn. Pretty nifty, huh?

# Creating the cNodeTree Class

It's time to do some programming. You start by creating a few structures to represent the vertices, polygons, nodes, and texture groups:

```
// The sVertex structure is a custom vertex structure that
// contains only the 3-D coordinates. This is used to
// retrieve coordinate info from a mesh's vertex buffer.
typedef struct sVertex { float x, y, z; } sVertex;

// The polygon structure maintains a texture group (by #)
// the time it was last drawn (so you don't redraw it
// many times over per frame), and the three vertices
// used to render the polygon (which you'll read about later).
typedef struct sPolygon {
  unsigned long  Group;       // Texture group
  unsigned long  Time;        // Time last drawn
  unsigned short Vertex[3];   // Vertex index #'s

  sPolygon() { Group = Time = 0; } // Clear data
} sPolygon;

// The node structure keeps count of the # of polygons in
```

```
// its 3-D space, an array of sPolygon structures, the
// 3-D coordinates of the node (as well as the size, which
// is the distance from the center to one edge making the node
// a perfect cube), and pointers to the child nodes.
typedef struct sNode {
  unsigned long   NumPolygons;        // # of polygons in node
  sPolygon        **PolygonList;      // List of polygon data
  float           XPos, YPos, ZPos;   // Center coordinate of node
  float           Size;               // Size of node
  sNode           *Nodes[8];          // Child nodes 4=quad, 8=oct

  // Constructor used to clear out variables
  sNode()
  {
    NumPolygons = 0;          // Set to no polygons in node
    PolygonList = NULL;       // Clear polygon list
    XPos = YPos = ZPos = Size = 0.0f; // Position and size
    for(short i=0;i<8;i++)    // Quadtrees only uses first 4
      Nodes[i] = NULL;        // Clear out child node pointers
  }

  // Destructor to clear child nodes and variables
  ~sNode()
  {
    delete [] PolygonList;    // Delete polygon list array
    for(short i=0;i<8;i++)
      delete Nodes[i];        // Delete child nodes
  }
} sNode;


// The texture group structure uses a cVertexBuffer class
// from the Graphics Core to store polygons that need to
// be rendered in a single frame, also it maintains the
// number of polygons in a texture group and how many
// polygons to draw each frame.
typedef struct sGroup {
  cVertexBuffer   VertexBuffer; // Vertex data to draw
  char            *VertexPtr;   // Pointer to vertex data
  unsigned long   NumPolygons;  // # polygons in group
  unsigned long   NumPolygonsToDraw; // # polygon to draw
```

```
    sGroup()  { NumPolygons = 0;      }  // Clear # polygons
    ~sGroup() { VertexBuffer.Free(); }  // Free vertex buffer
} sGroup;
```

Each structure stores the various kinds of information about the mesh or NodeTree structure. sVertex is the basic custom vertex structure; it maps directly to all other vertex structures. If you load a mesh from a disk, you can use the sVertex structure to retrieve the vertex coordinates.

You use the sPolygon structure to store information about each polygon in the scene. The structure stores the texture group number (textures are numbered from zero to the number of textures minus one), the time it was last drawn (to stop redraw), and the three vertices used to draw the polygon.

That's right; you directly poll the mesh object for the index number of each vertex used to draw each polygon. Accessing the mesh's vertices will have to wait until we can construct a NodeTree class later in this section. For right now, turn your attention to the sNode structure.

sNode maintains the number of polygons contained within a node's 3-D space. Each node has a coordinate that represents the center of the node, as well as a size variable that tells you the distance from the center of the node to one edge (making each node a perfect cube). For each polygon in the node, a pointer is kept to point back to the respective sPolygon structure used to store the polygon data. Last, there are pointers to eight child node pointers that construct the tree structure. Note that a quadtree uses only the first four child node pointers.

Last is the cGroup structure, which maintains the texture groups. Each texture group uses a cVertexBuffer object to contain exactly the number of polygons that uses the texture in the scene. As nodes are scanned, all visible polygons are added to their respective texture groups' vertex buffer. Once all nodes are scanned, each texture group is drawn out using the groups' vertex buffer render function.

Enough about the data structures; it's time to move on to the class code. Take a look at the following class, which takes a mesh as input and converts it to a tree structure of your choice, either a quadtree or an octree:

```
// Enumerate the two types of tree structures
enum TreeTypes { QUADTREE = 0, OCTREE };


class cNodeTreeMesh
{
  private:
    // .. insert previous sVertex, sPolygon, sNode, and
```

```
        // sGroup structures here.

        int             m_TreeType;       // Type of nodetree
                                          // QUADTREE or OCTREE

        cGraphics       *m_Graphics;      // Parent cGraphics object
        cFrustum        *m_Frustum;       // Viewing frustum

        unsigned long   m_Time;           // Time of current render

        float           m_Size;           // Size of world cube
        float           m_MaxSize;        // Maximum node size

        sNode           *m_ParentNode;    // Node linked list parent

        unsigned long   m_NumGroups;      // # of texture groups
        sGroup          *m_Groups;        // Texture groups

        unsigned long   m_NumPolygons;    // # of polygons in mesh
        unsigned long   m_MaxPolygons;    // Maximum polygons in node
        sPolygon        *m_PolygonList;   // Polygon data array

        sMesh           *m_Mesh;          // Parent mesh
        char            *m_VertexPtr;     // Pointer to mesh vertices
        unsigned long   m_VertexFVF;      // Mesh vertex FVF
        unsigned long   m_VertexSize;     // Size of mesh vertex

        // SortNode groups the polygons into nodes and splits
        // the nodes into child nodes as needed.
        void            SortNode(sNode *Node,                       \
                            float XPos, float YPos, float ZPos,  \
                            float Size);

        // AddNode adds a node into the list of nodes to draw.
        void            AddNode(sNode *Node);

        // IsPolygonContained return TRUE if a polygon's bounding
        // box intersects with the specified cube space.
        BOOL            IsPolygonContained(sPolygon *Polygon,     \
                            float XPos, float YPos, float ZPos, \
                            float Size);
```

```
      // CountPolygons returns the # of polygons in a 3-D cube.
      unsigned long  CountPolygons(                                \
                        float XPos, float YPos, float ZPos,  \
                        float Size);

  public:
      cNodeTreeMesh();    // Constructor
      ~cNodeTreeMesh();   // Destructor

      // Functions to create and free a node/tree mesh from
      // a source cMesh object, specifying the maximum # of
      // polygons in an area that is larger than a specific
      // size (forcing node splits).
      BOOL Create(cGraphics *Graphics, cMesh *Mesh,            \
              int TreeType = OCTREE,                           \
              float MaxSize = 256.0f, long MaxPolygons = 32);
      BOOL Free();

      // Render the current view using the current view
      // transformation and overloaded distance of view.
      // Also specify to use a pre-calculate frustum or
      // force a calculation of own frustum.
      BOOL Render(cFrustum *Frustum = NULL, float ZDistance = 0.0f);
};
```

The comments in the preceding class do a good job of explaining what each variable represents and what each function does. In the next few sections, I cover each function in more detail. First, check out Table 12.1, which lists and describes all the cNodeTree variables.

As you continue through this chapter, I'll point out when the class variables come into play, but now it's time to learn more about each function in the cNodeTree class.

# cNodeTreeMesh::Create and cNodeTreeMesh::Free

The cNodeTreeMesh::Create function is where the whole process starts. To create a NodeTree structure, you need a source mesh with which to work, and what better place to get one than from a cMesh object. The cMesh object maintains a list of meshes contained in a single .X file, and to make things easy, deals only with the first mesh in the list of contained meshes.

## Table 12.1 cNodeTree Variables

| Variable | Description |
| --- | --- |
| m_Graphics | A pointer to a pre-initialized cGraphics object. |
| m_Frustum | A pointer to the cFrustum viewing frustum class used during a render operation. |
| m_Time | The current time (used during rendering to stop redraw). |
| m_Size | The size of the world from the center (the origin) to the farthest edge in any of the three axes (making the world a cube). |
| m_MaxSize | The maximum size a node can be before being split (which happens when the node contains too many polygons). |
| m_ParentNode | The head of the node linked list. |
| m_NumGroups | The number of texture groups. |
| m_Groups | The texture group array. |
| m_NumPolygons | The number of polygons in the source mesh. |
| m_MaxPolygons | Holds the maximum number of polygons allowed in a node (before forcing a split on nodes that are too large). |
| m_PolygonList | An array of sPolygon structures holding the details for each polygon in the mesh. |
| m_Mesh | A pointer to the source mesh (the sMesh structure used by the Graphics Core). |
| m_VertexPtr | Used globally to access the source mesh vertex buffer. |
| m_VertexFVF | The source mesh FVF descriptor. |
| m_VertexSize | Holds the size of a single source mesh vertex (in bytes). |

By passing the Create function the pointers to your pre-initialized cGraphics object, the pre-loaded cMesh object, and the type of node tree you want to use (either QUADTREE or OCTREE), you set the entire class up so that it is ready to render. In addition to the function arguments just mentioned, you also need to specify the maximum number of polygons allowed per node and the maximum size of a node before it needs to be split (when it contains the maximum number of polygons per node).

```
BOOL cNodeTreeMesh::Create(cGraphics *Graphics, cMesh *Mesh,
                           int TreeType,
                           float MaxSize, long MaxPolygons)
{
  ID3DXMesh      *LoadMesh;
  unsigned short *IndexPtr;
  DWORD          *Attributes;
  unsigned long  i;
  float          MaxX, MaxY, MaxZ;

  // Free a prior mesh
  Free();

  // Error checking
  if((m_Graphics = Graphics) == NULL)
    return FALSE;
  if(Mesh == NULL)
    return FALSE;
  if(!Mesh->GetParentMesh()->m_NumMaterials)
    return FALSE;

  // Get source mesh info
  m_Mesh        = Mesh->GetParentMesh();  // Pointer to mesh
  LoadMesh      = m_Mesh->m_Mesh;         // ID3DXMesh pointer
  m_VertexFVF   = LoadMesh->GetFVF();     // Get FVF and size
  m_VertexSize  = D3DXGetFVFVertexSize(m_VertexFVF);
  m_NumPolygons = LoadMesh->GetNumFaces(); // Get # polygons
  m_MaxPolygons = MaxPolygons;            // Save max polygons

  // Create the polygon list and groups
  m_PolygonList = new sPolygon[m_NumPolygons]();
  m_NumGroups   = m_Mesh->m_NumMaterials;
  m_Groups      = new sGroup[m_NumGroups]();

  // Lock vertex, index, and attribute buffers
  LoadMesh->LockIndexBuffer(D3DLOCK_READONLY,(BYTE**)&IndexPtr);
  LoadMesh->LockAttributeBuffer(D3DLOCK_READONLY, &Attributes);
```

Here, you see something new. The `ID3DXMesh` uses vertex buffers; in addition, the `ID3DXMesh` uses what is called an *indexed vertex buffer*. Instead of storing vertices in the order they need to be drawn, you store all the vertices in the buffer (in any order) and create a second array that keeps track of which three vertices are used to draw each polygon. That array is called the *index array*.

Next, an `ID3DXMesh` object has what's called an *attribute buffer*, which is simply an array of values that states which texture each polygon uses. A one-to-one correlation exists between the array elements and the polygons. It's this attribute buffer that is used to assign polygons to their respective texture groups.

The following code starts by looping through each polygon in the mesh, pulling out the three vertices that are used to construct each polygon. Also, you store the texture used to draw the polygon within each polygon's data structure.

```
// Load polygon information into structures
for(i=0;i<m_NumPolygons;i++) {
  m_PolygonList[i].Vertex[0] = *IndexPtr++; // Store polygon
  m_PolygonList[i].Vertex[1] = *IndexPtr++; // index #'s
  m_PolygonList[i].Vertex[2] = *IndexPtr++; // in structure

  // Store the polygon texture group and count
  m_PolygonList[i].Group = Attributes[i];
  m_Groups[Attributes[i]].NumPolygons++;
}

// Unlock buffers and release them (including mesh)
LoadMesh->UnlockIndexBuffer();
LoadMesh->UnlockAttributeBuffer();

// Build the group vertex buffers
for(i=0;i<m_NumGroups;i++) {
  if(m_Groups[i].NumPolygons != 0)
    m_Groups[i].VertexBuffer.Create(m_Graphics,             \
                           m_Groups[i].NumPolygons * 3,     \
                           m_VertexFVF, m_VertexSize);
}
```

In the preceding code, you can see that the mesh's index array and attribute buffer are locked. At that point, you're merely building a list of polygon information (which vertices are used for each polygon, plus the texture group to use). When you finish building the list of polygon data, the index and attribute buffers are unlocked, and the actual texture groups are configured.

Each texture group contains a cVertexBuffer object to store the vertices that need to be drawn. This is the standard vertex buffer you've come to love, so working with it shouldn't be hard. Notice that each vertex buffer has enough space for exactly the number of polygons used for each texture in the mesh.

```
// Get the size of the bounding cube
MaxX = (float)max(fabs(Mesh->GetParentMesh()->m_Min.x),          \
                  fabs(Mesh->GetParentMesh()->m_Max.x));
MaxY = (float)max(fabs(Mesh->GetParentMesh()->m_Min.y),          \
                  fabs(Mesh->GetParentMesh()->m_Max.y));
MaxZ = (float)max(fabs(Mesh->GetParentMesh()->m_Min.z),          \
                  fabs(Mesh->GetParentMesh()->m_Max.z));
m_Size    = max(MaxX, max(MaxY, MaxZ)) * 2.0f;
m_MaxSize = MaxSize;

// Create the parent node
m_ParentNode = new sNode();
```

Here, the point farthest away from the center of the source mesh is calculated. In order to make calculations smoother, the world must be a perfect cube, so you use the distance from the center of the mesh to the outer edge as the size for the world bounding box. After creating the parent node (m_ParentNode), you then lock the mesh's vertex buffer in order to read in the vertex coordinates. Lastly, the nodes are sorted by calling the SortNode function.

```
// Sort polygons into nodes
LoadMesh->LockVertexBuffer(D3DLOCK_READONLY,                     \
                           (BYTE**)&m_VertexPtr);
SortNode(m_ParentNode, 0.0f, 0.0f, 0.0f, m_Size);
LoadMesh->UnlockVertexBuffer();

  return TRUE;
}
```

Once sorted, the mesh's vertex buffer is unlocked, and the function returns TRUE to signify success. At this point, the node tree mesh is ready to use. When you're done with the node tree mesh, you call cNodeTree::Free to free the mesh:

```
BOOL cNodeTreeMesh::Free()
{
  delete m_ParentNode; // Delete parent node and all child nodes
  m_ParentNode = NULL;
```

```
m_Graphics = NULL;

m_NumPolygons = 0;  // No more polygons
delete [] m_PolygonList; // Delete polygon array
m_PolygonList = NULL;

m_NumGroups = 0;  // No more texture groups
delete [] m_Groups;  // Delete texture groups
m_Groups = NULL;

return TRUE;
}
```

# cNodeTreeMesh::SortNode

cNodeTreeMesh::SortNode is a *recursive function* (one that calls itself) that counts the number of polygons contained in the node's 3-D space and decides whether the node needs to be split into four or eight child nodes (depending on the tree type). After the nodes are appropriately split, the SortNode function then builds a list of polygons contained with the node's 3-D space.

The code to the SortNode function starts off by ensuring that the arguments passed to the function are valid. From there, the function stores the node's coordinates and begins splitting the nodes.

```
void cNodeTreeMesh::SortNode(sNode *Node,                        \
                       float XPos, float YPos, float ZPos,  \
                       float Size)
{
  unsigned long i, Num;
  float         XOff, YOff, ZOff;

  // Error checking
  if(Node == NULL || m_PolygonList == NULL)
    return;

  // Store node coordinates and size
  Node->XPos = XPos;
  Node->YPos = (m_TreeType==QUADTREE)?0.0f:YPos;
  Node->ZPos = ZPos;
  Node->Size = Size;
```

> **NOTE**
>
> **If the node tree type is a quadtree, you can ignore the height used during clipping and split operations. Notice that the height values are ignored or handled differently, as you see in the cNodeTreeMesh class code.**

```
// See if there are any polygons in the node
if(!(Num = CountPolygons(XPos, YPos, ZPos, Size)))
  return;

// Split node if size > maximum and too many polygons
if(Size > m_MaxSize && Num > m_MaxPolygons) {
  for(i=0;i<(unsigned long)((m_TreeType==QUADTREE)?4:8);i++) {
    XOff = (((i % 2) < 1) ? -1.0f : 1.0f) * (Size / 4.0f);
    ZOff = (((i % 4) < 2) ? -1.0f : 1.0f) * (Size / 4.0f);
    YOff = (((i % 8) < 4) ? -1.0f : 1.0f) * (Size / 4.0f);

    // See if any polygons in new node bounding box
    if(CountPolygons(XPos+XOff,YPos+YOff,ZPos+ZOff,            \
                     Size/2.0f)) {

      Node->Nodes[i] = new sNode();   // Create new child node

      // Sort the polygons with the new child node
      SortNode(Node->Nodes[i],XPos+XOff,YPos+YOff,            \
               ZPos+ZOff,Size/2.0f);
    }
  }

  return;
}
```

Up to this point, all polygons that are within the node's bounding box are counted. If there are too many polygons and the node's bounding box is too large, the node is split. The subsequent split nodes are run through the same process. This time, however, empty nodes are skipped from further processing, and nodes with polygons are sent back to the SortNode function (thus, the recursion).

```
// Allocate space for polygon pointer list
Node->NumPolygons = Num;
Node->PolygonList = new sPolygon[Num];

// Scan through polygon list, storing pointers and
// assigning them.
Num = 0;
for(i=0;i<m_NumPolygons;i++) {
  // Add polygon to node list if contained in 3-D space.
```

```
      if(IsPolygonContained(&m_PolygonList[i],              \
                            XPos, YPos, ZPos, Size) == TRUE)
        Node->PolygonList[Num++] = &m_PolygonList[i];
    }
  }
}
```

The last bit of the SortNode code allocates an array of pointers that point back to the sPolygon array. When it comes time to render, that array of pointers is used to retrieve each polygon's information, which includes the vertex data and texture group to use. Those polygons to draw are added to the appropriate texture group's vertex buffer later by the AddNode function.

## cNodeTreeMesh::IsPolygonContained and cNodeTreeMesh::CountPolygons

You use this duo of functions to determine whether a polygon is within the specified 3-D bounding box space and to count the total number of polygons contained within the bounding box.

```
BOOL cNodeTreeMesh::IsPolygonContained(sPolygon *Polygon,        \
                          float XPos, float YPos, float ZPos, \
                          float Size)
{
  float    XMin, XMax, YMin, YMax, ZMin, ZMax;
  sVertex *Vertex[3];

  // Get the polygon's vertices
  Vertex[0] = (sVertex*)&m_VertexPtr[m_VertexSize *             \
                        Polygon->Vertex[0]];
  Vertex[1] = (sVertex*)&m_VertexPtr[m_VertexSize *             \
                        Polygon->Vertex[1]];
  Vertex[2] = (sVertex*)&m_VertexPtr[m_VertexSize *             \
                        Polygon->Vertex[2]];

  // Check the X-axis of specified 3-D space
  XMin = min(Vertex[0]->x, min(Vertex[1]->x, Vertex[2]->x));
  XMax = max(Vertex[0]->x, max(Vertex[1]->x, Vertex[2]->x));
  if(XMax < (XPos - Size / 2.0f))
    return FALSE;
  if(XMin > (XPos + Size / 2.0f))
    return FALSE;
```

The preceding code (as well as the following code) determines the farthest extents of a vertex in the X-axis. If the polygon is too far left or right from the bounding cube that's being checked, then FALSE is returned. The same goes for the next two axes.

```
// Check the Y-axis of specified 3-D space (if octree)
if(m_TreeType == OCTREE) {
  YMin = min(Vertex[0]->y, min(Vertex[1]->y, Vertex[2]->y));
  YMax = max(Vertex[0]->y, max(Vertex[1]->y, Vertex[2]->y));
  if(YMax < (YPos - Size / 2.0f))
    return FALSE;
  if(YMin > (YPos + Size / 2.0f))
    return FALSE;
}

// Check the Z-axis of specified 3-D space
ZMin = min(Vertex[0]->z, min(Vertex[1]->z, Vertex[2]->z));
ZMax = max(Vertex[0]->z, max(Vertex[1]->z, Vertex[2]->z));
if(ZMax < (ZPos - Size / 2.0f))
  return FALSE;
if(ZMin > (ZPos + Size / 2.0f))
  return FALSE;

  return TRUE;
}


unsigned long cNodeTreeMesh::CountPolygons(                    \
            float XPos, float YPos, float ZPos, float Size)
{
  unsigned long i, Num;

  // Return if no polygons to process
  if(!m_NumPolygons)
    return 0;

  // Go through every polygon and keep count of those
  // contained in the specified 3-D space.
  Num = 0;
  for(i=0;i<m_NumPolygons;i++) {
    if(IsPolygonContained(&m_PolygonList[i],XPos,YPos,ZPos,   \
                          Size) == TRUE)
```

```
      Num++;
  }

  return Num;
}
```

You can see that CountPolygons loops only through each polygon in the mesh and checks whether it falls inside the bounding cube. Each polygon contained is counted and a final tally is returned. You use this function to determine how many polygons are within a node when splitting and sorting the nodes.

## cNodeTreeMesh::AddNode

You use the cNodeTreeMesh::AddNode function in conjunction with the Render function. AddNode performs the frustum check on all nodes and recursively checks all child nodes. At first call to the AddNode function, the m_ParentNode variable is passed to AddNode to start the process from the root.

```
void cNodeTreeMesh::AddNode(sNode *Node)
{
  unsigned long i, Group;
  short         Num;

  // Perform frustum check based on tree type
  if(m_TreeType == QUADTREE) {
    if(m_Frustum->CheckRectangle(                              \
            Node->XPos,          0.0f,            Node->ZPos,   \
            Node->Size / 2.0f, m_Size / 2.0f,                   \
            Node->Size / 2.0f) == FALSE)
      return;
  } else {
    if(m_Frustum->CheckRectangle(                              \
            Node->XPos,          Node->YPos,       Node->ZPos,  \
            Node->Size / 2.0f, Node->Size / 2.0f,               \
            Node->Size / 2.0f) == FALSE)
      return;
  }
```

Again, you can see the frustum check I mentioned earlier. Here's where quadtree and octree modes differ. A quadtree, being a 2-D structure, checks only two dimensions (Y always falls into view for 2-D). As for an octree, a node might be anywhere in 3-D space, so at least one point must be in view.

The AddNode function now decides if child
nodes need to be added (as long as
there is a node with polygons). Adding
nodes stops whenever a node has no
more children. In this case, the next parent node is processed, with the process
continuing until all nodes are processed.

**NOTE**

If a node doesn't fall within the
viewing frustum, it and all its child
nodes are skipped. Here's where the
node tree speeds things up!

```
// Scan other nodes
Num = 0;
for(i=0;i<(unsigned long)((m_TreeType==QUADTREE)?4:8);i++) {
  if(Node->Nodes[i] != NULL) {
    Num++;
    AddNode(Node->Nodes[i]);
  }
}

// Don't need to go on if there are other nodes
if(Num)
  return;
```

From here, the AddNode function checks to see whether the node in question contains any polygons. If the node contains polygons, then each polygon in the node is
checked to see if it is visible (polygons that use a material alpha value of 0.0 are
considered invisible).

AddNode will add those polygons that are visible into the appropriate texture group's
vertex buffer as well as keep count of the number of polygons to draw in the node.
Each frame, the number of polygons to render in each texture group is reset by the
Render function. The following code increments the count of polygons to draw:

```
// Add contained polygons (if any)
if(Node->NumPolygons != 0) {
  for(i=0;i<Node->NumPolygons;i++) {

    // If a polygon hasn't yet been drawn and it has a
    // valid texture group value, then process it.
    if(Node->PolygonList[i]->Time != m_Time &&              \
      (Group = Node->PolygonList[i]->Group) < m_NumGroups) {

      // Only draw polygons that are visible
      // ie: have a material alpha value of > 0.0
```

```
        if(m_Mesh->m_Materials[                                    \
           Node->PolygonList[i]->Group].Diffuse.a != 0.0f) {

          // Copy over vertex data from source mesh
          memcpy(m_Groups[Group].VertexPtr,                        \
                &m_VertexPtr[m_VertexSize *                        \
                 Node->PolygonList[i]->Vertex[0]],                 \
                 m_VertexSize);
          m_Groups[Group].VertexPtr += m_VertexSize;

          memcpy(m_Groups[Group].VertexPtr,                        \
                &m_VertexPtr[m_VertexSize *                        \
                 Node->PolygonList[i]->Vertex[1]],                 \
                 m_VertexSize);
          m_Groups[Group].VertexPtr += m_VertexSize;

          memcpy(m_Groups[Group].VertexPtr,                        \
                &m_VertexPtr[m_VertexSize *                        \
                 Node->PolygonList[i]->Vertex[2]],                 \
                 m_VertexSize);
          m_Groups[Group].VertexPtr += m_VertexSize;

          m_Groups[Group].NumPolygonsToDraw++;
        }

        // Mark polygon as processed this time segment
        Node->PolygonList[i]->Time = m_Time;
      }
    }
  }
}
```

When completed, the AddNode function will
have built a complete set of texture group
vertex buffers ready to be rendered.

### NOTE

You assign each polygon a time
variable because once a polygon is
drawn for a given time, it doesn't
need to be redrawn (from other
nodes to which the polygon
belongs). For that reason, AddNode
checks the time value for each
polygon before it is added to the
texture group vertex buffer.

# cNodeTreeMesh::Render

You're coming down to the end of the cNodeTreeMesh class, and what better place than with the function that gives you the gratification of rendered polygons? The cNodeTreeMesh::Render function takes an optional viewing frustum to use in place of its internal frustum.

Also, because the rendering function works from the viewing frustum, you need a way to overload the distance of the field of view. This helps if you want to draw only portions of the mesh that are within a specific distance from the viewing point. For example, if the frustum can see 20,000 units in distance but you want to render only those polygons within 5,000 units, specify 5000.0 for ZDistance.

The Render function starts off by calculating the viewing frustum and locking the vertex buffers:

```
BOOL cNodeTreeMesh::Render(cFrustum *Frustum, float ZDistance)
{
  D3DXMATRIX Matrix;      // Matrix used for calculations
  cFrustum ViewFrustum;   // Local viewing frustum

  // Error checking
  if(m_Graphics==NULL || m_ParentNode==NULL || !m_NumPolygons)
    return FALSE;

  // Construct the viewing frustum (if none passed)
  if((m_Frustum = Frustum) == NULL) {
    ViewFrustum.Construct(m_Graphics, ZDistance);
    m_Frustum = &ViewFrustum;
  }

  // Set the world transformation matrix to identity so that
  // level mesh is rendered around the origin it was designed.
  D3DXMatrixIdentity(&Matrix);
  m_Graphics->GetDeviceCOM()->SetTransform(D3DTS_WORLD,&Matrix);

  // Lock vertex buffers
  for(unsigned long i=0;i<m_NumGroups;i++) {
    m_Groups[i].VertexBuffer.Lock(0,0);
    m_Groups[i].VertexPtr =                                    \
                  (char*)m_Groups[i].VertexBuffer.GetPtr();
```

```
    m_Groups[i].NumPolygonsToDraw = 0;
  }
  m_Mesh->m_Mesh->LockVertexBuffer(D3DLOCK_READONLY,               \
                                  (BYTE**)&m_VertexPtr);
```

At this point, the texture group vertex buffers are locked and ready to receive vertex information from the locked source mesh vertex buffer (recall the AddNode function). Each texture group has the number of polygons to draw zeroed out, and with the following lines of code, all polygons in view (via nodes) are added to the texture group vertex buffers. At that time, all locked vertex buffers are unlocked, and each texture group that contains polygons is drawn using the texture groups' vertex buffer Render function (while also setting the proper material and texture).

```
  // Store current time of render
  m_Time = timeGetTime();

  // Add all polygons to vertex buffer
  AddNode(m_ParentNode);

  // Unlock vertex buffers and draw
  m_Mesh->m_Mesh->UnlockVertexBuffer();
  for(i=0;i<m_NumGroups;i++) {
    m_Groups[i].VertexBuffer.Unlock();

    if(m_Groups[i].NumPolygonsToDraw) {
      m_Graphics->GetDeviceCOM()->SetMaterial(                  \
                                  &m_Mesh->m_Materials[i]);
      m_Graphics->GetDeviceCOM()->SetTexture(0,                 \
                                  m_Mesh->m_Textures[i]);

      m_Groups[i].VertexBuffer.Render(0,                        \
          m_Groups[i].NumPolygonsToDraw, D3DPT_TRIANGLELIST);
    }
  }

  return TRUE;
}
```

# Using cNodeTree

As long as you're using the Graphics Core in your project, using the cNodeTree class is as easy as including it in your project, giving it a source mesh with which to work, and rendering away! If, on the other hand, you're not using the Graphics Core, a little reworking is in order. In the code that follows, you can see the spots that use the Graphics Core classes (I kept them to a minimum), and at this point, you should be able to adjust the NodeTree engine according to your own graphics engine.

The NodeTree demo is on the CD-ROM at the back of this book. You can find it in BookCode\Chap12\NodeTree\. Right now, check out this code to see how quickly you can get a node tree up and running:

```
// Graphics = pre-initialized cGraphics object
cMesh         Mesh;
cNodeTreeMesh NodeTreeMesh;
cCamera       Camera;
cFrustum      Frustum;

// Load a mesh from disk
Mesh.Load(&Graphics, "mesh.x");
NodeTreeMesh.Create(&Graphics, &Mesh, OCTREE);

// Set a camera position and create the frustum
Camera.Point(0.0f, 100.0f, -200.0f, 0.0f, 0.0f, 0.0f);
Graphics.SetCamera(&Camera);
Frustum.Construct(&Graphics);

// Begin the scene, render the mesh, end scene, and display
// Render everything
Graphics.Clear(D3DCOLOR_RGBA(0,0,0,0));
if(Graphics.BeginScene() == TRUE) {
  NodeTreeMesh.Render(&Frustum);
  Graphics.EndScene();
}
Graphics.Display();

// Free everything
NodeTreeMesh.Free();
Mesh.Free();
```

# Adding 3-D Objects to the World

Three-dimensional worlds are not complete without objects. Because you're using 3-D worlds, 3-D meshes will suffice as game objects; however, as you saw in the section "Meshes as Levels," blindly drawing thousands of objects (without performing any clipping) causes some major lag time in the graphics-rendering pipeline.

What you need is to once again use the viewing frustum to quickly determine which objects are, or are not, within the view. In order to determine which objects are visible, you enclose each 3-D object within an invisible sphere, called a *bounding sphere*, that is used in conjunction with the viewing frustum class's CheckSphere function (see the section "The cFrustum Class," earlier in this Chapter).

Figure 12.7 illustrates the use of bounding spheres and the frustum. The figure shows a scene with three objects and the viewing frustum. Each mesh has an invisible bounding sphere that surrounds it. Recall that a sphere is considered visible if it lies in front of all six planes that construct the viewing frustum.

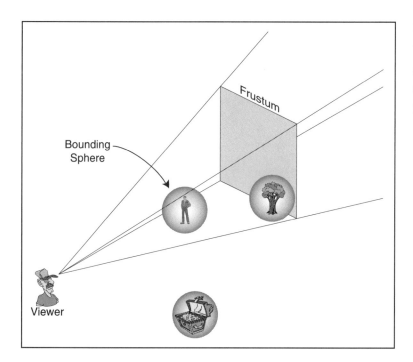

**Figure 12.7**

*You can test the three objects in the scene against the viewing frustum.*

In Figure 12.7, only two objects are visible in the viewing frustum. One object is completely outside the frustum. You want to be able to draw the visible objects and skip the one outside the frustum. To do that, you must calculate each object's bounding sphere and then test the spheres to see if they are within the frustum.

## Computing the Bounding Sphere

If you don't use the Graphics Core mesh class, you need to determine the bounding sphere of a mesh. Using D3DX, you can call the D3DXComputeBoundingSphere function (which is what the Graphics Core uses):

```
HRESULT D3DXComputeBoundingSphere(
    PVOID pvPointsFVF,      // Buffer containing vertices
    DWORD NumVertices,      // # of vertices in buffer
    DWORD FVF,              // FVF descriptor
    D3DXVECTOR3* pCenter,   // &D3DXVECTOR2(0.0f, 0.0f, 0.0f)
    FLOAT* pRadius);        // Pointer to radius variable
```

This function merely scans a vertex buffer, remembering which vertex is farthest away from the center. The distance from the center to the outermost vertex then becomes the radius. In order to call D3DXComputeBoundingSphere, you lock the vertex buffer with a call to the following:

```
HRESULT ID3DXMesh::LockVertexBuffer(
    DWORD Flags,       // Lock flags. Use D3DLOCK_READONLY
    BYTE **ppData);    // Pointer to vertex buffer data
```

With a mesh loaded, you are ready to compute its bounding sphere, as follows:

> **NOTE**
>
> ID3DXMesh and ID3DXSkinMesh share the same function for locking a vertex buffer, so the function calls for ID3DXMesh applied to ID3DXSkinMesh.

```
// pMesh = pre-loaded ID3DXMesh object
float Radius;   // Radius of object
BYTE **Ptr;     // Vertex buffer pointer

// Lock the vertex buffer
if(SUCCEEDED(pMesh->LockVertexBuffer(D3DLOCK_READONLY,    \
                    (BYTE**)&Ptr))) {

    // Compute bounding sphere radius
    D3DXComputeBoundingSphere((void*)Ptr,                 \
            pMesh->GetNumVertices(), pMesh->GetFVF(),
            &D3DXVECTOR3(0.0f, 0.0f, 0.0f), &Radius);
```

```
  // Unlock vertex buffer
  pMesh->UnlockVertexBuffer();
}
```

Notice that in the call to D3DXComputeBoundingSphere, you query the ID3DXMesh directly for the vertex count and vertex FVF descriptor. You follow the call to ID3DXMesh::LockVertexBuffer with a call to ID3DXMesh::UnlockVertexBuffer. You must unlock the vertex buffer when you're done with it, or further calls to lock or render the buffer will fail.

## Bounding Spheres and the Frustum

Now that you have the viewing frustum constructed and have a bounding sphere, you can call cFrustum::CheckSphere to check whether an object is visible, as shown here:

```
// cFrustum *Frustum = pre-constructed viewing frustum
// Radius = pre-calculated bounding sphere radius
// XPos, YPos, ZPos = Object world coordinates
if(Frustum->CheckSphere(XPos, YPos, ZPos, Radius) == TRUE) {
  // Object is in frustum, go ahead and render
} else {
  // Object is not in frustum, just skip rendering
}
```

# Collision Detection with Meshes

Even using a simple mesh to represent a game level can present some big problems, including when 3-D objects collide with other objects in the world, or when (and where) the user clicks on a mesh with the mouse (a mouse-to-mesh collision). For example, how do you know when your player or any other character walks around and bumps into a wall or when meshes collide into each other? Detecting these kinds of problems is referred to as *collision detection*. In this section, you find out how to determine when a mesh collides with another mesh, and how to determine when a mesh is being pointed at (with the mouse) by the user.

# Colliding with the World

I don't know about your games, but in mine, most of my characters are not superheroes, so they can't all go around walking through walls! For that reason, a 3-D engine needs to know when to block the path of a character that is about to collide with an object such as a wall.

## Casting a Ray

In order to check whether a polygon blocks the path from one point to another, you "cast" an imaginary ray between the two points and check to see whether it intersects with a plane. Remember planes? I spoke of them in the section, "Planes and Clipping." A polygon is nothing more than a finitely sized plane. By constructing a plane to represent the polygon, you can use algebra to determine the intersection (refer to Figure 12.7).

In the earlier section "Checking for Visibility with the Plane," you learned about dot products and calculating distance from points to planes. Using the same calculations, you can determine if, and where, a point intersects a plane as that point moves in 3-D space. The point, as it moves, creates a line that represents the path an object takes during some sort of movement.

Figure 12.8 illustrates these points. In the figure, you see a polygon and a line. The line represents the ray cast from a starting point to an ending point. The ray intersects with the polygon about halfway down the ray.

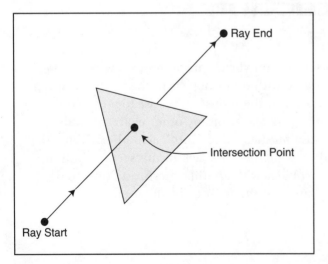

**Figure 12.8**

*A polygon blocks the path of the ray.*

Remember that a plane is infinite in size, so a ray will always intersect with the plane as long at it isn't parallel with the plane. For that reason, you must be able to tell whether the intersection is within the polygon's edges, and that's a little more difficult to do.

Here comes D3DX to the rescue! A single function performs an intersection test, ensures that the point of the ray-to-plane intersection lies within the polygon, gives the exact coordinates of the intersection, and, as a bonus, reveals the distance from the ray's starting point to the intersection point. Talk about one useful function! So, which function is it? It's the D3DXIntersect function, which has the following prototype:

```
HRESULT D3DXIntersect(
    LPD3DXBASEMESH      pMesh,    // Mesh to check intersection
    CONST D3DXVECTOR3 *pRayPos, // Ray origin
    CONST D3DXVECTOR3 *pRayDir, // Direction to cast ray
    BOOL              *pHit,    // Flag if intersection occurs
    DWORD             *pFaceIndex, // Which face ray intersects
    FLOAT             *pU,
    FLOAT             *pV,
    FLOAT             *pDist);  // Distance to intersection
```

Right off the bat, you can see that D3DXIntersect works with meshes (ID3DXBaseMesh), which is a boon because mesh objects are just what you're working with at this point. Next, you can see that you need to specify the starting origin of the ray (in pRayPos). For pRayPos (and pRayDir), you can use the D3DXVECTOR3 macro inline.

pRayDir represents a direction vector, much like a normal vector. For example, to cast a ray upward, you use a value of -1.0 for the Y value. The only other argument you need to deal with is pDist. pDist points to a FLOAT type variable that is filled with the distance from the ray origin to the intersection point.

## Blocking the Path

Now that you know the do-all intersection function, how about testing it? Here's a quick example that shows the D3DXIntersect function in action. The following function takes a pointer to a mesh (that represents your level) to check for intersections, plus a starting and ending point to check for intersections. In return, you receive the distance to the intersection and the exact coordinates of the intersection:

```
BOOL CheckIntersection(ID3DXMesh *Mesh, // Level mesh
        float XStart, float YStart, float ZStart,
        float XEnd,   float YEnd,   float ZEnd,
        float *Distance)
```

```
{
{
  BOOL         Hit;         // Flag if intersection occurred
  float        u, v, Dist;  // Misc. and distance to intersection
  float        XDiff, YDiff, ZDiff, Size; // Differences and size
  DWORD        FaceIndex;   // Face that was intersected
  D3DXVECTOR3 vecDir;       // Direction vector for ray

  // Calculate differences from start to end point
  XDiff = XEnd - XStart;
  YDiff = YEnd - YStart;
  ZDiff = ZEnd - ZStart;

  // Calculate the direction vector
  D3DXVec3Normalize(&vecDir, &D3DXVECTOR3(XDiff, YDiff, ZDiff));

  // Perform the intersection test
  D3DXIntersect(Mesh,
                &D3DXVECTOR3(XStart,YStart,ZStart), &vecDir,
                &Hit, &FaceIndex, &u, &v, &Dist);

  // If there was an intersection, see if it's within the
  // path of the ray (distance to intersection is less than
  // the length of the ray).
  if(Hit == TRUE) {
    // Get length of ray
    Size = (float)sqrt(XDiff*XDiff+YDiff*YDiff+ZDiff*ZDiff);

    // Ray did not intersect with polygon
    if(Dist > Size)
      Hit = FALSE;
    else {
      // Ray intersected, store distance to intersection
      if(Length != NULL)
        *Length = Dist;
    }
  }

  // Return TRUE if intersection occurred, FALSE if not
  return Hit;
}
```

## Moving Up and Down

One of the added benefits of using collision detection at a polygon level is that you can make objects follow the changing height of the polygons below the objects. In other words, you can make them walk on top of polygons! Talk about cool! Imagine being able to draw your levels in a 3-D model editor and not worry about defining which areas and object can "walk" on—the polygons are those areas! This makes dealing with quadtree and octree meshes even easier.

To perform ground-height based intersection tests, you create three functions, which I have added to the NodeTree engine. These three functions are GetClosestHeight, GetHeightAbove, and GetHeightBelow, as shown here:

```
float GetClosestHeight(ID3DXMesh *Mesh,                      \
                        float XPos, float YPos, float ZPos)
{
  float YAbove, YBelow;

  // Get height above and below point we're checking
  YAbove = GetHeightAbove(Mesh, XPos, YPos, ZPos);
  YBelow = GetHeightBelow(Mesh, XPos, YPos, ZPos);

  // See which height is closer to point we're checking
  // and return that value.
  if(fabs(YAbove-YPos) < fabs(YBelow-YPos))
    return YAbove;     // Height above is closest, return it.
  return YBelow;       // Height below is closest, return it.
}


float GetHeightBelow(ID3DXMesh *Mesh,                      \
                     float XPos, float YPos, float ZPos)
{
  BOOL  Hit;          // Flag if polygon hit
  float u, v, Dist;   // Misc. plus distance to intersection
  DWORD FaceIndex;    // Which face ray intersects with

  // Perform intersection test against mesh
  D3DXIntersect(Mesh,
                &D3DXVECTOR3(XPos,YPos,ZPos),
                &D3DXVECTOR3(0.0f, -1.0f, 0.0f),
                &Hit, &FaceIndex, &u, &v, &Dist);
```

```
  // Return closest height below if there was an intersection
  if(Hit == TRUE)
    return YPos-Dist;
  return YPos;  // Return height passed as no intersection
}


float GetHeightAbove(ID3DXMesh *Mesh,                        \
                        float XPos, float YPos, float ZPos)
{
  BOOL  Hit;          // Flag if polygon hit
  float u, v, Dist;   // Misc. plus distance to intersection
  DWORD FaceIndex;    // Which face ray intersects with

  // Perform intersection test against mesh
  D3DXIntersect(m_Mesh->m_Mesh,
                &D3DXVECTOR3(XPos,YPos,ZPos),
                &D3DXVECTOR3(0.0f, 1.0f, 0.0f),
                &Hit, &FaceIndex, &u, &v, &Dist);

  // Return closest height below if there was an intersection
  if(Hit == TRUE)
    return YPos+Dist;
  return YPos;  // Return height passed as no intersection
}
```

Each of the three preceding functions serves a specific purpose. GetClosestHeight
retrieves the height of the polygon (Y-coordinate) that is closest to the point in
question. For example, if you're checking a point in 3-D space (say, at Y=55) that
has a polygon 10 units above it and another polygon 5 units below it, the
GetClosestHeight function will return a value of 50 (because the polygon below is
closer to the point in question).

GetHeightAbove and GetHeightBelow scan in a specific direction (up or down) and
retrieve the height of the closest polygon. Using GetHeightBelow, you can tell where to
position your objects (in regard to height) anywhere in your world. As objects move,
you can update their height based on the height of the ground below them. In addition, you can tell whether a polygon is too steep to traverse. Check out the combined
quadtree and octree demo, NodeTree, on this book's CD-ROM to see this method
put to good use.

# Fast Intersection Checking

With rays flying all over the place and polygon counts pushing the limits, it's hard to keep things going at a fast pace. A 3-D engine's speed can lag severely when you start checking collisions between just a few objects. For that reason, you need to find ways to speed up your collision detection.

One of the most ingenious ways of speeding up collision checking that I've found (especially when dealing with quadtree and octree meshes) is to maintain separate meshes. That's right; by splitting a level into multiple meshes, you can perform collision detection against only the meshes that are necessary!

For example, try splitting your level mesh into three meshes: the ground (for tracking height), walls and obstacles (for collision detection so that characters don't walk through walls), and decorative (all those extra polygons that serve no purpose other than to make your levels look good). At the right time, you just check for intersections in the appropriate mesh

## Collisions with the cNodeTreeMesh Class

To enhance the `cNodeTreeMesh` class, you can add the intersection and height functions just mentioned. Now, using a couple of simple functions wrapped into an awesome class, you have at your disposal the ability to load any level mesh you want and allow characters to walk around, bumping into the walls and standing on a solid ground (as opposed to falling through the ground!).

# When Meshes Collide

In addition to detecting when object meshes will collide with the mesh that constructs the world, you want to know when smaller meshes will collide. For example, you don't want your characters to walk through each other, so you need to incorporate *object-to-object* collision detection.

Rather than use ray-casting and plane intersection tests as you did in the previous section on colliding with the world mesh, you can cut object-to-object collision down to one simple calculation. Remember the bounding spheres discussed in section "Computing the Bounding Sphere"? All you have to do is determine if the objects in question have intersecting bounding spheres.

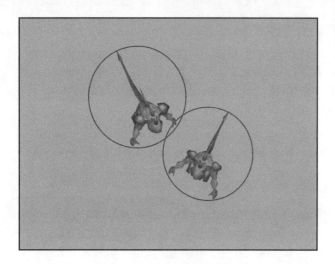

**Figure 12.9**

*Meshes that contain extruded parts (such as the monsters' tails) might use larger-than-needed bounding spheres during collision detection.*

Before you can do that, however, you need to understand a few things, including the downside to using bounding spheres. Take a look at Figure 12.9, which shows two monsters. They have tails—very long tails. Those tails affect the overall size of the bounding sphere for the mesh—the sphere would be overly large in order to encompass the entire mesh (including the tail). If you were to move the two monsters in Figure 12.9, you would see that the two bounding spheres would intersect, even though the monsters aren't close to each other.

Although you can get around the large bounding sphere problem many ways, there is one that you can quickly perform. Instead of using the mesh's bounding sphere, go ahead and compute your own bounding sphere radius for each mesh. By computing your own bounding sphere radius, you can quickly adjust it to cover the amount of space needed to safely cover the mesh.

With that problem aside, you can come up with a single function that checks whether two bounding spheres intersect:

```
BOOL CheckSphereIntersect(                                        \
        float XCenter1, float YCenter1, float ZCenter1,          \
        float Radius1,                                           \
        float XCenter2, float YCenter2, float ZCenter2,          \
        float Radius2)
{
  float XDiff, YDiff, ZDiff, Distance;

  // Calculate distance between center points
```

```
XDiff    = (float)fabs(XCenter2-XCenter1);
YDiff    = (float)fabs(YCenter2-YCenter1);
ZDiff    = (float)fabs(ZCenter2-ZCenter1);
Distance = (float)sqrt(XDiff*XDiff+YDiff*YDiff+ZDiff*ZDiff);

// Return TRUE if the two spheres intersect
if(Distance <= (Radius1+Radius2))
  return TRUE;

// No intersection
return FALSE;
}
```

When called with the two bounding sphere locations and radiuses, the preceding function returns TRUE if the spheres intersect or FALSE if the spheres do not intersect. The way to tell whether two spheres intersect is to calculate the distance between the center points; if the distance is less than or equal to the two radiuses combined, the spheres intersect.

> **TIP**
>
> To optimize the CheckSphereIntersect **function, you can drop the** sqrt
> **function call in the code, as in the following:**
>
> Distance = XDiff*XDiff+YDiff*YDiff+ZDiff*ZDiff;
>
> float RadiusDistance = (Radius1+Radius2)*(Radius1+Radius2)*3.0f;
>
> // Return TRUE if the two spheres intersect
>
> if(Distance <= RadiusDistance)
>
>   return TRUE;
>
> return FALSE;  // No intersection
>
> **The distance comparison factors the distance of the radiuses without using** sqrt **to calculate the actual distance from the center points.**

# Mouse Clicks and Meshes

In your final examination of mesh intersections, you focus on a feature that you're sure to want when dealing with 3-D graphics: the ability to click a mesh and know exactly which polygon face was selected. You already know how to scan a mesh to see which polygon a ray may intersect with (see the section "Casting a Ray," earlier in this chapter)—now you need to cast a ray from the mouse's cursor into the 3-D scene and see which polygon the mouse pointer is covering.

To determine exactly which polygon in a mesh was clicked, in addition to using the D3DXIntersect (see the section "Casting a Ray," earlier in this chapter), you use the D3DXIntersect function argument DWORD *pFaceIndex. This pointer to a DWORD variable contains the indexed polygon face that was intersected by the ray that you cast.

Note that if you cast a ray from an imaginary viewpoint (center of the screen) to the mouse cursor, you can check every polygon in the scene for a collision. The intersection closest to the viewpoint (the intersection with the least distance) is the polygon on which the user clicked. This can be calculated using the following code (which uses code from the DirectX 8.0 SDK samples):

```
// Graphics = pre-initialized cGraphics object
// Mouse = pre-initialized mouse cInputDevice object
D3DXVECTOR3 vecRay, vecDir;  // Ray's position and direction
D3DXVECTOR3 v;                // Temporary vector
D3DXMATRIX matProj, matView; // Projection and view matrices
D3DXMATRIX m;                 // Temporary matrix

// Get the current projection and view transformations
Graphics.GetDeviceCOM()->GetTransform(D3DTS_PROJECTION,       \
                                      &matProj);
Graphics.GetDeviceCOM()->GetTransform(D3DTS_VIEW,             \
                                      &matView);

// Inverse the view matrix
D3DXMatrixInverse(&m, NULL, &matView);

// Read mouse coordinates (to prepare for reading)
Mouse.Read();

// Compute the vector of the pick ray in screen space
v.x =  (((2.0f * Mouse.GetXPos()) / Graphics.GetWidth())  -   \
          1) / matProj._11;
v.y = -(((2.0f * Mouse.GetYPos()) / Graphics.GetHeight()) -   \
          1) / matProj._22;
v.z =  1.0f;

// Transform the screen space ray
```

```
vecRay.x = m._41;
vecRay.y = m._42;
vecRay.z = m._43;
vecDir.x = v.x*m._11 + v.y*m._21 + v.z*m._31;
vecDir.y = v.x*m._12 + v.y*m._22 + v.z*m._32;
vecDir.z = v.x*m._13 + v.y*m._23 + v.z*m._33;
```

To use the preceding code effectively, go ahead and load a mesh into an `ID3DXMesh` object. You can use the Graphics Core's `cMesh` object to make loading and containing the mesh easier:

```
// Mesh = pre-loaded cMesh object
ID3DXMesh *pMesh;
BOOL      Hit;
DWORD     Face;
float     u, v, Dist;

// Get pointer to cMesh ID3DXMesh object
pMesh = Mesh->GetParentMesh()->m_Mesh;

// call above code to get ray vectors and call intersect
ID3DXIntersect(pMesh, &vecRay, &vecDir, &Hit, &Face,           \
                &u, &v, &Dist);

// If Hit is TRUE, then user clicked on mesh
```

By determining the intersection with the least distance (using the preceding code), you can even check each mesh in the scene (or other meshes, such as characters) and find out which one was clicked.

# Using Sky Boxes

A *sky box* is a graphics technique in which a texture-mapped 3-D cube surrounds the viewer. When rendering a sky box, you always center it with the viewpoint so that the user always sees the inside texture-mapped faces of the box. This technique gives the effect that the world actually surrounds the user (as illustrated in Figure 12.10).

Sky boxes are easy to implement. You just need a cube mesh (with the faces pointed inward). Using a vertex buffer to store the cube mesh is perfect. As for textures, you

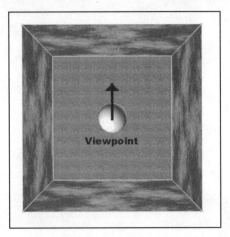

**Figure 12.10**

*A sky box gives users the illusion of being surrounded by a huge world.*

can have up six—giving you one per side. The mesh need not be large, only a cube 20.0 units in size. Textures should be $256 \times 256$, as anything smaller would appear stretched out and unappealing.

# Creating a Sky Box Class

What better way to implement sky boxes in your own game than to create a class that you can easily include for your project. This class, in this case named cSkyBox, needs to take control of every aspect of the sky box, from creating the vertex buffer used to render the box to containing the textures used when rendering. The following code for the sky box class is very compact and is a nice addition to any gaming library:

```
class cSkyBox
{
  private:
    typedef struct sSkyBoxVertex {
      float x, y, z;
      float u, v;
    } sSkyBoxVertex;
    #define SkyBoxFVF (D3DFVF_XYZ | D3DFVF_TEX1)

    cGraphics      *m_Graphics;      // Parent cGraphics object
    cTexture       m_Textures[6];    // Face textures (0-5)
    cVertexBuffer  m_VB;             // Mesh vertex buffer
    cWorldPosition m_Pos;            // Sky box orientation
```

```
public:
  cSkyBox();   // Constructor
  ~cSkyBox();  // Destructor

  // Create and free a sky box class object
  BOOL Create(cGraphics *Graphics);
  BOOL Free();

  // Set a specific side's texture map. Allow for
  // transparent and storage format changes.
  BOOL LoadTexture(short Side, char *Filename,
                   D3DCOLOR Transparent = 0,
                   D3DFORMAT = D3DFMT_UNKNOWN);

  // Rotate box to an absolute or relative rotation.
  BOOL Rotate(float XRot, float YRot, float ZRot);
  BOOL RotateRel(float XRot, float YRot, float ZRot);

  // Render the sky box (using optional alpha-blending)
  // and using current view transformation from Camera.
  BOOL Render(cCamera *Camera, BOOL Alpha = FALSE);
};
```

The upcoming sections cover each function in the preceding code in more detail.

## cSkyBox::Create and cSkyBox::Free

You use this duo of functions to retrieve the parent graphics object, create the sky box mesh, and release all the used cTexture objects (size in total). Take at look at their code bits:

```
BOOL cSkyBox::Create(cGraphics *Graphics)
{
  sSkyBoxVertex Verts[24] = {
    { -10.0f,  10.0f, -10.0f, 0.0f, 0.0f },  // Top vertices
    {  10.0f,  10.0f, -10.0f, 1.0f, 0.0f },
    { -10.0f,  10.0f,  10.0f, 0.0f, 1.0f },
    {  10.0f,  10.0f,  10.0f, 1.0f, 1.0f },

    { -10.0f, -10.0f,  10.0f, 0.0f, 0.0f },  // Bottom vertices
    {  10.0f, -10.0f,  10.0f, 1.0f, 0.0f },
    { -10.0f, -10.0f, -10.0f, 0.0f, 1.0f },
```

```
    {  10.0f, -10.0f, -10.0f, 1.0f, 1.0f },

    { -10.0f,  10.0f, -10.0f, 0.0f, 0.0f },   // Left vertices
    { -10.0f,  10.0f,  10.0f, 1.0f, 0.0f },
    { -10.0f, -10.0f, -10.0f, 0.0f, 1.0f },
    { -10.0f, -10.0f,  10.0f, 1.0f, 1.0f },

    {  10.0f,  10.0f,  10.0f, 0.0f, 0.0f },   // Right vertices
    {  10.0f,  10.0f, -10.0f, 1.0f, 0.0f },
    {  10.0f, -10.0f,  10.0f, 0.0f, 1.0f },
    {  10.0f, -10.0f, -10.0f, 1.0f, 1.0f },

    { -10.0f,  10.0f,  10.0f, 0.0f, 0.0f },   // Front vertices
    {  10.0f,  10.0f,  10.0f, 1.0f, 0.0f },
    { -10.0f, -10.0f,  10.0f, 0.0f, 1.0f },
    {  10.0f, -10.0f,  10.0f, 1.0f, 1.0f },

    {  10.0f,  10.0f, -10.0f, 0.0f, 0.0f },   // Back vertices
    { -10.0f,  10.0f, -10.0f, 1.0f, 0.0f },
    {  10.0f, -10.0f, -10.0f, 0.0f, 1.0f },
    { -10.0f, -10.0f, -10.0f, 1.0f, 1.0f },
  };

  Free(); // Free a prior sky box

  // Error checking
  if((m_Graphics = Graphics) == NULL)
    return FALSE;

  // Create the vertex buffer (and copy over sky box vertices)
  if(m_VB.Create(m_Graphics, 24, SkyBoxFVF,                      \
                 sizeof(sSkyBoxVertex)) == TRUE)
    m_VB.Set(0,24,(void*)&Verts);

  // Rotate sky box into default orientation
  Rotate(0.0f, 0.0f, 0.0f);

  return TRUE;  // Return success!
}
```

```
BOOL cSkyBox::Free()
{
  m_Graphics = NULL;        // Clear parent cGraphics object
  for(short i=0;i<6;i++)   // Release textures
    m_Textures[i].Free();
  m_VB.Free();             // Release vertex buffer

  return TRUE;  // Return success!
}
```

You can see that both functions get right to the point. From the start, Create creates a vertex buffer (a cube mesh with 12 faces and 6 sides). This vertex buffer is filled with the information defined locally in the Create function. Once the vertex buffer has been created, the Create function continues by setting the orientation of the sky mesh to a default rotation value.

Using rotation, you can layer multiple sky boxes to create a 3-D effect. For example, imagine layering a few sky boxes—one box with stars, another with clouds, and another with the sun and moon—and, just like that, creating a rotating sky complete with an orbiting sun and moon!

With the Create function complete, I move on to the Free function. The Free function frees the texture resources and vertex buffer using those objects' respective Free functions.

## cSkyBox::LoadTexture

The LoadTexture function loads a single texture, which is used to texture-map a single side of the sky box mesh, as illustrated here:

```
BOOL cSkyBox::LoadTexture(short Side, char *Filename,            \
                    D3DCOLOR Transparent, D3DFORMAT Format)
{
  // Error checking
  if(m_Graphics == NULL || Side < 0 || Side > 5)
    return FALSE;

  m_Textures[Side].Free(); // Free prior texture

  return m_Textures[Side].Load(m_Graphics, Filename,            \
                               Transparent, Format);
}
```

The LoadTexture function loads a single bitmap image into the texture you specify (using the supplied transparent color and storage format if you plan on using transparent blits or alpha blending). Finally, note the numbering order of the sky box faces. You can see which value corresponds to which face in Table 12.2.

## cSkyBox::Rotate and cSkyBox::RotateRel

You've already learned that the sky box can be rotated to give the illusion of the sky object orbiting the viewer. With these two functions, you can alter the rotation values of the sky box:

```
BOOL cSkyBox::Rotate(float XRot, float YRot, float ZRot)
{
  return m_Pos.Rotate(XRot, YRot, ZRot);
}


BOOL cSkyBox::RotateRel(float XRot, float YRot, float ZRot)
{
  return m_Pos.RotateRel(XRot, YRot, ZRot);
}
```

These two functions call the Graphics Core's cWorldPosition class functions in order to alter the rotation values (refer to Chapter 10, "Creating the Game Core," for more information on the cWorldPosition object).

## Table 12.2  Face Values for cSkyBox::LoadTexture

| Value | Face |
| --- | --- |
| 0 | Top |
| 1 | Bottom |
| 2 | Left |
| 3 | Right |
| 4 | Front |
| 5 | Back |

# cSkyBox::Render

Here's the real meat-and-potatoes function. This function centers the sky box with the supplied camera, enables alpha blending and alpha testing (if required), and renders the six sides of the sky box (or at least those that are texture-mapped):

```
BOOL cSkyBox::Render(cCamera *Camera, BOOL Alpha)
{
  D3DXMATRIX matWorld;
  short i;

  // Error checking
  if(m_Graphics == NULL || Camera == NULL)
    return FALSE;

  // Position sky box around viewer
  m_Pos.Move(Camera->GetXPos(), Camera->GetYPos(), Camera->GetZPos());
  m_Graphics->SetWorldPosition(&m_Pos);

  // Enable alpha testing and alpha blending
  m_Graphics->EnableAlphaTesting(TRUE);
  if(Alpha == TRUE)
    m_Graphics->EnableAlphaBlending(TRUE, D3DBLEND_SRCCOLOR, D3DBLEND_DESTCOLOR);

  // Draw each layer
  for(i=0;i<6;i++) {
    if(m_Textures[i].IsLoaded() == TRUE) {
      m_Graphics->SetTexture(0, &m_Textures[i]);
      m_VB.Render(i*4,2,D3DPT_TRIANGLESTRIP);
    }
  }

  // Disable alpha testing and alpha blending
  m_Graphics->EnableAlphaTesting(FALSE);
  if(Alpha == TRUE)
    m_Graphics->EnableAlphaBlending(FALSE);

  return TRUE;
}
```

To call the Render function, you must pass it the current cCamera object that is being used to render the scene. You can optionally set the Alpha argument to TRUE in order for the Render function to render the sky box using alpha blending techniques.

## Using the Sky Box

Now you get to see the sky box in action. In fact, if you've already looked at the NodeTree example program, you've seen the sky box in action. Basically, the NodeTree sample uses a single texture (stars) for the sky box. Although a simple example was used in the NodeTree sample, sky boxes can use up to six textures, which makes great looking 3-D scenes look even better.

# Wrapping Up 3-D Graphics

You will rarely need engines any more powerful than the ones this chapter provides. Some of you might want to improve on the NodeTree engine by using indexed vertex buffers, thus decreasing the number of memcpy's needed to draw the visible polygons. (Consult the DirectX SDK example and documents for more information on index vertex buffers if you're feeling brave!) You might also test each node for visibility; if a node is fully visible (with each of its eight corners in the viewing frustum), you can draw every polygon and child node in the fully visible node without further checking.

---

### Programs on the CD-ROM

Programs that demonstrate the code discussed in this chapter are located on the CD-ROM at the back of this book. You can find the following programs in the \BookCode\Chap12\ directory:

- **MeshLvl.** Shows how to use single meshes to construct levels. Location: \BookCode\Chap12\MeshLvl\.

- **NodeTree.** Demonstrates node tree level rendering. Location: \BookCode\Chap12\NodeTree\.

- **Objects.** See how to use viewing frustums to clip out unseen objects. Location: \BookCode\Chap12\Objects\.

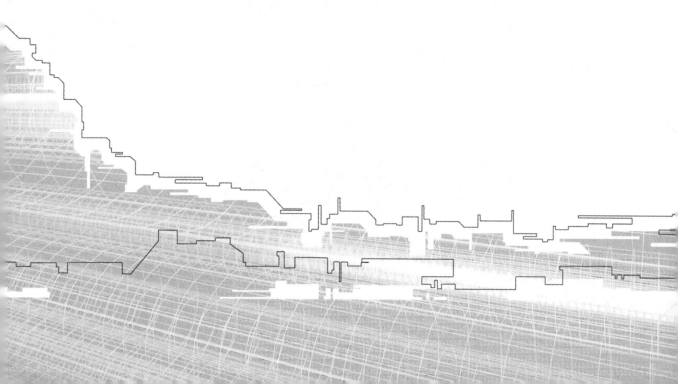

# CHAPTER 13

# MIXING 2-D AND 3-D GRAPHICS ENGINES

When it comes to graphics, there are neither limits nor rules to which you must abide; that is, you're not limited to using only 2-D graphics or only 3-D graphics. You can mix the two with impunity. This chapter is your guide to understanding the tricks behind mixing the two dimensions in order to achieve some awesome effects.

In this chapter, you learn how to do the following:

- Use 2-D graphics in 3-D engines
- Draw 3-D objects in a 2-D world

# Mixing the Two Dimensions

Imagine having 3-D characters able to walk around a 2-D image or using 2-D tiles inside a 3-D world. I know you're dying to know how to mix 3-D characters in your flat 2-D images, but you might be wondering why you would want to use 2-D tiles in a 3-D world.

Think of it like this: Using billboards (2-D objects) saves on using polygons to represent simple objects in your 3-D world—objects such as trees, rocks, and so on. These objects add to the visual flare of your game.

In fact, if you've been observant, you're probably aware that a lot of 3-D games use 2-D objects, and in such a way that you barely notice the effect. For example, in *Mario 64* for the N64 (a console gaming system), you can walk up to a tree and circle around it. Notice that the tree doesn't rotate. That's because it's 2-D.

Whatever your reasons for mixing 2-D and 3-D, you are about to get a firsthand look at a couple of engines I created that can help you on your way. You use the first engine, called 2Din3D, to draw 3-D meshes that represent a game level overlaid for 2-D tiles that represent game objects.

# Using 2-D Objects in a 3-D World

Chapter 6, "Drawing with DirectX Graphics," covers using billboards (2-D objects that are aligned so that they are always facing the viewer), but in this chapter, I'm also talking about using actual 2-D objects, such as tiles, in a 3-D scene.

To see 2-D objects in a game, you might want to check out *Paper Mario* for the N64. Mario (and all the other game denizens) is drawn as a flat image using the billboarding technique (textures mapped to flat polygons). The whole world surrounding Mario is 3-D, and as you move him around, the 3-D scene shifts to always show all the characters in the game from the proper viewing angle.

That's the effect you want to duplicate, which you can do by using billboarding to simulate 2-D objects or by using 2-D tile graphics. With billboards, you can easily introduce depth (such as having objects appear smaller as they move farther from the viewer). With 2-D tiles, you can achieve a similar effect by using scaling, but why bother when you can use billboards?

## Drawing Tiles in 3-D

As complicated as it might seem to mix 2-D tiles with 3-D meshes, there's really nothing new here. You learn how to load and draw 2-D tiles in Chapter 11, "Using 2-D Graphics," and how to work with 3-D meshes in Chapter 6. In this chapter, you find out how to intertwine the 2-D and 3-D components in order to draw a 3-D mesh that represents a game level and how to overlay the mesh with 2-D graphics tiles that represent the game's objects.

At this point, you need a 3-D mesh that represents the game level to use. Figure 13.1 shows one such mesh that is stored on this book's CD-ROM (look for \BookCode\ Chap13\2Din3D). In the Chapter 13 directory, you will also find a bitmap image that contains a series of 2-D tiles to use for drawing a character in the game.

Typically, a character moves around the 3-D world (usually running along a single axis), and as the character moves, so does the camera. The camera needs to stay a short distance from the character and needs to be offset a little higher than the character, just to give the full 3-D effect of the level. To see what I'm talking about, take a look at Figure 13.2, which shows the 2Din3D demo in action.

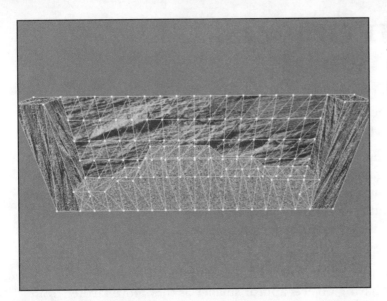

**Figure 13.1**

*A large mesh can represent the 3-D level within which you will draw the 2-D objects.*

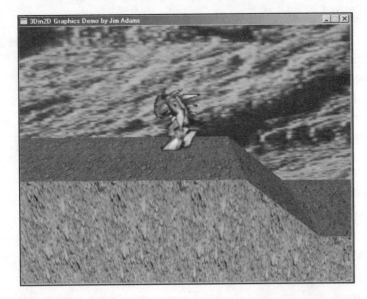

**Figure 13.2**

*The 2Din3D demo program demonstrates using 2-D tiles mixed with the complexity of 3-D levels. In this image, you can see a 2-D tile, the monster being drawn on a 3-D mesh that represents the level.*

Without further ado, please turn your attention to the code that you use to load a mesh that represents the level, to create a set of 2-D tiles that represent the objects (such as the player character), and to draw everything so that it is aligned correctly for each frame. You start by loading all the mesh that represents the level.

# Loading the Level Mesh

Because the Graphics Core is a useful library of functions, you can use it to load an .X file that contains the level's mesh. The Graphics Core object that handles loading .X files is cMesh. Once the mesh is loaded in the cMesh object, you create a cObject object used to render the level mesh. For this example, the mesh to use is Level.x, which you can find in the Chapter 13 directory on the CD-ROM (look for \BookCode\ Chap13\2Din3D).

```
// Graphics = pre-initialized cGraphics object
cMesh    LevelMesh;  // The level mesh
cObject LevelObj;    // The object used for rendering

// Load the .X file titled Level.x
LevelMesh.Load(&Graphics, "LevelMesh");

// Assign mesh to object
LevelObj.Create(&Graphics, &LevelMesh);
```

Using the Graphics Core really is handy; the preceding code is all that's needed at this point. Next comes loading the tiles.

# Loading the Tiles

The 2-D tiles in this example contain a series of images used to draw an animated, walking monster. These tiles are contained within a single bitmap image, which is loaded into a cTexture object. The bitmap image is Tiles.bmp, which is on the CD-ROM (again, look for \BookCode\Chap13\2Din3D).

```
// Graphics = pre-initialized cGraphics object
cTexture Tiles;

// Load the tile texture, assign a transparent color of 0
Tiles.Load(&Graphics, "Tiles.bmp", 0, D3DFMT_A1R5G5B5);
```

You're almost ready to start drawing the level—at this point, the level mesh and the tiles are loaded. Before you can draw the scene, however, you need to do a little preparation.

## Preparing to Draw

Before each frame is rendered, you must align the camera to the player and clear the display (and Z-buffer):

```
// Graphics = pre-initialized cGraphics object
// XPos, YPos, ZPos = coordinates of character to align with
cCamera Camera;

// Clear the display and Z-buffer to defaults
Graphics.Clear();

// Align camera (from a distance away and above position)
Camera.Point(XPos, YPos+50.0f, ZPos-500.0f,                    \
             XPos, YPos,        ZPos);
Graphics.SetCamera(&Camera);
```

You're getting closer; you can now draw the level mesh.

## Drawing the Level Mesh

A quick call to cObject::Render takes care of rendering the level mesh. As with all calls to render a mesh, you must be sure to enclose the call in a cGraphics::BeginScene/cGraphics::EndScene series of calls:

```
if(Graphics::BeginScene()==TRUE) {
  LevelObj.Render();
  Graphics::EndScene();
}
```

At this point, the level is rendered and all that's left is drawing the 2-D tiles.

## Drawing 2-D Objects

You are ready to draw the tiles onscreen in their appropriate locations. You do so by looping through each object and drawing it to the display. Advanced game programmers can even use a viewing frustum to reject objects that don't appear in the view. The following example builds on the code in the preceding section by drawing one object—the player character:

```
// Graphics = pre-initialized cGraphics object

// Begin the scene
if(Graphics::BeginScene()==TRUE) {
```

```
// Draw the level mesh
LevelObj.Render();

// Enable transparent drawing
Graphics.EnableAlphaTesting(TRUE);

// Disable z-buffering
Graphics.EnableZBuffer(FALSE);

// Begin the sprite drawing features
Graphics.BeginSprite();

// Draw the player character object (64x64 tiles) based on
// its middle coordinate of the bottom of the tile.
// Since the camera is centered on the object, you can just
// draw the tile in the middle of the screen (offset by the
// tile size a bit). Notice that 640 and 480 represent the
// dimensions of the display.
Tiles.Blit(0,0,(640-64)/2,480/2-64,64,64);

// End the sprite drawing
Graphics.EndSprite();

// Disable alpha testing
Graphics.EnableAlphaTesting(FALSE);
// End scene drawing
Graphics::EndScene();
}
```

> **TIP**
>
> Using 2-D tiles has a drawback. They don't use Z-buffers (at least not if you're using the ID3DXSprite interface, as I am), which means that you can't just draw them and expect them to mix correctly with a 3-D scene. Once drawn, a 2-D tile is fully visible until you draw something over it (such as a polygon or another tile).

# Moving in the 3-D World

A still picture has limited appeal, so you need to add a little motion to the demo—the characters need to walk around, for example. Because your characters are essentially represented by a set of 3-D coordinates and the level is really an ID3DXMesh object, why not just use the ID3DXIntersect function to test for height changes and character-to-wall intersections? In fact, why not use the intersection test functions? There is no reason not to do both, so go ahead and call up the functions developed in Chapter 12, "Creating 3-D Graphics Engines."

> **NOTE**
>
> Check out the complete 2Din3D sample program that comes on the CD-ROM at the back of this book (look for \BookCode\Chap13\2Din3D\) to see just how I added the intersection tests. You will also find some rudimentary movement features. With this sample program, you can use the arrow keys to move left and right throughout the level. Have fun!

# Adding 3-D Objects to a 2-D World

With games such as *Final Fantasy* and *Parasite Eve*, both created by Square Co., Ltd., you can enjoy the beauty of pre-rendered background images while at the same time, use 3-D models in the game. Mixing 2-D and 3-D graphics has been a highly guarded secret of game companies, and it's a secret that's worth exposing.

If you haven't seen the 3-D in 2-D graphics engines I'm talking about, take a look at Figure 13.3, which shows the engine that comes on this book's CD-ROM (look for \BookCode\Chap13\3Din2D). The figure shows a static 2-D backdrop with a 3-D object placed in it. The 3-D object moves around the backdrop, just as though the image were 3-D.

**Figure 13.3**

*A 3-D in 2-D graphics engine allows for great looking 2-D backdrops while using 3-D elements, such as the character graphics.*

Backdrops are represented by pre-rendered bitmaps drawn to the display for every frame using the 2-D blitting techniques in Chapter 11. Specifically, a ID3DXSprite object handles drawing the bitmap (which is loaded into an IDirect3DTexture8 object). Using an ID3DXMesh object is perfect for the 3-D objects in the engine, not to mention the Graphics Core cMesh and cObject classes that aid in loading and displaying those 3-D objects.

So, on one hand, you have a pre-rendered backdrop that is blitted to the screen for every frame, and on the other hand, you have 3-D objects drawn in the scene. Are things actually that easy? Not really—at least not at first glance.

How can you get 3-D depth information from a 2-D image? In fact, you can duplicate the 3-D–object–on–2-D–image backdrop effect in a number of ways. Here are some examples:

- Create pre-rendered backdrops in a 3-D modeler such as Caligari's trueSpace or discreet's 3D Studio Max and save the images along with the depth buffer that contains the Z-values for each pixel. For each frame of the game, copy the depth buffer of the image to the depth buffer of the back buffer and continue by drawing the 3-D objects.

- Create the backdrop in layers. Starting at the bottom layer, draw each image in succession and draw the 3-D characters on the appropriate layer, thus allowing succeeding layers to cover up portions of lower layers (and 3-D objects).

- Use a highly detailed pre-rendered backdrop and a simplified version of the mesh that you used to render the scene in the 3-D modeler. Use the mesh to render out the Z-values and for collision detection. Three-dimensional objects can then rely on the Z-buffer to handle drawing the right depth.

Here you have three viable ways to get 3-D depth information into a 2-D image. Option number one, storing an image in a format that includes each pixel's Z-value, sounds great and using it would be the best method except that doing so is not possible at this time with DirectX. Even though DirectX Graphics provides minimal functions to lock the depth buffer and manipulate it (note that DirectX doesn't allow blitting to the depth buffer), you have no guarantee that every video card supports the depth buffer locking mechanism. In addition, manually locking and unlocking the depth buffer in each frame puts a major demand on the system.

Option number two is to draw the backdrop in layers. This option is in many ways the easiest one to use. By separating sections of the backdrop, you can draw them in order, adding the 3-D objects as needed for each layer. If your backdrops don't include real areas that will cover up the 3-D objects, you can just draw the layers all at once and then draw the 3-D objects.

Last is option three, utilizing a simplified version of the mesh used to render the backdrop for creating Z-values of each pixel, which is the option I use in this book. Because the scenes will be pre-rendered in a 3-D modeler, you can take a simplified version of the scene mesh and use it to fill the Z-buffer for every frame, blit the backdrop image, and continue by drawing the 3-D objects onscreen. In addition, you can reuse the mesh for collision detection (and for determining height, as you do in Chapter 12 when using the NodeTree engine).

You're now ready to start constructing a 3Din2D demo; you begin by obtaining the backdrop image and mesh with which you will work.

## Dealing with 2-D Backdrops

As I mentioned in the previous section, you develop 2-D backdrops by means of a 3-D modeling program such as trueSpace (and not a painting program—because you need the polygon data from the modeler). Figure 13.4 exemplifies a simple mesh and final render.

When designing your scene, you can go crazy with the details because the only thing you really want is the final rendered image (although polygons that cover portions of the view become a bit tricky, as you see in the upcoming section, "Dealing with the Scene Mesh"). For now, just remember the exact location and orientation of the camera that you use to render the scene (it'll come in handy later).

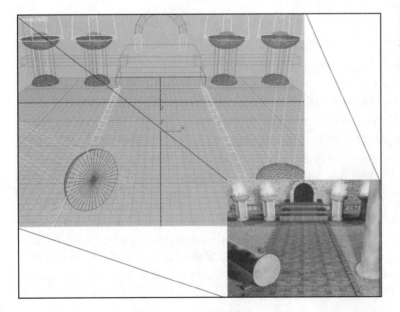

**Figure 13.4**

*A mesh you create in a 3-D modeler is rendered out as the backdrop.*

**Figure 13.5**

*The backdrops are split into six smaller rectangular chunks.*

Once the scene that you're modeling is rendered, you need to save it on a disk as a bitmap file. That bitmap file needs to be split up into smaller textures. Figure 13.5 shows the sample backdrop again, this time divided into six small rectangular chunks (textures).

You need to split the backdrop image in Figure 13.5 into multiple textures that Direct3D can handle. In this case, the backdrop image is 640 × 480, so the textures are 256 × 256 (for chunks 1, 2, 4, and 5) and 128 × 256 (for chunks 3 and 6). Notice that if a chunk is not large enough, you need to expand it to match the correct texture size (for example, chunks 4–6 need to be expanded in height to 256 pixels).

As you split the bitmap image into six chunks, save each chunk to its own bitmap file. You later load the six bitmap files into a Graphics Core cTexture object, which is used to render the chunks to the display. Assuming that the chunks are numbered 1–6 and prefixed with the filename Scene, you can do the following to load the textures:

**NOTE**

If you're feeling brave, try creating a class that will load any size bitmap and divide it into chunks. This way, you don't have to mess with paint programs to cut up the image, which will make it easier to load in bitmaps of different resolutions.

```
// Graphics = pre-initialized cGraphics object
char Filename[81];      // Filename of texture to load
```

```
cTexture Textures[6];  // Objects to holds textures

for(short i=0;i<6;i++) {
  // Construct the filename of the texture
  sprintf(Filename, "Scene%u.bmp", i+1);

  // Load the texture
  Textures[i].Load(&Graphics, Filename);
}
```

Once you load each of the six chunks in their respective texture objects, you can utilize the cTexture::Blit function to draw them to the screen. You find out how to do that in the section "Rendering the Scene," later in this chapter, but first focus your attention on the scene mesh.

## Dealing with the Scene Mesh

Your detailed level looks great, and now you want to include some 3-D objects in it. First, though, you need to construct a simplified version of your scene, which you will use in two ways—to fill in the depth buffer for every frame so that 3-D objects blend correctly with the 2-D backdrop and as a collision mesh for movement of objects.

When I say simplified, I mean really simplified. Because the mesh must be rendered out for every frame in order to create the Z-values in the scene, the fewer polygons you use the better. However, you must use enough polygons to make sure that the 3-D objects blend in correctly. To see what I'm talking about, look at Figure 13.6, which shows the final rendered image, the actual scene mesh, and the simplified scene mesh.

Earlier, I mentioned that you use just the right number of polygons to render the scene. If there are too many polygons, your engine slows down; if you have too few, you get graphical errors when playing your game. Think about it like this: A sphere mesh that uses 500 polygons is obviously too complex to use as a simplified mesh. In a simplified mesh,

> **TIP**
>
> When dealing with a simplified mesh, use only two materials (no textures). The first material represents the polygon areas that were actually drawn in the backdrop, whereas the second material hides polygons that are used in intersection tests. The second material, therefore, uses an alpha value of 0.0 (meaning that it's invisible and actually not rendered).

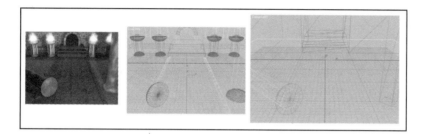

**Figure 13.6**

*The rendered image used as the backdrop (left). The actual mesh used to render the backdrop in the 3-D modeler (center). The simplified mesh used for Z-buffering and intersection tests (right).*

you need only enough polygons to represent the sphere and to make sure that it covers the same area on the screen when rendered. Figure 13.7 illustrates a common mistake when creating simplified meshes—that is, using far too few polygons.

## TIP

To cut back on the number of polygons in the simplified mesh, cut out the faces that will never be seen or used in intersection tests. Also, you draw only polygons that are actually going to cover up 3-D objects. For example, if you have a box in the background that the player's character is never going to get near, don't draw it in the simplified mesh. The 3Din2D demo (located in \BookCode\Chap13\3din2d) that is on the **CD-ROM** that comes with this book demonstrates using simplified meshes and 3-D objects to good effect because only one object in the foreground needs to be rendered.

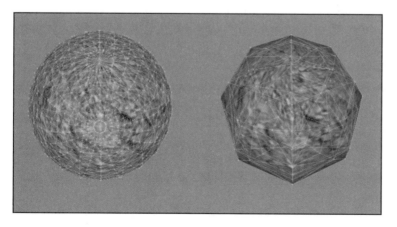

**Figure 13.7**

*The mesh on the left has numerous polygons and can be used to render the backdrop. The simplified mesh on the right doesn't have enough polygons to match the original mesh, so 3-D objects will incorrectly overwrite the excluded pixels.*

Okay, you've done the hard work and created your simplified scene mesh. The simplified mesh needs to make its way into your engine, so go ahead and convert it into an .X file. I export the mesh as a .3DS file (compatible with many modeling programs) and then use the Microsoft .X conversion utility (conv3ds.exe) that comes with the DirectX 8 SDK.

> **TIP**
>
> Using `conv3ds.exe` to convert from a .3DS file to an .X file is as easy as using the following commands at a DOS prompt:
>
> ```
> conv3ds -mx filename.3ds
> ```
>
> The preceding DOS command will convert the mesh file from filename.3ds to filename.x. This .X file contains a single mesh (all meshes combined into one) that is saved in text format. At this point, you can cut out all the mesh normal and texture-mapping data (that information isn't used) from the .X file to save space. You really need only the mesh vertices, faces, materials, and mesh material list templates.

Once you convert the .3DS file (or any other mesh file) to an .X file, you can utilize the cMesh and cObject classes to make it easier to load the simplified mesh:

```
// Graphics = pre-initialized cGraphics object
cMesh   SceneMesh;  // Contains mesh info
cObject SceneObj;   // Used to render mesh

SceneMesh.Load(&Graphics, "Scene.x");
SceneObj.Create(&Graphics, &SceneMesh);
```

# Rendering the Scene

You now have completed the last step required for ensuring that the backdrop image is capable of containing depth information (via the simplified mesh). If you load the backdrop images and simplified mesh, you can easily render a frame of your game by following these steps:

1. Clear the Z-buffer to 1.0 (and ensure that Z-buffering is enabled).
2. Render the simplified mesh (thus filling in the scene Z-buffer), skipping polygons that have a value of 0.0 (which signifies that they are invisible).
3. Disable the Z-buffer.
4. Blit out the backdrop textures using ID3DXSprite.
5. Enable the Z-buffer.

Because you have already loaded the backdrop image as a series of six textures and you now have a simplified mesh loaded and ready to use, get a jump on things and look at some code that renders the scene for you:

**CAUTION**

You need to do a few things before you can render the scene, such as creating and orienting a camera to match the camera that rendered the backdrop image.

You also need to match the perspective projection used in the modeling program when the backdrop image was rendered. If you're using 3D Studio Max, this is typically 34.516 degrees (or 0.6021124 radians). Last, be sure to match the aspect ratio, which is typically 1.333333.

```
// Graphics = pre-initialized cGraphics object
// Textures[6] = pre-loaded scene textures
// SceneObj = Scene mesh object (cObject)

// Clear the z-buffer and begin the scene
Graphics.ClearZBuffer();
if(Graphics.BeginScene() == TRUE) {

  // Render simplified mesh for z-values
  Graphics.EnableZBuffer(TRUE);
  SceneObj.Render();

  // Draw the backdrop (composed of six textures)
  Graphics.EnableZBuffer(FALSE); // Disable z-buffering
  Graphics.BeginSprite();
  for(long i=0;i<2;i++) {
    for(long j=0;j<3;j++)
      Textures[i*3+j].Blit(j*256,i*256);
  }
  Graphics.EndSprite();

  // End the scene
  Graphics.EndScene();
}

// Display the scene
Graphics.Display();
```

That's it for the backdrops. To recap: You first drew the simplified mesh (in order to set the appropriate scene Z-buffer values), and then you filled the screen with the backdrop image. Next comes the best part—adding 3-D objects to the scene!

# Adding 3-D Objects

After drawing the backdrop, nothing holds you back from drawing 3-D objects (meshes) in the scene—because the Z-buffer contains all the depth values for each relevant pixel. Don't be shy. Draw the characters, objects, and even enhancements to the background image. For example, use 3-D objects for the doors; they can open, close, and block the path of movement. Nothing is sacred here, so have fun!

# Collisions and Intersections

Now comes the point where the 3-D objects must know where they collide with the backdrop. If you need to brush up on how to detect mesh intersections, before continuing, refer to Chapter 12. All you want to do at this point is make sure that your characters don't walk through walls and determine the height in which to draw them at any point in the scene.

If you read the 3Din2D project source code referred to earlier in this chapter, you realize that I borrowed the intersection code from Chapter 12. In the 3Din2D demo, I strive to keep the character from walking through walls, and I allow him to move up and down the stairs. I'll leave it up to you to perfect the movement routines.

# Wrapping Up Mixed Engines

I really enjoyed writing this chapter, and I hope you enjoyed reading it. The real secret behind terrific graphics engines such as those from *Final Fantasy 7* is that there really is no secret. As you learned in this chapter, using the simple graphics techniques presented in this book, you can come up with some cool stuff. Just keep your mind open to the possibilities, and the ideas will start flowing.

Advanced readers can expand the 3Din2D sample by adding animation to the textures (using DirectShow, a DirectX multimedia component) and to the simplified mesh. Adding animation will bring the engine up to par with newer games such as *Final Fantasy 10.* As for the 2Din3D example, you can use the `cNodeTreeMesh` object developed in Chapter 12 to optimize rendering of the level and to let the player's character move around in complete 3-D freedom, rather than along the X- and Y-axes.

## Programs on the CD-ROM

Programs that demonstrate the code discussed in this chapter are located on the CD-ROM at the back of this book. You can find the following programs in the \BookCode\Chap13\ directory:

- **2Din3D.** A program that demonstrates using 2-D objects in a 3-D world. Location: \BookCode\Chap13\2Din3D\.

- **3Din2D.** On the flip side, this program shows how to use 3-D objects in a 2-D world (ala *Final Fantasy 7-9*). Location: \BookCode\Chap13\3Din2D\.

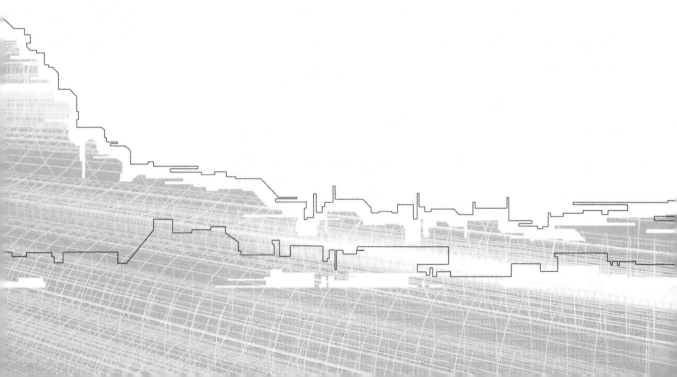

# CHAPTER 14

# IMPLEMENTING SCRIPTS

When creating projects as large as role-playing games, you will find it difficult (and foolhardy) to program game-related information in your source code. Your best course is to use external sources (that resemble programming code) called *scripts* for gaming data such as dialogue. In this way, you can control the flow of your game and save time because you don't have to recompile the project every time you make a change. In this chapter, you learn how to create and use a basic scripting system.

In this chapter, you do the following:

- Learn about scripts
- Create your own scripting system
- Use the scripting system
- Apply scripts to your game

# Understanding Scripts

When creating a game, you use scripts in much the same way that movie producers use scripts —to control every aspect of your "production." Game scripts are similar to the program code you write when creating your game, except that game scripts are *external* to the gaming engine. Because they are external, you can make quick changes to a script without having to recompile the entire game engine. Imagine having a project with more than one million lines of code and having to recompile the entire project just to change a single line of dialogue!

Scripts are not really difficult to work with, and just about every aspect of your game can benefit from the use of scripts. You can use scripts when navigating menus, controlling combat, handling a player's inventory, and so much more. For example, when developing a game, imagine that you want to present users in combat with a list of magic spells that they regularly use for attack. Say that over the course of developing the game, you decide to change some of those spells. If that spell information is hard-coded, you have a major problem; you must change every instance of the program code that controls the spell, not to mention having to debug and test that code until it's perfect. Why devote so much time on changes such as this one?

Instead, you can write the code for magic spells and their respective effects on the game denizens in several small scripts. Whenever combat commences, these scripts are loaded and the selection of magic spells shown. Once a magic spell is cast, a script processes the effects—from the damage done to the movement and animation of the spell's graphics.

For this book, I was torn between using two different types of scripting systems. One script system involves the use of a language much like C++. You type commands into a script file, compile the file, and execute the compiled script file from within your game. The second script system is an extremely simplified version of the first. Rather than allowing you to type the commands into a file, the system enables you to create scripts by selecting the commands from a predetermined set of commands.

Because I want to get you up and running with your scripting engine as quickly as possible, I opted to use the second script system. This system, which I call the *Mad Lib Scripting* system, works by using a set of predetermined commands, called *actions*, each of which has an associated game function. Take, for example, the actions in Table 14.1—each action has a specific function to perform.

With such a limited set of actions, you really don't need the power of complex compiled script languages; instead, you need the ability to tell the script system which action to use and what options the action should use to perform the gaming function. The great thing about this method is that instead of spouting out lines of code to specify a simple action, you reference the action and options by number.

For example, say that the Play Sound action is considered action number four, and the action requires only one entry, the sound number to play. There are only two

## Table 14.1  Example Command Actions

| Action | Function |
| --- | --- |
| Print | Prints a line of text to the screen. |
| End | Ends script processing. |
| Move Character | Moves the specified character in a specific direction. |
| Play Sound | Plays a specific sound effect. |

values to store in the script: one number for the action and one number that represents the sound. Using values to represent actions (instead of text) makes processing these types of scripts quick and easy.

# Creating a Mad Lib Script System

As I mentioned in the preceding section, I refer to my recommended scripting system as the Mad Lib Script system (or MLS for short) because it closely resembles the old pen-and-paper game of the same name. In Mad Libs (which is founded on the perfect concept for a basic scripting system), you receive a story that is missing numerous words, and your job is to fill in the blanks with hilarious text. While your game's actions represent something other than funny quotes, the idea is perfect for your needs.

In this section, I introduce the concepts of creating a Mad Lib Script system, from developing the actions you use in your scripts to creating a script system (complete with a script editor) that you can insert into your game project.

## Designing the Mad Lib Script System

Implementing your own MLS system is easy enough; just create the actions that you want in your game, complete with the blank spots (called *entries*) that need to be filled in by the person creating or editing the scripts. For each action, be sure to provide a list of choices for filling in the blank entries, which can vary in type from a line of text to a numerical value.

You number the actions and the blank entries so that the scripting system can reference them, as illustrated in the following example lists of actions:

1. Character (*NAME*) takes (*NUMBER*) damage.
2. Print (*TEXT*).
3. Play sound effect titled (*SOUND_NAME*).
4. Play music titled (*MUSIC_NAME*).
5. Create object (*OBJECT_NAME*) at coordinates (*XPOS*),(*YPOS*).
6. End script processing.

Each of the six actions has either zero or more blank entries enclosed within parentheses. Each of the blank entries holds either a text string or a number. This list of actions and possible entries (with the type of entry) is called an *action template* (see Figure 14.1 for an example).

Once action templates are in use, you can refer to actions by their numbers rather than by the actions' text (which exists only to make it easier for users to understand which function each action performs). For example, from now on, I can say that I want to implement action #4 using *title.mid* in the first blank entry. When you execute the script, the script system will see the number 4 (action #4) and know that it has only one entry—the filename of the song that you want to load and play.

I trust that you are beginning to see the ease with which you can use this system. Now, I will forgo any more theory so that you can jump right into programming your own MLS system.

> **NOTE**
>
> The **MLS** scripting system will work for **90** percent of your game. For example, take a look at the PlayStation console in the game *RPG Maker* (by Agetec, Inc.). In *RPG Maker*, you can create your own role-playing games, working off an **MLS**-type system such as the one I just described; believe me, you can create complex scripts in this game.

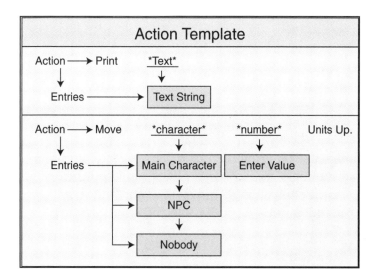

**Figure 14.1**

*An action template is divided into multiple actions, which in turn are split into entries.*

# Programming the Mad Lib Script System

In order to make your MLS system as powerful as possible, you need to design it so that it supports multiple action templates, with each action template containing an unlimited number of actions. In this way, you can reuse the system for just about any project your heart desires.

To make writing the scripts easier, utilize a script editor program (such as the one you see in the later section, "Working with the MLS Editor") with an action template that enables you to quickly piece together actions and change the blank entries for each action. When a script is complete, you can read the script file into your engine and process each individual action, using the specific entries for each action that was entered via the script editor.

The first order of business is to work with the action templates.

## Working with Action Templates

An action template needs to contain a list of actions, complete with text, number of entries, and each entry's data. Recall that each action is numbered by its index within a list, with each blank entry in each action numbered as well. You assign each entry a type (text, integer number, float number, Boolean value, or multiple choice). You also number types, as follows:

**0.** No entry type

**1.** Text entry

**2.** Boolean value

**3.** Integer number

**4.** Float number

**5.** Multiple choice (a choice from a list of text selections)

Each entry type has unique characteristics; strings can be of variable size, numbers can be between any range of two numbers, and Boolean values can either be TRUE or FALSE. As for multiple choices, each choice has its own text string (the scripts are given a choice from a list, and the index number of the selected choice is used rather than the text).

A sample action might then take this form:

```
Action #1: Spell targets (*MULTIPLE_CHOICE*).
```

Possible choices for blank entry #1:
1. Player character
2. Spell caster
3. Spell target
4. Nobody

Imagine that you are using the preceding action and instructing it to use choice #3 as the target. You instruct the script engine to use action #1 with choice #3 for the first blank spot (which is a multiple-choice entry). Using numbers to represent the actions and entries means that the script processor doesn't have to deal directly with code text, which makes processing the scripts easier.

To contain the actions and entries, I've come up with the following structures, which are heavily commented so that you can follow along:

```c
// Type of entries (for blank entries)
enum Types { _NONE = 0, _TEXT, _BOOL, _INT, _FLOAT, _CHOICE };

// Structure to store information about a single blank entry
typedef struct sEntry {
  long      Type;          // Type of blank entry (_TEXT, etc.)

  // The following two unions contain the various
  // information about a single blank entry, from
  // the min/max values (for int and float values),
  // and the number of choices in a multiple choice entry.
  //   Text and Boolean entries do not need such info.
  union {
    long    NumChoices;  // # of choices in list
    long    lMin;        // long min. value
    float   fMin;        // float min. value
  };
  union {
    long    lMax;        // long max. value
    float   fMax;        // float max. value
    char **Choices;      // text array for each choice
  };

  // Structure constructor to clear to default values
  sEntry()
  {
    Type      = _NONE;
    NumChoices = 0;
```

```
    Choices    = NULL;
  }


  // Structure destructor to clean up used resources
  ~sEntry()
  {
    // Special case for choice types
    if(Type == _CHOICE) {
      if(NumChoices) {
        for(long i=0;i<NumChoices;i++)
          delete [] Choices[i];  // Delete choice text
      }
      delete [] Choices; // Delete choice array
    }
  }
} sEntry;


// Structure that stores a single action and contains
// a pointer for using linked lists.
typedef struct sAction {
  long      ID;           // Action ID (0 to # actions-1)
  char      Text[256];    // Action text
  short     NumEntries;   // # of entries in action
  sEntry    *Entries;     // Array of entry structures
  sAction   *Next;        // Next action in linked list

  sAction()
  {
    ID         = 0;        // Set all data to defaults
    Text[0]    = 0;
    NumEntries = 0;
    Entries    = NULL;
    Next       = NULL;
  }

  ~sAction()
  {
    delete [] Entries;   // Free entries array
    delete Next;         // Delete next in list
  }
} sAction;
```

You use the two preceding structures, sEntry and sAction, in conjunction to store the action text as well as the type of each entry. For entries, you select from the enumerated list type (as described earlier in this section). The sEntry structure also holds the rules for each entry type (using the two unions).

Because text entries are only buffers of characters, you have no rules to follow for using text entry types. The same goes for Boolean values because they can be only TRUE or FALSE. Integer and float values need a minimum and maximum range of acceptable values (hence, the min/max variables). There are a number of multiple choices and an array of char buffers that holds the text for each choice.

sAction holds the action ID (the action number from the list of actions), the action text, and an array of entries to use for the action. To determine the number of entries in the action (as well as each type), you need to encrypt the action text a bit. To insert an action into the action text, use a tilde (~) character, as shown here:

```
Player ~ gains ~ hit points
```

The two tildes represent two entries. More information is needed about each entry, but how do you obtain information from only two tilde characters? You can't, so you must access the storage format of the action templates to determine what additional information is required for each action.

Action templates are stored as text files, with each action's text enclosed within quotes. Each action that contains entries (marked as tildes in the text) is followed by a list of entry data. Each entry begins with a word that describes the type of entry (TEXT, BOOL, INT, FLOAT, or CHOICE). Depending on the entry type, further information might follow.

No more information is needed for TEXT. The same goes for BOOL types. As for INT and FLOAT, a minimum value and a maximum value are required. At last, the CHOICE entry is followed by the number of choices to select from and then by each choice's text (enclosed in quotes).

After you define each entry, you can go on to the next action text. The following example action template file demonstrates each entry type:

```
"Print ~"
  TEXT

"Move character to ~, ~, ~"
  FLOAT 0.0 2048.0
  FLOAT 0.0 2048.0
  FLOAT 0.0 2048.0
```

```
"Character ~ ~ ~ ~ points"
  CHOICE 3
    "Main Character"
    "Caster"
    "Target"
  CHOICE 2
    "Gains"
    "Losses"
  INT 0 128
  CHOICE 2
    "Hit"
    "Magic"

"Set variable ~ to ~"
  INT 0 65535
  BOOL

"End Script"
```

Because the action template doesn't allow comments, I'll explain the actions and entries. The first action (Print ~) prints a single text string (using the first entry in the action, entry 0). The second action takes three float values, each ranging from 0 to 2,048. The third action gives three multiple-choice options as well as an integer value that can range from 0 to 128. Action four demonstrates integer values again, as well a single Boolean value. Last is action five, which takes no entries.

Loading the action template is a matter of processing a text file and setting up the appropriate structures, which consists of doing string comparisons on words loaded and storing text lines within quotes. This is really an easy process, and in the section, "Putting Together the cActionTemplate Class," you find out exactly how it is done.

The next step is to use the action templates in conjunction with another structure that stores the entry data (which text to display, what number or choice was selected, and so on), which is the purpose of the script entries.

## Creating Script Entries

Because the sEntry structure contains only the template (guidelines) of the actions and entries, you need another array of structures to store the data for each entry. These new structures include what text to use in a text entry, which Boolean value to use, and which multiple-choice selection to use. This new structure that contains an entry's data is sScriptEntry, and is defined as follows:

```
typedef struct sScriptEntry
{
  long    Type;            // Type of entry (_TEXT, _BOOL, etc.)

  union {
    long    IOValue;       // Used for saving/loading
    long    Length;        // Length of text (w/ 0 terminator)
    long    Selection;     // Selection in choice
    BOOL    bValue;        // BOOL value
    long    lValue;        // long value
    float   fValue;        // float value
  };
  char    *Text;           // Text buffer

  sScriptEntry()
  {
    Type = _NONE;   // Clear to default values
    IOValue = 0;
    Text = NULL;
  }

  ~sScriptEntry() { delete [] Text; }  // Delete text buffer
} sScriptEntry;
```

Much like sEntry, the sScriptEntry holds the actual values to use for each blank entry in the action. Here, you see Type again. It describes the type of entry (_TEXT, _BOOL, and so on). The single union of variables is where the good stuff is, including one variable for the length of the text, one for the multiple choice selection, and one for the integer and float values and the Boolean value.

Take note of two things about sScriptEntry. First, a character pointer is outside the union (because both Length and Text are used to store text data); second, an additional variable called IOValue is included in the union. You use IOValue to access the union variables to save and load the entry data.

To demonstrate how to store each action's entry data into an sScriptEntry structure (or structures if there is more than one entry), review the following action:

```
"~ player's health by ~"
  CHOICE 2
    "Increase"
    "Decrease"
  INT 0 65535
```

Depending on multiple choice selection, the preceding action either increases or decreases the player's health by a set amount ranging from 0 to 65535. Because there are two entries (a multiple choice and an integer), you need two sScriptEntry structures:

```
sScriptEntry Entries;

// Configure multiple choice - set to first choice
Entries[0].Type = _CHOICE;
Entries[0].Selection = 0; // Increase

// Configure integer - set to 128
Entries[1].Type = _INT;
Entries[1].lValue = 128;
```

When dealing with the script entries, the most difficult part crops up when many entries are in a complete script. Each action in the script requires a matching sEntry structure, which in turn might contain a number of sScriptEntry structures. Before you know it, you can become knee-deep in structures—talk about a mess! To better handle a script's structures, you need another structure that tracks each entry that belongs to the script actions:

```
typedef struct sScript
{
  long          Type;       // 0 to (number of actions-1)
  long          NumEntries; // # entries in this script action
  sScriptEntry *Entries;    // Array of entries

  sScript      *Prev;       // Prev in linked list
  sScript      *Next;       // Next in linked list

  sScript()
  {
    Type = 0;              // Clear to defaults
    NumEntries = 0;
    Entries = NULL;
    Prev = Next = NULL;
  }

  ~sScript()
  {
    delete [] Entries; // Delete entry array
    delete Next;       // Delete next in linked list
  }
} sScript;
```

You use the sScript structure to contain a single action, as well as maintain a linked list of further sScript structures that constitutes an entire script. The Type variable can range from zero to the number of actions in the action template minus one. If you have ten actions in the action template, Type can range from zero to nine.

To make processing easier, store the number of entries in the NumEntries variable. The value in NumEntries must match the number-of-entries variable in the action template. From there, allocate an array of sScriptEntry structures to store the data for each entry in the action template. If two entries are in the associated action, you need to allocate two sScriptEntry structures.

Lastly, there are the two pointer variables, Prev and Next, in sScript. These two pointers maintain a linked list of the entire script. To construct a linked list of sScript structures (much as illustrated in Figure 14.2), start with a root structure that represents the first action in the script. You then link sScript structures via the Next and Prev variables, as shown here:

```
sScript *ScriptRoot = new sScript();
sScript *ScriptPtr = new sScript;
ScriptRoot->Next = ScriptPtr;  // Point to second action
ScriptPtr->Prev = ScriptRoot;  // Point back to root
```

At this point, you can start at the root of the script and traverse down the entire script with the following code:

```
void TraverseScript(sScript *pScript)
{
  while(pScript != NULL) { // loop until no more script actions
    // Do something with pScript
    // pScript->Type holds the script action ID
    pScript = pScript->Next; // Go to next script action
  }
}
```

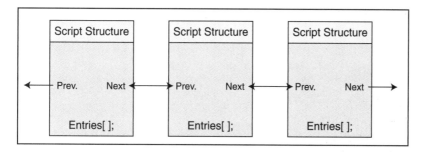

**Figure 14.2**

*A script-action linked list uses* Prev *and* Next *variables to link the entire script. Each script action has it own array of script entries.*

You can also quickly load and save scripts by using linked lists, as illustrated in the following two functions:

```c
BOOL SaveScript(char *Filename, sScript *ScriptRoot)
{
  FILE *fp;
  long i, j, NumActions;
  char Text[256];
  sScript *ScriptPtr;

  // Make sure there's some script actions
  if((ScriptPtr = ScriptRoot) == NULL)
    return FALSE;

  // Count the number of actions
  NumActions = 0;
  while(ScriptPtr != NULL) {
    NumActions++;                    // Increase count
    ScriptPtr = ScriptPtr->Next; // Next action
  }

  // Open the file for output
  if((fp=fopen(Filename, "wb"))==NULL)
    return FALSE;  // return a failure

  // Output # of script actions
  fwrite(&NumActions, 1, sizeof(long), fp);

  // Loop through each script action
  ScriptPtr = ScriptRoot;
  for(i=0;i<NumActions;i++) {

    // Output type of action and # of entries
    fwrite(&ScriptPtr->Type, 1, sizeof(long), fp);
    fwrite(&ScriptPtr->NumEntries, 1, sizeof(long), fp);

    // Output entry data (if any)
    if(ScriptPtr->NumEntries) {
      for(j=0;j<ScriptPtr->NumEntries;j++) {

        // Write entry type and data
```

```
                fwrite(&ScriptPtr->Entries[j].Type, 1,sizeof(long), fp);
                fwrite(&ScriptPtr->Entries[j].IOValue,1,sizeof(long),fp);

                // Write text entry (if any)
                if(ScriptPtr->Entries[j].Type == _TEXT &&              \
                   ScriptPtr->Entries[j].Text != NULL)
                  fwrite(ScriptPtr->Entries[j].Text, 1,                \
                         ScriptPtr->Entries[j].Length, fp);
            }
        }

        // Go to next script structure in linked list
        ScriptPtr = ScriptPtr->Next;
    }

    fclose(fp);

    return TRUE; // return a success!
}

sScript *LoadScript(char *Filename, long *NumActions)
{
    FILE *fp;
    long i, j, Num;
    char Text[2048];
    sScript *ScriptRoot, *Script, *ScriptPtr = NULL;

    // Open the file for input
    if((fp=fopen(Filename, "rb"))==NULL)
        return NULL;

    // Get # of script actions from file
    fread(&Num, 1, sizeof(long), fp);

    // Store number of actions in user supplied variable
    if(NumActions != NULL) *NumActions = Num;

    // Loop through each script action
    for(i=0;i<Num;i++) {

        // Allocate a script structure and link in
```

```
              Script = new sScript();
              if(ScriptPtr == NULL)
                ScriptRoot = Script;   // Assign root
              else
                ScriptPtr->Next = Script;
              ScriptPtr = Script;

              // Get type of action and # of entries
              fread(&Script->Type, 1, sizeof(long), fp);
              fread(&Script->NumEntries, 1, sizeof(long), fp);

              // Get entry data (if any)
              if(Script->NumEntries) {

                // Allocate entry array
                Script->Entries = new sScriptEntry[Script->NumEntries]();

                // Load in each entry
                for(j=0;j<Script->NumEntries;j++) {

                  // Get entry type and data
                  fread(&Script->Entries[j].Type, 1, sizeof(long), fp);
                  fread(&Script->Entries[j].IOValue, 1, sizeof(long), fp);

                  // Get text (if any)
                  if(Script->Entries[j].Type == _TEXT &&            \
                    Script->Entries[j].Length) {
                    // Allocate a buffer and get string
                    Script->Entries[j].Text =                       \
                            new char[Script->Entries[j].Length];
                    fread(Script->Entries[j].Text, 1,               \
                          Script->Entries[j].Length, fp);
                  }
                }
              }
            }

            fclose(fp);

            return ScriptRoot;
          }
```

Given the root script structure in a linked list, SaveScript will output each script structure's data, which includes the action number, the number of entries to follow, the entry data, and the optional text of a text entry. The entire linked list of sScript structure is written to the file.

The LoadScript function opens the script file in question and builds a linked list of sScript structures from the data it loads. sScriptEntry structures are allocated on-the-fly, as well as the sScript structures that construct the linked list. When complete, the LoadFile function sets NumActions to the number of script actions loaded and returns a pointer to the root script structure.

## Putting Together the cActionTemplate Class

You now understand the structure used for action templates and for containing the script data. Now, it's time to put them all together in order to create a working class that loads and processes scripts:

```
class cActionTemplate {
  private:
    long      m_NumActions;     // # of actions in template
    sAction *m_ActionParent;   // list of template actions

    // Functions for reading text (mainly used in actions)
    BOOL GetNextQuotedLine(char *Data, FILE *fp, long MaxSize);
    BOOL GetNextWord(char *Data, FILE *fp, long MaxSize);

  public:
    cActionTemplate();
    ~cActionTemplate();

    // Load and free an action template
    BOOL      Load(char *Filename);
    BOOL      Free();

    // Get # actions in template, action parent,
    // and specific action structure.
    long      GetNumActions();
    sAction *GetActionParent();
    sAction *GetAction(long Num);

    // Get a specific type of sScript structure
```

```
        sScript *CreateScriptAction(long Type);

        // Get info about actions and entries
        long    GetNumEntries(long ActionNum);
        sEntry  *GetEntry(long ActionNum, long EntryNum);

        // Expand action text using min/first/TRUE choice values
        BOOL    ExpandDefaultActionText(char *Buffer, sAction *Action);

        // Expand action text using selections
        BOOL    ExpandActionText(char *Buffer, sScript *Script);
};
```

The only functions in this code that you haven't seen in this chapter are
GetNextQuotedLine and GetNextWord. The GetNextQuotedLine function scans the file in
question for a line of text enclosed within quotes, while the GetNextWord function
reads in the next text word from a file. Both functions take a pointer to a data
buffer in which to store the text, the file access pointer, and the maximum size
of the data buffer (to avoid overflow):

```
BOOL cActionTemplate::GetNextQuotedLine(char *Data,                 \
                                        FILE *fp, long MaxSize)
{
  int c;
  long Pos = 0;

  // Read until a quote is reached (or EOF)
  while(1) {
    if((c = fgetc(fp)) == EOF)
      return FALSE;

    if(c == '"') {
      // Read until next quote (or EOF)
      while(1) {
        if((c = fgetc(fp)) == EOF)
          return FALSE;

        // Return text when 2nd quote found
        if(c == '"') {
          Data[Pos] = 0;
          return TRUE;
        }
```

```
          // Add acceptable text to line
          if(c != 0x0a && c != 0x0d) {
            if(Pos < MaxSize-1)
              Data[Pos++] = c;
          }
        }
      }
    }
  }
}


BOOL cActionTemplate::GetNextWord(char *Data, FILE *fp,           \
                                    long MaxSize)
{
  int   c;
  long Pos = 0;

  // Reset word to empty
  Data[0] = 0;

  // Read until an acceptable character found
  while(1) {
    if((c = fgetc(fp)) == EOF) {
      Data[0] = 0;
      return FALSE;
    }

    // Check for start of word
    if(c != 32 && c != 0x0a && c != 0x0d) {
      Data[Pos++] = c;

      // Loop until end of word (or EOF)
      while((c=fgetc(fp)) != EOF) {
        // Break on acceptable word separators
        if(c == 32 || c == 0x0a || c == 0x0d)
          break;

        // Add if enough room left
        if(Pos < MaxSize-1)
          Data[Pos++] = c;
      }
```

```
      // Add end of line to text
      Data[Pos] = 0;

      return TRUE;
    }
  }
}
```

Using the GetNextQuotedLine and GetNextWord functions, you can scan input files for
text that describes the actions, which is the purpose of the cActionTemplate::Load
function:

```
BOOL cActionTemplate::Load(char *Filename)
{
  FILE *fp;
  char Text[2048];
  sAction *Action, *ActionPtr = NULL;
  sEntry  *Entry;
  long i, j;

  // Free previous action structures
  Free();

  // Open the action file
  if((fp=fopen(Filename, "rb"))==NULL)
    return FALSE;

  // Keep looping until end of file found
  while(1) {
    // Get next quoted action
    if(GetNextQuotedLine(Text, fp, 2048) == FALSE)
      break;

    // Quit if no action text
    if(!Text[0])
      break;

    // Allocate an action structure and append it to list
    Action          = new sAction();
    Action->Next    = NULL;
    if(ActionPtr == NULL)
      m_ActionParent = Action;
```

```
else
  ActionPtr->Next = Action;
ActionPtr = Action;

// Copy action text
strcpy(Action->Text, Text);

// Store action ID
Action->ID = m_NumActions;

// Increase the number of actions loaded
m_NumActions++;

// Count the number of entries in the action
for(i=0;i<(long)strlen(Text);i++) {
  if(Text[i] == '~')
    Action->NumEntries++;
}

// Allocate and read in entries (if any)
if(Action->NumEntries) {
  Action->Entries = new sEntry[Action->NumEntries]();
  for(i=0;i<Action->NumEntries;i++) {
    Entry = &Action->Entries[i];

    // Get type of entry
    GetNextWord(Text, fp, 2048);

    // TEXT type, no data follows
    if(!stricmp(Text, "TEXT")) {
      // Set to text type
      Entry->Type = _TEXT;
    } else

    // INT type, get min and max values
    if(!stricmp(Text, "INT")) {
      // Set to INT type and allocate INT entry
      Entry->Type = _INT;

      // Get min value
      GetNextWord(Text, fp, 2048);
```

```
    Entry->lMin = atol(Text);

    // Get max value
    GetNextWord(Text, fp, 2048);
    Entry->lMax = atol(Text);
} else

// FLOAT type, get min and max values
if(!stricmp(Text, "FLOAT")) {
  // Set to FLOAT type and allocate FLOAT entry
  Entry->Type = _FLOAT;

    // Get min value
    GetNextWord(Text, fp, 2048);
    Entry->fMin = (float)atof(Text);

    // Get max value
    GetNextWord(Text, fp, 2048);
    Entry->fMax = (float)atof(Text);
} else

// BOOL type, no options
if(!stricmp(Text, "BOOL")) {
  // Set to BOOL type and allocate BOOL entry
  Entry->Type = _BOOL;
} else

// CHOICE type, get number of entries and entry's texts
if(!stricmp(Text, "CHOICE")) {
  // Set to CHOICE type and allocate CHOICE entry
  Entry->Type = _CHOICE;

    // Get the number of choices
    GetNextWord(Text, fp, 1024);
    Entry->NumChoices = atol(Text);
    Entry->Choices = new char[Entry->NumChoices];

    // Get each entry text
    for(j=0;j<Entry->NumChoices;j++) {
      GetNextQuotedLine(Text, fp, 2048);
      Entry->Choices[j] = new char[strlen(Text)+1];
```

```
                strcpy(Entry->Choices[j], Text);
            }
          }
        }
      }
    }

    fclose(fp);

    return TRUE;
}
```

Using the `cActionTemplate::Load` function, you can open a text file and begin scanning through it. With the beginning of each iteration, the next line of text enclosed in quotes (an action) is loaded in a new `sAction` structure and then examined for tilde characters. If tilde characters are found, the remaining information is loaded and parsed. This process continues until the end of the file is found.

Moving on, the next questionable function in `cActionTemplate` is `CreateScriptAction`; it takes an action number and returns an initialized `sScript` structure that is set up to store the number of entries to match the action. You can directly parse the `sScript` structure from this point on to access data contained within the actions and entries (which is how the MLS editor and samples do it):

```
sScript *cActionTemplate::CreateScriptAction(long Type)
{
    long i;
    sScript *Script;
    sAction *ActionPtr;

    // Make sure it's a valid action - Type is really the
    // action ID (from the list of actions already loaded).
    if(Type >= m_NumActions)
        return NULL;

    // Get pointer to action
    if((ActionPtr = GetAction(Type)) == NULL)
        return NULL;

    // Create new sScript structure
    Script = new sScript();
```

```
// Set type and number of entries (allocating a list)
Script->Type        = Type;
Script->NumEntries = ActionPtr->NumEntries;
Script->Entries     = new sScriptEntry[Script->NumEntries]();

// Set up each entry
for(i=0;i<Script->NumEntries;i++) {
  // Save type
  Script->Entries[i].Type = ActionPtr->Entries[i].Type;

  // Set up entry data based on type
  switch(Script->Entries[i].Type) {
    case _TEXT:
      Script->Entries[i].Text = NULL;
      break;

    case _INT:
      Script->Entries[i].lValue = ActionPtr->Entries[i].lMin;
      break;

    case _FLOAT:
      Script->Entries[i].fValue = ActionPtr->Entries[i].fMin;
      break;

    case _BOOL:
      Script->Entries[i].bValue = TRUE;
      break;

    case _CHOICE:
      Script->Entries[i].Selection = 0;
      break;
  }
}

  return Script;
}
```

## NOTE

I didn't include the script saving or loading functions because they are not part of the action templates. However, you can modify the saving and loading functions for each application as you see fit. This is also the case for this chapter's two sample programs, MlsEdit and MlsDemo, which you can find on the CD-ROM at the back of this book (both programs are in the \BookCode\Chap14 directory).

Last in cActionTemplate are the two final functions: ExpandDefaultActionText and ExpandActionText. Both functions take the action text and replace the tilde characters inside with more understandable text, such as an integer number or the selected multiple-choice text. The difference between the functions is that ExpandDefaultActionText expands text with any entry data; it simply picks the minimum values or first multiple-choice entry. ExpandActionText, expands the action text using the data contained in the supplied sScript structure. Both functions are used only in the script editor to make sense of the data contained with the action template and script structures—you can find the code for them on the CD-ROM (in the MLS Script Editor project).

With an understanding of the action templates and script structures, you can start piecing them together and putting MLS to good use, which all starts with the Mad Lib script editor.

# Working with the MLS Editor

An MLS system works only with numbers: the number that represents an action, the number of entries to follow, and numbers to represent the entry data. Computers work well with numbers, but we need more. You need to construct scripts in comprehensible lines of text and let a script editor convert the text you enter into a series of numerical representations that a script system can handle.

During the editing of a script, dealing with numbers is not for us, so the editor also has the job of loading and converting those numbers back into lines of text that is easy for us to read. So, to clear up matters, you only need to construct a script using a series of text commands, and let the script editor and engine convert those commands into their numerical representations and vice versa.

The Mad Lib script editor imports the text that represents the actions and provides the user with the ability to edit a list of actions and modify the blank entry spots with each action. Figure 14.3 shows the MLS editor I created for the book. The script list box, which contains the currently edited script, is at the top of the MLS application window. The actions from the action template are listed at the bottom of the window. The various buttons used to construct the scripts are spread around the window.

You will find using the script editor to be very intuitive. You have options for loading a set of actions, loading and saving a script, creating a new script, and adding, removing, and modifying script entries (as well as for moving their entries up or down the list). The actions used by the editor are stored in action template files.

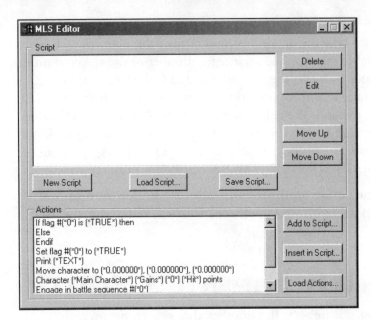

**Figure 14.3**

*This MLS editor contains all
the essentials for creating and
editing scripts.*

As for the actual script entries, the editor makes use of the sScript and sScriptEntry structures to store the current script being edited, and are saved and loaded just as you have already seen.

To start your MLS editing session, go ahead and load up an action template or use the default action template, which is titled default.mla (you can find it in the \BookCode\ Chap14\Data directory). Then you can begin adding, inserting, and editing script entries by using the respective buttons in the editor's application window. Table 14.2 explains what each button does in the script editor.

As you begin adding actions to the script (using Add to Script, or Insert in Script), notice that the action text is expanded and added to the script list box (the list box at the top of the script editor). The script actions are stored from the top down, with the root of the script being the topmost script action. Processing of the scripts starts at the top and continues downward, much like typical C/C++ code.

Notice that each time you add, insert, or edit a script entry, the Modify Action Entry dialog box appears (see Figure 14.4). You use this dialog box to modify the script action entries.

In the Modify Action Entry dialog box, you see various controls for modifying the script action entries. The dialog box provides two places to type text. You use the first one (at the top of the dialog box) to type an entry's text or the minimum and maximum

## Table 14.2  The MLS Editor Buttons

| Button | Function |
| --- | --- |
| Delete | Deletes the currently selected line from the script list box. |
| Edit | Edits the entries from the currently selected line from the script list box. |
| Move Up | Moves the currently selected script action up in the list box. |
| Move Down | Moves the currently selected script action down in the list box. |
| New Script | Removes all script actions from memory and starts with a fresh slate. |
| Load Script | Loads a script file from disk (files with an .MLS extension). |
| Save Script | Saves a script file to disk (files with an .MLS extension). |
| Add to Script | Adds the currently selected action (from the action list) to the end of the script list. This automatically opens the Modify Action Entry dialog box as well. |
| Insert in Script | Inserts the currently selected action (from the action list) into the selected line in the script list. Also opens the Modify Action Entry dialog box. |
| Load Actions | Loads a new action template file (files with an extension .MLA). This also forces the current script to be cleared. |

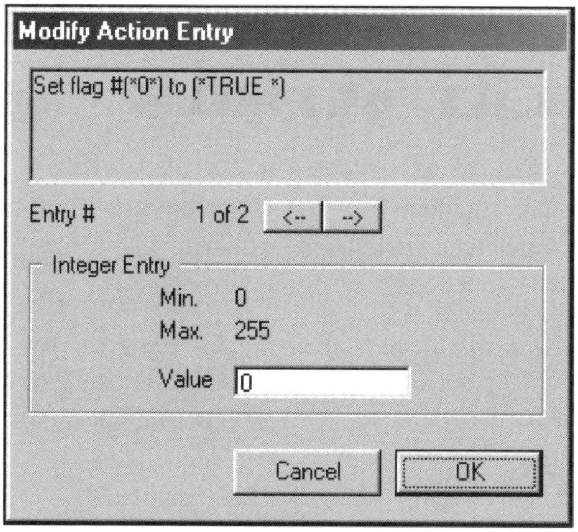

**Modify Action Entry**

Set flag #(*0*) to (*TRUE *)

Entry #　　1 of 2　<-- | -->

Integer Entry
Min.　0
Max.　255
Value　0

Cancel | OK

**Figure 14.4**

*Use the Modify Action Entry dialog box to quickly navigate and modify the script's action entries.*

ranges for values; in the second one, you type values relevant to the entry. Boolean values have two radio buttons, one to select a TRUE value and another to select a FALSE value. The dialog box provides a list box for multiple-choice selections.

A few controls that are common to each type of entry are at the top of the Modify Action Entry dialog box. First is the box that displays the action text (with the selected entries expanded in the text). Next is an Entry #, a text box that displays the entry number currently being editing, as well as the number of entries in the action. To navigate the entries, you use two buttons—the previous entry button (represented by an arrow pointing left) and the next entry button (represented by an arrow pointing right). Clicking either button forces the current entry to be updated and the next entry's data to be displayed.

At the bottom of the Modify Action Entry dialog box are two more buttons—OK and Cancel. The Cancel button is displayed only when you add an action. When you select an action to edit from the list, the Cancel button is not shown, which means that all the changes you make to an entry are used whenever OK is clicked, so make sure that you don't modify anything if that's not your intention. Clicking OK accepts all entry data and adds, inserts, or modifies the action selected in the MLS Editor dialog box.

The script editor comes with a sample action template and script to help you get started. The real power comes when you start constructing your own action templates, tailored for your game project. After you create the action templates and construct your script, you are ready to start using them in your own project.

> **NOTE**
> The code for the MLS editor is on the **CD-ROM** at the back of this book (look for \BookCode\Chap14\MLSEdit\).

# Executing Mad Lib Scripts

Whew! I can honestly say the hardest part is over, as executing the scripts is child's play at this point. You can now toss the action templates out the door because you work with only the sScript and sScriptEntry structures from here on out.

The first step to working with a script is to load it into memory, which you accomplish using the LoadScript function (refer also to the section "Creating Script Entries" for more on this function):

```
long NumActions;
sScript *LoadedScript = LoadScript("Script.mls", &NumActions);
```

From this point on, your game engine just iterates the script-linked list in order to execute each action. This requires a bit of hard-coding because the actions are known only by numbers at this point (so you must know what each action does). Here's an example that iterates the preceding loaded script and looks for Print actions (action 0), which contain a single entry (the text to print):

```
sScript *ScriptPtr = LoadedScript; // Start at root

// Loop through all script actions in list
while(ScriptPtr != NULL) {
  // Is it an action 0?
  if(ScriptPtr->Type == 0) {
    // This action definitely has one entry, the text.
    // Display the text in a message box
    MessageBox(NULL, ScriptPtr->Entries[0].Text, "TEXT", MB_OK);
  }

  // Go to next action in script
  ScriptPtr = ScriptPtr->Next;
}
```

Although the preceding is nothing more than a few lines of code, it demonstrates the awesome potential of processing the scripts. With a little ingenuity, you could use MLS to handle some major scripting duties.

How about using conditional if...then...else statements? You know, those statements that determine whether a condition is true or false and, depending on the outcome, process a different sequence of actions. Take for example the following C code:

```
BOOL GameFlags[256];  // Some game flags defined in the game

if(GameFlags[0] == TRUE) {
  // Print a message and set flag to FALSE
  MessageBox(NULL, "It's TRUE!", "Message", MB_OK);
  GameFlags[0] = FALSE;
} else {
  // Print a message
  MessageBox(NULL, "It's FALSE.", "Message", MB_OK);
}
```

Based on the value contained in the GameFlags array, a different block of code is processed. By creating a few actions and a slight reworking of the script processing code, you could enjoy the benefits of using if...then...else statements in MLS as well. First, check out the action template:

```
"If GameFlag ~ equals ~ then"
  INT 0 255
  BOOL
"Else"
"EndIf"
"Set GameFlag ~ to ~"
  INT 0 255
  BOOL
"Print ~"
  TEXT
```

There is nothing special here because the real work is done in the script-processing code:

```
// pScript = pre-loaded script that contains the following:
//   "If GameFlag (0) equals (TRUE) then"
//      "Print (It's TRUE!)"
//      "Set GameFlag (0) to (FALSE)"
//   "Else"
//      "Print (It's FALSE.)"
//   "EndIf"

// Action processing functions
sScript *Script_IfThen(sScript *Script);
sScript *Script_Else(sScript *Script);
sScript *Script_EndIf(sScript *Script);
sScript *Script_SetFlag(sScript *Script);
sScript *Script_Print(sScript *Script);

// The script action execution structure
typedef struct sScriptProcesses {
  sScript *(*Func)(sScript *ScriptPtr);
} sScriptProcesses;

// List of script action function structures
sScriptProcesses ScriptProcesses[] = {
  { Script_IfThen      },
  { Script_Else        },
  { Script_EndIf       },
```

```
    { Script_SetFlag    },
    { Script_Print      }
};

BOOL GameFlags[256];   // The games flags array

void RunScript(sScript *pScript)
{
  // Clear the GameFlags array to FALSE for this example
  for(short i=0;i<256;i++)
    GameFlags[i] = FALSE;

  // Scan through script and process functions
  while(pScript != NULL) {
    // Call script function and break on NULL return value.
    // Any other return type is the pointer to the next
    // function, which is typically pScript->Next.
    pScript = ScriptProcesses[pScript->Type].Func(pScript);
  }
}


sScript *Script_IfThen(sScript *Script)
{
  BOOL Skipping; // Flag is skipping script actions

  // See if a flag matches second entry
  if(g_Flags[Script->Entries[0].lValue % 256] ==              \
             Script->Entries[1].bValue)
    Skipping = FALSE;
  else
    Skipping = TRUE;

  // At this point, Skipping states if the script actions
  // need to be skipped due to a conditional if..then statement.
  // Actions are further processed if skipped = FALSE, looking
  // for an else to flip the skip mode, or an endif to end
  // the conditional block.

  // Go to next action to process
  Script = Script->Next;
```

```
    while(Script != NULL) {
      // if Else, flip skip mode
      if(Script->Type == 1)
        Skipping = (Skipping == TRUE) ? FALSE : TRUE;

      // break on EndIf
      if(Script->Type == 2)
        return Script->Next;

      // Process script function in conditional block
      // making sure to skip actions when condition not met.
      if(Skipping == TRUE)
        Script = Script->Next;
      else {
        if((Script = ScriptProcesses[Script->Type].Func(Script)) == NULL)
          return NULL;
      }
    }
  return NULL; // end of script reached
}


sScript *Script_SetFlag(sScript *Script)
{
  // Set a Boolean flag
  GameFlags[Script->Entries[0].lValue % 256] =                    \
            Script->Entries[1].bValue;
}


sScript *Script_Else(sScript *Script) { return Script->Next;  }
sScript *Script_EndIf(sScript *Script) { return Script->Next; }

sScript *Script_Print(sScript *Script)
{
  MessageBox(NULL, Script->Entries[0].Text, "Text", MB_OK);
  return Script->Next;
}
```

You can see that the real magic is in the Script_IfThen statement, which is a recursive
function that processes all script actions contained within a pair of if...then and EndIf
actions. The Else action does a simple job of switching processing modes (from no
processing to processing), based on the original value of the Skipping variable.

Now that is power, and if you need a little more convincing, I suggest that you check out some later chapters that use the MLS system, such as Chapter 16, "Controlling Players and Characters," and Chapter 20, "Putting Together a Full Game." Both chapters demonstrate the use of scripts when interacting with game characters.

# Applying Scripts to Games

From the beginning of your project, expect to implement scripts in every game-related detail. For example, scripts come in handy when dealing with dialogue and cinemas all the way down to spell effects and inventory handling. In fact, creating your game engine to accept scripts for the majority of in-game data produces a very open-source and efficient project.

In Chapter 20, you learn just how to apply the scripts to your various game components, such as the combat and inventory system. As for now, you might want to become familiar with the whole script concept by checking out the sample program MlsDemo, which is on this book's CD-ROM.

# Wrapping Up Scripting

The scripting method introduced in this chapter is very powerful when used correctly, and in most cases, will be just the right system for your game project. Advanced readers who want to develop their own "real" script language (one that resembles C++, for example) might want to acquire a good book on compilers, specifically one that utilizes lexx and yacc (two programs that process text and grammar). One such book, aptly titled *lexx & yacc,* is a great guide to learning the basics on creating a script-parsing language processor. Turn to Appendix C, "Recommended Reading," for more information on the book.

If you are intrigued by the power behind the MLS system, before beginning your project, you might create a set of action templates that will carry you through the entire game. In this chapter, I discussed some of the simpler techniques for doing so, but I'm sure that you can build on this information and come up with other great uses for MLS.

## Programs on the CD-ROM

Two programs that demonstrate the code discussed in this chapter are located on the CD-ROM at the back of this book. You can find the following programs in the \BookCode\Chap14\ directory:

- ◆ **MlsEdit.** A Mad Lib Script editor program that is perfect for putting together scripts for your project.
  Location: \BookCode\Chap14\MlsEdit\.

- ◆ **MlsDemo.** A small project that demonstrates the parsing of Mad Lib Scripts created with the MLS editor.
  Location: \BookCode\Chap14\MlsDemo\.

# CHAPTER 15

# Defining and Using Objects

**B**ig things, little things, round things, and all other sorts of things—the world is full of objects of every size, shape, and description. I'm not just talking about any world here—your gaming world needs to be packed with useful items. Trying to keep track of those useful objects and what they actually do in your role-playing game is a major chore, but with a little knowledge, you can tackle this job blindfolded!

In this chapter, you learn how to do the following:

- Define objects in your game
- Create a master list of items
- Use inventory systems to manage items

# Defining Objects for Your Game

Frantically I dig through my sack. I know that I put that healing potion in there yesterday; where could it have gone? What a time to lose something—in the midst of a battle, taking hits from all sides, and now that I have a moment, I can't recover my health!

Let's see, there's my dagger, that extra shield, a handful of gold pieces, something I don't recognize, and . . . oh, there it is—my healing potion! How in the world did I manage to collect all this junk? Oh well, I'll worry about that later; for now, I need to take a gulp of elixir and get back to the job of slaying monsters.

Thankfully my ordeal wasn't really life threatening; I really only had to pause the game for a moment, sort my inventory list, and locate the appropriate potion. Fully refreshed and game resumed, I managed to fight on in true warrior spirit!

During the course of a game, you're bound to pick up a few items (also called *objects*), each serving its unique purpose. When creating your game, each object must be accounted for, each designed for a specific use. Weapons, armor, or even healing items, all need definition. They need form and function.

Form and function—two words to live by when defining an object. *Form* refers to appearance and identity—what an object looks like, what it feels like, how big it is, how much it weighs, and so on. *Function* refers to purpose; every object has a purpose —money buys things, swords aid in an attack, and healing potions heal wounds.

In this section, you learn how to define an object's form and function in a format readily usable in your game project.

## Using Form in Objects

Although essential in order for us to visually comprehend an object, form means nothing to a computer—for which an object just needs to be represented by a graphics image or a 3-D model. In Chapter 6, "Drawing with DirectX Graphics," you learn how easy it is to load a bitmap image or an .X file that contains a 3-D mesh, so why not go with using those bitmaps or meshes to define the form of an object?

Assume that you want to create a weapon, or more specifically, a sword. In a 3-D game (for example, the one I describe at the beginning of this chapter), you want players to be able to see the characters holding swords and to examine the swords closely by zooming in. In addition, to show which weapon is equipped (being held), you want to display a bitmap of the sword onscreen. You need only a single mesh and a single bitmap image (see Figure 15.1) to represent the sword.

I know what you're thinking—that's a big, heavy sword in Figure 15.1! In the real world, a sword is "big and heavy." For that matter, you don't want just anyone to be able to wield it. A sword might weigh about five pounds and be about four feet

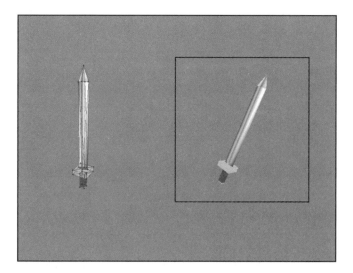

**Figure 15.1**

*You can use the mesh on the left for in-game play (with the player holding it) and in an inventory list (to examine the sword). The bitmap image on the right is displayed during the game to signify that the player is indeed holding a sword.*

long. If your game is concerned with the physical properties of an object, each item in the game can be assigned dimensions and weight. I opt to measure size in cubic feet.

With this bit of information, you can start entering the item information into your game. Start by creating a structure that will hold the information for the sword (and every other item for that matter):

**NOTE**
Why would you bother with weight and size in your game? For one thing, do you want a tiny guy or gal wielding a huge sword? What about when the little character tries to put a four-foot sword in a one-cubic foot backpack? Quite a few games dismiss these problems, but if you want a realistic edge in your game, consider weight and size.

```
typedef struct sItem
{
  char Name[32];           // A short name for the item
  char Description[128];   // A description of item
  float Weight;            // Weight (in lbs.)
  float Size;              // Size (in cubic feet)
  char MeshFilename[16];   // .X mesh filename
  char ImageFilename[16];  // .BMP filename
} sItem;
```

To quickly define the Sword object, declare it as follows:

```
sItem Sword = {
  "Sword", "A big heavy sword.",
  5.0f, 4.0f,
  "Sword.x", "Sword.bmp" };
```

At this point, the sword is ready for use! Well, not really, because at this point, you've only assigned the physical properties of the sword (along with the filenames to use for the mesh and image). The game engine doesn't have enough information about the item in order to use it. That's where function comes in.

# Defining the Functions of Objects

If you were to hand an object to a child (or to anyone for that matter), the child would be able to find some use for it, even if it's not the correct use. Although it might be great to be able to do all kinds of things with objects in a game, that just will not do for your purposes. The items (objects) in your game will be used for specific purposes, which can be in one of the following categories (note that the list is not comprehensive, but is a starting place for ideas):

- **Accessory.** Rings, necklaces, belts, and any other form of wearable equipment that can aid an adventurer are classified as accessories. Sometimes an accessory is a magical piece of equipment that helps boost the abilities of the wearer.

- **Armor.** Taking a blow is nothing—if you're wearing the proper protection, that is. Armor can be any form of protective gear, from a full suit of armor to a pair of boots.

- **Collection.** Any item that doesn't serve an actual purpose is considered to be a collection piece. These can be items that are important to the game story in some way or that really have no definitive use. Items such as a picture, small ornamental figurine, or chair are considered collection items.

- **Edible.** Clam cakes, clam pies, clam alamode, creamed clam, or BBQ clam— whatever your fancy. Your gaming denizens are bound to get hungry, and whatever they can find and consume is classified as edible, even potions and herbs.

- **Money.** Everybody deals with the big M, no matter what form it takes—coins, bills, clam shells, and so on. Games do not require denominations—one gold coin is as good as the next, and the more coins you have, the better.

- **Transportation.** Whether by bus, boat, plane, or hang glider, people sure know how to get around, and items that can transport belong to characters in the game. A boat can't be lugged around, but your game recognizes a character as the item's owner by noting so in the character's inventory.

- **Weapon.** Whether it's a sword, rock, or piece of lint, some things are just more suitable for dealing out damage.

- **Other.** Anything that doesn't fit into the preceding categories is considered "other."

Your game engine determines what each item does, based on each item's category. For example, weapons can be equipped (worn), whereas edible items can be consumed. You can add subcategories to each as needed to make dealing with items even easier. For example, a healing potion, although edible, can be categorized as a healing item. When your game engine sees a healing item, it knows immediately to restore some level of health to the character.

Each item has additional information for usage, however, so you can't stop here. Weapons have a strength attribute, which increases a character's ability to deal out damage, a healing potion restores heath, and a piece of armor reduces damage to a character during attacks. Now, take a look at what each category of items accomplishes.

# Weapons

Characters have the potential to deal out damage with their bare hands. The more powerful the character, the more damage he can administer. Put a weapon in that character's hands and the amount of damage meted out increases. Some weapons do more damage than others, so finding the perfect weapon is more than enough reason to keep adventuring.

Weapons can also have more than one use. In the mythical sense, an enchanted sword can slash through demon hides and, at the same time, cast a potent fireball spell. I refer to such extra functions of an item as *specials*.

Not just everybody can wield every weapon, however; there are some restrictions. Size and weight is one restriction, and how much fun would it be to hand a beginner the most powerful weapon in the game? For that reason, you introduce usage restrictions (you find out more on usage restrictions in the section "Usage Restrictions," later in this chapter).

Getting back on track, some weapons can do more damage than others. The amount of damage a weapon can cause is measured as a number, called an *attack modifier*. The higher the number, the more damage the weapon does. Also, some weapons are easier to wield, so you can hit your targets more often. To measure just how much easier a weapon can hit its target, you use a *to-hit modifier*. The higher a weapon's to-hit modifier, the better chance a character has to hit a target using that weapon. You'll read more about using modifiers and how those modifiers relate to characters in Chapter 16, "Controlling Players and Characters."

Some weapons can also be classified in special groups, called *weapons groups*. Certain weapons tend to do more damage to certain creatures than other weapons—for example, using a fire-enchanted sword against an ice-based monster.

> **NOTE**
>
> A *modifier* is something that changes a character's attributes in some way. A *damage modifier*, for example, increases or decreases the amount of damage they do.

Finally, weapons can be categorized into subgroups such as *hand-to-hand* or *ranged*. Regardless of the type of weapon, each one has a *range of use*. Swords can hit the targets in front of them, while a crossbow may hit a target 40 feet away. In addition, weapons may be able to hit more than one target at once. These are all things to take into consideration when designing weapons.

# Armor

The more protection, the better, and in your game every little piece of armor helps. Armor helps add resistance to damage. This resistance amount is called the *defense modifier*. Just like weapons, armor has special uses and usage restrictions and belongs to *armor groups*.

Armor can be split into multiple subcategories, such as helmets, chest and abdomen protection, leggings, boots, gloves, and so on.

# Accessories

As mentioned earlier, accessories usually have a specific use. A magic ring can be worn to gain the ability to become invisible. This ability might always be in use once the ring is donned, or it may have to be activated. Accessories can also act like armor; they can increase the resistance to some aspect of the game—for example, making it harder for the wearer to be poisoned.

# Edibles

Edible items usually come in a few flavors (pun intended). Food items sustain life, healing items increase health, and poisonous items decrease health. Again, special uses are in effect, but because there are few uses for edible items, you can hard-code those into your game engine.

# Collections

A collectable object is usually docile; it's needed only for some small aspect of the game. For example, if a character gives you a picture of himself to deliver to a girl in a neighboring town (and for no other purpose), the picture is considered a collection item. Collection items simply move some part of the game story forward. Perhaps the character delivering the picture will receive, in turn, a special item from the girl in the next town.

# Transportation

Getting around on foot is slow and tiring, so other forms of transportation might be needed. The purpose of transportation items is to change the way the characters move around (typically around the map). Transportation can also open up new areas in the game that were previously not accessible. For instance, your character's newly acquired boat can now be used to sail across the lake to an isolated island, or maybe that horse you saw in a nearby town will help you cross a barren desert safely.

## Others

"Other" items are pretty much useless because they don't have a defined use. However, don't throw them out. At the least, they can perform some type of action as defined by the engine. For instance, depending on how well you do in combat, your character could be awarded medals. While these medals are cool to look at, they serve no purpose in the game.

# Adding Function to Objects

In the earlier section "Defining the Functions of Objects," you can see how much is needed to define the function of an object. Luckily, because each object is categorized as one thing or another, not all the information is needed—swords do damage, whereas armor prevents it—so there's no need to mix damage and protection data.

## Item Categories and Values

In reality, you'll want to categorize each item specifically to fit your game engine, just as I did in the section "Defining the Functions of Objects." Each category of item is numbered for reference (1 is a weapon, 2 is armor, and so on). Each category has a value associated with it, one that determines the modifier (attack or defend), the special use, the healing or damaging value, and an attached script. That's right. Items can use scripting to increase their capabilities.

Except for an attached script, you can represent all values with a single variable, one that represents the modifier amount, healing value, and so on. At this point, the following two variables can then be added to the sItem structure previously created:

```
// ... previous sItem info
long Category;   // 1-5 representing item category shown above
long Value;      // Modifier, health increase, etc.
// .. More sItem info
```

**TIP**

You can use an enumerator value to represent the categories in the sItem structure:

```
enum ItemCategories { WEAPON=0,ARMOR,SHIELD,HEALING,OTHER };
```

## Assigning Value to Items

Everything in the game is of value. Assigning each item a monetary value helps to determine what a player can buy or sell and at what price. You don't want to clutter each item with multiple amounts; just pick a single amount that the character should pay to buy the item. When being sold, the same item will have an amount lower than what your character would pay to buy it. For instance, an item can be sold for half the price your character paid for it.

An item's value can be inserted in the sItem structure as follows:

```
// ... previous sItem info
long Price;  // Buying price of item
```

## Item Flags

Sometimes, you will not want the character to be able to sell an item—important magic items, for example. A bit flag will take care of this, and while you're at it, add a few more bit flags. Table 15.1 contains a list of possible flags you can use.

Each bit flag is contained within a variable in the sItem structure:

```
long Flags; // Item bit flags
// ... more sItem data
```

### Table 15.1   Item Bit Flags

| Flag | Description |
| --- | --- |
| SELLABLE | These items can be sold in shops. |
| CANDROP | These items can be dropped. Don't use this flag with important items if you don't want characters to drop those items. |
| USEONCE | These items can be used only once. Once used, they disappear. |
| UNKNOWN | These items are unknown. You must identify them in order to use them correctly. You can find examples of this kind in Sega's online masterpiece game, *Phantasy Star Online*. |

You can then represent each flag as an enum value (with a maximum of 32 flags). To set, clear, or check a flag, use the following macros (using the macros, v represents the item flag variable, and f is the flag):

```
enum {
  SELLABLE = 0,  // Bit 0
  CANDROP,       // Bit 1
  USEONCE,       // Bit 2
  UNKNOWN        // Bit 3
};

#define SetItemFlag(v,f)   (v |= (1 << f))
#define ClearItemFlag(v,f) (v &= ~(1 << f))
#define CheckItemFlag(v,f) (v & (1 << f))

// Example using macros and flags
long ItemFlags = 0;

// Set item flags to sellable and item can be dropped
SetItemFlag(ItemFlags, SELLABLE);
SetItemFlag(ItemFlags, CANDROP);

// Check if the item is dropable and display a message
if(CheckItemFlag(ItemFlags, CANDROP))
  MessageBox(NULL, "Can Drop Item", "Item", MB_OK);

ClearItemFlag(ItemFlags, SELLABLE); // Clear sellable flag
```

## Usage Restrictions

Certain characters in your game might not be able to use a specific item. A magic user, for example, can't wield a huge two-handed battleaxe, and a barbarian can't wield a wizard's staff. In such cases, where only certain characters are allowed to use certain items, you need to restrict usage to specific character classes.

> **NOTE**
>
> A *character class* is a classification or grouping of characters based on their race or profession. For example, all humans belong to the same class, but to be more specific, human fighters are considered a separate class from human wizards (or just fighters and wizards—who says they all have to be human).

To represent the usage restrictions of an item, another variable is introduced to the sItem structure, one that tracks 32 bits of information. Each bit represents a single class, which means that you can track up to 32 classes. If an item is usable by a certain class, that respective bit is set; if an item is restricted in use by the character's class, the appropriate bit is cleared.

Here's the addition to the sItem structure, which handles usage restrictions:

```
long Usage;  // Usage restrictions
// ... other sItem data
```

To make setting, clearing, and retrieving a usage restriction class bit easier, you can use the following macros (v represents the flag variable, and c is the class number ranging from 0 to 31):

```
#define SetUsageBit(v,c)   (v |= (1 << c))
#define ClearUsageBit(v,c) (v &= ((~(1 << c))
#define CheckUsageBit(v,c) (v & (1 << c))


// Examples using macros
long Flags = 0;
SetUsageBit(Flags, 5);        // Set class 5 bit
if(CheckUsageBit(Flags, 5)) // Check class 5 bit
  MessageBox(NULL, "Usage Set", "Bit", MB_OK);
ClearUsageBit(Flags, 5);     // Clear class 5 bit
```

Using the preceding macros (SetUsageBit, ClearUsageBit, and CheckUsageBit), you can quickly check whether a character is allowed to use or equip the item based on his character class. For example, this game places wizards in class 1 and fighters in class 2. When the wizard tries to equip a broadsword (one that has the class 1 bit clear), the game engine informs the player that the wizard cannot use the item.

## Attaching Scripts to Items

To make items more versatile, you can attach scripts to items. A script is triggered any time an item is used, whether it is a potion being consumed, a sword being used in a round of combat, or a user activating the special usage of an item (by using a magic wand, for example).

> **TIP**
>
> When using scripts, it's good form to use a specialized action template better suited for items. Refer to Chapter 14, "Implementing Scripts," for more information on creating action templates and using the script editor.

At this point, you need to store only the script's filename in the sItem structure:

```
// .. previous sItem data
char ScriptFilename[16];  // .mls script filename
```

## Meshes and Images

You want your game's players to see what an item looks like, which means that you need to load a 2-D image or a 3-D mesh to represent the object. You achieve this using the following additions to the sItem structure:

```
// .. previous sItem data
char MeshFilename[16];   // .X mesh filename
char ImageFilename[16];  // .bmp image filename
} sItem;  // Close structure
```

## The Final Item Structure

At this point, the sItem structure is ready for use! Here it is again in its entirety (including supporting macros):

```
enum ItemCategories { WEAPON=0,ARMOR,SHIELD,HEALING,OTHER };


#define SetUsageBit(v,c)    (v |= (1 << c))
#define ClearUsageBit(v,c) (v &= ((~(1 << c))
#define CheckUsageBit(v,c) (v & (1 << c))


enum {
  SELLABLE = 0,  // Bit 0
  CANDROP,       // Bit 1
  USEONCE,       // Bit 2
  UNKNOWN        // Bit 3
};


#define SetItemFlag(v,f)    (v |= (1 << f))
#define ClearItemFlag(v,f) (v &= ~(1 << f))
#define CheckItemFlag(v,f) (v & (1 << f))


typedef struct sItem
{
```

```
    char Name[32];              // A short name for the item
    char Description[128];   // A description of item
    float Weight;              // Weight (in lbs.)
    float Size;                // Size (in cubic feet)
    long Category;             // Category of item
    long Value;                // Modifier, health increase, etc.
    long Price;                // Buying price of item
    long Flags;                // Item bit flags
    long Usage;                // Usage restrictions

    char ScriptFilename[16];   // .mls script filename
    char MeshFilename[16];     // .X mesh filename
    char ImageFilename[16];    // .bmp image filename
} sItem;
```

With the complete sItem structure in place, it's time to get back to building the
sword item. Say that the sword item uses a +10 modifier on damage (which means
that you add 10 to the damage factor in combat). The sword normally sells for 200
monetary units in the game, and only fighter classes (class two) can use it:

```
// Character class definitions
#define WIZARD    1
#define WARRIOR   2

sItem Sword = {
  "Sword", "A big heavy sword",        // name and description
  5.0f, 4.0f,                          // weight and size
  WEAPON, 200, SELLABLE | CANDROP,   // category, price, and flags
  (1 << WARRIOR),                      // usage class 2 (warrior)
  "", "Sword.x", "Sword.bmp"          // Script, mesh, image files
};
```

Now that the sword item is
defined, you can use it in the
game. But what good is a single
item? Your game world is going
to be packed with items! How
can you possibly deal with all
those objects?

> **NOTE**
>
> The script, mesh, and image filenames are
> limited to 16 bytes, which means that the
> sItem structure will store only the actual
> filename and not the path to the appropri-
> ate file. Also, although the sItem structure
> stores the filenames, you are responsible
> for loading the files to use in the game.

# The Master Item List

Every item in your game needs to be defined, and to keep things tidy, you need to keep all item descriptions in a *master item list* (*MIL*). Think of the MIL as a catalog of objects, much like the one shown in Figure 15.2. Each object is numbered for reference, and only one of each item is shown.

Anytime you need a new object or need to retrieve the attributes of a specific object, you consult the MIL. At a basic level, your game's MIL can be stored as an array of sItem structures or a single sequential file composed from a list of item structures (similar to the one shown in Figure 15.3). How can you go about creating your own MIL? Well, let's take a closer look.

## Constructing the MIL

The following code bit creates a small item structure that contains the item's name, weight, and size. You will use this structure to construct a simple MIL:

```
typedef struct sItem
{
  char Name[32];   // Name of item
  float Weight;    // Weight (in lbs.)
  float Size;      // Size (in cubic ft.)
};
```

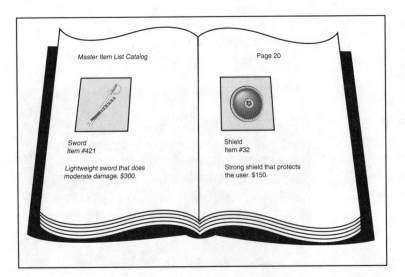

**Figure 15.2**

*Much like a department store catalog, a master item list helps you keep every object in the world in order.*

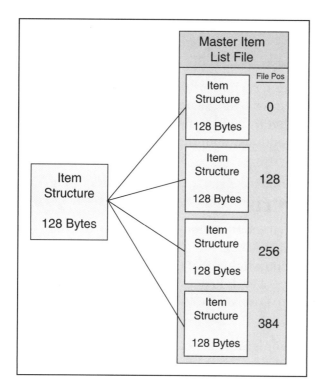

**Figure 15.3**

*A sequential MIL file keeps track of every item in your game. Each item's data is fixed in size, ensuring that you can quickly access the file when you need to retrieve data.*

From here, say that you want to store five items in the MIL, all represented in an array of sItem structures:

```
sItem Items[5] = {
   { "Big Sword",   5.0f, 4.0f },
   { "Small Sword", 2.0f, 2.0f },
   { "Magic Wand",  0.5f, 1.0f },
   { "Rock",        1.0f, 0.5f },
   { "Potion",      0.5f, 0.5f }
};
```

Now that you have defined your MIL (using an array of sItem structures), you may want to save the list out to a file for later retrieval. Such is the case if you are using a separate program that creates the MIL file for you, much like the program you'll see in the upcoming section, "Using the MIL Editor." As for here, take a look at the following bit of code that will create a file (called items.mil) and save the Items array to the file:

```
FILE *fp=fopen("items.mil", "wb");

for(short i=0;i<5;i++)
```

```
      fwrite(&Items[i], 1, sizeof(sItem), fp);
   fclose(fp);
```

Although short and to the point, the preceding example for creating a MIL file is wholly unusable in a real-world application such as a role-playing game. Item descriptions need to contain much more information, and you could theoretically work with thousands of items. Doing all that by hand is a waste of time. What you need is an item editor to help you create and maintain the MIL . . . and, so, behold the *MIL Editor*.

## Using the MIL Editor

The need for quick-and-easy item creation gave birth to the Master Item List Editor (MIL). Much like the MLS Editor discussed in Chapter 14, "Implementing Scripts," the MIL Editor consists of a single application window that enables you to navigate through a list of items, editing the attributes of each item as you go. You can save and load MILs, but the list of item attributes remains fixed (until you reprogram them for your own purposes).

The complete source code to the MIL Editor is included on the CD-ROM that comes with this book (look for \BookCode\Chap15\MILEdit). When you start the MIL Editor found on the CD, the Master Item List Editor dialog box appears as shown in Figure 15.4. The Master Item List Editor dialog box consists of a list box that contains each item in the list, plus buttons to edit each item's information and to save and load an item list. The list provides room for 1,024 items, which means that you can store an item number within a 16-bit variable (ranging from 0 to 1,023).

To begin using the Master Item List Editor, locate and execute the MILEdit.exe file (look in \BookCode\Chap15\MILEdit). At the Master Item List Editor dialog box, you can perform the following steps to add or edit items, and then save them to disk:

1. Select an item from the Item List by double-clicking the item (or selecting the item and clicking the Edit button), or add an item by clicking the Add button. The Modify Item dialog box appears (shown in Figure 15.5).

2. Edit the appropriate fields in the Modify Item dialog box.

3. When you finish editing, click OK to apply the changes and return to the Master Item List Editor dialog.

4. To make the changes permanent, click Save on the Master Item List Editor dialog box, and in the Save MIL File dialog box, enter a filename and save the MIL to disk.

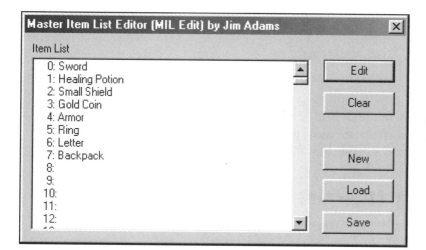

**Figure 15.4**

*The Master Item List Editor is used to create and edit your game's objects. The list of items shown here has eight items defined.*

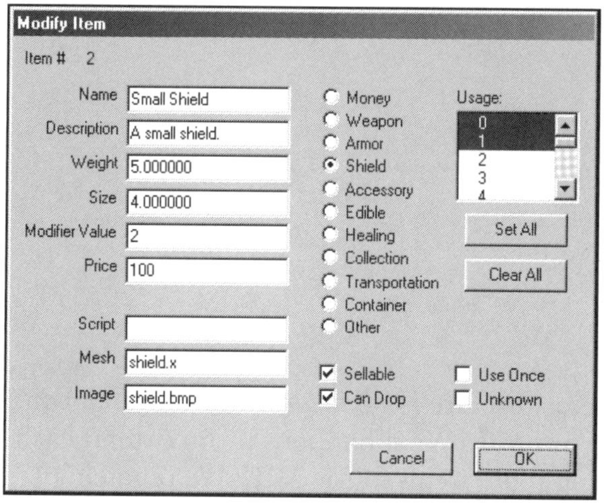

**Figure 15.5**

*The Modify Item dialog box enables you to modify each item's vital information.*

> **NOTE**
>
> Loading a MIL is just as easy as saving one; just click the Load button on the Master Item List Editor dialog box. When the Load MIL File dialog box appears, select the file you want to load.
>
> MIL files typically use a .MIL file extension. You can use a different extension for your lists, but the sample programs for this book use .MIL.

The MIL Editor uses the same version of the sItem structure shown earlier in this chapter, but I added some extra item categories. Those extra categories are *Shield, Healing,* and *Container* (a container object such as a backpack). Here these extra categories are added to the ItemCategories enum list, shown previously in the section "Items Categories and Values":

```
enum ItemCategories
{
```

```
MONEY = 0, WEAPON,     ARMOR,
SHIELD,    ACCESSORY,  EDIBLE,
HEALING,   COLLECTION, TRANSPORTATION,
CONTAINER, OTHER
};
```

If you decide to modify the MIL Editor to use different item attributes or categories, modify the sItem structure as well. When you're ready, you can start using the item data you created in your game project.

# Accessing Items from the MIL

Once you have a MIL, you can load the entire list into an array of sItem structures using the following code:

```
sItem Items[1024];   // Array of sItem structures

// Open the Default.mil file
FILE *fp = fopen("Default.mil", "rb");

// Read in all items
for(short i=0;i<1024;i++)
  fread(&Items[i], 1, sizeof(sItem), fp);

// Close file
fclose(fp);
```

At this point, I'm assuming that your item structure is relatively small and that you are using no more than 1,024 items in your MIL. What happens if you extend each item's sItem structure or you begin storing more items in the MIL? We're talking about some serious memory usage.

To avoid loading each and every single item in memory from the MIL at once, you can access individual items directly from the MIL. Because the size of each item structure is fixed, you can access each item's data by moving the file pointer to the appropriate position and reading in the structure, as in the following code bit:

```
// ItemNum = reference # of item to load
sItem Item;

// Open the MIL file titled items.mil
FILE *fp=fopen("items.mil", "rb");
```

```
// Seek to the appropriate position in file
// based on the size of the sItem structure and
// the number of the item to load.
fseek(fp, sizeof(sItem) * ItemNum, SEEK_SET);

// Read in the item structure
fread(&Item, 1, sizeof(sItem), fp);

// Close the file
fclose(fp);
```

And there you go—quick and easy access to every item in the MIL! Now, it's time to do something with those items.

# Managing Items with Inventory Control Systems

With your items ready to be scattered around the world, it's only a matter of time before players start trying to pick up everything that isn't nailed down. When that happens, the players will need a way of managing the items, which includes using an *inventory control system* (an ICS for short) to sort things out.

Don't be fooled; an ICS doesn't just apply to player characters. It applies to the entire world. Items can belong to a map, a character, or even to a different item (a backpack with other items inside it, for example). That means items need to be assigned *ownership*. In addition, an owner can have *multiple instances* of an object—coins, for example.

An owner's collection of items is called an *inventory list*, and any object can belong within this list (and as many instances of the object as well). The relationships between owners, inventory lists, and quantities are illustrated in Figure 15.6. (*Note:* Don't think of items as belonging to an owner; rather, think of owners as having a collection of items.)

The ICS works hand in hand with the master item list. Where the MIL contains only a single, unique instance of each object in the world, the ICS works with many instances of any object. Anytime the ICS needs information about an item, it can refer to the MIL for the specifics. In that way, you can conserve memory by using only the ICS to store reference numbers to objects in the MIL (as illustrated in Figure 15.7).

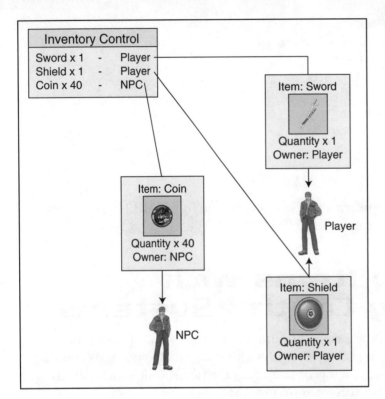

**Figure 15.6**

*An inventory control system keeps track of each owner's items, including the number of items.*

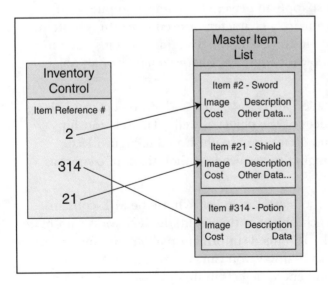

**Figure 15.7**

*Assuming that the ICS contains only item references, you can save massive amounts of memory by letting the MIL store the rest of the item's information.*

For your game's maps and levels, a simple ICS (called a *map ICS*) consists of only a list of items and their locations within the map, which is just fine because you can place objects throughout—ready for characters to pick them up. The real problem comes when those characters pick them up and add them to their inventory. Multiple instances pile up, new items are added, and other items are used or dropped. Things quickly become a real jumble. Handling a collection of character's objects is the job of a character ICS, which is a little more complicated than its map counterpart.

# Developing a Map ICS

The map ICS tracks items that are placed within levels, including items that are contained within other items—a sword contained within a treasure chest, for example. The type of map you use determines how you position items within the map. In 3-D maps, you use three coordinates for positioning an item—the X-, Y-, and Z- coordinates. Because each map is also unique (each part of the world has different maps), you can track each map's items in separate files.

You can represent the map ICS with a structure and a class:

```
typedef struct sMapItem
{
  long      ItemNum;          // MIL item number
  long      Quantity;         // Quantity of item (ie coins)
  float     XPos, YPos, ZPos; // Map coordinates

  sMapItem  *Prev, *Next;     // linked list pointers

  long      Index;            // This item's index #
  long      Owner;            // Owner index #
  sMapItem  *Parent;          // Parent of a contained item

  sMapItem()
  {
    Prev = Next = Parent = NULL;
    Index = 0; Owner = -1;
  }

  ~sMapItem() { delete Next; }
} sMapItem;
```

```
class cMapICS
{
  private:
    long        m_NumItems;    // # items in map
    sMapItem *m_ItemParent;    // Linked list parent map item

    // Functions to read in next long or float # in file
    long  GetNextLong(FILE *fp);
    float GetNextFloat(FILE *fp);

  public:
    cMapICS();    // Constructor
    ~cMapICS();   // Destructor

    // Load, save, and free a list of map items
    BOOL Load(char *Filename);
    BOOL Save(char *Filename);
    BOOL Free();

    // Add and remove an item on map
    BOOL Add(long ItemNum, long Quantity,                    \
             float XPos, float YPos, float ZPos,             \
             sMapItem *OwnerItem = NULL);
    BOOL Remove(sMapItem *Item);

    // Retrieve # items or parent linked list object
    long        GetNumItems();
    sMapItem *GetParentItem();
    sMapItem *GetItem(long Num);
};
```

First, you see the sMapItem structure, which holds the information for every item in the map. ItemNum is the MIL item reference number (which ranges from 0 to 1,023 if you used the MILEdit program), and Quantity is the number of ItemNums (to allow things like a horde of coins to be represented as a single object). Then you see the item's map coordinates XPos, YPos, and ZPos.

Next comes the Prev and Next pointers. You insert them to track a linked list of sMapItem structures. The next couple of variables, Index and Owner, are used when loading and saving the items in a map. Index stores the current index number of an item in the linked list. If an item is owned by another item, the Owner variable holds the index number of the parent object (otherwise, Owner is set to -1). When loading (or adding) an object, you set the final variable in sMapItem (Parent) to point to the actual owner item's structure. You can see the sMapItem structure link list concept illustrated in Figure 15.8.

The sMapItem uses both a constructor and destructor function called whenever a structure instance is allocated or reallocated. Both functions ensure that the linked list pointers are in check, and whenever a structure is deleted, all subsequent sMapItem structures in the linked list are deleted as well.

The cMapICS class has two private functions (GetNextLong and GetNextFloat) used to read in text and convert it into a long or float value. The cMapICS class also has eight usable public functions. Take a closer look at those public functions.

> **CAUTION**
>
> If you're removing only a single instance of sMapItem from the linked list, you first have to set the instance's Next variable to NULL. Doing so ensures that all subsequent instances in the linked list are not deleted as well.

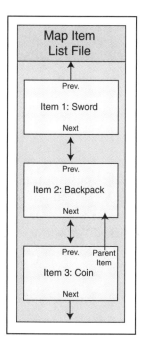

**Figure 15.8**

*You store the map's list of items as a linked list. Items are numbered as they are read in from disk, which helps to match child-to-parent objects.*

# cMapICS::Load, cMapICS::Save, and cMapICS::Free

As their names suggest, this trio of functions loads, saves, and frees a list of items that belong to a map. The first of the three, Load, loads and creates a list of items. For simplicity, store all items in a text file, using the following format:

```
MIL_ItemNum
Quantity
XPos
YPos
ZPos
ParentID
```

Each item uses six lines of text, and each entry (group of six lines) is numbered sequentially (the first item in the file is item #0, the second item is #1, and so on). Here's a sample file that contains two items:

```
// Item #0 as follows:
10          // MIL Item # (long value)
1           // Quantity (long value)
10.0        // XPos (float value)
0.0         // YPos (float value)
600.0       // ZPos (float value)
-1          // Owner (-1 = none, index # otherwise)
// Item #1 as follows:
1           // MIL Item #
1           // ...
10.0
0.0
600.0
0           // belongs to item #0 (first item in file)
```

The preceding comments are for clarification; the actual storage file does not use them. When reading in a list of items such as the preceding ones, the Load function converts the text into usable numbers. Using those numbers, it creates a sMapItem structure for each item in the map to be loaded, constructing a linked list as the items are loaded. After every item is read in, all objects that belong to another are matched up (using the Parent pointer in the sMapItem structure).

There's really nothing too difficult here, so jump right into the cMapICS::Load code:

```
BOOL cMapICS::Load(char *Filename)
{
```

```
FILE *fp;
long LongNum;
sMapItem *Item, *ItemPtr = NULL;

Free();  // Free a prior set

// Open the file
if((fp=fopen(Filename, "rb"))==NULL)
  return FALSE;

// Loop forever reading in items
while(1) {
  // Get next item number (break if no more items,
  // which is represented by a return value of -1).
  if((LongNum = GetNextLong(fp)) == -1)
    break;

  // Create a new map pointer and link it in
  Item = new sMapItem();
  if(ItemPtr == NULL)
    m_ItemParent = Item;
  else {
    Item->Prev = ItemPtr;
    ItemPtr->Next = Item;
  }
  ItemPtr = Item;

  // Store MIL item number
  Item->ItemNum = LongNum;

  // Get quantity
  Item->Quantity = GetNextLong(fp);

  // Get coordinates
  Item->XPos = GetNextFloat(fp);
  Item->YPos = GetNextFloat(fp);
  Item->ZPos = GetNextFloat(fp);

  // Get owner #
  Item->Owner = GetNextLong(fp);
```

```
      // Save index # and increase count
      Item->Index = m_NumItems++;
   }

   // Close the file
   fclose(fp);

   // Match objects that belong to others
   ItemPtr = m_ItemParent;
   while(ItemPtr != NULL) {

      // Check if this item belongs to another
      if(ItemPtr->Owner != -1) {

         // Find matching parent item
         Item = m_ItemParent;
         while(Item != NULL) {

            if(ItemPtr->Owner == Item->Index) {
               // A match, point to parent
               ItemPtr->Parent = Item;
               break; // Stop scanning for parents
            }

            Item = Item->Next;
         }
      }

      // Go to next item
      ItemPtr = ItemPtr->Next;
   }

   return TRUE;
}
```

> **NOTE**
>
> Much like all the code in this book, the cMapICS class functions return a value of TRUE if the function call succeeded or a value of FALSE if the call failed.

Save takes an internal list of items and, using the filename you specify, saves that list to a file on disk. The Save function is typically used to update the game data, because players might consistently pick up and drop items.

The Save function first assigns an index value to each sMapItem structure in the linked list (based on their order). The first item in the linked list is 0 (zero), the second item is 1, and so on. Each child item's `Owner` variable is updated as well at this point, and finally all data is written to a file:

```
BOOL cMapICS::Save(char *Filename)
{
  FILE *fp;
  sMapItem *Item;
  long Index = 0;

  // Open the file
  if((fp=fopen(Filename, "wb"))==NULL)
    return FALSE;

  // Assign index numbers to items
  if((Item = m_ItemParent) == NULL) {
    fclose(fp);
    return TRUE; // no items to save
  }
  while(Item != NULL) {
    Item->Index = Index++;
    Item = Item->Next;
  }

  // Match child items to parents
  Item = m_ItemParent;
  while(Item != NULL) {
    if(Item->Parent != NULL)
      Item->Owner = Item->Parent->Index;
    else
      Item->Owner = -1;
    Item = Item->Next;
  }

  // Save 'em out
  Item = m_ItemParent;
  while(Item != NULL) {
    // Item number
    fprintf(fp, "%lu\r\n", Item->ItemNum);

    // Quantity
    fprintf(fp, "%lu\r\n", Item->Quantity);
```

```
    // Coordinates
    fprintf(fp, "%lf\r\n%lf\r\n%lf\r\n", Item->XPos, Item->YPos, Item->ZPos);

    // Owner #
    fprintf(fp, "%ld\r\n", Item->Owner);

    // Next item
    Item = Item->Next;
  }

  fclose(fp); // Close the file

  return TRUE; // Return success!
}
```

Finally, you use the Free function when destroying the class (thus, deleting the linked list of items). Here's the code for Free:

```
BOOL cMapICS::Free()
{
  m_NumItems = 0;
  delete m_ParentItem;
  m_ParentItem = NULL;
  return TRUE;
}
```

You're just deleting the item linked list and getting the class ready for further use.

## cMapICS::Add and cMapICS::Remove

As items are added to the map (as the result of a player dropping them, for example), you need to call Add to make sure those dropped items make it into the list of map objects. The Add function does this by first allocating a sMapItem structure, filling it with the appropriate item information that you give it and then linking it into the map's list of items:

```
BOOL cMapICS::Add(long ItemNum, long Quantity,              \
                  float XPos, float YPos, float ZPos,        \
                  sMapItem *OwnerItem)
{
  sMapItem *Item;

  // Create a new item structure
```

```
Item = new sMapItem();

// Insert into top of list
Item->Next = m_ItemParent;
if(m_ItemParent != NULL)
  m_ItemParent->Prev = Item;
m_ItemParent = Item;

// Fill the item structure
Item->ItemNum  = ItemNum;
Item->Quantity = Quantity;
Item->XPos     = XPos;
Item->YPos     = YPos;
Item->ZPos     = ZPos;
Item->Parent   = OwnerItem;

return TRUE;
}
```

Just as the Add function is used to add objects to the map's list of items, you'll need to use Remove to remove items from a map. You call Remove using the item's identifier that you wish to remove from the map's list. Remove also deletes the allocated item structure and takes care of items that belong to the removed item:

```
BOOL cMapICS::Remove(sMapItem *Item)
{
  sMapItem *ItemPtr, *NextItem;

  // Remove child objects first
  if((ItemPtr = m_ItemParent) != NULL) {
    while(ItemPtr != NULL) {
      NextItem = ItemPtr->Next;
      if(ItemPtr->Parent == Item)
        Remove(ItemPtr);
      ItemPtr = NextItem;
    }
  }

  // Remove from linked list and reset root
  // if it's the current head of list.
  if(Item->Prev != NULL)
    Item->Prev->Next = Item->Next;
```

```
  else
    m_ItemParent = Item->Next;
  if(Item->Next != NULL)
    Item->Next->Prev = Item->Prev;

  // Clear link list
  Item->Prev = Item->Next = NULL;

  // Free memory
  delete Item;

  return TRUE;
}
```

## cMapICS::GetNumItems, cMapICS::GetParentItem, and cMapICS::GetItem

You use these three functions to retrieve the number of items that belong to the map and to retrieve the parent sMapItem or specified item structure in the linked list. The first two of the following three functions return a single variable while the third function does the hard work by scanning through the linked list of objects, returning the specified item in the list:

```
long cMapICS::GetNumItems()        {   return m_NumItems;   }
sMapItem cMapICS::GetParentItem() {   return m_ParentItem; }

sMapItem *cMapICS::GetItem(long Num)
{
  sMapItem *Item;

  Item = m_ItemParent;  // Start at parent item
  while(Num--) {         // Loop until reached item num
    if(Item == NULL)
      return NULL;       // no more items to scan, return error
    Item = Item->Next;  // go to next item in linked list
  }
  return Item;           // return resulting item
}
```

> **NOTE**
>
> With the parent item structure pointer returned from GetParentItem, you can scan the entire linked list of items by utilizing each item structure's Next pointer. If you want a specific item structure based on its index into the list, use the GetItem function.

## Using the cMapICS Class

Every map in your game will have an associated list of items that belongs to it. The map ICS will load those items and provide them to your engine whenever it needs to render the map or add a specific item to a player's inventory (when an item contained in the map is picked up).

Take a look at the following code bit, which loads a sample list of items, adds a single item, removes another item, and saves the list of items:

```
cMapICS MapICS;

MapICS.Load("sample.mi");  // Load the file

// Add 1 of item # 10
MapICS.Add(10, 1, 0.0f, 0.0f, 100.0f, NULL);

// Remove 2nd item from list
MapICS.Remove(MapICS.GetItem(1));

// Save list back out
MapICS.Save("sample.mi");
```

Although this is a simple example of modifying a map's item list, why not go ahead and see just how complicated it can become.

The MapICS demo (see Figure 15.9) contains the full cMapICS class shown in this chapter and the sItem structure from the MIL edit program. You can load the MapICS demo from the CD-ROM at the back of this book (look for \BookCode\ Chap15\MapICS). You use the map ICS and MIL to render a list of objects spread around a simple level.

The MapICS loads the map items and uses their coordinate data to draw a generic item mesh in the scene. Whenever you approach an item, a targeting icon appears and displays the name of the item.

Nothing in the MapICS should be new to you, so I'll skip the code at this point. Basically, the MapICS demo is like the NodeTree demo shown in Chapter 12, "Creating 3-D Graphics Engines."

> **NOTE**
>
> The MapICS demo allows you to walk around a simple level by using the arrow keys and mouse. You can pick up items by standing in front of one and pressing the left mouse button. Pressing the right mouse button causes you to drop a random item.

Small Shield x 1

**Figure 15.9**

*The MapICS demo allows you to walk around a simple level, picking up and dropping items.*

Once the level is rendered out, each item in the map is scanned and drawn if in view. The closest item is detected, and its name is printed to the screen. The code is well commented, so you should have no problem breezing through it.

## Developing a Character ICS

Although developing a character's inventory system might make you cringe at first, let me reassure you that it's not much different from developing a map inventory control system. You have the ability to add and remove items, but you don't have the problem of dealing with the item coordinates on the map. Instead, a player's ICS keeps track of order, which means that players can rearrange the items as they see fit.

Of course, this ordering is just a matter of arranging the linked list, but what about the items that can hold other items, such as backpacks? As long as you properly categorize the items as containers in the MIL Editor, you don't need to worry.

Speaking of categorizing, the real magic happens when you want to equip or use an item. Because each item is categorized, the character ICS can quickly determine what to do with the item in question. If the item is a weapon, the character ICS can ask to equip the item. If it's a healing item, the player can consume it. Beginning to get the idea?

Finally, a character ICS should allow the player to examine objects, which is the reason for the mesh and image parameters in the MIL Editor. Whenever the game's player examines the object, the specific mesh or image is loaded and displayed.

Now, turn your attention to putting together a character ICS and example by using the ICS.

## Defining the cCharICS Class

The character ICS class and supporting structure developed for this book are defined as follows:

```
typedef struct sCharItem
{
  long      ItemNum;         // MIL item number
  long      Quantity;        // Quantity of item (i.e. coins)

  sCharItem *Prev, *Next;    // linked list pointers

  long      Index;           // This items index #
  long      Owner;           // Owner index #
  sCharItem *Parent;         // Parent of a contained item

  sCharItem()
  {
    Prev = Next = Parent = NULL;
    Index = 0; Owner = -1;
  }

  ~sCharItem() { delete Next; }
} sCharItem;

class cCharICS
{
  private:
    long      m_NumItems;      // # items in inventory
    sCharItem *m_ItemParent;   // Linked list parent item

    // Functions to read in next long or float # in file
    long  GetNextLong(FILE *fp);
    float GetNextFloat(FILE *fp);
```

```
public:
  cCharICS();   // Constructor
  ~cCharICS();  // Destructor

  // Load, save, and free a list of items
  BOOL Load(char *Filename);
  BOOL Save(char *Filename);
  BOOL Free();

  // Add and remove an item
  BOOL Add(long ItemNum, long Quantity,
           sCharItem *OwnerItem = NULL);
  BOOL Remove(sCharItem *Item);

  // Retrieve # items or parent linked list object
  long      GetNumItems();
  sCharItem *GetParentItem();
  sCharItem *GetItem(long Num);

  // Re-ordering functions
  BOOL Arrange();
  BOOL MoveUp(sCharItem *Item);
  BOOL MoveDown(sCharItem *Item);
};
```

Much like the cMapICS class, the cCharICS class uses a special structure (sCharItem) that tracks the MIL item numbers and quantity and maintains a linked list. Unlike the sMapItem structure, however, sCharItem doesn't care about the item's coordinates.

The cCharICS class, again, is much like its cMapICS counterpart, except for the addition of three more public functions—Arrange, MoveUp, and MoveDown. You use these functions to sort the character's list of items. Their code is as follows:

```
BOOL cCharICS::Arrange()
{
  sCharItem *Item, *PrevItem;

  // Start at top of linked list and float
  // each item up that has a lesser ItemNum.
  // Break if past bottom of list
  Item = m_ItemParent;
  while(Item != NULL) {
```

```
      // Check previous item to float up
      if(Item->Prev != NULL) {

        // Keep floating up while prev item has
        // a lesser ItemNum value or until top
        // of list has been reached.
        while(Item->Prev != NULL) {
          PrevItem = Item->Prev;  // Get prev item pointer

          // Break if no more to float up
          if(Item->ItemNum >= PrevItem->ItemNum)
            break;

          // Swap 'em
          if((PrevItem = Item->Prev) != NULL) {
            if(PrevItem->Prev != NULL)
              PrevItem->Prev->Next = Item;

            if((PrevItem->Next = Item->Next) != NULL)
              Item->Next->Prev = PrevItem;

            if((Item->Prev = PrevItem->Prev) == NULL)
              m_ItemParent = Item;

            PrevItem->Prev = Item;
            Item->Next = PrevItem;
          }
        }
      }

      // Go to next object
      Item = Item->Next;
    }

  return TRUE;
}

BOOL cCharICS::MoveUp(sCharItem *Item)
{
  sCharItem *PrevItem;

  // Swap item and item before it
```

```
    if((PrevItem = Item->Prev) != NULL) {
      if(PrevItem->Prev != NULL)
        PrevItem->Prev->Next = Item;

      if((PrevItem->Next = Item->Next) != NULL)
        Item->Next->Prev = PrevItem;

      if((Item->Prev = PrevItem->Prev) == NULL)
        m_ItemParent = Item;

      PrevItem->Prev = Item;
      Item->Next = PrevItem;
    }

    return TRUE; // Return success
}

BOOL cCharICS::MoveDown(sCharItem *Item)
{
  sCharItem *NextItem;

  // Swap item and item after it
  if((NextItem = Item->Next) != NULL) {
    if((Item->Next = NextItem->Next) != NULL)
      NextItem->Next->Prev = Item;

    if((NextItem->Prev = Item->Prev) != NULL)
      Item->Prev->Next = NextItem;
    else
      m_ItemParent = NextItem;

    NextItem->Next = Item;
    Item->Prev = NextItem;
  }

  return TRUE; // Return success
}
```

Arrange sorts the linked list of items based on each item's MIL item number, from lowest to highest. If, on the other hand, you want to specifically order the list yourself, you can utilize the MoveUp and MoveDown functions, which take a pointer to a sCharItem structure that is already contained in the list.

The MoveUp function moves the specified sItem structure up in the linked list, and MoveDown moves the specified structure down in the linked list. Figure 15.10 illustrates the concept of using the Arrange, MoveUp, and MoveDown functions on a sample linked list of items.

The rest of the functions in cCharICS are identical in their functionality to the cMapICS class, with the obvious exclusion of the item coordinates used when adding an item to the list. Even the storage format for character items is identical to the map item format, except for the coordinates.

## Using the cCharICS Class

To demonstrate the use of the character ICS system, I created a demo application named CharICS that maintains a list of items contained in the default.mil master item list file. You can find the demo on the CD-ROM at the back of this book (look for \BookCode\Chap15\CharICS). When you start the demo, you'll see the Inventory dialog box (shown in Figure 15.11). In the Inventory dialog box, the list box contains an imaginary character's inventory, which you can manipulate by using the buttons on the dialog box.

To use the CharICS demo, follow these steps:

1. Click the Add Item button. The CharICS demo will add a random item from the MIL to the inventory list.

2. Select an item from the list. Items are classified, so the Use and Equip buttons are enabled or disabled depending on which item you select from the list. Clicking Equip has no effect; it comes into play later when you deal with characters. Clicking Use, however, removes an item if it is flagged as USEONCE.

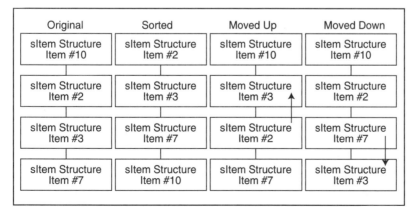

**Figure 15.10**

*From left to right, you see the original unsorted list, the arranged (sorted) list, the list after moving an item up, and the list after moving an item down.*

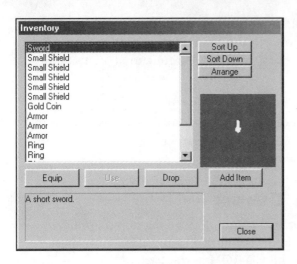

**Figure 15.11**

*The CharICS demo allows you to peruse an imaginary character's inventory, adding, dropping, or sorting items as you see fit.*

3. Click the Drop button to drop an item (remove the item from the inventory list) if it is flagged as CANDROP.

4. In order to arrange the items in the inventory, you can click an item and then click either Sort Up or Sort Down. The selected item then moves up or down in the list. To arrange the items by their item number in the list, click Arrange.

As a last, special treat, items that have matching meshes appear in the box on the right in the demo. The 3-D object spins around slowly so that you have a full view of all sides. Now, that's cool!

# Wrapping Up Objects and Inventory

Don't let the complexity of working with objects in your game fool you. The simple fact is that items in your game are actually small, easily handled bits of data. It's when characters start using those items that things become a bit more complicated. In this chapter, you saw just how you use inventory control systems to handle items belonging to a map and a character.

To expand the usefulness of the MIL Editor (and for your own game's items), I recommend adding your own item attributes. This involves a little Windows programming knowledge, because you must modify the dialog box that handles the modifications. In addition, you have to rewrite the sItem structure to hold the new attributes that you're adding. Of course, you don't have to worry about that challenge; you're becoming a role-playing game programming wizard.

## Programs on the CD-ROM

The \BookCode\Chap15\ directory contains these three programs, which demonstrate how to use a master item list and how to use the two inventory control systems developed in this chapter:

- ◆ **MILEdit.** The Master Item List Editor program discussed in this chapter. The editor aids in the creation of items you can use in your own game project. Location: \BookCode\Chap15\MILEdit\.

- ◆ **MapICS.** An example of a map inventory control system. Items loaded from disk are scattered about a map that the user can scroll around using the mouse and arrow keys. Location: \BookCode\Chap15\MapICS\.

- ◆ **CharICS.** An example character inventory control system that enables you to view a list of items. Items can be examined, used, or equipped. Location: \BookCode\Chap15\CharICS\.

# CHAPTER 16

# CONTROLLING PLAYERS AND CHARACTERS

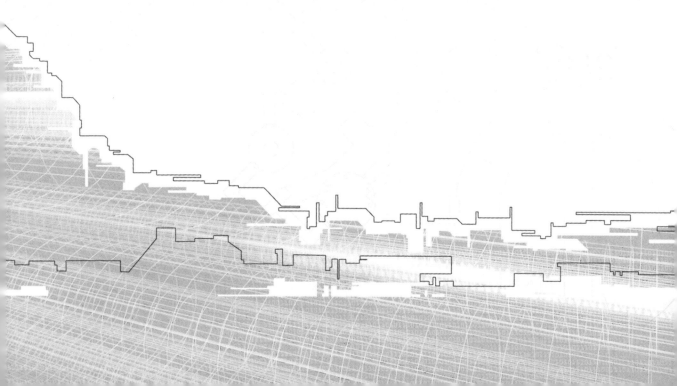

A gaming world is nothing without players and monsters running around. Nevertheless, creating them can be a little daunting at first. But don't worry. In this chapter, you can find the basic information you need to create characters and give them a life of their own in your game—all in an easy-to-follow format.

In this chapter, you learn how to do the following:

- Define characters
- Control characters in play
- Use spells with characters
- Deal with interaction between the player character and NPCs

# Players, Characters, and Monsters, Oh My!

Prior to this chapter, the game components are pretty standard. Those components—graphics engines, object handling, and using scripts—are easy to handle. Now you come to what can seem like an impasse because fashioning characters can be difficult or easy depending on your game's needs. You must handle the player characters (from now on referred to as PCs) that are under the control of the player, the non-player characters (from now on called NPCs) that are running around populating the world and carrying on with their own lives, and the monster characters (from now on called MCs) that want nothing more than to strike you down.

In this section, I introduce you to the various topics that help you design and define your game's characters, ranging from a character's controls, abilities, and features.

Talk about pressure! How do you handle every little aspect of these

> **NOTE**
>
> A *player character* is your player's alter ego. *Non-player characters* are the characters for whom your player has no direct control. NPCs are often townsfolk, shopkeepers, bankers, healers, and monsters. Yes, even monsters are NPCs, but for this book, I like to make a clear distinction between an NPC and an MC. NPCs do not attack players, whereas MCs do attack.

three types of characters? You might first break those aspects into the following categories and then determine how to proceed:

- **Definition.** You determine everything that a character can accomplish in a game by using a set of rules. Those rules need to establish exactly what a character is capable of accomplishing. Character definition includes a character's abilities (such as physical strength and agility) and a character's graphical appearance (as defined by 3-D meshes, for example).

- **Navigation.** Characters need to navigate through the world, whether on foot, by horse, or in an airship.

- **Conversation.** PCs interact with other PCs and with NPCs by talking or via other communication channels. The course of your game can change with a single spoken word, or the story can be permanently laid out by means of canned responses from talking dummies.

- **Resource management.** Resource management plays a large part in role-playing games. You have a PC inventory that consists of armor, weapons, potions, keys, and whatever else the PCs can fit into their virtual pockets. Those items, of course, are used at some point in the game, and it's the job of PCs to figure out each object's use. Spells and magic also fall into this category.

- **Combat.** Combat is a PC's means of ridding the world of evildoers, who take the form of NPCs or other PCs, and of giving PCs a chance to gain experience and power. Remember that a major element of role-playing games is to take your big, bad characters and build them into even bigger, badder characters!

- **Character building.** As I just mentioned, the purpose of typical role-playing games is to consistently increase your characters' powers and experiences so that they are better prepared to take on the more challenging aspects of the game. As characters' experiences increase, they gain knowledge of new skills, powers, spells, and abilities.

- **Character actions and appearance.** Characters can do only so much in a game. They can walk around, attack, cast spells, use items, and what have you. Each action that a character can perform is matched by a graphical representation, such as a 3-D mesh displayed on the screen.

# Defining Characters in Your Game

Employing characters into your game is one of the most difficult jobs you'll face. Even at a basic level, the code needed to control gaming characters can be convoluting. What's a lowly programmer to do? Just take it slow, work from the beginning, and all will be well.

In this section, I introduce you to some basic concepts common to most role-playing games. These concepts include defining a character's basic *abilities* (which include strength, intelligence, agility, and so on), how characters navigate through the game world, and how characters can interact with each other. Let's start by looking at how you can define a character's abilities.

## Character Abilities

Characters need particular abilities in order to affect the outcome of certain actions that take place within the game—combat for example. If a character swings a sword, what is the chance it will hit its intended target, and for that matter how much damage will the sword produce?

Typical role-playing games assign values to abilities—the higher the value, the better the character in terms of a particular ability. Using numbers also makes calculations easier. For example, a typical ability in a role-playing game is strength. Say that strength is measured from 0 (total weakling) to 999 (super-hero). An average human could then have strength of 100 to 150.

Now, go one step further and assume that a character must be a certain strength in order to perform a specific feat. Pushing open a jammed door, for example, requires a person to have strength of 100 or more. Lifting a boulder requires strength of 500 or more. Beginning to get the idea?

What other types of abilities can a character possess? For your game, that is the big question, so think about it carefully. Just what is going to happen in your game that requires an ability to be assigned to a character? Generally speaking, you can get by with the abilities shown in Table 16.1.

Each ability in your game is assigned a number, and each ability has a different use for the numbers. Attack is the amount of damage characters deal out without weapons in their hands. If this value is 100, the character can cause 100 points of damage per attack. At this point, let me just say that a character can experience only so many points of damage before dying.

> **TIP**
>
> To keep things fair, whenever a weak character attacks a character with high defense without the ability to do damage, you still want to apply some level of damage. Later, in the section "Combat and Characters," you see how to modify a weak character's attack ability in order to apply some sort of damage to a character with a high defense ability.

## Table 16.1  Character Abilities

| Ability | Description |
| --- | --- |
| Attack | This is the amount of damage a character can deal out. The attack value is based on how much damage characters can do with their bare hands, but add a weapon and the attack value increases (based on the type of weapon). |
| Defense | With a full set of armor you feel invincible. With just your blue jeans and T-shirt you are very vulnerable. Defense is the level of protection you have—the higher the defense, the less damage you take. Each character has a natural defense, whether it is weak skin or a tough hide. Using armor or other types of equipment can raise defense. |
| Agility | The ability to move around quickly and sure-footed. Characters with high agility can move quicker and even dodge attacks with greater ease. |
| Mental | The character's ability to control his mind. Total control over one's mind is a requirement of magical characters who cast spells and the like. The higher the mental ability, the greater the chance a character's spells will hit the intended target. |
| Resistance | Whereas defense ability helps reduce physical damage from physical attacks, resistance ability reduces damage from magic-based attacks. The higher the resistance, the lower the damage from spells. A 100 percent resistance makes a character invulnerable to magic! |
| To hit | Some characters aim right on; others have a little trouble. Characters' to-hit abilities detail just how well characters can hit their targets during an attack. This ability is raised or lowered depending on the type of weapon or other equipment donned. |

Defense, on the other hand, reduces the amount of damage points taken from an attack. If a character has a defense value of 50, the damage from an attack is reduced by 50 points, so the higher the defense, the lower the damage.

You also can modify attack and defense abilities by using items. Specific items, such as weapons, have a value that can multiply the attack value of a character (again, see the later section "Combat and Characters" for more on these modifier values).

In terms of agility, characters have an innate chance of dodging attacks, which increases as the characters grow stronger. Agility is measured from 0 to 999—the higher the value, the greater the chance of dodging an attack. To determine the chances of dodging an attack, a random number is figured and compared to the agility value. If the random number is equal to or lower than the agility ability, the attack is dodged.

The mental ability ranges anywhere from zero and up. The mental ability determines the chances of a spell affecting its target. Spells normally have a chance for success, but when you add mental ability, those chances increase. If a spell has a mental value of 100, the spell has a 100 percent greater chance for working.

Resistance is the character's ability to reduce damage from spells. This value can range from 0 to 100 percent. The percentage is applied to the spell's damage amount and used as a final value to cause damage to a target character.

Finally, the to-hit ability can range from 0 to 999 as well. Again, a random value is compared to the to-hit ability; a random number higher than the to-hit value means that the attack missed its target.

In addition to character abilities, other types of information can define a character—for example, the player's health. A few extra details about each character are needed at this point to determine just how healthy and powerful a character is. Enter character attributes.

## Character Attributes

Character's attributes are much like abilities, except that attributes define a different aspect of a character. Your physical health is an attribute, for example; it varies depending on how much injury a character sustains. These injuries can be healed and, as such, the health of the character is increased.

You need only a few attributes in a game. Table 16.2 describes four attributes that I use throughout this chapter.

A character's health is measured in health points (HP), and mana is measured in mana points (MP). A character needs MPs in order to cast spells. Each time a spell is cast, a set amount of MPs are taken away; if no mana remains, no spells can be cast.

Experience and experience levels enable players to track the progress and increase the power of their characters. Dealing with experience relates to PCs only, which is discussed in the section "Increasing in Experience and Power," later in this chapter.

## Table 16.2  Character Attributes

| Attribute | Description |
|---|---|
| Health | The health of a character ranges from zero and up. The higher the number, the more damage the character can take. A value of zero means that the character is dead. |
| Mana | Mana applies to the amount of magic power a character has in reserve. Every spell requires a set amount of mana that is depleted each time a spell is cast. |
| Experience points | Think of assigning a number to the amount of experiences you've had in life. As characters in a game experience more, they grow stronger and learn more. A character's experiences are measured in numerical form. |
| Experience level | Every so often, a character's abilities and attributes increase. Experience levels are those instances of increase. Experience levels are determined by a set amount of experience points, as you soon see in the section "Increasing in Experience and Power." |

## Status Ailments in Characters

Abilities and attributes are a great way to determine the capabilities of a character. Of course, those abilities and attributes describe a character at his peak performance. Certain ailments can dog characters, causing them to weaken or strengthen. Characters can be poisoned or inflicted with an ailment that causes them to become clumsy.

These *status ailments* are magical in nature and help turn the tide at critical points. Table 16.3 lists several status ailments used in many games (and in this book) and their effect on the afflicted character.

As you can see, certain status ailments aid characters rather than affect them badly. Later, in the sections "The Function of Spells" and "Using Combat Rules for Attacking," you see how to incorporate these ailments into your project.

## Table 16.3 Status Ailments and Their Effects on Characters

| Ailment | Effect |
|---|---|
| Poison | Poison slowly saps the health of a character until the calamity is dispelled. In this book, characters that are poisoned lose two health points every four seconds. |
| Sleep | Characters who are asleep can't do anything until they wake up. The only ways to wake up are to be hit by another character or to wait until the effect wears off (a 4-percent chance). |
| Paralyze | Paralyzed characters can't do anything, which is much like the Sleep ailment. However, paralyzed characters will recover only when the magic is dispelled or the effect wears off (a 2-percent chance). |
| Weak | The attack and defense abilities of weak characters are reduced by half. |
| Strong | The attack and defense abilities of strong characters are increased by 50 percent. |
| Enchanted | The magical resistance ability of enchanted characters is reduced by half. |
| Barrier | A magical barrier ailment increases the character's resistance ability by 50 percent. |
| Dumbfounded | Dumbfounded characters lose half their mental ability when afflicted. |
| Clumsy | The agility of clumsy characters is reduced by 25 percent, making them less able to dodge physical attacks. |
| Sure-footed | Being quick on their feet is the name of the game, and the agility of sure-footed afflicted characters is raised by 50 percent. |
| Slow | Normally, characters have a set rate of walking speed (measured in units per second), but being afflicted by the slow ailment reduces this walking speed by half. |
| Fast | Increases the character's walking speed by 50 percent. |
| Blind | Blind characters are 25 percent more likely to miss their targets when attacking. |
| Hawkeyed | Hawkeyed characters are 50 percent more likely to hit their targets when attacking. |
| Silenced | Silenced character are unable to cast spells until this ailment is dispelled. |

# Character Classes

Characters come in all shapes and sizes—big ones, little ones, even short and furry ones. The fact is that some characters have different attributes that make them special.

For every different type of character in your game, there is a matching character class. You can think of character classes as being a way to differentiate the different species of characters in your game. Going even further, classes can determine a specific type of character in a species.

Classifying a character simply as human isn't enough. Instead, the classification of human fighter might be appropriate in certain cases. This applies to all characters. For example, you might classify a dragon as an ice dragon, or a fire dragon, or a rock dragon, and so on.

The reasons for determining class are important to your game design (refer to Chapter 15, "Defining and Using Objects," for more information on using classes in relation to items and characters). The items in your game are assigned a class usage variable that states which classes can harness a particular item. Broadswords can be wielded only by human or dwarf warrior characters, whereas only a wizard class can use a spell scroll.

Character classes also come into play when you are handling combat situations. Certain attacks, whether physical or magical, have either a strong or weak effect on specific character classes. Consider, for example, a fireball spell. Although a fireball is heat-based, it will do much more damage to an ice-based monster than to a fire-based monster (in fact, it might heal a fire-based monster).

Character classes are assigned by number and are entirely up to your design.

# Character Actions

Every character in your game has an associated set of actions that the character can perform, and with action, an associated animation is played out on the screen. Taking a swing with a weapon, casting a spell, or talking to another character—they're all actions, and it's your job to determine what actions your game's characters can perform.

Each action in the game also has a resulting effect. A walking action moves a character, whereas an attack action involves swinging a weapon and determining who or what is hit. Internally, one effect is taking place; externally, the player is treated to a graphical animation to represent the action.

Table 16.4 shows the actions I implement in this book.

## Table 16.4  Character Actions

| Action | Description |
|--------|-------------|
| Attack | Swinging with their weapons, characters strike forth at any character in front of them. Although only one type of attack is implemented in this book, you should be able to add different types of attacks in your game. |
| Cast spell | The ancient art of magic is brought forward as characters perform a small ritual with the intention of calling forth a damaging or beneficial spell. |
| Movement | Walking, flying, running—all are ways of getting around in your gaming world. Your character needs a typical method of motion, and for this book, that method is to walk around. |
| Idle | When characters stand still, they are idle. Characters might appear to be bored, alert, or constantly looking around, but no matter what they're doing, they are considered idle. |
| Use item | When a character decides to harness the use of the items they have collected, a use item action is initiated. |
| Talk | Conversing with the gaming denizens is a talk action. Instead of just standing still, gamers want their characters to appear as though they are interacting with each other—waving their arms, moving their mouths, or what have you. |
| Hurt | A character hit by an attack, whether magical or physical, usually requires a second to recover. This period of recovery is considered a hurt action, and during this action, the player cannot perform any actions. |
| Die | After enough damage is received, a character can die. Not just any death will do, however; an over-dramatized animation of the downfall is followed by the character's removal from the game. |

Certain actions can be performed only at specific times. Maybe characters can't attack during navigation sequences, leaving combat actions to a separate battle sequence. Even when those actions are acceptable to use, another factor limits when some actions can be performed.

Take the attack action for example. Assuming that it can be performed at any time during the game doesn't mean that the player can sit and constantly hack away. You use a limiting factor called the *charge* to delay the time between attacks. In fact, all actions except idle and movement work off the character's charge.

Whenever one of those actions is used, the character's charge is reset. Slowly, that charge refills until the character is once again able to perform another action. The rate at which this charge increases is specific to each type of character.

Although every character in the game can perform the actions shown in Table 16.4, different types of characters use only certain actions. PCs are the only ones who use items, for example, so a monster will never be assigned that action.

To better understand what each character type is capable of performing, take a brief look at each one of them.

# The Player Character

The world revolves around your PC, so most of your game development will go into controlling him. PCs have the most actions and options available to them. Other than those character actions previously mentioned, PCs have the option of managing their game resources, which includes items and magic spells. In addition, character building is used to build up the strength of the character.

The following sections show how each aspect comes into play when working with PCs.

## Player Navigation

The most important ability of your PCs is navigation. It's a huge world, and half the fun of the game is exploring every nook and cranny in it. You must give PCs as many ways as possible to navigate the world, whether they walk, fly, swim, or teleport.

Again, staying with the basics, the characters' most important navigation method is walking around the world. Each character in your game is assigned a value that gauges the character's speed of movement, and for your player, the faster the movement rate, the better.

## Resource Management

Resources are the items and objects that litter your gaming world. They make the game worth playing.

Chapter 15 introduces you to creating items, but it doesn't fully cover the use of those items. The fact is that items are nothing unless there's somebody to use them, so now is a good time to review how your game players can interact with those items. Potions can be consumed, weapons and armor worn, and gold spent—it's all up to how you design those items (see Chapter 15) and how your players use them!

Not only are items resources, but they also can be magic spells. Spells are tremendously useful tools, and in order to make it anywhere in the world, your PC needs to learn to use as many spells as possible. How does a player learn to use spells? Through ever-increasing experience, that's how!

## Increasing in Experience and Power

True to typical role-playing game design, characters can grow in experience—every treasure they find and every battle they win increase their abilities. Think of experience as a number, and the higher the number, the more powerful the character. As specific levels of experience are reached, a character gains certain benefits.

For example, imagine that George, a game character, has just finished slaying his one-thousandth Ogre. Throughout all his combat experiences, he has grown increasingly stronger. He can now deal out three times the amount of damage with his sword than he could when he started his adventure. His physical strength has increased, and he is more agile and more able to dodge attacks. His mental abilities have increased, and he has learned some powerful new spells.

Characters have what's called *experience points* and *experience levels*. Every experience increases the experience points of a character. At specific intervals of experience points, a character's experience level is raised. When an experience level raises, a character gains benefits, which generally include an increase in abilities and spells.

For this book, gaining experience points comes from killing monsters. The amount of experience points gained is coded into a character's definitions. Killing a homely little imp might give your character a measly 10 experience points, whereas slaying a level-200 red dragon might give your character a whopping 20,000! It's up to you to designate the amount of experience gained for killing monsters.

Designating experience levels and rewarding advances are part of your work as a game designer. A character designated as level 1 might need 500 experience points to go to level 2, and going up to experience level 3 might require 1,200 experience points.

When determining the experience points needed for a specific level, you might gauge those levels of advancement by the average experience given from killing monsters in a specific area in the game. For example, if your character is in "imp-land" and each imp gives your PC 10 experience points when killed, you want the player to kill at least 20 monsters to go up to level 2, which means that level 2 requires 200 experience points.

In addition to benefits going up, abilities and attributes also increase as experience levels go up. The PC's maximum amount of health and mana points increase; the player becomes stronger and able to take more damage. Spells become easier to cast, and with the addition of more mana points, your PC can cast more spells before running out of juice. What really happens to PCs as levels increase is a matter of a game's design. In this chapter, I don't delve too deeply into it (but you can find out how I increase a PC's abilities because of an increase in experience in the full-game example in Chapter 20, "Putting Together a Full Game").

# Non-Player Characters

You contend with NPCs much as you contend with PC controls, except that the game engine handles all aspects of an NPC's controls. This difference creates some tough design and programming situations, and you must develop an artificial intelligence system that can mimic believable behavior.

Reviewing the characters' aspects, you can see that even NPCs need quite a bit of managing:

- **Navigation.** Although not as complicated as PCs, NPCs do need to get around in the world. With the help of scripting, this becomes much easier, but problems still arise because of terrain obstacles and PC interaction.

- **Conversation.** Again, although not at the same level as PCs, NPCs need to act "human," and part of acting human is using communication skills.

- **Combat.** NPCs make up the majority of characters against whom PCs do combat, so the NPCs need to be worthy adversaries. Even the lowliest NPC has self-preservation skills and needs to exhibit them in a battle to the death!

Other major control aspects, such as resource management, don't apply to NPCs. The items that NPCs carry are written into the design of the characters. Rarely do they have free choice of what they carry or use. Also, because the players do not control most NPCs, they have their "entire lives" to develop, so character building doesn't affect them either.

Because it applies only to MCs (and not all NPCs), leave combat at this point and turn your attention to navigation and conversation, which have a great effect on NPCs. These two actions require a plausible artificial intelligence in order for the characters to become semi-sentient beings in a game. Actually, NPCs only need to *appear* intelligent. Under all the fluff, they follow a small set of instructions and rules that govern their actions.

For example, *Phantasy Star Online,* a popular game created by Sega, uses minimal NPC interactions. It has a couple of shopkeepers who sell items, a bank to hold money and other items, a healer to cure wounds, and a guild to embark on quests. The game's monsters are dumb by many standards; they simply walk around until they see the PC, at which point they home in for an attack. This group of NPC control aspects is perfect for fast-action role-playing games, but not good enough for more serious gamers.

On the other hand, a game such as Origin's *Ultima Online* is packed with NPCs. How do these two games compare? The NPCs in *Ultima Online* are limited in terms of their artificial intelligence—they can only wander around, follow a character, remain still, attack, heal, guard, or act as a banker or shopkeeper. In *Ultima Online,* the scripts that the NPCs use are their real magic. Each NPC can have a script attached that enables the NPC to perform additional actions. For example, talking to an NPC yields nothing special until the player gives the NPC a special item, at which point the NPC bequeaths the player a magic sword.

Which is the way to go? If you want a super complex artificial intelligence, so be it, but your gaming world can be literally packed with hundreds of NPCs, so the easier it is to handle them, the better.

In this book, I model the *Ultima Online* NPC control scheme. NPCs are assigned specific movements and are allowed to utilize scripts. To keep things simple, a PC must interact with an NPC before a script is activated.

# Monster Characters

Monster characters are really NPCs in disguise. An MC is programmed just like an NPC, but with monsters, they take on an additional form of intelligence—hunting and attacking PCs.

Monsters can wander around, follow, evade, follow a route, and even stand still—just like normal NPCs. However, when a PC comes within range of a monster's attack range (physical or magical), that player becomes fair game. The monster will consistently attack nearby PCs until either the PCs are dead or the PCs leave the monster's attack range.

Monsters also have a sense of self-preservation. If a monster loses half its health points and has the ability to perform a healing spell, it will attempt to heal itself using the healing spell. Likewise, if a monster has an ailment, it will attempt to dispel the ailment. Finally, a monster will attempt to enhance itself by casting beneficial status ailment spells upon itself.

Monsters are the only type of character that a PC can attack (or should be able to attack for that matter). Because a PC gains experience only by killing monsters, you want to provide your game with a sufficient number of monsters.

## Character Graphics

Up to this point, only the functionality of a character has been discussed. The reality is that functionality is the only part that really matters, but game players will want some sort of visual representation of their digital alter ego. With the power of a 3-D modeler and the Graphics Core, you'll have no problem tackling the graphics portion of your characters.

Each character in your game can perform specific actions. These actions (or at least those actions used in this book) are as follows: to walk, stand still, swing a weapon, cast a spell, be hurt, and die. Each of these actions has a specific animation, which is used in conjunction with a mesh to create a character's graphics component.

As you learn in the later section "Creating a Character Controller Class," each character's mesh is loaded into a cMesh object, and each animation

> **NOTE**
>
> Two great models and supporting action animations are included on the CD-ROM at the back of this book (look for \Resources\Models\Yodan and Spawn). You use these meshes in later chapters. Take some time to load these models into MilkShape 3-D and check out how each model is animated and how you can modify and use the models and animations in your project.

is loaded into a cAnimation object. Those two Graphics Core objects are unique to each character in your game (with multiple instances of the same character using only one mesh and animation object). Your job is to load those meshes and animations and to render the characters to the display at each frame.

## Navigating Characters

Now that you've defined your characters, it is time to put them in the world and move them around. This is where you separate control systems between PCs and NPCs. PCs, being the characters directly controlled by the players, have the most options.

If you've checked out the demo programs in Chapter 12 and Chapter 13 that are on this book's CD-ROM, you have already witnessed the player control system (which I like to call *direct control*) that I created. Those demos enable you to move the player around using arrow keys and the mouse.

For the first-person demos (such as the NodeTree demo in Chapter 12), pushing the up arrow moves the player forward, pushing the down arrow moves the player backward, and pushing the left and right arrows moves the player left and right, respectively. Moving the mouse rotates the viewpoint. As for a non-first-person demo (such as the 3Din2D demo in Chapter 13), the arrows move the character in the appropriate direction (press the up arrow to move up, press the left arrow to move left, and so on).

> **NOTE**
>
> First person and non-first person describes the viewpoint of the player. For first-person games, the player's viewpoint is from the character's eyes. Non-first-person games take a different viewpoint— from above, the side, or any other such angle.

Rarely does anything become more complicated than using these control systems when dealing with a PC. Things do get complicated, however, whenever your player starts walking around bumping into other characters and objects (such as doors). You've already seen how to perform collision detection of sorts, so that's really not a big problem.

Things tend to get a little more complicated for NPCs. No longer is the player responsible for moving a character around the map; the game engine takes over. You also can enable NPCs to walk around according to simple directions, but instead of moving around the world like the PC, NPCs perform a basic set of movement behaviors, as follows:

- Stand still
- Wander aimlessly around the entire level or specific area
- Walk along a specified route
- Follow a character
- Evade a character

The preceding list of actions is all you ever need to start, and because you have to start somewhere, start at the most logical place—with the PC controls.

# Controlling Player Characters

Your player is the most important character in the game, so you need complete control of him. Typical games utilize a simple directional control scheme, similar to the scheme you read about in the section "Player Navigation."

A direct control scheme enables you to manually move a character forward, backward, left, right, up, and throughout the map. Nothing can be more direct, so I tend to use the direct control method to control characters in this book.

There are two types of direct controls—*directional control* and *rotational control,* which are covered in the following two sections.

## Using Directional Control

Directional control uses controls such as arrow keys or a joystick to move characters in a single direction. Directional control is best suited to third-person games in which the camera is viewing the character from above and from the side (as illustrated in Figure 16.1).

To move a character by using directional controls, you need to know the camera's angle (along the Y-axis), the character's position, and the direction in which the character wants to move (0.0 being up or away from the camera, 1.57 being right, 3.14 being down, and 4.71 being left).

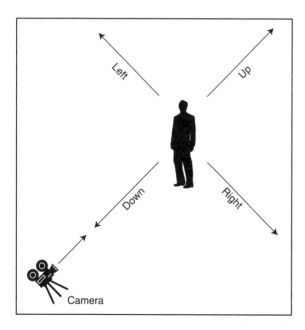

**Figure 16.1**

*With a directional control, a character walks in the direction directed by the key pressed— the up arrow moves the character up the screen (away from the camera), the left arrow moves the character left, and so on. This control method takes into account the camera's position when moving the character so that the up arrow always moves a character up (away), regardless of the camera's viewing angle.*

Assume that the character's coordinates are represented in a pair of variables:

```
float XPos, ZPos; // YPos = height and is not required yet.
```

Now the camera's angle (along the Y-axis) is represented with a variable:

```
float CameraYAngle; // The angle of view
```

Last, you have the direction you want to move the character and the distance to move in that direction:

```
float Direction;  // Direction to move
float Distance;    // How far to move
```

Next, set up a sample in which a character is located at the origin of the world and wants to walk up (relative to the camera view); the camera is positioned to the right of the origin along the X-axis and is pointed left, as illustrated in Figure 16.2.

Here are the variables to set up and the calculations to perform:

> **CAUTION**
>
> Using distance values can be a problem because you're not controlling how fast each frame is updated in your engine. When a game is running full speed on one computer and is updated 100 times a second, the game's characters will move much faster on that computer than they will on a computer that is updating the game 30 times a second. You need to limit the number of times your game updates each frame, much as I do later in the section "Using cCharacterController" and in Chapter 20.

```
XPos = ZPos = 0.0f;      // The character's position
CameraYAngle = -1.57f;   // The camera angle
Direction = 0.0f;        // Direction to move
float Distance = 4.0f;   // The distance to move character

// The new direction (angle) to move
float NewAngle = CameraYAngle + Direction - 1.57f;

// Move character
XPos += (float)cos(NewAngle) * Distance;
ZPos += (float)-sin(NewAngle) * Distance;
```

At this point, the character has moved 4.0 units away from the camera, which means that the character is now located at X=-4.0, Z=0.0, which is just where you want the character to be. The only problem now is determining the character's height (for those using a 3-D engine).

That really isn't a problem. Chapter 12 explains how to use the respective intersection tests to determine the height of a point in a polygon, which you use as the

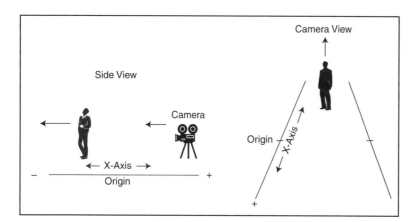

**Figure 16.2**

*The camera is pointing left, whereas the character points up.*

Camera View

Side View

Camera

X-Axis

Origin

Origin

X-Axis

Y-coordinate for the characters. Chapter 12 covers utilizing the `GetHeight` functions to determine the Y-coordinates required to place characters in 3-D space.

## Rotational Control

Rotational control allows the player to rotate the character using the left and right arrow keys and forward and backward using the up and down arrow keys.

Rotational control is better than directional control is some aspects, because the movement calculations are more basic. Characters need to store a directional value now, however, that represents the direction they are facing (with 0.0 pointing along the positive Z-axis, 1.57 pointing along the positive X-axis, 3.14 pointing along the negative Z-axis, and 4.71 pointing along the negative X-axis). Assume that the direction variable is as follows:

```
float Facing = 0.0f;  // Direction character is facing
```

At this point, you can say that pushing the left control (the left arrow key or left on a joystick) rotates the character to the left (negative rotation), and pushing right rotates the character to the right (positive rotation):

```
// using the Input Core:
// Keyboard = pre-created cInputDevice object for keyboard
Keyboard.Read();

// Rotating left?
if(Keyboard.GetKeyState[KEY_LEFT] == TRUE)
  Facing -= 0.01f; // Rotate left .01 radians
```

```
// Rotating right
if(Keyboard.GetKeyState[KEY_RIGHT] == TRUE)
  Facing += 0.01f; // Rotate right .01 radians
```

From the `Facing` angle variable, movement forward and backward becomes a matter
of the following:

```
// Move forward?
if(Keyboard.GetKeyState[KEY_UP] == TRUE) {
  XPos += (float)cos(Facing-1.57f) * Distance;
  ZPos += (float)-sin(Facing-1.57f) * Distance;
}


// Move backward?
if(Keyboard.GetKeyState[KEY_DOWN] == TRUE) {
  XPos += (float)-cos(Facing-1.57f) * Distance;
  ZPos += (float)sin(Facing-1.57f) * Distance;
}
```

## First Person Control

The last type of directional control I like to use is one for a first-person style game
in which you see the world through the eyes of the character. This form of control
uses the arrow keys to move characters left, right, forward, and backward and the
mouse to rotate the view (much like turning your head as you look around).

Pressing the up arrow moves characters forward in the direction they are looking,
whereas pressing the down arrow moves characters backward. The left and right
arrows move left and right. First-person control is similar to the rotational control
you just read about, but with first-person control, the mouse turns the character.

This time however, it's not characters that rotate, but the camera (because the camera view represents the view from the character's eyes). This introduces a couple of
new variables that represent the camera angles:

```
float XAngle = 0.0f, YAngle = 0.0f; // Character viewing angles
```

The two preceding variables will now hold the viewing angle, which is modified as
the player moves the mouse. Here's the code to modify the viewing angles:

```
// Assuming using the Input Core
// Mouse = pre-created cInputDevice for mouse
// same for keyboard
Mouse.Read();
Keyboard.Read();
```

```
// Rotate the character based on mouse angle
XAngle += Mouse.GetYDelta() / 200.0f;
YAngle += Mouse.GetXDelta() / 200.0f;

// Move character
if(Keyboard.GetKeyState[KEY_UP] == TRUE) {
  XPos += (float)cos(YAngle-1.57f) * Distance;
  ZPos += (float)-sin(YAngle-1.57f) * Distance;
}
if(Keyboard.GetKeyState[KEY_DOWN] == TRUE) {
  XPos += (float)-cos(YAngle-1.57f) * Distance;
  ZPos += (float)sin(YAngle-1.57f) * Distance;
}
if(Keyboard.GetKeyState[KEY_LEFT] == TRUE) {
  XPos += (float)cos(YAngle-3.14f) * Distance;
  ZPos += (float)-sin(YAngle-3.14f) * Distance;
}
if(Keyboard.GetKeyState[KEY_RIGHT] == TRUE) {
  XPos += (float)cos(YAngle) * Distance;
  ZPos += (float)-sin(YAngle) * Distance;
}
```

Notice that whenever the user moves the mouse, a delta value (the amount of movement) is used to rotate the view. From there, calculating which direction to move the character is easy.

# Controlling Non-Player Characters

As you've been able to surmise from the past few sections, controlling the player is relatively simple. Now comes the tough part—controlling the game's NPCs. This section shows you the various methods of navigating your game's NPCs.

Although games might trick you into thinking some elaborate scheme is moving the NPCs around the world, that just isn't the case.

Do you remember the five general types of NPC movements that I mentioned earlier—standing still, wandering around an area, walking along a route, following a character, and evading a character? With these in mind, you might want to take a closer look at your favorite role-playing games to find out which control schemes they use.

As for *your* role-playing game, take a moment to examine the following controls and how to implement them.

## Standing Still

There's not much to think about here—just place a character and he stands still facing a specific direction. That direction is an angular rotation.

## Wandering an Area

Games such as *Ultima Online* allow NPCs to wander around a set area, whether it is the entire level or a section that you define. To keep things simple, you can specify the range in which you want a character to wander, within a specific range of coordinates (as illustrated in Figure 16.3). These coordinates can be stored in variables such as these:

```
float WanderMinX, WanderMinY, WanderMinZ;
float WanderMaxX, WanderMaxY, WanderMaxZ;
```

Now, assuming that you are tracking a character's coordinates in the level in a trio of variables, you can move them around randomly and check whether a move is valid:

```
float CharXPos, CharYPos, CharZPos; // Character coordinates
float XMove, ZMove;  // Movement amounts - skip YMove movements

// Distance to move character
float Distance;

// Determine a random direction to move - loop until found
while(1) {
  float Direction = 6.28f / 360.0f * (float)(rand() % 360);
  XMove = cos(Direction) * Distance;
  ZMove = sin(Direction) * Distance;

  // Check if move is valid - ignore height for now
  if(CharXPos+XMove >= WanderMinX &&                        \
     CharXPos+XMove <= WanderMaxX &&                        \
     CharZPos+ZMove >= WanderMinZ &&                        \
     CharZPos+ZMove <= WanderMaxZ) {
    // Movement allowed, update coordinates
    CharXPos+=XMove;
    CharZPos+=ZMove;

    break; // break out of loop
  }
```

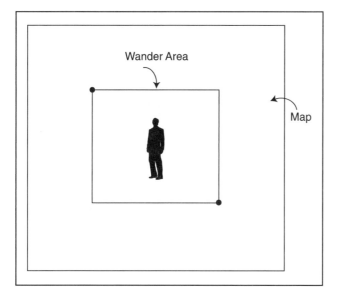

**Figure 16.3**

*A character needs to know its limits when wandering around. By specifying a small area within a map (as shown here), you can limit just where a character can go.*

> ## CAUTION
>
> **Don't randomly move a character around at every frame, or you'll find yourself with characters that look like they're having a conniption fit. Instead, update a character's direction only every few seconds or so.**

## Walking a Route

Although NPCs aren't intelligent enough to know their way around the level, you can assign them routes to travel. These routes include coordinates that must be reached in order to proceed to the next coordinates. Once the last set of coordinates is reached, the character returns to the first set of coordinates and starts the path all over again.

## Using Route Points

Route points are defined as a set of coordinates, and keeping with the 3-D concept that you're accustomed to, you can use the following structure to store those coordinates:

```
typedef struct sRoutePoint {
  float XPos, ZPos;
} sRoutePoint;
```

In order to construct a route, you pick the points you want a character to walk and construct an array of sRoutePoint structures to store the coordinates. Figure 16.4, for example, shows a simple map, with five points marked.

Because each point in the route is marked with coordinates, you can see how to construct the sRoutePoint structures array:

> **NOTE**
>
> Note that there's no need for a Y-coordinate when using a 3-D engine because the height is determined by the height of the ground below the character.

```
sRoutePoint Route[5] = {
    { -200.0f, -100.0f },
    {  100.0f, -300.0f },
    {  300.0f, -200.0f },
    {  200.0f,  100.0f },
    {    0.0f,  400.0f }
};
long NumRoutePoints = 5;   // To make it easier to know # points
```

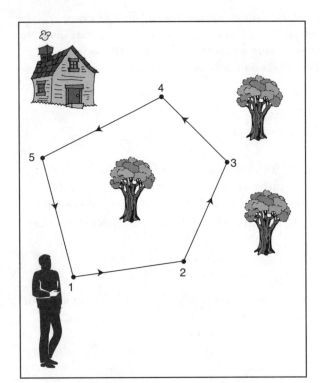

**Figure 16.4**

*This imaginary map shows five route points. The character starts at point 1 and proceeds directly to point 2, and then to point 3, and so on until point 5 is reached. At that point, the character goes back to point 1 and starts the routine again.*

## Walking from Point to Point

In order to proceed from point to point, a character walking a route needs to compare its current coordinates to the point where it's headed. You use this, combined with the character's walking speed, to compute a pair of movement variables that update the character's position.

Start by assuming that the character's coordinates are kept in the following variables (along with the character's walking speed):

```
float CharXPos, CharZPos; // No Y-coordinate needed
float WalkSpeed;          // Walking speed per frame
```

At this point, assume that you've already retrieved the coordinates you want the character to walk to and placed them into another pair of variables:

```
float RouteXPos, RouteZPos; // Again, no Y-coordinate
```

Now, to start the character moving, you calculate the movement variables:

```
// Calculate distance from character to route point
float XDiff = (float)fabs(RouteXPos - CharXPos);
float ZDiff = (float)fabs(RouteZPos - CharZPos);
float Length = sqrt(XDiff*XDiff + ZDiff*ZDiff);

// Calculate movement towards point
float MoveX = (RouteXPos - CharXPos) / Length * WalkSpeed;
float MoveZ = (RouteZPos - CharZPos) / Length * WalkSpeed;
```

Whenever you update the character per frame from now on, you'll need to add MoveX and MoveZ to the character's coordinates, as in the following:

```
CharXPos += MoveX;
CharZPos += MoveZ;
```

With that aside, go back and see just how to track which route point a character is walking toward. When one route point is reached, the character must walk toward the next. To determine when a route point is reached, you check the distance from the character to the route point; if the distance is within a certain limit, the character has reached the point and is allowed to continue on to the next route point.

## Faster than the Speed of Pythagoras

To determine the distance away from a route point, you can use the standard Pythagorean Theorem, but in order to speed things up, you can toss the sqrt operation out the door and use the sum of the squares of the lengths instead. To see what I mean, take a look at the following two lines of code:

```
float Distance = sqrt(Length1*Length1 + Length2*Length2);
float Distance = Length1*Length1 + Length2*Length2;
```

Notice that the preceding two lines of code are almost identical, except the second line omits the sqrt function, making the second line execute much faster. The downside is that you don't get the exact length, which really isn't a problem.

For example, imagine that you are measuring the distance between two points and

> **NOTE**
>
> The *Pythagorean Theorem* is probably the most famous theorem in geometry. It states that the square of the length of the hypotenuse of a right triangle is equal to the sum of the squares of the lengths of the sides. Basically, it means that the square root of the lengths of two sides (when both are squared and added together) equals the length of the third side of a right triangle.

you want to see whether that distance is less than 40. If the coordinates of the two points are 0,0 and 30,20, the faster distance calculation will give you a distance of 1,300 (because the length of the two sides are 30 and 20, respectively).

How can you determine the distance now? By calculating the square (the number times itself) of the distance, that's how! So, by taking 40 times 40, you get 1,600. By comparing the distance of 1,300 between the points, you can see that indeed the distance is less than 1,600 and, thus, less than the original distance of 40 you were checking.

To get back to what I was originally talking about, you can use the faster method of distance calculation to determine when a character is close enough to a route point. Say that you want a route point considered as being touched by a character if that character comes within so many units from it. Utilizing the faster method of distance calculation, you can use the following function to determine whether that is the case:

```
BOOL TouchedRoutePoint(
    float CharXPos, float CharZPos,    // Character coordinates
    float RouteXPos, float RouteZPos,  // Route point coordinates
    float Distance)                    // Distance to check
{
    // Square the distance to adjust for faster distance checking
    Distance *= Distance;
```

```
// Now calculate the distance
float XDiff = (float)fabs(RouteXPos - CharXPos);
float ZDiff = (float)fabs(RouteZPos - CharZPos);
float Dist = XDiff*XDiff + ZDiff*ZDiff;

// Return results
if(Dist <= Distance)  // Within range being checked
  return TRUE;
return FALSE;  // Out of distance range
}
```

When calling `TouchedRoutePoint` with the character coordinates, the coordinates of the route point, and the distance from the point to check, you will receive a value of TRUE if the character is within `Distance` units from the route point coordinates. A return value of FALSE means that the character is not within `Distance` units from the route point.

## Walking the Route

At long last, you can put everything together and force a character to walk from one route point to the next. Here's a small program that takes the five route points defined previously and puts a character at point one, forcing the character to walk from point to point forever:

```
sRoutePoint Route[5] = {
  { -200.0f, -100.0f },
  {  100.0f, -300.0f },
  {  300.0f, -200.0f },
  {  200.0f,  100.0f },
  {    0.0f,  400.0f }
};
long NumRoutePoints = 5;

// Character coordinates and movement variables
float CharXPos = Route[0].XPos;
float CharZPos = Route[0].ZPos;
float MoveX, MoveZ;
float Speed;  // Walking speed of character

// Start track to 2nd point
long TargetRoutePoint = 1;
SetupMovement(TargetRoutePoint);
```

```
// Loop forever, moving and checking for route points reached
while(1) {
  // Is character within range of route point?
  if(TouchedRoutePoint(TargetRoutePoint, 32.0f) == TRUE) {
    // Move to next route point
    TargetRoutePoint++;
    if(TargetRoutePoint >= NumRoutePoints)
      TargetRoutePoint = 0;
    SetupMovement(TargetRoutePoint);
  }


  // Move character
  CharXPos += MoveX;
  CharZPos += MoveZ;
}

// Function to check if within range of route point
BOOL TouchedRoutePoint(long PointNum, float Distance)
{
  Distance *= Distance;
  float XDiff = (float)fabs(CharXPos - Route[PointNum].XPos);
  float ZDiff = (float)fabs(CharZPos - Route[PointNum].ZPos);
  float Dist = XDiff*XDiff + ZDiff*ZDiff;

  if(Dist <= Distance)
    return TRUE;
  return FALSE;
}

// Function to calculate movement variables
void SetupMovement(long PointNum)
{
  float XDiff = (float)fabs(CharXPos - Route[PointNum].XPos);
  float ZDiff = (float)fabs(CharZPos - Route[PointNum].ZPos);
  float Length = sqrt(XDiff*XDiff + ZDiff*ZDiff);
  MoveX = (Route[PointNum].XPos - CharXPos) / Length * Speed;
  MoveZ = (Route[PointNum].ZPos - CharZPos) / Length * Speed;
}
```

# Following Another Character

Although following another character might seem complicated at first, don't worry too much. Remember that keeping it simple is the solution. Following a character is as easy as walking a route. Because a character already knows its own coordinates and the coordinates of the character it is following, you can use previously seen functions to move the character toward another one.

The only difference at this point is that you might want a character to get within a specific distance from the followed character, as illustrated in Figure 16.5.

Knowing each character's coordinates (the character being followed and the character doing the following), you can construct a single function that determines which direction the "following" character should move:

```
void CalculateFollowMovement(
  float CharXPos, float CharZPos,     // Coordinate of character
  float WalkSpeed,                    // Walking speed of char.
  float FollowXPos, float FollowZPos, // Coords of followed char.
  float FollowDistance,               // Distance to follow at
  float *MoveX, float *MoveZ)         // Variables for movement
{
  // Fix for faster distance checking
  FollowDistance *= FollowDistance;

  // Get distance between characters
  float XDiff = (float)fabs(FollowXPos - CharXPos);
  float ZDiff = (float)fabs(FollowZPos - CharZPos);
  float Length = XDiff*XDiff + ZDiff*ZDiff;

  // If distance between characters is less than allowed,
  // then just stand still.
  if(Length < FollowDistance) {
    *MoveX = *MoveZ = 0.0f;
    return;
  }

  // Calculate rate to move based on character walking speed
  Length = sqrt(Length);
  *MoveX = (CharXPos - FollowXPos) / Length * WalkSpeed;
  *MoveZ = (CharZPos - FollowZPos) / Length * WalkSpeed;
}
```

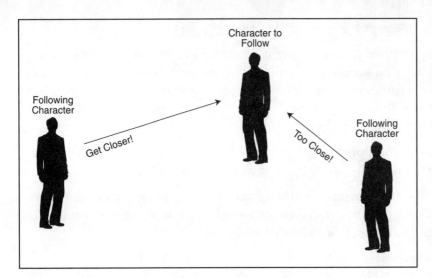

**Figure 16.5**

*One character has picked another character to follow. If the character being followed is closer than an assigned distance, the following character stands still. If the distance is greater, the character that is following the other one needs to move closer.*

Whenever you want to update a character that is following another one, you merely pass along the required data and move the character using the returned movement variables.

## Evading Another Character

Evading means to move a character away from another one. If the character to be avoided is closer than the minimum set distance, the evading character moves in the opposite direction through the use of the CalculateEvadeMovement function:

```
void CalculateEvadeMovement(
    float CharXPos, float CharZPos,      // Coordinate of character
    float WalkSpeed,                     // Walking speed of char.
    float FollowXPos, float FollowZPos,  // Coords of evaded char.
    float EvadeDistance,                 // Distance to evade
    float *MoveX, float *MoveZ)          // Variables for movement
{
    // Fix for faster distance checking
    FollowDistance *= FollowDistance;

    // Get distance between characters
    float XDiff = (float)fabs(FollowXPos - CharXPos);
    float ZDiff = (float)fabs(FollowZPos - CharZPos);
    float Length = XDiff*XDiff + ZDiff*ZDiff;
```

```
// If distance between characters is more than allowed,
// then just stand still.
if(Length > EvadeDistance) {
  *MoveX = *MoveZ = 0.0f;
  return;
}

// Calculate rate to move based on character walking speed
Length = sqrt(Length);
*MoveX = -((CharXPos - FollowXPos) / Length * WalkSpeed);
*MoveZ = -((CharZPos - FollowZPos) / Length * WalkSpeed);
}
```

# Automatic Control of Characters

Ever get the feeling you aren't in control? With your role-playing game that just might seem like the case. However, when scripting comes into play, you want to control the PCs at times—for example, to advance the story in some way. This involves automatic control.

*Automatic control* of a character means that the game decides which control method to use and where to move the character. Automatic control takes place in the artificial intelligence settings. To temporarily control a PC, you can use the following steps:

1. Change the PC to an NPC.
2. Change the artificial intelligence setting of the PC (now an NPC) to follow a route (or other movement type).
3. Perform movements and continue updating until the last route point is reached or until you want to stop using automatic control.
4. Switch the character back to a PC type.

# Conversation among Characters

That's right, chat it up! Character interaction is also a major part of a role-playing game, but have you seriously thought about how to implement conversation into a game? Thankfully, there are easy ways to make your characters talk to each other, and not wanting to stray from the easy path, let me show you some of the basic character conversation methods.

# The Talking Dummy

The easiest conversation method to use has got to be the *talking dummy*. Every role-playing game has at least one character (the talking dummy) that says the same thing again and again; no intelligence is involved. Programming a talking dummy into your game is as easy as assigning a line of text that is displayed whenever a character is spoken to.

The problem is that the talking dummy can say only one thing at a time, which isn't very useful. Also, rather than inserting the code for a character's dialogue into the game engine, you can use an external source for the conversation text, which takes us to the next topic, how to improve the basic talking dummy design.

## Script-Driven Talking Dummies

You knew this was coming, didn't you? Scripting is the heart and soul of computer role-playing games, so you should try to use it to the fullest degree, including when your characters converse with each other. By assigning a script to each character in your game, the scripting engine can take the basic talking dummy concept and expand it.

Adding the ability to use conditional code in the script enables talking dummies to decide what to say based on internal flags and variables. Say that you have a script that tracks the status of a flag, a flag that states whether you've visited a nearby town.

When it comes to a script-driven talking dummy, your script engine decides which text to display based on the flag it receives. That character (the dummy) tells you to visit the nearby town, or if you've been to the town, the dummy might comment on the town's population. One such script might look something like this (in a textual format):

```
If flag 0 is TRUE then
   Print message "I see you've visited GranWell to the south!"
Else
   Print message "You should head south to the town GranWell."
Endif
```

As you can see in the preceding script, a flag (flag 0) tracks a TRUE or FALSE value (the flag is set to TRUE whenever the player visits the town GranWell).

The script-talking dummy is relatively easy to create and process, and I use this conversation method throughout the rest of the book. In the later section "Demonstrating Characters with the Chars Demo" and in Chapter 20, you see the script process in action and how to use script-driven talking dummies in your game.

# Displaying Conversational and Other Text

No matter which way you look at it, you need to display the conversation among characters in one way or another. You know the routine—whenever your player talks to another character, a small window pops up and displays text. Every once in a while, the character can choose from a list of actions displayed, and the conversation goes on.

Using 2-D techniques, you can display a *conversation window* (or *text window* to be more precise), with the conversation text displayed inside the window. Because only so many text characters can fit within the window at one time, multiple windows are displayed with each page holding a portion of the complete conversation. A player pushes a button to navigate through each page of text that is displayed in the window. When the text finishes, the conversation ends.

To keep things simple, I developed a system (a text window class called cWindow) that can render a text window of any size anywhere on the display. This window can be moved at any time, and may contain any string of text you assign. As a bonus, the window can act as a text-bubble of sorts, whereas the window has a pointer to a talking character. Figure 16.6 shows the text window class in action.

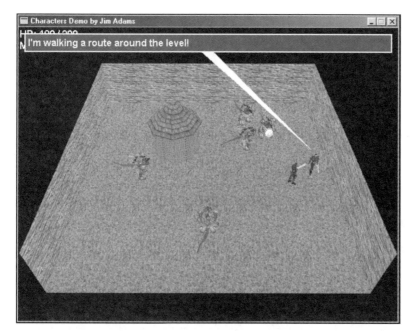

**Figure 16.6**

*The* cWindow *text window class enables you to open windows of any height and width to display any type of text (usually conversation text).*

Technically, the window is two rectangles drawn on top of each other, with both rectangles contained within a vertex buffer. One rectangle is white and is slightly larger than the inner colored rectangle. When you draw them in order (from the larger white rectangle to the smaller colored window), you achieve a bordered window look as shown in Figure 16.6.

The window text is drawn on top of the two windows. Text can be set at any time, but presetting a string of text gives you the extra ability of calculating a window size that's guaranteed to fit the entire string of text within the window. Once you define a window's size, you can dynamically change the string of text drawn without re-creating the vertex buffer defining the window.

Realistically, you can use the text window for anything. Say that you want to open a window to display an image using a text window class and texture object. It becomes a matter of drawing one and then the other. In fact, in Chapter 20, you find out how the text window class is put to good use for things other than conversations.

## The cWindow Class

To get things rolling, take a look at the following cWindow class definition:

```
class cWindow
{
  private:
    typedef struct sVertex {  // Custom vertex
      float    x, y, z;  // Coordinates in screen space
      float    rhw;      // RHW value
      D3DCOLOR Diffuse;  // Diffuse color
    } sVertex;
    #define WINDOWFVF (D3DFVF_XYZRHW | D3DFVF_DIFFUSE)
```

Remember that the text window uses a vertex buffer to contain a couple of rectangles (with two triangles defined per rectangle). The vertex buffer uses only transformed vertices that are assigned a diffuse color (white for the larger rectangle in the back and your color of choice for the smaller rectangle in the front). Each vertex is stored within the preceding sVertex structure (and matching vertex descriptor).

> **CAUTION**
>
> At this time, you hard-code the size of the font required; the font must be 16 pixels or some spacing issues will arise. I'll leave it to you to alter the code a bit, but for all further examples, I suggest sticking with an Arial font using a size of 16.

From here, you define a set of parent cGraphics and cFont object pointers. A text window must have a pre-initialized graphics object and font object in order to work. Also, you instance the text window vertex buffer object.

```
cGraphics      *m_Graphics;  // Parent cGraphics object
cFont          *m_Font;      // Font object
cVertexBuffer  m_WindowVB;   // Vertex buffer for window

char           *m_Text;      // Text to display
D3DCOLOR       m_TextColor;  // Color to draw text
```

The text string is contained within the class (that is, inside an allocated char buffer), along with a matching text color used to draw the text. Following these text string definitions are the window coordinates and dimensions and a single variable that states whether the text-bubble pointer needs to be drawn (as defined by a later call to position the window).

```
long           m_XPos, m_YPos;     // Window coordinates
long           m_Width, m_Height;  // Window dimensions

BOOL           m_DrawTarget;  // Flag to draw bubble pointer
```

Next come the public class function declarations. (I cover the details of the function prototype descriptions after showing them. At that point, I show the code for each function separately.)

```
public:
  cWindow();   // Constructor
  ~cWindow();  // Destructor

  // Functions to create/free a text window
  BOOL Create(cGraphics *Graphics, cFont *Font);
  BOOL Free();

  // Set the text and window coordinates/dimensions/colors
  BOOL SetText(char *Text, D3DCOLOR TextColor = 0xFFFFFFFF);

  // Move the window
  BOOL Move(long XPos, long YPos, long Width,long Height=0, \
            long TargetX = -1, long TargetY = -1,           \
            D3DCOLOR BackColor = D3DCOLOR_RGBA(0,64,128,255));

  long GetHeight();  // Get window height after set
```

```
      // Render window and text to display
      BOOL Render(char *Text = NULL);
};
```

## cWindow::cWindow and cWindow::~cWindow

The constructor and destructor are small and to the point, merely clearing and releasing the class resources:

```
cWindow::cWindow()
{
  // Clear class data
  m_Graphics  = NULL;
  m_Font      = NULL;
  m_Text      = NULL;
  m_TextColor = 0xFFFFFFFF;
}


cWindow::~cWindow()
{
  Free();   // Free class data
}
```

## cWindow::Create and cWindow::Free

You use the Create and Free functions to prepare the class for use (by assigning the cGraphics and cFont objects used for rendering) and to free the internal class data:

```
BOOL cWindow::Create(cGraphics *Graphics, cFont *Font)
{
  Free();   // Free previous class data

  // Error checking
  if((m_Graphics = Graphics) == NULL || (m_Font = Font) == NULL)
    return FALSE;

  // Create new vertex buffer (w/11 vertices to use)
  m_WindowVB.Create(m_Graphics, 11, WINDOWFVF, sizeof(sVertex));

  return TRUE; // Return success
}
```

```
BOOL cWindow::Free()
{
  m_WindowVB.Free();   // Free vertex buffer

  delete [] m_Text;    // Delete text buffer
  m_Text = NULL;

  return TRUE;
}
```

A window vertex buffer uses 11 vertices to store the two window rectangles and a pointer graphic to a target location on the screen. You get to see how the vertex buffer is constructed and used coming up in the section "cWindow::Move." As for the window text, merely allocating an array and copying the string into it is sufficient, so freeing the class involves deleting the array in use.

### cWindow::SetText

As I just mentioned, you store the window text by creating an array of bytes and copying the window text into that array. Setting the window text is the purpose of the SetText function, which takes two parameters—the text to use (char *Text) and the color to use to draw the text (D3DCOLOR TextColor).

```
BOOL cWindow::SetText(char *Text, D3DCOLOR TextColor)
{
  // Delete previous text
  delete [] m_Text;
  m_Text = NULL;

  m_Text = strdup(Text);        // Copy text string
  m_TextColor = TextColor;      // Store text color

  return TRUE;
}
```

For efficiency, use the strdup function to allocate and copy the text string at the same time. The strdup function takes a text string as an argument and returns a pointer to an allocated buffer that contains the text in question. From now on, the text is ready to use in the class, and any time you want to change the text, just make another call to SetText.

## cWindow::Move

The biggest of the bunch, cWindow::Move has the job of constructing the vertex buffer used to render the window (and supporting pointer, if needed). The function takes as arguments the position to place the window (screen coordinates), the dimensions (in pixels), a pair of coordinates at which to point the text-bubble pointer, and a color to use for the smaller frontmost window.

```
BOOL cWindow::Move(long XPos, long YPos,                          \
                   long Width, long Height,                       \
                   long TargetX, long TargetY,                    \
                   D3DCOLOR BackColor)
{
  sVertex Verts[11];
  long i;
```

After declaring the few local variables in use, you store the position and dimensions of the window within the class variables. The Move function prototype defaults the Height argument to 0, which means that you want the class to calculate the height required to display all text contained within the already created text buffer.

Having the Move function calculate the height of the text is perfect. If you're displaying text of unknown lengths, you merely set Height to 0 and let the class do the hard work. Speaking of this hard work, the code that stores the position and dimensions are as follows (including the code to calculate the height):

```
// Save the coordinates and calculate height if needed
m_XPos  = XPos;
m_YPos  = YPos;
m_Width = Width;
if(!(m_Height = Height)) {
  RECT Rect;
  Rect.left   = XPos;
  Rect.top    = 0;
  Rect.right  = XPos + Width - 12;
  Rect.bottom = 1;

  m_Height = m_Font->GetFontCOM()->DrawText(m_Text, -1,    \
             &Rect, DT_CALCRECT | DT_WORDBREAK,            \
             0xFFFFFFFF) + 12;
}
```

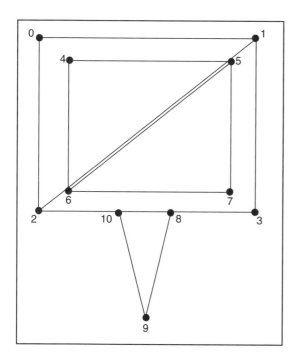

**Figure 16.7**

*Two windows, each using four vertices are defined by use of triangle strips. The last triangle in the vertex buffer (the pointer) uses three vertices of its own and is stored as a triangle strip.*

From here on in, the code is dedicated to constructing the vertex buffer to display the window. As I've mentioned, you use two rectangles, with each rectangle using four vertices (arranged in a triangle strip to conserve memory and improve rendering time).

Using the previously stored position and dimensions, the windows are constructed as shown in Figure 16.7.

Additionally, the vertex buffer may contain three more vertices that construct the pointer at either the top or the bottom of the text window. Setting the TargetX and TargetY arguments to a value other than -1 informs the Move function to draw a pointer. Continue on in the code to set the vertices for the window:

```
// Clear the vertex data
for(i=0;i<11;i++) {
    Verts[i].z = 0.0f;
    Verts[i].rhw = 1.0f;
    Verts[i].Diffuse = 0xFFFFFFFF;
}

// Set up the white outline
Verts[0].x = (float)m_XPos;
Verts[0].y = (float)m_YPos;
```

```
          Verts[1].x = (float)(m_XPos+m_Width);
          Verts[1].y = (float)m_YPos;
          Verts.x = (float)m_XPos;
          Verts.y = (float)(m_YPos+m_Height);
          Verts.x = (float)(m_XPos+m_Width);
          Verts.y = (float)(m_YPos+m_Height);

          // Set up the text window
          Verts.x = (float)m_XPos+2.0f;
          Verts.y = (float)m_YPos+2.0f;
          Verts.Diffuse = BackColor;
          Verts[5].x = (float)(m_XPos+m_Width)-2.0f;
          Verts[5].y = (float)m_YPos+2.0f;
          Verts[5].Diffuse = BackColor;
          Verts[6].x = (float)m_XPos+2.0f;
          Verts[6].y = (float)(m_YPos+m_Height)-2.0f;
          Verts[6].Diffuse = BackColor;
          Verts[7].x = (float)(m_XPos+m_Width)-2.0f;
          Verts[7].y = (float)(m_YPos+m_Height)-2.0f;
          Verts[7].Diffuse = BackColor;

          // Set up the target pointer
          if(TargetX != -1 && TargetY != -1) {
            m_DrawTarget = TRUE;

            if(TargetY < m_YPos) {
              Verts[8].x  = (float)TargetX;
              Verts[8].y  = (float)TargetY;
              Verts[9].x  = (float)(m_XPos+m_Width/2+10);
              Verts[9].y  = (float)m_YPos;
              Verts[10].x = (float)(m_XPos+m_Width/2-10);
              Verts[10].y = (float)m_YPos;
            } else {
              Verts[8].x  = (float)(m_XPos+m_Width/2-10);
              Verts[8].y  = (float)(m_YPos+m_Height);
              Verts[9].x  = (float)(m_XPos+m_Width/2+10);
              Verts[9].y  = (float)(m_YPos+m_Height);
              Verts[10].x = (float)TargetX;
              Verts[10].y = (float)TargetY;
            }
          } else {
            m_DrawTarget = FALSE;
```

```
  }

  m_WindowVB.Set(0,11,&Verts);  // Set the vertices

  return TRUE;
}
```

## cWindow::GetHeight

Because you don't have to specify a height value in the call to Move, you might need to retrieve the actual height of the text window used. GetHeight does just that; it returns the height of the text window as defined from Move:

```
long cWindow::GetHeight()
{
  return m_Height;
}
```

## cWindow::Render

Last comes the Render function, which you call with a cGraphics::BeginScene and cGraphics::EndScene code block. Render merely sets the required rendering states and draws the required polygons that form the pointer and text window. Then it draws the text string (if the window height is greater than 12, which is the size of the border used to surround the smaller frontmost window).

```
BOOL cWindow::Render(char *Text, D3DCOLOR Color)
{
  // Error checking
  if(m_Graphics == NULL || m_Font == NULL)
    return FALSE;

  // Set rendering states
  m_Graphics->SetTexture(0, NULL);
  m_Graphics->EnableZBuffer(FALSE);

  // Draw window
  m_WindowVB.Render(0,2,D3DPT_TRIANGLESTRIP);
  m_WindowVB.Render(4,2,D3DPT_TRIANGLESTRIP);

  // Draw target pointer if needed
  if(m_DrawTarget)
    m_WindowVB.Render(8,1,D3DPT_TRIANGLELIST);
```

```
    // Only draw text if height > 12
    if(m_Height > 12) {
      // Draw the text
      if(Text == NULL)
        m_Font->Print(m_Text, m_XPos+6, m_YPos+6,              \
                              m_Width-12,m_Height-12,           \
                              m_TextColor, DT_WORDBREAK);
      else
        m_Font->Print(Text, m_XPos+6, m_YPos+6,                \
                            m_Width-12,m_Height-12,             \
                            Color, DT_WORDBREAK);
    }

    return TRUE;
}
```

Render takes two optional arguments. The first argument, Text, overrides the class's text that was already set using the SetText function. Overriding the text to draw is great for dynamically updating what needs to be shown. The second argument, Color, specifies the color you want to use to draw the text to the display.

## Using cWindow

To quickly demonstrate using cWindow, let me show you how to display a short message (assuming that you've already initialized a cGraphics object):

```
// Graphics = pre-initialized cGraphics object
cFont Font;
cWindow Window;

// Create a font to use
Font.Create(&Graphics, "Arial", 16);

Window.Create(&Graphics, &Font);  // Prepare class for use
Window.SetText("The cWindow class in action!");
Window.Move(4,4,632);

Graphics.BeginScene();  // Begin the scene
Window.Render();        // Draw the window and text
Graphics.EndScene();    // End the scene
Graphics.Display();     // Display the scene

Window.Free();  // Free window class data
```

The usefulness of the `cWindow` class really comes into use later in the section "Demonstrating Characters with the Chars Demo" when you display dialogue, so put conversations and text windows on the back burner for a moment.

# Scripting and Characters

Scripting keeps popping its head up throughout these last few chapters, and true to form, scripting plays a major role when dealing with characters. Scripts work with conversations, spells, character movement, and much more.

What you need at this point is a clean-cut method of processing the game scripts. The best way to do this is to create a class to entwine into your character and other application processing.

## The Script Class

Rather than developing a class to process scripts earlier in the book, I waited until you have a real need for doing so. In Chapter 14, "Implementing Scripts," you learn how easy it is to work with the Mad Lib Script (MLS) system and how easy it is to process scripts created using the MLS editor. However, it becomes even easier to execute scripts when you put the whole script processing in a class. Here is the `cScript` class, defined in the Script.cpp and Script.h files (found on the CD in the \BookCode\Chap16\Chars directory):

```
class cScript
{
  private:
    long      m_NumActions;    // # of script actions loaded
    sScript *m_ScriptParent;   // Script linked list

    // Overloadable functions for preparing for script
    // processing and when processing completed
    virtual BOOL Prepare() { return TRUE; }
    virtual BOOL Release() { return TRUE; }

    // Process a single script action
    virtual sScript *Process(sScript *Script)
            { return Script->Next; }

  public:
    cScript();    // Constructor
```

```
    ~cScript();    // Destructor

    BOOL Load(char *Filename);              // Load a script
    BOOL Free();                             // Free loaded script
    BOOL Execute(char *Filename=NULL);  // Execute script
};
```

Although deceptively small, the cScript class packs a punch. Loading a script is accomplished via the Load function. Once it's loaded, you can process the script with a call to Execute. If you don't want to hassle with loading a script before processing, a call to the Execute function takes a script file to load and execute in the same function call (plus it frees the script when execution is complete).

The way the cScript class processes scripts is ingenious. You actually have to derive the cScript class to parse each script action as it is processed. That's the purpose of the Process function. Once a script is loaded, the Process function is called for every script action to process.

Each script pointer is queried for the script action number, and you must decide what to do with the action. Then you need to update the script pointers by returning the pointer to the next script action in the linked list. (Refer to Chapter 14 for information on how scripts are processed.)

> **TIP**
>
> Using the Load function to load a script is useful if the script is processed many times because you don't have to free it between uses. Loading a script within the Execute function forces the script to be loaded and freed every time, wasting precious time.

The entire cScript class code is shown in Chapter 14, so turn now to finding out how to derive a class that is used to process a script.

## Creating a Derived Script Class

I'm going to assume that you are comfortable working with action templates and scripts at this point. The following action template provides an example of using a derived script class:

```
"End"
"If flag ~ equals ~ then"
  INT 0 255
  BOOL
"Else"
"EndIf"
```

```
"Set flag ~ to ~"
  INT 0 255
  BOOL
"Print ~"
  TEXT
```

Now, using the preceding action template, include the following script (I list it in text form here to make it easier to understand):

```
If flag 0 equals TRUE then
  Print "Flag is TRUE"
  Set flag 0 to FALSE
Else
  Print "Flag is FALSE"
  Set flag 0 to TRUE
EndIf
```

A brief reading shows that the pre-ceding script displays the message "Flag is FALSE" first (because all script flags are reset to FALSE when initialized); when executed again, the script displays "Flag is TRUE".

> **CAUTION**
>
> Remember that the example script shown here is in text form, but when used as a Mad Lib Script, the format is based on values. For example, the if...then action is represented by the value 1, whereas the EndIf action uses the value 3.

## The Derived Class

The next step to processing the script is to derive a class from cScript:

```
class cGameScript : public cScript
{
  private:
    BOOL m_Flags[256];  // The internal flags

    // The script function prototypes
    sScript *Script_End(sScript*);
    sScript *Script_IfFlagThen(sScript*);
    sScript *Script_Else(sScript*);
    sScript *Script_EndIf(sScript*);
    sScript *Script_SetFlag(sScript*);
    sScript *Script_Print(sScript*);

    // The overloaded process function
    sScript *Process(sScript *Script);
```

```
  public:
    cGameScript();
};
```

The derived class shown here (cGameScript) uses an array of BOOL values that represents the internal flags the scripts can use. Following the single variable declaration is a list of function prototypes.

The script function prototypes are the bread and butter of the script processor. Each script action has an associated function that is called during the Process function. The Process function is overridden to call upon those script functions, as you soon see in this section.

Aside from those private function calls, there is the constructor, which clears the m_Flags array to all FALSE values.

```
cGameScript::cGameScript()
{
  // Clear all internal flags to FALSE
  for(short i=0;i<256;i++)
    m_Flags[i] = FALSE;
}
```

Jumping back a bit, take a look at the overridden Process function. As you can see from the following code, cGameScript::Process takes only the current script action type and jumps to the appropriate function. Upon the return of each action function, a pointer to the next script action is returned. If a value of NULL is returned, script execution halts.

```
sScript *cGameScript::Process(sScript *Script)
{
  // Jump to function based on action type
  switch(Script->Type) {
    case  0: return Script_End(Script);
    case  1: return Script_IfFlagThen(Script);
    case  2: return Script_Else(Script);
    case  3: return Script_EndIf(Script);
    case  4: return Script_SetFlag(Script);
    case  5: return Script_Print(Script);
  }

  return NULL; // Error executing
}
```

Now that you've overridden the Process function (and filled in the switch statement with the action's function calls), you can continue by programming all of the actions' functions, as follows:

```
sScript *cGameScript::Script_End(sScript *Script)
{
  return NULL;  // Force script to stop processing
}


sScript *cGameScript::Script_IfFlagThen(sScript *Script)
{
  BOOL Skipping;  // Flag for if...then condition

  // See if a flag matches second entry
  if(m_Flags[Script->Entries[0].lValue % 256] ==          \
            Script->Entries[1].bValue)
    Skipping = FALSE;  // Don't skip following actions
  else
    Skipping = TRUE;   // Skip following actions

  // At this point, Skipping states if the script actions
  // need to be skipped due to a conditional if..then statement.
  // Actions are further processed if skipped = FALSE, looking
  // for an else to flip the skip mode, or an endif to end
  // the conditional block.

  Script = Script->Next;  // Go to next action to process

  while(Script != NULL) {
    // if else, flip skip mode
    if(Script->Type == 2)
      Skipping = (Skipping == TRUE) ? FALSE : TRUE;

    // break on end if
    if(Script->Type == 3)
      return Script->Next;

    // Process script function in conditional block
    // making sure to skip actions when condition not met.
    if(Skipping == TRUE)
```

```
      Script = Script->Next;
    else {
      if((Script = Process(Script)) == NULL)
        return NULL;
    }
  }

  return NULL; // End of script reached
}

sScript *cGameScript::Script_Else(sScript *Script)
{
  return Script->Next;  // Go to next script action
}

sScript *cGameScript::Script_EndIf(sScript *Script)
{
  return Script->Next;  // Go to next script action
}

sScript *cGameScript::Script_SetFlag(sScript *Script)
{
  // Set boolean value
  m_Flags[Script->Entries[0].lValue % 256] =                    \
          Script->Entries[1].bValue;

  return Script->Next;  // Go to next script action
}

sScript *cGameScript::Script_Print(sScript *Script)
{
  // Display some text in a message box
  MessageBox(NULL, Script->Entries[0].Text, "Text", MB_OK);

  return Script->Next;  // Go to next script action
}
```

# Using the Derived Class

To test the cGameScript class, instance it and run the example script that I showed you earlier in the section "Creating a Derived Script Class." Assuming that you saved that script to a file named test.mls, the following example shows the script class functionality:

```
cGameScript Script;

Script.Execute("test.mls");  // Prints a Flag is FALSE message

// At this point, the script's internal flags are maintained,
// so the next call would take the new flag states into account.
Script.Execute("test.mls");  // Prints a Flag is TRUE message
```

Although this is a quick and dirty example of the derived cGameScript class, there really isn't much difference between this class and a full-fledged script parser that uses a huge action template. You merely need to add each action-processing function into the class and call that function via the Parse function. Throughout the rest of the book, you see this script class put to good use; it actually forms the backbone of many projects.

# Resource Management

Resource management plays a major role in your game. For characters to really get anywhere or achieve anything, they may need the aid of the items, spells, and other objects you've constructed for your game.

In Chapter 15, "Defining and Using Objects," you see how to design your game's items and place those items into a master item list. Now is the time to see what you can do with those items.

Resources also include spells that your game's characters can learn through the course of the game. You read more about spells later in this chapter in the section "Magic and Spells," but for now, here is a glimpse of what resources can do for you.

## Using Items

You've already seen how to control items in your game using a character inventory control system. If you have played with the CharICS demo, you have noticed the lack of function for the Equip and Use buttons. Now is the time to understand just what will happen when the functionality is put into place in that demo.

A character can keep track of whatever armor, weapons, and accessories they can equip. Because those equipped items are contained within an sItem structure, you can query for the associated modified value (stored as sItem::Value) that is used to modify a character's abilities.

Say that item 1 is a sword. That sword is defined as a weapon and has a modified value of 10. If a character is allowed to equip the weapon (as determined by the class flags), the appropriate modified value is added to the character's attack ability value. Tracking which item is equipped can be as simple as storing the item number in the character definition. Also, because you want to visually display the weapon that a character is holding, you might also load a weapon mesh to attach to the character.

As for using items, that's just as easy as equipping items. Remember that you predetermined what each item can be and what it can do. Say that you have a healing potion and your player decides to drink it. Once you have checked the usage restriction, you can determine that the healing potion is a healing item, and as such, adds the item modifier value to the player's health points.

## Using Magic

Magic spells, much like items, are an essential resource for a player's survival. Magic aids the users in some way; stronger attacks, adding better defenses, and the ability to heal are typical magic spell fare. Although spells are not needed, they sure do help.

Magic spells are defined just like items. They have an assigned feature. Some spells alter the character's health, although other spells cause certain status ailments (such as Poison). Any character can harness magic; they just need to "know" the spell and have the matching mana points to cast it.

In order for characters to know a spell, they must learn it by working through experience levels. You can track learned spells by using the bit flags. You can use a 32-bit variable to store known spells, with each bit in the variable representing a specific spell. By setting a bit in the variable, the spell is learned. Once a spell is learned, it is typically known forever.

Managing spell usage is just like managing items; by displaying a list of spells known by a character, the player can determine which spells to cast when and where. As for this book, there are no restrictions to when or where a character can cast a spell.

In the section "Working with Magic and Spells," you find more on including spells in your project.

# Shops and Bartering

Resources are commodities, so characters will want to buy and sell their wares from and to each other. Only specific characters in a game are open to bartering. These characters are commonly called "shopkeepers" because they tend to appear only in stops. You know the drill—enter a shop, approach the counter, and begin dealing.

There are specific types of shops for each type of resource dealt with—item shops, weapon shops, armor shops, and so on. You can use a standard approach to shops in all instances.

Character inventory control systems are not just for PCs; here the inventory control system (ICS) developed in Chapter 15 comes in great for shops and shopkeepers. Shopkeeper characters have a unique ICS attached to them, one that determines which items a given shopkeeper character can sell. You don't have to worry about a shopkeeper buying items; all shopkeepers can buy all items marked as sellable (for a reduced cost as defined in the item definition, that is).

Buying an item from a shopkeeper is a matter of displaying the shopkeeper's list of items and their cost. Normally, shopkeepers never run out of stock, no matter how many items the player buys; but occasionally you'll want a shopkeeper to sell only one instance of an item.

Some tinkering with the ICS is in order, but only in terms of quantity of items. If a shopkeeper has an unlimited amount of an item, you set the quantity of that item in the ICS as 2 or more (refer to Chapter 15 to see how to set the item quantity). A quantity value of 1 means that the shopkeeper can sell the item only once. Ingenious, isn't it?

You will find it better to work with shops outside the character code and in the game's main application code. Check out Chapter 20 to see how I was able to implement a bartering system.

# Working with Magic and Spells

Naturally, a first-rate role-playing game must have characters capable of harnessing the mysterious magical powers of the unknown in order to reduce the game's denizens to small piles of charred flesh. Even if you're not into the deadly side of magic, don't just dismiss the benefits of a well-timed healing spell. Magic plays a major part in role-playing games, and now is the time to find out how to blast your game's players with awesome spells and their inevitable effects on the targets.

From a gamer's point of view, a spell is a fancy flash of graphical goodness, although from the game engine side, a spell is nothing more than a function that alters character data. Your game engine can separate graphics and functionality, the two components of a spell, thus making each component easier to handle.

## Spell Graphics

Using 3-D meshes, you can easily deal with the graphical portion of a spell. These spells originate from the spell caster and journey forth to their intended targets, at which point, the spell takes full effect on some poor character. This happens in three steps—origination of the spell mesh, traveling of the mesh, and when the mesh reaches the target. With each step, you can assign an animated mesh, which means that a spell can have up to three meshes graphically representing it.

To increase the choices in creating your game's spell effects, the position and motion of those three meshes are not fixed. In fact, any of the three meshes can hover over the caster or target, move from caster to target or target to caster, or stretch out between the caster and target.

> **NOTE**
>
> Each mesh is displayed separately. Two spell meshes can never be displayed at once. When one mesh completes its cycle, it is released, and the new mesh takes its place.

Whenever a mesh is hovering over the caster or target (or stretching out between the two), it remains there for a fixed amount of time (measured in milliseconds). This gives your mesh the chance to complete its animation cycle (or multiple cycles).

As for moving meshes (moving from caster to target or vice versa), a mesh is assigned a speed of movement (measured in units per second). Once a mesh reaches a target, that mesh is dismissed, and the next mesh takes over (if any meshes are to follow).

Say that you have a fireball spell. Only two meshes are required. The first mesh, a fireball, originates from the caster and moves toward the target, as illustrated in Figure 16.8.

The second mesh, an explosion, takes over when the first mesh reaches its target. The explosion mesh hovers over the target and cycles a few times to give the appearance of some real damage taking place. You're probably wondering about

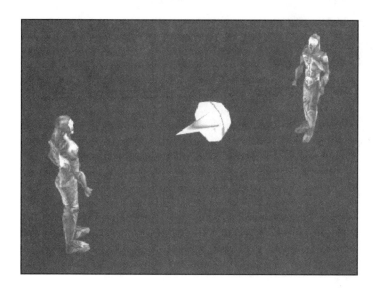

**Figure 16.8**

*A spell caster has unleashed a fireball toward an intended target. The mesh travels at a set speed until it reaches its destination.*

those times when you don't want a spell to move but still want it to extend toward your target. That's the reason for the stretch positioning of meshes.

If you define a mesh that extends outward in the positive Z-axis (which you should always do), that mesh can hover over the caster and scale so that the farthest extent of the mesh touches the target. This stretching (or rather *scaling*) is perfect for spells such as *lightning* or (as the Chars demo program from this chapter uses) a *groundball* spell that ruptures the ground between the caster and the victim (as illustrated in Figure 16.9). You can find the Chars demo program on the CD-ROM in the \BookCode\Chap16\Chars directory. Although not apparent at first glance, the groundball spell described in Figure 16.9 shows a small brownish-colored mesh that is stretched out from the spell caster to the target character.

As you can tell, tracking the three meshes of the spell graphics component is just a matter of loading the appropriate meshes and rendering the correct one at its proper position over a period of time. Upon completion of the required mesh cycles, the graphics segment of spells is complete, and it's time for the functional portion to take over.

## The Function of Spells

The functional component of a spell does the real work. Once a spell runs through its animation and reaches its intended target, the damaging or beneficial effects need to be dealt with.

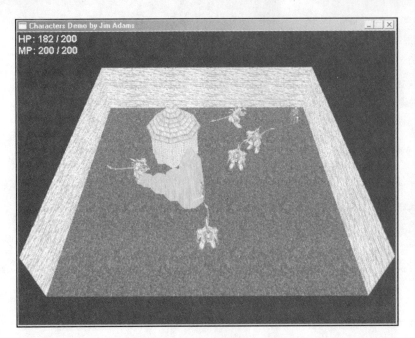

**Figure 16.9**

*The groundball spell from the Chars demo program demonstrates the stretch/scale mesh positioning technique. Whatever the distance between caster and target, the mesh is scaled down to always originate from the caster and touch the target.*

Healing spells need to restore health to an injured character, whereas damaging spells need to take away health. In fact, just about any aspect of a character can be altered from a spell, ranging from characters' health and mana to their abilities such as attack or defense. In Table 16.5, I define the effects that can be used as a spell effect, according to how I use them in this book.

Each spell effect has a supporting value defined in the source code as an `enum` object that is defined as follows:

```
enum SpellEffects {
  ALTER_HEALTH = 0,
  ALTER_MANA,
  CURE_AILMENT,
  CAUSE_AILMENT,
  RAISE_DEAD,
  INSTANT_KILL,
  DISPEL_MAGIC,
  TELEPORT
};
```

## Table 16.5  Possible Spell Effects

| Effect | Description |
| --- | --- |
| Alter health | Increases or decreases target's health points by a set amount. |
| Alter mana | Increases or decreases target's mana points by a set amount. |
| Cure ailment | Cures a target's specified ailment (such as poison or slow). |
| Cause ailment | Causes a target to have an ailment (poison, and so on). |
| Raise dead | Brings the PC back to life. |
| Instant kill | Kills the target character instantly. |
| Dispel magic | Cures all the target character's status ailments. |
| Teleport | Teleports a PC to a specific location on a map. |

Each spell effect is assigned a number. In that way, you can contain the processing of a spell effect within a single switch statement, as in the following:

```
switch(SpellEffect) {
  case ALTER_HEALTH:
    // do health altering processing
  case ALTER_MANA:
    // do mana alter processing
  ...
}
```

Each spell effect is pretty straightforward. Now, take a closer look at just what each of these effects do.

## Alter Health and Mana

A spell can cause damage or rob characters of their stored mana, or it can, on the other hand, restore health or mana. Alteration of health is probably the most widely used spell effect.

A health altering spell has an associated value that determines how much health is removed or added to the target character. The same applies to mana points, which can be restored or drained away with the mere flick of a wizard's hand.

## Cure and Cause Ailment

Status ailments are the bane and bonus of a character's abilities and attributes. The duo of curing and causing spell effects gives you great freedom in devising how to curse or what to bestow upon a character.

When you alter an ailment (cause or cure), you must use a bit-encoded number to define the ailment. By using bit flags, more than one status ailment can be caused or cured at once. Each ailment has an associated macro defined as follows (defined in the Chars.h file):

```
#define AILMENT_POISON          1
#define AILMENT_SLEEP           2
#define AILMENT_PARALYZE        4
#define AILMENT_WEAK            8
#define AILMENT_STRONG          16
#define AILMENT_ENCHANTED       32
#define AILMENT_BARRIER         64
#define AILMENT_DUMBFOUNDED     128
#define AILMENT_CLUMSY          256
#define AILMENT_SUREFOOTED      512
#define AILMENT_SLOW            1024
#define AILMENT_FAST            2048
#define AILMENT_BLIND           4096
#define AILMENT_HAWKEYE         8192
#define AILMENT_SILENCED        16384
```

Character ailments are stored within a single 32-bit variable, and all characters have an ailment variable associated with them. That's right, any character in your game can be burdened with status ailments, but it is harder to afflict characters that have a higher resistance.

## Raise Dead and Instant Kill

At times, your poor characters are going to die, and except for MCs, you want the ability to raise them from the dead. The raise dead spell effect does just that—raises PC or NPC characters from death and gives them exactly one health point.

On the flip side, there will be times when you just want to strike a monster down in one blow. That's the purpose of the instance kill effect. Although having little chance of working, the instant kill ability is still a force to be reckoned with.

## Dispel Magic

Forget all those status ailment-curing spells; why not just get rid of them all in one shot! The dispel effect clears a target character's ailments, whether good or bad, and although this effect can be represented as a cure ailment effect, it becomes much easier to not use bit flags.

## Teleport

Other than walking around, the best way to travel is to magically teleport around. Only PCs can use this spell. Teleporting can move a PC to any position on a map.

# Spell Targeting, Cost, and Chances

Spell effects usually target a single player, but this is not always the case. At times, the spell is either targeted at the spell caster or all the characters within an area. Also, not all characters can be affected by a spell. A spell cast by a monster, for example, should not hurt other monsters, just PCs. In the same vein, spells cast by PCs should be directed only toward monsters.

Each spell has a range of attack; that is, any target within this range can be targeted by the spell. Once a spell is launched and takes effect, the spell has a specific distance at which the effect extends outward from the impact point. A spell targeting multiple characters can then affect those characters under the spell's distance of effect.

Assuming that a character knows a spell (dictated by tracking a bit-encoded variable for each character), you can determine how much mana is required to cast the spell. Each spell has an associated cost assigned—a character must have that much mana to cast the spell. Once cast, the spell's cost in mana is deducted from the casting character's mana points.

Merely casting a spell doesn't mean it will work, however; there are chances of failure. The chance of the spell working or failing is called the *spell effect chance*, and this chance ranges from 0 percent (never works) to 100 percent (always works).

# The Master Spell List

Every aspect of a spell that you've read about can be stored within a single structure, making it much easier to work with.

> **NOTE**
>
> The sSpell structure is defined within the msl.h include file included in the Char project directory (look for \BookCode\Chap16\Chars on this book's CD-ROM). Consult the end of this chapter for more information on the Char project.

This structure, sSpell, is as follows:

```
typedef struct sSpell
{
  char  Name[32];         // Name of character
  char  Description[128]; // Description of spell

  long  DmgClass;         // Class that spell does 2x dmg
  long  CureClass;        // Class that spell aids

  long  Cost;             // Spell casting cost in MP

  float Distance;         // Max. distance to target

  long  Effect;           // Spell effect
  long  Chance;           // % of effect occurring
  float Value;            // Misc. values

  long  Target;           // Target of spell
  float Range;            // Range (in game units)

  long  MeshNum;          // Mesh # to use
  long  MeshPos;          // Positioning of mesh
  float MeshSpeed;        // Speed of mesh movement
  long  MeshSound;        // Sound effect # to play
  BOOL  MeshLoop;         // Loop animation
} sSpell;
```

As you can see, each spell is assigned a name and a description, both of which are contained with small buffers. Your game engine will display the name of each spell in anticipation of the player selecting one to cast when the time comes.

Earlier in this chapter, I mentioned character classes. With spells, those classes come into effect. Certain spells can do double damage to characters that have a weak defense against them, which is the reason for the sSpell::DmgClass variable. If the character's class and DmgClass variables match, the spell does double damage.

On the other hand, if a character's class is based on the spell's class, that spell actually heals the character. Imagine casting an ice spell at an ice dragon. Instead of hurting the dragon, it heals him for half the damage amount of the spell. Thus, the purpose of sSpell::CureClass becomes apparent; if the character's class and CureClass match, the spell heals rather than hurts.

Moving on, you can see the spell casting cost (sSpell::Cost), measured in mana points. A character must have at least this amount of mana (Cost) in reserve to cast the spell. Once the spell is cast, the value in the Cost variable is deducted from the character's mana.

Remember that spells have an assigned range and distance; range (sSpell::Range) is the distance away from the caster that a spell can reach and strike a target, whereas distance (sSpell::Distance) is the parameter around the targeted position at which the spell's effects can take place.

Once a spell finds its mark, the cSpell::Target variable determines who or what is affected—either the spell caster, a single target caught in the parameter of the spell, or all characters caught in the parameter. Each type of target is defined in the engine as follows:

```
enum SpellTargets {
  TARGET_SINGLE = 0,
  TARGET_SELF,
  TARGET_AREA
};
```

The spell's effect (sSpell::Effect) has an associated chance of success, which is stored in sSpell::Chance. Each value has an associated trio of variables (sSpell::Value) at its disposal. The first value in the array is the amount of damage caused or cured or the bit values of the ailment to be used.

The values' only other use is for the teleport spell effect; for NPCs and monsters, the first three values are those of the coordinates inside the current level that the character is moved to whenever the teleport spell is cast. As for PCs, the fourth variable is used to specify which map the player will be switched to when the spell is cast. Because of the complexity of teleporting PCs, let the game script engine handle such teleporting situations.

You use the final group of variables (MeshNum, MeshPos, MeshSpeed, MeshSound, and MeshLoop) for the graphical portion of the spell. Rather than reference the spell meshes by name, it is much more efficient to use numbers. The MeshNum stores a mesh number that the spell control engine uses for drawing the spell's graphics.

MeshPos is the array of variables that contains the position of each mesh. Remember that a mesh can hover over the caster or target, move to or from them, and even stretch out between the two characters. You can set the MeshPos variables to one of the following values:

```
enum AnimPositions {
    POSITION_NONE = 0,
    POSITION_CASTER,
    POSITION_TOTARGET,
    POSITION_TOCASTER,
    POSITION_TARGET,
    POSITION_SCALE
};
```

Again, each mesh has an associated speed of travel or time that it remains in place (as it hovers over a character or stretches out between two positions). Both speed and time are stored in the MeshSpeed variable, as only one of those values is used (depending on the movement of the mesh).

In speed calculations, MeshSpeed determines the distance in 3-D units that the mesh travels in one second. For time, the MeshSpeed variable is converted into a long value that represents the amount in milliseconds that the mesh remains in place.

If the mesh is able to complete its animation cycle before it reaches its target or before its time of display is up, the MeshLoop variables tell the spell control engine to loop the animation over and over until the mesh cycle is complete.

As a final bonus, each one of the three meshes has the ability to emanate a sound when the mesh is initialized (positioned). Imagine that your fireball spell is sizzling toward its target, only to blast forth in a speaker-shattering sound! You also reference each sound by a number and have your game engine play those sounds.

## The Spell List

You use an array of sSpell structures to contain the information about every spell in a game. This array of structures is called the *master spell list* (referred to as MSL from now on), which is stored as a sequential data file. The spell data structure is relatively small, which means that the list can be completely loaded at the start of the game in order to save you time when accessing the data.

Looking back, you can see I've designated that each character has the ability to use 64 spells, so the MSL should hold only 64 sSpell data structures, each representing a single spell that is available for use by all characters.

As I mentioned previously, it becomes a matter of loading each sSpell structure with the appropriate spell data needed. Even with only 64 spells at your disposal, trying to hard-code that many spell structures is too much work.

## Defining Spells with the MSL Editor

Defining your game's spells by manually constructing a bunch of sSpell structures can quickly become tedious. Instead, you need an editor that is better suited to quickly change every aspect of your game's spells. Welcome to the MSL Editor!

The MSL Editor (located on this book's CD-ROM; look for \BookCode\Chap16\ MSLEdit) has a straightforward interface, as shown in Figure 16.10.

The MSL Editor has room for 64 spells (limited only by the flags used to store the character's known spells). Once you start the editor, you can follow these steps to create or edit your spells:

1. Double-click a spell in the list to open the Modify Spell dialog box.
2. In the Modify Spell dialog box (see Figure 16.11), enter the spell's data. Click OK to close the Modify Spell dialog box and return to the Master Spell List Editor dialog box.
3. To save your spell list, click the Save button.
4. In the Save MSL File dialog box, enter a filename and click OK. To load a spell file, click the Load button in the Master Spell List Editor dialog box, enter the filename of the spell file to load, and click OK.

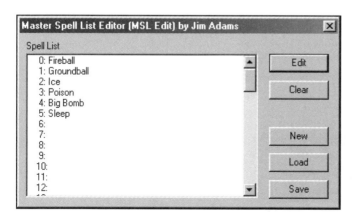

**Figure 16.10**

*The MSL Editor main screen maintains a list of the spells currently loaded, as well as buttons controlling the adding, removing, saving, and loading of MSL files.*

Modifying a spell can be a little daunting at first because of all the data involved, but earlier in this chapter, you learned what each piece of data does for a spell. Now, refer to Figure 16.11 as you follow this brief example of defining the fireball spell shown in the figure.

The fireball spell is hitting a single target with a ball of fire. Costing 5 MP to cast, this spell has no damage or cure classes assigned (as denoted by the value of -1). The spell alters health by -10 (as denoted in the Value 1 edit box), and has a 100 percent chance of affecting the target.

Characters within 256 units of distance from the caster can be targets of the spell, with only a single target being hurt by the spell (the first character found within the 30 unit distance parameter).

Two meshes are in use; the first is mesh 0, which moves from the caster to the target at a speed of 256 units per second. This mesh loops in its animation until the mesh hits the intended target, at which time the second mesh takes over. The second mesh uses mesh 1, which hovers over the target for 400 milliseconds. The third mesh is not in use (which you set by selecting N/A as the position). At this point, the spell is completed.

Take your time and check out the example spells included with this chapter's demo program (Chars). Try adding some of your own spells and test their visual effects and functions on the demo's characters.

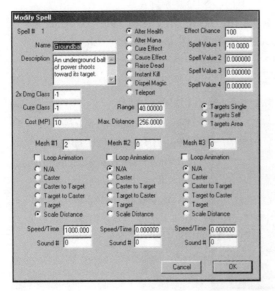

**Figure 16.11**

*The Modify Spell dialog box is packed with graphics and all the information you need to describe a spell's effects.*

# Creating a Spell Controller

Controlling spells is a matter of tracking the meshes and animations that represent the spell and then processing the spell's effects on their intended targets. Because the spell's effects are really related to the characters, it's best to let the engine that controls the characters handle the spell effects and leave the spell animation up to a spell controller class object.

You want to create a spell controller class that maintains a list of currently cast spells and displays them onscreen. When a spell is complete, this controller class calls an outside function to process the spell's effects.

This spell controller class, cSpellController, uses supportive structures that make tracking the spell meshes and animation easier. These structures are sSpellMeshList and sSpellTracker.

> **NOTE**
>
> The cSpellController class, the sSpellMeshList structure, and the sSpellTracker structure are contained within the spell.h and spell.cpp files on the CD-ROM at the back of this book (look for \BookCode\Chap16\Chars).

## Meshes with sSpellMeshList

Reviewing the sSpell spell structure, you can see that meshes are referenced by number rather than by name. That mesh reference number is actually the index to an array of meshes. You store this array of meshes in a collection of sSpellMeshList structures:

```
typedef struct sSpellMeshList {
  char       Filename[MAX_PATH];  // Filename of mesh/anim
  long       Count;               // # Spells using mesh
  cMesh      Mesh;                // Mesh object
  cAnimation Animation;           // Animation object

  // Construct and destructor to prepare and release data
  sSpellMeshList()  { Count = 0;                          }
  ~sSpellMeshList() { Mesh.Free(); Animation.Free(); }
} sSpellMeshList;
```

For each mesh in use in your engine, you have a matching sSpellMeshList structure. Each structure instance stores the filename of the mesh to use, a cMesh and a cAnimation object for the mesh, and a variable (Count) that keeps count of how many instances of the mesh are currently in use.

For each spell that needs a mesh, the appropriate .X file is loaded into the mesh and animation objects (both using the same filename and the animation using a single animation set called anim).

Meshes are only loaded from disk whenever the spell controller requires them, and because the structure maintains a count of the times the mesh is in use, the spell controller can quickly determine whether the mesh is loaded.

As spells complete their animation cycle, the appropriate mesh count is reduced, and when the number of spells that use the mesh is reduced to zero, the mesh and animation objects are released (to save memory).

## Tracking Spells Using sSpellTracker

Whereas the sSpellMeshList structure maintains the meshes used by spells, the actual list of active spells is maintained by the sSpellTracker structure. The sSpellTracker structure is allocated and inserted into a linked list of the same structures any time a spell is cast:

```
typedef struct sSpellTracker
{
  long   SpellNum;                    // Spell #

  sCharacter *Caster;                 // Character casting spell
  long   Type;                        // Character type to affect

  long   CurrentAnimation;            // Animation: 0-2
  float SourceX, SourceY, SourceZ;    // Source coordinates
  float TargetX, TargetY, TargetZ;    // Target coordinates

  float XPos, YPos, ZPos;             // Current coordinates
  float XAdd, YAdd, ZAdd;             // Movement values
  float Distance;                     // Distance to target

  union {
    float Speed;                      // Speed of movement
    long  Time;                       // Timer to continue
  };

  cObject Object;                     // Graphics object

  sSpellTracker *Prev, *Next;         // Linked list
```

```
    sSpellTracker()  { Caster = NULL; Prev = Next = NULL; }
    ~sSpellTracker() { delete Next;                        }
} sSpellTracker;
```

For each spell cast, a sSpellTracker structure is used to contain the information to track the mesh, animation, movement, timing, and which character cast the spell. The structure starts off with the spell number (SpellNum), which relates directly to the MSL.

To later help determine the effects of a spell, a pointer to a character (Caster) is maintained as well as the type of characters the spell can affect (PCs, NPCs, or MCs). You can define each type of character as follows:

```
#define CHAR_PC          0
#define CHAR_NPC         1
#define CHAR_MONSTER     2
```

Notice that a spell has no target character defined, but a trio of target coordinates. In fact, a spell has a trio of source coordinates. Remember that a spell mesh can stay in place over the caster or victim, move between the two, or stretch between them. Setting the source and target coordinates ensures that the tracker knows how to position the mesh in use.

Speaking of the mesh in use, CurrentAnimation is used to track which of the three meshes to use. As you may recall, a mesh movement takes place in three steps, and once the current animation passes the third step, the spell takes effect.

To track the motion of the spell meshes (if they are indeed moving), you use a set of values (XAdd, YAdd, and ZAdd) that tells the spell controller which direction to move the mesh at each update. As for the current position of the mesh in use, the variables XPos, YPos, and ZPos contain the current coordinates at which to render the mesh.

The speed in which a mesh moves is contained in Speed, and the total distance the mesh can move is contained in Distance. If a mesh stays in place, the Time variable does a countdown of the number of milliseconds until the cycle is complete.

Rounding off sSpellTracker, Object is the graphics object you use to render the meshes, and Prev and Next maintain the linked list of structures.

## The cSpellController Class

Because the spell controller is needed only for tracking the spell meshes and animation, the class definition is relatively small:

```
class cSpellController
{
```

```
private:
  cGraphics   *m_Graphics;          // Parent graphics object
  cFrustum    *m_Frustum;           // Viewing frustum

  sSpell m_Spells[NUM_SPELL_DEFINITIONS];  // Spell data

  sSpellTracker *m_SpellParent;     // List of active spells

  long            m_NumMeshes;      // # meshes in use
  sSpellMeshList *m_Meshes;         // Meshes list

  char m_TexturePath[MAX_PATH];     // Mesh texture path

  cCharacterController *m_Chars;    // Character controller

  // Setup the mesh movement
  BOOL SetAnimData(sSpellTracker *SpellPtr, long Num);

  // Function to override for playing sounds
  virtual BOOL SpellSound(long Num) { return TRUE; }
```

Now check the private data of the spell controller before examining the public functions. The spell controller uses a graphics and frustum object. The graphics object (m_Graphics) must be pre-initialized for use with the class, whereas the frustum object (m_Frustum) can be supplied from outside code or calculated from within the spell-rendering function.

Next comes the MSL, which is contained in the array m_Spells. Notice that the macro NUM_SPELL_DEFINITIONS defines the size of the MSL array, which means that you can easily adjust the size for later enhancements.

Following the MSL is the linked list pointer m_SpellParent, which tracks the spells that have been cast and are being displayed. Next comes m_NumMeshes (which stores the number of meshes used) and m_Meshes (a list of meshes).

Because this example uses 3-D meshes to represent the spells, you need to load textures, and in order for the spell controller to find those textures, you must store a directory path that indicates the location of the bitmaps to be used as textures.

Something you haven't seen up to now is the m_Chars pointer, which points to the character controller class object in use. This class pointer triggers the spell effects (you find more on this topic in the section "Creating a Character Controller Class," later in this chapter).

cSpellController contains two private functions: SetAnimData and SpellSound. The
SetAnimData function sets up the mesh to use as well as the movement of the mesh.
SpellSound is called whenever a spell mesh is used; it's your job to override this func-
tion to play the appropriate sound as specified in the function's argument list.

With private data and functions covered, you can move on to the class's public functions (the Constructor, Destructor, Init, Shutdown, Free, GetSpell, Add, Update, and Render):

```
public:
    cSpellController();   // Constructor
    ~cSpellController();  // Destructor

    // Functions to init/shutdown controller class
    BOOL Init(cGraphics *Graphics, char *DefinitionFile,        \
              long NumSpellMeshes, char **MeshNames,            \
              char *TexturePath,                                \
              cCharacterController *Controller);
    BOOL Shutdown();

    // Free class
    BOOL Free();

    sSpell *GetSpell(long SpellNum);

    // Add a spell to the list
    BOOL Add(long SpellNum,                                     \
             sCharacter *Caster, long TargetType,               \
             float SourceX, float SourceY, float SourceZ,       \
             float TargetX, float TargetY, float TargetZ);

    // Update all spells based on elapsed time
    BOOL Update(long Elapsed);

    // Render all spell meshes within viewing frustum
    BOOL Render(cFrustum *Frustum=NULL, float ZDistance = 0.0f);
};
```

Because this chapter is becoming a bit lengthy, I will now just list each function and
describe what it does. You might like to load the class code from the CD-ROM at the
back of this book (look for \BookCode\Chap16\ Chars\Spell.cpp) and follow along.

## cSpellController::cSpellController and cSpellController::~sSpellController

Typical in C++ classes, the constructor and destructor clear the class data and free all used resources, respectively. The destructor relies on a separate function (the Shutdown function) to clear the data.

## cSpellController::Init and cSpellController::Shutdown

Before using the spell controller class, you must initialize it. When you finish with the class, you call Shutdown to free up the resources. Having the longest argument list of all the controller functions, Init takes the following arguments:

> A pointer to the pre-initialized graphics object (cGraphics)
>
> The filename of the MSL (DefinitionFile)
>
> Number of spell meshes to use (NumSpellMeshes)
>
> An array of spell mesh .X filenames to use (MeshNames)
>
> The texture-directory path (TexturePath)
>
> A pointer to the yet unseen character controller class (Controller)

## cSpellController::Free

When you're done with a spell controller class instance but want to reuse it without having to shut it down, a call to cSpellController::Free is in order. Free releases the spell tracking list as well as the mesh list.

## cSpellController::GetSpell

Outside code might need access to the MSL, and GetSpell fills that need. Providing the MSL reference number returns a pointer into the array of the loaded MSL.

## cSpellController::Add

Now the real fun begins! Add is the function you use the most because it initiates a spell. The argument list includes the MSL reference number (from 0 to 63), the casting character structure pointer, the type of characters to target, and the source and target coordinates.

### cSpellController::SetAnimData

The private function SetAnimData initializes the three meshes in use by a spell. If one of the meshes is not used (as specified by the POSITION_NONE value in MeshPos), the next mesh in the three is used. After all three meshes are used up, the spell's effects are triggered.

### cSpellController::Update

Spells need to move, have their timing updated, and have their mesh initiated at the various steps. Update is responsible for all those functions. To use Update, just pass the amount of time (in milliseconds) that has elapsed from the last call to Update (or the amount of time you want the controller to update the spells).

### cSpellController::Render

The last of the functions, Render, is used to render all spell meshes that are in effect. Providing the Render function with an optional frustum and viewing distance helps alter the way the meshes are rendered.

## Determining Victims and Processing Spell Effects

After a spell triggers and the effects are processed, what happens? As I've previously mentioned, spells only affect characters, so only the character controller engine should modify the character's data. In the section "Creating a Character Controller Class," later in this chapter, you find out how to process spells in regard to characters.

## Using the Spell Controller

At this point, the spell controller is fully functional, but without the aid of the character controller, the spell controller won't work. However, for the moment, hold that thought and observe the following example, which shows how to use the spell controller. Begin by instancing the spell controller and declaring an array of mesh filenames:

```
// Graphics = pre-initialized cGraphics object

// Use two meshes
char *g_SpellMeshNames[] = {
    { "Fireball.x"   },
    { "Explosion.x"  }
  };
```

Next, instance and initialize the spell controller:

```
cSpellController Controller;

// Initialize the controller
Controller.Init(&Graphics, "default.msl",              \
                sizeof(g_SpellMeshNames)/sizeof(char*),  \
                g_SpellMeshNames, "..\\", NULL);
```

Now you're ready for action. Assuming that you have a single spell in the MSL (spell 0), you can cast it with the following code:

```
Controller.Add(0, NULL, CHAR_MONSTER,                  \
                0.0f, 0.0f, 0.0f, 100.0f, 0.0f, 100.0f);
```

The spell will now travel from the coordinates 0,0,0 to the coordinates 100,0,100 using the settings specified in the MSL Editor. When you finish with the spell controller, always be sure to call the controller's `Shutdown` function:

```
Controller.Shutdown();
```

> **NOTE**
>
> The call to `Init` loads the MSL named default.msl and also uses the current directory as the texture path. No character controller is passed to the spell controller at this point; that comes later.

# Combat and Characters

There are times when characters just can't get along. For those special moments, you need to teach those critters just who the boss is. Handling combat in your game is a necessity that, fortunately, is easy to carry out.

Although the flashy graphics and cool special effects are something you want in combat sequences, you need to start with the basics. Behind every combat action is a set of rules (called the *combat rules*) that determines the outcome of every swing of a weapon, every deflected blow, and the result of each magic spell.

Earlier in the chapter, you learned about character abilities—those abilities that determine a character's strength, agility, and so on. The abilities that most concern you at this point are those to determine whether an attack hits its mark and how much damage it does. Following a succinct set of rules, you can use those character abilities to determine the outcome of combat.

# Using Combat Rules for Attacking

Your game depends greatly on a set of underlying rules for handling combat, much like traditional pen-and-paper role-playing games. Those rules are a set of mathematical equations, which, when applied with a little randomness, determine the outcome of attacks, damage, and defense.

The *combat rule set (CRS)* of your game works off the character's abilities, attributes, and skills that you've already seen in this chapter. Remember how those abilities, skills, and attributes are assigned a numerical value? Guess what? Those values are used to generate a few values that determine the outcome of combat actions.

For example, a character's to-hit attribute is used in a random number calculation to see whether an attack lands. Then a check against the agility of the attacker's opponent determines whether the attack was dodged. If the opponent was not so lucky, the attacker's attack values come into play to determine the damage. Remember that the character being hit also has a defense ability that helps reduce the amount of damage.

Once the decision to attack is made, a few steps determine the outcome.

## Taking a Swing

When a character takes a swing at another character, this action triggers the process that determines whether the blow hit the target. Determining whether the attack hit involves an attacking character's to-hit ability and a defending character's agility ability. Remember that the higher the ability values, the better the chance to hit or dodge the attack.

The to-hit ability can range from 0 (always misses) to 999 (always hits). By taking a random number and comparing it to the to-hit value, you can quickly determine whether a hit was accomplished. If the random number is equal to or less than the to-hit attribute, the blow lands. The following code illustrates how to determine whether a hit is successful:

```
// ToHit = character's to-hit attribute value
long RandomValue = rand() % 1000;
BOOL HitFlag = (RandomValue <= ToHit) ? TRUE : FALSE;
```

In the preceding code, HitFlag is set to TRUE if the blow lands, or rather if the blow should land. In order to improve the chances of hitting a target, the attacker can have specific status ailments that decrease or increase the to-hit value. Two status ailments in use that affect the attacker's to-hit ability are Blind and Hawkeye. The Blind status ailment reduces the to-hit chance ability by 25 percent, whereas Hawkeye increases the chances to hit by 50 percent.

To apply either status ailment modifiers, multiply the determined to-hit value:

```
if(Ailments & AILMENT_BLIND)
  ToHit = (long)((float)ToHit * 0.75f);
if(Ailments & AILMENT_HAWKEYE)
  ToHit = (long)((float)ToHit * 1.5f);
long RandomValue = rand() % 999;
BOOL HitFlag = (RandomValue <= ToHit) ? TRUE : FALSE;
```

## Dodging an Attack

Remember that a victim's agility ability comes into play when being attacked. The greater the defender's agility, the greater the chance the victim dodges the attack. You calculate whether the defender dodges the attack in the same way that you check whether the attacker makes a hit:

```
// Agility = character's agility ability
RandomValue = rand() % 999;
BOOL DodgeFlag = (RandomValue <= Agility) ? TRUE : FALSE;
```

In order to decrease or increase the chances of dodging an attack, you can use the Clumsy and Surefooted status ailments. Clumsy decreases the chances of dodging and attack by 25 percent, whereas Surefooted increases the chances by 50 percent (meaning that characters that are affected by both the Clumsy and Surefooted ailments have their chances of dodging an attack increased by 25%):

> ### CAUTION
>
> **You can determine from the agility dodging calculations that the higher the agility, the higher the chance of dodging the attack. For that reason, you generally don't set a character's agility too high because they can become untouchable.**

```
if(Ailments & AILMENT_CLUMSY)
  Agility = (long)((float)Agility * 0.75f);
if(Ailments & AILMENT_SUREFOOTED)
  Agility = (long)((float)Agility * 1.5f);
long RandomValue = rand() % 999;
BOOL DodgeFlag = (RandomValue <= Agility) ? TRUE : FALSE;
```

# Dealing Damage

When it is determined that the blow hit the victim, it's time to calculate how much damage was done, which is where the character's attack and defense abilities come into play. Damage is usually variable, which means that rarely does the same attack do the same damage each time. Again, you use a little randomness.

To keep things simple, you can take the attacker's attack ability value (or at least 90 percent to 110 percent of it) and subtract the victim's defense value (at least 80 percent to 100 percent of it). Note that status ailments are an issue here as well, along with the use of items to increase the attack and defense abilities.

That's right. Equipped items add a multiplier to the attack and defense abilities. The item modifier value is the key. The value represents a value from 0 and up that, when divided by 100 and increased by one, gives you a multiplier value to use in conjunction with the ability value. For example, a weapon with a modifier value of 150 increases the attack ability by 50 percent:

```
// Attack = character's attack ability value
// Item[] = master item list array
long Attack = (long)((float)Attack *                    \
            (((float)Item[Weapon].Value / 100.0f) + 1.0f));
```

Getting back to status ailments, two affect both attack and defense—Weak and Strong. `Weak` reduces attack and defense by half whereas `Strong` increases the values by 50 percent. Here's how everything works to determine the amount of damage to apply:

```
// Attack = attacker's attack ability value
// Defense = defenders defense ability value
// Item[] = master item list array
// Weapon = weapon # in item list (or -1 if none)
// Armor = armor # in item list (or -1 if none)
// Shield = shield # in item list (or -1 if none)

// Determine attack amount
// Start with adding equipping weapon modifier
if(Weapon != -1)
  long Attack = (long)((float)Attack *                  \
            (((float)Item[Weapon].Value / 100.0f) + 1.0f));

// Adjust by status ailments
if(Ailments & AILMENT_WEAK)
```

```
    Attack = (long)((float)Attack * 0.5f);
if(Ailments & AILMENT_STRONG)
    Attack = (long)((float)Attack * 1.5f);


// Determine defense amount

// Apply armor and shield modifiers
if(Armor != -1)
  Defense = (long)((float)Defense *                              \
              (((float)Item[Armor].Value / 100.0f) + 1.0f);
if(Shield != -1)
  Defense = (long)((float)Defense *                              \
              (((float)Item[Shield].Value / 100.0f) + 1.0f);


// Apply status ailments
if(Ailments & AILMENT_WEAK)
  Defense = (long)((float)Defense * 0.5f);
if(Ailments & AILMENT_STRONG)
  Defense = (long)((float)Defense * 1.5f);


float DamagePercent = ((float)(rand() % 70) + 50.0f) / 100.0f;
long DamageAmount = (long)((float)Attack * DamagePercent);


// Determine damage amount (use some randomness in there)
float Range      = (float)((rand() % 20) + 90) / 100.0f;
long DmgAmount = (long)((float)Attack * Range);
Range            = (float)((rand() % 20) + 80) / 100.0f;
DmgAmount        -= (long)((float)Defense * Range);
```

At long last, the DmgAmount variable will contain the amount of damage that is dealt. You're not done at this point, however, because now character class comes into play. If an attack is strong against the character's class type, damage is doubled. If the victim is of the same class as the attack, that attack cures the victim for half the amount of damage dealt! I'll let you work those into the calculations.

**CAUTION**

Again, the defense ability of a character shouldn't be so high that the defending character rarely takes any damage when an attack hits.

# Spells in Combat

Now, you can put all the neat spells that your game has to offer to good use. You know how spells work, but you need to know how the spells affect the characters. Remember that the spell controller tracks only the meshes that create the visual side of spells; the character controller determines the effects of the spells.

Spells in combat are used mainly to damage an opponent. A spell uses a series of calculations to determine the outcome of the spell's effects, just as physical attacks do. Spells have a chance of failing, which is determined by the spell's chance value in the spell definition.

The chance of a spell working is increased by the caster's mental ability, which uses the following calculation to determine the multiplier to apply to the chance value:

```
// Chance = spell's chance of working
// Mental = caster's mental ability
Chance = (long)(((float)Mental / 100.0f + 1.0f) * (float)Chance);
```

The last line shows that the mental value can range from 0 and up. A value of 150 means to increase the chance by 50 percent, whereas a value of 200 means to double the chances. To aid victims of a spell, the target characters have their associated resistance abilities factored in as well:

```
// Resistance = target's resistance ability
Chance = (long)((1.0f - (float)GetResistance(Target) /           \
                                 100.0f) * (float)Chance);
```

When it is determined that the spell took effect, the appropriate actions can be taken to handle the results. The only spell effect you want to contend with at this time is damage. Whenever damage is dealt to a victim, the victim's resistance ability is used to reduce the amount of damage. Resistance is a percentage value, which means that a value of 0 does not reduce spell damage, whereas a value of 100 completely dispels damage.

Status ailments also work their way into spell casting. An ailment of Silenced means a character can't even cast magic spells, whereas an ailment of Dumbfounded reduces a character's mental ability by half. Finally, the Enchanted and Barrier ailments reduce the victim's resistance by half or increase the resistance by 50 percent, respectively.

You can use the following code to determine whether a spell affects the victim and just how much damage is dealt:

```
// Chance = Magic spell's chance of working
// Mental = Spell caster's mental ability
```

```
// Resistance = victim character's resistance amount
// Amount = base damage amount spell causes

// Apply status ailments to mental and resistance
if(Ailments & AILMENT_DUMBFOUNDED)
  Mental /= 2;
if(Ailments & AILMENT_ENCHANTED)
  Resistance = (long)((float)Resistance * 0.5f);
if(Ailments & AILMENT_BARRIER)
  Resistance = (long)((float)Resistance * 1.5f);

// Check chance of working and calculate damage
Chance=(long)(((float)Mental / 100.0f + 1.0f) * (float)Chance);
if((rand() % 100) < Chance) {
  float Resist = 1.0f - ((float)Resistance / 100.0f);
  long DmgAmount = (long)((float)Amount * Resist);

  // Apply extra class damage or cure-class amounts here
}
```

After a spell has hit its target, the proper amount of damage to apply is calculated. Remember that certain classes of spells can cause twice as much damage as the spell normally would to a character, whereas other spells can cure half the damage dealt.

Because you create a feasible character controller in the section "Creating a Character Controller Class," later in this chapter, you can wait until then to finish working with spells.

# Intelligence in Combat

Although your game's players are completely capable of controlling their player characters, it's up to you to control the NPCs. In order to make your game worthy, the NPCs' artificial intelligence needs to be up to par for combating. Their actions need to mimic yours, from choosing to attack, healing themselves, or casting a spell.

Characters are given a rudimentary intelligence when it comes to combat. If a character has lost over half of his health or is under the effects of a status ailment, that character will attempt to heal himself or dispel the ailments. This means it will search through its list of known spells (if any) and cast the appropriate spell for aid.

If, on the other hand, a PC comes into another character's range, a hostile character then chooses to either perform a physical attack or a magical attack (if any spells are known). You need to assign the chances that a character will perform either type of attack. Note that attacks are based on the built-up charge of the attacking creature—the charge must be full in order for the creature to attack.

When the decision is made to attack a nearby character, either the attack is performed or a magic spell is chosen. Only spells that hurt other characters are cast. If a character does not have a viable target character in range, the game randomly decides that the character in question will attempt to enhance itself by using a status ailment-causing spell, in this way raising its strength, agility, or other beneficial ailment.

The specifics on performing the preceding actions come into play when you create a character controller that will make such decisions for your characters. You will find that discussion later in the section "Creating a Character Controller Class."

# Building the Master Character List

You create and use a *master character list* (MCL) much like you use the master item list (MIL) to define objects in your game. Before using them in your game, you need to design every character, complete with appearance (3-D mesh) and functionality (abilities and attributes). This character information is stored in the sCharacterDefinition structure.

The MCL is stored just as the MIL, as a sequential data file (see Figure 16.12). Whenever a character is needed within the game, the MCL is referenced; each

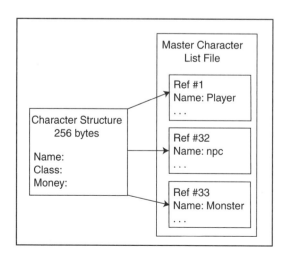

**Figure 16.12**

*The MCL file is divided into sections (structures), each the same size, which makes it easy to seek out and load a specific structure by its reference number.*

character is assigned a number that tells which character to use. As a character is needed, you load the specific data structure.

Now take a look at the sCharacterDefinition structure:

```
typedef struct sCharacterDefinition
{
    // Misc data
    char   Name[32];              // Name of character
    long   Class;                 // Class # of character
    long   Money;                 // Amount of money
    float  Speed;                 // Movement speed
    long   MagicSpells;       // Bit flags to mark known spells
    long   MeshNum;               // Mesh/anim # to load

    // Abilities
    long   Agility;               // Agility ability
    long   Attack;                // Attack ability
    long   Defense;               // Defend ability
    long   Resistance;            // Magic resistance ability
    long   Mental;                // Mental ability

    // Attributes
    long   HealthPoints;          // # health points (maximum)
    long   ManaPoints;            // # mana points (maximum)
    long   ToHit;                 // Chance to hit
    long   Level;                 // Experience level
    long   Experience;            // Experience points

    // Inventory
    char   ItemFilename[MAX_PATH]; // CharICS filename
    long   Weapon;                // Equipped Weapon
    long   Armor;                 // Equipped Armor
    long   Shield;                // Equipped Shield
    long   Accessory;             // Equipped Accessory

    // Dropping item data
    long   DropChance;            // % of dropping item when killed
    long   DropItem;              // Item # to drop when killed

    // Attack/Magic chances and effects
    float  Range;                 // Attack range
```

```
    float ChargeRate;        // Countdown rate to attack
    long  ToAttack;          // Percent to attack
    long  ToMagic;           // Percent to use magic
    long  EffectChance;      // Chance of attack effect occurring
    long  Effects;           // Bit flags of attack effects
} sCharacterDefinition;
```

Just like the master item list, the MCL stores only minimal information about a character. Because multiple characters of the same type can exist in the game world at one time (for example, ten instances of a Goblin character), the per-instance data is kept separate. This per-instance data includes the coordinates of the characters, their current health and mana points, and so on.

**NOTE**

You can find the cCharacterDefinition structure in the mcl.h include file located in the Chars demo program on this book's **CD-ROM** (look for **\BookCode\Chap16\Chars\**).

The sCharacterController structure stores the template to use when instancing a character. This template encompasses all characters, including the PCs.

Although the structure is well commented, a few things might not make immediate sense. In addition to the abilities and attributes that you've already read about, you have the miscellaneous, inventory, dropping item, and attack/magic chances and effects. Table 16.6 describes what these variables do for the character definition.

### Table 16.6  Various sCharacterDefinition Structure Variables

| Variable | Description |
| --- | --- |
| Name | Name of character (limited to 32 bytes, including the trailing string terminator). |
| Class | The character's class number. Characters are assigned classes, and only items marked as the same class can be used by that character. Also, certain attacks and spells affect different classes differently. |
| Money | The amount of money the character is carrying. |

*(continued)*

## Table 16.6 Various sCharacterDefinition Structure Variables *(continued)*

| Variable | Description |
| --- | --- |
| MagicSpells | This array of two long variables contains the bit flags detailing the spells known by a character. Starting with the first byte in the array, the lowest bit represents spell 0, the second bit represents spell 1, and so on until the sixty-fourth bit is reached, which represents spell 63. |
| MeshNum | An external array of meshes is maintained that details the mesh and animation to use for the character. The value stored in MeshNum is the index into that array for which mesh to use. |
| ItemFilename | This is the character inventory control system filename used for PCs. NPCs use only an ICS if they are going to barter with the player. |
| Weapon | This is the index number into the MIL of the weapon currently equipped by the character. If this value is -1, nothing is equipped (same applies to the following equipable items). |
| Armor | The index number in the MIL of the armor currently equipped by the character. |
| Shield | Same as weapon and armor. This is the index into the item list of the currently equipped shield. |
| Accessory | Rounding off the bunch, this is the index into the item list of the currently equipped accessory. |
| DropChance | This is the percentage chance of the character dropping an item when killed. |
| DropItem | When a character is killed and it is determined that the character is dropping an item (via DropChance), this is the number of the item to drop. |
| Range | Characters have a normal range of attack that extends from their outermost bounding edge. This value is that range and should be set to a value higher than 0 to be effective. |
| ChargeRate | After a character performs an action such as attacking, using an item, equipping an item, or casting a spell, that character is unable to perform another such move for a short period of time. ChargeRate is the speed at which the countdown to the time that a character can perform another action is reached. |

**Table 16.6** *(continued)*

| Variable | Description |
|----------|-------------|
| ToAttack | Characters have two choices of attacking—physical and magical. ToAttack is the percentage rate of the character using a physical attack when given the chance. |
| ToMagic | ToMagic is the percentage rate in which a character will cast a spell given the chance. |
| EffectChance | If the character attacks, this is the percentage rate of a magical effect occurring. |
| Effects | These are the effects of the character attack given the effect has occurred. This is a bit flag encoded value, and you decide what each bit represents. |

Configuring a single character definition is as simple as filling in the blanks, but when it comes to defining 100 characters, things can quickly become complicated. What you need is an MCL Editor.

# The MCL Editor

You're probably used to these editors by now, and this one is just as easy to use as other editors. If you haven't done so already, go ahead and run the MCLEdit application (found on this book's CD-ROM in the \BookCode\Chap16\MCLEdit directory). Figure 16.13 shows the MCL Editor dialog box.

Working with the MCL is similar to working with the MSL Editor earlier in this chapter and with the MIL Editor in Chapter 15. The MCL Editor can handle up to 256 characters—each numbered from 0 to 255. Each character is shown in the list box. To work with the MCL Editor, follow these steps:

1. Double-clicking a character in the list or clicking the New button brings up the Modify Character dialog box, as shown in Figure 16.14.

2. In the Modify Character dialog box, enter the appropriate character information in each field. You can alter a character's Name, Class, Health Points,

Mana Points, Level, Experience, Money, ability values, known Spells, and Mesh information.

3. Once you finish filling in a character's information in the Modify Character dialog box, click OK. You'll return to the Master Character List Editor dialog box.

4. Click the Save button to bring up the Save MCL File dialog box.

5. Enter a filename and click the Save button to write the MCL file to disk.

6. To Load a file, click the Load button (in the Master Character List Editor dialog box), enter a filename, and click OK.

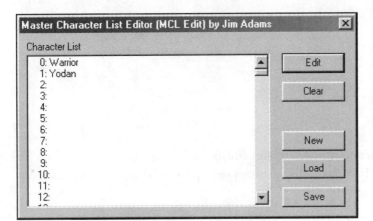

**Figure 16.13**

*The Master Character List Editor dialog box contains the list of characters and some buttons laid out around the application window—buttons that let you add new characters to the list, clear a character definition, and edit, save, and load the character lists.*

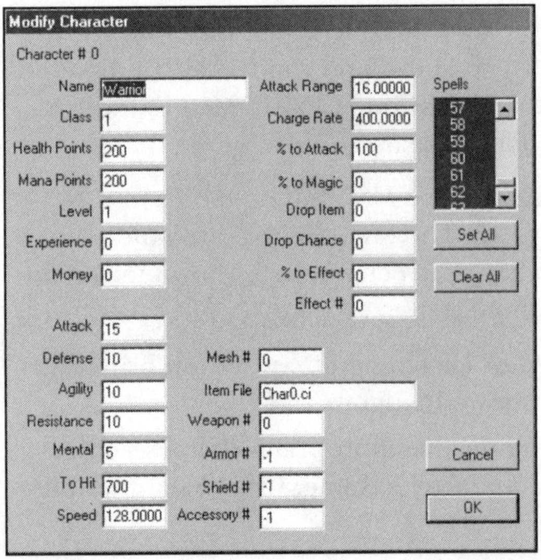

**Figure 16.14**

*The Modify Character dialog box is packed with every bit of information about a character found in the* sCharacterDefinition *structure.*

You've read about each bit of the character definition. Now, it's time to enter that information into the appropriate places. When it comes to spells, highlight the spell number you want the character to know automatically. Those spell numbers relate directly to your MSL, so you might want to run the MSL Editor and MCL Editor side by side to compare the information.

## Using the Character Definitions

The character definitions are templates by nature, so you really need to load up the definitions and work with them on a per-instance basis. This means that you need to come up with a controller that loads the definitions and tracks each instance of a character in your game. What you need is a character controller class.

# Creating a Character Controller Class

Now that you've seen what is involved in controlling and defining your game's characters, you can focus on constructing a controller class that takes care of everything for you, including adding, removing, updating, and rendering the characters, as well as handling the spell effects from the spell controller previously developed.

Because so much is involved in tracking characters, the job is split into a few structures and a single class. Much like spells, a mesh list is required to hold the list of used meshes. This time however, the looping information of the animations is not contained in the character definitions; another structure is needed to contain the character animations that need to be looped.

When working in artificial intelligence, you create a single structure to store the coordinates of route points. Finally, another structure maintains a linked list of characters in use. Now, examine each structure just mentioned and the information they contain.

## Meshes with sCharacterMeshList

Earlier, in section "Meshes with sSpellMeshList," you read about the spell controller and how the controller maintains a list of meshes. For the character controller, you also have to provide a list of meshes that are used to render the characters. The sCharacterMeshList structure contains the mesh and animation objects and filenames.

```
typedef struct sCharacterMeshList {
```

```
char        Filename[MAX_PATH];  // Filename of mesh/anim
long        Count;               // # characters using mesh
cMesh       Mesh;                // Mesh object
cAnimation Animation;            // Animation object

sCharacterMeshList()  { Count = 0;                            }
~sCharacterMeshList() { Mesh.Free(); Animation.Free(); }
} sCharacterMeshList;
```

# Animation Loops and sCharAnimationInfo

The animations used by the characters are set in their ways; either they can or cannot loop. Certain actions, such as standing, require a character's mesh to constantly repeat, giving the appearance of constant motion, whereas other animations such as swinging the sword only need be performed once.

By storing a list of the animations that need be looped, the character controller can pass the information on to the Graphics Core so that it can handle the hard work for you. You store this animation loop information in the sCharAnimationInfo structure, as follows:

```
typedef struct {
  char Name[32];     // Name of animation
  BOOL Loop;         // To loop flag
} sCharAnimationInfo;
```

To use the structure, you must store the name of the animation (matching the animation set name in the .X file) and a flag that tells whether to loop the associated animation. You see more on this in the section "Using cCharacterController," later in the chapter.

# Moving with sRoutePoint

As previously discussed, you use the sRoutePoint structure to store the coordinates of a route point that characters move toward in their never-ending movement through the levels.

```
typedef struct {
  float XPos, YPos, ZPos;   // Target position
} sRoutePoint;
```

# Tracking Characters with sCharacter

Things are about to become more complicated because tracking each character involves quite a bit of data. In fact, so much data is involved in tracking characters (within an sCharacter structure) that you need to see it in pieces:

```
typedef struct sCharacter
{
  long  Definition;       // Character definition #
  long  ID;               // ID # of character

  long  Type;             // PC, NPC, or MONSTER
  long  AI;               // STAND, WANDER, etc

  BOOL  Enabled;          // Enabled flag (for updates)
```

To start, each character needs a definition, which is pulled from the master character list. You store this definition value in the Definition variable. To tell similar characters apart, you assign a unique identification number (ID) to each one. Think of using identification numbers as you use names. Instead of adding a character named "George" into the game during play, you refer to that same character as character 5.

Each character being tracked is of a specific type, either a PC, an NPC, or a monster. To determine the value for Type, use the following three macros:

```
#define CHAR_PC         0
#define CHAR_NPC        1
#define CHAR_MONSTER    2
```

Next are the character's artificial intelligence settings. Remember that a character can stand in place, wander around, walk a route, follow another character, or evade another character. The artificial intelligence of each character is stored in the AI variable and can be set to one of the following macro values:

```
#define CHAR_STAND      0
#define CHAR_WANDER     1
#define CHAR_ROUTE      2
#define CHAR_FOLLOW     3
#define CHAR_EVADE      4
```

Finally, each character needs to be enabled in order to be updated. The Enabled flag determines this, and setting it to TRUE lets the controller update the character every frame, whereas setting the flag to FALSE means that the character is never updated (until enabled, that is).

You need to store the character's MCL definition for referencing, and for characters with an inventory, you contain the ICS. The following structure variables store that information, along with the filename of a script file that is called when the player activates the character:

```
sCharacterDefinition Def;  // Loaded definition
cCharICS *CharICS;         // PC character's ICS

char ScriptFilename[MAX_PATH]; // Associated script
```

Because the character's definition stores only the maximum values of the abilities and attributes, the sCharacter structure needs a way to track the current values as they change through game-play. This includes the health points, mana points, status ailment flags, and the current charge of the character.

> **NOTE**
>
> Remember that characters can perform specific actions (attacking or casting a spell, for example) only when their charges are at full peak. This charge rate increases at the rate defined within the MCL.

```
long  HealthPoints;    // Current health points
long  ManaPoints;      // Current mana points
long  Ailments;        // Ailments against character
float Charge;          // Attack charge
```

As characters move around performing their various actions (moving, idling, attacking, and so on), you need to provide a way for their actions and positions to be tracked. In addition, their last known animation needs to be maintained (in order to update their animation), as well as the last time their animation was updated.

You use the following structure variables to track a character's action, coordinates, direction of movement, and animation data:

```
long  Action;              // Current action
float XPos, YPos, ZPos;    // Current coordinates
float Direction;           // Angle character is facing
long  LastAnim;            // Last animation
long  LastAnimTime;        // Last animation time
```

You also need to provide a way to prevent characters that perform specific actions from being updated until the completion of those actions. When a character is attacking, for example, there's no need to update the character any further until the character finishes swinging the weapon. What is needed is a countdown timer to lock a character's actions; this countdown timer is ActionTimer.

To permanently prevent a character from being updated, you use a second variable, called Locked. If you set Locked to TRUE, the character controller will not update the character until you set Locked to FALSE.

You define both ActionTimer and Locked in the sCharacter structure as follows:

```
BOOL   Locked;              // Specific action lock
long   ActionTimer;         // Lock action countdown timer
```

The next set of variables take care of the combat side of characters:

```
sCharacter *Attacker;       // Attacking character (if any)
sCharacter *Victim;         // Character to attack

long   SpellNum;            // Spell to cast when ready
long   SpellTarget;         // Target type of spell
float  TargetX, TargetY, TargetZ; // Spell target coords
```

When a character attacks another one, the pointers to both the attacking character and victim character are stored in their respective sCharacter structures. The attacker remembers the victim while the victim remembers the attacker. Also, when a character uses a spell, the MSL spell number is stored, along with the spell's target coordinates and the type of character to target (CHAR_PC, CHAR_NPC, or CHAR_MONSTER).

Recall that characters have actions, and those actions have a set of associated animations. The reason for storing the attacker, victim, and spell information (as well as the following item information) is that a character's action and animation must be completed before the results of the action take place. Once an attacking character swings a weapon, the results of the attack are calculated. The same goes for spell; once a character casts a spell, the spell information in the sCharacter structure is used to determine who, or what, is affected.

The same goes for using items; the pointer to the item used during a use item action is stored, as well as the pointer to the ICS cCharItem structure of the character (in order to remove the item if it was marked as USEONCE):

```
long   ItemNum;             // Item to use when ready
sCharItem *CharItem;        // Item to remove from inventory
```

You're about halfway through the structure. Now, you store the information about the character's artificial intelligence. You've already read about most of the following data. You have the distance to follow or evade a character, along with the pointer to the character to follow or evade.

For characters that use a bounding area, you store the minimum and maximum coordinates, followed by the route information:

```
float  Distance;          // Follow/Evade distance
sCharacter *TargetChar;   // Character to follow
float  MinX, MinY, MinZ;  // Min bounding coordinates
float  MaxX, MaxY, MaxZ;  // Max bounding coordinates

long   NumPoints;         // # points in route
long   CurrentPoint;      // Current route point
sRoutePoint *Route;       // Route points
```

Moving on, you use a trio of variables to store a simple message that is overlaid on top of a character during game-play (as illustrated in Figure 16.15).

```
char   Message[128];      // Text message
long   MessageTimer;      // Text message timer
D3DCOLOR MessageColor;    // Color of text message
```

Character messages help relate tiny bits of information, as Figure 16.15 shows. To set a message, copy the message string (up to 128 characters) into the Message buffer, set the amount of time (in milliseconds) to display the message, and assign a color to the text to be displayed.

**Figure 16.15**

*A message mechanism displays the outcome of certain actions, such as shown here. A character attacking another character discovers that the intended victim dodged the attack.*

Finishing up the sCharacter class variables is the Graphics Core cObject object that maintains the character's mesh and animation. To enhance the visual appearance of the characters, a separate mesh and object are used to represent a character's weapon. This weapon mesh and object are configured any time a new weapon is equipped. Last comes the linked list pointers Prev and Next:

```
cObject Object;         // Character object class
cMesh   WeaponMesh;     // Weapon mesh
cObject WeaponObject;   // Weapon object

sCharacter *Prev, *Next;  // Linked list of characters
```

That's a lot of information to store for each character, and to help the controller prepare a structure every time a new character is added to the fray, the sCharacter structure comes complete with a constructor and destructor in order to prepare the data and help release its resources.

```
sCharacter()
{
  Definition = 0;        // Set to definition #0
  ID = -1;               // Set to no ID
  Type = CHAR_NPC;       // Set to NPC character
  Enabled = FALSE;       // Set to not enabled

  Ailments = 0;          // Set no ailments
  Charge = 0.0f;         // Set no charge

  // Clear definition
  ZeroMemory(&Def, sizeof(sCharacterDefinition));
  CharICS = NULL;        // Set no ICS

  ScriptFilename[0] = 0; // Set no script

  Action = CHAR_IDLE;    // Set default animation
  LastAnim = -1;         // Reset animation

  Locked = FALSE;        // Set no lock
  ActionTimer = 0;       // Set no action timer

  Attacker = NULL;       // Set no attacker
  Victim = NULL;         // Set no victim
```

```
        ItemNum = 0;              // Set no item to use
        CharItem = NULL;          // Set no item to decrease

        Distance = 0.0f;          // Set distance
        TargetChar = NULL;        // Set no target character

        // Clear bounding box (for limiting movement)
        MinX = MinY = MinZ = MaxX = MaxY = MaxZ = 0.0f;

        NumPoints = 0;            // Set no route points
        Route = NULL;             // Set no route

        Message[0] = 0;           // Clear message
        MessageTimer = 0;         // Set no message timer

        Prev = Next = NULL;       // Clear linked list pointers
    }

    ~sCharacter()
    {
        if(CharICS != NULL) {     // Release character ICS
            CharICS->Free();
            delete CharICS;
        }

        delete [] Route;          // Release route

        WeaponObject.Free();      // Release weapon object
        WeaponMesh.Free();        // Release weapon mesh
        Object.Free();            // Release character object

        delete Next;              // Delete next character in list
    }
} sCharacter;
```

And that's it! I told you sCharacter was a big structure, but it is nothing compared to the character controller class that uses the structures.

# The cCharacterController Class

The brains of the character operation is the cCharacterController class (contained in the Chars.h and Chars.cpp files), which is probably the biggest non-game core class you'll work with. Because of space constraints, rather than showing the class declaration here, I put the class code on the CD-ROM that comes with this book (look for \BookCode\Chap16\Chars).

The cCharacterController class maintains a list of active characters, each character being stored within a sCharacter structure. For each type of character, there is a matching entry into an array of sCharacterMeshList structures (and a matching sCharAnimationInfo structure).

A macro is defined at the beginning of the Chars.h file.

```
// Number of characters in file
#define NUM_CHARACTER_DEFINITIONS   256
```

Following this definition are the macros you've already seen—character types, artificial intelligence types, and status ailments. The macros after that trio are ones you haven't seen, but you should understand them by now; they are the actions that a character can perform (and the matching animations). Take a look at the macros:

```
// Character types
#define CHAR_PC          0
#define CHAR_NPC         1
#define CHAR_MONSTER     2

// AI types
#define CHAR_STAND       0
#define CHAR_WANDER      1
#define CHAR_ROUTE       2
#define CHAR_FOLLOW      3
#define CHAR_EVADE       4

// Status ailments
#define AILMENT_POISON        1
#define AILMENT_SLEEP         2
#define AILMENT_PARALYZE      4
#define AILMENT_WEAK          8
#define AILMENT_STRONG        16
#define AILMENT_ENCHANTED     32
#define AILMENT_BARRIER       64
#define AILMENT_DUMBFOUNDED   128
#define AILMENT_CLUMSY        256
#define AILMENT_SUREFOOTED    512
#define AILMENT_SLOW          1024
```

```
#define AILMENT_FAS          2048
#define AILMENT_BLIND        4096
#define AILMENT_HAWKEYE      8192
#define AILMENT_SILENCED    16384

// Action/Animation types
#define CHAR_IDLE            0
#define CHAR_MOVE            1
#define CHAR_ATTACK          2
#define CHAR_SPELL           3
#define CHAR_ITEM            4
#define CHAR_HURT            5
#define CHAR_DIE             6
#define CHAR_TALK            7
```

From here, it's all left up to the controller class.

```
class cCharacterController
{
  private:
    cGraphics   *m_Graphics;          // Parent graphics object
    cFont       *m_Font;              // Font object to use
    cFrustum    *m_Frustum;           // Viewing frustum
```

The class begins its private data with a pointer to the parent cGraphics object and a pointer to a cFont object (used to draw text to the display). You must pre-initialize both objects before the character controller can use them. You use the frustum object as you use the one in the spell controller.

Next comes the filename of the MCL, the pointers to the MIL and MSL, and finally a pointer to the spell controller:

```
    char m_DefinitionFile[MAX_PATH];   // Filename of def. file

    sItem      *m_MIL;                 // Master item list
    sSpell     *m_MSL;                 // Master spell list

    cSpellController *m_SpellController; // Spell controller
```

As characters are added to the game, a counter (m_NumCharacters) keeps track of how many are in use. Following the counter is the pointer to the parent (root) sCharacter structure in the linked list of structures:

```
    long         m_NumCharacters;      // # characters in list
    sCharacter *m_CharacterParent;     // List of characters
```

You use a list of mesh and animation structures much like you use the spell controller. This time, in addition to storing the texture path, you also create a directory path where the meshes are located. Why use a mesh directory? In the case of attaching weapons to a character, the sItem structure stores only the filename, not the path. This means that weapon meshes must be located in the same directory as the character meshes.

```
long          m_NumMeshes;          // # meshes in use
sCharacterMeshList *m_Meshes;       // Meshes list
char m_MeshPath[MAX_PATH];          // Weapon mesh path
char m_TexturePath[MAX_PATH];       // Mesh texture path

long          m_NumAnimations;      // # animations
sCharAnimationInfo *m_Animations;   // Animation data
```

That wraps up the internal data of the sCharacterController class. Now, you can turn your attention to the private functions. You use the first function, GetXZRadius, to calculate the maximum bounding radius along the X- and Z-axes.

```
// Return X/Z radius of character
float GetXZRadius(sCharacter *Character);
```

You use the X/Z radius to enhance the reliability of bounding sphere collision detection. To see what I mean, take a look at Figure 16.16.

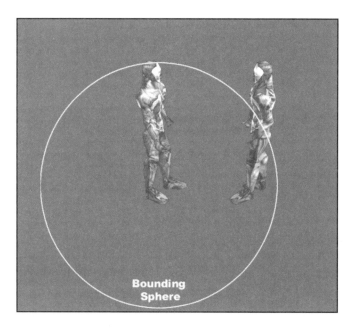

**Figure 16.16**

*The character on the left is a tall lad. The entire character object's bounding sphere extends far out in each direction based on his height, causing some false collision detection results when two characters collide.*

Taller characters in the game have the unfortunate side effect of having large bounding spheres. To remedy this, only the farthest point of the character in the X- and Z-axes is used to compute the bounding sphere size, because those two axes represent the character's width and depth, not height.

Getting on with the functions, you insert a virtual function that is used to play a sound effect whenever an action is initiated. It's your job to derive the cCharacterController class in order to override the function to make it do something useful:

```
// Function to override for playing sounds
virtual BOOL ActionSound(sCharacter *Character)
        { return TRUE; }
```

The next two functions to come along work in conjunction with the update functionality of the class. At every frame that a character needs updating, a specific function is called to update the character's actions. This specific function is dependent on the type of character being updated; for PCs, that specific function is PCUpdate (which is overridden by you in order to control your player).

For NPCs and monsters, the update function called is CharUpdate. PCUpdate does nothing at this point because you need to write the code in the main application to control the player. Monsters and NPCs already have their AIs sets, and the controller knows how to handle them with CharUpdate.

```
// Move function for player characters (need to override)
virtual BOOL PCUpdate(                                       \
                sCharacter *Character, long Elapsed,         \
                float *XMove, float *YMove, float *ZMove)  \
        { return TRUE; }


// Character update function for all non-PC characters
BOOL CharUpdate(sCharacter *Character, long Elapsed,         \
                  float *XMove, float *YMove, float *ZMove);
```

The steps taken for initiating an update and processing all of a character's actions is a long one. First, you iterate each character in the list of active characters. The appropriate character's update function is called (PCUpdate or CharUpdate).

Once it is determined what action each character wants to perform, that action must be validated. Characters moving around can't walk through other players (except for PCs, who can walk through other PCs). Also, depending on your levels, you use a function to determine character-to-map collisions. These two validation functions are as follows:

```
// Check for valid movements. Bounds check to other
// characters and call ValidateMove (overridden).
BOOL CheckMove(sCharacter *Character,                    \
              float *XMove, float *YMove, float *ZMove);

// Virtual ValidateMove for outside bounds checking
// against character movements.
virtual BOOL ValidateMove(sCharacter *Character,         \
              float *XMove, float *YMove, float *ZMove)  \
              { return TRUE; }
```

Both of the preceding functions (CheckMove and ValidateMove) take a pointer to the character being updated, as well as the character's intended amount of movement in each direction. Each function modifies these values appropriately. When the character's moves and actions have been validated, another function wraps up the actions and actually updates the character positions and actions.

```
// Finish movement by setting direction, animation, etc
BOOL ProcessUpdate(sCharacter *Character,               \
              float XMove, float YMove, float ZMove);
```

Whenever characters start battling it out, some are sure to die. The controller can quickly handle dying NPCs and monsters by removing their respective structures from the list. As for PCs though, death can mean the end of the game, so it's up to the main application to handle them. That's the reasoning behind PCDeath, which takes a single argument, the pointer to the dying PC:

```
// Process death of a player character
virtual BOOL PCDeath(sCharacter *Character)             \
              { return TRUE; }
```

Speaking of characters dying, any time a monster dies, it has a chance of dropping an item, as well as all the money it is carrying. Because your main application handles all items in the maps, it's your job to determine when a monster drops an item or gold and to add the appropriate item to the map's list of items. Overriding the following two functions will help you out anytime a monster drops something by giving you the exact coordinates where the monster perished, the item dropped, and the amount of money dropped.

```
// Functions to drop money and item when character dies
virtual BOOL DropMoney(float XPos,float YPos,float ZPos, \
                      long Quantity)
              { return TRUE; }
```

```
virtual BOOL DropItem(float XPos, float YPos, float ZPos, \
                           long ItemNum)
                { return TRUE; }
```

You're coming to the end of the long haul. You've finished the private data and functions, and the public functions are left:

```
public:
    cCharacterController();   // Constructor
    ~cCharacterController();  // Destructor

    // Functions to init/shutdown controller class
    BOOL Init(cGraphics *Graphics, cFont *Font,            \
             char *DefinitionFile, sItem *MIL, sSpell *MSL, \
             long NumCharacterMeshes, char **MeshNames,    \
             char *MeshPath, char *TexturePath,            \
             long NumAnimations, sCharAnimationInfo *Anims, \
             cSpellController *SpellController);
    BOOL Shutdown();
```

In addition to the typical class constructor and destructor are the Init and Shutdown pair of functions. For the controller to operate, it must first be initialized with a call to Init. When you're done with the character controller class, a call to Shutdown is in order.

The arguments are plenty, but each is understandable. You have the parent graphics and font objects followed by the MCL definition filename. Next come the pointers to the master item list and MSL. Remember that the spell controller maintains the MSL, so a call to sSpellController::GetSpell is needed to obtain the pointer to the list.

Next is the number of character meshes to use, along with the mesh list, mesh path directory, and texture path directory. Rounding up the Init function arguments are the number of animation loop structures to set, the respective animation structure array pointer, and the pointer to the spell controller class object in use.

Somewhat similar in nature to shutdown, the following Free function completely removes all characters in the list of active characters. This function is useful for clearing the list when a character leaves a level and a whole new set of characters need to be added to the list:

```
// Free class
BOOL Free();
```

Speaking of adding characters to the list, here comes the function that does it all:

```
// Add a character to the list
```

```
BOOL Add(long IDNum, long Definition, long Type, long AI, \
         float XPos, float YPos, float ZPos,              \
         float Direction = 0.0f);

// Remove a character from list
BOOL Remove(long IDNum);
BOOL Remove(sCharacter *Character);
```

With the `Add` function, you need to provide a unique identification number, the MCL character definition number to use, the character's type to assign (`CHAR_PC`, `CHAR_NPC`, or `CHAR_MONSTER`), the artificial intelligence to use, and the character's coordinates and Y-axis angle used to point the character in a specific direction.

Following `Add` are two functions that remove a character in the list. The first version of the `Remove` function takes a character's unique identification number as an argument, and the second version of the `Remove` function takes a pointer to the character structure.

Notice that I keep talking about removing characters from the list. What about all the hard work you've put into your PCs—how are you ever going to store their achievements for later loading? With the following set of saving and loading functions, of course!

```
// Save or load an individual character
BOOL Save(long IDNum, char *Filename);
BOOL Load(long IDNum, char *Filename);
```

Both of the two preceding functions take the character's identification number to save or load, as well as the filename to use.

That about rounds up the functions used to prepare, add, and remove the characters from the game. Now it's time to get them all moving around performing their actions. Previously you saw the functions used to update the individual character types; now comes the single function you'll call to update all characters at once:

```
// Update all characters based on elapsed time
BOOL Update(long Elapsed);
```

The `Update` function is called once every frame. Taking a single argument (the time elapsed since the last update), the `Update` function calls upon each character's respective update function, validates each character's movements and actions, and wraps up by processing the actions. Then a call to `Render` is in order to display all characters visible within the specified frustum.

```
// Render all objects within viewing frustum
```

```
BOOL Render(long      Elapsed = -1,                    \
            cFrustum  *Frustum = NULL,                 \
            float     ZDistance = 0.0f);
```

With Render, you have a few optional arguments. You use the first one to control the animation timing of the characters. In a task-switchable environment such as Windows, merely using the time elapsed from the last processed frame is unacceptable; you must instead specify a fixed amount of time passed and ensure that your game engine sticks to updates at that rate. In this book, I use a typical update rate of 30 frames per second (33-millisecond delays between frames).

As for the viewing frustum pointer, the application can provide its own pre-created object, or pass NULL (and an optional Z-distance) to create its own frustum.

Whenever a character needs updating, rendering, or what have you, a pointer to the linked list of characters is needed in order to iterate the list. Either that or maybe your application needs access to the character data. Either way, the following functions will help you out:

```
// Retrieve an sCharacter structure
sCharacter *GetParentCharacter();
sCharacter *GetCharacter(long IDNum);
```

During specific functions, it becomes necessary for characters (such as monsters) to make sure that they can see another character before attacking or casting a spell. A function of your design is required to verify that such a line of sight is clear. Returning a value of TRUE states that a character is in sight of another one:

```
// Make sure there's a line of sight to attack/cast spell
virtual BOOL LineOfSight(                              \
            sCharacter *Source, sCharacter *Target,    \
            float SourceX, float SourceY, float SourceZ, \
            float TargetX, float TargetY, float TargetZ)  \
            { return TRUE; }
```

When the character controller (or outside code) needs one of the character's abilities, it needs to retrieve it with the following group of functions. These functions take into account the various modifiers such as status ailments and equipped items:

```
// Function to retrieve adjusted ability/other info
float GetSpeed(sCharacter *Character);
long  GetAttack(sCharacter *Character);
long  GetDefense(sCharacter *Character);
long  GetAgility(sCharacter *Character);
```

```
long  GetResistance(sCharacter *Character);
long  GetMental(sCharacter *Character);
long  GetToHit(sCharacter *Character);
float GetCharge(sCharacter *Character);
```

Coming up is a huge collection of functions you use to retrieve and set the specific information about a character (related to the artificial intelligence functionality or actions):

```
// Get pointer to the character ICS
cCharICS *GetICS(long IDNum);


// Set lock and action timer
BOOL SetLock(long IDNum, BOOL State);
BOOL SetActionTimer(long IDNum, long Timer);


// Set evade/follow distance
BOOL  SetDistance(long IDNum, float Distance);
float GetDistance(long IDNum);


// Set route points
BOOL SetRoute(long IDNum,                                    \
              long NumPoints, sRoutePoint *Route);


// Set script
BOOL SetScript(long IDNum, char *ScriptFilename);
char *GetScript(long IDNum);


// Set enable flags
BOOL SetEnable(long IDNum, BOOL Enable);
BOOL GetEnable(long IDNum);


// Functions to move and get character coordinates
BOOL Move(long IDNum, float XPos, float YPos, float ZPos);
BOOL GetPosition(long IDNum,                                 \
                 float *XPos, float *YPos, float *ZPos);


// Functions to Set/Get character bounds
BOOL SetBounds(long IDNum,                                   \
               float MinX, float MinY, float MinZ,           \
               float MaxX, float MaxY, float MaxZ);
BOOL GetBounds(long IDNum,                                   \
```

```
                              float *MinX, float *MinY, float *MinZ,      \
                              float *MaxX, float *MaxY, float *MaxZ);


       // Functions to Set/Get character type
       BOOL SetType(long IDNum, long Type);
       long GetType(long IDNum);


       // Functions to Set/Get character AI
       BOOL SetAI(long IDNum, long Type);
       long GetAI(long IDNum);


       // Set a target character
       BOOL SetTargetCharacter(long IDNum, long TargetNum);
```

Skipping the details on the preceding functions (refer to the section "Navigating Characters," for information on their functionality), you now encounter the function used to set up the data that displays a message over a character:

```
       // Set text messages to float up from character
       BOOL SetMessage(sCharacter *Character, char *Text,          \
                  long Timer, D3DCOLOR Color=0xFFFFFFFF);
```

SetMessage allows you to temporarily overlay a string of text for Timer milliseconds, drawing the text in the color specified. You set a character message to inform the player of an event, such as how many health points were reduced because of an attack.

Coming next is the function that processes the damage taken from an attack, whether it's physical or magical (as denoted by the PhysicalAttack flag, set to TRUE for physical attacks or FALSE for magical):

```
       // Process attack damage from spells and physical attacks
       BOOL Damage(sCharacter *Victim,                            \
                  BOOL PhysicalAttack, long Amount,               \
                  long DmgClass, long CureClass);
```

Damage takes a pointer to the character taking damage, the type of damage (physical or magical), the amount of damage to apply, and the double damage and cure classes of the attack. You adjust the damage amount based on the defense and resistance abilities of the victim.

Once characters take enough damage, they die, and when that happens, the following function is called:

```
       // Process death of an NPC/Monster
       BOOL Death(sCharacter *Attacker, sCharacter *Victim);
```

Taking the pointer to the victim, the controller is able to handle its death appropriately. If the victim is a monster, you use the attacking character pointer to apply the experience points. Also, if a monster dies, the Death function determines how much gold the monster drops and what item (if any) is dropped and calls the appropriate controller function to handle such dropped items.

Leading into the next function, whenever a PC kills a monster, that PC gains the experience stored in the monster's MCL definition. To apply the experience, use the following function:

```
// Process experience up
virtual BOOL Experience(sCharacter *Character,          \
                        long Amount)                     \
    { Character->Def.Experience += Amount; return TRUE; }
```

Notice that the Experience function can be overridden. This can occur when you're using a separate battle sequence engine; you don't want experience added to the PC until the battle is over. Consequently, you use your own function to keep track of how much experience to apply when the battle is over.

The overridden function can also occur when the character needs to go up in experience levels once he gains a certain number of experience points. The Experience function is the place to determine just when a character goes up an experience level and to take the appropriate actions to increase their abilities.

One note about the Experience function: The character controller normally displays the number of experience points that a PC gains when killing a monster. To stop the controller from displaying this number (as in the case of the separate battle sequences), return a value of FALSE from the Experience function.

The next couple of functions are the ones responsible for processing attacks and spells. Both functions take pointers to the attacking characters (if any) as well as their intended victims. For spells, a sSpellTracker structure is required to tell the controller which spell to process, as well as the sSpell structure that contains the information about the spell effects to use:

```
// Resolve a physical attack from attacker to victim
BOOL Attack(sCharacter *Attacker, sCharacter *Victim);

// Process spell ailments when spell completed
BOOL Spell(sCharacter *Caster,                          \
           sSpellTracker *SpellTracker, sSpell *Spells);
```

Each of the preceding functions takes into account the attacking and defending characters' abilities and adjust their values accordingly. When an attack connects, damage is dealt. When a spell is found to have affected the target (remember, there's a chance it might fail), the next function is called to process the effects:

```
// Apply spell effects
BOOL SpellEffect(sCharacter *Caster, sCharacter *Target, \
                 sSpell *Spell);
```

Things are winding down with the controller at this point. You use the following functions to equip, use, and drop an item:

```
// Process equipping/unequipping of item
BOOL Equip(sCharacter *Character, long ItemNum,          \
           long Type, BOOL Equip);

// Process item being used on character
BOOL Item(sCharacter *Owner, sCharacter *Target,          \
          long ItemNum, sCharItem *CharItem = NULL);

// Process dropping an item
BOOL Drop(sCharacter *Character,                          \
          sCharItem *Item, long Quantity);
```

With Equip, you must specify the character to modify and the item number (from the MIL) of the item being equipped. You use the Type argument to specify which item type to equip (WEAPON, ARMOR, SHIELD, or ACCESSORY) and the Equip flag to tell the controller to equip the specified item (set Equip to TRUE) or just to unequip the currently used item (by setting Equip to FALSE).

As for the use item function (Item), two characters are required: the owner of the item and the character on which the item is being used. In that way, one character can use a healing potion on another character. Specify the MIL item number being used, as well as a pointer to the owner's ICS CharItem structure so that the quantity of the item can be decreased.

The next function is required to process the teleport spell effect on PCs. Whenever a teleport spell is used on a PC, the character controller calls the following function to handle the effects. Both the pointer to the target character and spell structure are passed:

```
// Process a PC teleport spell
virtual BOOL PCTeleport(sCharacter *Character,           \
```

```
                              sSpell *Spell)                          \
            { return TRUE; }
```

Finishing up the character controller class functions is the one that is responsible for preparing a character to perform an action. You use this function mostly when controlling your PC via the PCUpdate function:

```
    // Set action (w/timer)
    BOOL SetAction(sCharacter *Character,                         \
                   long Action, long AddTime = 0);
};
```

When a PC (or any character for that matter) does something, a matching action is performed. Walking is an action, attacking is an action, and so on. Previously, actions were defined as CHAR_IDLE, CHAR_MOVE, CHAR_ATTACK, and so on, for example. You need to set the Action argument to one of those values in order to initiate a character action.

For each action that a character can perform, there is a matching animation in the sCharAnimationInfo structure array used to initialize the controller. When a character performs an action, the appropriate animation is set, as well as the action timer used to count down the time until the animation is complete. Remember that no further actions can be performed until the current action is complete.

The last argument in the list, AddTime, is used to add additional milliseconds to the action timer. Specifying a value of -1 for AddTime, forces SetAction to not use the action timer, which means that the action clears on the next update.

## Using cCharacterController

You find loads of functions in the cCharacterController class, and although you've already read about their functionality, it's difficult to comprehend just what everything does. Perhaps an example will help.

Start by setting up the mesh and animation information for each character mesh. This example uses two meshes.

```
char *g_CharMeshNames[] = {
    { "..\\Data\\Warrior.x" },    // Mesh # 0
    { "..\\Data\\Yodan.x"   }     // Mesh # 1
  };
```

Each mesh contains a list of animations representing the actions each character can perform. Each action animation in the two meshes shares the same animation set names. You map these names using the cCharAnimationInfo structure (which stores the name of the animation in the .X file, as well as a flag to determine whether the animation loops) as follows:

```
sCharAnimationInfo g_CharAnimations[] = {
    { "Idle",  TRUE  },   // CHAR_IDLE action
    { "Walk",  TRUE  },   // CHAR_MOVE action
    { "Swing", FALSE },   // CHAR_ATTACK action
    { "Spell", FALSE },   // CHAR_SPELL action
    { "Swing", FALSE },   // CHAR_ITEM action
    { "Hurt",  FALSE },   // CHAR_HURT action
    { "Die",   FALSE },   // CHAR_DIE action
    { "Idle",  TRUE  }    // CHAR_TALK action
  };
```

Now that you have determined which meshes to use and how to animate them, you can initialize the character controller and begin adding characters:

> **NOTE**
>
> Notice that in the animation info structures I reused some of the animations, which is perfectly fine. Just make sure that you don't set the loop flag to TRUE in an animation if you later set the loop flag to FALSE, or else things just won't work out. The same applies when you first set the loop flag to FALSE and later set it to TRUE for another action.

```
// Graphics = pre-initialized cGraphics object
// Font = pre-initialized font object
// MIL = master item list array (sItem MIL[1024])
// SpellController = pre-instanced spell controller
cCharacterController Controller;

// Initialize the controller
Controller.Init(&Graphics, &Font, "..\\Data\\Default.mcl",    \
      (sItem*)&MIL, SpellController.GetSpell(0),              \
      sizeof(g_CharMeshNames)/sizeof(char*), g_CharMeshNames, \
      "..\\Data\\", "..\\Data\\",                             \
      sizeof(g_CharAnimations) / sizeof(sCharAnimationInfo),  \
      (sCharAnimationInfo*)&g_CharAnimations,                 \
      &SpellController);

// Add an NPC (MCL definition #0) that wanders inside an area
// from -256,0,-256 to 256,0,256
Controller.Add(0, 0, CHAR_NPC, CHAR_WANDER,           \
               0.0f, 0.0f, 0.0f, 0.0f);
Controller.SetBounds(0, -256.0f, 0.0f, -256.0f,       \
                        256.0f, 0.0f,  256.0f);
```

Now that you've added an NPC to the list, you can continuously update and render him each frame:

```
long UpdateCounter = timeGetTime();  // Record current time

// For example, set an attack action
Controller.GetCharacter(0)->Victim = FALSE;
Controller.SetAction(Controller.GetCharacter(0), CHAR_ATTACK);

// Attach a weapon to the NPC (item #0 - a sword)
Controller.Equip(Controller.GetCharacter(0), 0, WEAPON, TRUE);

while(1) {
  // Limit updates to every 33 milliseconds
  while(timeGetTime() < UpdateCounter + 33);
  UpdateCounter = timeGetTime();  // Record new time

  Controller.Update(33);  // Force a 33 millisecond update

  Graphics.Clear();
  if(Graphics.BeginScene() == TRUE) {
    // Update character animations by 33 milliseconds and
    // render them to the display.
    Controller.Render(33);
  }
  Graphics.Display();
}
```

This brief example demonstrates the basics for using the controller. For a more advanced example, check out the Chars demo program.

# Demonstrating Characters with the Chars Demo

All your hard work is about to pay off with a demonstration of the character and spell controllers seen in this chapter. Now is the time to check out the Chars demo program included on this book's CD-ROM (look for \BookCode\Chap16\Chars\). Upon executing the program, you see the scene shown in Figure 16.17.

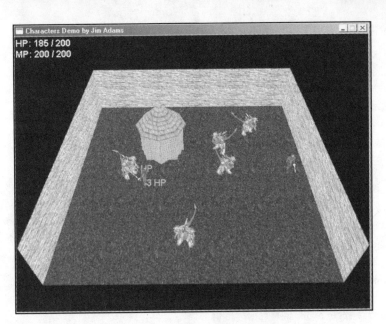

**Figure 16.17**

*The Chars demo contains only the essentials—characters interacting with each other. They walk, talk, and fight it out in this demo.*

In the Chars demo, you take control of the PC, using the arrow keys to turn and move him. The controls are straightforward—use the space bar to interact with the closest character (either to speak to an NPC or to attack a monster). Pressing the number keys 1 through 3 casts a few spells at the closest monster.

Each character in the game demonstrates a single artificial intelligence. Speaking to another character conveys which artificial intelligence a particular character uses (except for monsters, which either stand still or follow the player character). It's best to quickly dispatch the monsters before they take your player character out.

Everything in the Chars demo has been explained in this chapter. A script class determines which characters to place in the map during startup (as detailed in the startup script) and what each character does or says when spoken to.

The demo's action template, default.mla, contains a number of script actions that directly modify a character's type, artificial intelligence, position, and direction. Adding characters to the world is as easy as using an add character script action, and from there, you modify the character's attributes accordingly.

As for the main application, the system core's cApplication class is being used to control the flow of the demo; each frame update is regulated to 33-millisecond lapses, giving a 30-frames-per-second update rate. At each and every frame, keyboard input is read in and stored, waiting to be used during the PC update function. A fixed camera renders out the action, with each character fully animated inside a single level (both characters and the level represented by meshes).

The code to the demo is well commented, so enjoy exploring it, and find out how quickly you can create characters running around in your game project. Be sure to check out the scripts and script action template using the Mad Lib Script editor, as well as the items and character definitions using the MIL and MCL Editors.

# Wrapping Up Characters

You can do a great deal with characters in your game, and this chapter only touches on the basics for doing so. Programming a superior artificial intelligence system, one that better handles the decisions a character can make during gameplay is the place to start enhancing the characters. Then add path-finding abilities, and suddenly characters will become aware of their surroundings and know just where to go and how to get there.

Also, when working with monsters, a basic structure is in place for determining what actions to perform—heal thyself, attack, or cast a spell against an opponent. The percentages of doing any of those actions are fixed. To improve upon a character's intelligence, try assigning percentages that a monster will use for a specific action or magic spell.

Always remember the cardinal rule, however—just keep it simple. Although the character class presented in this chapter is simplistic in nature, it becomes a powerful addition to your game project when you need to control characters.

## Programs on the CD-ROM

The \BookCode\Chap16\ directory contains the following programs, which demonstrate how to use and edit characters and spells:

- **MCLEdit**. The Master Character List Editor discussed in this chapter. Use this program to edit the lists of characters in your game. Location: \BookCode\Chap16\MCLEdit\.

- **MSLEdit**. The Master Spell List Editor discussed in this chapter. Use this program to edit the spells and effects in your game. Location: \BookCode\Chap16\MSLEdit\.

- **Chars**. Using this application, find out how to control characters, including PCs and NPCs. As the player, you control the PC's actions by using the arrow keys, the space bar, and the 1, 2, and 3 numerical keys (to cast spells). Location: \BookCode\Chap16\Chars\.

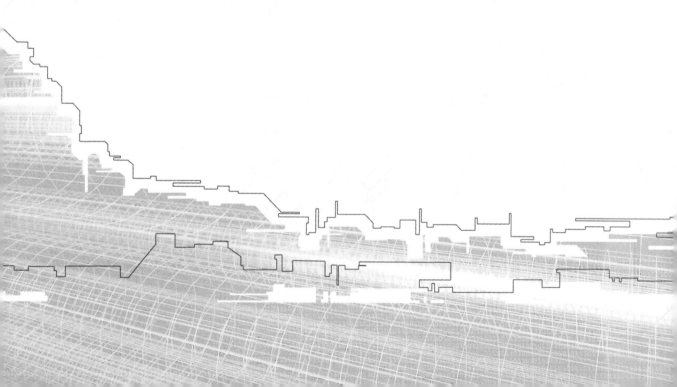

# CHAPTER 17

# WORKING WITH MAPS AND LEVELS

In Chapter 12, "Creating 3-D Graphics Engines," you learn how to construct and display your maps and levels in full 3-D graphics glory. However, drawing those pretty little maps is just the beginning. You also need to place characters in the world, mark spots that will trigger specific actions, place doors and other barriers, and design a way to track where players have been. Well, don't fret; this chapter is just what you need to tackle those tasks.

In this chapter, you learn how to do the following:

- Populate maps with characters
- Use triggers and barriers
- Edit maps, in and out of the game
- Use auto mapping to track character movement

# Placing Characters on the Map

While going through the examples in the book, I placed characters on the map in a direct, hard-coded manner. However, remember that hard-coding game data is a no-no. You need to have as much flexibility as possible when designing your maps, and this includes placement of characters in a level.

Two methods for placing characters in maps that provide the flexibility you want involve character map lists and scripts.

## Character Map Lists

In numerous chapters, such as Chapter 14, "Implementing Scripts," I use external data files that store a list of numbers and text. Those data files are loaded and parsed into some useful information to the engine loading the data. Action templates, for example, contain the action text plus the entry data for each action, all in one easy-to-read-and-edit file.

To adhere to the simple nature of using text data files, you can create lists of characters to place within a map when the map is loaded. Because players are placed in a map using only a set of coordinates and a direction to face, this data file might look something like the following:

```
0    100.0 0.0 450.0 0.0
21     0.0 0.0 -82.0 1.57
18   640.0 10.0  0.0 3.14
```

At first appearance, the preceding three lines of numbers are just that—a list of numbers—but the trained eye sees that each number represents something. Starting with the first number on each line, you have the following:

- The character's type (for example: 0=Main Character, 21=Ogre, 18=Child)
- The X-coordinate, Y-coordinate, and Z-coordinate
- The angle that the character is facing (in radians)

Now knowing what each number means, you can see that I defined three characters and placed them through the map at their respective locations and pointed them in a certain direction. This data is compact, easy to edit, and can be loaded and processed quickly.

## Loading Character Map Lists

To process the data files as just described, you need only two functions (which you also find in Chapter 14). These functions are as follows:

```
long GetNextLong(FILE *fp)
{
  char Buf[1024];
  long Pos = 0;
  int c;

  // Read until EOF or EOL
  while(1) {
    if((c = fgetc(fp)) == EOF)
      break;
    if(c == 0x0a || (c == ' ' && Pos))
      break;
    if((c >= '0' && c <= '9') || c == '.' || c == '-')
      Buf[Pos++] = c;
  }
  if(!Pos)
    return -1;
  Buf[Pos] = 0;
```

```
    return atol(Buf);
}

float GetNextFloat(FILE *fp)
{
  char Buf[1024];
  long Pos = 0;
  int c;

  // Read until EOF or EOL
  while(1) {
    if((c = fgetc(fp)) == EOF)
      break;
    if(c == 0x0a || (c == ' ' && Pos))
      break;
    if((c >= '0' && c <= '9') || c == '.' || c == '-')
      Buf[Pos++] = c;
  }
  Buf[Pos] = 0;

  return (float)atof(Buf);
}
```

Both functions take a file pointer (fp) as an argument and return the next long type number or float type number found in the specified file. You arrange the character map list data file so that the first number (the character type) is a long, although the remaining numbers are float.

Using GetNextLong and GetNextFloat, you can parse an entire character map list as follows:

```
// fp = file pointer to open character map data file
long Type;   // Character type to load
float XPos, YPos, ZPos, Direction;
long NumCharactersLoaded = 0;   // # characters loaded

while(1) {
  // Break if no more characters to process
  if((Type = GetNextLong(fp)) == -1)
    break;

  // Get coordinates and angle
  XPos = GetNextFloat(fp);
```

```
    YPos = GetNextFloat(fp);
    ZPos = GetNextFloat(fp);
    Direction = GetNextFloat(fp);

    // Do something with data - insert a character

    NumCharactersLoaded++; // Increase # characters loaded
}

// Done loading NumCharactersLoaded # of characters
```

## Using Character Map Lists in Your Game

Using character map lists is a quick way to place characters in a map. When you load a map into memory, load the matching character map list and insert the characters. Although this method of adding characters to a map seems desirable, you'll need a bit more flexibility at times, and that's when using scripts comes into play.

# Script Placement

As I said earlier in this section, you can also use scripts to insert characters into a map. Scripts give you more control over where and when a character is placed on a map than using direct placement does.

For example, imagine that you want to track time in your game. At nighttime, all town vendors are at home, so the marketplace is empty. Guards are in the vendors' places, so your game needs to know which characters to place—the vendors or the guards.

You might notice that I'm coming up empty here by not defining a class for loading character placements on maps. How are your characters going to know where to be placed on your maps? As you might have guessed, you can use the Mad Lib Script system presented in Chapter 14 to create and incorporate an action template and a script processor into your project—the script processor then assumes the task of adding characters to the map based on the scripts you write for your game.

A sample action template that adds characters to the map might look like this:

```
"Add character # ~ to map at coordinates ~, ~, ~"
  INT 0 65535
  FLOAT -5000 5000
  FLOAT -5000 5000
  FLOAT -5000 5000
```

With that single action defined, you can construct small scripts that place a character (by a unique identification number) on the map based on the X-, Y-, and Z-coordinates you provided. Quick, clean, and right to the point, scripting is definitely the way to go, and is the method I use to add characters to the map in the complete role-playing game in Chapter 20, "Putting Together a Full Game."

# Using Map Triggers

Cause and effect—two words that say it all. In your world, nothing happens unless you specifically tell it to. Most events in your game happen when a character picks up an item, walks past a certain spot, or even tries to talk to another character. Those events are called *triggers*, and once a trigger has been signaled, a series of effects are sure to follow. Those effects usually take the form of a script being processed.

The problem at this point isn't dealing with the scripts, but figuring out how to trigger them. Programming a trigger for things like picking up an item is easy enough; just assign a number to the item description and process the appropriate script if that item is picked up. The same goes for talking to characters.

Maps are a whole new deal. Maps come in all shapes and sizes, and trying to figure out when a character touches a certain spot on a map is the problem at this point. Well, I'm kidding, as that's not really a problem. The trick is to mark sections of the map with geometric shapes that are used to quickly check whether a character steps inside the shape.

The geometric shapes you want to use are spheres, boxes, cylinders, and triangles. Take a look at each one and how they all work out in the whole trigger scheme.

## Sphere Triggers

You define sphere triggers (see Figure 17.1) by a set of coordinates and a radius. Sphere triggers have two unique benefits:

- Spheres are perfect for defining large areas of a map as a trigger, only using the center coordinates and a radius to define the location of the sphere.
- The sphere trigger is one of the fastest ways to check for character-to-trigger collisions in the map trigger engine.

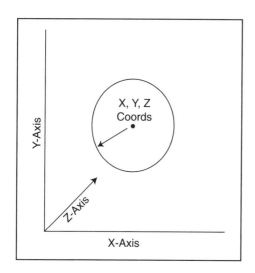

**Figure 17.1**

*You can locate a sphere trigger in 3-D space by using a trio of coordinates and the radius of the sphere.*

# Box Triggers

A box trigger uses bounding boxes to work its magic. Box triggers are the fastest triggers to process when looking for character-to-trigger collisions, but on the downside, box triggers can exist only parallel to the world's axis (the boxes can't be rotated to fit your needs). You define box triggers by the coordinates of its opposing corners, as illustrated in Figure 17.2.

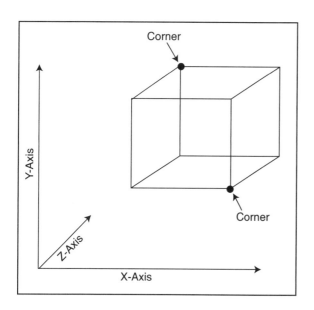

**Figure 17.2**

*Define a box trigger by the coordinates of the opposing corners.*

# Cylinder Triggers

Cylinder triggers are much like sphere triggers, except that with a cylinder trigger, you can limit the height of the covered area (unlike a sphere trigger, which extends higher as the radius increases). Cylinder triggers are most effective when used for circular areas in which you want to keep the height of the trigger from extending into higher or lower levels. Check out an illustration of cylinder triggers in Figure 17.3.

# Triangle Triggers

A triangle trigger is similar to a polygon in that both are defined by three points; however, a triangle trigger's three points are defined only by their X- and Z-coordinates. This makes the triangle two-dimensional. To make the triangle work in a 3-D world, you must assign a single Y-coordinate at which all three points of the triangle are placed, as well as the height in which the triangular area extends upward. It helps to think of a triangle trigger as a three-sided box, as shown in Figure 17.4.

# Triggering a Trigger

After you place the trigger shapes on the map, it's a simple matter to determine which trigger is touched by a character. Each trigger has its special way of determining these character-to-trigger collisions. A sphere uses distance checks, a box uses

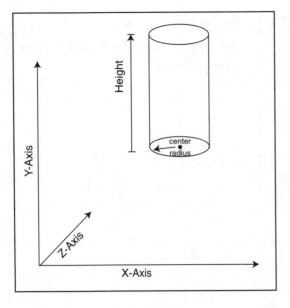

**Figure 17.3**

*Define a cylinder trigger by the coordinates of its lower-center point, radius, and height.*

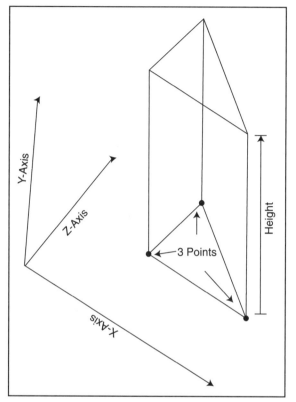

**Figure 17.4**

*Because they use a flat 2-D triangle that extends upward from their placement in the world, triangle triggers are the most versatile shape you can use for defining triggers.*

bounding box calculations, and a cylinder uses bounding and distance checks—although the triangle trigger uses bounding checks and also makes sure that the point in question is contained within the triangle.

When you determine that a trigger has sprung, what do you do? Because each trigger is assigned an identification number, you can use that number to determine which action to perform. You can execute a matching script or perform another hard-coded function. In fact, in the later section "Using Triggers," you find out how useful it is to use triggers.

# Creating a Trigger Class

Adhering to object-oriented programming techniques, create a class that will handle a list of triggers and determine which (if any) has been touched by a character. The class uses a structure to store the information of each trigger—the coordinates, type, and so on. Each trigger is also assigned an identification number that it uses to refer back to itself. The entire list is maintained as a linked list of structure.

The cTrigger class can load and save a trigger file, which makes editing lists of triggers easier. This file is text-based, making it easier to read and edit. Each trigger in the map uses a single line of text written in this order: an identification number, the type of trigger (0=sphere, 1=box, 2=cylinder, 3=triangle), and the default enabled status (if the trigger is enabled when loaded). A value of 0 means that the trigger is disabled, and a value of 1 means that the trigger is enabled.

Depending on the type of trigger you are defining, the trigger must include a few more values. Spheres require the X-, Y-, and Z-coordinates and the radius, as shown in the following:

```
ID 0 ENABLED X Y Z RADIUS
```

Boxes have the coordinates of the opposing corners:

```
ID 1 ENABLED X1 Y1 Z1 X2 Y2 Z2
```

You define cylinders by the lower-center coordinates plus the radius and height:

```
ID 2 ENABLED X Y Z RADIUS HEIGHT
```

Finally, you define triangles by the X- and Z-coordinates of the three corners, in a clockwise order, as seen from above the triangle on the Y-axis (much as a polygon face is defined in Chapter 6, "Drawing with DirectX Graphics"). The Y-coordinate for all three points of the triangle and the height of the trigger round out this definition:

```
ID 3 ENABLED X1 Z1 X2 Z2 X3 Z3 Y HEIGHT
```

I'll get back to the trigger data file in a moment. For now, take a look at the class definition of the trigger class. The class (with the header declared in the Trigger.h file and the full source to the trigger class declared in the Trigger.cpp file) starts out with an enum list that defines each type of trigger shape that you can use:

```
// An enum for type of triggers
enum TriggerTypes { Trigger_Sphere = 0, Trigger_Box,          \
                    Trigger_Cylinder,   Trigger_Triangle };
```

Each trigger you define requires a structure that contains the information pertinent to the trigger—the trigger's location, enabled state, and unique identification number. Each type of trigger uses a set of coordinates to define its location on the map, as well as additional data to define the trigger's radius, opposing corner coordinates, and so on. The structure that contains the information about each trigger created is as follows:

```
typedef struct sTrigger {
  long Type;          // Sphere, Box, etc
```

```
    long ID;            // Trigger ID
    BOOL Enabled;       // Flag if enabled

    float x1, y1, z1;  // Coord 1
    float x2, y2, z2;  // Coord 2
    float x3, z3;       // Coord 3
    float Radius;       // Radius of bounds

    sTrigger *Prev, *Next; // Linked list of triggers

    sTrigger()  { Prev = Next = NULL; }
    ~sTrigger() { delete Next; }
} sTrigger;
```

Notice that the sTrigger structure maintains a set of linked list pointers, as well as a constructor and a destructor that clear the linked list pointers and free the linked list, respectively.

In order to utilize the sTrigger structure, you use the trigger class, which manages the linked list of triggers and enables you to save and load lists of those triggers. Take a look at the trigger class declaration:

```
class cTrigger
{
  private:
    long        m_NumTriggers;     //# triggers in linked list
    sTrigger *m_TriggerParent;  // Linked list parent

    long        GetNextLong(FILE *fp);  // Get next long
    float       GetNextFloat(FILE *fp); // Get next float

    // Function that adds a trigger to linked list
    sTrigger *AddTrigger(long Type, long ID, BOOL Enabled);

  public:
    cTrigger();
    ~cTrigger();

    // Functions to load/save a trigger list
    BOOL Load(char *Filename);
    BOOL Save(char *Filename);
```

```
// Functions to add a specific trigger to list
BOOL AddSphere(long ID, BOOL Enabled,                      \
               float XPos, float YPos, float ZPos,         \
               float Radius);

BOOL AddBox(long ID, BOOL Enabled,                         \
            float XMin, float YMin, float ZMin,            \
            float XMax, float YMax, float ZMax);

BOOL AddCylinder(long ID, BOOL Enabled,                    \
                 float XPos, float YPos, float ZPos,       \
                 float Radius, float Height);

BOOL AddTriangle(long ID, BOOL Enabled,                    \
                 float x1, float z1,                       \
                 float x2, float z2,                       \
                 float x3, float z3,                       \
                 float YPos, float Height);

// Remove a specific trigger by ID
BOOL Remove(long ID);

// Free all triggers
BOOL Free();

// Find first trigger at location (returns 0 if none)
long GetTrigger(float XPos, float YPos, float ZPos);

// Get state of trigger by ID
BOOL GetEnableState(long ID);

// Enabled/Disable a trigger by ID
BOOL Enable(long ID, BOOL Enable);

// Return the # of triggers and parent of linked list
long GetNumTriggers();
sTrigger *GetParentTrigger();
};
```

Most of the functions deal with only a linked list of sTrigger structures—add a structure, remove a structure, find a structure and modify it, and so on. For a closer look at what's going on, take a minute or two to review the following sections, which provide the code for each function.

## cTrigger::cTrigger and cTrigger::~cTrigger

Just as does every C++ class, cTrigger has a constructor and a destructor that set up and free the data contained within the class. The only data tracked by the trigger class that is not contained with the linked list is the number of triggers currently held in the linked list and a pointer to that linked list. The constructor and destructor ensure that the class is prepared for using those two variables to free the class's data when destroyed (by calling the Free function), as seen here:

```
cTrigger::cTrigger() { m_NumTriggers = 0;
                       m_TriggerParent = NULL; }
cTrigger::~cTrigger() { Free(); }
```

## cTrigger::Load and cTrigger::Save

You typically design maps with a set of triggers all in their proper locations. Loading a list of those triggers is the main priority of the trigger class. Once a list of triggers is created or loaded, you also have the option to save that list of triggers (to save the game state, for example).

The Load function opens a text file and repeatedly reads in lines of text that define the type, identification, location, and special properties of each trigger (as described in the earlier section "Creating a Trigger Class"). When the end of file is reached, the Load function returns. Take a look at the Load function code to see just what I'm talking about:

```
BOOL cTrigger::Load(char *Filename)
{
  FILE *fp;
  long Type, ID;
  BOOL Enabled;
  float x1, y1, z1, x2, y2, z2, x3, z3, Radius;

  Free();  // Remove all current triggers

  // Open file
  if((fp=fopen(Filename, "rb"))==NULL)
    return FALSE;
```

At this point, the trigger data file is open and ready to begin reading in a list of trigger definitions. For each trigger, remember that the text line uses the following order: the trigger identification number, the type (0=sphere, 1=box, and so on), the default enabled status (0=trigger disabled, 1=enabled), and the specific data based on the type of trigger being read. Keep that order in mind as you read on:

```
// Start looping, reading in until EOF reached
while(1) {
  // Get ID of trigger
  if((ID = GetNextLong(fp)) == -1)
    break;

  Type = GetNextLong(fp);  // Get type

  // Get enabled status
  Enabled = (GetNextLong(fp)) ? TRUE : FALSE;

  // Read in rest depending on type
  switch(Type) {
    case Trigger_Sphere:  // Load a sphere
      x1 = GetNextFloat(fp); y1 = GetNextFloat(fp);
      z1 = GetNextFloat(fp); Radius = GetNextFloat(fp);
      AddSphere(ID, Enabled, x1, y1, z1, Radius);
      break;

    case Trigger_Box:  // Load a box
      x1 = GetNextFloat(fp); y1 = GetNextFloat(fp);
      z1 = GetNextFloat(fp); x2 = GetNextFloat(fp);
      y2 = GetNextFloat(fp); z2 = GetNextFloat(fp);
      AddBox(ID, Enabled, x1, y1, z1, x2, y2, z2);
      break;

    case Trigger_Cylinder:  //Load a cylinder
      x1 = GetNextFloat(fp); y1 = GetNextFloat(fp);
      z1 = GetNextFloat(fp); Radius = GetNextFloat(fp);
      y2 = GetNextFloat(fp);
      AddCylinder(ID, Enabled, x1, y1, z1, Radius, y2);
      break;

    case Trigger_Triangle:  // Load a triangle
      x1 = GetNextFloat(fp); z1 = GetNextFloat(fp);
```

```
        x2 = GetNextFloat(fp); z2 = GetNextFloat(fp);
        x3 = GetNextFloat(fp); z3 = GetNextFloat(fp);
        y1 = GetNextFloat(fp); y2 = GetNextFloat(fp);
        AddTriangle(ID, Enabled, x1, z1, x2, z2, x3, z3, y1, y2);
        break;

      default: fclose(fp);      // Some error occurred
               Free();
               return FALSE;
    }
  }


  // Close file and return results
  fclose(fp);
  return (m_NumTriggers) ? TRUE : FALSE;
}
```

Once past reading in the identification number, type, and enabled flag of each trigger, a single switch...case code block takes care of loading in each trigger type's data. As each trigger's data is read in, a separate function is called (based on the trigger's type) to insert the trigger into the linked list. Those functions are AddSphere, AddBox, AddCylinder, and AddTriangle.

Moving past the Load function, you see the Save function, which scans the linked list of triggers and saves each trigger's data to a file, using the same format for each line of text that defines a trigger. Take a look:

```
BOOL cTrigger::Save(char *Filename)
{
  FILE *fp;
  sTrigger *TriggerPtr;

  // Error checking
  if(!m_NumTriggers)
    return FALSE;
  if((TriggerPtr = m_TriggerParent) == NULL)
    return FALSE;

  // Open file
  if((fp=fopen(Filename, "wb"))==NULL)
    return FALSE;
```

```
        // Write out all triggers in linked list
        while(TriggerPtr != NULL) {
          // Write out ID, Type, and enabled flag
          fprintf(fp, "%lu ", TriggerPtr->ID);
          fprintf(fp, "%lu ", TriggerPtr->Type);
          fprintf(fp, "%lu ", (TriggerPtr->Enabled) ? 1 : 0);

          // Write out remaining data depending on type
          switch(TriggerPtr->Type) {
            case Trigger_Sphere:  // Write out sphere
              fprintf(fp, "%lf %lf %lf %lf\r\n",
                      TriggerPtr->x1, TriggerPtr->y1, TriggerPtr->z1,
                      TriggerPtr->Radius);
              break;

            case Trigger_Box:  // Write out box
              fprintf(fp, "%lf %lf %lf %lf %lf %lf\r\n",
                      TriggerPtr->x1, TriggerPtr->y1, TriggerPtr->z1,
                      TriggerPtr->x2, TriggerPtr->y2, TriggerPtr->z2);
              break;

            case Trigger_Cylinder:  // Write out cylinder
              fprintf(fp, "%lf %lf %lf %lf %lf\r\n",
                      TriggerPtr->x1, TriggerPtr->y1, TriggerPtr->z1,
                      TriggerPtr->Radius, TriggerPtr->y2);
              break;

            case Trigger_Triangle:  // Write out triangle
              fprintf(fp, "%lf %lf %lf %lf %lf %lf %lf %lf\r\n",
                      TriggerPtr->x1, TriggerPtr->z1,
                      TriggerPtr->x2, TriggerPtr->z2,
                      TriggerPtr->x3, TriggerPtr->z3,
                      TriggerPtr->y1, TriggerPtr->y2);
              break;
          }
        }

        // Close file and return success
        fclose(fp);
        return TRUE;
    }
```

# cTrigger::AddTrigger

`AddTrigger` is the heart of all the other functions that add a trigger. This function allocates a `sTrigger` structure, sets its type, identification number, and enable flag, and then links the structure into the linked list of triggers. Once you allocate your program using the `AddTrigger` function, the program can fill in the returned `sTrigger` structure with the coordinates, radius, height, or whatever other information the trigger needs to have defined.

Keeping in mind that the `AddTrigger` function allocates only a `sTrigger` structure and fills it with the minimal data as just mentioned, take a look at the code:

```
sTrigger *cTrigger::AddTrigger(long Type, long ID, BOOL Enabled)
{
  // Allocate a new trigger structure and link in
  sTrigger *Trigger = new sTrigger();
  Trigger->Prev = NULL;
  if((Trigger->Next = m_TriggerParent) != NULL)
    m_TriggerParent->Prev = Trigger;
  m_TriggerParent = Trigger;

  // Set trigger Type, ID, and Enabled flag
  Trigger->Type = Type;
  Trigger->ID = ID;
  Trigger->Enabled = Enabled;

  m_NumTriggers++;   // Increase trigger count

  return Trigger;    // Return structure pointer
}
```

# cTrigger::AddSphere, cTrigger::AddBox, cTrigger::Cylinder, and cTrigger::AddTriangle

This group of functions adds a trigger of a specific type to the linked list of triggers. Each function has its own list of arguments to use for creation (you can check the comments preceding each function to see what each argument does). Regardless of the type of trigger, each function first calls the `AddTrigger` function to get a `sTrigger` structure with which to work.

Let's start with the AddSphere function, which takes, in addition to the trigger's identification number and default enabled state (as each of the four functions here do), the sphere's radius and the X-, Y-, and Z-coordinates for the sphere:

```
BOOL cTrigger::AddSphere(long ID, BOOL Enabled,              \
                         float XPos, float YPos, float ZPos, \
                         float Radius)
{
  // Create a new trigger structure and link in
  sTrigger *Trigger = AddTrigger(Trigger_Sphere, ID, Enabled);

  // Set up trigger data
  Trigger->x1 = XPos;
  Trigger->y1 = YPos;
  Trigger->z1 = ZPos;
  Trigger->Radius = Radius * Radius;

  return TRUE;
}
```

Short and to the point, the AddSphere function calls on the AddTrigger function to allocate and link in a sTrigger structure to the linked list. Once created, the sTrigger structure instance is filled with the sphere trigger's coordinates and radius.

AddBox, AddCylinder, and AddTriangle operate in much the same way the AddSphere function does. The AddBox function takes the identification number and default enabled state, as well as the coordinates for the opposing corners of the box:

```
BOOL cTrigger::AddBox(long ID, BOOL Enabled,                   \
                      float XMin, float YMin, float ZMin,      \
                      float XMax, float YMax, float ZMax)
{
  // Create a new trigger structure and link in
  sTrigger *Trigger = AddTrigger(Trigger_Box, ID, Enabled);

  // Set up trigger data (fix for min/max values)
  Trigger->x1 = min(XMin, XMax);
  Trigger->y1 = min(YMin, YMax);
  Trigger->z1 = min(ZMin, ZMax);
  Trigger->x2 = max(XMin, XMax);
  Trigger->y2 = max(YMin, YMax);
  Trigger->z2 = max(ZMin, ZMax);
```

```
    return TRUE;
}
```

The AddCylinder function uses the lower-middle coordinates of the cylinder, the radius, and height for the trigger. Take a look at the AddCylinder code:

```
BOOL cTrigger::AddCylinder(long ID, BOOL Enabled,              \
                           float XPos, float YPos, float ZPos,    \
                           float Radius, float Height)
{
  // Create a new trigger structure and link in
  sTrigger *Trigger = AddTrigger(Trigger_Cylinder, ID, Enabled);

  // Set up trigger data
  Trigger->x1     = XPos;
  Trigger->y1     = YPos;
  Trigger->z1     = ZPos;
  Trigger->Radius = Radius * Radius;
  Trigger->y2     = Height;

  return TRUE;
}
```

Wrapping up the bunch is AddTriangle, which takes the three pairs of X- and Z-coordinates that define each of the triangle's three corners. The Y-coordinate to use for those three corners, as well as the height of the triangular trigger shape, follows. By now, the following code should be a snap:

```
BOOL cTrigger::AddTriangle(long ID, BOOL Enabled,              \
                           float x1, float z1,                 \
                           float x2, float z2,                 \
                           float x3, float z3,                 \
                           float YPos, float Height)
{
  // Create a new trigger structure and link in
  sTrigger *Trigger = AddTrigger(Trigger_Triangle, ID, Enabled);

  // Set up trigger data
  Trigger->x1 = x1;
  Trigger->z1 = z1;
  Trigger->x2 = x2;
  Trigger->z2 = z2;
  Trigger->x3 = x3;
```

```
Trigger->z3 = z3;
Trigger->y1 = YPos;
Trigger->y2 = Height;

return TRUE;
}
```

**NOTE**

All functions that use a radius as an argument square the value when it is stored in the structure. This speeds up distance checks later on. How does the trigger class speed up distance checks? A standard distance check uses a sqrt call to calculate the correct distance. Tossing out the sqrt speeds up the engine, but then you must square the values to match the distance.

## cTrigger::Remove and cTrigger::Free

These two functions remove triggers from the linked list by referring to the identification number of the trigger to remove in the Remove function or by allowing the class to remove all triggers in the list using the Free function.

The Remove function operates by scanning the entire linked list—for each trigger that shares the same identification number as the number passed in the ID argument, the Remove function removes the structure from the linked list and frees the structure's memory:

```
BOOL cTrigger::Remove(long ID)
{
  sTrigger *TriggerPtr, *NextTrigger;
  long Count = 0;

  // Scan through list of triggers
  if((TriggerPtr = m_TriggerParent) != NULL) {
    while(TriggerPtr != NULL) {
```

At this point, the linked list of sTrigger structures is being scanned. Now you store a pointer to the next structure in the linked list and check the currently iterated sTrigger structure for a match in the identification number being removed:

```
      // Remember which is next
      NextTrigger = TriggerPtr->Next;

      // Matched?
      if(TriggerPtr->ID == ID) {
```

Once it is determined that a structure needs to be removed, the following code alters the linked list's pointers and releases the structure's memory resources:

```
            // Remove from list
            if(TriggerPtr->Prev != NULL)
              TriggerPtr->Prev->Next = TriggerPtr->Next;
            else
              m_TriggerParent = TriggerPtr->Next;
            if(TriggerPtr->Next != NULL)
              TriggerPtr->Next->Prev = TriggerPtr->Prev;
            if(TriggerPtr->Prev==NULL && TriggerPtr->Next==NULL)
              m_TriggerParent = NULL;

            // Release memory
            TriggerPtr->Prev = TriggerPtr->Next = NULL;
            delete TriggerPtr;
```

From this point on, the number of triggers stored in the linked list is reduced and the
loop that scans for structures to remove continues until all structures are scanned:

```
            // Decrease number of triggers and increase # removed
            m_NumTriggers--;
            Count++;
          }

        // Go to next trigger
        TriggerPtr = NextTrigger;
      }
    }

  // Return TRUE if any found and removed
  return (Count) ? TRUE : FALSE;
}
```

Whereas the Remove function removes triggers according to their identification numbers, the Free function can skip all the hoopla and delete the entire linked list in
one fell swoop using the following code:

```
BOOL cTrigger::Free()
{
  delete m_TriggerParent;
  m_TriggerParent = NULL;
  m_NumTriggers = 0;

  return TRUE;
}
```

# cTrigger::GetTrigger

GetTrigger is the function in the trigger class that you call every time the player's character moves. GetTrigger will take the coordinates of the character you are checking and return the identification number of the first trigger found at that location (if any). If no triggers are found at the specified location, GetTrigger returns a value of zero.

A great deal is going on in GetTrigger, but things are not too complicated. As the linked list of triggers is scanned, each trigger in question is checked to see whether it and the specified coordinates share the same map space. If so, the trigger's identification number is returned.

**CAUTION**

Never assign a value of zero to a trigger because the trigger class uses zero to signify that no trigger is found when the GetTrigger function is called.

```
long cTrigger::GetTrigger(float XPos, float YPos, float ZPos)
{
  float XDiff, YDiff, ZDiff, Dist;
  D3DXVECTOR2 vecNorm;
  sTrigger *Trigger;

  // Scan through list of triggers
  if((Trigger = m_TriggerParent) != NULL) {
    while(Trigger != NULL) {

      // Only bother if enabled
      if(Trigger->Enabled == TRUE) {
```

At this point, you check a trigger that is enabled to see whether it intersects with the coordinates passed in the XPos, YPos, and ZPos arguments of the GetTrigger function. Each trigger has a special way of determining whether the specified coordinates are within the trigger space, and by using a switch statement, the following code can determine how to process that intersection check:

```
        // Check based on type
        switch(Trigger->Type) {
          case Trigger_Sphere:
```

For spheres, you use a distance check. If the coordinates have a distance equal to or less than the radius of the sphere, the trigger is touched:

```
            // Check distance from sphere (using radius)
            XDiff = (float)fabs(Trigger->x1 - XPos);
```

```
      YDiff = (float)fabs(Trigger->y1 - YPos);
      ZDiff = (float)fabs(Trigger->z1 - ZPos);
      Dist = XDiff*XDiff+YDiff*YDiff+ZDiff*ZDiff;
      if(Dist <= Trigger->Radius)
        return Trigger->ID;
      break;

    case Trigger_Box:
```

Box triggers use typical bounding boxes to compare the coordinates of the opposing corners to the coordinates being checked to see whether they intersect:

```
      // Check if inside box
      if(XPos >= Trigger->x1 && XPos <= Trigger->x2) {
        if(YPos >= Trigger->y1 && YPos <= Trigger->y2) {
          if(ZPos >= Trigger->z1 && ZPos <= Trigger->z2)
            return Trigger->ID;
        }
      }
      break;

    case Trigger_Cylinder:
```

Cylinder triggers use a mixture of spheres and bounding boxes.

```
      // First make sure within height bounds
       if(YPos >= Trigger->y1 &&                              \
          YPos <= Trigger->y1 + Trigger->y2) {
         // Check distance from cylinder
         XDiff = (float)fabs(Trigger->x1 - XPos);
         YDiff = (float)fabs(Trigger->y1 - YPos);
         ZDiff = (float)fabs(Trigger->z1 - ZPos);
         Dist = XDiff*XDiff+YDiff*YDiff+ZDiff*ZDiff;
         if(Dist <= Trigger->Radius)
           return Trigger->ID;
       }
      break;

    case Trigger_Triangle:
```

The triangle trigger code shown here checks whether the coordinate in question is in front of all three edges of the triangle by using what's called a *dot-product*. For each edge of the triangle, the dot-product is calculated and checked to see whether the coordinates in question are on the inside or the outside of the triangle.

You can think of the dot-product as the distance of the coordinates in question from a triangle edge. A negative distance means that the coordinates in question are on the outside of the triangle, whereas a positive distance means that the coordinates in question are inside the triangle.

If all three dot-product checks come up with positive values, the coordinates in question must be inside the triangle. You use one last test to determine whether the coordinates in question fall within the height range defined in the sTrigger structure:

```
// First make sure within height bounds
if(YPos >= Trigger->y1 &&                              \
   YPos <= Trigger->y1 + Trigger->y2) {

  // Check if point in front of all lines

  // x1,z1 to x2,z2
  D3DXVec2Normalize(&vecNorm,                          \
        &D3DXVECTOR2(Trigger->z2 - Trigger->z1,  \
                     Trigger->x1 - Trigger->x2));
  if(D3DXVec2Dot(&D3DXVECTOR2(XPos-Trigger->x1,   \
                              ZPos-Trigger->z1),  \
                              &vecNorm) < 0)
    break;

  // x2,z2 to x3,z3
  D3DXVec2Normalize(&vecNorm,                          \
        &D3DXVECTOR2(Trigger->z3 - Trigger->z2,  \
                     Trigger->x2 - Trigger->x3));
  if(D3DXVec2Dot(&D3DXVECTOR2(XPos-Trigger->x2,   \
                              ZPos-Trigger->z2),  \
                              &vecNorm) < 0)
    break;

  // x3,z3 to x1,z1
  D3DXVec2Normalize(&vecNorm,                          \
        &D3DXVECTOR2(Trigger->z1 - Trigger->z3,  \
                     Trigger->x3 - Trigger->x1));
  if(D3DXVec2Dot(&D3DXVECTOR2(XPos-Trigger->x3,   \
                              ZPos-Trigger->z3),  \
                              &vecNorm) < 0)
    break;
```

```
            return Trigger->ID;
          }
        break;
      }
    }

    // Go to next trigger
    Trigger = Trigger->Next;
  }
}

return 0; // return no trigger found
}
```

## cTrigger::GetEnableState and cTrigger::Enable

The GetEnableState function checks the current status of a trigger; by passing the trigger identification number, you get in return the state of the trigger. If a trigger is disabled, a call to GetEnableState returns a value of FALSE. If enabled, the return value is TRUE. To enable or disable a trigger, call on the Enable function, using the trigger's identification number as the only argument.

Each of the two functions scans the linked list of sTrigger structures. For GetEnableState, the enabled flag value of the first structure found in the list that has a matching identification number as the number provided in the ID argument is returned.

For the Enable function, the linked list is scanned, and every instance of a structure with a matching identification number as passed in the ID argument has its enabled flag set to the value as provided in the Enable argument. Take a look at each function's code:

```
BOOL cTrigger::GetEnableState(long ID)
{
  sTrigger *TriggerPtr;

  // Loop through all triggers looking for ID
  if((TriggerPtr = m_TriggerParent) != NULL) {
    while(TriggerPtr != NULL) {

      // If matched ID then set return state
      if(TriggerPtr->ID == ID)
```

```
                    return TriggerPtr->Enabled;


        // Go to next flag
        TriggerPtr = TriggerPtr->Next;
      }
    }


    // Return FALSE for none found
    return FALSE;
  }


  BOOL cTrigger::Enable(long ID, BOOL Enable)
  {
    sTrigger *TriggerPtr;
    long Count = 0;

    // Loop through all triggers looking for ID
    if((TriggerPtr = m_TriggerParent) != NULL) {
      while(TriggerPtr != NULL) {

        // If matched ID then set flag and increase count
        if(TriggerPtr->ID == ID) {
          TriggerPtr->Enabled = Enable;
          Count++;
        }

        // Go to next flag
        TriggerPtr = TriggerPtr->Next;
      }
    }

    // Return TRUE if any triggers changed
    return (Count) ? TRUE : FALSE;
  }
```

## cTrigger::GetNumTriggers and cTrigger::GetParentTrigger

As I like to do with all my classes, I have included two functions that you can use to retrieve the number of sTrigger structures in the linked list as well as the pointer to the first structure (the root, or parent, structure) contained with the list. You program these two functions, GetNumTriggers and GetParentTrigger, as follows:

```
long cTrigger::GetNumTriggers()
{
  return m_NumTriggers;
}

sTrigger *cTrigger::GetParentTrigger()
{
  return m_TriggerParent;
}
```

# Using Triggers

As I promised in the section, "Using Map Triggers," you now revisit using files to store triggers on a map, this time using the cTrigger class created in the section "Creating a Trigger Class." In this section, you find out how to define and load a trigger file effectively.

> **NOTE**
>
> The Mapping example that comes on this book's **CD-ROM** (look for **\BookCode\ Chap17\Mapping\**) demonstrates using triggers much better than this small example does. Be sure to check it out!

## Defining a Trigger File

You start with a sample trigger data file (called test.trg):

```
1 0 1 -900 0 900 620
2 1 0 0   0 0 100 100 100
3 2 1 100 10 200 20 100
4 3 0 10 10 10 -100 -50 0 0 100
```

The first trigger (ID# 1) is a sphere located at -900,0,900 with a radius of 620. The second trigger (ID# 2) is a box that covers the area from 0,0,0 to 100,100,100. The third trigger (ID# 3) is a cylinder; its lower-middle point is at 100,10,200, it has a radius of 20, and it extends up 100 units. The fourth trigger (ID# 4) is a triangle that encloses the area from 10,10 to 10,-100 to -50,0; it has a Y-coordinate (the bottom of the triangle) of 0 and extends 100 units upward. Notice that all other triggers are disabled by default.

## Loading a Trigger File

To load the trigger file, instance the cTrigger file and call Load:

```
cTrigger Trigger;
Trigger.Load("test.trg");
```

## Touching a Trigger

Finally, to see whether a trigger is touched by a character, call GetTrigger with the character's coordinates:

```
long TriggerID;
TriggerID = Trigger.GetTrigger(CharXPos, CharYPos, CharZPos);
if(TriggerID)
  MessageBox(NULL, "Trigger touched!", "Message", MB_OK);
```

With this admittedly simplified example of loading and using the cTrigger class under your belt, you might want to work through the Mapping example program to get more experience with creating, loading, and checking for character-to-trigger collisions using the cTrigger class.

# Blocking the Path with Barriers

In Chapter 12, I explain the basics for using collision detection. You know—detecting when your character is walking around the map bumping into walls or standing on solid ground. What about objects such as doors blocking your character's way? Because a door is not part of the terrain, I didn't include a door when I constructed the collision detection code. Now is the time to remedy that situation.

Anything that bars clear passage of a character's movement is called a *barrier*. Barriers can exist in two states—open (disabled) or closed (enabled). Characters are allowed to pass through a barrier when it is open, but they cannot pass through when the barrier is closed.

You can treat barriers much as you do triggers. You can define a barrier similar to the way you define a trigger on a map. You can define barriers as spheres, boxes, cylinders, and triangles. Barriers can also have an enabled state, with TRUE meaning that the barrier is blocking the character's passage and FALSE meaning that the way through the barrier is clear.

The big difference between barriers and triggers is that barriers can have meshes and animation assigned to them. This relieves you of the burden of drawing the barrier and gives the job to the barrier engine. All you have to do is assign the meshes and animations.

You start off using barriers with the barrier class declaration (as found in the Barrier.h and Barrier.cpp files located on the CD-ROM in the Chapter 17 directory), which looks very similar to the trigger class declaration. Notice that I also define an `enum` list and structure (sBarrier) used to contain each barrier's data:

```
enum BarrierTypes { Barrier_Sphere = 0, Barrier_Box,            \
                    Barrier_Cylinder,    Barrier_Triangle };

typedef struct sBarrier {
  long Type;           // Sphere, Box, etc
  long ID;             // Barrier ID
  BOOL Enabled;        // Flag if enabled

  float XPos, YPos, ZPos; // Coordinates
  float XRot, YRot, ZRot; // Rotation

  float x1, y1, z1;    // Coord 1
  float x2, y2, z2;    // Coord 2
  float x3, z3;        // Coord 3
  float Radius;        // Radius of bounds
```

Here's where the similarities between the triggers and barrier end. A barrier needs a graphical representation (a 3-D mesh), so the following code adds a Graphics Core cObject object that is used to contain the barrier's mesh and animation data:

```
  cObject Object;      // Graphics object
```

Getting back to the similarities of the trigger and barrier classes, notice the pointers that maintain the linked list as well as the sBarrier structure constructor and destructor:

```
  sBarrier *Prev, *Next;  // Linked list

  sBarrier()  { Prev = Next = NULL; }
  ~sBarrier() { delete Next; Object.Free(); }
} sBarrier;
```

The similarities between triggers and barrier continue with the declaration of the barrier class:

```
class cBarrier
{
  private:
    cGraphics *m_Graphics;       // Parent cGraphics object
    long       m_NumBarriers;    // # barriers in linked list
    sBarrier  *m_BarrierParent;  // Linked list of barriers

    long       GetNextLong(FILE *fp);  // Get next long in file
    float      GetNextFloat(FILE *fp); // Get next float in file

    // Get a sBarrier structure and linked into list
    sBarrier *AddBarrier(long Type, long ID, BOOL Enabled,    \
                         float XPos, float YPos, float ZPos,  \
                         float XRot, float YRot, float ZRot);
```

Shift your focus for a moment to the arguments that the AddBarrier function is taking. Aside from the position in which to position the barrier (using the XPos, YPos, and ZPos arguments), the AddBarrier function takes the rotational values in which to draw the barrier's mesh (using the XRot, YRot, and ZRot arguments that represent the X-, Y-, and Z-rotational values, in radians, respectively).

Notice that the addition of rotational values throughout the barrier class, as well as the addition of an extra trio of coordinates that define the mesh's position in the world. As you come upon these additional values, I'll be sure to point them out.

Continue now with the cBarrier class declaration:

```
  public:
    cBarrier();   // Constructor
    ~cBarrier();  // Destructor

    // Functions to load and save a barrier list
    BOOL Load(char *Filename);
    BOOL Save(char *Filename);

    // Functions to set a mesh and animation for a barrier
    BOOL SetMesh(long ID, cGraphics *Graphics, cMesh *Mesh);
    BOOL SetAnim(long ID, cAnimation *Anim,                  \
                 char *Name, long Time);
```

When you need to assign a mesh to a barrier, use the SetMesh function, passing the barrier's identification number to set, as well as the Graphics Core cGraphics and cMesh objects to use. For setting an animation for a barrier, you pass the barrier's identification number, cAnimation object, the name of the animation to use, and the time the animation is set (using a timer function such as timeGetTime).

After you assign a mesh and animation, you can render a barrier to the display using the following Render function. The Render function takes as arguments the current time to update the animations (again using timeGetTime) and the viewing frustum to use for clipping out the barriers that are out of the viewpoint:

```
// Render barriers out using specified frustum
BOOL Render(unsigned long Time, cFrustum *Frustum);
```

When it comes time to start adding barriers to the linked list, the cBarrier class comes packed with as many functions to do so as cTrigger. Take a look at those functions' prototypes (I show you how they each work after showing the entire cBarrier class declaration):

```
BOOL AddSphere(long ID, BOOL Enabled,                    \
               float XPos,  float YPos,  float ZPos,     \
               float XRot,  float YRot,  float ZRot,     \
               float CXPos, float CYPos, float CZPos,    \
               float Radius);

BOOL AddBox(long ID, BOOL Enabled,                       \
            float XPos,  float YPos,  float ZPos,        \
            float XRot,  float YRot,  float ZRot,        \
            float XMin, float YMin, float ZMin,          \
            float XMax, float YMax, float ZMax);

BOOL AddCylinder(long ID, BOOL Enabled,                  \
                 float XPos,  float YPos,  float ZPos,   \
                 float XRot,  float YRot,  float ZRot,   \
                 float CXPos, float CYPos, float CZPos,  \
                 float Radius, float Height);

BOOL AddTriangle(long ID, BOOL Enabled,                  \
                 float XPos,  float YPos,  float ZPos,   \
                 float XRot,  float YRot,  float ZRot,   \
                 float x1, float z1,                     \
                 float x2, float z2,                     \
```

```
                        float x3, float z3,                          \
                        float CYPos, float Height);

    BOOL Remove(long ID);
    BOOL Free();

    long GetBarrier(float XPos, float YPos, float ZPos);

    BOOL GetEnableState(long ID);
    BOOL Enable(long ID, BOOL Enable);

    long GetNumBarriers();
    sBarrier *GetParentBarrier();
};
```

Again, the barrier class is so similar to the trigger class you saw in the section "Creating a Trigger Class" that I would be wasting space by providing the complete code to the cBarrier class here. Instead, just refer to the cTrigger class for the specifics on the majority of functions and read on to see the breakdown of the functions that are exclusive to the barrier class.

# cBarrier::SetMesh and cBarrier::SetAnim

With the addition of graphics objects, you need to assign meshes and animations. Each barrier has a dedicated cObject to use for orientation, but first a mesh must be assigned via the SetMesh function. Animations are sure to follow using the SetAnim function. Take a look at each of the functions responsible for setting those meshes and animations:

```
BOOL cBarrier::SetMesh(long ID,                              \
                       cGraphics *Graphics, cMesh *Mesh)
{
    sBarrier *BarrierPtr;
    long Count = 0;

    // Loop through all Barriers looking for ID
    if((BarrierPtr = m_BarrierParent) != NULL) {
        while(BarrierPtr != NULL) {

            // If matched ID then set mesh
```

```
        if(BarrierPtr->ID == ID) {
          BarrierPtr->Object.Create(Graphics, Mesh);
          Count++;
        }

        // Go to next flag
        BarrierPtr = BarrierPtr->Next;
      }
    }

  // Return TRUE if any meshes set
  return (Count) ? TRUE : FALSE;
}

BOOL cBarrier::SetAnim(long ID, cAnimation *Anim,                 \
                       char *Name, long Time)
{
  sBarrier *BarrierPtr;
  long Count = 0;

  // Loop through all Barriers looking for ID
  if((BarrierPtr = m_BarrierParent) != NULL) {
    while(BarrierPtr != NULL) {

      // If matched ID then set animation
      if(BarrierPtr->ID == ID) {
        BarrierPtr->Object.SetAnimation(Anim, Name, Time);
        Count++;
      }

      // Go to next flag
      BarrierPtr = BarrierPtr->Next;
    }
  }

  // Return TRUE if any animations set
  return (Count) ? TRUE : FALSE;
}
```

After you've loaded or created barriers, assign the meshes by their respective barrier identification numbers. Notice that the SetAnim function is just like the

cObject::SetAnimation function—you have the name of the animation and the starting time of the animation.

Both functions simply scan through the linked list of barriers looking for a matching identification number, at which point, the class records the mesh or animation being set and moves on through the rest of the linked list.

# cBarrier::Render

The only other exclusive function in cBarrier (as opposed to cTrigger) is Render, which takes a time value that is used to update the barriers' animations and a viewing frustum that is used to clip out unseen barrier objects. Take a look at the Render function code:

```
BOOL cBarrier::Render(unsigned long Time, cFrustum *Frustum)
{
  sBarrier *BarrierPtr;
  float Radius;

  // Error checking
  if(Frustum == NULL)
    return FALSE;

  // Loop through all Barriers looking for ID
  if((BarrierPtr = m_BarrierParent) != NULL) {
    while(BarrierPtr != NULL) {

      // Get radius and perform frustum check
      BarrierPtr->Object.GetBounds(NULL,NULL,NULL,NULL,         \
                                   NULL,NULL,&Radius);
      if(Frustum->CheckSphere(BarrierPtr->XPos,                 \
                              BarrierPtr->YPos,                 \
                              BarrierPtr->ZPos, Radius)) {

        // Position object
        BarrierPtr->Object.Move(BarrierPtr->XPos,               \
                                BarrierPtr->YPos,               \
                                BarrierPtr->ZPos);
        BarrierPtr->Object.Rotate(BarrierPtr->XRot,             \
                                  BarrierPtr->YRot,             \
                                  BarrierPtr->ZRot);
```

```
        // Update animation
        BarrierPtr->Object.UpdateAnimation(Time, TRUE);

        // Render object
        BarrierPtr->Object.Render();
      }

      // Go to next flag
      BarrierPtr = BarrierPtr->Next;
    }
  }


  return TRUE;
}
```

In the preceding Render function, the linked list of barriers is scanned, and for each barrier, a frustum check is performed. If a barrier is in the view, its respective animation is updated and the mesh is rendered.

# Adding Barriers with cBarrier

Even though the barrier class marks areas on the map using geometric shapes in exactly the same way as the trigger class does, the barrier class also positions meshes. Looking again at the cBarrier class declaration, notice that each of the add barrier functions—AddSphere, AddBox, AddCylinder, and AddTriangle—have a set of coordinates that position and rotate the barrier's mesh before being rendered.

To determine where the mesh is positioned, set the XPos, YPos, and ZPos arguments of the add barrier functions to where you want the mesh rendered. You also need to set the XRot, YRot, and ZRot arguments to the rotational values to draw the mesh.

For example, say that you want to add a spherical barrier that already has a mesh assigned. The barrier is positioned at coordinates 10,20,30 (with a radius of 40), while the mesh is positioned at 10,0,30 using no rotational values. To add the barrier, you call the AddSphere function as follows:

```
cBarrier::AddSphere(1, TRUE,                                \
                    10.0f, 0.0f, 30.0f, 0.0f, 0.0f, 0.0f,   \
                    10.0f, 20.0f, 30.0f, 40.0f);
```

You get a better understanding of adding and using barriers in the next section.

# Using the Barrier Class

Using the barrier class is not difficult; it's much like using the trigger class. The biggest difference is that you have to add object placement data to the barrier data files and assign the appropriate meshes and animations.

## Creating the Barrier Data File

The barrier data files are arranged just like trigger data files, except that you start each barrier definition with the identification number, type, enabled flag, placement coordinates (X, Y, Z), and rotations (X-rotation, Y-rotation, and Z-rotation) to place the barrier graphics object. Finish each definition with the respective barrier type's data.

The following defines two barriers to use (contained in a file called test.bar). Note that the coordinates and rotational values of the barrier are shown in bold:

```
1 1 1 -900 0 0 0 0 0 -1154 0 10 -645 100   -10
2 1 0 0 0 -900 0 1.57 0 -10 0 -1154 10 100 -645
```

Here are two barriers, both using a box shape. The first barrier's graphics object is placed at -900,0,0 and has rotational values of 0,0,0. The first box covers the area from -1154,0,10 to -645,100, -10.

The second barrier has a graphics object placed at 0,0, -900 and has rotational values of 0,1.57,0. The second barrier covers the area from -10,0,-1154 to 10,100,-645.

## Loading the Barrier Data

In order to load and use a barrier data file, instance the cBarrier class, load the data file and appropriate meshes, and assign the meshes:

```
// Graphics = pre-initialized cGraphics object
cBarrier Barrier;

// Load a barrier data file
Barrier.Load("test.bar");

// Load a mesh and animation to use
cMesh Mesh;
cAnimation Anim;
Mesh.Load(&Graphics, "barrier.x");
Anim.Load("barrier.x", &Mesh);
```

```
// Assign mesh and animation to both barriers loaded
Barrier.SetMesh(1, &Graphics, &Mesh);
Barrier.SetMesh(2, &Graphics, &Mesh);
Barrier.SetAnim(1, &Anim, "AnimationName", 0);
Barrier.SetAnim(2, &Anim, "AnimationName", 0);
```

## Checking Barrier Collisions

To see whether an area on the map is blocked, call GetBarrier with the character coordinates. If a value of TRUE is returned, passage is blocked, and you should take appropriate actions. Take the following example that checks a character's coordinates against all barriers loaded from the barrier list.

You use a trio of values that represents the direction the character is moving in each axis to determine beforehand whether the movement is blocked by a barrier. Say that a character is moving 10 units in the position Z-axis, meaning that the upcoming ZMove variable will be set to 10. That ZMove variable is added to the character's current position, and if intersecting with a barrier, that ZMove variable is cleared out, thus not allowing such a movement along the axis, as shown here:

```
// XPos, YPos, ZPos = character coordinates
// XMove, YMove, ZMove = character movement values
if(Barrier.GetBarrier(XPos+XMove,YPos+YMove,ZPos+ZMove)==TRUE) {
  // Passage not allowed, clear movement variables
  XMove = YMove = ZMove = 0.0f;
}
```

## Rendering Barriers

Last, you only need to call cBarrier::Render to draw all barrier objects within view:

```
// Frustum = pre-initialize cFrustum object
Barrier.Render(timeGetTime(), &Frustum);
```

# Using Auto Maps

Your game world is a huge place, and when players start exploring their surroundings, you may want to make things easier on them by providing a miniature version of your map for their reference. Not just any map mind you—a map that is smart enough to know where the player has been and the places he still needs to explore.

You need to display only those portions of the map that a player has explored. Sections never visited do not need to be shown—that is, not until discovered by players. In that way, players can look back to where they've been and maybe plot out their paths to future destinations. This is the magic of *auto mapping*.

## Auto Maps in Action

One of my favorite games, *Phantasy Star Online,* by Sega Corp., uses auto mapping in a seamless fashion. Check out Figure 17.5, which shows the auto map at work in the upper-right corner of the screen.

In *Phantasy Star Online,* the main player and other important characters in the game are displayed on the auto map as well as small arrows. As the main player walks around, the map scrolls to show the area around the player. As the player visits new rooms (sections), the rooms are revealed on the auto map.

This auto-mapping feature, much like the other features shown in this book, are easy to re-create for your own game project.

## Big Map, Small Map

The challenge here is to change your large game level into a small map suitable for display in your game. Figure 17.6 shows a screen shot of the Mapping example

**Figure 17.5**

*Phantasy Star Online uses a flat 2-D version of the level as seen from above.*

**Figure 17.6**

*The Mapping example uses auto mapping to display sections of the map that the player has visited.*

program. Notice the map in the upper-right corner of the screen. It uses alpha blending (refer to Chapter 6 for more on this topic) to show the game action underneath.

The easiest way to make a smaller version of the in-game level is to go into your 3-D editor and load up the level of the small map that you want to construct. Figure 17.7 shows a sample level loaded up into MilkShape 3-D and ready to work with.

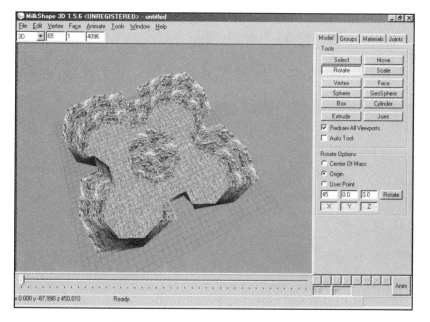

**Figure 17.7**

*A sample level is loaded into the MilkShape 3-D editor and is ready to be converted into a smaller map.*

To start off, select all polygon faces by pressing Ctrl+A. Click the Groups tab and choose Regroup to create a single mesh. Next click the Materials tab and keep clicking Delete until all materials are deleted. At this point, you should have a single mesh that does not use texture maps.

**CAUTION**

Milkshape 3-D is unable to display large meshes, so in order to view an entire level at once you might have to scale down the mesh to work with, then scale it back up when ready to save.

Now for the hard part: Go through the entire mesh and delete all nonessential polygons. This includes polygons that will never be seen from above, that are used for decoration, or that represent walls. You want to keep only those polygons that construct the ground. To delete a face, select it (although you have the Select, Face options selected) and press the Delete key.

If needed, create new faces to match the level mesh as best possible, but avoid overlapping polygons. If you are alpha-blending a small map onto the display, overlapped polygons are darkened and create a bad effect (as you can see in Figure 17.8).

After a little reworking, as you can see in Figure 17.9, my loaded level mesh is reduced to only those polygons on which the characters are capable. I've added a few new polygon faces that are going to be useful when splitting the mesh into multiple sections.

At last, the map needs to be split into smaller sections (which are basically the separate rooms on the map) that are revealed as the character discovers them. Begin by clearing the selection (press Shift+Ctrl+A). Now click the Model tab, click Select, and choose Face.

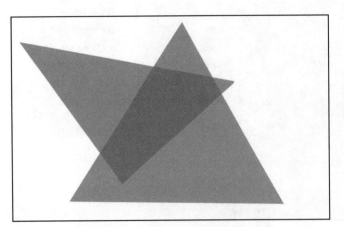

**Figure 17.8**

*Overlapping polygons in the small map can create strange color artifacts when rendered using alpha blending.*

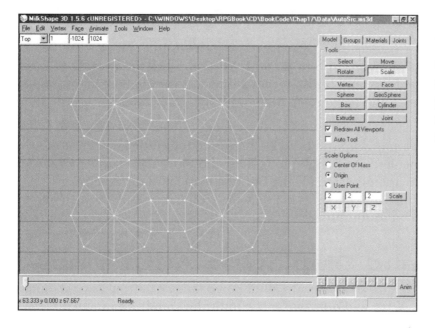

**Figure 17.9**

*The small map mesh contains significantly fewer polygons. The polygons are ready to be grouped into individual sections.*

Start clicking the faces that you want to include in a single map section. You can see in Figure 17.10 that I selected a group of faces in the upper-left corner of the mesh. These faces will form the first map section.

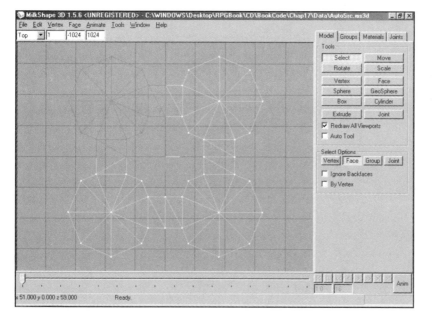

**Figure 17.10**

*Selecting faces is the first step to building the various map sections.*

Now that the faces have been selected, click the Groups tab again and choose Regroup. Notice that a new group is created (as shown in Figure 17.11).

Congratulations! You have created your first map section. Click the Regroup01 group, deselect all the faces, and begin selecting the faces for the next map section. Continue selecting faces and regrouping them until the whole map is split into the various groups.

For the sample map, I ended up splitting the mesh into four individual groups, representing the upper-left, upper-right, lower-left, and lower-right corners of the level. Check out the mapping demo for the finished map file. At this point, go ahead and save your map and export it as an .X file (using the .X file exporter created by myself that comes with this book).

# Loading and Displaying Auto Maps

Okay, the small auto map is created and waiting to be used. What you need to do at this point is load the .X file and query it for the individual meshes contained within. Using the Graphics Core's cMesh object is perfect for loading the mesh.

Now, you construct an array of vertex buffers—one for each mesh in the auto map. You fill each vertex buffer with the triangle face data from each mesh in the cMesh object. The trick at this point is that although you are copying the vertex data from

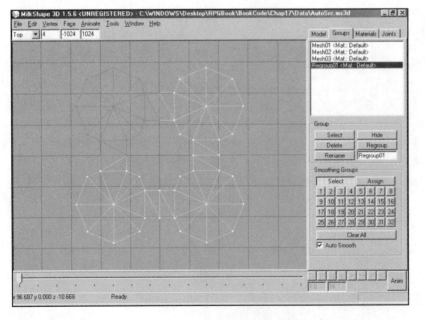

**Figure 17.11**

*A new group of faces has been created.*

the mesh to the vertex buffer, the Y-coordinate is tossed out so that the resulting vertex buffer mesh is flat, and thus the 2-D look of the auto map.

To display the loaded map, you just position a camera, set up a viewport to render to on the display, and render each vertex buffer. With auto mapping in place, you can skip rendering the vertex buffers that represent sections of the map that have not been visited by the character.

Although the concept sounds simple, get a jump on things by looking at some working code.

## Creating the Auto Map Class

The auto map class I've developed for the book will load a cMesh object and compress it into a flat version of the map. The flattened map is stored in a series of vertex buffers. These vertex buffers use only the X-, Y-, and Z-coordinates of each vertex plus a single diffuse color. This means that auto maps are compact and easy to render. This also means that you can use alpha blending to overlay the map on the screen without covering the crucial gaming action going on.

Each map section has an associated flag that defines whether it is visible. The class allows you to enable or disable those visibility flags, and to make sure that the player's hard work is not in vain, save and load those visibility flags.

Enough talk; now check out the class declaration:

```
class cAutomap
{
  private:
    typedef struct {
      float x, y, z;  // 3D coordinates
    } sGenericVertex;

    typedef struct {
      float x, y, z;      // Coordinates
      D3DCOLOR Diffuse;   // Map color
    } sVertex;
    #define AUTOMAPFVF (D3DFVF_XYZ | D3DFVF_DIFFUSE)

    cGraphics     *m_Graphics;    // Parent cGraphics object

    long          m_NumSections;  // # sections in map
```

```
        char          *m_Visible;        // Visibility of sections
        cVertexBuffer *m_MapVB;          // Map vertex buffer

        cVertexBuffer  m_PointerVB;      // Pointer vertex buffer

        D3DVIEWPORT8   m_Viewport;       // Area to draw map
        cCamera        m_Camera;         // Camera used to render map

        float          m_Scale;          // Scale used to draw map

    public:
        cAutomap();    // Constructor
        ~cAutomap();   // Destructor

        // Functions to create and free a map
        BOOL Create(cGraphics *Graphics, char *Filename,             \
                    long Color = D3DCOLOR_RGBA(64,64,64,255));
        BOOL Free();

        // Functions to load/save enabled map sections
        BOOL Load(char *Filename);
        BOOL Save(char *Filename);

        // Return number of map sections
        long GetNumSections();

        // Enable/disable a map section's visibility flag
        BOOL EnableSection(long Section, BOOL Enable);

        // Define an area to draw the map
        BOOL SetWindow(long XPos, long YPos,                         \
                       long Width, long Height);

        // Render the map to display
        BOOL Render(cCamera *OldCamera,                              \
                    float MXPos, float MYPos, float MZPos,           \
                    float NumPositions,                              \
                    float *XPos, float *ZPos, float *Angle);
    };
```

From the start, you can see that I've defined two vertex structures. You use the first, sGenericVertex, to access the vertex coordinates from the source meshes. You use the second vertex structure, sVertex, to store the map sections.

Following the vertex structures are a collage of variables. Notice the cGraphics object to use for loading meshes, the number of map sections in use, an array of vertex buffers, an array of char variables used to mark sections of the map that are visible, a viewport structure, a cCamera, a scaling factor variable, and a pointer vertex buffer.

You should be comfortable with everything except the pointer vertex buffer and the scaling factor. To make things easier on you, a map being loaded is scaled down to a workable size. When you render the auto map, you need to specify coordinates from the large map scale, but the auto map class will scale them down to fit the small map.

For example, a map that is 1,024 units in width and depth is scaled down to 256 units in width and depth. In fact, all maps are scaled down to a size of 256 x 256, regardless of their size in the .X file.

As for the pointer vertex buffer, I've added the capability to display an arrow pointer that represents each character on the map. The arrow pointer points in the direction each character is facing. This vertex buffer simply contains three points and is rendered using a red diffuse color.

In addition to the class's private variables, you must deal with the functions.

## cAutomap::cAutomap and cAutomap::~cAutomap

The constructor and destructor of the cAutomap class ensure that all data is placed within a known state and that all used resources are released. The constructor does nothing more than clear some variables and orient a camera to point downward. You later use that camera to render the map. The destructor calls on the Free function to release all used resources. Take a look at each function's code:

```
cAutomap::cAutomap()
{
  m_Graphics = NULL;

  // Set section data and vertex buffer
  m_NumSections = 0;
  m_Visible = NULL;
  m_MapVB = NULL;
```

```
    // Point the camera down
    m_Camera.Rotate(1.57f, 0.0f, 0.0f);

    // Set a default window for displaying map
    SetWindow(0,0,100,100);

    m_Scale = 1.0f;  // Set a default scale
}


cAutomap::~cAutomap()
{
    Free();
}
```

# cAutomap::Create and cAutoMap::Free

All right, take a deep breath for this part. The Create function is the biggest of the
bunch. It loads an .X file and converts each mesh within into a separate vertex
buffer. Starting with its variable declarations, examine the variable in pieces to
better understand what's going on:

```
BOOL cAutomap::Create(cGraphics *Graphics,                           \
                      char *Filename, long Color)
{
  cMesh            Mesh;       // The .X file being loaded
  sMesh            *MeshPtr;   // Pointer to meshes in cMesh
  ID3DXMesh        *IMeshPtr;  // Direct3D mesh pointer
  sGenericVertex   *GenVert;   // Vertex source
  sVertex          Vertex, *VBPtr;  // Vertex destination
  long             i, j, Num;
  long             VertexSize, NumFaces;
  unsigned short   *IndexPtr;  // Pointer into mesh index buffer
  char             *VertexPtr; // Mesh vertex buffer pointer
  float            Radius;     // Radius of all meshes in .X
  // Pointer vertex buffer definition
  sVertex          PointerVerts = {
      {    0.0f, 0.0f,  10.0f, D3DCOLOR_RGBA(128,64,0,255) },
      {    5.0f, 0.0f, -10.0f, D3DCOLOR_RGBA(128,64,0,255) },
      {   -5.0f, 0.0f, -10.0f, D3DCOLOR_RGBA(128,64,0,255) }
    };
```

```
// Free a prior automap
Free();

// Error checking
if((m_Graphics = Graphics) == NULL || Filename == NULL)
  return FALSE;
```

At this point, some variables are declared, a prior auto map is freed (via a call to
Free), and some error checking is being performed. Notice that the variable declarations include the vertex definitions for the pointer vertex buffer.

Now move on, starting with the code that loads the map mesh that is used to create
the vertex buffers:

```
// Attempt to load the mesh
if(Mesh.Load(Graphics, Filename) == FALSE)
  return FALSE;

// Get mesh pointer
if((MeshPtr = Mesh.GetParentMesh()) == NULL) {
  Mesh.Free();
  return FALSE;
}

// Get size of vertices from source mesh
VertexSize = D3DXGetFVFVertexSize(MeshPtr->m_Mesh->GetFVF());

// Get a bounding radius to scale by
Mesh.GetBounds(NULL,NULL,NULL,NULL,NULL,NULL,&Radius);
m_Scale = 128.0f / Radius;

// Get # of sections in map mesh
if(!(m_NumSections = Mesh.GetNumMeshes())) {
  Mesh.Free();
  return FALSE;
}
```

The first order of business is to load the actual .X file from disc. The first sMesh
structure is grabbed from the cMesh object (remember from the Graphics Core that
the cMesh class stores meshes in a linked list of sMesh structures).

Next, you calculate the size of the vertex structure used by the .X file and calculate
the scaling factor to alter the meshes being loaded. Finally, you store the number

of map sections in a class variable. Notice that the number of map sections happens to be the number of meshes in the .X file.

Moving on, you allocate an array of char variables, with each element in the array representing whether a map section is visible. Each map section has a matching element in the array. You also create an array of vertex buffers (using the Graphics Core's cVertexBuffer class). These vertex buffers will be used to store the map sections. Take a look at the code that creates those arrays and begins scanning through the list of meshes:

```
// Allocate the visibility buffer and clear it
m_Visible = new char[m_NumSections];
ZeroMemory(m_Visible, m_NumSections);

// Allocate the vertex buffers
m_MapVB = new cVertexBuffer[m_NumSections]();

// Go through each mesh in the cMesh object and
// construct a matching vertex buffer. Make sure
// to start with last section in map to compensate
// for linked list ordering of meshes in cMesh.
Num = m_NumSections - 1;
while(MeshPtr != NULL) {
   // Get a pointer to the mesh
   IMeshPtr = MeshPtr->m_Mesh;
```

Remember that the meshes are contained with a linked list of structures. Now is the time to iterate through each structure in the linked list and query each structure for the pointer to the actual Direct3D ID3DXMesh object that contains the mesh information for a single map section.

Next, you lock the index and vertex buffers (just as in Chapter 12) and start pulling out the vertex data:

```
// Lock index and vertex buffers
IMeshPtr->LockIndexBuffer(D3DLOCK_READONLY,            \
                          (BYTE**)&IndexPtr);
IMeshPtr->LockVertexBuffer(D3DLOCK_READONLY,           \
                          (BYTE**)&VertexPtr);

// Create the vertex buffer
NumFaces = IMeshPtr->GetNumFaces();
m_MapVB[Num].Create(Graphics, NumFaces*3,              \
```

```
                    AUTOMAPFVF, sizeof(sVertex));

    // Lock the vertex buffer
    m_MapVB[Num].Lock(0,0);
    VBPtr = (sVertex*)m_MapVB[Num].GetPtr();
```

A vertex buffer is being created to match the number of polygon faces in the source mesh. The vertex buffer is being locked and a pointer is being retrieved to start storing the vertices:

```
    // Pull out vertices and construct vertex list
    for(i=0;i<NumFaces;i++) {
      for(j=0;j<3;j++) {
        // Get pointer to vertex
        GenVert=(sGenericVertex*)                            \
                &VertexPtr[VertexSize * (*IndexPtr++)];

        // Create new vertices
        Vertex.x = GenVert->x * m_Scale;
        Vertex.y = 0.0f;
        Vertex.z = GenVert->z * m_Scale;
        Vertex.Diffuse = Color;

        memcpy(VBPtr++, &Vertex, sizeof(sVertex));
      }
    }
```

Two loops now go through every polygon face in the source mesh, and three vertices for each face are copied over to the map vertex buffers. Notice that you use only the X- and Z-coordinates, although the Y-coordinate is set to 0 (again to flatten the map). Last, you set the diffuse color to the color value provided (used to render the map).

```
    // Unlock the vertex buffer
    m_MapVB[Num].Unlock();

    // Unlock buffers
    IMeshPtr->UnlockVertexBuffer();
    IMeshPtr->UnlockIndexBuffer();

    // Go to next mesh
    Num--;
    MeshPtr = MeshPtr->m_Next;
  }
```

You wrap up the process by unlocking the index and vertex buffers of the source mesh and then proceeding to the next map section mesh in the linked list of meshes loaded from the .X file. Notice that the Num variable is tracking the vertex buffer that is being created, and the preceding code decrements it with each mesh being processed.

You decrement rather than increment the Num variable because the meshes in the cMesh object are stored in reverse order (to make loading faster), so you must compensate to make sure that each map section is numbered sequentially to match the order those meshes are stored in the .X file.

The Create function finishes up by creating the pointer vertex buffer and copying over the vertex definition data defined earlier. The source mesh is freed and control returns to the caller.

```
// Create a character pointer vertex buffer
m_PointerVB.Create(Graphics,3,AUTOMAPFVF, sizeof(sVertex));
m_PointerVB.Set(0,3,&PointerVerts);

Mesh.Free();  // Free loaded mesh

return TRUE;
}
```

In order to free the map sections from memory, you provide a Free function that releases all the allocated resources and prepares the class to load another map class:

```
BOOL cAutomap::Free()
{
  long i;

  // Free map vertex buffers
  if(m_MapVB != NULL) {
    for(i=0;i<m_NumSections;i++)
      m_MapVB[i].Free();
    delete [] m_MapVB;
    m_MapVB = NULL;
  }

  m_NumSections = 0;    // Reset # of sections

  delete [] m_Visible;  // Release visibility array
  m_Visible = NULL;
```

```
    m_PointerVB.Free();    // Free pointer vertex buffer

    return TRUE;
}
```

## cAutomap::Load and cAutomap::Save

Recall that you need to enable each map section in order for it to be visible when rendered. The m_Visible array tracks the visibility of each map section; if an array element is set to 0, the respective map section is not displayed. If the element is set to 1, the map section is drawn.

In your game, once the map sections are marked as visible, you save those flags so that a player can track his progress through the game and later load his map progression to continue the game-play. The load and save functions do just that:

```
BOOL cAutomap::Load(char *Filename)
{
  FILE *fp;
  long Num;
  BOOL ReturnVal = FALSE;

  // Open the file
  if((fp=fopen(Filename, "rb"))==NULL)
    return FALSE;

  // Get the number of sections in file
  fread(&Num, 1, sizeof(long), fp);

  // Make sure they match and load in visible flags
  if(m_NumSections == Num && m_Visible != NULL) {
    fread(m_Visible, 1, Num, fp);
    ReturnVal = TRUE;
  }

  fclose(fp);

  return ReturnVal;
}

BOOL cAutomap::Save(char *Filename)
{
```

```
FILE *fp;

// Error checking
if(m_NumSections && m_Visible == NULL)
  return FALSE;

// Create the file
if((fp=fopen(Filename, "wb"))==NULL)
  return FALSE;

// Write out number of sections
fwrite(&m_NumSections, 1, sizeof(long), fp);

// Write out visible flags
fwrite(m_Visible, 1, m_NumSections, fp);

fclose(fp);  // Close file

return TRUE;  // Return success
}
```

The storage format for the visibility array is simple: The file starts with a `long` variable that states how many elements are in the array. Following that, the entire map visibility array is written out. To load the visibility array back up, read in the number of elements, ensure that they match the currently loaded map, and load in the array.

## cAutomap::GetNumSections and cAutomap::EnableSection

These two functions return the number of map sections loaded and allow you to set the visibility of each map section. Each map section is numbered sequentially from the order stored in the .X file. Using an argument of `TRUE` for `Enable` makes sure that a map section is visible, although using `FALSE` ensures that the map section is not displayed. Keep that in mind as you read the following code:

```
long cAutomap::GetNumSections()
{
  return m_NumSections;
}


BOOL cAutomap::EnableSection(long Section, BOOL Enable)
{
```

```
  if(Section >= m_NumSections || m_Visible == NULL)
    return FALSE;

  m_Visible[Section] = (Enable==TRUE) ? 1 : 0;

  return TRUE;
}
```

## cAutomap::SetWindow and cAutomap::Render

You use SetWindow to define the area in which you want the auto map displayed (specified in screen coordinates plus height and width in pixels). As you can see, the function is small—it only sets up the viewport structure declared in the cAutomap class:

```
BOOL cAutomap::SetWindow(long XPos, long YPos,                    \
                         long Width, long Height)
{
  m_Viewport.X = XPos;
  m_Viewport.Y = YPos;
  m_Viewport.Width  = Width;
  m_Viewport.Height = Height;
  m_Viewport.MinZ = 0.0f;
  m_Viewport.MaxZ = 1.0f;

  return TRUE;
}
```

As for the Render function, this is where your hard work shows. To display a map, you have to provide a pointer to a camera that you are currently using (to restore it after changing the view matrix), the coordinates of the map camera to use when rendering, the number of characters to display on the map, and three arrays that define each character's coordinates and facing angle to draw on the auto map:

```
BOOL cAutomap::Render(cCamera *OldCamera,                         \
                 float MXPos, float MYPos, float MZPos,           \
                 float NumPositions,                              \
                 float *XPos, float *ZPos, float *Angle)
{
  cWorldPosition Pos;
  D3DVIEWPORT8 OldViewport;
```

```
long i;

// Error checking
if(m_Graphics == NULL || !m_NumSections ||
   m_MapVB == NULL    || m_Visible == NULL)
   return FALSE;

// Move camera
m_Camera.Move(MXPos*m_Scale, MYPos, MZPos*m_Scale);
m_Graphics->SetCamera(&m_Camera);
```

The Render function starts off by defining a few variables, performing some error-checking, and setting up a camera to render the map sections. That's right. The map sections are still 3-D meshes, just flat and viewed from above (which is the reason for the camera being rotated down earlier in the code).

Next you create the rendering viewport (with the old viewport settings saved for later restoring). You set the rendering states (no Z-buffering and no textures) and a transformation matrix to center the auto map in the world:

```
// Get old viewport and set new viewport
m_Graphics->GetDeviceCOM()->GetViewport(&OldViewport);
m_Graphics->GetDeviceCOM()->SetViewport(&m_Viewport);

// Set rendering states and texture
m_Graphics->EnableZBuffer(FALSE);
m_Graphics->SetTexture(0, NULL);

// Render vertex buffers
m_Graphics->SetWorldPosition(&Pos);
```

Next you render every map section. Actually, only those map sections that are flagged as visible are rendered. The code to render those map sections is small, so you can wrap it up with the code that renders the pointers (which represent the characters' positions on the map):

```
for(i=0;i<m_NumSections;i++) {
   if(m_Visible[i])
     m_MapVB[i].Render(0, m_MapVB[i].GetNumVertices()/3,      \
                       D3DPT_TRIANGLELIST);
}
```

```
    // Display alpha blending to render pointers
    m_Graphics->EnableAlphaBlending(FALSE);

    // Draw the character positions
    if(NumPositions) {
      for(i=0;i<NumPositions;i++) {
        Pos.Move(XPos[i] * m_Scale, 0.0f, ZPos[i] * m_Scale);
        Pos.Rotate(0.0f, Angle[i], 0.0f);
        m_Graphics->SetWorldPosition(&Pos);
        m_PointerVB.Render(0, 1, D3DPT_TRIANGLELIST);
      }
    }
```

After rendering the map sections, you disable alpha blending (in case it was used to render the map) and position and render the pointer vertex buffer for each character that was passed to the Render function.

Last, you restore the camera and viewport settings that were used prior to rendering the auto map:

```
    // Restore old camera if passed
    if(OldCamera != NULL)
      m_Graphics->SetCamera(OldCamera);

    // Restore old viewport
    m_Graphics->GetDeviceCOM()->SetViewport(&OldViewport);

    return TRUE;
}
```

# Using cAutomap

The mapping demo for this chapter contains a perfect example of using the auto map class, but to give you a clear idea of its use, here is an example. Start by instancing the cAutomap class and call Create to load an .X file:

```
// Graphics = pre-initialized cGraphics object
cAutomap Automap;

Automap.Create(&Graphics, "Map.x", D3DCOLOR_RGBA(64,64,64,255));
```

At this point, the map is loaded and ready to go. The map uses a color of dark gray for rendering (which is the reason for the D3DCOLOR_RGBA macro). To start rendering the map, you must first set the position of the window to which you are rendering:

```
Automap.SetWindow(0,0,200,200); // Use 0,0 to 200,200 for map
```

Next, you mark a map section as visible:

```
Automap.EnableSection(0); // Set 1st section to visible
```

All that's left to do is to render the map:

```
Automap.Render(NULL, 0.0f, 200.0f, 0.0f, 0, NULL, NULL, NULL);
```

The preceding call positions the camera at the coordinates 0,200,0 (200 units above the map) and renders the single visible map section. Now, what about the other map sections? How is your game going to know which map sections to flag as visible? By using triggers; that's how!

By instancing a cTrigger class, you can embed triggers into your map that signal which map sections have been entered, and thus marked as visible. You just mark those map triggers using the same identification numbers as the map section mesh contained with the map .X file (the first mesh in the file needs a trigger with an identification number of 1, the second mesh needs a trigger identification number of 2, and so on).

The Mapping example uses triggers to mark sections of the map to display as characters enter them—be sure to check out the example to see just what I'm talking about.

# Wrapping Up Maps and Levels

In this chapter, you learned how to use external files to store the locations of character on your map, how to use map triggers and barriers, and how to use auto maps. That's a lot of information to swallow, and I managed to fill your head with more code than you could possibly absorb at once.

Be sure to go over the code carefully to see exactly what is going on, especially regarding the auto maps. The code is simple at its core, but trying to take in the class code all at once is overwhelming. Make sure you're comfortable using the Graphics Core as well; the code shown in this chapter depends on the various components of the Graphics Core to make your programming task easier.

If you're feeling adventurous, try creating a character class that handles loading of characters much like the map inventory control class in Chapter 15, "Defining and Using Objects."

## Programs on the CD-ROM

In the \BookCode\Chap17\ directory, you can find the following program, which demonstrates what you've read about in this chapter:

♦ **Mapping.** A program that demonstrates auto maps, triggers, and barriers. Move your character around using the mouse and arrow keys, and use the spacebar to open and close the doors. Location: \BookCode\Chap17\Mapping\.

# CHAPTER 18

# CREATING COMBAT SEQUENCES

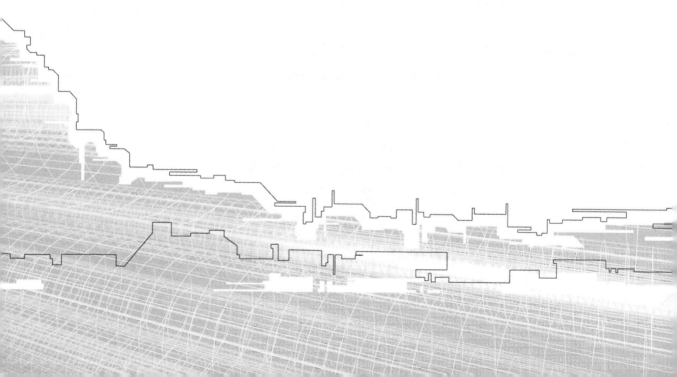

With swords swinging and magic blasting, you manage to wade through wave after wave of demonic creatures. With every victory, you feel yourself growing stronger; new spells are learned, and stronger weapons are usable. The enemy is beginning to lose ground, and here you are standing tall on the mountain you created.

That is, until you encounter the Red Dragon that has been razing the countryside. All your hard work comes crashing down in the ten seconds it takes for the huge beast to turn you into small, charred chunks of flesh.

Ah, but what fun it is—the power and exhilaration you feel from beating down countless evildoers, and the agony of defeat that comes from the hands, or in this case the claws, of stronger foes. Awesome combat sequences make some games what they are (or at least the sequences boost the fun of playing the games). Now is your chance to add combat sequences to your game.

In this chapter, you learn how to do the following:

- Design external combat sequences
- Construct a simple combat sequence

# Designing External Combat Sequences

Some of my fondest memories of role-playing games are those of combat. Not just any type of combat, mind you. I'm talking about those incredible combat sequences that pit you against evil hordes in close-quarter strategic warfare. If you've ever played *Final Fantasy 7*, you know the kind of combat sequences I'm referring to.

Games such as *Final Fantasy 7* take combat in a whole different direction. Rather than battling it out in real time, such as you do in the Chars demo (located on this book's CD-ROM; look for \BookCode\Chap16\Chars\) in Chapter 16, "Controlling Players and Characters", *Final Fantasy 7* switches to an external battle sequence screen in which the view is much closer to the action. Figure 18.1 shows a typical external combat sequence game (from the Battle demo designed in this chapter; look for \BookCode\Chap18\Battle\ on the CD-ROM).

**Figure 18.1**

*The camera views the action from a fixed position that encompasses all engaged characters. In this figure, a monster has cast a powerful spell at the player.*

External combat sequences generally follow similar designs and patterns. First, you have the arena, which is the area representing a small section of the level on which the characters are fighting. The characters are spread around the arena—players on the right, monsters on the left.

Each character has an associated timer (the charge timer) tracking how often the character can perform an action. This timer slowly increases until it tops off at maximum, at which point the character can decide which action to perform. No more hand-twitching, button-pounding combat here—just deliberate, decisive selections.

> **NOTE**
>
> *External combat sequence means that the combat sequence is separated from the game's navigation sequences. For example, a player walking within a level enters combat, and the game-play, in turn, switches to a combat sequence screen.*

Once an action and the action's victim are selected, the characters slowly carry out the results. When casting spells, the characters perform long, mundane rituals that bring forth amazing spells and graphical effects. Whenever a character attacks another character, the two quickly engage, regardless of their distance from each other.

After a character completes an action, the character's charge timer is reset, and the character must once again wait for it to be fully charged before performing another action. Combat continues in the same manner as previously described until all monsters or players are dead (or the PC runs away).

Once combat is complete, the combat sequence engine divides the booty, and the regular game-play continues (until the next combat sequence that is). Of course, this style of combat proceeds more slowly than real-time combat, but all in all, it's worth the wait.

> **NOTE**
>
> Most actions require the player to have a fully charged timer in order to perform the action, such as using items, equipping new weapons and armor, attacking, and using spells.

## The Technical Side

The arena is represented by a single mesh, as are the characters and the spells. In fact, the character and spell controllers developed in Chapter 16 are perfect for the combat sequences here. You need to tweak only a few things to make those controllers work for you.

Only the attack and spell ranges need reworking. Characters are allowed to attack any other character, regardless of the distance between them. Similarly, spells are allowed to target any character, regardless of the distance between the target character and the spell caster.

To handle the differences in distances, you alter the master character and master spell data. Characters need a very high attack range, so you'll need to run the Master Character List Editor and increase the attack range for each character. Figure 18.2 shows one such character's Attack Range being set to 1,024.

As for the spells, the Master Spell List Editor is where you'll want to go to increase the maximum distance of each spell. In Figure 18.3, you'll see one such spell in which I increased the Max. Distance value to 1,024.

In addition to setting appropriate distances, you need to alter each character's AI settings when using the character controller. In combat sequences, you must force characters to stand in place using a CHAR_STAND AI setting; otherwise, they'll just wander around the combat level and possibly get lost! If you do let your characters walk around the level, it's best to use the route-walking AI setting (CHAR_ROUTE) to ensure that the characters walk specifically along the route you want. Consult Chapter 16 for more information on using AI settings and moving characters.

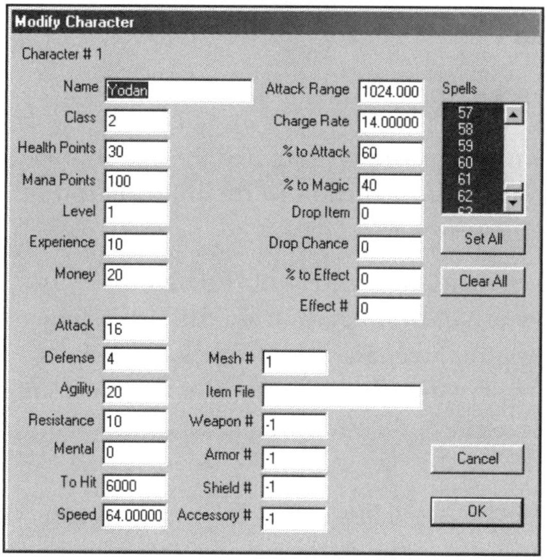

## Figure 18.2

*Each character's Attack Range setting in the MCL Editor should be high enough that all characters in the battle can hit each other, regardless of the distance between them.*

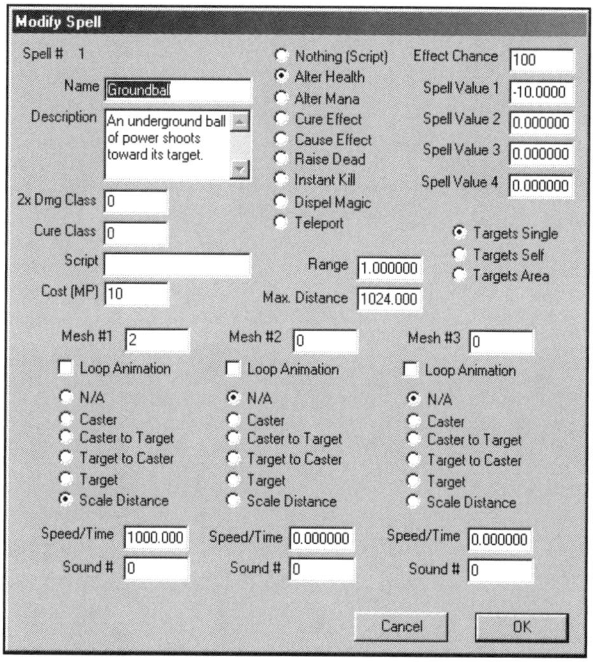

## Figure 18.3

*The MSL Editor enables you to adjust the range of a spell. Be sure to set the Max. Distance to a high level, such as the range in this figure.*

# Developing the Combat Sequence

What better way to learn how to create your own combat sequence than to follow by example. In this section, I'm going to show how you can use the information in Chapter 16 to create your own combat sequence engine.

To see how I developed a combat sequence engine, copy the Battle demo project from the CD-ROM and read along as I show you each function from the WinMain.cpp file. Those functions are relatively small, because the character and spell controllers handle the majority of the work. Your combat engine adds characters to the fray using the character controller's Add function, collects and processes the player's actions, and updates the characters accordingly.

The entire project is contained within a cApplication class object from the System Core. Here's the cApplication class declaration (derived as cApp):

```
class cApp : public cApplication
{
  friend class cChars;

  private:
    cGraphics       m_Graphics;    // cGraphics object
    cCamera         m_Camera;      // cCamera object
    cFont           m_Font;        // cFont object

    cWindow         m_Stats;       // Window for HP/MP stats
    cWindow         m_Options;     // Window for spells

    cInput          m_Input;       // cInput object
    cInputDevice    m_Keyboard;    // Keyboard input object
    cInputDevice    m_Mouse;       // Mouse input object

    cMesh           m_TerrainMesh;    // Terrain mesh
    cObject         m_TerrainObject;  // Terrain object

    cVertexBuffer   m_Target;      // Target object
    cTexture        m_Buttons;     // Buttons and more pics.

    // Character and spell animation controllers
```

```
cCharacterController m_CharController;
cSpellController      m_SpellController;

sItem               m_MIL[1024]; // The master item list

// See which character mouse is pointing at
long GetCharacterAt(long XPos, long YPos);

public:
   cApp();

   BOOL Init();
   BOOL Shutdown();
   BOOL Frame();
};
```

The application class (cApp) seems fairly small for an ambitious project such as a combat sequence, but don't let the size fool you. This project packs a punch! Remember that the previously developed character and spell controllers do most of the work. The character and spell controllers are identical to those in Chapter 16; even the code to initialize each object is the same.

The only differences between these characters and spells and those in previous examples in the book are the attack and spell ranges. All spell and attack ranges have been raised to 1,024 in the master lists, so there's no need to bother modifying them in the application class.

In the Battle project, I constructed a simple, small mesh for the arena (see Figure 18.4) and loaded it into the m_TerrainMesh and m_TerrainObject objects. You do not need a node tree because the level meshes typically fit perfectly in the display. The combat sequence level meshes don't have to be large, so when designing your own levels, keep the meshes just small enough to fit in the display.

The controls are straightforward. For your character to attack or cast a spell, you must first select a target character at which to direct the attack or spell. Selecting a target character is accomplished by clicking any character in the battle. Two small triangles that spin around the target character represent the target (which is contained within the vertex buffer m_Target). The player can target any character at any time.

When the player is fully charged (the charge is denoted by a bar that slowly fills up at the lower-right corner of the screen), he can select the type of action to perform. Click Attack to cause the player to strike the selected target (thus damaging it). Click Spell to open a list of known spells; clicking a spell casts it at the targeted character.

**Figure 18.4**

*The arena mesh in use for the Battle project.*

Other than the addition of the targeting mechanism, there's really nothing new here. So why not breeze through the application code at this point?

# Global Data

The application class uses three global variables to contain the data about the character and spell meshes, and the character animation information:

```
#include "Core_Global.h"

#include "Window.h"
#include "Chars.h"
#include "WinMain.h"

// Global names of character meshes
char *g_CharMeshNames[] = {
    { "..\\Data\\Warrior.x" },    // Mesh # 0
    { "..\\Data\\Yodan.x"   }     // Mesh # 1
  };
sCharAnimationInfo g_CharAnimations[] = {
    { "Idle",  TRUE  },
    { "Walk",  TRUE  },
    { "Swing", FALSE },
    { "Spell", FALSE },
    { "Swing", FALSE },
    { "Hurt",  FALSE },
    { "Die",   FALSE },
```

```
    { "Idle",  TRUE  }
  };

char *g_SpellMeshNames[] = {
    { "..\\Data\\Fireball.x"   },
    { "..\\Data\\Explosion.x"  },
    { "..\\Data\\Groundball.x" },
    { "..\\Data\\ice.x" },
    { "..\\Data\\bomb.x" },
  };
```

The characters and spells used here are the same as those in Chapter 16. Refer to that chapter for more information on setting new character and spell meshes.

## cApp::cApp

You use the constructor of the application class only to set up the class data, which includes configuring the application window:

```
cApp::cApp()
{
  m_Width  = 640;
  m_Height = 480;
  m_Style  = WS_BORDER|WS_CAPTION|WS_MINIMIZEBOX|WS_SYSMENU;
  strcpy(m_Class, "BattleClass");
  strcpy(m_Caption, "Battle Demo by Jim Adams");
}
```

## cApp::Init

Init, the first overloaded function in the application class, initializes the graphics and input systems, loads all graphics, fonts, items, and other data needed for the program:

```
BOOL cApp::Init()
{
  long i;
  FILE *fp;

  // Initialize the graphics device and set display mode
  m_Graphics.Init();
  m_Graphics.SetMode(GethWnd(), TRUE, TRUE);
```

```
m_Graphics.SetPerspective(D3DX_PI/4, 1.3333f, 1.0f, 10000.0f);
ShowMouse(TRUE);

// Create a font
m_Font.Create(&m_Graphics, "Arial", 16, TRUE);
```

As is typical in a graphics project, the graphics system is initialized and an Arial font is created. Next comes initialization of the input system and devices:

```
// Initialize input and input devices
m_Input.Init(GethWnd(), GethInst());
m_Keyboard.Create(&m_Input, KEYBOARD);
m_Mouse.Create(&m_Input, MOUSE, TRUE);
```

As I mentioned, you need to target a character in order to attack or cast a spell on the character. A pair of red, spinning triangles contained within a triangle list vertex buffer with six vertices represents the target (as illustrated in Figure 18.5).

At this point in the Init function, create the vertex buffer that contains the two triangles that represent the target:

```
// Create the target vertex buffer
typedef struct {
    float x, y, z;
    D3DCOLOR Diffuse;
} sVertex;
sVertex Vert[6] = {
    { -20.0f,  40.0f, 0.0f, 0xFFFF4444 },
    {  20.0f,  40.0f, 0.0f, 0xFFFF4444 },
    {   0.0f,  20.0f, 0.0f, 0xFFFF4444 },
    {   0.0f, -20.0f, 0.0f, 0xFFFF4444 },
    {  20.0f, -40.0f, 0.0f, 0xFFFF4444 },
    { -20.0f, -40.0f, 0.0f, 0xFFFF4444 }
};
m_Target.Create(&m_Graphics, 6, D3DFVF_XYZ|D3DFVF_DIFFUSE,
                sizeof(sVertex));
m_Target.Set(0,6,&Vert);
```

Once the target vertex buffer is created, the various graphics need to be loaded from disk. First, you load the button graphics used to select an action. You can see the button graphics image in Figure 18.6. The images used to draw the charge timer are included with the button graphics image. Next, you load the arena mesh and object.

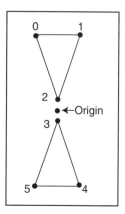

**Figure 18.5**

*By design, the target vertex buffer rotates its center coordinate (the origin).*

**Figure 18.6**

*The button image contains the Attack and Spell buttons as well as the Charge Timer bar.*

```
// Load the buttons and other graphics
m_Buttons.Load(&m_Graphics, "..\\Data\\Buttons.bmp");

// Load the terrain mesh and set object
m_TerrainMesh.Load(&m_Graphics, "..\\Data\\Battle.x",          \
                   "..\\Data\\");
m_TerrainObject.Create(&m_Graphics, &m_TerrainMesh);
```

In order to display the player character's status (including health and mana points as defined in Chapter 16), you create a text window (m_Stats—a cWindow object from Chapter 16) below the character. Create a second window (m_Options) to contain the names of all known spells from which players can select spells as needed. As you can see in Figure 18.7, this second window covers the top of the display.

```
// Create text windows
m_Stats.Create(&m_Graphics, &m_Font);
m_Stats.Move(508, 400, 128, 48);
m_Options.Create(&m_Graphics, &m_Font);
m_Options.Move(4, 4, 632, 328);
```

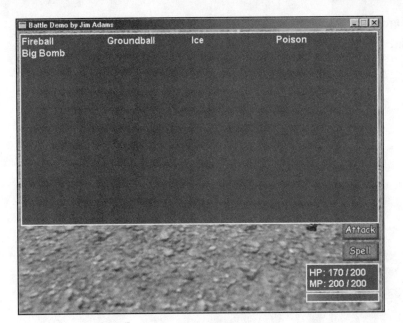

**Figure 18.7**

*The text windows allow the application to show players their status and all known spells.*

Next, you need to load the master item list and initialize the character and spell controller classes. The code to initialize the controllers is identical to the code used in the Chars demo project in Chapter 16.

```
// Load the master item list
  for(i=0;i<1024;i++)
    ZeroMemory(&m_MIL[i], sizeof(sItem));
  if((fp=fopen("..\\Data\\Default.mil", "rb")) != NULL) {
    for(i=0;i<1024;i++)
      fread(&m_MIL[i], 1, sizeof(sItem), fp);
    fclose(fp);
  }

  // Initialize the character controller
  m_CharController.Init(&m_Graphics, NULL, &m_Font,          \
      "..\\Data\\Default.mcl", (sItem*)&m_MIL,               \
      m_SpellController.GetSpell(0),                         \
      sizeof(g_CharMeshNames)/sizeof(char*), g_CharMeshNames, \
      "..\\Data\\", "..\\Data\\",                            \
      sizeof(g_CharAnimations) / sizeof(sCharAnimationInfo), \
      (sCharAnimationInfo*)&g_CharAnimations,                \
      &m_SpellController);
```

```
// Initialize the spell controller
m_SpellController.Init(&m_Graphics, NULL,                     \
    "..\\Data\\Default.msl",                                   \
    sizeof(g_SpellMeshNames)/sizeof(char*),g_SpellMeshNames, \
    "..\\Data\\", &m_CharController);
```

To finish the Init function, you position a few characters (players and monsters) within the arena. (I was a little lazy here; hard-coding the characters encountered and their positions in the arena should be a bit randomized, but I'll leave that up to you.) To add and position characters in the battle, use the character controller's Add function, as shown here:

```
// Add the character player
m_CharController.Add(0, 0, CHAR_PC, CHAR_STAND,              \
                        200.0f, 0.0f, 0.0f, 4.71f);

// Hardcoded - add some other characters
m_CharController.Add(1, 1, CHAR_MONSTER, CHAR_STAND,         \
                        -200.0f, 0.0f, 0.0f, 1.57f);
m_CharController.Add(2, 1, CHAR_MONSTER, CHAR_STAND,         \
                        -100.0f, 0.0f, -200.0f, 1.57f);
m_CharController.Add(3, 1, CHAR_MONSTER, CHAR_STAND,         \
                        0.0f, 0.0f, 100.0f, 1.57f);

// Give an axe to one of the monsters
m_CharController.Equip(m_CharController.GetCharacter(1),     \
                        8, WEAPON, TRUE);

return TRUE;
}
```

Notice that a total of four characters are added to the fray. To make things a little harder for the player, I went ahead and equipped the second character (a monster) with an ax weapon. To equip characters with a weapon, you use the character controller's Equip function, as I did.

## cApp::Shutdown

cApp::Shutdown (which is opposite cApp::Init) frees all used resources (from the meshes, objects, and controllers) as shown here:

```
BOOL cApp::Shutdown()
{
```

```
    // Free controllers
    m_CharController.Free();
    m_SpellController.Free();

    // Free objects and meshes
    m_TerrainMesh.Free();
    m_TerrainObject.Free();

    // Free windows
    m_Stats.Free();
    m_Options.Free();

    // Free target vertex buffer
    m_Target.Free();
    m_Buttons.Free();

    // Shut down input
    m_Keyboard.Free();
    m_Mouse.Free();
    m_Input.Shutdown();

    // Shut down graphics
    m_Font.Free();
    m_Graphics.Shutdown();

    return TRUE;
}
```

## cApp::Frame

The cApp::Frame function is a little crowded in its current incarnation. Here, Frame has the job of collecting and processing player input. The only input used is that of the mouse; the left mouse button selects a target character, a spell to cast, or an attack to perform. The right mouse button closes the spell selection window if it is currently open. Once a target and an action are picked, the appropriate action is performed.

Besides processing input, the Frame function renders everything to the display, including the arena, characters, spell animations, status window (which displays the player's health and mana points), charge bar, spell list, and action buttons:

```
BOOL cApp::Frame()
{
```

```
static DWORD UpdateCounter = timeGetTime();
static sCharacter *PCChar=m_CharController.GetCharacter(0);
static BOOL SelectSpell = FALSE;
static long TargetID = -1;
cWorldPosition Pos;
sCharacter *CharPtr;
sSpell     *SpellPtr;
char Text[128];
long   x, y, Num, i;
float MinY, MaxY, YOff;

// Lock to 30 fps
if(timeGetTime() < UpdateCounter + 33)
   return TRUE;
UpdateCounter = timeGetTime();
```

A frame timer governs the speed in which the game plays. Currently, the battle project is locked at 30 frames per second. If an update is allowed, execution continues by reading in the player input:

```
// Read in input
m_Keyboard.Acquire(TRUE);
m_Keyboard.Read();
m_Mouse.Acquire(TRUE);
m_Mouse.Read();

// Exit if ESC pressed
if(m_Keyboard.GetKeyState(KEY_ESC) == TRUE)
   return FALSE;
```

Frame next determines what to process if the player presses the left mouse button. Remember that this includes selecting a target, a spell, or an attack:

```
// Get selected character if left button pressed
if(m_Mouse.GetButtonState(MOUSE_LBUTTON) == TRUE) {
   // Get mouse coordinates
   x = m_Mouse.GetXPos();
   y = m_Mouse.GetYPos();

   // Lock the mouse button
   m_Mouse.SetLock(MOUSE_LBUTTON, TRUE);
   m_Mouse.SetButtonState(MOUSE_LBUTTON, FALSE);
```

From here, Frame determines what to process. If the player clicks the Spell button, the spell list window (m_Options) opens displaying all known spells. When the spell list window opens, the SelectSpell flag (which is set to FALSE by default) is set to TRUE, and Frame waits for a spell to be selected or for the window to be closed (by the player clicking the right mouse button).

```
// See if selecting a spell
    if(SelectSpell == TRUE) {

        // Get pointer to spell
        Num = ((y-8)/20) * 4 + ((x-8)/150);
```

You select a spell by calculating the coordinates that were clicked onscreen and comparing those coordinates to the location where each spell name was printed to the window. Each spell name consumes a 150 x 20 pixel section of the window (which is located at the screen coordinates 8,8), and there is room for 64 spell names in the window.

```
// Make sure player knows spell (and has enough MP)
    if(Num >= 0 && Num < 64) {
      SpellPtr = m_SpellController.GetSpell(Num);
      if(PCChar->Def.MagicSpells[Num/32] & (1<<(Num&31)) && \
        SpellPtr->Name[0] &&                                \
        PCChar->ManaPoints >= SpellPtr->Cost) {
        PCChar->SpellNum = Num;   // Set spell number to cast
        PCChar->SpellTarget = CHAR_MONSTER;  // Set target
        m_CharController.SetAction(PCChar, CHAR_SPELL);
        SelectSpell = FALSE;  // Close selection window
```

Once the player selects a spell from the spell selection window, the appropriate spell is cast, and the control classes process the effects. The spell selection window is flagged as closed, and execution continues. If a spell is not being selected, the Frame function continues execution by determining whether the player clicked either the attack or spell buttons.

```
        }
      }
    } else {
      // See if a button pressed (if target picked and charged)
      if(TargetID != -1 && PCChar->Charge >= 100.0f) {
        // Set victim and attacker info
        CharPtr = m_CharController.GetCharacter(TargetID);
```

```
            PCChar->Victim = CharPtr;
            CharPtr->Attacker = PCChar;
            PCChar->TargetX = CharPtr->XPos;
            PCChar->TargetY = CharPtr->YPos;
            PCChar->TargetZ = CharPtr->ZPos;

            // Determine if attack selected
            if(x >= 572 && x < 636 && y >= 328 && y < 360)
              m_CharController.SetAction(PCChar,CHAR_ATTACK);

            // Determine if spell selected
            if(x >= 572 && x < 636 && y >= 364 && y < 396)
              SelectSpell = TRUE;
```

After an action is selected (and if a target character has been chosen and the player's charge timer is fully charged), the attack information is set up. If the player clicked the Attack button, the attack action initiates. If the player clicked the Spell button, the spell window opens.

Regardless of what is clicked, the code continues to the next line that determines whether a target character has been selected via a call to GetCharacterAt:

```
        // See if a character picked
        TargetID = GetCharacterAt(x, y);
      }
    }

    // Clear spell state if right mouse button clicked
    if(m_Mouse.GetButtonState(MOUSE_RBUTTON) == TRUE) {
      // Lock the mouse button
      m_Mouse.SetLock(MOUSE_RBUTTON, TRUE);
      m_Mouse.SetButtonState(MOUSE_RBUTTON, FALSE);
      SelectSpell = FALSE;
    }

    // Update controllers
    m_CharController.Update(33);
    m_SpellController.Update(33);
```

If the player clicked the right mouse button, the spell selection window closes, and execution continues with the Frame function updating the characters and spell controllers (by calling each controller's Update function). At this point, all input processing is complete and rendering begins.

```
// Set the camera
m_Camera.Point(300.0f, 300.0f, -340.0f, 0.0f, 0.0f, 0.0f);
m_Graphics.SetCamera(&m_Camera);

// Render everything
m_Graphics.Clear(D3DCOLOR_RGBA(0,32,64,255));
if(m_Graphics.BeginScene() == TRUE) {
```

To begin, the camera is positioned, the scene cleared, and the scene rendering begins by drawing the arena, characters, and spells.

```
    // Render terrain
    m_Graphics.EnableZBuffer(TRUE);
    m_TerrainObject.Render();

    // Render all characters
    m_CharController.Render();

    // Render spells
    m_SpellController.Render();

    // Check if target needs rendering
    if(TargetID != -1) {
      // Move target to target character position
      CharPtr = m_CharController.GetCharacter(TargetID);
      Pos.EnableBillboard(TRUE);
      Pos.Move(CharPtr->XPos,CharPtr->YPos,CharPtr->ZPos);
      Pos.Rotate(0.0f, 0.0f, (float)timeGetTime() / 100.0f);

      // Offset to half of character height
      CharPtr->Object.GetBounds(NULL,&MinY,NULL,
                                NULL,&MaxY,NULL,NULL);
      YOff = MinY + ((MaxY-MinY)*0.5f);
      Pos.MoveRel(0.0f, YOff, 0.0f);

      // Render the target
      m_Graphics.SetTexture(0, NULL);
      m_Graphics.EnableZBuffer(FALSE);
      m_Graphics.SetWorldPosition(&Pos);
      m_Target.Render(0,2,D3DPT_TRIANGLELIST);
      m_Graphics.EnableZBuffer(TRUE);
    }
```

After the arena, characters, and spells have been rendered, it comes time to render the target vertex buffer (only if a target character is selected). You center the target in the middle of the character (based on the character's height) and draw the target (using a billboard world transformation matrix so that the target always faces the camera).

Next comes the player character's status window, which you update to display the player's current health and mana points:

```
// Display stats screen
sprintf(Text, "HP: %ld / %ld\r\nMP: %ld / %ld",               \
        PCChar->HealthPoints, PCChar->Def.HealthPoints,    \
        PCChar->ManaPoints, PCChar->Def.ManaPoints);
m_Stats.Render(Text);
```

Next, you display the charge timer. The charge timer ranges anywhere from 0 to 100, and using the buttons image previously loaded into the m_Buttons object, blit only a small portion of the image that represents the current level of charge:

```
// Display charge meter
m_Graphics.BeginSprite();
m_Buttons.Blit(508,450,0,64,128,16);
m_Buttons.Blit(510,452,0,80,(long)(1.24f*PCChar->Charge),12);
m_Graphics.EndSprite();
```

Now, you draw the action buttons (only if the charge timer is fully charged):

```
// Display attack options
if(m_CharController.GetCharacter(0)->Charge >= 100.0f) {
  m_Graphics.BeginSprite();
  m_Buttons.Blit(572,328,0,0,64,32);
  m_Buttons.Blit(572,364,0,32,64,32);
  m_Graphics.EndSprite();
}
```

To wrap up the render, draw the spell selection window if needed, and display each known spell for the player's selection:

```
// Display spell list
if(SelectSpell == TRUE) {
  m_Options.Render();

  // Display known spells
  for(i=0;i<64;i++) {
    SpellPtr = m_SpellController.GetSpell(i);
```

```
            if(PCChar->Def.MagicSpells[i/32] & (1<<(i&31)) &&       \
                SpellPtr->Name[0] &&                                 \
                PCChar->ManaPoints >= SpellPtr->Cost) {
                x = i % 4 * 150;
                y = i / 4 *  20;
                m_Font.Print(m_SpellController.GetSpell(i)->Name,    \
                             x+8, y+8);
            }
        }
    }

    m_Graphics.EndScene();
  }
  m_Graphics.Display();

  return TRUE;
}
```

## cApp::GetCharacterAt

One of the coolest functions is GetCharacterAt, which scans through the list of characters and determines which one is positioned at the specified display coordinates. Although doing this might be as easy as performing a bounding check on the character's display coordinates, go the extra mile and make the selection work on a polygon face level:

```
long cApp::GetCharacterAt(long XPos, long YPos)
{
D3DXVECTOR3 vecRay, vecDir;
  D3DXVECTOR3 vecMeshRay, vecMeshDir;
  D3DXVECTOR3 vecTemp;
  D3DXMATRIX  matProj, matView, *matWorld;
  D3DXMATRIX  matInv;
  DWORD       FaceIndex;
  BOOL        Hit;
  float       u, v, Dist;
  sCharacter  *CharPtr;
  sMesh       *MeshPtr;

  // Get parent character object
  if((CharPtr = m_CharController.GetParentCharacter()) == NULL)
    return -1;
```

You want to check every character to see which one was clicked, so GetCharacterAt starts by first determining whether any characters exist. At that point, you need to compute a ray to test for polygon intersections from the mouse cursor to each mesh.

```
// Get the project, view, and inversed view matrices
  m_Graphics.GetDeviceCOM()->GetTransform(D3DTS_PROJECTION,   \
                                     &matProj);
  m_Graphics.GetDeviceCOM()->GetTransform(D3DTS_VIEW,         \
                                     &matView);
  D3DXMatrixInverse(&matInv, NULL, &matView);

  // Compute the vector of the pick ray in screen space
  vecTemp.x =  (((2.0f * (float)XPos) /                       \
               (float)m_Graphics.GetWidth()) - 1.0f) /        \
               matProj._11;
  vecTemp.y = -(((2.0f * (float)YPos) /                       \
               (float)m_Graphics.GetHeight()) - 1.0f) /       \
               matProj._22;
  vecTemp.z =  1.0f;

  // Transform the screen space ray
  vecRay.x = matInv._41;
  vecRay.y = matInv._42;
  vecRay.z = matInv._43;
  vecDir.x = vecTemp.x * matInv._11 +                         \
               vecTemp.y * matInv._21 +                       \
               vecTemp.z * matInv._31;
  vecDir.y = vecTemp.x * matInv._12 +                         \
               vecTemp.y * matInv._22 +                       \
               vecTemp.z * matInv._32;
  vecDir.z = vecTemp.x * matInv._13 +                         \
               vecTemp.y * matInv._23 +                       \
               vecTemp.z * matInv._33;
```

Now that the ray is configured (in exactly the same way you configured them in Chapter 12, "Creating 3-D Graphics Engines"), you continue the execution by entering a loop that iterates through all characters. For each character, the GetCharacterAt function scans through each contained mesh to check for a ray-to-polygon intersection:

```
// Scan through each character and intersect check
  while(CharPtr != NULL) {
```

```
// Scan through character meshes
MeshPtr = CharPtr->Object.GetMesh()->GetParentMesh();
while(MeshPtr != NULL) {

  // Transform ray and direction by object's
  // world transformation matrix
  matWorld = CharPtr->Object.GetMatrix();
  D3DXMatrixInverse(&matInv, NULL, matWorld);
  D3DXVec3TransformCoord(&vecMeshRay, &vecRay, &matInv);
  D3DXVec3TransformNormal(&vecMeshDir, &vecDir, &matInv);

  // Check for intersection
  D3DXIntersect(MeshPtr->m_Mesh, &vecMeshRay,&vecMeshDir, \
                &Hit, &FaceIndex, &u, &v, &Dist);
```

Note that for each character in question, you have to offset the ray's coordinates by the character's orientation in the world (obtained from the character object's transformation matrix). You do so because the intersect function doesn't take the world transformation of each character into mind; you do that.

If a polygon is intersected, the function returns the identification number of the character. On the other hand, if no intersection is found, you check the next character mesh, followed by the next character in the list. If no characters are found, the function returns an error (signified by -1).

```
  // Check if ray hit character and return ID if so
  if(Hit == TRUE)
    return CharPtr->ID;

  // Go to next mesh
  MeshPtr = MeshPtr->m_Next;
}

// Go to next character
CharPtr = CharPtr->Next;
}

return -1;  // Return no hit
}
```

# Using Battle Arrangements

Although I intentionally hard-coded the functions that determine the characters to use in the combat sequence in the Battle demo, in a real game application, you base the selection of monsters on the map region in which the player is currently located.

For example, players in a haunted house will encounter ghosts and zombies. In the countryside, players might encounter large beasts native to the area. You need to determine each type of monster that players can encounter (and where).

The best way to determine which monsters to battle in each sequence is to use *battle arrangements,* pre-configured sets of monsters. In a haunted house, you could have one arrangement with two ghosts and another arrangement with three zombies. When combat starts, one arrangement is picked at random by the game.

How do you store the arrangements? With scripts, of course! In Chapter 16, you learn how to load a startup script. All you do is determine which script to load and then process it, allowing the script to add the arrangement of monsters to the sequence.

The great thing is that you can force a specific battle sequence to take place. For example, if it is time to fight a boss monster, you can specifically load that script. Within the script, you can load a song to play signifying that a major battle is occurring. There are no limits when using scripting!

The full-game demo, entitled *The Tower,* found in Chapter 20, "Putting Together a Full Game," demonstrates how to use battle arrangements in an actual game application. Be sure to check it out for more details on using scripting in your combat sequences (on the CD-ROM, look for \BookCode\Chap20\Game).

# Wrapping Up Combat Sequences

If you're like me, you believe that combat sequences make role-playing games fun. What better way to unload your daily stress than by slashing through hordes of evil doers? That feeling I get when my ultimate spell unleashes and wipes clear the battlefield is all I need to lift my spirits.

When dealing with combat in your game, just remember to keep it simple enough to hold the interest of the gamers. Nobody wants to become bogged down with useless features or details; just get to the fun stuff and let 'em rip.

Although the combat-sequence project developed in this chapter is a relatively simple one, it provides you with a good foundation on which you can expand—and then show everyone what you can do. Try adding the ability to change inventory mid-combat or the ability for your character to run away. Change the arena mesh depending on the player's location in the world. Also, track which items and money the monsters drop when killed, and add those to the player's inventory when combat is over.

With a little work, you can change the battle project into a full-fledged combat sequence engine!

## Programs on the CD-ROM

The \BookCode\Chap18\ directory contains the following program, which demonstrates external combat sequences:

- **Battle.** A 3-D combat engine demo. Click the target creatures; then wait for the battle options to appear and select how to attack. Location: \BookCode\Chap18\Battle\.

# CHAPTER 19

# GETTING ONLINE WITH MULTIPLAYER GAMING

Although beating down the endless hordes of evil and saving countless worlds is interesting enough to rob you of precious sleep, it can get pretty boring after a while. No matter how hard we try, game developers just can't nail down the intrigue and challenge of human intelligence that gamers want in virtual opponents.

Enter the world of Internet gaming—where real-life opponents with real thoughts and reactions await your participation in a realm of gaming action that is reshaping the way people play games. No longer do you just sit there beating on mindless minions. Now you are faced with hundreds of cunning gamers waiting to either come to your aid or stand in your way.

Your game needs to give players the ability to hook up to the Internet and find other gamers willing to join forces and duke it out in true multiplayer style. This chapter is your guide to accomplishing that feat.

In this chapter, you learn about the following:

- The basics of multiplayer gaming
- How to design a multiplayer game architecture
- The network game sample design
- How to work with game servers and client applications

# Maddening Multiplayer Mayhem

With a puff of smoke and glitter of light, my hero materializes behind a small building located within a small town. Circling around the corner, a large chapel comes into view. The stench of death fills the air, obviously emanating from the cursed chapel that lies ahead. My hero's goal is clear—to delve into the now-evil temple and remove the curse deep within its bowels.

To his left stand two other ominous figures, both scarred from countless battles. As he approaches the grizzly duo, he realizes that they are none other than two comrades-in-arms, all ready to join him in his adventure into the depths. After a quick jaunt to the local item shop for some healing potions, they delve into the chapel.

Hordes of evil creatures of every size immediately sense the adventurers' presence. The creatures take it upon themselves to rid their world of the newcomers. But the worthy adventurers have other plans, and through strength and cunning, they defeat every last monster that stands in their way. Their goal is close at hand, and they feel good to have made it this far.

As you can see in the preceding scenario, my gaming buddies and I had an almost perfect adventure (thanks to *Diablo* by Blizzard Entertainment). I say almost because even though our group was victorious in its fights against the computerized demons, we weren't a match against a new arrival—a mysterious fellow who just joined the game. Within moments of being magically transported to our current location, the new arrival proceeded to make mincemeat of us.

Lying on the ground, I (the hero) watch the would-be robber sift through my belongings, taking the glorious treasures I worked so hard to discover. How could anyone be so vicious, so deceiving—and so powerful? Apparently, this chap has been around a lot longer than I have; his power is staggering, and I vow to reach that level of power so that I, too, can venture forth and illustrate just who is the boss!

Leaving the current adventure, I once again connect to Blizzard Entertainment's *Diablo* lobby-server and initiate a new game. This time, however, I'm going solo. With every kill, I grow stronger; with every treasure I find, I buy better weapons. Soon I will be ready to hunt down the savage who earlier decimated my fellow adventurers and me.

These adventures are among the many that I have been privileged to experience. Those of you who have "wasted" (that is to say, *invested*) precious hours playing *Diablo* can attest to how much fun the game can be. *Diablo's* online gaming features make the game worth playing, and you'll want to duplicate those features in your projects. So, with this teaser under your belt, you're ready to start doing just that.

# Multiplayer Game Design

Online gaming has given players a whole new way to match up with other human players, and as the narrative in the preceding section illustrates, these encounters can be fun or a wake-up call to the deftness of other players.

When dealing with multiplayer games, a little extra design effort must go into the mix. With single-player gaming, the player takes control of the game's hero and so takes it upon himself to save the world. Multiplayer gaming can have thousands of other players, each wanting to be the one true hero, which is obviously impossible.

When you move from single-player to multiplayer gaming, the goals begin to change. Consider a game like Origin's *Ultima Online*, for example. If you've played the game, you realize it has no real goal. There are no supreme bosses to defeat, no lead-you-by-the-hand story, and no sense that a single person can change the world.

So why would anybody want to play *Ultima Online?* For one thing—it's fun. No longer can you expect to be the most powerful being in the universe, because you are now joined by thousands of other gamers with the same thoughts of glory. *Ultima Online* gives people the ability to join forces to combat endless hordes of evil, to conquer small quests, or even to lay in ambush against each other.

With the human intellect and the power of the *Ultima Online* gaming engine, gamers can accomplish whatever they can imagine, making the experience truer to real life. Although *Ultima Online* does not provide a storyline (nor the ability to beat the game), it still remains an online gaming juggernaut.

On the other hand, take a look at a game such as Sega's *Phantasy Star Online*, which forces players to join forces against the ultimate evil of a supreme being. *Phantasy Star Online* also has the benefit of a storyline (although it's rather vague and seems almost thrown in). The other great thing about *Phantasy Star Online* is that you can beat it. That's right, with each new game session, the story begins anew, waiting for your characters to slash through thousands of monsters on their way to killing the supreme bad guy.

The differences between *Ultima Online* and *Phantasy Star Online* are significant, yet they both draw gamers by the thousands. What is it that players enjoy the most, and what features do they demand of their online games? Those are tough questions, but look at what each game has to offer and consider which features you want to incorporate into you own game project:

- **Character building.** Why waste time playing a game if your accomplishments can't be reflected? The reason you go out into the world slaying hordes of beasts is that your character is going to get "bigger and badder" and will go on to even more achievements.

- **An evolving world.** A world that never changes is bland; once explored, it stays the same no matter what. Popular games allow changes in the world, with new levels to explore or new quests to undergo.

- **Cooperative and opposing players.** Humans need to interact with other humans; it's a part of life. With the Internet at your disposal, joining players for multiplayer action is just what you need, even if those players are at war with one another.

- **New, secret, and cool items to discover.** What good is consistently exploring the world unless you can pick up a couple of things along the way—stronger weapons, wicked armor, and maybe a super-secret magical item that will really turn the tide in combat.
- **An actual storyline.** Whether the storyline runs throughout the entire play of the game or only in quests within the game, a good storyline gives games that extra little pizzazz.
- **Ability to win.** Games like *Phantasy Star Online* and *Diablo* give players the ability to actually beat the game. Of course, a typical game can run for hours, but it is still possible to defeat the last big boss and save the world.

Just remember that whatever features you have in your game, you want to make the game fun and worth playing again and again. Take a look at games currently on the market to see what they have going for them and try to make your project as entertaining.

To help you create your multiplayer games, I wrote a demonstration game, appropriately named Network Game. In the upcoming section, you find out how I designed the game, and throughout the rest of this chapter, you find the specifics on programming the game.

# The Network Demo

The *Network Game* demonstration program included on this book's CD-ROM (look in the \BookCode\Chap19 directory) is basic in design. The game has a single large level that players are allowed to join and in which they can begin moving and attacking each other as they like (although no damage is done and nobody can die).

The game level is a large mesh (as illustrated in Figure 19.1) and utilizes the NodeTree class object for rendering (see Chapter 12, "Creating 3-D Graphics Engines," for more on using the NodeTree class).

A single mesh defines the players (and a mesh defines their weapons). Take a look at Figure 19.2, which shows the character and weapon meshes in use.

As far as the demonstration game's mechanics go, players are allowed to join the game in play and begin moving throughout the level. Locally, players use

> **NOTE**
>
> In Figure 19.2, the impressive character mesh is a slightly modified version of Scarecrow's great Spawn model. *Thanks to Scarecrow for allowing me to use the models!*

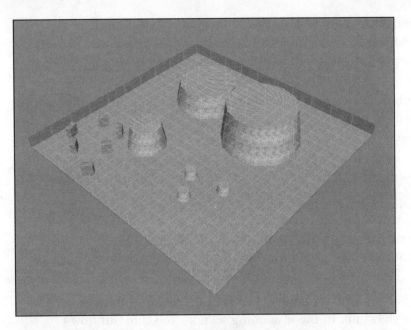

**Figure 19.1**

*The network demo level. A few obstacles provide cover for players to hide from each other.*

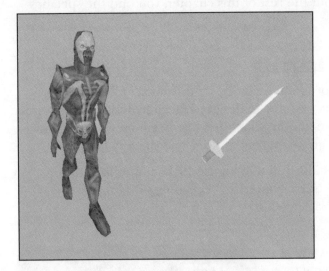

**Figure 19.2**

*The game characters are represented by a fully animated 3-D character (on the left) who bears the weapon on the right.*

meshes to render a 3-D view of the game world. Each player's view is oriented slightly above and away from his character, as you can see in Figure 19.3.

To move their character, players use the arrow keys; pressing in a specific direction moves the character relative to the camera. Moving the mouse left and right changes the camera-viewing angle to give players a full 360-degree view. Players are

**Figure 19.3**

*The demo game shows off some snazzy 3-D terrain and animated virtual players.*

allowed to attack each other by pressing the spacebar, which, in turn, makes their characters swing their swords in hopes of knocking another character off of his feet.

Although the demo game is very basic, it does give you the foundation you need to begin creating your own game. Remember though that all roads will eventually lead down one road—getting your multiplayer game ready, and to do that, you must first create an underlying game architecture.

# Creating a Multiplayer Game Architecture

When creating your game, if you were to stop mid-stream and try to add multiplayer features (features you hadn't planned on including) chances are you would have a hard time making everything work out correctly. Let's face it—you need to be prepared ahead of time, and if your game is going to be multiplayer-compatible, you must make sure that you have a solid foundation on which to work.

You start by understanding what you're up against when using networks and what you can do to ensure that everything works correctly. It will be helpful to look at how to use a client/server network architecture. Chapter 9, "Networking with DirectPlay," covers the basics on working with client and server network communications, but now is the time to see how the server and clients can work together effectively from a gaming perspective.

> **NOTE**
> A client application is the program the player interacts with during a networked gaming session. A server is the network application that serves as the central processing hub of the gaming world. Client applications connect to servers and begin communicating player actions back and forth. However, ultimately, the server handles the majority of the game-processing functionality.

## Working Together: The Client and the Server

The client and the server communicate back and forth continuously. As players (the clients) perform actions in the game, those actions are sent as messages to the server for verification. The server, in order to maintain synchronization, takes the players' actions, updates the game world, and then sends game updates to the clients. In this way, the server maintains the entire gaming world, whereas the clients are merely systems for collecting the players' actions (and displaying their eventual outcomes on the clients' screens).

The types of messages sent between the server and clients are numerous, but with some well thought-out design, those messages are easily manageable. The messages can be the following:

- **Connection requests.** Joining in a game means connecting to a server. Not just anyone can join, however; the server might be operating at its limit or the player might not have a valid account. Once a client is connected, the real action(s) begin!

- **Navigation.** Players can move around maps, usually by pressing an arrow on the keyboard or clicking their destination on the map. Clients send in movement requests and leave it up to the server to return game update messages.

- **Combat.** With swords swinging and spells erupting, it seems too much to deal with. If you were to strip away the fluff, however, you would discover that combat is nothing more than an attacker with his form of attack and a defender with his form of defense. Clients are the only ones to request combat; it's the job of the server to take combat requests and work them into the game updates.

- **Resource management.** With a world full of goods, players want to be able to buy, sell, find, and use just about any resource that they can get their hands on. I'm beginning to repeat myself, because resource management comes from the client, and requests are sent to the server to use for updates.

- **Conversation.** What fun is a multiplayer game without the social interaction? Characters talk to each other in order to learn vital information or just to shoot the breeze. Either way, this is a simple matter of displaying a few lines of text. This conversation works both ways, from clients sending in text to the server returning text to display.

- **Game updates.** As mentioned, the server needs to let all clients know the state of the game periodically, and the game update messages are just the ticket. Game updates usually include the positions of all characters in the game, plus information about items and other game resources.

A couple of things quickly come to mind when using the type of network communications just mentioned. First, because the server is the only system responsible for maintaining the game state, all connected clients would have to wait for those periodic updates to keep the game flowing.

Unfortunately, network transmission speeds don't allow instantaneous transmissions, so some of the data passing from client to server and back again are delayed. This delay in transmission is called *latency*, and it's this latency that can cause havoc in your game.

> **NOTE**
>
> Latency is measured in milliseconds (ms).

Because the server is the only system allowed to make changes to the game world, the server must validate players' actions before they can occur. As you can see from Figure 19.4, players trying to issue actions will experience a delay from the time the actions are initiated to the time they take place. This delay of action, called *lag*, can cause the game-play to be choppy (and thus unplayable).

To keep things running smoothly and help alleviate the effects of latency and lag, clients are allowed to make small changes to the world between server updates. Those small changes are typically only to update the movement of characters. In that way, clients don't have to wait for server updates in order to move characters; clients can just guess how to update all characters based on their last known state (as you can see in Figure 19.5). This form of guessing is called *dead reckoning*, and it is used in network gaming.

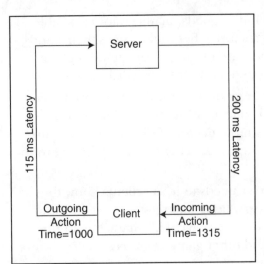

**Figure 19.4**

*A client sending out a message and waiting for a response from the server experiences a delay in transmission (lag).*

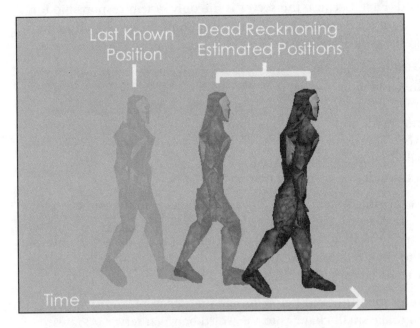

**Figure 19.5**

*With dead reckoning, a character that is walking continues to walk until the server tells that character to stop.*

When more serious actions, such as combat actions, come into play, using dead reckoning is unacceptable. The server is the authority, and if a system needs to determine who hits whom and how much damage is done, that system needs to query the server for resolution.

As mentioned, when using a networking system, the second problem is game timing. Let's face it—trying to synchronize possibly dozens of clients is almost impossible. Each computer hooked on the network has a different latency; some clients take longer sending messages to the server and receiving them back from the server.

> **CAUTION**
>
> If you leave any of the major decisions (such as combat) up to a client, you're inviting trouble, because game hackers and cheaters will take full advantage of any loopholes. Remember that the server is the only system responsible for keeping track of the game; the clients are merely portals into the game world.

On the client side, one player might make a move at the exact time as another player, but because their actions take a moment to reach the server, the client with the faster connection will have the advantage (as illustrated in Figure 19.6).

All messages received by the client and server are recorded with the time of their receipt. The server uses that time to determine how to update the players. For example, if a message received by the server isn't processed within 100 milliseconds (ms), the server compensates for that amount of time during updates. The same goes for clients. If an action message needs to be updated (especially during the use of dead reckoning), that time (the time the messages are received) is used to move characters appropriately.

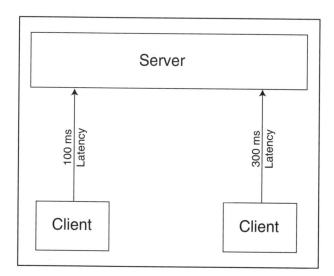

**Figure 19.6**

*The client on the left has a lower latency than the player on the right, so the left player's action will reach the server first and will be processed first.*

Now that you have an overview of how the clients and server work together, take a closer look at each one.

## Looking at the Server

**TIP**

To help improve synchronization, the client and server both calculate latency into the time that a message is received. You see how to calculate the latency in the section "Calculating Latency," later in this chapter.

The game server is a specialized piece of software. It doesn't need fancy graphics, kicking tunes, or even dedicated input functions. The server merely needs to process the actions received from connected players and, every so often, send updates to the clients.

Once the server begins executing, it enters into a tight loop, continuously processing incoming network messages, updating all connected players based on their last known movement actions, and sending updates.

Few network messages are received from the server—connection requests, disconnect notifications, and player actions. Those player actions are solely up to the game design, and with the demo game for this chapter, those actions include only players walking, standing still, or attacking with a weapon.

**NOTE**

To keep things processing quickly, the server updates players only every 33ms, whereas client updates are sent approximately every 100ms. Incoming messages (contained in the message queue) are processed every frame, however.

As network messages are received from clients, the messages are stuffed into a *message queue.* Using a message queue speeds up network operations and leaves the majority of the work up to the main application (rather than the network code thread). The server maintains a message queue (a stack of messages) that holds all incoming messages. As a message comes in, it is added to the queue. The server continuously pulls out the oldest message and sends it off to various functions for processing. This process of message handling is illustrated in Figure 19.7.

The server deals with player connection requests by first checking whether there are any open slots for players. If so, the player data is requested from the client and saved in a local structure. All players in the game are notified that another player has joined the fray, and play goes on. A slot is freed up whenever a player disconnects.

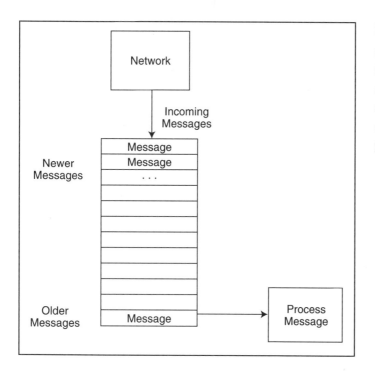

**Figure 19.7**

*Network messages are inserted into the queue in the order those messages are received. The message queue ensures that the oldest messages are next to be processed by the server.*

Player actions are quickly dealt with; all player actions simply change the state of the player. At this point, the only states used are those for walking, standing still, attacking, and being hurt. At every frame, those states are used to update the player. As player actions are received, the server sends them out to all other connected players so that the players can update their game states (between server updates, of course).

Aside from dealing with network messages, the server updates the state of the players. If a player character's last known state was walking in a certain direction, that player's character continues to walk in that direction. The server, in all its authority, will perform collision detection to make sure those moving characters can't walk through walls!

**NOTE**

By allowing only the server to update the game world, you eliminate cheaters (players who try to alter the game-play to their advantage). Cheaters typically work by sending bogus data to the server in the hope that they can move their player in impossible ways.

For every action and state you add to your game, you add the logic to the server to process the characters. For example, the attack state requires the server to refuse further state changes from a player until the attack state has cleared (after one second). At the same time the attack is initiated by a client, the server will calculate which other clients were hit and the level of damage.

Implementing the server is easy. After you create a sound base from which to work, you can easily begin adding more features to the server. Besides adding new actions that players can perform, you can also add features such as player account management. However, now it's time to take a quick peek at the client side of things.

> **NOTE**
>
> I left out the damage portion of the server demo for this chapter, but you can still harm other players. I'll leave adding the damage up to you.

## Looking at Clients

Once connected, clients just need to collect local player control information and send it up to the server. Between the updates received from the server, the clients guess (using dead reckoning) how to handle all the game characters based on their last known state.

For example, all characters that were walking at the last update keep walking until the server signals them to stop. In this way, the game-play appears smooth, and with a good network connection, server updates are received fast enough for the game to stay entirely in sync.

As illustrated in Figure 19.8, whenever a client makes a change in action (such as walking in a different direction than in the last known state), that change in state is immediately relayed to the server, which immediately sends that action to all connected clients. In that way, synchronization is much better.

Speaking of changes in player actions, exactly what actions can a player perform? Navigation for one. As players walk around the map, their direction of travel is sent up to the server. Notice that only the direction of travel is sent.

If you allow clients to specify their coordinates when they move, you're inviting cheaters to mess with the values. Instead, the server will modify the coordinates of the player and send those coordinates back to the clients (at which time, it doesn't matter whether cheaters modify the values, because the server can't be affected).

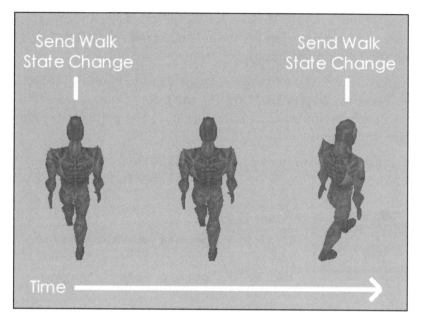

**Figure 19.8**

*The client sends state changes to the server only when the player makes a move that's different from the last move, which saves time because the same move does not have to be resent again and again.*

For specific actions, such as walking, clients are allowed to change their own states. As a result, players can move between server updates. For actions such as attacking, only the state change is sent to the server, which in turn processes the attack and sends out the appropriate state changes to all clients.

Players can be updated only every 33ms. The updates are time-limited in order to make sure the clients don't flood the server with thousands of actions. By keeping actions to a minimum, the server can process things more quickly, and the game-play stays smooth.

Whenever the server does send those crucial updates to the client, the client will immediately change the state of the characters (or characters) in question (no need for a message queue here). This update can also include the local player, so as you're moving around, some jumps in the action can occur due to the client synchronizing to the server.

Well, enough of the explanations; let's get on to making an actual network game!

# Working with Game Servers

You've already read about how simple the server can be. To put theory into practice (and help you create your multiplayer games), I put together a server application, which you can find on this book's CD-ROM (look for \BookCode\Chap19\Server). In this section, you discover how to develop the underlying server-network-game architecture and create the server application.

The game server is basic in nature. You can use the Game Core to handle graphics, networking, and input. Because Chapter 10, "Creating the Game Core," covers how to use the Game Core, I'll skip the formalities and get right to the point. To use the server application, follow these steps:

1. Locate the Server application on this book's CD-ROM. When you open the application, the Configure Server dialog box appears (see Figure 19.9).

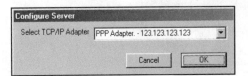

**Figure 19.9**

*The Configure Server dialog box, which appears first when you run the server application, enables you to select the TCP/IP adapter to use for hosting a game.*

2. In the Configure Server dialog box, select the TCP/IP Adapter that you'll be using to host the game.

3. Click OK to start the game.

   The Network Server Demo window opens (see Figure 19.10). This window displays the server's IP address, number of players, and a list of the players connected to the server (if any).

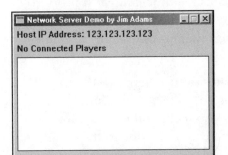

**Figure 19.10**

*The Network Server Demo window displays the host's IP address, the number of connected players, and each player's name.*

Players can now connect to the server and play the game. Only eight players can join the game at any given time, but you can increase that number in the source code.

4. To close the server (and disconnect all players), press Alt+F4.

Once you've had a chance to play with the server, go ahead and load up the source code.

The real work is done behind the scenes where messages are processed, characters are moved around, and the entire game world is maintained. The application uses a derived cApplication class, named cApp; you see portions of the server's application class throughout this section.

Skipping the standard application setup functions (such as initializing the graphics and input systems), let's go through the server's functionality step-by-step, starting with handling players.

# Storing Player Information

Players in the game are only allowed to move around and swing their weapons (hitting other players). The server will want to track every player's current state (walking, standing still, swinging their weapons, or being hurt), the coordinates in the world, the direction they are facing, and the speed they are walking (if they are walking).

This player data is stored inside a structure called sPlayer. Because all connected players in the game need their own set of unique data, an array of sPlayer structures are allocated to store the information. Both the number of player structures to allocate and the number of players to allow to join the game session are stored in the macro MAX_PLAYERS, which is currently set to 8.

The sPlayer structure is as follows (with supporting state definition macros):

```
// Player states
#define STATE_IDLE          1
#define STATE_MOVE          2
#define STATE_SWING         3
#define STATE_HURT          4

typedef struct sPlayer {
  BOOL  Connected;         // TRUE if player connected

  char  Name[256];         // Name of player
  DPNID dpnidPlayer;       // DirectPlay Player ID #

  long  State;             // Last known state (STATE_*)
  long  Time;              // Time of last state update
  long  Latency;           // Half of roundtrip latency in ms

  float XPos, YPos, ZPos; // Player coordinates
```

```
    float Direction;        // Angle facing
    float Speed;            // Movement speed

    // Constructor
    sPlayer() { Connected = FALSE; Latency = 0; }
} sPlayer;
```

There's not much to the sPlayer structure; you have a flag if the player is connected, the name of the player, the player's DirectPlay identification number, the
player's current state (as defined by the state macros), time of last state change,
network latency value, the player's coordinates, direction, and walking speed.

The variables in sPlayer are self-explanatory, except for Latency. Remember that
latency is the delay resulting from network transmission. By storing the time it takes
for a message to go from the server to the client (and vice versa), time-based calculations become more synchronized between the server and client.

Speaking of time-based calculations, that's the purpose of the Time variable. Whenever
the server updates all players, it needs to know the time that has elapsed between
updates. Every time a player state is changed (from the client), the Time variable is set
to the current time (minus the latency time).

Time is also used to control actions. If a player swings a weapon, the server refuses
to accept further state changes from the client until the swing weapon state is
cleared. How does the state clear? After a set amount of time, that's how! After one
second passes, the update player cycle clears the player's state back to idle, allowing
the client to begin sending new state-change messages.

On the subject of sending messages, take a look at how the server deals with the
incoming network messages.

# Handling Messages

You've already seen DirectPlay messages in action, but now you focus on the game
action messages (state changes). Because DirectPlay has only three functions of
interest when handling incoming network messages (CreatePlayer, DestroyPlayer, and
Receive), the server will need to convert the incoming networking message to messages more suited to game-play.

The server receives messages from clients via the DirectPlay network's Receive function. Those messages are stored in the pReceiveData buffer contained within the
DPNMSG_RECEIVE structure passed to the Receive function. That buffer is cast into a
more usable game message, which is stuffed into the game message queue.

The server game code doesn't deal directly with network messages. Those are handled by a small subset of functions that take the incoming messages and convert them into game messages (which are entered into the message queue). The server game code works with those game messages.

Because there can be many different types of game messages, a generic message container structure is needed. Each message starts with a header that stores the type of message, the total size of the message data (in bytes) including the header, and a DirectPlay player identification number that is usually set to the player sending the message.

I've taken the liberty of separating the header into another structure, making it possible to reuse the header in every game message:

> **NOTE**
>
> `IDirectPlay8Server::Receive` is not the only function that can store messages in the server message queue, however; so can `CreatePlayer` and `DestroyPlayer`. In the upcoming section, "DirectPlay Messages to Game Message," you see how those two functions are used to inform the server that players are joining and leaving the game session.

```
// The message header structure used in all messages
typedef struct {
  long   Type;               // Type of message (MSG_*)
  long   Size;               // Size of data to send
  DPNID PlayerID;            // Player performing action
} sMessageHeader;
```

Because there can be many different game messages, you first need a generic message container capable of holding all the different game messages. This generic message container is a structure as follows:

```
// The message queue message structure
typedef struct {
  sMessageHeader Header;   // Message header

  char Data[512];            // Message data
} sMessage;
```

Pretty basic, isn't it? The `sMessage` structure needs to contain only the message header and an array of `char`s used to store the specific message data. To use a specific message, you can cast the `sMessage` structure into another structure to access the data.

For example, here is a structure that represents a state-change message:

```
// Change in state message
typedef struct {
  sMessageHeader Header;   // Message header

  long  State;             // State message (STATE_*)
  float XPos, YPos, ZPos;  // Player coordinates
  float Direction;         // Player facing direction
  float Speed;             // Walking speed of player

  long  Latency;           // Latency value of connection
} sStateChangeMessage;
```

To cast the sMessage structure that contains a state-change message into a usable sStateChangeMessage structure, you can use this code bit:

```
sMessage Msg;  // Assuming message contains data
sStateChangeMessage *scm = (sStateChangeMessage*)Msg;

// Access state-change message data
scm->State = STATE_IDLE;
scm->Direction = 1.57f;
```

In addition to the state-change message, the following message structures are used in the network game:

```
// Request a player DPNID from server message
typedef struct {
  sMessageHeader Header;   // Message header
} sAssignPlayerIDMessage;

// Create a player message
typedef struct {
  sMessageHeader Header;   // Message header

  float XPos, YPos, ZPos;  // Create player coordinates
  float Direction;         // Direction of player
} sCreatePlayerMessage;

// Request player information message
typedef struct {
  sMessageHeader Header;   // Message header

  DPNID PlayerID;          // Which player to request
```

```
} sRequestPlayerInfoMessage;

// Destroy a player message
typedef struct {
  sMessageHeader Header;  // Message header
} sDestroyPlayerMessage;
```

Each message also has a related macro that both the server and client use. Those message macros are the values store in the `sMessageHeader::Type` variable. Those message type macros are as follows:

```
// Types of messages
#define MSG_CREATE_PLAYER   1
#define MSG_PLAYER_INFO     2
#define MSG_DESTROY_PLAYER  3
#define MSG_STATE_CHANGE    4
#define MSG_ASSIGNID        256
```

You see each message in action in the sections "Processing Game Messages" and "Working with Game Clients," later in this chapter, but for now, check out how the server maintains these game-related messages.

## DirectPlay Messages to Game Messages

As I've mentioned before, the server needs to convert the DirectPlay network messages into the game-related messages you've just read about. You accomplish this by processing incoming player *connection, disconnection,* and *receive* data messages from DirectPlay and converting those messages into game messages.

To accomplish this conversion of messages, you derive a class from `cNetworkServer` and override the `CreatePlayer`, `DestroyPlayer`, and `Receive` functions:

```
class cServer : public cNetworkServer
{
  private:
    BOOL CreatePlayer(DPNMSG_CREATE_PLAYER *Msg);
    BOOL DestroyPlayer(DPNMSG_DESTROY_PLAYER *Msg);
    BOOL Receive (DPNMSG_RECEIVE *Msg);
};
```

Because I'm using the System Core to handle application processing, a problem quickly arises when dealing with the network. The network component and application component are two separate entities, which means that neither component is allowed to modify the other's private data.

As Figure 19.11 illustrates, the network component needs a way to siphon incoming messages into the application, which by chance is handled by creating three public functions that match the network class's functions.

To use the three message functions in the application component, you construct a derived cApplication class that contains the three public functions as follows:

```
class cApp : public cApplication
{
  // Previous cApp data and functions
  private:
    cServer m_Server; // Include derived server network class

  public:
    // Functions to siphon network messages to application
    BOOL CreatePlayer(DPNMSG_CREATE_PLAYER *Msg);
    BOOL DestroyPlayer(DPNMSG_DESTROY_PLAYER *Msg);
    BOOL Receive(DPNMSG_RECEIVE *Msg);
};
```

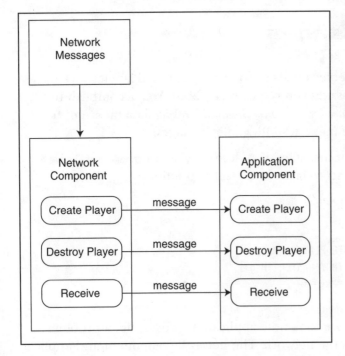

**Figure 19.11**

*The network component sends incoming messages from the overridden* CreatePlayer, DestroyPlayer, *and* Receive *functions to the matching public functions in the application component.*

To start sending DirectPlay messages to the application class, you code the overridden cServer functions to call upon the matching application functions. In order for the server to know which application class instance to send messages to, you need to declare a global variable that points to the current application class instance in use:

```
cApp *g_Application = NULL;
```

Inside the derived application class's constructor, you then point the global g_Application variable to the application class instance:

```
cApp::cApp()
{
  // Other constructor code

  g_Application = this;  // Set application instance pointer
}
```

Now, you can code the network server component to send incoming messages to the application object defined by the global g_Application pointer:

```
BOOL cServer::CreatePlayer(DPNMSG_CREATE_PLAYER *Msg)
{
  // Send message to application class instance (if any)
  if(g_Application != NULL)
    g_Application->CreatePlayer(Msg);

  return TRUE;
}


BOOL cServer::DestroyPlayer(DPNMSG_DESTROY_PLAYER *Msg)
{
  // Send message to application class instance (if any)
  if(g_Application != NULL)
    g_Application->DestroyPlayer(Msg);
  return TRUE;
}


BOOL cServer::Receive(DPNMSG_RECEIVE *Msg)
{
  // Send message to application class instance (if any)
  if(g_Application != NULL)
    g_Application->Receive(Msg);
  return TRUE;
}
```

The server component is now complete and is forwarding network messages to the application class. To convert those network messages to game-related messages, the application class must contain the following public functions:

```
BOOL cApp::CreatePlayer(DPNMSG_CREATE_PLAYER *Msg)
{
  sCreatePlayerMessage cpm;

  // Set up message data
  cpm.Header.Type     = MSG_CREATE_PLAYER;
  cpm.Header.Size     = sizeof(sCreatePlayerMessage);
  cpm.Header.PlayerID = Msg->dpnidPlayer;

  QueueMessage(&cpm); // Queue the message

  return TRUE;
}

BOOL cApp::DestroyPlayer(DPNMSG_DESTROY_PLAYER *Msg)
{
  sDestroyPlayerMessage dpm;

  // Setup message data
  dpm.Header.Type     = MSG_DESTROY_PLAYER;
  dpm.Header.Size     = sizeof(sDestroyPlayerMessage);
  dpm.Header.PlayerID = Msg->dpnidPlayer;

  QueueMessage(&dpm); // Queue the message

  return TRUE;
}

BOOL cApp::Receive(DPNMSG_RECEIVE *Msg)
{
  sMessageHeader *mh = (sMessageHeader*)Msg->pReceiveData;

  // Make sure it's a valid message type and queue it
  switch(mh->Type) {
    case MSG_ASSIGNID:
      // Store player ID before continuing
      mh->PlayerID = Msg->dpnidSender;
```

```
        case MSG_PLAYER_INFO:
        case MSG_STATE_CHANGE:
          // Add message to queue
          QueueMessage((void*)Msg->pReceiveData);
          break;
    }

    return TRUE;
}
```

You can see that in each of the three functions, I'm constructing a game-related message using the data from the DirectPlay messages provided. When a player tries to connect to the server, a *create-player* message is created that stores the connecting player's DirectPlayer identification number (along with the message type and size). That create-player message is then queued.

As for players disconnecting from the game, a *disconnect-player* message is constructed and queued. Last, whenever data (other than a system message) is received from a client, the cApp::Receive function checks it to see whether it's a valid message type, and if so, the message is queued.

If the player has sent an MSG_ASSIGNID message (you see one such message later in the section "Handling Player Data"), the requesting player's DirectPlayer identification number is stored before the cApp::Receive function queues the message (for reasons you'll soon see).

I keep mentioning the message queue and how the previously shown function adds messages to the queue. Next, you find out what the queue is and how it works.

## The Message Queue

The server never deals directly with incoming messages; instead, the server pulls messages from the queue. If a message needs to be processed, it must be inserted into the queue. Using a queue ensures that the server never gets bogged down with processing incoming network data.

The queue is just an array of sMessage structures that is allocated when the application class is initialized. I set a limit of 1,024 messages to be allocated for the server, but you can change that amount just by altering the NUM_MESSAGE macro in the source code.

To track messages being added and removed from the queue, use two variables—m_MsgHead and m_MsgTail. Check out Figure 19.12 to see how the queue uses those two variables to track which messages are to be inserted or removed.

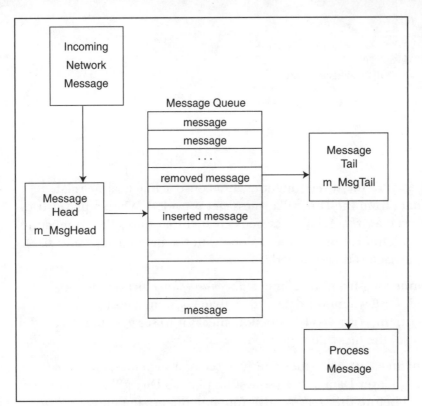

**Figure 19.12**

*The* m_MsgHead *variable marks the next position in the message queue to insert a message.* m_MsgTail *is the position where messages are pulled out.*

Whenever a message needs to be added to the message queue, a special function is called. That function is cApp::QueueMessage, and it takes a single argument: the sMessage structure to add to the queue.

Remember the incoming message functions of cApp (covered in the section "DirectPlay Messages to Game Messages")? Those functions built a message structure and added the message to the queue via QueueMessage. Look at the QueueMessage code to see what's going on:

```
BOOL cApp::QueueMessage(void *Msg)
{
  sMessageHeader *mh = (sMessageHeader*)Msg;

  // Error checking - make sure there's a message array
  if(m_Messages == NULL)
    return FALSE;
```

```
// Return if no room left in queue
if(((m_MsgHead+1) % NUM_MESSAGES) == m_MsgTail)
  return FALSE;

// Stuff message into queue
if(mh->Size <= sizeof(sMessage)) {
  // Start the critical section
  EnterCriticalSection(&m_MessageCS);

  memcpy(&m_Messages[m_MsgHead], Msg, mh->Size);

  // Go to next empty message (flip around if at end)
  m_MsgHead++;
  if(m_MsgHead >= NUM_MESSAGES)
    m_MsgHead = 0;

  // Leave the critical section
  LeaveCriticalSection(&m_MessageCS);
}

return TRUE;
}
```

As you can see, QueueMessage merely copies the supplied sMessage structure into the
next available element in the message array (pointed to by m_MsgHead). Two things
you haven't seen are the EnterCriticalSection and LeaveCriticalSection functions.
Windows uses these two functions to restrict the application's access to memory
(using the EnterCriticalSection function), only allowing a single process to modify
that memory. Once you finish modifying the memory, you need to inform Windows
by calling LeaveCriticalSection.

Although this may not make sense at first, think about it like this—the network
component (a process) is running in the background at the same time as the application (another process). If the network component is adding messages to the
array while the application is trying to remove messages or modify the messages,
the program data can become corrupt. Critical sections ensure that only one
process gets sole access to data for a short time.

## Processing Game Messages

Now that the game messages have made their way into the message queue, the next
step is to remove the messages at each frame and process them. To keep things

running quickly, only 64 messages at a time are processed (as defined by the MESSAGE_PER_FRAME macro in the server source code).

Message processing takes place within the cApp::ProcessQueuedMessages function:

```
void cApp::ProcessQueuedMessages()
{
  sMessage *Msg;
  long Count = 0;

  // Pull out messages to process
  while(Count != MESSAGES_PER_FRAME && m_MsgHead != m_MsgTail) {

    // Get pointer to 'tail' message
    EnterCriticalSection(&m_MessageCS);
    Msg = &m_Messages[m_MsgTail];
    LeaveCriticalSection(&m_MessageCS);

    // Process a single message based on type
    switch(Msg->Header.Type) {
      case MSG_ASSIGNID: // Send users their player ID
        PlayerID(Msg, Msg->Header.PlayerID);
        break;

      case MSG_PLAYER_INFO:    // Request player info
        PlayerInfo(Msg, Msg->Header.PlayerID);
        break;

      case MSG_CREATE_PLAYER:  // Add a player
        AddPlayer(Msg);
        break;

      case MSG_DESTROY_PLAYER: // Remove a player
        RemovePlayer(Msg);
        break;

      case MSG_STATE_CHANGE:   // Change state of player
        PlayerStateChange(Msg);
        break;
    }
```

```
    Count++; // Increase processed message count

    // Go to next message in list
    EnterCriticalSection(&m_MessageCS);
    m_MsgTail = (m_MsgTail + 1) % NUM_MESSAGES;
    LeaveCriticalSection(&m_MessageCS);
  }
}
```

As ProcessQueuedMessages iterates through the next 64 messages, it calls upon a separate set of functions to handle the various game messages. Those message-handling functions are described in the following sections.

### cApp::PlayerID

The PlayerID function is used whenever clients are requesting their own DirectPlayer identification numbers. Those identification numbers are crucial to the clients for maintaining their lists of connected players (as illustrated in Figure 19.13).

When a client receives a message from the server, it consults the list of players to match the identification number; in this way, the client knows which client the message affects. Remember that the cApp::Receive function stores the requesting player's identification number in the sMessage being passed; that number is vital for this function.

```
BOOL cApp::PlayerID(sMessage *Msg, DPNID To)
{
  sAssignPlayerIDMessage apidm;

  apidm.Header.Type     = MSG_ASSIGNID;
  apidm.Header.Size     = sizeof(sAssignPlayerIDMessage);
  apidm.Header.PlayerID = To;
  SendNetworkMessage(&apidm, DPNSEND_NOLOOPBACK, To);

  return TRUE;
}
```

### cApp::AddPlayer

Let's face it—your game is going to be cool, and before long you'll have players joining the game left and right. When a player joins the game (or at least tries to join), a player message is added to the queue, and when that message is processed, the AddPlayer function is called to find room for the player. If no room exists, that player is disconnected.

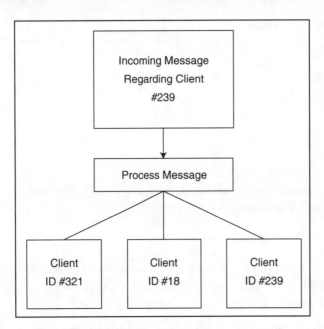

**Figure 19.13**

*Clients maintain a list of connected players, each identified by server-assigned DirectPlay identification number.*

```
BOOL cApp::AddPlayer(sMessage *Msg)
{
  long i;
  DWORD Size = 0;
  DPN_PLAYER_INFO *dpi = NULL;
  HRESULT hr;
  DPNID PlayerID;

  // Error checking
  if(m_Players == NULL)
    return FALSE;

  PlayerID = Msg->Header.PlayerID;

  // Get the player information
  hr = m_Server.GetServerCOM()->GetClientInfo(PlayerID, dpi,  \
                                              &Size, 0);

  // Return on error or if adding server
  if(FAILED(hr) && hr != DPNERR_BUFFERTOOSMALL)
    return FALSE;
```

```
// Allocate player data buffer and try again
if((dpi = (DPN_PLAYER_INFO*)new BYTE[Size]) == NULL)
  return FALSE;
ZeroMemory(dpi, Size);
dpi->dwSize = sizeof(DPN_PLAYER_INFO);
if(FAILED(m_Server.GetServerCOM()->GetClientInfo(              \
                              PlayerID, dpi, &Size, 0))) {
  delete [] dpi;
  return FALSE;
}
```

Up to this point, the server has polled DirectPlay for the client's information (as set from the client), which includes the client's name. From now on, the server will scan the array of sPlayer structures looking for one that has the Connected flag set to FALSE (and also to make sure that the player isn't already connected), which means that the spot is open to joining players.

```
// Make sure not already in list
for(i=0;i<MAX_PLAYERS;i++) {
  if(m_Players[i].dpnidPlayer == PlayerID &&              \
     m_Players[i].Connected == TRUE) {
    delete [] dpi;
    m_Server.DisconnectPlayer(PlayerID);
    return FALSE;
  }
}

// Search for an empty slot to put player
for(i=0;i<MAX_PLAYERS;i++) {
  if(m_Players[i].Connected == FALSE) {

    m_Players[i].Connected = TRUE; // Flag as connected

    // Save DirectPlay DPNID # and name of player
    m_Players[i].dpnidPlayer = PlayerID;
    wcstombs(m_Players[i].Name, dpi->pwszName, 256);

    // Setup player data
    m_Players[i].XPos      = 0.0f;
    m_Players[i].YPos      = 0.0f;
    m_Players[i].ZPos      = 0.0f;
    m_Players[i].Direction = 0.0f;
```

```
            m_Players[i].Speed     = 512.0f;
            m_Players[i].State     = STATE_IDLE;
            m_Players[i].Latency   = 0;
```

If an empty slot is found in the player array, the client information is stored and the player's structure is reset to known values. Continuing, the rest of the function will send a MSG_CREATE_PLAYER game message to all other connected players, informing them of a new player.

> **NOTE**
>
> All server network messages are sent via the SendNetworkMessage function, which basically forwards the message to the DirectPlay network's IDirectPlay8Server::SendTo function to handle. To see the exact code, check out the full source code on this book's **CD-ROM** (again, look for the **Server** demo in the **\BookCode\Chap19\Server** directory).

```
        // Send add player info to all players in area
        sCreatePlayerMessage cpm;
        cpm.Header.Type     = MSG_CREATE_PLAYER;
        cpm.Header.Size     = sizeof(sCreatePlayerMessage);
        cpm.Header.PlayerID = PlayerID;
        cpm.XPos            = m_Players[i].XPos;
        cpm.YPos            = m_Players[i].YPos;
        cpm.ZPos            = m_Players[i].ZPos;
        cpm.Direction       = m_Players[i].Direction;
        SendNetworkMessage(&cpm, DPNSEND_NOLOOPBACK, -1);

        ListPlayers();          // List all players

        delete [] dpi;          // Free player data

        return TRUE;            // Return success
      }
    }

    delete[] dpi;  // Free player data

    // Disconnect player - not allowed to connect
    m_Server.DisconnectPlayer(PlayerID);

    return FALSE;  // Return failure
  }
```

## cApp::RemovePlayer

Just as players join the game, so do players quit, and that's the purpose of the RemovePlayer function. In the RemovePlayer function, the server will scan the list of connected players for a match of a DirectPlay identification number (from the disconnecting player) and remove that player from the list. After the scan is complete and the appropriate player is removed from the list, all clients are notified of the disconnecting player, and the server rebuilds a list of existing players.

```
BOOL cApp::RemovePlayer(sMessage *Msg)
{
  long i;

  // Error checking
  if(m_Players == NULL)
    return FALSE;

  // Search for player in list
  for(i=0;i<MAX_PLAYERS;i++) {
    if(m_Players[i].dpnidPlayer == Msg->Header.PlayerID &&   \
       m_Players[i].Connected == TRUE) {

      m_Players[i].Connected = FALSE;  // Disconnect player

      // Send remove-player message to all players in area
      sDestroyPlayerMessage dpm;
      dpm.Header.Type     = MSG_DESTROY_PLAYER;
      dpm.Header.Size     = sizeof(sDestroyPlayerMessage);
      dpm.Header.PlayerID = Msg->Header.PlayerID;
      SendNetworkMessage(&dpm, DPNSEND_NOLOOPBACK, -1);

      // List all players
      ListPlayers();

      return TRUE;
    }
  }

  return FALSE;  // Return failure
}
```

## cApp::PlayerInfo

Unfortunately, in network gaming, game messages sometimes get lost along the way. What if one of those lost messages intended to inform the client application that a player had joined the game? Furthermore, what if the client started receiving messages related to a player that the client didn't know existed (because of a lost message)?

In cases where the client has no knowledge of a player and is receiving messages related to that player, the client will request the appropriate player's data from the server in order to continue. The server, in turn, will send the requested player's information to the client using the PlayerInfo function:

```
BOOL cApp::PlayerInfo(sMessage *Msg, DPNID To)
{
  sRequestPlayerInfoMessage *rpim;
  sCreatePlayerMessage cpm;
  long i;

  // Error checking
  if(m_Players == NULL)
    return FALSE;

  // Get pointer to request info
  rpim = (sRequestPlayerInfoMessage*)Msg;

  for(i=0;i<MAX_PLAYERS;i++) {
    // Only send if found in list
    if(m_Players[i].dpnidPlayer == rpim->PlayerID &&          \
       m_Players[i].Connected == TRUE) {

      // Send player info to requesting player
      cpm.Header.Type     = MSG_PLAYER_INFO;
      cpm.Header.Size     = sizeof(sCreatePlayerMessage);
      cpm.Header.PlayerID = rpim->PlayerID;

      cpm.XPos            = m_Players[i].XPos;
      cpm.YPos            = m_Players[i].YPos;
      cpm.ZPos            = m_Players[i].ZPos;
      cpm.Direction       = m_Players[i].Direction;
```

```
        SendNetworkMessage(&cpm, DPNSEND_NOLOOPBACK, To);

        break;
      }
  }

  return TRUE;
}
```

## cApp::PlayerStateChange

The major message-processing function in the server must be PlayerStateChange, which takes incoming actions from the clients and updates the internal player data.

```
BOOL cApp::PlayerStateChange(sMessage *Msg)
{
  sStateChangeMessage *scm, uscm;
  long i, PlayerNum;
  BOOL AllowChange;
  float XDiff, ZDiff, Dist, Angle;

  // Error checking
  if(m_Players == NULL)
    return FALSE;

  // Get pointer to state-change message
  scm = (sStateChangeMessage*)Msg;

  // Get player number in list
  PlayerNum = -1;
  for(i=0;i<MAX_PLAYERS;i++) {
    if(m_Players[i].dpnidPlayer == Msg->Header.PlayerID &&     \
      m_Players[i].Connected == TRUE) {
      PlayerNum = i;
      break;
    }
  }
  if(PlayerNum == -1)
    return FALSE;
```

Up to this point, the server has looked for the player that uses the state-change message. If a message is coming from a player who is not connected, the message is ignored. From now on, the game's logic takes over.

Players are allowed to walk, stand still, or swing their weapons. Players whose states are already set as swinging their weapons or being hurt are not allowed to update their states (until those states are cleared).

```
AllowChange = TRUE;  // Flag to allow changes in state

// Refuse to update player if swinging sword
if(m_Players[PlayerNum].State == STATE_SWING)
  AllowChange = FALSE;

// Refuse to update player if hurt
if(m_Players[PlayerNum].State == STATE_HURT)
  AllowChange = FALSE;

// Only change state if allowed
if(AllowChange == TRUE) {

  // Update selected player
  m_Players[PlayerNum].Time      = timeGetTime();
  m_Players[PlayerNum].State     = scm->State;
  m_Players[PlayerNum].Direction = scm->Direction;

  // Adjust action time based on latency
  m_Players[PlayerNum].Time -= m_Players[PlayerNum].Latency;

  // Send player data to all clients
  uscm.Header.Type     = MSG_STATE_CHANGE;
  uscm.Header.Size     = sizeof(sStateChangeMessage);
  uscm.Header.PlayerID = scm->Header.PlayerID;
  uscm.State           = m_Players[PlayerNum].State;
  uscm.XPos            = m_Players[PlayerNum].XPos;
  uscm.YPos            = m_Players[PlayerNum].YPos;
  uscm.ZPos            = m_Players[PlayerNum].ZPos;
  uscm.Direction       = m_Players[PlayerNum].Direction;
  uscm.Speed           = m_Players[PlayerNum].Speed;
  SendNetworkMessage(&uscm, DPNSEND_NOLOOPBACK);
```

Now the player's state is updated (if allowed) and sent out to all other connected players. Next, if the player has swung his weapon, all players are scanned to see whether the attacker hit them. If so, the states of those hurt are changed to HURT.

Also, notice that I offset the state's time variable (`sPlayer::Time`) by the player's latency value (`sPlayer::Latency`). This adjusts for network transmission delays and improves synchronization. If you remove the latency offset, you'll see a jumping effect when players are moving around the level.

```
// If swinging sword, determine who's hurt
if(scm->State == STATE_SWING) {

  // Check all players
  for(i=0;i<MAX_PLAYERS;i++) {

    // Only check against other players who are connected
    if(i != PlayerNum && m_Players[i].Connected == TRUE) {

      // Get distance to player
      XDiff = (float)fabs(m_Players[PlayerNum].XPos -          \
                          m_Players[i].XPos);
      ZDiff = (float)fabs(m_Players[PlayerNum].ZPos -          \
                          m_Players[i].ZPos);
      Dist = XDiff*XDiff + ZDiff*ZDiff;

      // Continue if distance between players acceptable
      if(Dist < 10000.0f) {

        // Get angle between players
        Angle = -(float)atan2(                                \
                      (m_Players[i].ZPos -                    \
                      m_Players[PlayerNum].ZPos),             \
                      (m_Players[i].XPos -                    \
                      m_Players[PlayerNum].XPos)) +           \
                      1.570796f;
        // Adjust for attacker's direction
        Angle -= m_Players[PlayerNum].Direction;

        Angle += 0.785f; // Adjust for FOV

        // Bounds angle value
        if(Angle < 0.0f)
          Angle += 6.28f;
        if(Angle >= 6.28f)
          Angle -= 6.28f;
```

```
          // Player hit if in front of attacker (90 FOV)
          if(Angle >= 0.0f && Angle <= 1.57f) {
```

Note that players who are swinging their swords have a chance to hit the players in front of them. To check whether another player was hit during an attack, you first perform a distance calculation, and if any characters are considered close enough, the angles between the players are checked. If the players being attacked are within a 90-degree field of view in front of the attackers (as illustrated in Figure 19.14), they are considered hit, at which point, those victims' states are changed to HURT.

```
          // Set victim's state to hurt (if not already)
          if(m_Players[i].State != STATE_HURT) {
            m_Players[i].State = STATE_HURT;
            m_Players[i].Time = timeGetTime();

            // Send network message
            uscm.Header.Type = MSG_STATE_CHANGE;
            uscm.Header.Size = sizeof(sStateChangeMessage);
            uscm.Header.PlayerID = m_Players[i].dpnidPlayer;
            uscm.State = m_Players[i].State;
            uscm.XPos = m_Players[i].XPos;
            uscm.YPos = m_Players[i].YPos;
            uscm.ZPos = m_Players[i].ZPos;
            uscm.Direction = m_Players[i].Direction;
            uscm.Speed = m_Players[i].Speed;
            SendNetworkMessage(&uscm, DPNSEND_NOLOOPBACK);
          }
        }
      }
    }
  }

  return TRUE;
}
```

And that's it for dealing with the game messages and state changes in players. Although the PlayerStateChange function is responsible for parsing the queued game messages, it's really up to another function to move players and clear their swinging or hurt states, as you see in the following section.

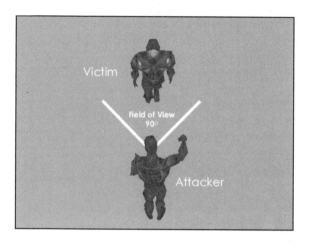

**Figure 19.14**

*In order for a player to hit another player, the attacker must be close enough and must be facing the intended victim. The server checks to see whether the victim is within a 90-degree field of vision of the attacker.*

# Updating Players

In order to synchronize itself with clients, the server needs to maintain a simplified version of the game running internally. This version of the game doesn't include graphics, sound, or any other fancy features; it only needs to track player's actions.

The server tracks those actions by updating the player's actions every 33ms (just as the client application will do). Those actions include walking and waiting for other specific states to clear (such as sword swinging and being hurt).

The `cApp::UpdatePlayers` function is responsible for updating all players:

```
void cApp::UpdatePlayers()
{
  long i;
  float XMove, ZMove, Speed;
  sStateChangeMessage scm;
  long Elapsed;

  // Loop through all players
  for(i=0;i<MAX_PLAYERS;i++) {

    // Only update connected players
    if(m_Players[i].Connected == TRUE) {

      // Get elapsed time from now and state time
      Elapsed = timeGetTime() - m_Players[i].Time;
```

As the server scans the list of players, it determines which players are connected and calculates the time since the last server update for all connected players. Next, if a player's state is set to STATE_MOVE, the elapsed time is used to move the player:

```
// Process player movement state
if(m_Players[i].State == STATE_MOVE) {
  // Calculate amount of movement by time passed
  Speed = (float)Elapsed / 1000.0f * m_Players[i].Speed;
  XMove = (float)sin(m_Players[i].Direction) * Speed;
  ZMove = (float)cos(m_Players[i].Direction) * Speed;

  // Check for movement collisions -
  // can't walk past anything blocking path.
  if(CheckIntersect(&m_LevelMesh,                          \
                    m_Players[i].XPos,                     \
                    m_Players[i].YPos + 16.0f,             \
                    m_Players[i].ZPos,                     \
                    m_Players[i].XPos + XMove,             \
                    m_Players[i].YPos + 16.0f,             \
                    m_Players[i].ZPos + ZMove) == TRUE)
    XMove = ZMove = 0.0f;

  // Update player coordinates
  m_Players[i].XPos += XMove;
  m_Players[i].YPos = 0.0f;     // Stay on ground
  m_Players[i].ZPos += ZMove;

  m_Players[i].Time = timeGetTime();  // Reset time
}
```

Next, the server deals with the STATE_SWING and STATE_HURT states. Those states are cleared only after one second has passed (as determined by the elapsed time):

```
// Clear swing status after 1 second
if(m_Players[i].State == STATE_SWING) {
  if(Elapsed > 1000) {
    m_Players[i].State = STATE_IDLE;

    // Send network message to player to clear
    scm.Header.Type    = MSG_STATE_CHANGE;
    scm.Header.Size    = sizeof(sStateChangeMessage);
```

```
                scm.Header.PlayerID = m_Players[i].dpnidPlayer;
                scm.XPos            = m_Players[i].XPos;
                scm.YPos            = m_Players[i].YPos;
                scm.ZPos            = m_Players[i].ZPos;
                scm.Direction       = m_Players[i].Direction;
                scm.Speed           = m_Players[i].Speed;
                scm.State           = m_Players[i].State;

                // Send the message over network
                SendNetworkMessage(&scm, DPNSEND_NOLOOPBACK, -1);
              }
            }

            // Clear hurt status after 1 second
            if(m_Players[i].State == STATE_HURT) {
              if(Elapsed > 1000) {
                m_Players[i].State = STATE_IDLE;

                // Send network message to player to clear
                scm.Header.Type     = MSG_STATE_CHANGE;
                scm.Header.Size     = sizeof(sStateChangeMessage);
                scm.Header.PlayerID = m_Players[i].dpnidPlayer;
                scm.XPos            = m_Players[i].XPos;
                scm.YPos            = m_Players[i].YPos;
                scm.ZPos            = m_Players[i].ZPos;
                scm.Direction       = m_Players[i].Direction;
                scm.Speed           = m_Players[i].Speed;
                scm.State           = m_Players[i].State;

                // Send the message over network
                SendNetworkMessage(&scm, DPNSEND_NOLOOPBACK, -1);
              }
            }
          }
        }
      }
    }
```

Surprisingly, that's it for cApp::UpdatePlayers! Remember that the UpdatePlayers function is called every 33ms, so keeping the function quick and to the point is crucial. Once all players are updated, you need to notify other players.

# Updating the Network Clients

Throughout earlier sections in this chapter, I mentioned periodic server updates that are sent to the client in order to synchronize game-play. That's the purpose of the cApp::UpdateNetwork function. The UpdateNetwork function is quick and to the point, sending out the current state of all connected clients every 100ms.

```
void cApp::UpdateNetwork()
{
  long i;
  sStateChangeMessage scm;

  // Send all player updates
  for(i=0;i<MAX_PLAYERS;i++) {

    // Only send data about connected players
    if(m_Players[i].Connected == TRUE) {
      scm.Header.Type     = MSG_STATE_CHANGE;
      scm.Header.Size     = sizeof(sStateChangeMessage);
      scm.Header.PlayerID = m_Players[i].dpnidPlayer;
      scm.XPos            = m_Players[i].XPos;
      scm.YPos            = m_Players[i].YPos;
      scm.ZPos            = m_Players[i].ZPos;
      scm.Direction       = m_Players[i].Direction;
      scm.Speed           = m_Players[i].Speed;
      scm.State           = m_Players[i].State;
      scm.Latency         = m_Players[i].Latency;

      // Send the message over network
      SendNetworkMessage(&scm, DPNSEND_NOLOOPBACK);
    }
  }
}
```

# Calculating Latency

The server periodically calculates the time it takes a message to be received from a client and uses the latency in the timed calculations to update clients, all of which is crucial to maintaining the synchronization of the game. The function that calculates the latency is UpdateLatency, and it is called every 10 seconds from the main application loop (cApp::Frame).

```
void cApp::UpdateLatency()
{
  long i;
  DPN_CONNECTION_INFO dpci;
  HRESULT hr;

  // Go through all players
  for(i=0;i<MAX_PLAYERS;i++) {

    // Only process connected players
    if(m_Players[i].Connected == TRUE) {

      // Request player connection settings
      hr = m_Server.GetServerCOM()->GetConnectionInfo(          \
                  m_Players[i].dpnidPlayer, &dpci, 0);

      if(SUCCEEDED(hr)) {
        m_Players[i].Latency = dpci.dwRoundTripLatencyMS / 2;

        // Bounds latency to 1 second
        if(m_Players[i].Latency > 1000)
          m_Players[i].Latency = 1000;

      } else {
        m_Players[i].Latency = 0;
      }
    }
  }
}
```

To calculate the latency, the server queries DirectPlay for the connection statistics
via the IDirectPlay8Server::GetConnectInfo function. That function call takes a structure (DPN_CONNECTION_INFO) as an argument, and inside the structure is a variable that
represents the roundtrip latency time in milliseconds. The server divides that
latency value in half and stores it in each player's data structure.

# The Hard Part Is Over!

You've been through the guts of the server. Now you just need to wrap everything into
a fully functional application. Other than the code for the server, there's not much left
to do. To see how the application is set up, check out the server code on the CD-ROM.

Things are really getting exciting! Now, it's time to focus on the other side of the network game—the client!

# Working with Game Clients

The client application (referred to as the *client*) is the conduit between the gaming server and the player. The client accepts the user's input and forwards it to the server. Between updates from the server, the client updates itself based on what little information it has—the player's movement, other players' movements, NPC actions, and so on.

The client uses graphics, sound, and input-processing to work its magic. However, if you were to strip away the graphics and sound, you would be left with a rather bland application. This "dumb" client structure might look unworthy, but believe me, it will work perfectly for your game project.

To use the Client application (located on this book's CD-ROM in the \BookCode\ Chap19\Client directory), you can follow these steps:

1. Locate and run the Client application. The Connect to Server dialog box (shown in Figure 19.15) appears.

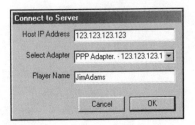

**Figure 19.15**

*Besides picking an adapter and entering a player name, you'll need to know the server's IP address in order to connect and play the game.*

2. In the Connect to Server dialog box, enter the host's IP address, select an adapter, and enter your player's name.

3. Click OK to begin the game and connect to the server.

The client works almost identically to the server in some respects, the first of which is dealing with players.

# Handling Player Data

The client, much like the server, uses an sPlayer structure that contains the information about each connected player in the game. This time, however, information is needed to track the 3-D object for drawing the player (as well as the weapon) and the player animation being played. Other than that, you can see many similarities between the sPlayer structure being used by the client and server. Take a look at the declaration of the client's sPlayer structure (along with supporting macros):

```
// Player states
#define STATE_IDLE          1
#define STATE_MOVE          2
#define STATE_SWING         3
#define STATE_HURT          4

// Animations
#define ANIM_IDLE           1
#define ANIM_WALK           2
#define ANIM_SWING          3
#define ANIM_HURT           4

typedef struct sPlayer {
  BOOL  Connected;          // TRUE if player active

  DPNID dpnidPlayer;        // DirectPlay Player ID #

  long  State;              // Last known state (STATE_*)
  long  Time;               // Time of last state update
  long  Latency;            // Half of roundtrip latency in ms

  float XPos, YPos, ZPos;   // Player coordinates
  float Direction;          // Angle facing
  float Speed;              // Movement speed

  cObject Body;             // Character 3-D object
  cObject Weapon;           // Weapon 3-D object
  long    LastAnim;         // Last known animation

  // Constructor and destructor
  sPlayer()
  {
    Connected = FALSE;
    dpnidPlayer = 0;
    LastAnim = 0;
    Time = 0;
  }

  ~sPlayer() { Body.Free(); Weapon.Free(); }
} sPlayer;
```

Again, an array of sPlayer structures is allocated to hold the player information. Each player is allowed to use a separate Graphics Core object for the character's body and weapon mesh. The local player uses the first element in the player data array (defined as m_Players in the application class), although joining players are stuffed into the first empty slot found.

As the application class for the client is initialized, all character and weapon meshes are loaded and assigned to each of the player data structures. This is your first chance to customize your network game; by loading different meshes, you can have each player appear differently. For example, one character can be a warrior, another character a wizard, and so on.

A list of animations is also loaded. Those animations represent the various states of players: a walking animation, standing still (idle), swinging a weapon, and finally a hurt animation. Those animations are set by the UpdatePlayers function, which you see in a bit in the section "Updating Local Players."

One extra tidbit in the sPlayer structure is a DirectPlay identification number. Clients normally don't have access to their identification numbers; those are left for the server to track. However, clients are designed so that their identification numbers track all players, and in order to start playing, all clients must request their identification number from the server.

Remember the MSG_ASSIGNID game message that I mentioned earlier in the section "Handling Messages"? Clients use the MSG_ASSIGNID message to request their identification from the server. Upon receiving it, clients can determine which incoming update messages go to which connected players.

When a game message is received from the server, the client application scans through the list of connected players. When the player identification number from the local list of players and from the server is matched, the client knows exactly which player to update.

The client uses a function called GetPlayerNum to scan the list of players and return the index number of the matching player (or -1 if no such match is found):

```
long cApp::GetPlayerNum(DPNID dpnidPlayer)
{
  long i;

  // Error checking
  if(m_Players == NULL)
    return -1;
```

```
    // Scan list looking for match
    for(i=0;i<MAX_PLAYERS;i++) {
      if(m_Players[i].dpnidPlayer == dpnidPlayer &&                    \
         m_Players[i].Connected == TRUE)
        return i;
    }

    return -1;  // Not found in list
}
```

From now on, the client will always use the GetPlayerNum function to determine which player to update. If a player is not found in the list but is known to exist, the client must send a MSG_PLAYER_INFO message, which requests the player's information from the server. In response, the server will return a create-player message to the requesting client.

But I'm getting a little ahead of myself, so let's slow things down a bit. Much like the server, the client uses the Network Core to handle network communications. Now, take a look at the client component I'm using for the client application.

# The Network Component

To use a client component, you have to derive a class from it and, in that derived class, override the necessary functions. Those functions are few and are needed only to convey when a connection to the server is achieved or to receive incoming game messages.

To use the client network component, begin by deriving your own class from cNetworkClient:

```
class cClient : public cNetworkClient
{
  private:
    BOOL ConnectComplete(DPNMSG_CONNECT_COMPLETE *Msg);
    BOOL Receive(DPNMSG_RECEIVE *Msg);
};
```

To pass messages to the application, the derived application object needs only one public function to siphon in received messages. Why only one? The client needs to know when a connection is established to the server, which is the purpose of the ConnectComplete function.

By using a global variable (g_Connected) that represents the connection status, the client network component can update the state of the connection as follows:

```
cApp                *g_Application; // Global application pointer

BOOL cClient::ConnectComplete(DPNMSG_CONNECT_COMPLETE *Msg)
{
  // Save connection status
  if(Msg->hResultCode == S_OK)
    g_Connected = TRUE;
  else
    g_Connected = FALSE;

  return TRUE;
}
```

Use the matching cApp::Receive function for the cClient::Receive function:

```
BOOL cApp::Receive(DPNMSG_RECEIVE *Msg)
{
  sMessage *MsgPtr;

  // Get pointer to received data
  MsgPtr = (sMessage*)Msg->pReceiveData;

  // Handle packets by type
  switch(MsgPtr->Header.Type) {
    case MSG_ASSIGNID:        // Assign local player ID
      AssignID(MsgPtr);
      break;

    case MSG_PLAYER_INFO:     // Add a player to list
    case MSG_CREATE_PLAYER:
      CreatePlayer(MsgPtr);
      break;

    case MSG_DESTROY_PLAYER:  // Remove a player from list
      DestroyPlayer(MsgPtr);
      break;
```

```
     case MSG_STATE_CHANGE:     // Change state of player
       ChangeState(MsgPtr);
       break;
   }

   return TRUE;
}
```

Notice that the Receive function immediately processes incoming messages appropriately by calling separate functions for each type of game message.

## Message Handling

The client application uses the same message structures as the server, but the client has no need for queuing messages. As Figure 19.16 demonstrates, incoming messages are immediately parsed by the client.

Now that you've seen the Receive function that handles incoming message, it's time to examine each message handling function.

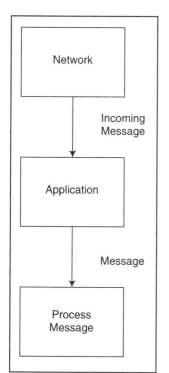

**Figure 19.16**

*The client receives messages from the client network component in much the same way as the server. However, with the client, incoming messages are cast into game-related messages and processed immediately.*

## cApp::AssignID

Recall that the client needs to first know its own DirectPlay identification number from the server. AssignID is the function that sets this identification number as it is received.

```
void cApp::AssignID(sMessage *Msg)
{
  sAssignPlayerIDMessage *apidm;

  // Error checking
  if(m_Players == NULL || m_Players[0].dpnidPlayer)
    return;

  // Get pointer to message data
  apidm = (sAssignPlayerIDMessage*)Msg;

  EnterCriticalSection(&m_UpdateCS);
  m_Players[0].dpnidPlayer = apidm-
>Header.PlayerID;
  LeaveCriticalSection(&m_UpdateCS);
}
```

> **NOTE**
> Because the network compo-
> nent and the application are
> in constant struggles over the
> same player data structures,
> critical sections are in full
> abundance in the client.

## cApp::CreatePlayer

As clients join the game, the server informs other connected clients of those new arrivals. The purpose of the following CreatePlayer function is to find room in the sPlayer structure and store the player data:

```
void cApp::CreatePlayer(sMessage *Msg)
{
  sCreatePlayerMessage *cpm;
  long PlayerNum, i;

  // Error checking
  if(m_Players == NULL || !m_Players[0].dpnidPlayer)
    return;

  // Get pointer to message data
  cpm = (sCreatePlayerMessage*)Msg;

  // Don't add local player to list
```

```
    if(cpm->Header.PlayerID == m_Players[0].dpnidPlayer)
      return;

    // Make sure player not already in list while at
    // same time finding an empty slot.
    PlayerNum = -1;
    for(i=1;i<MAX_PLAYERS;i++) {
      if(m_Players[i].Connected == TRUE) {
        if(m_Players[i].dpnidPlayer==cpm->Header.PlayerID)
          return;
      } else
        PlayerNum = i;
    }

    // Return error if no open slots
    if(PlayerNum == -1)
      return;

    // Enter critical section
    EnterCriticalSection(&m_UpdateCS);

    // Add player data
    m_Players[PlayerNum].Connected    = TRUE;
    m_Players[PlayerNum].dpnidPlayer = cpm->Header.PlayerID;
    m_Players[PlayerNum].XPos         = cpm->XPos;
    m_Players[PlayerNum].YPos         = cpm->YPos;
    m_Players[PlayerNum].ZPos         = cpm->ZPos;
    m_Players[PlayerNum].Direction    = cpm->Direction;
    m_Players[PlayerNum].Speed        = 0.0f;
    m_Players[PlayerNum].State        = STATE_IDLE;

    m_NumPlayers++;

    // Leave critical section
    LeaveCriticalSection(&m_UpdateCS);
}
```

## cApp::DestroyPlayer

The server notifies clients when a player is leaving a session. The clients, in turn, signal the player as being disconnected and skips updating the player during the update cycle. The following code determines which client is disconnected and takes the appropriate steps:

```
void cApp::DestroyPlayer(sMessage *Msg)
{
  sDestroyPlayerMessage *dpm;
  long PlayerNum;

  // Error checking
  if(m_Players == NULL || !m_Players[0].dpnidPlayer)
    return;

  // Get pointer to message data
  dpm = (sDestroyPlayerMessage*)Msg;

  // Don't remove local player from list
  if(dpm->Header.PlayerID == m_Players[0].dpnidPlayer)
    return;

  // Get player number in list
  if((PlayerNum = GetPlayerNum(dpm->Header.PlayerID)) == -1)
    return;

  // Enter critical section
  EnterCriticalSection(&m_UpdateCS);

  // Set player as disconnected
  m_Players[PlayerNum].Connected = FALSE;
  m_NumPlayers--;

  // Leave critical section
  LeaveCriticalSection(&m_UpdateCS);
}
```

## cApp::ChangeState

The client processes changes of state in players by pulling out the message data and putting it in the player's structure. If a player isn't found in the list of players, the client requests that player's information via a MSG_PLAYER_INFO message and exits the ChangeState function without further ado.

This is the only situation in which a player's coordinates can be directly modified by a state change—clients are not allowed to make direct changes to their coordinates (to avoid cheating), so it's up to the server to tell players just where they are in the world during the updates:

```
void cApp::ChangeState(sMessage *Msg)
{
  sStateChangeMessage *scm;
  sRequestPlayerInfoMessage rpim;
  long PlayerNum;

  // Error checking
  if(m_Players == NULL || !m_Players[0].dpnidPlayer)
    return;

  // Get pointer to message data
  scm = (sStateChangeMessage*)Msg;

  // Get player number in list
  if((PlayerNum = GetPlayerNum(scm->Header.PlayerID)) == -1) {
    // Unknown player - request info
    if(PlayerNum == -1) {
      // Construct message
      rpim.Header.Type = MSG_PLAYER_INFO;
      rpim.Header.Size = sizeof(sRequestPlayerInfoMessage);
      rpim.Header.PlayerID = m_Players[0].dpnidPlayer;
      rpim.PlayerID = scm->Header.PlayerID;

      // Send message to server
      SendNetworkMessage(&rpim, DPNSEND_NOLOOPBACK);

      return;
    }
  }

  // Enter critical section
  EnterCriticalSection(&m_UpdateCS);

  // Store new sytate info
  m_Players[PlayerNum].Time      = timeGetTime();
  m_Players[PlayerNum].State     = scm->State;
```

```
m_Players[PlayerNum].XPos      = scm->XPos;
m_Players[PlayerNum].YPos      = scm->YPos;
m_Players[PlayerNum].ZPos      = scm->ZPos;
m_Players[PlayerNum].Direction = scm->Direction;
m_Players[PlayerNum].Speed     = scm->Speed;
m_Players[PlayerNum].Latency   = scm->Latency;

  // Bounds latency to 1 second
  if(m_Players[PlayerNum].Latency > 1000)
    m_Players[PlayerNum].Latency = 1000;

  // Adjust time based on latency
  m_Players[PlayerNum].Time -=
m_Players[PlayerNum].Latency;

  // Leave critical section
  LeaveCriticalSection(&m_UpdateCS);
}
```

Just like the server, the client has a
SendNetworkMessage to send the game-related
network messages to the server (for details
on this function, check out the client's source
code on this book's CD-ROM).

> **NOTE**
> The client also depends on the latency time to modify the timing calculations. The server sends this latency time to the client, but to make things safe, the client application is allowed to cut the latency down to one second if the server states that it is higher.

# Updating the Local Player

Between updates from the server, the clients need to update all players to keep the game running smoothly. The client application limits updates to every 33ms (30 times a second), which matches the server update rate. Between these player updates, the client is allowed to collect input from the player who is used to change their actions.

The cApp::Frame function is generally used to update the local player. The players use the keyboard and mouse to control their characters, so I included a few Input Core objects (m_Keyboard and m_Mouse):

```
BOOL cApp::Frame()
{
  static DWORD UpdateCounter = timeGetTime();
  static long MoveAction = 0, LastMove = 0;
  static BOOL CamMoved = FALSE;
  BOOL AllowMovement;
```

```
long Dir;
float Angles[13] = { 0.0f, 0.0f, 1.57f, 0.785f, 3.14f,        \
                     0.0f, 2.355f, 0.0f, 4.71f, 5.495f,       \
                     0.0f, 0.0f, 3.925f };

// Get local input every frame
m_Keyboard.Acquire(TRUE);
m_Mouse.Acquire(TRUE);
m_Keyboard.Read();
m_Mouse.Read();

// Pressing ESC quits program
if(m_Keyboard.GetKeyState(KEY_ESC) == TRUE)
  return FALSE;
```

At every frame, the input devices are restored (in case a device's focus has been lost), and input is read in. If the user presses Esc, the game-play quits by returning a value of FALSE from the Frame function.

From here, game-play may only continue if the client is connected to the server. If no such connection exists, a message displays to that effect. Also, if a player is still waiting for a DirectPlay identification number from the server, a message displays, and a request is periodically sent to the server for the correct identification number. You use the following code to display those messages and wait for the identification number from the server:

```
// Handle connection and waiting for data screen
if(g_Connected == FALSE || !m_Players[0].dpnidPlayer) {

  // Display message(s)
  m_Graphics.Clear();
  if(m_Graphics.BeginScene() == TRUE) {
    m_Font.Print("Connecting to server...", 0, 0);
    if(!m_Players[0].dpnidPlayer)
      m_Font.Print("Waiting for server data...", 0, 20);
    m_Graphics.EndScene();
  }
  m_Graphics.Display();

  // Request player ID from server every 2 seconds
  if(timeGetTime() > UpdateCounter + 2000) {
    UpdateCounter = timeGetTime();  // Update counter
```

```
        sAssignPlayerIDMessage apidm;
        apidm.Header.Type = MSG_ASSIGNID;
        apidm.Header.Size = sizeof(sAssignPlayerIDMessage);
        SendNetworkMessage(&apidm, DPNSEND_NOLOOPBACK |          \
                                   DPNSEND_GUARANTEED);
    }


    return TRUE;
}
```

From here on, player input is parsed. A single variable tracks player actions (MoveAction), and each bit in the variable represents a specific action (as shown in Figure 19.17). The user's actions are move up, move down, move left, move right, and attack. Also, camera angle changes are recorded (and flagged for later updating).

The following code determines which keys the player is currently pressing and sets the appropriate bits in the MoveAction variable:

```
// Store movements every frame
if(m_Keyboard.GetKeyState(KEY_UP) == TRUE)
  MoveAction |= 1;
if(m_Keyboard.GetKeyState(KEY_RIGHT) == TRUE)
  MoveAction |= 2;
if(m_Keyboard.GetKeyState(KEY_DOWN) == TRUE)
  MoveAction |= 4;
if(m_Keyboard.GetKeyState(KEY_LEFT) == TRUE)
  MoveAction |= 8;

// Store attack action
if(m_Keyboard.GetKeyState(KEY_SPACE) == TRUE)
  MoveAction |= 16;
```

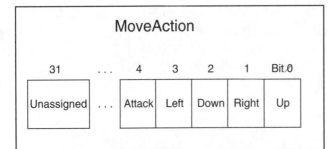

**Figure 19.17**

*Each bit in the* MoveAction *variable is used to define a specific move action.*

```
if(m_Mouse.GetButtonState(MOUSE_LBUTTON) == TRUE)
  MoveAction |= 16;

// Rotate camera
if(m_Mouse.GetXDelta() > 0) {
  m_CamAngle -= 0.1f;
  CamMoved = TRUE;
}
if(m_Mouse.GetXDelta() < 0) {
  m_CamAngle += 0.1f;
  CamMoved = TRUE;
}

// Only update players every 33ms (30 times a second)
if(timeGetTime() < UpdateCounter + 33)
  return TRUE;
```

Remember that player updates are limited to 30 times per second, so the last bit of the preceding code will return control if that amount of time has not passed.

```
// Set flag to allow player movement
AllowMovement = TRUE;

// Don't allow movement if still swinging weapon
if(m_Players[0].State == STATE_SWING)
  AllowMovement = FALSE;

// Don't allow movement if still being hurt
if(m_Players[0].State == STATE_HURT)
  AllowMovement = FALSE;
```

Normally, players are allowed to move around the world, but if a player is currently swinging his weapon or being hurt, that player is not allowed to move. You use the AllowMovement flag to signify when a player's actions can be processed, as shown here:

```
// Handle movements if allowed
if(AllowMovement == TRUE) {

  // Process attack
  if(MoveAction & 16) {
    MoveAction = 0;  // Clear movement
    LastMove = 0;    // Clear last movement
```

```
        // Send attack message - let server signal swing
        sStateChangeMessage Msg;
        Msg.Header.Type     = MSG_STATE_CHANGE;
        Msg.Header.Size     = sizeof(sStateChangeMessage);
        Msg.Header.PlayerID = m_Players[0].dpnidPlayer;
        Msg.State           = STATE_SWING;
        Msg.Direction       = m_Players[0].Direction;

        // Send message to server
        SendNetworkMessage(&Msg, DPNSEND_NOLOOPBACK);
    }
```

If a player chooses to attack, you need to construct a state-change message and send that message to the server. After you send the state-change message, clear the player's movement actions. Notice that the client does not change its own state at this point; the server determines when to change the player's state.

If the player did not attack, his actions are checked to see whether the player is moving:

```
    // Process local player movements
    if((Dir = MoveAction) > 0 && Dir < 13) {
        // Set new player state (w/time and direction)
        EnterCriticalSection(&m_UpdateCS);
        m_Players[0].State     = STATE_MOVE;
        m_Players[0].Direction = Angles[Dir] - m_CamAngle + 4.71f;
        LeaveCriticalSection(&m_UpdateCS);

        // Reset last move if camera moved since last update
        if(CamMoved == TRUE) {
            CamMoved = FALSE;
            LastMove = 0;
        }
```

After the player's state and movement direction is set, the Frame function continues by resetting the camera's movements (by setting the CamMoved flag to FALSE). The player's controls are relative to the camera-viewing angle (if the player is pressing the up arrow key, he is walking away from the camera). If you change the camera's angle while the player is walking, you force the player's direction to change as well. The client takes this change of the player's direction into consideration when the camera is rotated.

The Frame function now determines whether the player has changed the direction of movement (from the movement in the last frame):

```
// Send actions to server if changed from last move
if(MoveAction != LastMove) {
  LastMove = MoveAction;  // Store last action

  m_Players[0].Time = timeGetTime();

  // Construct message
  sStateChangeMessage Msg;
  Msg.Header.Type     = MSG_STATE_CHANGE;
  Msg.Header.Size     = sizeof(sStateChangeMessage);
  Msg.Header.PlayerID = m_Players[0].dpnidPlayer;
  Msg.State           = STATE_MOVE;
  Msg.Direction       = m_Players[0].Direction;

  // Send message to server
  SendNetworkMessage(&Msg, DPNSEND_NOLOOPBACK);
}
```

Once a player has moved, the client sends a state-change message to the server. Notice that the state-change message is sent only if the player's movement is different from the last move he performed (as recorded in the LastMove variable).

If the player hasn't moved, his state is changed to standing still (STATE_IDLE), and a state-change message is sent to the server using the following code:

```
} else {
  // Change to idle state
  EnterCriticalSection(&m_UpdateCS);
  m_Players[0].State = STATE_IDLE;
  LeaveCriticalSection(&m_UpdateCS);

  // Send update only if player moved last update
  if(LastMove) {
    LastMove = 0;

    sStateChangeMessage Msg;
    Msg.Header.Type     = MSG_STATE_CHANGE;
    Msg.Header.Size     = sizeof(sStateChangeMessage);
    Msg.Header.PlayerID = m_Players[0].dpnidPlayer;
```

```
          Msg.State            = STATE_IDLE;
          Msg.Direction        = m_Players[0].Direction;

          // Send message to server
          SendNetworkMessage(&Msg, DPNSEND_NOLOOPBACK);
        }
      }
  }
```

At this point, the local player's actions have been recorded and sent to the server. Next, all players are updated, the scene is rendered, and the movement actions are reset for the next frame:

```
// Update all players
UpdatePlayers();

// Render the scene
RenderScene();

MoveAction = 0; // Clear action data for next frame

UpdateCounter = timeGetTime(); // Reset update counter

return TRUE;
}
```

## Updating All Players

Whereas the local player's input is processed in the cApp::Frame function, the UpdatePlayers (which you saw in the code in the previous section) processes the players according to their respective states.

Unlike the server's UpdatePlayers function, the client's UpdatePlayers function is simple. The client is allowed to move players based only on their last known positions, directions, and elapsed time since their last update.

Remember, only the server can clear the weapon-swinging and being-hurt states, so the client has nothing to do at this point except update the various animations to show the player what is going on:

```
void cApp::UpdatePlayers()
{
  long  i;
```

```
float XMove, ZMove, Dist, Speed;
long Elapsed;

// Process all active player movements
for(i=0;i<MAX_PLAYERS;i++) {
  if(m_Players[i].Connected == TRUE) {

    // Get elapsed time from now and state time
    Elapsed = timeGetTime() - m_Players[i].Time;

    // Process player movement state
    if(m_Players[i].State == STATE_MOVE) {
      // Calculate amount of movement by time movement processed
      Speed = (float)Elapsed / 1000.0f * m_Players[i].Speed;
      XMove = (float)sin(m_Players[i].Direction) * Speed;
      ZMove = (float)cos(m_Players[i].Direction) * Speed;

      // Check for movement collisions -
      // can't walk past anything blocking path
      if(m_NodeTreeMesh.CheckIntersect(
                          m_Players[i].XPos,
                          m_Players[i].YPos + 16.0f,
                          m_Players[i].ZPos,
                          m_Players[i].XPos + XMove,
                          m_Players[i].YPos + 16.0f,
                          m_Players[i].ZPos + ZMove,
                          &Dist) == TRUE)
        XMove = ZMove = 0.0f;

      // Update coordinates
      EnterCriticalSection(&m_UpdateCS);
      m_Players[i].XPos += XMove;
      m_Players[i].YPos = 0.0f;
      m_Players[i].ZPos += ZMove;

      m_Players[i].Time = timeGetTime(); // Reset time

      LeaveCriticalSection(&m_UpdateCS);
    }
```

```
         // Set new animations as needed
         if(m_Players[i].State == STATE_IDLE) {
           if(m_Players[i].LastAnim != ANIM_IDLE) {
             EnterCriticalSection(&m_UpdateCS);
             m_Players[i].LastAnim = ANIM_IDLE;
             m_Players[i].Body.SetAnimation(                      \
                   &m_CharacterAnim, "Idle", timeGetTime() / 32);
             LeaveCriticalSection(&m_UpdateCS);
           }
         } else
         if(m_Players[i].State == STATE_MOVE) {
           if(m_Players[i].LastAnim != ANIM_WALK) {
             EnterCriticalSection(&m_UpdateCS);
             m_Players[i].LastAnim = ANIM_WALK;
             m_Players[i].Body.SetAnimation(                      \
                   &m_CharacterAnim, "Walk", timeGetTime() / 32);
             LeaveCriticalSection(&m_UpdateCS);
           }
         } else
         if(m_Players[i].State == STATE_SWING) {
           if(m_Players[i].LastAnim != ANIM_SWING) {
             EnterCriticalSection(&m_UpdateCS);
             m_Players[i].LastAnim = ANIM_SWING;
             m_Players[i].Body.SetAnimation(                      \
                   &m_CharacterAnim, "Swing", timeGetTime() / 32);
             LeaveCriticalSection(&m_UpdateCS);
           }
         } else
         if(m_Players[i].State == STATE_HURT) {
           if(m_Players[i].LastAnim != ANIM_HURT) {
             EnterCriticalSection(&m_UpdateCS);
             m_Players[i].LastAnim = ANIM_HURT;
             m_Players[i].Body.SetAnimation(                      \
                   &m_CharacterAnim, "Hurt", timeGetTime() / 32);
             LeaveCriticalSection(&m_UpdateCS);
           }
         }
       }
     }
   }
```

Character animations are updated only if they differ from the last known animation. The `sPlayer::LastAnim` variable tracks the last known animation, although the various `ANIM_*` macros define which animations to play.

## The Client's Full Glory

The hard work is over! The only requirements for running the client are processing the local player's input and updating the players. Now, all you have to do is spruce up your project with some 3-D graphics, and you'll almost have a game.

The graphics portion of the client application uses the Graphics Core to draw the various connected players in the game. You use a `NodeTree` object to render the game's level. The client loads all meshes when the application class is initialized. As previously mentioned, all players receive an assigned mesh to represent their characters and weapons. Animations are also used and are set by the various update messages.

You limit rendering of a scene to 30 times a second, and to ensure that everything runs as quickly as possible, you use a viewing frustum to render the level and to clip unseen characters out of the rendering loop.

To wrap up the Client application, you deal with the different kinds of application code, such as selecting an adapter and connecting to the server. You can find this code on the CD-ROM at the back of this book (look for \BookCode\Chap19\Client).

# Wrapping Up Multiplayer Gaming

The game server and client discussed in this chapter are powerful (regardless of how bland they might appear). With a little reworking, you can fine-tune them to match the needs of your gaming project. If you want to create games that can handle thousands of players at once, I suggest researching a multiserver setup that uses lobbies and connection servers. For a huge game world, you could use 100 computers to host a single, persistent game session. Wouldn't that be awesome!

For further study on the topic of multiplayer gaming, I highly suggest picking up a copy of Todd Barron's book, *Multiplayer Game Programming*. Check out Appendix C, "Recommended Reading," for more information on Todd's book.

In addition, you could brave the multiplayer frontier by downloading the code to *Quake* and *Quake II* (two games from id Software, Inc., that helped revolutionize the multiplayer genre). *Quake* and *Quake II* are perfect examples of multiplayer gaming in action, and by reading through the source code of those two games, you'll learn a good deal about using networking with games. To download the source code for *Quake* and *Quake II,* point your browser (or ftp client) to ftp://ftp.idsoftware.com/idstuff/source/q1source.zip and ftp://ftp.idsoftware.com/idstuff/source/quake2.zip.

## Programs on the CD-ROM

Two projects that harness the multiplayer features shown in this chapter are located on the CD-ROM at the back of this book. You can find the following programs in the \BookCode\Chap19\ subdirectory:

* **Server.** A multiplayer game server that allows eight clients to connect and play. Location: \BookCode\Chap19\Server\.

* **Client.** The client application that allows a player to connect to a remote server and join up to seven other players in multiplayer gaming action. The server must be running in order to play the game. Location: \BookCode\Chap19\Client\.

# Part Five

# The Finishing Touches

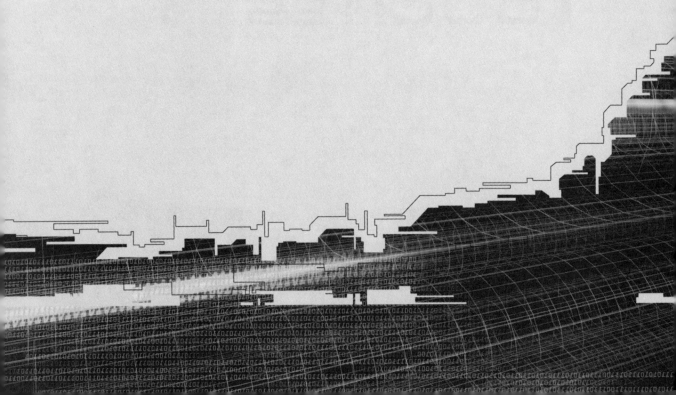

# CHAPTER 20

# PUTTING TOGETHER A FULL GAME

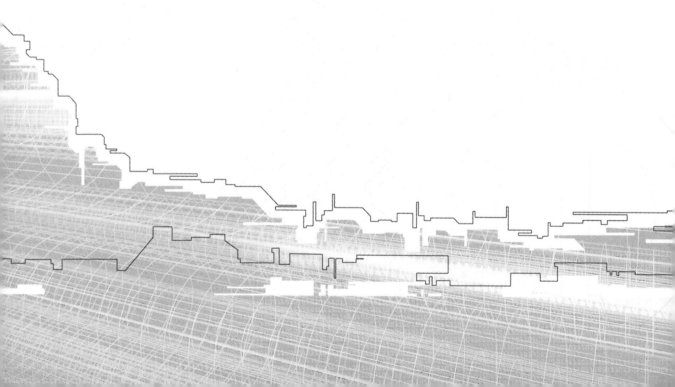

In this chapter, you put all the pieces of a game together. If you've followed the book sequentially, you now have fully developed core engines, maps, characters, items, scripts, and a story. All that's left is to put everything in place and call the result a game! In this chapter, you build a small game that I developed especially for this book.

In this chapter, you learn how to do the following:

- Design a sample game
- Assemble gaming components
- Program the game

# Designing the Sample Game

Now comes the time to commence creating the book's sample game—*The Tower*. Although its title is not too ingenious, the game does put together all the gaming pieces you need to complete a game. The purpose of *The Tower* is to show every component in its proper place, including tech engines, map and level management, character control, and scripting.

The game's creation starts with the design. You need to write the story, create the levels, develop characters, design items, and devise spells. To help set a context, I will kick off the design process with a short story describing what occurs up to the time the player enters the game. This story explains how the player came to be within the vicinity of the game, what set the mood, and so on.

## Writing the Game's Story

Part of the experience of picking up a new game is to delve into the game's instruction booklet to read up on the game's controls, characters, and the pre-game story. That's right, not only do you need a story for your game, but also you generally write a small pre-game story that precedes the action that takes place at the start of your game.

The pre-game story, much like the following one, sets the mood for your game (or at least for the beginning of the game), introduces the player to his alter-ego, and thrusts the player right into the actual story. For *The Tower*, I wrote the following pre-game story to let the player know his role and the kind of situation he is in at the beginning of the game.

The day's travel has gone well. After a quick stop in the quaint village of Dunsberry, our hero once again sets off to explore the rolling plains of the Eastern Lands. Thrice before he had adventured forth to those Lands—they were quickly becoming his favorite romping grounds, and for good reason. With each visit, our hero has found thrilling adventures, amazing treasures, and the most intriguing people he has ever had the pleasure of encountering.

> **NOTE**
>
> For your game, instead of writing a pre-game story in the game's instruction booklet, you might choose to include the story in your game. For example, when the player begins his first game, you might display the pre-game story immediately before the game commences.

With high hopes on his mind and the setting sun at his back, our lone adventurer journeys onward. If he makes good time, he should reach the village of Grandere before dawn. Once there, he will take a break for some well-deserved rest and relaxation before entering the center plains of the Lands, where he hopes to find a grand quest upon which to embark.

With a sudden, loud clap of thunder, the glorious dreams of conquest are swept from his mind. The day is ending—the sun setting. A shrill wind arises, bringing forth dark, rolling clouds. The night grows darker, and with every passing moment the wind grows stronger and the clouds thicken. A heavy hit of thunder echoes in the air, and a brief flash of lightning illuminates the plains in a sickly blue hue.

The storm forming over the plains is quickly building in strength. With one last deafening clap of thunder, clouds pour forth their watery innards. Relentlessly, the clouds unleash their fury—driving rain drenches the land, making further travel impossible. Our adventurer needs to find shelter, or this storm will claim his life.

Staggering forward, he comes upon a small clump of trees within which he hoists his tent. With his remaining energy, the now-exhausted adventurer closes the flap to his hastily erected tent and buries himself in his makeshift bed of water-logged hay and cloth. Unconsciousness soon comes over him, pulling him into a deep, restless sleep. Visions of hideous scaled demons fill his dreams. A grand tower looms over him, casting a dark shadow over the surrounding land. A small village appears in front of the hero—the way is clear; the village beckons him forth.

As you can see, although the story starts off fairly well for the would-be hero, circumstances turn everything upside down. A mysterious storm appears and forces him to take shelter. At the completion of this part of the story, the game-play begins. What the preceding story does not detail is what happens to the hero as he enters the village in his dream. What you need to do now is define the purpose of the story—that is, what the player (as the game's hero) needs to do from this point on in the story.

# The Purpose of *The Tower* Game

The story in the preceding section helps to set the mood for *The Tower* and provides a way for the player to be in a small village located by a dark, ominous tower. The purpose of the player of *The Tower* is to free a cursed village from the evil demons that inhabit the nearby tower. It turns out that the inhabitants of the village are forever trapped, only to be sacrificed one by one to the tower's evil demon lord. It is the job of the player to go into the tower and destroy the evil creatures.

Along the way, the player can harness various weapons and spells. Killing monsters increases the player's experience points. At specific points, the player's experience level and abilities are increased. At certain experience levels, the player is also able to use a newly learned spell.

Those items and spells will come in handy because the player must fight through five monster-packed levels (including the local village where the player can regain health and buy items). Each unique level demonstrates briefly what you can accomplish using the components created in this book. So, it's time to get a move on and see how those levels are designed.

# Designing the Levels

*The Tower* consists of five game levels (also referred to as *scenes*)—the village, the bridge, the ground level of the tower, the tower ledge, and the Evil Lord's room. A pre-rendered backdrop bitmap image represents each level, much like the backdrops developed in Chapter 13, "Mixing 2-D and 3-D Graphics Engines." All the game levels have a single bitmap that is split into six smaller textures. Each level also has a simplified mesh used to render each level's depth buffer.

The first scene, the village, is shown in Figure 20.1. The village is the starting point of the adventure and is where the character will find a place to heal and buy items. At the start of the game, when the player arrives, a single monster inhabits the village. Once the monster is dispatched, the village becomes safe enough for the villagers to come out of hiding.

**Figure 20.1**

*The village level, complete with locals, is where the player begins his adventure.*

Figure 20.2 shows the second level of the game, the bridge. Upon the player's first visit to the bridge, the village guard blocks travel across the bridge. Once the guard leaves his post, the player is free to move across the bridge and into the tower. Monsters randomly inhabit this level once the guard returns to the village.

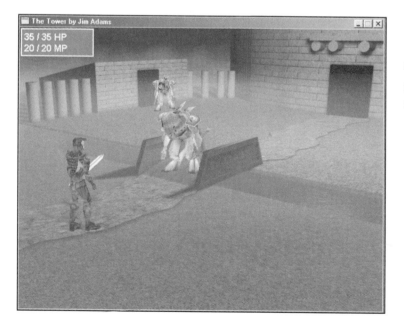

**Figure 20.2**

*The bridge to the tower is sometimes wrought with perils. Here, two monsters close in for the kill.*

The third level of the game, shown in Figure 20.3, is the ground level of the tower. The first time the player enters the tower, he sees two guards. As one guard attacks, the other one goes to warn his master of the player's intrusion. Subsequent visits to the tower's ground level leads to a random number of guards attacking.

In Figure 20.4, you see the fourth level, the tower ledge. The action moves outside as the player moves along a ledge leading to the last level. Here, the player engages in combat against Granite, the magically altered guard with the unfortunate duty of warning his lord of the player's arrival.

The last level of the game, the Evil Lord's room (see Figure 20.5) is where the game comes to an end. Within the round walls of this last level is the Evil Lord, demon supreme, and the beast responsible for the curse placed upon the village. The player must kill the Evil Lord in order to win the game.

Although limited in the number of characters, this sample game does a fine job of demonstrating characters. Check out the next section to see how to define the characters in the game, and the section "Controlling Characters in the Game," later in this chapter, to see how those characters are programmed in the project.

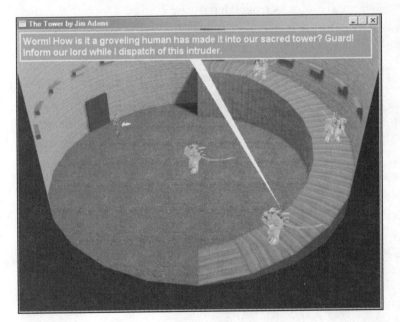

**Figure 20.3**

*Two or more guards initially patrol the tower's ground level. Here, one guard issues a command to another guard.*

**Figure 20.4**

*The tower ledge is home to the strong demon beast, Granite. Be careful; he packs a punch and is ready to make quick work of the player.*

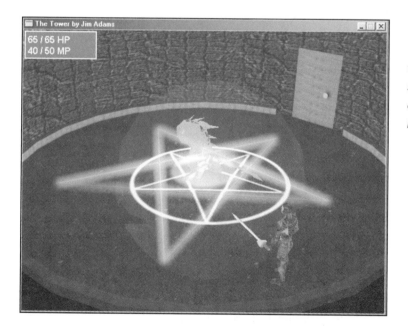

**Figure 20.5**

*The Evil Lord lies in wait for the player to visit his inner sanctum. Here, the Lord casts a power-up spell on himself.*

# Defining the Characters

Including the player of the game, a total of eight types of characters are in *The Tower* (with the game using multiple instances of those types of characters). Table 20.1 defines those eight types of characters. To understand those definitions, use the following legend:

- **Class.** The character's class.
- **HP.** Health points. The maximum number of health points of a character.
- **MP.** Mana points. The maximum number of mana points of a character.
- **Exp.** The amount of experience gained when a character is killed.
- **Gold:** The amount of gold a character is carrying (and drops when killed).
- **Atk.** Attack ability.
- **Def.** Defense ability.
- **Agl.** Agility ability.
- **Res.** Magical resistance ability.
- **Mnt.** Mental ability.
- **ToH.** A character's to-hit ability.
- **Speed.** Speed of movement measured in units per second.
- **Range.** Attack range measured in units.
- **Charge.** The charge rate of a character. This is in units per second. Once a character's charge is at 100, that character can perform an attack or magic spell.
- **Atk%.** Percentage of chance that a character will attack a nearby player.
- **Mag%.** Percentage of chance that a character will use a spell on a nearby player.
- **Spells.** The magic spells a character knows.

As an example for using the character definitions and the legend, take character #3. Granite (the character's name) is class 3, has 70 health points, 100 mana points, 200 experience points (given to the player when Granite is killed), no gold, and the following ability values:

| | |
|---|---|
| Attack: 20 | Movement speed: 16 units per second |
| Defense: 15 | Attack range: 16 units |
| Agility: 5 | Charge rate: 15 per second |
| Magic resistance: 10 | Percentage to attack: 80% |
| Mental: 10 | Percentage to use magic: 20% |
| To Hit: 800 | Knows spells: #4 (Groundball) |

## Table 20.1 *The Tower's Game Characters*

| Character #/Name | Description |
| --- | --- |
| 0: **Player** | The player of the game. Statistics listed are those at the beginning of game. Class 1, HP:25, MP:10, Atk:6, Def:3, Agl:2, Res:2, Mnt:2, ToH:800, Speed:150, Range:16, Charge:40. The player can learn spells 0 through 4 at the gain of each experience level, starting at level 2. Experience levels increase at 10, 30, 80, 150, 350, and 500 experience points. |
| 1: **Yodan Peon** | A weak demon. Class 2, HP:14, Exp:10, Gold:10, Atk:8, Def:1, Agl:1, Res:0, Mnt:0, ToH:700, Speed:64, Range:8, Charge:30. |
| 2: **Yodan Guard** | A stronger version of the Peon. Class 2, HP:28, MP:20, Exp:50, Gold:20, Atk:10, Def:5, Agl:3, Res:2, Mnt:2, ToH:800, Speed:64, Range:10, Charge:30, Atk%:80, Mag%:20, Spells:0, 2. |
| 3: **Granite** | Born from magic, this stone monster packs a wallop! Class 3, HP:70, MP:100, Exp:200, Gold:0, Atk:20, Def:15, Agl:5, Res:10, Mnt:10, ToH:800, Speed:16, Range:16, Charge:15, Atk%:80, Mag%:20, Spells:4. |
| 4: **The Evil Lord** | The king of chaos, this demon is the purpose of the player being trapped in the cursed village. Class 4, HP:150, MP:200, Exp:1000, Gold:500, Atk:25, Def:25, Agl:10, Res:40, Mnt:50, ToH:900, Speed:16, Range:16, Charge:40, Atk%:70, Mag%:30, Spells:0, 5, 6. |
| 5: **Elder** | The village elder. He heals you whenever spoken to. |
| 6: **Guard** | The village guard. He blocks passage across the bridge to the tower. |
| 7: **Villager** | This is the shopkeeper of the village. He sells magical items as well as healing potions. |

To make better sense of the character's definitions, I suggest loading up the MCLEdit project and using it to edit the Game.mcl file (both are on this book's CD-ROM; look for \BookCode\Chap16\MCLEdit). The only character in the list that you really need to be concerned about is the game's player, character #0.

The character statistics listed in Table 20.1 (and in the master character list used in the demo game—look for \BookCode\Chap20\ Data\ Game.mcl) represent the statistics when the game starts.

> **NOTE**
>
> You can edit the master character list (the MCL) using the MCL Editor program covered in Chapter 16, "Controlling Players and Characters."
>
> **Maximum health points: +10**
> **Maximum mana points: +10**
> **Attack: +2**
> **Defense: +1**
> **Agility: +1**
> **Magic Resistance: +1**
> **To Hit: +5**

Whenever the player kills a monster, the player's experience points rise a bit (based on the monster's experience points), and as the player reaches specific levels of experience points, his statistics increase by the following amounts:

As well as increased statistics, the player might learn a spell, depending on the experience level gained. The levels of experience points at which those experience "level-ups" occur are listed here, along with the spell learned:

- **10 experience points for level 2.** The player learns the Fireball spell (spell #0).
- **30 experience points for level 3.** The player learns the Ice spell (spell #1).
- **80 experience points for level 4.** The player learns the Heal Self spell (spell #2).
- **150 experience points for level 5.** The player learns the Teleport spell (spell #3).
- **350 experience points for level 6.** The player learns the Groundball spell (spell #4).
- **500 experience points for the level 7 (the final level).** No spells learned.

Notice that the last experience level achievable by the player is level 7. At that point, the player should be powerful enough to take on the Evil Lord at the end of the game.

# Assigning Characters

During the design of the sample game, it is necessary to assign each character a unique identification number. For example, the player is assigned the identification #0, whereas the village elder uses the identification #1. By assigning these identification numbers, the script engine knows which characters to use for performing certain actions, such as displaying dialogue or tracking flags in order to alter in–game-play. These pre-assigned identification numbers are as follows:

    0: Player character

    1: Village elder

    2: Village guard

    3: Village shopkeeper

    4: Monster in village at start of game

    5: Demon in tower who runs to warn the Evil Lord

    6: Granite, the rock demon

    7: Evil Lord

The only characters in the list shown here that do not have identification numbers assigned are the monsters the player encounters throughout the game. You assign these monsters identification numbers from 256 and up—there's really no reason at this point to predetermine these numbers. Think of the numbering order as a first-come, first-serve order of assigning monsters' identification numbers.

# Creating the Items and Spells

*The Tower* has eight items, each of which is shown in Table 20.2. Only a few of the items are for sale; the player receives the rest from other characters. Items with a price listed (shown by a number followed by *gp*) are for sale in the village level.

You use seven spells in the sample game—numbered from 0 to 6. Table 20.3 lists and describes each spell. You can also confer with the Master Spell List Editor program from Chapter 16 for the specifics on each spell. The game's spells are contained in the Game.msl file (located on this book's CD-ROM; look for \BookCode\Chap20\Data\ Game.msl).

## Table 20.2 *The Tower's* Game Items

| Item #/Name | Description |
| --- | --- |
| 0: **Gold** | The monetary unit of *The Tower* in gold pieces. |
| 1: **Sword** | A weapon that increases damage dealt from attacks by 15%. The player starts the game with the Sword. |
| 2: **Magic Sword** | A strong sword that increases damage from attacks by 50%. Price: 100gp. |
| 3: **Leather Armor** | A weak piece of leather-studded armor that reduces damage taken from attacks by 10%. Obtain from village guard. |
| 4: **Magic Plate** | A superior armor made from enchanted metals. Reduces damage taken from attacks by 50%. Price: 100gp. |
| 5: **Buckler** | A small weak shield that reduces damage taken from attacks by 5%. Obtain from village guard. |
| 6: **Magical Shield** | An awesome shield made from the scales of a red dragon. Reduces damage taken from attacks by 20%. Price: 100gp. |
| 7: **Healing Potion** | One quaff from this elixir cures 50 health points. Price: 10gp. |

To better understand the spells in Table 20.3, use the following legend:

- **Cost.** This is the amount of mana points it takes to cast a spell.
- **Cure.** A spell can cure characters with a specific class assigned to them. If a cure class is listed, casting the spell on a character instead heals that character for half the amount of intended damage.
- **2xDmg.** Much like cure, this is the class of character to which the spells cause twice as much damage as the spell normally would cause. For example, an ice spell will cause twice the normal amount of damage to a fire-based monster, such as the Evil Lord.

> **NOTE**
>
> You can view and edit the spells in *The Tower* by using the Master Spell List (MSL) Editor program covered in Chapter 16.

- **Effect.** This is the effect of the spell on the intended character. The four effects used in *The Tower* are alter health, teleport, cure ailment, and cause ailment. Each effect (except teleport) is followed by a number that represents the modifier value. Alter health is the amount to subtract or add to the target's health points. Cure ailment and cause ailment refer to the bit-flags used.

- **Target.** This is the spell's target type, which can be a single character (Single), self (the character casting the spell), or an area.

- **EffectRange.** This is the radius in which the spell's effect hits nearby targets.

- **TargetDistance.** This is the maximum distance the spell will travel to hit a target character. The character casting the spell must be within this distance to cast the spell at a target character.

## Table 20.3 *The Tower's* Game Spells

| Spell #/Name | Description |
|---|---|
| 0: **Fireball** | Hurls a ball of fire at a single enemy for light damage. Cost:5, Cure:4, Effect: Alter Health -10, Target:Single, EffectRange:32, TargetDistance:512. |
| 1: **Ice** | Chunks of ice encase the victim for moderate damage. Cost:10, 2xDmg:4, Effect: Alter Health -20, Target: Single, EffectRange: 40, TargetDistance:512. |
| 2: **Heal Self** | Restore 50 health points to caster. Cost:8, Effect:Alter Health +50, Target:Self. |
| 3: **Teleport** | Teleports the player to a nearby town. Cost:10, Effect:Teleport, Target:Self. |
| 4: **Groundball** | A rush of underground power that sends up chunks of rock. Cost:10, Cure:3, Effect: Alter Health -30, Target:Single, EffectRange:40, TargetDistance:512. |
| 5: **Concussion** | A huge blast of power that causes major damage. Cost:20, Effect: Alter Health -40, Target:Area, EffectRange:1024, TargetDistance:1024. |
| 6: **Evil Force** | The caster increases in power after being surrounded by a ball of darkness. Cost:10, Effect:CauseAilment 10832, Target:Self. |

Some of the preceding spells are unique to certain characters. For example, the Evil Force spell is used only by the Evil Lord—he casts it upon himself to increase his power (specifically raising his statistics and increasing his speed). Consult the game's master character list (\BookCode\Chap20\Data\Game.mcl) to determine which characters know which spells.

That's about it for the game's contents, spells, or characters, so now you can turn your attention to the game's scripts.

## Developing the Scripts

You control all *The Tower*'s game content, such as dialogue, through the use of scripts. The Mad Lib Script system covered in Chapter 14, "Implementing Scripts," is in use here. A single action template, Game.mla (see \BookCode\Chap20\Data\Game.mla), contains a number of actions that will be useful in your project. More than 200 lines in length, the game's action template is a little too long to list here, so I highly suggest that you open the action template while reading through this section.

The action template is split into the following six groups of actions:

- **Script flow.** Much like a standard program, scripts execute actions starting at the beginning of the script. The script flow continues until the end of the script. Scripts also use conditional if...then checking (checking the status of internal flags and variables) to change the flow of the script's execution.

- **Character control.** This includes adding, removing, moving, and setting the character's AI settings.

- **Item controls.** These check whether items exist and add and remove items in a character's inventory.

- **Barriers and triggers.** This group of actions enable you to add, enable, and remove map triggers.

- **Sound and music.** You can play various sound effects and songs using this group of actions.

- **Miscellaneous.** A group of actions that doesn't fit into the previously listed groups.

You use the preceding actions to construct the game's scripts. Once you construct the scripts, you can use them to control the flow of the game. You trigger the scripts used by the game in six ways—the player talking to another character, the player touching a map trigger, and a character reaching the last route point in an assigned route, entering a level, starting combat, or ending combat.

You name the scripts that are called when the player talks to another character according to the character's identification number, which you append to the word char. For example, character #2 has a script file named char2.mls that is executed any time the player clicks that character with the mouse.

You place map triggers in each level by using the script actions. Whenever a trigger is touched, a script executes. You name the map triggers by using the word trig followed by the trigger's identification number—such as trigger #4 using the script filename of trig4.mls.

When entering a level, use the word scene followed by the map level's assigned number. For example, when the character enters map #4, the script file scene4.mls is executed.

The final three methods of executing a script use a three-letter script filename that is appended with the associated character's identification number or map level number. For end-of-route scripts, you use eor followed by the character's identification number. For example, when character #2 reaches the last point on a route, the script named eor2.mls is executed.

> **NOTE**
>
> *End-of-route scripts* are processed whenever a character reaches the last point of a route assigned to that character.

For the start of combat, use soc followed by the map level number for the filename of the script. The same applies to the end-of-combat method, except you use eoc— for example, eoc3.mls, which is executed when combat ends in map level #3.

With the six script file-naming methods in mind, check out the following list of scripts used in *The Tower* (again, you can find the scripts on the CD-ROM):

- **Char1.mls, Char2.mls, Char3.mls, Char6.mls, and Char7.mls.** These are the scripts that are executed whenever the player clicks a character with the mouse. Characters 1, 2, and 3 are villagers, whereas characters 6 and 7 are Granite and the Evil Lord, respectively.

- **SOC1.mls, SOC2.mls, SOC3.mls, SOC4.mls, and SOC5.mls.** These are the start-of-combat scripts for each level. These play only the third assigned song in the game.

- **EOC1.mls, EOC2.mls, EOC3.mls, EOC4.mls, and EOC5.mls.** The end-of-combat scripts typically restore the music to the level's original song.

- **EOR0.mls, EOR4.mls, and EOR5.mls.** Only three characters in the game walk along routes—the player during the first level of the game, the demon that is attacking the player in the village at the start of the game, and the guard that runs to warn his Evil Lord.
- **Scene1.mls, Scene2.mls, Scene3.mls, Scene4.mls, and Scene5.mls.** Each scene starts by playing music and setting up all characters that belong in that level.
- **Trig1.mls, Trig2.mls, Trig3.mls, Trig4.mls, Trig5.mls, Trig6.mls, Trig7.mls, and Trig8.mls.** You use the map triggers solely to move the player from one level to another whenever the player tries to leave a particular level.

The majority of the scripts are basic. For example, check out the trig2.mls script:

```
Set character id=(*0*) direction to (*0.000000*)
Teleport character id=(*0*) to map (*1*) at
               (*100.000000*) (*0.000000*) (*-170.000000*)
```

The purpose of the trig2.mls, which is placed in the second scene (the bridge), is to teleport the character to the first map (the village) and to change the player's direction. To see a more advanced script, check out scene4.mls, which is executed when the player enters the fourth level:

```
// (*Store scene #*) //
Set variable (*1*) to (*4*)
_____

// (*Play scene music *) //
Play music (*1*)
_____

// (*Add teleporter triggers *) //
Add triangle trigger id=(*6*) at
              (*-177.00000*) (*200.000000*) (*-144.000000)
Add triangle trigger id=(*7*) at
              (*177.00000*) (*200.000000*) (*210.000000)

_____

// (*Add Granite is not killed already *) //
if flag (*8*) equals (*FALSE*) then
  Add character id=(*6*) definition=(*3*) type=(*NPC*) at
    XPos=(*170.000000*) YPos=(*0.000000*) ZPos=(*-60.000000*)
    direction=(*3.925000*)
  Set character id=(*6*) AI to (*Stand*)
EndIf
```

Although it's certainly much longer than the other scripts in the game, the scene4.mls script is fairly simple. The script starts much like the other scene scripts do—by storing the scene's map number in variable #1 and playing the level's associated song. From there, two triggers are placed in the scene that teleport the player back down to the ground level of the tower or to the Evil Lord's chamber.

Finishing up the script, flag #8 is checked, and if set to FALSE, a character is added to the level. This character, Granite, is character #3 in the master character list. In the game engine, Granite is assigned the character identification number 6. At first, Granite begins as an NPC (non-player character), merely standing still and waiting for the player to speak to him.

When he is spoken to, Granite's script is processed—some words are exchanged between Granite and the player, and then Granite's type is changed to Monster. When the player dispatches Granite, the end of combat script sets flag #8 to TRUE, thereby skipping the portion of the scene4.mls script that adds Granite to the map when the player reenters scene #4. Ingenious, isn't it?

In the section "Processing Scripts," later in this chapter, you find out how the scripts in *The Tower* are processed. As for now, move on to defining how the player interacts with the game.

## Defining the Controls

The player interacts with *The Tower* by using the keyboard and mouse. When working in the main menu (see Figure 20.6), the player uses the mouse to select an option. The options available on the main menu are as follows:

- **New Game**. Select this option to begin a new game.
- **Back to Game**. Return to a game already in progress.
- **Load Game**. Load and continue a previously saved game.
- **Save Game**. Save a game that's in progress.
- **Quit**. Quit the game.

To select an option, the player positions the mouse over one of the displayed options and presses the left mouse button to select that option. When playing the game, the controls are a little trickier.

The player uses the arrow keys to move a character and the mouse to home in on a character that will be the target of a spell or an attack. Pressing the up arrow key moves the player forward, whereas the left and right arrow keys rotate him. Position the mouse cursor over a nearby monster and left-click in order to attack. Note that

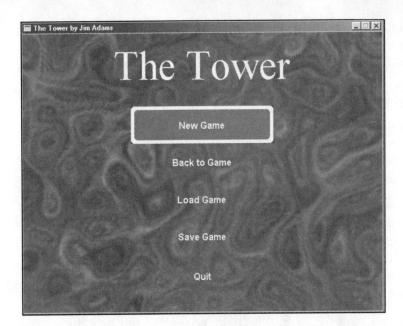

**Figure 20.6**

*The main menu enables the player to begin a new game, return to a game in progress, load a saved game, and quit the current game.*

the player must be close enough to a monster in order to attack the monster. Left-clicking an NPC effectively "talks" to that character. The player doesn't have to be close to talk to a character—simply clicking the character from anywhere on the screen does the job.

Pressing a number key from 1 to 5 while the cursor is over a character (other than NPCs) casts a spell with that character as the target. Pressing the number 1 casts the Fireball spell, 2 casts Ice, 3 casts Heal Self, 4 casts Teleport, and 5 casts Groundball. Spells 3 and 4 target only the player, so no matter which character you cast it on, it will always affect the player. Note that only known spells can be cast, and to determine which spells the player knows, enter the character status window.

During game-play, you can right-click to bring up the character status window. To use, equip, or unequip an item, left-click it. Right-clicking again closes the status window. On the lower-right side of the status window, you see the numbers 1 through 5, each representing a known spell.

To exit the game and return to the main menu, press the Esc key during game-play. If you're speaking to a character, left-click or press the space bar to continue the conversation; if you're bartering with the shopkeeper, left-click an item to buy it or right-click to exit the window.

# Laying Out the Flow

With all the design aspects in place, it's time to piece them into the whole game. The game is fairly linear—everything that will happen in the game is already laid out. The player has a straightforward path from the beginning to the end of the game, mainly because of the game's small size.

The game begins with the player walking into the village. With a few words to himself, the player catches glimpses of a demon walking through the town. A sacrifice appears to be in order this night, and the demon is in the village to escort the poor soul to his doom. Confused and curious, the player speaks up, only to be attacked by the monster.

After the player dispatches the vile demon, the villagers feel safe enough to come out and congratulate him for his heroic deed. It seems that the villagers believe the player is the savior of an old legend—a legend in which a liberator sets them free from the curse that traps all inhabitants within the neighboring lands (mainly the village and the nearby tower).

Not to let the good people down, the player heads off to the tower in the East. Along the way, the village's guard blocks the player's access across the only bridge to the tower. Only doing his duty, the guard refuses to grant the player passage across the bridge until the player returns to the village and obtains permission to cross the bridge from the village elder. The guard returns to town, leaving the bridge unguarded and accessible. If the player returns to town and speaks with the guard, the guard will give the player a piece of armor and a shield.

Back on track, the player continues back across the bridge and into the tower, where he encounters a few demons. This area's head demon orders another one to run and inform their master (the Evil Lord) of the player's arrival. Their master is not very happy with this news and apparently kills the messenger. Whenever the player enters this area, monsters are sure to attack.

The player moves up the ramp and through the second-level door, which leads to the tower's ledge where a seemingly unmovable stone creature (Granite) is waiting. Once spoken to, this creature attacks the player. Upon the creature's death, the way to the Evil Lord's chamber is open.

Entering the next chamber, the player finds the root of all the villager's troubles— the Evil Lord. After spitting out a few angry words, the Evil Lord attacks the player. This is the final battle, and once the Lord is destroyed, the game ends.

To create the preceding flow in the game, you must carefully lay out scripts that take control whenever the player speaks to certain characters, enters a specific area on the map, or enters a level. (Aspects that trigger the script are described in the earlier section "Developing the Scripts.")

Most of the scripts are easy to understand. There are the map triggers that transport the player to another map whenever the player tries to exit the current map. Clicking a character triggers another script. The more ingenious uses of scripts are those for checking whether a route point has been reached.

For example, at the start of the game, the scene1.mls script is executed. The player's type changes to an NPC and a route is assigned. This forces the player to walk into the village, and once he reaches the end of the assigned route, a new script takes over that adds the monster to the level. The monster then follows a route. When the monster finishes, another script takes over, displaying dialogue between the player and the monster. When the dialogue is over, the player once again changes into a PC character and combat begins.

At the end of combat in the village, the player walks to the center of town, triggering a script that teleports the player back into the town—at which time, another portion of the scene1.mls script runs adding the villagers to the town. The same style of scripting that processes scripts based on characters' routes is used in the ground level of the tower, where the demon runs to inform his master of the player's arrival.

The remaining scripts randomly add monsters to the maps, sometimes based on certain script flags. If the player kills Granite, for example, a flag is set that informs further scripts not to add Granite back in the level when the character enters the tower ledge map.

Using flags is perfectly demonstrated in *The Tower*—be sure to check out every script file in use to get an understanding of the flags in use. Again, you can find the game's scripts on this book's CD-ROM.

# Programming the Sample Game

The game design is relatively simple. The majority of the work is assembling all the pieces so that they work together. Imagine a game split into its major components, much as illustrated in Figure 20.7. If you've read the book sequentially, you learned how to deal with the components of your game in earlier chapters. Now, you just need to amass those components into a useable form.

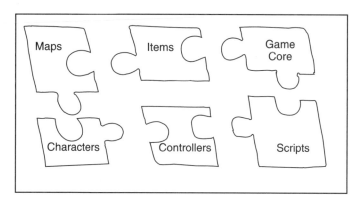

**Figure 20.7**

*Your game project is split into pieces, much like a puzzle. Each piece has its own purpose, and all pieces must be in place in order to create a full game.*

Throughout this book, I separated each game component and did not intermix them from chapter to chapter (with the exception of characters, which depend on a few components from various chapters). I didn't want you to be dependent on each and every component working together. In this way, you can pick the components that suit the needs for your project and apply what you learn quickly and easily.

Finally, in this chapter, you discover how easy it is to take all the separate components and paste them together to form a complete game. With the game's design, which is outlined in the earlier section "Designing the Sample Game" under your belt, you can focus on the programming side of creating the sample game.

Table 20.4 describes the components used in *The Tower* and the chapters in which those components are developed.

The sample game project (\BookCode\Chap20\Game\) consists of the following files, which represent the gaming components in Table 20.4.

- **Core_Graphics.h, Core_Graphics.cpp, Core_Input.h, Core_Input.cpp, Core_Sound.h, Core_Sound.cpp, Core_System.h, Core_System.cpp, and Core_Global.h.** These files compose the Graphics Core.
- **Frustum.h, Frustum.cpp, Window.h, and Window.cpp.** These files represent the viewing frustum and text viewing window objects.
- **Script.h, Script.cpp, Game_Script.h, and Game_Script.cpp.** The MLS system and derived processor class objects are in these files.
- **Charics.h and Charics.cpp.** The character inventory control system is in this duo of files.
- **Chars.h, Chars.cpp, Game_Chars.h, and Game_Chars.cpp.** These four files hold the character controller and derived character controller code for the sample game.

- **Spell.h, Spell.cpp, Game_Spell.h, and Game_Spell.cpp.** These four files contain the spell controller and derived spell controller class.

- **Barrier.h, Barrier.cpp, Trigger.h, and Trigger.cpp.** Barriers and triggers are handled through these files.

- **MCL.h, MIL.h, and MSL.h.** These are the master character, item, and spell list include files.

- **WinMain.h and WinMain.cpp.** These are the main application files that contain the application class code.

Don't be overwhelmed by the number of files in use here. You become familiar with the majority of the files throughout the book. To better understand how the files all work together, however, take them one at a time, starting with the main application class.

## Table 20.4 The Game Components

| Component | Description |
| --- | --- |
| Game Core | Except for the Network Core, every component of the Game Core is in use. Specifically, those components are the Graphics Core, System Core, and Input Core. The entire Game Core is outlined in Chapter 10, "Creating the Game Core." |
| Frustum and text windows | A viewing frustum component from Chapter 12, "Creating 3-D Graphics Engines," is used to clip unseen objects before they are rendered. Also, the text window class from Chapter 16 is used to display dialogue and other text in the game. |
| Mixed 2-D/3-D graphics engine | The same graphics engine developed in Chapter 13. This engine allows you to render 3-D meshes onto a pre-rendered 2-D backdrop. |
| Script and script controller | The Mad Lib Script system developed in Chapter 14 is used to develop the game's scripts. A script controller class from Chapter 16 is used to load and process those scripts. |

**Table 20.4** *(continued)*

| Component | Description |
|---|---|
| Items and inventory | A master item list combined with a character inventory control system, both from Chapter 15, "Defining and Using Objects." |
| Characters and character controller | A complete character controller (with supporting master character list), as seen in Chapter 16, is used to control and render characters in the game. |
| Spells and spell controller | The spell controller from Chapter 16 is used to manage and display spells. The master spell list (also covered in Chapter 16) is used to define the spells in the game. |
| Barriers and triggers | Barriers to block movement and triggers that execute scripts when touched, both systems are discussed in Chapter 17, "Working with Maps and Levels." |

# Structuring the Application

The main application is relatively small (if you can call just under 1,500 lines of code small). It has the job of initializing all the required components and tracking the game state (that's right, state-based processing is even used here).

First, you declare the application class. Although the class is incomplete at this point, throughout the rest of this chapter, the pieces fall into place, and the application class becomes complete. Now, check out the sections of the application class that set up the class data and initialize the game system:

```
class cApp : public cApplication
{
  friend class cSpells;
  friend class cChars;
  friend class cGameScript;
```

The application class begins by setting three friend class references. Those three classes, cSpells, cChars, and cGameScript, are the derived controllers for the spells, characters, and scripts, respectively. Each of those classes need special access to the application class, so you can make them friends.

The next portion of the cApp class declares a list of Game Core specific objects, all of which are private to the cApp class:

```
private:
    // Graphics device, camera, and font
    cGraphics       m_Graphics;
    cCamera         m_Camera;
    cFont           m_Font;

    // Input system and devices
    cInput          m_Input;
    cInputDevice    m_Keyboard;
    cInputDevice    m_Mouse;

    // Sound system, sound and music channels, and sound data
    cSound          m_Sound;
    cSoundChannel   m_SoundChannel;
    cMusicChannel   m_MusicChannel;
    cSoundData      m_SoundData;
```

> **NOTE**
>
> In Chapter 4, "Starting with C++," you read about using *friend classes.* When one class declares another one as a friend class, that friend class gains unrestricted access to the declaring class's data.

From the Graphics Core, you can see the use of the graphics, font, and camera objects. For input, there's the input system object, plus a device for each the keyboard and mouse. Rounding off the lot are objects for using the sound system, a single sound and music channel, and a sound data object for loading sounds.

A small bitmap stores the graphics used to display the player's charge bar (the amount of charge built up for attacking). You store this bitmap using a texture object. Following that, you include three text window objects to display various dialogue and screen text:

```
    // The options bitmap texture image
    cTexture        m_Options;

    // Text windows
    cWindow         m_Stats;
    cWindow         m_Window;
    cWindow         m_Header;
```

At this point in the application class declaration, you define a couple of miscellaneous private functions:

```
BOOL WinGame();  // Process win-game scenario

// Get the character where mouse is pointed
sCharacter *GetCharacterAt(long XPos, long YPos);
```

The WinGame function is called whenever a script encounters the win-game action. This action triggers the end of game, which returns play back to the main menu. GetCharacterAt is the function (discussed in Chapter 18, "Creating Combat Sequences") that determines which character a user clicks with the mouse.

Completing cApp are the class constructor and the overridden Init, Shutdown, and Frame functions, all of which you declare with public accessibility:

```
public:
    cApp();

    // Overridden functions
    BOOL Init();
    BOOL Shutdown();
    BOOL Frame();
};
```

At this point, the private variables are nothing without supporting functions. The functions you want to concentrate on now are the four public functions—the cApp class constructor, Init, Shutdown, and Frame.

## The cApp Constructor

You generally use the constructor for the application class to define the application window's class, style, size, class name, and application name, and the same applies here. The constructor sets define only the width and height of the window, the style of the window, the class name, and application title:

```
cApp::cApp()
{
  m_Width  = 640;
  m_Height = 480;
  m_Style  = WS_BORDER | WS_CAPTION |                    \
             WS_MINIMIZEBOX | WS_SYSMENU;
  strcpy(m_Class, "GameClass");
  strcpy(m_Caption, "The Tower by Jim Adams");
}
```

## The Application Init Function

As the starting point of the game, the Init function initializes the system (including the graphics, sound, and input systems), sets up the character and spell controllers, loads the master item list, pushes the main menu state, and carries out a few miscellaneous functions. Take a look at the Init function piece by piece to see what's going on:

```
BOOL cApp::Init()
{
  // Initialize the graphics device
  m_Graphics.Init();

  // Determine to use fullscreen mode or not
#ifdef FULLSCREENMODE
  m_Graphics.SetMode(GethWnd(), FALSE, TRUE, 640, 480);
#else
  m_Graphics.SetMode(GethWnd(), TRUE, TRUE);
#endif

  // Set perspective
  m_Graphics.SetPerspective(0.6021124f,1.33333f,1.0f,20000.0f);

  // Enable cursor
  ShowMouse(TRUE);

  // Create a font
  m_Font.Create(&m_Graphics, "Arial", 16, TRUE);
```

Graphics is the first order of business here—you initialize the graphics system and set the video mode. A macro definition at the beginning of the WinMain.cpp file determines whether to use a full-screen mode—just comment out the line to use a windowed mode. You then set the perspective to match that of the 3-D modeler used to render the backdrops. Finally, you create a font to use throughout the game and display the mouse cursor.

Next, you initialize the input system and create two device interfaces—one for the keyboard and the other for the mouse:

```
  // Initialize input and input devices
  m_Input.Init(GethWnd(), GethInst());
  m_Keyboard.Create(&m_Input, KEYBOARD);
  m_Mouse.Create(&m_Input, MOUSE, TRUE);
```

Rounding out the Graphics Core initialization code, you initialize the sound system and create the sound and music channels:

```
// Initialize the sound system and channels
m_Sound.Init(GethWnd(), 22050, 1, 16);
m_SoundChannel.Create(&m_Sound, 22050, 1, 16);
m_MusicChannel.Create(&m_Sound);
```

Now, you initialize the game-specific data and interfaces. You load the master item list from the CD-ROM (located in \BookCode\Chap20\Data) and initialize the character controller and spell controllers:

```
// Load the master item list
FILE *fp;
for(long i=0;i<1024;i++)
  ZeroMemory(&m_MIL[i], sizeof(sItem));
if((fp=fopen("..\\Data\\Game.mil", "rb")) != NULL) {
  for(i=0;i<1024;i++)
    fread(&m_MIL[i], 1, sizeof(sItem), fp);
  fclose(fp);
}


// Initialize the character controller
m_CharController.SetData(this);
m_CharController.Init(&m_Graphics, &m_Font,              \
    "..\\Data\\Game.mcl", (sItem*)&m_MIL,               \
    m_SpellController.GetSpell(0),                      \
    sizeof(g_CharMeshNames)/sizeof(char*), g_CharMeshNames, \
    "..\\Data\\", "..\\Data\\",                        \
    sizeof(g_CharAnimations) / sizeof(sCharAnimationInfo), \
    (sCharAnimationInfo*)&g_CharAnimations,            \
    &m_SpellController);

// Initialize the spell controller
m_SpellController.SetData(this);
m_SpellController.Init(&m_Graphics,                     \
    "..\\Data\\Game.msl",                              \
    sizeof(g_SpellMeshNames)/sizeof(char*),g_SpellMeshNames, \
    "..\\Data\\", &m_CharController);
```

The controllers have a lot of arguments in their initialization calls (refer to Chapter 16 to see just what each argument does).

You're about halfway through the Init function. At this point, you load a bitmap that contains the graphics that display the player's charge meter, and you create and position the text windows:

```
// Get the options bitmap
m_Options.Load(&m_Graphics, "..\\Data\\Options.bmp");

// Create the main, header, and stats windows
m_Window.Create(&m_Graphics, &m_Font);
m_Header.Create(&m_Graphics, &m_Font);
m_Stats.Create(&m_Graphics, &m_Font);

// Position all windows
m_Window.Move(2,2, 636, 476);
m_Header.Move(2,2,128,32,-1,-1,D3DCOLOR_RGBA(128,16,16,255));
m_Stats.Move(2,2,128,48);
```

Rounding off the Init function, you make a call to the derived script class that tells the script which application class interface to use. Following that, you push the first of the game states, the main menu, onto the state stack:

```
// Set script application pointer
m_Script.SetData(this);

// Push the main menu state, setting menu options first
g_MenuOptions = MENU_LOAD;
m_StateManager.Push(MenuFrame, this);

return TRUE;
}
```

## The Shutdown Function

What good is the Init function without a matching Shutdown function to shut down and free used resources in the game? The cApp::Shutdown function does just that; it clears the controllers, frees the states from the state stack, releases the script, and so much more:

```
BOOL cApp::Shutdown()
{
// Pop all states
m_StateManager.PopAll(this);
```

```
    // Free controllers
    m_CharController.Free();
    m_SpellController.Free();

    // Free script object
    m_Script.Free();

    // Free level data
    FreeLevel();

    // Free the options texture
    m_Options.Free();

    // Free the text windows
    m_Window.Free();
    m_Header.Free();
    m_Stats.Free();

    // Shut down sound
    m_MusicChannel.Free();
    m_SoundChannel.Free();
    m_Sound.Shutdown();

    // Shut down input
    m_Keyboard.Free();
    m_Mouse.Free();
    m_Input.Shutdown();

    // Shut down graphics
    m_Font.Free();
    m_Graphics.Shutdown();

    return TRUE;
}
```

## Processing Frames with the Frame Function

For every frame that the game is updated, the application class's Frame function is called. To limit how often the game actually updates, however, a timer is maintained that limits further frame processing to 30 frames a second. This process of limiting the updates takes up the first half of the Frame function, as shown here:

```
BOOL cApp::Frame()
{
  static DWORD UpdateTimer = timeGetTime();

  // Limit all frame updates to 30 fps
  if(timeGetTime() < UpdateTimer + 33)
    return TRUE;
  UpdateTimer = timeGetTime();
```

As I mentioned, the game is updated 30 times a second. Each frame that the game is updated, the keyboard and mouse's states are read in, and the current state is processed:

```
  // Acquire input devices and read input for all states
  m_Keyboard.Acquire(TRUE);    // Read keyboard
  m_Keyboard.Read();
  m_Mouse.Acquire(TRUE);       // Read mouse
  m_Mouse.Read();

  // Process state, returning result
  return m_StateManager.Process(this);
}
```

Chapter 5, "Programming with Windows and Application Basics," covers how state-based processing works. As states are inserted into the state stack, the uppermost state executes when cStateManager::Process is called, as shown in the Frame function.

# Using State-Based Processing

I developed the sample game to use state-based processing in order to effectively use the application class's processing structure. The game uses these four states:

- **Main menu state.** When executed, the game displays a main menu giving the player the option to start a new game, load a game, return to or save a game in progress, or to quit the game.

- **In-game state.** This state is used most often because it takes care of updating and rendering each frame of the game.

- **Character status window state.** Whenever the player right-clicks during game-play, he accesses the character status window. Here, the player can use, equip, or unequip items just by clicking them, as well as check on the character's statistics and known spells.

- **Barter window state.** When the player talks to the villager, the barter window opens in order to buy items. Click items to buy or press Esc or the right mouse button to exit.

You use a state manager object (refer to Chapter 5) to control the processing of these four states. Each state has an associated function that you declare in the cApp class:

```
// State-based processing manager and state functions
cStateManager m_StateManager;
static void MenuFrame(void *Ptr, long Purpose);
static void GameFrame(void *Ptr, long Purpose);
static void StatusFrame(void *Ptr, long Purpose);
static void BarterFrame(void *Ptr, long Purpose);
```

The four states control processing the user's input and rendering the results to the screen. The code for each state function is a little too much to list here, so rather than show each function's code, I will focus on the most important state function, GameFrame (which is called at every frame to update the player and monsters and to render the scene):

```
void cApp::GameFrame(void *Ptr, long Purpose)
{
  cApp    *App = (cApp*)Ptr;
  sCharacter *CharPtr;
  BOOL       MonstersInLevel;
  long       TriggerNum;
  char       Filename[MAX_PATH], Stats[256];
  float      MaxY;

  // Only process frame states
  if(Purpose != FRAMEPURPOSE)
    return;
```

Because this is a frame state, you can call the GameFrame function for one of three purposes—the state being initialized, the frame being processed, and the state being shut down. The GameFrame function uses only the update-frame purpose, so processing is returned if any other calling purpose is used.

> **NOTE**
>
> In Chapter 5, you read about using *calling purposes*. When using state-based functions, a calling purpose informs the state function about why it was called, whether to initialize data, process a frame, or shut down and release resources.

At the beginning of the GameFrame function is a quick check to see whether the Esc key has been pressed. If so, the main menu state is pushed onto the stack:

```
// Quit to menu screen if ESCAPE pressed
if(App->m_Keyboard.GetKeyState(KEY_ESC) == TRUE) {
  // Setup menu options
  g_MenuOptions = MENU_BACK | MENU_SAVE | MENU_LOAD;
```

In order for the main menu to know which options to display, you declare a global variable at the beginning of the application. This global variable, g_MenuOptions, is bit-encoded and uses the following macros to define them—MENU_BACK to display the back to game option, MENU_SAVE to display the save game option, and MENU_LOAD to display the load game option. Once you define the options, the state is pushed:

```
  // Push main menu state
  App->m_StateManager.Push(App->MenuFrame, App);

  return;
}

// If teleporting, then handle that first and return
if(App->m_TeleportMap != -1) {
  // Free level and process a new one
  App->FreeLevel();
  App->LoadLevel(App->m_TeleportMap);

  App->m_TeleportMap = -1;  // Clear out teleport map #

  return;  // No more processing this frame
}
```

Whenever the player needs to move from one map to another (such as calling the SetupTeleport function with the map number and coordinates to which to move the player), you set a global variable called m_TeleportMap to the correct map number for teleporting. The preceding bit of code checks each frame to see whether that variable has been set and teleports the player to the appropriate map.

Now comes the real bulk of the GameFrame function. At the start of the following block of code, you set a flag that records whether any monsters are in the map is cleared. From there, scan the entire list of loaded characters. If you find a monster character in the list, set the MonstersInLevel flag. Also, for each monster in the map, change its AI settings based on its action charge. For charges less than 70, set the monster's AI to wander (to let the monster wander around the map). If the charge is over 70, set the monster's AI type to follow the player (so that the monster is attempting to attack the player):

```
// Mark no monsters in level
MonstersInLevel = FALSE;

// See if any characters are in level. If any monsters,
// flag as such and change their AI to wander if their
// charge is less than 70, follow AI otherwise.
// Also, process whenever a character reaches a route point.
CharPtr = App->m_CharController.GetParentCharacter();
while(CharPtr != NULL) {

  // Alter monster's AI based on charge
  if(CharPtr->Type == CHAR_MONSTER) {
    MonstersInLevel = TRUE;

    // Change AI based on charge
    if(CharPtr->Charge >= 70.0f) {
      CharPtr->AI = CHAR_FOLLOW;
      CharPtr->TargetChar = g_PCChar;
      CharPtr->Distance = 0.0f;
    } else {
      CharPtr->AI = CHAR_WANDER;
    }
  }
```

If, on the other hand, an NPC is found on the map and that character has its AI set to follow a route, a separate function is called to determine whether that character has reached the last route point assigned. If the last point on the route has been touched, that character's end-of-route script is executed:

```
// Check if an NPC character has reached last route point
if(CharPtr->Type==CHAR_NPC && CharPtr->AI==CHAR_ROUTE) {

  // Was last point reached?
  if(App->LastPointReached(CharPtr) == TRUE) {
    // Process the route point script for character.
    sprintf(Filename,"..\\Data\\EOR%lu.mls", CharPtr->ID);
    App->m_Script.Execute(Filename);
```

```
        // Don't process any more this frame
        return;
    }
  }

  // Go to next character
  CharPtr = CharPtr->Next;
}
```

Once you are past the scan-for-characters phase of GameFrame, you compare the MonstersInLevel flag to the same flag that was stored from the last frame. If they do not match, either combat has started or ended, and the appropriate script is called:

```
// Handle start of combat stuff
if(MonstersInLevel==TRUE && App->m_MonstersLastFrame==FALSE)
  App->StartOfCombat();

// Handle end of combat stuff if combat over
if(MonstersInLevel==FALSE && App->m_MonstersLastFrame==TRUE)
  App->EndOfCombat();

// Remember if monsters were in this frame
// And reset player's charge to full if no monsters
if((App->m_MonstersLastFrame = MonstersInLevel) == FALSE)
  g_PCChar->Charge = 100.0f;

// Update controllers
App->m_CharController.Update(33);
App->m_SpellController.Update(33);
```

Next comes the point at which all characters and spells are updated. Because the cApp::Frame function is locked to update the game 30 times a second, all controllers use an update time of 33 milliseconds. Notice that before being updated, the player's charge meter is set to full if no monsters are in the level.

After the characters are updated, the trigger object comes into play. If the player walks into an active trigger, the appropriate script is executed:

```
// Check for triggers and execute script
if((TriggerNum = App->m_Trigger.GetTrigger(g_PCChar->XPos,  \
                                    g_PCChar->YPos,         \
                                    g_PCChar->ZPos))) {
```

```
sprintf(Filename, "..\\Data\\Trig%lu.mls", TriggerNum);
App->m_Script.Execute(Filename);

return;  // Don't process any more this frame
}
```

From this point on, you render the scene by calling the RenderFrame function from the application class. The RenderFrame function renders only the backdrop and character in the map—it's up to the rest of this function's code to draw the status window and charge meter:

```
// Position the camera for the scene
App->m_Graphics.SetCamera(&App->m_Camera);

// Render everything
App->m_Graphics.ClearZBuffer();
if(App->m_Graphics.BeginScene() == TRUE) {
  App->RenderFrame(33);
```

Again, you first render the scene by using the RenderFrame function, which takes as an argument the amount of time (in milliseconds) that the animations should be updated. You then draw the player's charge meter, but only if monsters are present on the map (as determined by the MonstersInLevel flag):

```
// Render the player's charge bar, but only during combat
if(MonstersInLevel == TRUE) {
  D3DXMATRIX matWorld, matView, matProj;
  D3DVIEWPORT8 vpScreen;
  D3DXVECTOR3 vecPos;

  // Get the world, projection, and view transformations
  D3DXMatrixIdentity(&matWorld);
  App->m_Graphics.GetDeviceCOM()->GetTransform(          \
                        D3DTS_VIEW, &matView);
  App->m_Graphics.GetDeviceCOM()->GetTransform(          \
                        D3DTS_PROJECTION, &matProj);

  // Get viewport
  App->m_Graphics.GetDeviceCOM()->GetViewport(&vpScreen);
  // Offset charge bar by character's height
  g_PCChar->Object.GetBounds(NULL,NULL,NULL,             \
                            NULL,&MaxY,NULL,NULL);
```

```
                // Project coordinates to screen
                D3DXVec3Project(&vecPos, &D3DXVECTOR3(                    \
                                         g_PCChar->XPos,                 \
                                         g_PCChar->YPos + MaxY,          \
                                         g_PCChar->ZPos),                \
                           &vpScreen, &matProj, &matView, &matWorld);


                // move 4 pixels right before displaying
                vecPos.x += 8.0f;
```

There are numerous matrix- and vector-related functions at work here—you use them to calculate the screen coordinates in which to draw the charge meter. To determine where to draw the meter, using the preceding D3DXVec3Project function, calculate the 2-D coordinates based on the 3-D world space coordinates of the player.

Now, you disable the Z-Buffer and draw the charge meter using the m_Option texture object as the source for the charge meter bitmap:

```
                // Display charge bar below player (flash when full)
                App->m_Graphics.EnableZBuffer(FALSE);
                App->m_Graphics.BeginSprite();
                App->m_Options.Blit((long)vecPos.x,(long)vecPos.y,        \
                                  0,0,16,4);
                if(g_PCChar->Charge >= 100.0f) {
                  if(timeGetTime() & 1)
                    App->m_Options.Blit((long)vecPos.x,(long)vecPos.y,    \
                                      0,4,16,4);
                } else {
                  App->m_Options.Blit((long)vecPos.x,(long)vecPos.y,      \
                          0,4,(long)(g_PCChar->Charge/100.0f*16.0f),4);
                }

                App->m_Graphics.EndSprite();
              }
```

During the game-play, you display the player's statistics at the upper-left corner of the screen—this includes the health and mana points, at their current levels and at their maximum level:

```
              // Draw the player's stats at top-left
              sprintf(Stats, "%ld / %ld HP\r\n%ld / %ld MP",              \
                g_PCChar->HealthPoints, g_PCChar->Def.HealthPoints,       \
                g_PCChar->ManaPoints, g_PCChar->Def.ManaPoints);
```

```
        App->m_Stats.Render(Stats);

        App->m_Graphics.EndScene();
    }
    App->m_Graphics.Display();
}
```

The GameFrame function ends up by calling EndScene and displaying the frame to the user. The remaining state frame functions are basic in nature, so I briefly explain them here, leaving it up to you to explore them as you work with the sample game on the CD-ROM.

You use the MenuFrame function to display the main menu, which, in all its glory, has a spinning texture-mapped polygon overlaid with the main menu options. The purpose of the MenuFrame function is to track which option is being selected and to handle the appropriate functions.

You use the StatusFrame function to display the player's statistics (health points, mana points, known spells, and so on) when the player's status window is displayed. This function handles equipping items and checking on the player's statistics. The last of the state functions, BarterFrame displays the store clerk's wares and allows the player to click-and-buy those items for sale.

## Dealing with Maps

The sample game is divided into five maps (scenes). Each scene uses six bitmaps, each of which is loaded as textures that are drawn to the display for each frame. The game also uses an underlying simplified mesh for each scene. These simplified meshes (as explained in Chapter 13) aid in properly drawing the 3-D characters that inhabit each scene.

To load and use the six textures, declare an array of cTexture objects (to contain the six bitmaps), a cMesh object (that contains the scene's simplified mesh), and a cObject object (that is used to render the simplified mesh):

```
long      m_SceneNum;           // The current scene number, 1-5
cTexture  m_SceneTextures[6];   // The six scene textures
cMesh     m_SceneMesh;          // The simplified scene mesh
cObject   m_SceneObject;        // The simplified scene object
```

A total of four functions are contained within the application class that is used to work with scenes. These functions are LoadLevel, FreeLevel, GetHeightBelow, and CheckIntersect. You use the GetHeightBelow and CheckIntersect functions, which are presented in Chapter 12, to check for mesh-to-mesh intersections. In the case of the game, those mesh intersections are used to determine when characters intersect with the simplified scene mesh.

The LoadLevel function loads the six scene textures and the simplified mesh and executes the script associated with loading the scene. An external file, which you see in just a moment, stores the position of the camera within each scene. Here is the code for LoadLevel:

```
BOOL cApp::LoadLevel(long Num)
{
  char Filename[MAX_PATH];
  FILE *fp;
  long i;
  float XPos, YPos, ZPos, XAt, YAt, ZAt;

  FreeLevel(); // Free a prior level

  // Record scene number
  m_SceneNum = Num;
```

The previously loaded level is now freed, and the new scene number is recorded. Now, you load the scene textures and simplified mesh:

```
  // Load the backdrop textures
  for(i=0;i<6;i++) {
    sprintf(Filename, "..\\Data\\Scene%u%u.bmp", Num, i+1);
    if(m_SceneTextures[i].Load(&m_Graphics, Filename) == FALSE)
      return FALSE;
  }

  // Load the scene mesh and configure object
  sprintf(Filename, "..\\Data\\Scene%u.x", Num);
  if(m_SceneMesh.Load(&m_Graphics, Filename) == FALSE)
    return FALSE;
  m_SceneObject.Create(&m_Graphics, &m_SceneMesh);
```

After you load the scene's mesh and create the scene's object, you are ready to determine the placement of the camera used to render the 3-D graphics. You place the camera in each scene by first creating a text file for each scene. Name these files cam1.txt, cam2.txt, cam3.txt, cam4.txt, and cam5.txt—each named according to its respective scene number (scenes being numbered 1 through 5).

Place a scene's camera by opening the appropriate text file and reading in six numbers, each of which is used to determine the camera's orientation in the scene. The first three numbers represent the position of the camera in the world, and the last three numbers are the coordinates to which the camera is pointed.

After you load the six numbers and orient the camera, call the cGraphics::SetCamera function to inform Direct3D of the new view transformation being used by the camera:

```
// Load the camera data
sprintf(Filename, "..\\Data\\Cam%u.txt", Num);
if((fp=fopen(Filename, "rb"))==NULL)
  return FALSE;
XPos = GetNextFloat(fp);
YPos = GetNextFloat(fp);
ZPos = GetNextFloat(fp);
XAt  = GetNextFloat(fp);
YAt  = GetNextFloat(fp);
ZAt  = GetNextFloat(fp);
fclose(fp);
m_Camera.Point(XPos, YPos, ZPos, XAt, YAt, ZAt);

// Position the camera for the scene
m_Graphics.SetCamera(&m_Camera);
```

After you position the camera in the file, the class clears a flag that determines whether monsters are currently in the scene (for combat processing) and then executes the script associated with the scene:

```
// Set no monsters in last frame
m_MonstersLastFrame = FALSE;

// Execute the script for loading this scene
sprintf(Filename, "..\\Data\\Scene%lu.mls", Num);
m_Script.Execute(Filename);

return TRUE;
}
```

There's not much to do in LoadLevel as you can see. The FreeLevel function is rather trouble-free as well. It frees the scene's textures and simplified mesh, removes every character from the character controller (except for the player, that is), and clears all spells currently being processed. Here is the complete FreeLevel function code (sans comments because the function gets right to the point):

```
BOOL cApp::FreeLevel()
{
  sCharacter *CharPtr, *NextChar;
  long i;

  // Free scene mesh and textures
  m_SceneMesh.Free();
  m_SceneObject.Free();
  for(i=0;i<6;i++)
    m_SceneTextures[i].Free();

  // Free triggers and barriers
  m_Barrier.Free();
  m_Trigger.Free();

  // Free all non-pc characters
  if((CharPtr=m_CharController.GetParentCharacter()) != NULL) {
    while(CharPtr != NULL) {
      // Remember next character
      NextChar = CharPtr->Next;

      // Remove non-PC character
      if(CharPtr->Type != CHAR_PC)
        m_CharController.Remove(CharPtr);

      // Go to next character
      CharPtr = NextChar;
    }
  }

  // Free all spell effects
  m_SpellController.Free();

  return TRUE;
}
```

# Using Barriers and Triggers

Both barriers and triggers are used in *The Tower*. Those components remain exactly as shown in Chapter 17, so you might want to refer to that chapter for details on using them. Only scripts have the ability to add barriers and triggers in the game.

You declare the barrier and trigger objects in the cApp class declaration as follows:

```
cTrigger        m_Trigger;
cBarrier        m_Barrier;
```

Again, nothing has changed in these interfaces, so now you can focus on how to control the characters in the game.

# Controlling Characters

The characters are the heart and soul of your game. The character and spell controllers developed in Chapter 16 are perfect for the sample game in this chapter. If you read Chapter 16, you probably recall that the controllers must be derived, so let's make that the first order of business here.

You derive the character controller in order to control the player of the game and to collision-check a character's movements against the maps. For *The Tower,* you can use a derived character controller, first pre-sented in Chapter 16, to manage all your game's characters. The first step to using the character controller in a game is to derive your own class from cCharacterController:

> **NOTE**
>
> You store the derived charac-ter controller class in the pair of files entitled **Game_Chars.h** and **Game_Chars.cpp.**

```
class cChars : public cCharacterController
{
  private:
    cApp        *m_App;

    BOOL PCUpdate(sCharacter *Character, long Elapsed,       \
                  float *XMove, float *YMove, float *ZMove);
    BOOL ValidateMove(sCharacter *Character,                 \
                  float *XMove, float *YMove, float *ZMove);

    BOOL Experience(sCharacter *Character, long Amount);

    BOOL PCTeleport(sCharacter *Character, sSpell *Spell);
```

```
        BOOL ActionSound(sCharacter *Character);

        BOOL DropMoney(float XPos, float YPos, float ZPos,        \
                        long Quantity);
        BOOL DropItem(float XPos, float YPos, float ZPos,         \
                        long Item, long Quantity);

    public:
        BOOL SetData(cApp *App) { m_App = App; return TRUE; }
};
```

The cChars class comes with only one public function, SetData. You use the SetData function to set the application class pointer in the cChars class instance. In addition, the cChars class overrides only the functions used to move the player and to validate all character movements. The remaining functions come into play when the player gains experience points from combat or teleports the character with a spell, when the character controller plays a sound, when a monster drops some money, or when a monster drops an item after being killed.

Because the derived character controller class requires access to the application class, you must precede all calls to the cChars class with a call to the SetData function. The SetData function takes one argument—the pointer to the application class.

The other functions, such as Experience, DropMoney, and DropItem tell the game engine that a monster was killed and that the game needs to reward the player with experience, money, and items dropped from a dying monster. These rewards are pushed aside until combat ends, at which point, the application class's EndOfCombat function processes them.

The PCUpdate is the main function of interest here. It determines which keys the player is pressing and what mouse button is being pressed. Now, take this function apart to see what makes it tick:

```
BOOL cChars::PCUpdate(sCharacter *Character, long Elapsed,        \
                        float *XMove, float *YMove, float *ZMove)
{
  float Speed;
  sCharacter *TargetChar;
  float XDiff, YDiff, ZDiff;
  float Dist, Range;
  char Filename[MAX_PATH];
  long Spell = -1;
```

The PCUpdate function starts off with the prototype and a few variable declarations. The PCUpdate function uses five arguments—the pointer to the character to update, the elapsed time (in milliseconds) since the last update, and three pointers to the variables that are to be filled with the directional movements in each axis of the character.

PCUpdate starts by first determining whether an update is in order (based on whether any time has elapsed) and continues by determining which keys (if any) are pressed on the keyboard. If the up arrow key is pressed, the character moves forward, whereas if the left or right arrow keys are pressed, the character's direction is modified, as shown here:

```
// Don't update if no elapsed time
if(!Elapsed)
  return TRUE;

// Rotate character
if(m_App->m_Keyboard.GetKeyState(KEY_LEFT) == TRUE) {
  Character->Direction -= (float)Elapsed / 1000.0f * 4.0f;
  Character->Action = CHAR_MOVE;
}

if(m_App->m_Keyboard.GetKeyState(KEY_RIGHT) == TRUE) {
  Character->Direction += (float)Elapsed / 1000.0f * 4.0f;
  Character->Action = CHAR_MOVE;
}

if(m_App->m_Keyboard.GetKeyState(KEY_UP) == TRUE) {
  Speed = (float)Elapsed / 1000.0f *                        \
                   m_App->m_CharController.GetSpeed(Character);
  *XMove = (float)sin(Character->Direction) * Speed;
  *ZMove = (float)cos(Character->Direction) * Speed;
  Character->Action = CHAR_MOVE;
}
```

For each movement that the player performs, such as walking forward or turning left and right, you need to assign the CHAR_MOVE action to the player's character. Notice that even though pressing left or right immediately rotates the player's character, the code does not immediately modify the character's coordinates. Instead, you store the direction of travel in the XMove and ZMove variables.

You then determine whether the player has clicked the left mouse button. Remember from the design of the sample game that clicking the left mouse button on a nearby character either attacks the character (if the character is a monster) or speaks to the character (if the character is an NPC):

```
// Process attack/talk action
if(m_App->m_Mouse.GetButtonState(MOUSE_LBUTTON) == TRUE) {

  // See which character is being pointed at and make
  // sure it's a monster character.
  if((TargetChar = m_App->GetCharacterAt(                \
                     m_App->m_Mouse.GetXPos(),           \
                     m_App->m_Mouse.GetYPos())) != NULL) {
```

The portion of code just shown calls upon the GetCharacterAt function, which scans for the character that is positioned under the mouse cursor. If a character is found, you determine which type of character it is; if it is an NPC, you execute the appropriate character's script:

```
// Handle talking to NPCs
if(TargetChar->Type == CHAR_NPC) {
  // No distance checks, just process their script
  sprintf(Filename, "..\\Data\\Char%lu.mls",             \
          TargetChar->ID);
  m_App->m_Script.Execute(Filename);

  return TRUE; // Don't process anymore
}
```

On the other hand, if the character clicked is a monster and that monster is within attack range, you initiate an attack action:

```
// Handle attacking monsters
if(TargetChar->Type == CHAR_MONSTER) {

  // Get distance to target
  XDiff = (float)fabs(TargetChar->XPos-Character->XPos);
  YDiff = (float)fabs(TargetChar->YPos-Character->YPos);
  ZDiff = (float)fabs(TargetChar->ZPos-Character->ZPos);
  Dist = XDiff*XDiff + YDiff*YDiff + ZDiff*ZDiff;

  // Offset dist by target's radius
  Range = GetXZRadius(TargetChar);
  Dist -= (Range * Range);
```

```
      // Get maximum attack range
      Range = GetXZRadius(Character);
      Range += Character->Def.Range;

      // Only perform attack if target in range
      if(Dist <= (Range * Range)) {

        // Set target/victim info
        TargetChar->Attacker = Character;
        Character->Victim    = TargetChar;

        // Face victim
        XDiff = TargetChar->XPos - Character->XPos;
        ZDiff = TargetChar->ZPos - Character->ZPos;
        Character->Direction = (float)atan2(XDiff, ZDiff);

        // Set action
        m_App->m_CharController.SetAction(Character,         \
                                          CHAR_ATTACK);
      }
    }
  }
}
```

Coming up to the end of the PCUpdate function, the controller needs to determine whether a spell has been cast at a nearby character. In the game, positioning the mouse cursor over a character and pressing one of the number keys (from 1 through 5) casts a spell:

```
// Cast magic spell based on # pressed
if(m_App->m_Keyboard.GetKeyState(KEY_1) == TRUE) {
  m_App->m_Keyboard.SetLock(KEY_1, TRUE);
    Spell = 0;  // Fireball
}
if(m_App->m_Keyboard.GetKeyState(KEY_2) == TRUE) {
  m_App->m_Keyboard.SetLock(KEY_2, TRUE);
  Spell = 1;  // Ice
}
if(m_App->m_Keyboard.GetKeyState(KEY_3) == TRUE) {
  m_App->m_Keyboard.SetLock(KEY_3, TRUE);
  Spell = 2;  // Heal Self
}
```

```
if(m_App->m_Keyboard.GetKeyState(KEY_4) == TRUE) {
  m_App->m_Keyboard.SetLock(KEY_4, TRUE);
  Spell = 3;  // Teleport
}
if(m_App->m_Keyboard.GetKeyState(KEY_5) == TRUE) {
  m_App->m_Keyboard.SetLock(KEY_5, TRUE);
  Spell = 4;  // Groundball
}


// Cast spell if commanded
if(Spell != -1) {
```

If a spell was cast, the controller determines whether the player knows the spell and has enough mana to cast the spell and whether the target character is in range:

```
// Only cast if spell known and has enough mana points
if(g_PCChar->Def.MagicSpells[Spell/32]&(1<<(Spell&31)) && \
        g_PCChar->ManaPoints >=                            \
        m_App->m_SpellController.GetSpell(Spell)->Cost) {

    // See which character is being pointed
    if((TargetChar = m_App->GetCharacterAt(               \
                    m_App->m_Mouse.GetXPos(),             \
                    m_App->m_Mouse.GetYPos())) != NULL) {

      // Don't target NPCs
      if(TargetChar->Type != CHAR_NPC) {

        // Get distance to target
        XDiff = (float)fabs(TargetChar->XPos-Character->XPos);
        YDiff = (float)fabs(TargetChar->YPos-Character->YPos);
        ZDiff = (float)fabs(TargetChar->ZPos-Character->ZPos);
        Dist = XDiff*XDiff + YDiff*YDiff + ZDiff*ZDiff;

        // Offset dist by target's radius
        Range = GetXZRadius(TargetChar);
        Dist -= (Range * Range);

        // Get maximum spell range
        Range = GetXZRadius(Character);
        Range +=                                          \
```

```
             m_App->m_SpellController.GetSpell(Spell)->Distance;

        // Only perform spell if target in range
        if(Dist <= (Range * Range)) {
```

At this point, the controller has determined that the spell can be cast. You need to store the coordinates of the target, the number of the spell being cast, and the player's action in the structure pointed to by the Character pointer:

```
// Set spell data
        Character->SpellNum    = Spell;
        Character->SpellTarget = CHAR_MONSTER;

        // Store target coordinates
        Character->TargetX = TargetChar->XPos;
        Character->TargetY = TargetChar->YPos;
        Character->TargetZ = TargetChar->ZPos;

        // Clear movement
        (*XMove) = (*YMove) = (*ZMove) = 0.0f;

        // Perform spell action
        SetAction(Character, CHAR_SPELL);

        // Face victim
        XDiff = TargetChar->XPos - Character->XPos;
        ZDiff = TargetChar->ZPos - Character->ZPos;
        Character->Direction = (float)atan2(XDiff, ZDiff);

        // Set action
        m_App->m_CharController.SetAction(Character,         \
                                        CHAR_SPELL);
      }
    }
   }
  }
 }
```

To finish up the player character update, the controller determines whether the player clicked the right mouse button, which opens the character's status window (by pushing the character-status state onto the state stack):

```
// Enter status frame if right mouse button pressed
```

```
    if(m_App->m_Mouse.GetButtonState(MOUSE_RBUTTON) == TRUE) {
      m_App->m_Mouse.SetLock(MOUSE_RBUTTON, TRUE);
      m_App->m_StateManager.Push(m_App->StatusFrame, m_App);
    }

    return TRUE;
}
```

In order to use the derived character class, the game instances the cChars class within the cApp declaration:

```
cChars              m_CharController;
```

With the derived character controller class out of the way, you are ready to derive the spell controller. But keep your eyes open; this is going to be quick.

> **NOTE**
>
> You store the derived spell controller in the files Game_Spells.h and Game_Spells.cpp.

```
class cSpells : public cSpellController
{
  private:
    cApp *m_App;

  public:
    BOOL SetData(cApp *App) { m_App = App; return TRUE; }
    BOOL SpellSound(long Num);
};
```

Much like the derived character controller, the derived spell controller has the SetData function, which tells the controller which application class to access. In the case of the SpellSound function, you use the application pointer to call the cApp::PlaySound function.

I hope you didn't blink because that's all there is to the derived spell controller! The only overridden function is the one that plays sounds; the base cSpellController class handles the rest of the functions. In order to use the derived class in the game, you declare an instance of it within the application class declaration:

```
cSpells             m_SpellController;
```

# Handling Bartering

Previously you read about how the BarterFrame state is used to render the bartering scene (see Figure 20.8) in which the player can buy items from a character.

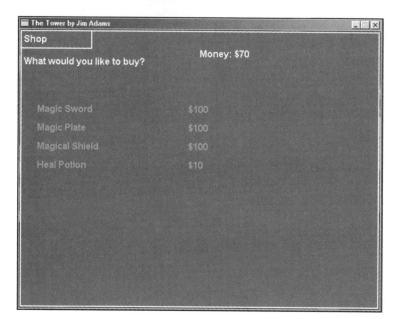

**Figure 20.8**

*The bartering interface displays items for sale at the left and the amount of money to spend on the item at the upper-right.*

How does that state know what items to sell? The only way the game initiates the bartering state is when a script triggers it via the Barter-with-Character script action. That action, in turn, calls cApp::SetupBarter, which configures the information needed for the BarterFrame function. This information includes the character that is selling the items, as well as the filename of the character inventory control system (ICS) item file:

```
BOOL cApp::SetupBarter(sCharacter *Character, char *ICSFilename)
{
  g_BarterChar = Character;
  strcpy(g_BarterICS, ICSFilename);
  m_StateManager.Push(BarterFrame, this);

  return TRUE;
}
```

The BarterFrame state function scans the ICS that was loaded, displaying every item contained with the character's inventory list on the screen. If the player clicks an item and the player has the appropriate amount of money, that item is bought. Once the player finishes dealing with the shopkeeper, the barter state is popped from the state stack, and game-play returns.

# Playing Sounds and Music

Music and other sounds are played during the game. Those game sounds, although somewhat cheesy (as you can tell, I'm no recording artist!), are played by a call to PlaySound. The only argument to PlaySound is an index number to an array of sound files that you declare at the beginning of the application code:

```
// Global sound effect filenames
#define NUM_SOUNDS 9
char *g_SoundFilenames[NUM_SOUNDS] = {
    { "..\\Data\\Attack1.wav" },
    { "..\\Data\\Attack2.wav" },
    { "..\\Data\\Spell.wav"   },
    { "..\\Data\\Roar.wav"    },
    { "..\\Data\\Hurt1.wav"   },
    { "..\\Data\\Hurt2.wav"   },
    { "..\\Data\\Die1.wav"    },
    { "..\\Data\\Die2.wav"    },
    { "..\\Data\\Beep.wav"    }
  };
```

Notice that the number of sound filenames is determined by the NUM_SOUNDS macro. You must ensure that a sound that doesn't exist isn't trying to be played—because trying to play a non-existent sound would crash the system. To play one of the valid sounds, you use the following function:

```
BOOL cApp::PlaySound(long Num)
{
  if(Num >=0 && Num < NUM_SOUNDS) {
    m_SoundData.Free();

    if(m_SoundData.LoadWAV(g_SoundFilenames[Num]) == TRUE)
      m_SoundChannel.Play(&m_SoundData);

    return TRUE;
  }

  return FALSE;
}
```

The PlaySound function needs to load the sound to play, using the cSoundData object. From there, the sound is played from memory. In much the same way that you call the PlaySound function, you can play different songs using the PlayMusic function.

The PlayMusic function also takes an index number into an array of song filenames, which you declare as follows:

```
char *g_MusicFilenames[] = {
    { "..\\Data\\Cathedral_Sunrise.mid" },
    { "..\\Data\\Distant_tribe.mid"     },
    { "..\\Data\\Escape.mid"            },
    { "..\\Data\\Jungle1.mid"           },
    { "..\\Data\\Magic_Harp.mid"        },
    { "..\\Data\\Medi_Strings.mid"      },
    { "..\\Data\\Medi_techno.mid"       },
    { "..\\Data\\Song_of_the_sea.mid"   },
    { "..\\Data\\Storm.mid"             }
};
```

No need for tracking the number of songs here (we're living on the wild side!), so you can jump right into the PlayMusic function:

```
BOOL cApp::PlayMusic(long Num)
{
  // Don't bother changing song if same already playing
  if(g_CurrentMusic == Num)
    return TRUE;
```

Before continuing, you want to check whether a song is currently playing. A global variable keeps track of which song was last played, and if that song is still playing, you don't need to start playing the same song again (the current song continues to play). If a new song is to be played, fade out the volume, free the current song, load the new song, and start playing the music playing:

```
  // Stop and free current song
  m_MusicChannel.Stop();
  m_MusicChannel.Free();

  // Fade music out, giving DirectMusic enough time
  // to finish up last song (or else new song doesn't
  // play correctly.  The 700 is based on play volume
  // of music, so adjust ahead.
  DWORD Timer = timeGetTime() + 700;
  while(timeGetTime() < Timer) {
    DWORD Level = (Timer - timeGetTime()) / 10;
    m_MusicChannel.SetVolume(Level);
  }
```

```
    // Load and play new song
    m_MusicChannel.Load(g_MusicFilenames[Num]);
    m_MusicChannel.Play(70,0);

    // Remember new song #
    g_CurrentMusic = Num;

    return TRUE;
}
```

# Rendering the Scene

During game-play, various states are pushed onto the stack—you use those states to determine which graphics to render to the scene. One thing common to most of those states is that their graphics are rendered over the map and characters. To keep things simple, you create one function that renders only the backdrop and character on the screen, leaving the remaining graphics to be drawn by the state functions. The RenderFrame function renders the map and character:

```
BOOL cApp::RenderFrame(long Elapsed)
{
    long i, j;

    // Render simplified mesh for z-values
    m_Graphics.EnableZBuffer(TRUE);
    m_SceneObject.Render();

    // Draw the backdrop (composed of six textures)
    m_Graphics.EnableZBuffer(FALSE);
    m_Graphics.BeginSprite();
    for(i=0;i<2;i++) {
        for(j=0;j<3;j++)
            m_SceneTextures[i*3+j].Blit(j*256,i*256);
    }
    m_Graphics.EndSprite();

    // Draw the 3-D objects
    m_Graphics.EnableZBuffer(TRUE);
    m_CharController.Render(Elapsed);
    m_SpellController.Render();

    return TRUE;
}
```

The map rendering is identical to that in Chapter 13 (refer to that chapter for more information on using the 3Din2D graphics engine). What's new here is rendering of the characters. A call to cCharacterController::Render updates the characters' animations and draws out their respective meshes. The function ends with a call to render the spells.

# Processing Scripts

Script processing controls the entire game's content. The content includes adding characters to the maps, displaying dialogue, and other functions not hard-coded into the game engine.

The sample uses the script and derived script class developed in Chapter 16. Whereas that script class is stored in the files script.h and script.cpp, *The Tower* stores the derived version of the script class that is used in the files game_script.h and game_script.cpp. Skipping the script class (because it remains the same as in Chapter 16), examine the derived script class, called cGameScript:

```
class cGameScript : public cScript
{
  private:
    // The internal flags and variables array
    BOOL         m_Flags[256];
    long         m_Vars[256];

    // The parent application object
    cApp         *m_App;

    // A text window for displaying messages
    cWindow      m_Window;
```

The scripts use an array of flags and variables (m_Flags and m_Vars), both arrays being 256 elements in size. Several script actions use these flags and variables to store and perform condition-checks to control the flow of script processing. Also, a pointer to the application class instance is stored (to call the application's functions), and a text window object is created to display the character's dialogue and other text.

Next in the cGameScript function, you define a sRoutePoint object that is used by the scripts to construct and assign a route to a character:

```
    // Route points for constructing a character route
    long         m_NumRoutePoints;
    sRoutePoint *m_Route;
```

From here on in, the majority of functions to follow are the script action process-ing functions. These functions are called when an action from the script is being processed—for example, the Script_SetFlag function is called when the SetFlag action is being processed from a script. Take a look at these function prototypes:

```
// Standard processing actions
sScript *Script_End(sScript*);
sScript *Script_Else(sScript*);
sScript *Script_EndIf(sScript*);
sScript *Script_IfFlagThen(sScript*);
sScript *Script_IfVarThen(sScript*);
sScript *Script_SetFlag(sScript*);
sScript *Script_SetVar(sScript*);
sScript *Script_Label(sScript*);
sScript *Script_Goto(sScript*);
sScript *Script_Message(sScript*);

// Character related actions
sScript *Script_Add(sScript*);
sScript *Script_Remove(sScript*);
sScript *Script_Move(sScript*);
sScript *Script_Direction(sScript*);
sScript *Script_Type(sScript*);
sScript *Script_AI(sScript*);
sScript *Script_Target(sScript*);
sScript *Script_NoTarget(sScript*);
sScript *Script_Bounds(sScript*);
sScript *Script_Distance(sScript*);
sScript *Script_Script(sScript*);
sScript *Script_CharMessage(sScript*);
sScript *Script_Enable(sScript*);
sScript *Script_CreateRoute(sScript*);
sScript *Script_AddPoint(sScript*);
sScript *Script_AssignRoute(sScript*);
sScript *Script_AlterHPMP(sScript*);
sScript *Script_Ailment(sScript*);
sScript *Script_AlterSpell(sScript*);
sScript *Script_Teleport(sScript*);
sScript *Script_ShortMessage(sScript*);
sScript *Script_Action(sScript*);
sScript *Script_IfExpLevel(sScript*);
```

```
// Shop/barter action
sScript *Script_Barter(sScript*);

// Item related actions
sScript *Script_IfItem(sScript*);
sScript *Script_AddItem(sScript*);
sScript *Script_RemoveItem(sScript*);

// Barrier related actions
sScript *Script_AddBarrier(sScript*);
sScript *Script_EnableBarrier(sScript*);
sScript *Script_RemoveBarrier(sScript*);

// Trigger related actions
sScript *Script_AddTrigger(sScript*);
sScript *Script_EnableTrigger(sScript*);
sScript *Script_RemoveTrigger(sScript*);

// Sound related actions
sScript *Script_Sound(sScript*);
sScript *Script_Music(sScript*);
sScript *Script_StopMusic(sScript*);

// Win game action
sScript *Script_WinGame(sScript*);

// Comment and separator actions
sScript *Script_CommentOrSeparator(sScript*);

// Wait action
sScript *Script_Wait(sScript*);

// Random number generation
sScript *Script_IfRandThen(sScript*);

// Force a frame to render
sScript *Script_Render(sScript*);
```

Whew! That's a lot of functions—and as I said, they directly relate to the script actions. Thankfully, the script action processing functions are brief and easy to process.

Chapter 14 presents the scripts, and Chapter 16 presents the script class, so you can refer to those chapters as needed, but now refocus on the cGameScript declaration:

```
// If/then processing function
sScript *Script_IfThen(sScript *ScriptPtr, BOOL Skip);
```

With all the if...then-related functions in the action template, it's easier to develop a single function that deals with the conditional processing. This function (Script_IfThen) takes a pointer to the next script function after the if...then action and a flag that determines the conditional state. If Skip is set to TRUE, all proceeding script actions are skipped until an Else or End script action is found, whereas if Skip is set to FALSE, the condition was met, and all script actions are processed until an Else or End script action is found. Note that the Else script action toggles the Skip flag (from TRUE to FALSE, and vice versa), allowing for true if...then...else processing.

The cGameScript declaration finishes with two more private functions—the first, Release, is called to free the script's internal data whenever a script completes processing. The second function, Process, contains a large switch statement that sends off the script actions to be processed by their respective functions (exactly as shown in Chapter 16):

```
// The overloaded processing functions
BOOL     Release();
sScript *Process(sScript *Script);

public:
  cGameScript();
  ~cGameScript();

  BOOL SetData(cApp *App);
  BOOL Reset();

  BOOL Save(char *Filename);
  BOOL Load(char *Filename);
};
```

The cGameClass finishes with the public function prototypes—you have the constructor, the destructor, the SetData function that records the application class instance pointer, a function to reset all flags and variables, and a duo of functions to save and load the flags and variables to a file.

You insert the derived script class, `cGameScript`, into the `cApp` declaration for the main application's use:

```
cGameScript      m_Script;
```

Even though the `m_Script` object is declared using private accessibility, most of the objects in the game use the script object. Now the reasons for declaring those friend classes in the application class declaration make sense!

## Assembling the Pieces

You are now more than familiar with the individual pieces of the puzzle. With the sample game on this book's CD-ROM, you'll get a true hands-on experience putting those pieces together! You learned about how the components are defined, developed, and coded. With a call to the `cApp::Init` function, followed by repeated calls to `cApp::Frame`, the game comes alive! The scripts execute, characters interact, spells and attacks go flying. Each component pulls its weight, and they all work together to form the whole.

When exploring the game project, I suggest starting with the WinMain.h and WinMain.cpp files; those files contain the application class that forms the application framework. As detailed in this chapter, you can follow the flow of the program, from initialization to shutdown.

# Wrapping Up Creating Games

Despite its size and simplicity, the example program in this chapter demonstrates the potential use of all the information I've shared in this book. Just imagine what you can do with your game project using the methods shown in this and other chapters! By understanding how each piece works individually and then by assembling the pieces and understanding how they all work together, you are prepared to create any kind of role-playing game.

By using an underlying library of functions to handle the graphics, sound, and input, your game-creation process can really take off. No longer must you worry about the low-level stuff. Instead, the components used to control the game-play take precedence; you can spend *your* time controlling characters, loading and drawing maps, and using items and scripts. When you develop these components, you will have created your own sample game.

Your next step is to take the sample game and modify it. Dig into its roots. Find out how it works. Change the scripts, add new NPCs and monsters, and add more levels. When you understand exactly how and why everything works, you'll realize just how easy it is to design and assemble a viable—and winning—game.

## Program on the CD-ROM

The following program is located on this book's CD-ROM. It contains the entire source code for *The Tower* game:

◆ **The Tower.** The sample game, *The Tower,* is a complete game project that takes everything you've learned in this book and puts it all together in an easy-to-understand package. Location: \BookCode\Chap20\The Tower\.

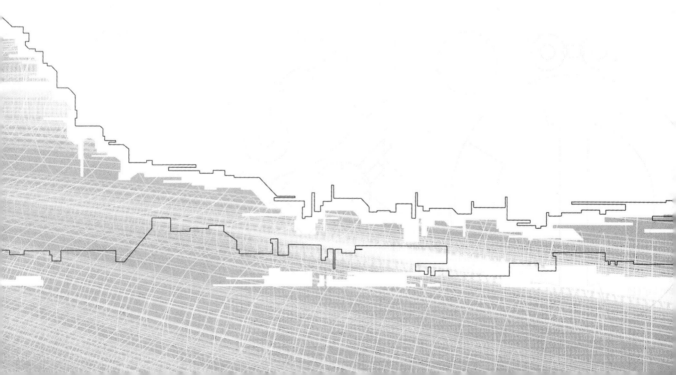

# CHAPTER 21

# Marketing and Publishing Your Game

Your game is complete, and the gaming world eagerly awaits its release. What's that? You don't know how to get your game published. Don't worry; this chapter tells you how to present your game to prospective publishing companies and how to put your product on the market yourself.

In this chapter, you learn about the following:

- How to prepare a proposal
- How to contact and deal with publishing companies
- How to manage do-it-yourself publishing

## Submitting Your Game

The question is, do you create your game before or after you contact a publisher? If creating games is your sole source of income, there's no choice. You want to receive your money upfront—to keep you going while you're developing your game. If you program as a hobby, you will probably do the majority of the work and then look for a publisher. Whichever choice you make, one point stands— you have to pitch your wares.

Preparing your game for submission (whether it's nearly complete or just a concept) is a major deal. Here are the elements that I suggest including in your submission packet:

- Proposal letter
- Marketing analysis
- Design document
- Budget
- Schedule
- Game demo (with uninstaller)

Although you can include much more information in a game submission, the preceding list covers the basics. Now, take a closer look at each element.

# Writing the Proposal Letter

The first place to start is with the *proposal letter*. This letter should contain the following components:

- A table of contents
- An introduction of your company or team
- Product highlights
- An overview of the product
- Non-Disclosure Agreement (NDA)

The *table of contents* enables the publisher to navigate quickly through the various aspects of your game submission (the marketing analysis, design document, and so on).

The *introduction* of your company or team should include contact information, history (if you've published previous games), available licensing that you have obtained, and names of team members. Then you disclose some of the key points of your project—licensing rights (say that you have the license for *The Matrix*!), graphics effects, marketing fringes, and so on.

You don't have to go into much detail in these highlights; that's what the *product overview* is for. Think of the product overview as a scaled-down version of the design document. You are showing the best points of the game in more detail, while not overloading the reader with useless details.

Finally (and this is optional), you can provide a standard NDA *(Non-Disclosure Agreement)* that the publisher signs in order to continue procuring an agreement with you. However, don't hold up the transaction waiting for the publisher to sign the NDA (and don't worry; publishers are not in the practice of stealing games). Just remember that in your submission packet, you want to include enough to whet publishers' appetites, but not anything that will hinder their vision of your game. God Games has an excellent NDA form that you can download and incorporate into your proposal (go to http://www.godgames.com).

# Performing Marketing Analysis

Next in line for your gaming proposal is the *marketing analysis*. The purpose of the marketing analysis is to check out the market to see who wants what, what is already on the market, and how your product might appeal to the gaming world. Don't skimp here. A publishing company will not research the market for you, so you'll have to tell them what's already out there and why your product is worth publishing.

For example, imagine that you're creating a first-person shooter game. Anyone who has played games has probably seen more than 20 first-person shooters, each one just like the others. How will your game stand out in the crowd? Will marketing it be worth pursuing in such a flooded market? These are some of the issues that you need to convey in your marketing analysis.

Assume that you think your game has some great features that will make it better than the rest. You must capitalize on those features, and you must help the publisher appreciate those features. Now, you need to find out whether other games have features in common with your game's features. Write down those games noting their features, publishers, retail prices, and why your game beats them hands down.

Finally, throw in testimonials such as letters and e-mails from players who have seen or tested your game. You want a publisher to see a typical reaction from the marketplace.

# Including Your Design Document

You've done the deed and written your design document, haven't you? Well, if you haven't then now is the time! A game submission must include a design document. Although Chapter 2, "Exploring RPG Design Elements," discusses how to write a design document, it deals only with the programming aspects of designing a document. Now, you are ready for a more detailed discussion on actually designing a document.

When designing your game, a major goal is to keep your "audience" in mind. You need to provide enough information on every aspect of the game so that anyone can understand how to create it (from their point of view, of course). This includes the game's story, controls, characters, items, technology engines, and so on.

# Calculating Budgets and Determining Schedules

As with anything, creating games require costs and schedules. You must develop a budget sheet as well as a development schedule. Your budget is very important; if you're just starting your project, you will need to sustain yourself during the entire development time. In addition, you might need to consider the compensation of teammates.

Your budget should include the following information (at a minimum):

- Payments to team members (per hour, salary, or total)

- Special packaging costs (extras that you want to package with your game, for example)
- Total cost of development

With your budget in hand, it's time to construct your schedule. This is your timetable, and you want to maintain it as best you can. The main elements in your schedule are the *milestones*. The milestones mark the major developmental targets, from the completion of one component to another. For example, imagine that your first milestone is completion of your sound engine within two weeks. In that case, two weeks from the start of development, you expect the sound engine to be completely ready to go.

Although that is a simple example, your real milestone markers should be quite detailed and include every aspect of your game, including engines, art, music, and test runs. That's right; you are expected to provide test runs of your game to demonstrate the quality of your game. You typically provide three test runs: *alpha*, *beta*, and *final beta*.

The alpha test version demonstrates the basics of your game, such as how the engines work, how specific graphics look, and whether the game development is going in the direction the design document dictates. You can have multiple alpha versions, each demonstrating various aspects of your game. Just remember that the alpha version represents a very early version of your game.

The beta represents your game after it is well under way. The majority of the underlying game should be in place, with some minor, cosmetic issues still being resolved. In this version, beta testers begin testing your game for bugs. Essentially, they check for actions or conditions that might cause your game to crash or to do something else that it isn't intentionally designed to do.

Using the information received from the first beta, you construct and test the final beta. At this point, all known bugs should have been eliminated, and the game is close to completion. Remaining issues should be only very minor ones, such as title credits and the like. This is the version that you give to your publisher and that the publisher uses to begin marketing your game.

# Including a Game Demo

Before dedicating resources to help you create your game, a publisher might ask you for a small demo version of your game. This demo needs to focus on certain important aspects of your game. For example, a publisher might want to see the combat engine in action, so you demonstrate your game by creating a menu of the things shown in your game. To show off the combat sequence, you might wow the publisher with the biggest, "baddest" monster and the coolest combat effects.

Don't overload the demo with useless game-play. You want publishers to be able to instantly get into the game and play or demonstrate it. Even better at times is to create a self-playing demo that demonstrates the best parts, skipping an interactive approach.

> **CAUTION**
>
> Whether you create an interactive or self-running demo, always make sure that you carefully check it for viruses and be sure to include an uninstall program. Nothing will get your name drop-kicked out the door faster than sending a publisher a virus-infested game demo.

# Communicating with Companies

Once you have your submission complete, grab a list of companies to contact regarding your proposal (you can find a list in the section "Considering Which Publishers to Contact," later in this chapter). Starting at the top of the list, call or e-mail each company.

Your first goal is to find the right person to contact; just ask for the name of the person in charge of submissions. This is the person you want to deal with—no one else. When communicating with that person, always use his name, never something as generic as Dear Sir/Madame or the like. Professionalism is the key here; in your approach, show that you are a qualified person worth dealing with.

After you know whom to contact, your next step is to send a letter explaining what you are presenting. Keep this letter short and succinct. Raise major points about your product, spelling out the key features. This letter is the teaser that determines the publisher's initial interest in (or lack of interest in) dealing with you. Don't worry if you're shot down at first; just keep moving down the list of publishers.

> **NOTE**
>
> Try imagining yourself as the publisher. Publishers want a product that they perceive as desirable and that you will deliver on their time. To them, games are merchandise, and they want to be able to sell this merchandise as quickly and cleanly as possible. Meet their criteria, and things should go smoothly.

When you receive a nibble from a publisher, it's time to start showing what you have to offer. Mail your submission packet (see the earlier section " Submitting Your Game" for items to include in the packet) and keep in touch with the publisher. You want to know the process your submission is going to take from mailing it to them to final approval.

# Dealing with Rejection

When a publishing company rejects your submission, trust me—it's not the end of the world. In fact, you are likely to be rejected a number of times, and it's even possible that your game will go unpublished.

Think of rejection as a way to learn from your mistakes (even if you're not making mistakes). You have to see it from the company's viewpoint. The publisher wants a product that is going to make money. If your game has market appeal, the company will most likely consider publishing your game. If they think that your game doesn't fit their marketing model, they'll pass it by.

If your game isn't accepted—and if you're otherwise lucky—you'll receive a good explanation about why not. Take that explanation for all it's worth—determine exactly why it was rejected. If your graphics weren't fancy enough, the story was lagging, or the concept was too plain, adjust that aspect of your game and resubmit it. Beware! Don't change one small aspect of your submission and then resubmit it; that would be wasting your time and the publisher's.

# Receiving the Acceptance Letter

All right! You've received your acceptance letter (or at least a letter that furthers the publishing company's interest in your game), and you've got some celebrating to do! Actually, don't count your chickens before they hatch. You still must deal with quite a few things before your game hits the shelf. You need to nail down contracts, schedules, and budgets (if that's part of the deal), and so on. You need to pay close attention to the contracts and how they are negotiated.

# Negotiating Your Contract

Behind every deal is a contract, and negotiating the terms of your contract is important. Your first step is to consider hiring a lawyer to examine your contract. The legalese in contracts can be confusing at times, and you need to understand all the fine lines. Remember the old saying, "What the big print gives, the small print takes."

Typical contracts will outline (usually in full detail) exactly what is expected of you, from start to finish. A good contract should outline the schedule, budget, and product expectations. You should also try to get marketing details in the contract, such as what the publishing company will do to advertise your game.

> **CAUTION**
>
> Take your time perusing the contract. Some of the fine print might contain something that you won't like. Most contracts are not written in stone, so try to get what you don't like changed, but don't go too far. Remember that each publishing company has a set way of doing certain things—for example, the publisher may have the right to set milestones, payment arrangements may be different than expected, or your licensing rights to the game may need to be transferred to the publishing company.

# Considering Which Publishers to Contact

This section contains a few game publishing companies that you might like to contact about your commercial game. Each listing contains a general description of the company and its contact information.

- **Activision.** One of the big boys that helped start it all, Activision publishes, develops, and distributes around the world, targeting a number of gaming platforms from PCs to home gaming consoles such as PlayStation 2, Dreamcast, GameBoy Advance, and Xbox. Several development companies call Activision "home," and with hard work, so can you.

    Activision, Incorporated
    3100 Ocean Park Boulevard
    Santa Monica, California 90405
    310-255-2000
    http://www.activision.com

- **Electronic Arts.** This conglomerate is one of the largest game publishing companies with which you're likely to deal. Its list of labels includes Origin

Systems, Fox Interactive, and Westwood Studios. This is the big leagues, and getting a deal with a company like this one is a godsend.

> Electronic Arts, Inc.
> 209 Redwood Shores Parkway
> Redwood City, CA 94065-1175
> 650-628-1500
> http://www.ea.com

- **Gathering of Developers.** Gathering of Developers is a publishing company that caters to the independent developers *(indies)*. These are the guys responsible for bringing you games such as *Oni, Railroad Tycoon II, Age of Wonders, 4x4 Evolution, Heavy Metal: F.A.K.K.2,* and *Rune.*

> Gathering of Developers
> 2700 Fairmount Street
> Dallas, TX 75201
> 212-696-2000
> http://www.godgames.com
> submissions@godgames.com

- **Infogrames.** With powerhouse games such as *Alone in the Dark, Unreal Tournament,* and *Driver,* Infogrames is a major contender worth checking out! Not only does it have great games, but also it has the licensing rights behind major names and productions—for example, Warner Bros., Inc.; "Looney Toons," and "Mission Impossible."

> Infogrames, Inc.
> 417 Fifth Avenue
> New York, NY 10016
> 212-726-6500
> http://www.infogrames.com

- **Microsoft Corp.** That's right, even the big M publishes games, and with the recent release of its Xbox gaming console, the company's reach into the gaming market expands. Getting a deal with Microsoft might seem like a dream, but one that is certainly achievable.

> Microsoft Corp.
> One Microsoft Way North Office 2211
> Redmond, WA 98052-6399
> 425-882-8080
> http://www.microsoft.com

- **Take2 Interactive.** Take2 is a large publisher that currently owns development studios such as TalonSoft, Tarantula Studios, and Alternative Reality. Take2 has business relationships with the Gathering of Developers. It publishes games for the PC, Dreamcast, PlayStation 2, N64, and GameBoy Color.

    Take2 Interactive Software, Inc.
    575 Broadway
    New York, NY 10012
    212-334-6633
    http://www.take2games.com

- **Wizard Works.** Another value-ware publisher, Wizard Works has a vast distribution channel that makes it easy for games to be seen. If you're working on a small- to mid-size project and you think value (discount) software is the way to go, give Wizard Works a jingle.

    The Wizard Works Group
    2155 Niagara Lane North, Ste. 150
    Plymouth, MN 55447
    763-249-7600
    http://www.wizardworks.com

- **Xtreme Games, LLC.** Xtreme games is a value-ware (discount software) game publishing company led by André LaMothe and crew. It not only publishes games, but also offers services such as access to its collection of gaming code, including 2-D and 3-D engines, tools, and DirectX add-ons, plus the company can hook you up with the resources you need—music, art, sound, and much more!

    Xtreme Games, LLC
    P.O. BOX 641744
    San Jose, CA 95164-1744
    925-736-2098
    http://www.xgames3d.com
    questions@xgames3d.com

# Do-It-Yourself Publishing

In addition to publishing through a large commercial company, you can distribute your game as shareware. In fact, major gaming companies such as id Software, Inc. (the creators of *Doom*) made shareware distribution a major part of their mainstream commercial marketing and distribution.

With shareware, you give your prospective buyers a chance to try out your game before they buy it. If they like it, they can buy it direct from you. There's no need for fancy boxing, marketing, or other such sales tactics; your game sells itself. Moreover, add the power of Internet distribution to your arsenal, and you'll have it made!

If you're interested in trying the do-it-yourself route, you begin by getting the word out.

# Advertising

The key to selling your game is advertising it to your potential customers. While you can find many ways to advertise, some of those methods work like a charm and others fail miserably.

If you're serious about advertising your game, you'll need to publish ads in magazines and on Web sites; you can also package ads with other products (for example, include a small pamphlet with your game's advertisement). Of course, these media can involve considerable expense. You might go to your favorite gaming zones and check out their advertising rates—those Web sites might be a cheaper alternative. You might even be able to work with a banner company to randomly display your ads on, possibly, millions of Web sites!

Gaming magazines are solid ground for getting results, but at a high cost. Some printed advertisements can cost you thousands, but they might be worth it. Again, check out the magazines' advertisement indexes; you should find information on contacting prospective magazine publishing companies to work out a deal for your ads.

Last, there's always word of mouth. If you belong to a gaming zone that has a message forum, why not "pitch" your game? You might generate thousands of visits to your gaming Web page with this single advertising technique.

Once your advertising is in place, it's time to give potential buyers a "taste" of your product.

# Using a Try-Before-You-Buy Approach

True to the nature of shareware, your game needs a scaled down (or shortened) demo version that is free for all to try. Design the demo so that players can finish a single mission or go on a quest to kill the first major bad guy in the game. You want to give the player a sufficient idea of how the game works and what it has to offer.

In do-it-yourself, shareware publishing, don't forget that your game demo is an additional medium for selling your game, so make it good. Include instructions on ordering the full product, perhaps along with a few incentives, such as an offer to buy two games and get the third one free. The bottom line is to sell your game!

> **TIP**
>
> A game demo is the perfect place for advertising! You can include messages about your other game projects and information about the full version of the demo they are trying out.

# Selling Your Product

Now comes the best part—selling your game! If you've done your duty, players are demanding your product. They've had a taste of the game and are ready for the full course; now, it's your job to feed them. To do so, however, you must distribute it.

> **TIP**
>
> If you decide that the shareware route is for you, I suggest checking out the Association of Shareware Professionals (www.asp-shareware.com). The Association of Shareware Professionals, or *ASP* for short, was formed in April 1987 to aid members in their goal of getting their products marketed and published.

You can distribute your game a number of ways. Of course, there's the traditional box-on-shelf method that you decided to skip when you decided to self-publish. You can record your games on discs, package them (minimal packaging, of course), and mail them as you receive orders. Another method is to allow players to download the games directly—that is, order, pay, and download the games from your Web site. Which way is best?

Directly downloading has problems because of high-bandwidth transfers. Can you find an affordable Internet server that allows you to transfer large volumes of data? In addition, customers might have difficulties downloading a 500MB game. Although smaller games don't present that problem, you still face problems such as downloads being cut off before they are complete.

The best methods at this point are to produce the discs yourself, via a couple of CD-ROM writers, or to send your product to a *mastering house,* which will take your disc and whip out a sufficient number of copies in no time flat, plus label the discs in a more professional manner than you might be able to do at home. Add in the jewel cases and maybe a small information booklet (instruction book), and your product is ready to mail.

You must also deal with various payment options—checks, credit cards, and cash. Setting up a business banking account enables you to take credit card payments, and doing so comes in handy when it comes time to pay taxes (sorting out business expenses and income). Ask your

> **CAUTION**
>
> Before selling your product, be sure to secure your business and tax licenses; the government frowns on back-door dealings, and it's best to do this the right way.

friendly banker (or an accountant) for more details on setting up financially. Before you know it, the money will be pouring in, and you'll have to keep up with orders!

# Wrapping Up Marketing and Publishing

The world of creating games is an exciting one. Imagine the joy that you'll feel seeing your very own game on store shelves! Gaming magazines will rave about your game, while players will line up by the hundreds to buy your game. Do you believe that can be true for your game? Sure it can, but only if you make it happen!

In this chapter, you found out how to prepare your game for submission to potential publishers, what to expect when dealing with publishing companies, and what other paths you can take in order to get your game on the market.

My final comment on marketing and publishing of your game is *good luck!* The key to getting your game published in this huge gaming world is to start contacting companies and looking for the one that will take your project and propel it into the market. In fact, companies solely devoted to independent developers are beginning to spring up all over the Internet, waiting to help you publish your game.

# Epilogue

Well, it's come to an end. Your journey through your game's creation was long and wrought with perils, but you prevailed through thick and thin. Creating a complete game is by no means an easy task, and if you're still having trouble, don't worry. It takes many resources, a lot of time, and dedication to finish even the simplest role-playing game. At this point, I will try to help you organize your thoughts by highlighting what you covered in this book.

In the Epilogue, you do the following:

- Review what you've learned from this book
- Consider what's next in your game-creating endeavors

## Looking Back

Getting into the game industry is a bit of a misnomer—to land a great job, you have to already have some game-making experience. How do you get that experience if you haven't worked for a company? The answer is via your mind and your hands. With books like this one as your guide, you can build a solid understanding of what goes into creating games. Nothing impresses a potential employer or publisher more than a programmer who knows his business and is able to deliver a quality product.

What did you discover during your quest through this book? All along your quest, you learned the following:

- **How to design the technical aspects of your game.** With a little forethought and planning, your project becomes easier to manage. Coupling technology with design, you are able to foresee all that your game needs, and with proper planning all goes smoothly.

- **The basics of C++ and Windows programming.** Learn the basics and jump right into programming your applications (in easy-to-follow formats). Basic programming techniques such as modular programming and state-based processing lead to shortened development times.

- **How to utilize DirectX to build the various game engine components.** This includes using DirectX Graphics, DirectX Audio, DirectInput, and DirectPlay.

- **How to use the game engines.** You learned the backbone of RPG game engines, from scripting systems, combat sequences, character AI, and inventory management.

- **How to improve your story-writing abilities.** With structure and plausibility, your stories bring your creation to life.

- **How to prepare your game for Internet play.** Networking is the new life of games, and you don't want to be left behind.

- **How to market and publish your game.** Although they're just the tip of the iceberg, the ideas introduced in this book will start you on your way to marketing and publishing your game.

Using what you've learned in this book, you should now be "up to snuff" on the latest tools and techniques needed for creating games. I have complete confidence that with the information in this book and a liberal dose of dedication, you can create a complete role-playing game.

# What's Next?

So where do you go with your newfound knowledge? Into the world my friend. With the recent release of so many powerful home-gaming consoles, you can even port your games to the console world. Imagine seeing your game in full Microsoft Xbox or Nintendo Game Cube glory! The basics behind each console are the same as those for your computer, and with a little more altering of your game project's libraries and source code (so that they work with the consoles' development kits), you can accomplish the dream of programming games for home consoles.

Perhaps you don't plan to create a complete game on your own. That's okay. Gaming companies need bright, intelligent, well-informed (now that you've read this book) individuals like you to keep the world of gaming going. You might use your new RPG programming powers to land your next job—and, hey, give my book a thought when you land that awesome job!

# PART SIX

# APPENDIXES

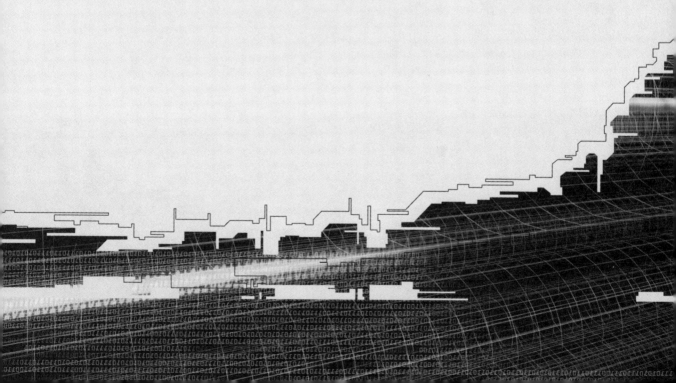

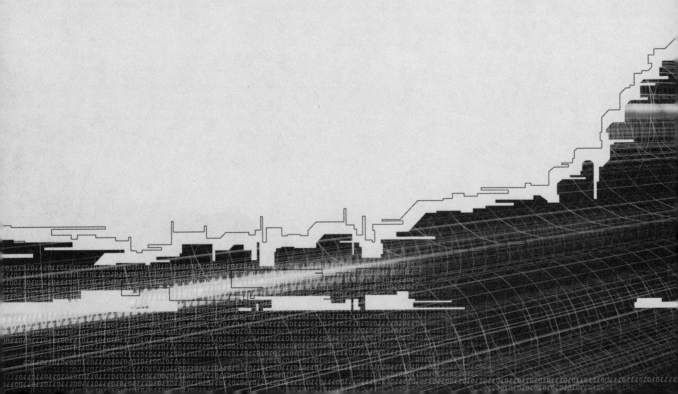

# APPENDIX A

# SETTING UP DIRECTX 8.0 AND CONFIGURING THE COMPILER

**B**efore working with the code and examples in this book, you must install and set up the Microsoft DirectX 8.0 Software Developer's Kit (SDK) on your computer. During the installation process, the DirectX installer will try to configure your compiler to use the appropriate SDK paths, but in order to complete the configuration of the compiler, you'll need to make some manual configuration changes, which I explain in this appendix.

> **NOTE**
>
> You will find the DirectX 8.0 SDK on this book's **CD-ROM**; check out Appendix E, "What's on the CD," for information on the install program. You can also download the SDK from Microsoft's Web site at http://msdn.microsoft.com/directx/.

# Setting Up DirectX 8.0

The first step in game programming is to install the Microsoft DirectX Run-Time Libraries and Software Developers Kit; both are packaged in the SDK installation on the CD-ROM at the back of this book.

Typically, new versions of DirectX are released annually. The new versions generally provide improvements on older features and other new enhancements. Because DirectX is based on COM, you never have to worry about someone using a newer version of DirectX—the matching components of the different versions remain the same (see Chapter 5, "Programming with Windows and Application Basics," for more on COM).

With each new release, you also retain access to earlier components and features, although the newer and older components are not interchangeable. For example, you cannot use the features of Direct3D 8.0 with the 2-D drawing features of DirectDraw 7. That's not a problem, however, because newer interfaces usually contain the functionality of the lacking features (for example, Direct3D can draw 2-D graphics, just in a slightly different manner than in earlier versions).

DirectX comes in two parts: the Run-Time Libraries and the SDK. As a developer, you need to install both (end users need to install only the Run-Time Libraries).

# Using Run-Time Libraries and the SDK

The Run-Time Libraries are the heart and sole of the DirectX components. The libraries contain the code that is specific for your system's hardware. Created by their respective manufacturers, these libraries are either packaged as part of the standard DirectX distribution or are available from the manufacturers (via an installation disk or the Internet).

Developers will find the source code, headers, and libraries packaged in the SDK. All you do is install these files, set up your compiler, and you're off and running. For developers, the device libraries come in two versions: the debug version and the retail version. End users (such as those people playing your game) need only the retail version. What's the difference between the debug and retail versions, you ask? Read on to find out.

# Using the Debug Version Versus the Retail Version

When you install the SDK, you are asked whether you want to use the retail or debug version of the DX device libraries. This is a judgment call, so you need to understand what each version does for you.

On one hand, debugging gives you the ability to see what is going on behind the scenes, but at the cost of speed and size. You can work at full speed with the retail version, but you might be left clueless when your programs start crashing.

I recommend using the debug version while becoming familiar with DirectX and the retail version if you're more experienced and want the fastest speed possible.

# Installing DirectX 8.0

It's time to get down to the business at hand. Insert this book's CD-ROM into your computer's CD-ROM drive. The *Programming Role Playing Games with DirectX* license page will appear. Click I Agree to continue. If the CD-ROM interface does not immediately appear, you can start it manually by following these steps:

1. Go to the Windows taskbar and click Start, Run and then type **d:\start_here.html** (where *d:* is your CD-ROM drive) in the textbox.

2. When the *Programming Role Playing Games with DirectX* license page appears, click I Agree to continue.

   The CD-ROM's main interface will appear (see Figure A.1). From this interface, you can choose a number of options, from browsing the source code to installing programs.

3. To start the installation process, click DirectX and then click Install DirectX 8.0 SDK.

## Installing DirectMusic Producer

Although DirectMusic Producer is not part of the standard DirectX SDK install package, you will find it on this book's CD-ROM (check Appendix E for more details on the package's location). This package is your tool for producing DirectMusic native song files (which includes importing Midi files) that can be played using the information in Chapter 8, "Playing Sound with DirectX Audio."

To install DirectMusic Producer, you can use the CD-ROM installation program, or you can go to your D drive, open the \DirectX\DirectMusic Producer directory, and run the Setup.exe program. Again, follow the instructions and configure the installation to your liking.

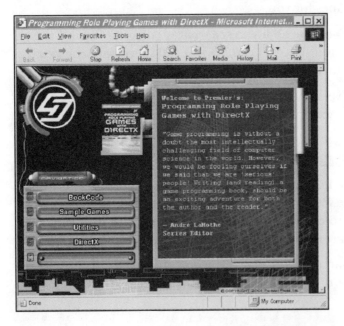

**Figure A.1**

*Use the CD-ROM interface to navigate the programs on the disc. Browse the source code or install one of the many utility applications or games.*

# Include Files and Libraries

When DirectX 8.0 and the SDK are installed and properly working (which you might check by executing some of the DX demo programs packaged with this book), you are ready to include the proper libraries and header files in your projects.

In the next section, you learn how to adjust the settings for your compiler, but first take a look at Table A.1, which provides a list of the DirectX components used in the book and the include files and libraries that you include in the compiler settings when creating a new project.

# Setting Up the Compiler

Microsoft's Visual C/C++ compiler is a powerful tool that is essential when writing Windows applications using the C and C++ languages. Currently in release 6 (with release 7 coming out as this book is being written), Visual C/C++ is the program of choice for developers worldwide (and the choice for this book). Before jumping into the book's code and examples, you need to set up a few options to ensure that everything works properly.

### Table A.1   DirectX Components, Include Files, and Libraries

| Component | Include File(s) | Library File(s) |
| --- | --- | --- |
| Direct3D | d3d8.h | d3d8.lib |
| D3DX | d3dx8.h | d3dx8.lib |
| DirectInput | dinput.h | dinput8.lib |
| DirectSound | dsound.h | dsound.lib |
| DirectMusic | dmusici.h | dsound.lib |
| DirectPlay | dpaddr.net, dplay8.h | dpnaddr.lib, dpnet.lib, dplayx.lib |

# Directory Settings for DirectX

In order for your compiler to find the DirectX SDK libraries and header files, you must add those elements to the directory lists, as follows:

1. To access the lists, go to the main menu and click Tools, Options. The Options dialog box appears.

2. Click the Directories tab (see Figure A.2).

3. In the Show directories for drop-down box, choose Include files.

4. If the DirectX directory is not listed in the Directories list, you need to add it. Do so by clicking the New button and entering the DirectX include file directory selected during the DX installation (refer to the section "Installing DirectX 8.0"). This directory typically ends with \include.

5. Repeat Step 4 to set the DirectX library directory. This time, however, click the Show Directories for drop-down box and choose Library files. If the library path is not shown, click the New button again and follow the procedure in Step 4 to find the library directory (typically ending with \lib).

# Linking to Libraries

The next step to using DirectX (and some Windows features) is to add the libraries to the project. You can accomplish this in two ways. You can add the libraries to the source file list or to the compiler link Object/libraries modules in the Project Settings dialog box.

To add the libraries to the source file list, follow these steps:

1. Open a project file and right-click the Source Files header under the Workspace navigator (it is typically on the left side of the screen and contains the files included in your project). A small menu appears (see Figure A.3).

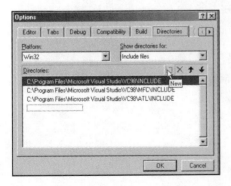

**Figure A.2**

*The Visual C/C++ version 6 Directories tab, located in the Options dialog box, contains the search paths for including header, library, and other source code files.*

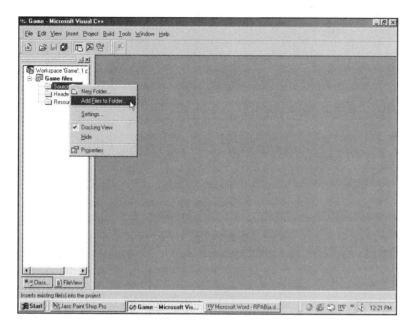

**Figure A.3**

*You will find it easy to add library files to the source files list.*

2. Click Add Files to Folder. The Insert Files into Project dialog box appears.

3. Locate and choose the libraries you want to include and click OK.

You can also add libraries inside the Project Settings dialog box, by following these steps:

1. To access the settings, with a project file open, click Project, Settings. The Project Settings dialog box opens.

2. Click the Link tab.

3. If the Link tab is not visible, make sure that your project's workspace is selected in the Settings For list box (see Figure A.4)—the project's workspace is the topmost option in the Settings For list box.

4. In the Category drop-down box, choose General. In the Object/library modules textbox, you'll see a list of libraries that Visual C/C++ links to your project when the application is compiled.

5. At the end of the text in the Object/library modules textbox, type the specific libraries you want to link to your project.

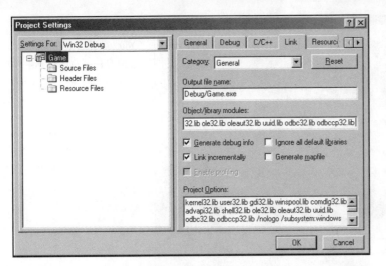

**Figure A.4**

*To add library files in the Project Settings dialog box, type the library filenames in the Object/library modules textbox.*

# Setting Default char Behavior

Strangely, Visual C/C++ lacks an option for selecting unsigned chars by default, which means whenever you type

```
char Variable;
```

the compiler will expand the variable declaration to

```
unsigned char Variable;
```

For many years, this was a typical coding convention, because most programs used unsigned chars to store a value from 0 to 255. Typing unsigned char every time was a waste of space, so by default, the compiler expanded a single char declaration to unsigned char when a program was compiled. Normally, this option was set by default inside the com-

**NOTE**

If you don't want to go through the hassle of setting the compiler option for using unsigned chars by default, use the BYTE macro to declare an unsigned char in your program code.

piler's configuration. However, for some reason, Microsoft's Visual C/C++ compiler does not set this option as the default, and trying to set it yourself can be daunting.

To force the compiler to use unsigned chars by default, do the following:

1. Open the Project Settings dialog box and click the C/C++ tab.
2. In the Category drop-down box, choose General.

3. In the Project Options textbox, add the characters /J to the end of the text (see Figure A.5).

# Release and Debug Versions

In every new project, Visual C/C++ creates a debug and a release version of your project, each with its own settings. Visual C/C++ does so because during development you might want to specify different settings to help debug the application—as opposed to those settings you use for the final release of your application. These settings determine which options the compiler sets by default, as well as which libraries the compiler uses (such as the debug Run-Time libraries).

Which version (release or debug) to use is entirely up to you. In this book, I use the debug version and its default options (with the exception of the modifying options that I include in this appendix).

# Multithreaded Libraries

Certain DirectX components (such as DirectSound) use the Windows multithreaded libraries, so you have to notify the compiler to use them. You do so in the Project Settings dialog box (boy, what a busy box!), as follows:

1. Open the Project Settings dialog box and click the C/C++ tab.
2. In the Category drop-down list, choose Code Generation.
3. In the Use run-time library drop-down list, choose Multithreaded (see Figure A.6).

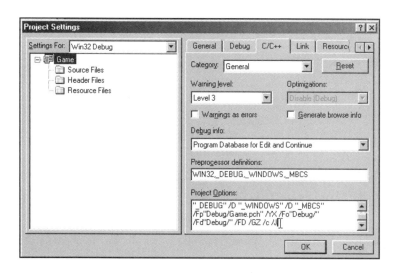

**Figure A.5**

*The compiler can modify compiler options, or you can type them in the Project Settings dialog box—in the Project Options textbox, as shown here.*

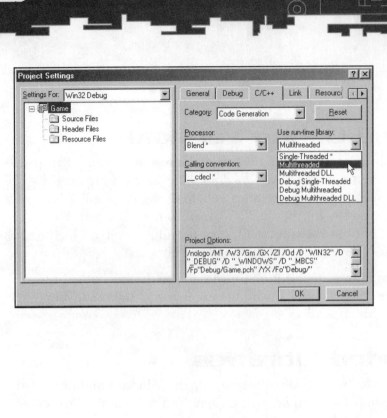

**Figure A.6**

*With so many options to choose from, the Use run-time library drop-down list might confuse the uninitiated. Select the Multithreaded option, and you'll be set to go.*

# APPENDIX B

# GETTING HELP ON THE WEB

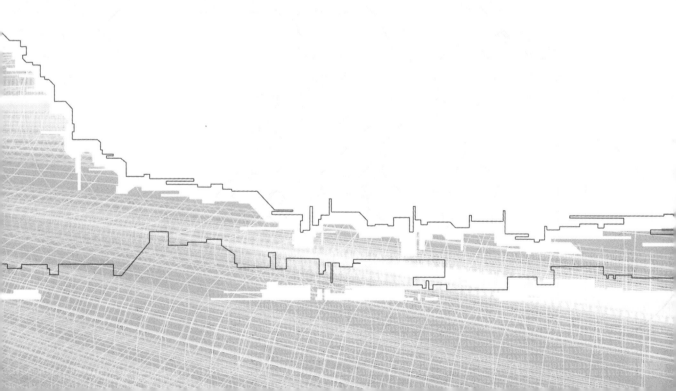

In this day and age, many (if not most) people turn to the Internet for information. In this appendix, you will find Web sites that I use for finding information on RPGs, including information on programming, designing, and playing games.

# Programming Role-Playing Games with DirectX

I shamefacedly begin with my Web site at http://home.att.net/~rpgbook. This site contains updated information about this book, as well as resources on designing and programming your RPGs. With its new articles, code updates, and information on upcoming releases, you'll want to keep an eye on this site!

# www.GameDev.net

This is the definitive site for programming enthusiasts. Point your browser in this direction for articles, tutorials, message forums, news, book reviews, and much more. I tend to hang out in the DirectX message forum, so feel free to drop me a line.

# XTreme Games

Home for André LaMothe, author of several popular books on game programming (and series editor for Premier's Game Development series), this Web site is the portal to XTremeGames, LLC. This site's goal is to help independent developers publish their games, mainly through the value software motif. If you want a start in the gaming industry and have a game you want to publish, visit this site at http://www.XGames3D.com.

# Flipcode

Here is another great programming resource site. It contains news, resources, source code, and all the other little goodies that keep people glued to their screens. Check them out at http://www.flipcode.com.

# MilkShape 3-D Home Page

This is the home of MilkShape 3-D, a low-cost, low-polygon modeler that you can find on the CD-ROM at the back of this book. Check this site for frequent updates to the program, as well as plug-ins you can use to import from and export to various model formats (including .X files). Point your browser at http://www.swissquake.ch/chumbalum-soft/ to visit the MilkShape 3-D homepage.

# Agetec

Agetec, Inc. (at http://www.agetec.com) is the maker of the cool RPG Maker software for the Sony PlayStation. With RPG Maker, you can design your own SNES-like RPGs, starting from the ground up. With graphics, scripts, and combat, this program has it all. This site is a good starting point for those who want to create RPGs without the hassles of programming.

# Wizards of the Coast

This is the home for Wizards of the Coast, Inc., makers of *Dungeons & Dragons*. Check this site (at http://www.Wizards.com) for resources on the granddaddy of RPGs—D&D, and while you're there, check out their full line of RPG products.

# White Wolf Publishing

This is the site of the makers of *Vampire the Masquerade* and numerous other RPG systems. This site (at http://www.white-wolf.com) contains great resources for starting you on the path to darkness (in the wicked creature of the night sort of way).

# Steve Jackson Games

Located at http://www.sjgames.com/gurps, this is Steve Jackson's GURPS home page. Steve's company is responsible for bringing you famous games such as *GURPS, OGRE, Car Wars, Illuminati: New World Order,* and many others. Check out this site for all the information you need on the Generic Universal RolePlaying System, including a list of books and free downloads of the core rules.

# Polycount

This site is loaded with models for just about every 3-D shooter out there. This site is a must for finding artists and models for your own projects. Go to http://www.polycount.com to check out those models. Be sure to install MilkShape 3-D, which you need to edit those models!

# RPG Planet

Packed with reviews, articles, and discussions on the newest in computer RPGs, this site (located at http://www.rpgPlanet.com) is a definite must-visit for all you RPG fanatics! If you're into the computer side of role-playing and want to keep up on current events in the RPG industry, you'll want to keep an eye out at this site.

# RPG Host

Host for many RPG Web sites, RPG Host is the definitive directory of RPG-related materials. This site packs in games, downloads, resources, news, and message forums—all related to your favorite game genre. Check out RPG Host at http://www.rpghost.com, and while you're there, check out the huge list of hosted RPG-related Web sites.

# www.gamedev.net/ reference/articles/frpg/site

Although I've mentioned GameDev.net, this section contains a plethora of information about RPG design. A definite look-see for those who need a little help or some direction. Chris Bennett of Dwarfsoft maintains this site.

# www.excite.com/ games/role_playing

Here you find Excite's page to RPG resources galore! Check out the various sections, such as scenario writing, guides, plots and stories, and much more! A great place to start when beginning your game project, this site will help guide you to design-related materials.

# APPENDIX C

# RECOMMENDED READING

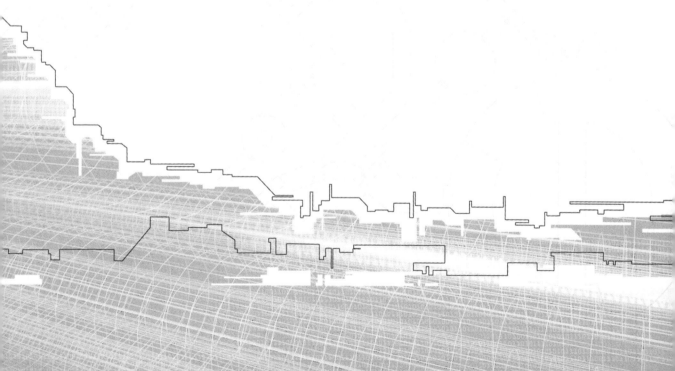

**B**ehind every great programmer is a great set of books. All programmers have to start at the bottom, learn the basics, build their knowledge, and struggle through every bit and piece of code. Having a good set of books at your disposal is a sure-fire way to kick-start your programming endeavors. In this appendix, I share my favorite books on programming. I have used these books in my work as a programmer and as general references to topics covered in this book. Each book in this appendix has bits of information that relate to the material in this book.

# Dragon Magazine

Periodical. (Wizards of the Coast, Inc.)

This magazine is devoted to role-playing games. Each issue is packed with adventures, stories, tips and tricks, letters, and so much more role-playing game goodness. If you're a fan of traditional RPGs, this is the magazine for you.

# Dungeon Adventures

Periodical. (Wizards of the Coast, Inc.)

This is *the* source for *Dungeons & Dragons* adventures. Each new issue brings you the most creative adventures developed by readers and professionals worldwide.

# Dungeons & Dragons 3rd Edition Player's Handbook

Authors: Monte Cook, Jonathan Tweet, and Skip Williams (Wizards of the Coast, Inc., 2000. ISBN: 0-7869-1550-1)

Every serious RPG player has heard of the big *Dungeons & Dragons* franchise—*Dungeons & Dragons* pretty much gave life to the RPG world. This book is the latest edition of the rules for the game.

# Dungeons & Dragons 3rd Edition Dungeon Master's Guide Handbook

Authors: Monte Cook, Jonathan Tweet, and Skip Williams (Wizards of the Coast, Inc., 2000. ISBN: 0-7869-1551-X)

This book, which is the companion book to the *Dungeons & Dragons 3rd Edition Player's Handbook*, is targeted to DMs (referees of the game). If you want to keep up with the D&D universe, this is the book to acquire.

# Isometric Game Programming with DirectX 7.0

Author: Ernest Pazera (Premier Press, Inc., 2001 ISBN: 0-7615-3089-4)

A must for those serious about breaking into isometric game-programming techniques. Although *Programming Role Playing Games with DirectX* covers using isometric graphics in general, Ernest Pazera's book does a great job of showing the whole iso-gaming phenomenon in detail.

# lexx & yacc

Authors: John R. Levine, Tony Mason, and Doug Brown (O'Reilly & Associates, Inc., 1995. ISBN: 1-56592-000-7)

In my book, I detail the use of a simple scripting system, called the Mad Lib Scripting system. In order to develop a much more advanced script system that uses program-like code (somewhat like C++), you'll need to delve into topics such as lexical analyzer and grammar structure. One book that's sure to help you out is *lexx & yacc*, which covers the basic steps to creating your own script language and compiler.

# Multiplayer Game Programming

Author: Todd Barron (Premier Press, Inc., 2001 ISBN: 0-7615-3298-6)

As you learn in the book you are now reading, multiplayer gaming is a major topic. Todd Barron's book is a great place to turn for in-depth information on multiplayer gaming that is beyond the scope of *Programming Role Playing Games with DirectX*. Ranging from networking basics to creating actual multiplayer games, *Multiplayer Game Programming* might be just the book you need.

# Programming Windows, Fifth Edition

Author: Charles Petzold (Microsoft Press, 1998 ISBN: 1-57231-995-X)

Anyone who is serious about Windows programming must have this tome. Covering nearly all the basics on Windows ideology, this book remains one of my most frequently used references.

# Schaum's Quick Guide to Writing Great Short Stories

Author: Margaret Lucke (McGraw-Hill, 1999. ISBN: 0-07-039077-0)

That's right. Even short stories can build to grand proportions, and this book is a straightforward guide to working with the basics of every story—plot development, story structure, and character creation. Learn the do's and don'ts of story writing, how to create colorful characters—each with its unique personality and history—how to develop unique plots, and much more.

# Swords & Circuitry: A Designers Guide to Computer Role-Playing Games

Authors: Neal Hallford and Jana Hallford (Premier Press, Inc., 2001 ISBN: 0-7615-3299-4)

Ever wanted to see the other side to creating a game—you know, the design aspect of gaming? The book you are now reading focuses mainly on the programming side of RPGs (with a smidgen of design topics), so you might want to pick up a copy of *Swords & Circuitry*, which details the secret world behind RPG design, from plot trees to game scripting.

# The Zen of Direct3D Game Programming

Author: Peter Walsh (Premier Press, Inc., 2001 ISBN: 0-7615-3429-6)

Who wouldn't want a book devoted solely to Direct3D? This book provides a detailed look at the features that Direct3D offers. Whereas my book gives you a whirlwind tour of Direct3D (from using the graphics system to drawing 3-D polygons and meshes), *The Zen of Direct3D Game Programming* digs deeper into the basics of Direct3D. It is a definite beginner's guide to getting into Direct3D programming.

# APPENDIX D

# GLOSSARY

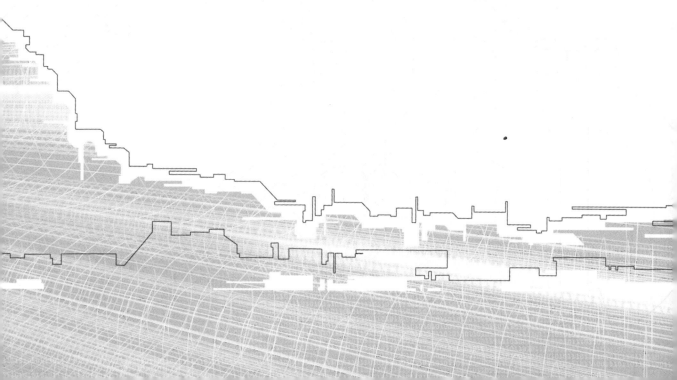

**Abilities.** *See Attributes.*

**Action template.** A list of script actions and their appropriate structure and use.

**Actions.** Script commands.

**Alpha blending.** The combination of colors or alpha values during rendering.

**Alpha channel.** The opacity of an image defined by an alpha value per pixel interleaved with the color components (for example, ARGB), an alpha value per pixel stored in a separate alpha surface, or a constant alpha value for the entire surface.

**Alpha testing.** A rendering state that skips the drawing of completely transparent pixels.

**Ambient light.** A constant level of light that illuminates all objects in a scene equally.

**Antagonist.** The character (or characters) who brings chaos and disarray into the story, typically by intruding in the hero's (the protagonist) attempts to achieve goals and intentions. *See also Protagonist.*

**Application framework.** An application structure (in regard to layout and processing).

**Application message queue.** A queue that stores Windows messages related to the application.

**Application Programming Interface (API).** The middleman in the programming world. The API provides the programmer with an interface to the underlying functionality of separate program code.

**Armor.** A generalized description of any piece of equipment that a player can wear to raise his defensive level against attacks. This can include pieces of armor to shields or boots.

**Artificial Intelligence (AI).** Describes the intelligence or processing control of non-player characters within a game in order to simulate specific behaviors or actions.

**ASCII.** An acronym for American Standard Code for Information Interchange. It is a code in which the numbers from 0 to 255 stand for letters, numbers, punctuation marks, and other characters. ASCII code is standardized to facilitate transmitting text among computers or between a computer and a peripheral device.

**Attributes.** Define the stature and abilities of characters in games. These attributes (and abilities) can range from physical details such as height to gauged estimates of strength.

**Attribute buffer.** An array of values used by the `ID3DXMesh` object for rendering meshes. Each element in the array corresponds to every polygon face in the mesh. Each element holds the material identification number used to render the respective polygon face.

**Audio path.** Controls the flow of data from the performance object, a segment, synthesizer, and sound buffers.

**Auto map (auto-mapping).** The function of a game engine to automatically track and display previously visited sections of gaming maps and levels. This feature enables players to see where they've already been.

**Backbuffer.** A nonvisible surface to which bitmaps and other images can be drawn while the front buffer displays the currently visible image.

**Backface culling.** The removal (or skipping) of polygons (that face away from the viewpoint) during the rendering process.

**Bandwidth.** The measure or amount of data that can pass through a network connection.

**Barrier.** A blockage on a map that halts a character's passage.

**Base class.** Used to describe a parent class of a derived class.

**Battle arrangements.** The predetermined arrangement of characters during a combat sequence.

**Big bitmap.** Describes large pre-rendered levels used within a specialized style of graphics engine called a Big Bitmap Engine.

**Billboard.** A polygon that is aligned to face the viewpoint.

**Billboarding.** A technique of simulating the appearance of a 3-D object in a scene.

**Bitmap.** A pattern of pixels that form a larger image. Bitmap is also the name of Microsoft's proprietary image storage format (signified by the .BMP file extension).

**Bounding box.** A rectangular area that completely encloses an object.

**Bounding sphere.** A spherical area that completely encloses an object.

**Calling purpose.** The reason for calling a state function.

**Camera.** In graphical terms, the representation of a free-moving viewpoint used to view maps and levels.

**Character building.** The process of increasing a character's abilities and attributes through the course of a game.

**Character class.** A character's classification, which is determined by the game's design.

**Child template (or child frame).** A template (or frame) that belongs to another template.

**Circular buffer.** A buffer that loops around in order to join the end and beginning of the buffer.

**Class.** In programming terms, a collection of program code and data unique to an object instance. In respect to RPGs, a class is the category or profession of a character (such as a ranger, warrior, or magic user).

**Class visibility.** The declaration of a class's data and functions that limits or restricts access to said data and functions.

**Client.** A client application is the program that the player of a game interacts with during a networked gaming session.

**Climax.** The point of greatest intensity in a story.

**Clipping planes.** Remove objects from rendering pipeline based on the side (front or back) that the object is in relation to each plane.

**Coding conventions.** A set of rules or definitions that determines the format or structure of program code.

**Color key.** A color that represents a transparent pixel. Pixels colored the same as the color key are skipped during rendering.

**Combat.** Describes any sequence of actions that involves attacking or defending player characters.

**Combat rule set.** The rules that govern combat.

**Compile.** The act of compiling, which converts your program code into executable code.

**Compiler.** The program you use to convert your program code into executable applications.

**Complications.** Obstacles that stand in the way of reaching a resolution.

**Component Object Module (COM).** A form of modular programming adopted by Microsoft. It is the heart of DirectX components.

**Console.** Console has two meanings. It is a special screen that allows users to modify, read, or type game information or messages. It also is a home-gaming unit, such as the Sony PlayStation.

**Constructor.** A function that shares the same name as the declaring class.

**Cooperative level.** A setting that defines how to share access to a device or object.

**Creature.** Describes a non-friendly or non-intelligent character. This includes any character you might fight (such as a skeleton) or an animal (such as a horse).

**Critical section.** An object used to synchronize the threads of a single process.

**Cut-scenes.** A temporary break in the story-flow; used to change scenes.

**D&D.** Abbreviation for the game *Dungeons & Dragons*.

**Data router.** A device that directs network data.

**Dead reckoning.** A form of updating game content based on known data.

**Decibels (dB).** A unit of comparison between two levels of sound intensity.

**Denouement.** The final portion of a story.

**Depth sorting.** Sorting of objects based on their depth in a scene.

**Derived class.** A class that borrows the structure of a base class and expands its functionality by adding or modifying existing functions and data.

**Design document.** This is the bible of a game design; it contains the layout of a game to be created.

**Destructor.** A function called by an object when destroyed.

**DirectInput (DI).** The DirectX component responsible for dealing with input devices (such as a keyboard, mouse, or joystick).

**Directional light.** A light that points in a specific direction.

**DirectMusic (DM).** The DirectX component used to play music and sound files (such as Midi and wave files).

**DirectPlay (DP).** The DirectX component used for networking functionality.

**DirectSound (DS).** The DirectX component used to play digital sounds.

**DirectX.** The brainchild of Microsoft, DirectX is a gaming API that allows programmers to create games without worrying about the details involved in using the underlying hardware.

**DirectX Audio.** With the release of DirectX 8.0, DirectX Audio represents the combination of all audio components, namely DirectSound and DirectMusic.

**DirectX Graphics.** Starting with DirectX 8.0, all previous graphics functionality from DirectDraw and Direct3D were merged into a single component named DirectX Graphics.

**Downloadable Sounds (DLS).** A digitally sampled sound (or set of sounds) that is downloaded into a synthesizer.

**Dot product (or scalar product).** The product of the lengths of two vectors and the angle between them.

**Dungeon Master (DM).** The referee that manages all gaming aspects and controls the flow of the game.

**Experience level.** Used to track major levels of advancement in a character. For example, a character might have 10,000 experience points, but be considered at level 5. Usually, each advancement in experience levels comes with bonuses, such as learning new spells or skills.

**Experience points (EXP).** Describe the amount of growth (in numerical values) of a character's advancement in experiences (much like experience level).

**Extended ASCII.** An extension of the ASCII standard that defines the use of 256 characters, as opposed to ASCII's 128-character limit.

**Falloff.** The reduction of a light's intensity over distance.

**Field of View (FOV).** The visible portion of a viewer's sight.

**Final beta.** The final test version of a software product before release.

**Flashback.** A look back in time, in the form of a story's cut-scene.

**Flexible Vertex Format (FVF).** Describes the contents of a vertex, ranging from a vertex's color to its coordinates.

**Flip.** Switching the visible and non-visible portions of the display.

**Foreshadowing.** Looking back to introduce the reasoning of a story's incident.

**Frame (also known as a reference frame).** Used in .X files to group related templates together for easier access.

**Frame hierarchy.** Categorized list of frames.

**Frame template.** A template that contains a frame.

**Frame transformation.** A transformation applied to a frame.

**Friend class.** A class allowed to freely access the declaring class's data and function.

**Frustum (or viewing frustum).** The visible portion of a viewer's sight contained within six planes (in the shape of a pyramid).

**Function overloading.** The method of providing multiple prototypes of the same function, each with a different set of calling arguments.

**Game engine.** The group of program code and functions that runs the actual game application.

**Game Master (GM).** *See Dungeon Master.*

**Gaming core.** A library of functions that controls the basic aspects of game programming, ranging from graphics processing and drawing to processing user input from devices such as the mouse and keyboard.

**Gaming system.** The set of rules that govern a role-playing game.

**Genre.** A style or classification. For example, role-playing games and action games are two separate genres of games.

**Global queue.** A queue of messages waiting to be processed by the operating system.

**Global Unique Identification (GUID).** A guaranteed unique number 128 bits in size.

**GM/GS set.** General Midi/General Synth set of instruments.

**GURPS.** Acronym for Generic Universal Role-Playing System.

**Hit points (HP).** Describe either a character's level of health or the amount of damage that a character can take before being considered dead.

**Hungarian Notation.** A coding convention that prefixes a variable or a function with its defined data type.

**Inciting incident.** The event that triggers a major event that drives a story.

**Index array.** An array of values that constructs a series of polygon faces.

**Indexed vertex buffer.** A vertex buffer that stores vertices in any order, using an index array to define which vertices construct polygons.

**Indies.** Independent developers.

**Inheritance.** In programming terms, describes the capability of derived classes to adopt their base class's functionality (including functions and variables).

**Instrument collections.** A collection of instruments used to play music.

**Inventory control system (ICS).** An engine used to manage a character's or a map's list of objects.

**Inventory list.** A list of objects belonging to a character or map.

**IP address.** A networking address that takes the form of four numbers—for example, 255.255.255.255.

**Key.** An object's orientation at a single point in time. Used in animation sequences.

**Key frame.** A sequence of keys used in an animation.

**Lag.** The delay between the time an action is requested and the time that it occurs. Lag is typically associated with networked games in which network congestion is so high that players' commands take much longer than usual to be processed. The result is sluggish gaming control.

**LARPS (Live Action RolePlaying System).** Used to describe any game system in which players dress up and act out their roles, much as in a stage play. *Vampire, the Masquerade* is one such game.

**Latency.** The time it takes a network message to travel from the source to the destination. The higher the latency, the longer it takes a message to reach the destination, and usually the higher the lag time in game-play.

**Level.** Either the level of experience a character achieves during game-play or an in-game map that characters inhabit and explore.

**Library.** In programming terms, a library is a collection of programming functions grouped into a single entity. You use libraries by means of APIs.

**Lobby server.** A network server object that manages multiple connections and directs users for a game session.

**Local space.** A 3-D object's local coordinate space.

**Mad Lib Script or Mad Lib Scripting (MLS).** A term I coined to describe the method of scripting in which you utilize prewritten actions that use a multiple choice format for obtaining required data.

**Magic.** Describes paranormal abilities that might or might not be harnessed by gaming characters.

**Magic points (MP).** Much like hit points, magic points describe a character's level of magic power or the amount of magic a character can use. Magic points are usually depleted with every magic spell cast, but are later regained with rest or restoration.

**Map (or level).** Location or locations in which a game takes place.

**Master character list (MCL).** List of characters used in a game.

**Master item list (MIL).** List of items used in a game.

**Master spell list (MSL).** List of spells used in a game.

**Master tempo.** The tempo used by the sound system during music playback.

**Material.** Describes the look and texture of a 3-D object; it is used to render such objects, including color, bumpiness, and spectacular highlights.

**Matrix concatenation.** The combination of two matrices.

**Mesh.** A grouping of polygons.

**Message pump.** A function that constantly pulls messages from the application message queue and processes them.

**Midi.** A music storage format.

**Model.** A mesh and assigned materials that are used to render the mesh.

**Model space.** *See Local space.*

**Modifier.** A value that alters another one.

**Modular.** Modular programs or libraries can be inserted into projects quickly and easily. Typical modular libraries consist of reusable functions, such as device input routines.

**Monster.** The term given to any gaming denizen opposing the player. Do not confuse a monster with a non-player character. Monsters have few roles in games other than for combat, whereas NPCs usually are important to the game's story or progress.

**Multithreading.** The processing of multiple threads.

**Network.** A series of connected computers that share or exchange data.

**Nodes.** A single entity contained with a tree. *See also Tree.*

**Non-Player Character (NPC).** Any character in the game that the player does not control. An NPC can be anything from the friendly shopkeeper to the lowliest demon of the underworld.

**Normal.** A vector that describes the direction in which a vertex, plane, light, or polygon is pointing.

**Painter's algorithm.** The order in which objects are rendered. Objects are rendered based on their distance from the viewpoint, farthest to nearest.

**Particle.** Represents any free-roaming object that is strictly used in the graphical sense to enhance the visual quality of a game. Particles can be used to represent trails of smoke, sparks of light, and even non-sentient bugs that flitter around aimlessly.

**Pass-along network.** A network or data router that passes network data onto another network or data router.

**Patch number.** An instrument's identification number.

**Patches.** Instruments.

**Peer-to-peer.** A direct network connection from one computer to another.

**Performance.** The main object used to control the playback of a music object.

**Player character (PC).** Character that is under the player's control (who is usually the hero of the game).

**Player killer (PK).** Character that does the dirty work of killing off other player characters.

**Plot points (also called plot twists).** Major turning points in a story.

**Point light.** An object (a light) that sheds light in every direction.

**Polygon.** A closed shape formed by a grouping of vertices connected by edges. Polygons form the basis of 3-D graphics (because all 3-D graphics are rendered as polygons). A polygon can be as small as a single pixel or large enough to cover the entire screen.

**Polymorphism.** The capability of a derived class to call on its base class's functions as though the derived class were the same class as the base.

**Port.** A virtual dock that directs incoming networking data. A port takes the form of a number, usually in the range of 0 to 10,000. Data targeted for a specific port of an IP address is sent directly to that port, so no other ports can interfere with that data.

**Primary sound buffer.** The main object that contains sounds before being played by the sound system.

**Processes.** A single-threaded block of execution. You can think of your game as a process that can be broken into other processes such as an input process, a graphics rendering process, and so on.

**Program flow.** The flow in which a program executes or is structured.

**Project.** In programming terms, a project is a collection of code, libraries, and any other programming aspects assembled into a single collection.

**Projection matrix.** Matrix used to convert from untransformed coordinates to transformed coordinates.

**Projection transformation.** The transformation that converts untransformed coordinates into transformed coordinates.

**Protagonist.** The hero of the story or the character around whom the story revolves.

**Race.** Much like real life, characters in role-playing games belong to races (for example, human, elf, or even ogre).

**Recursive function.** A function that calls on itself during execution.

**Render.** To draw an object or objects.

**Role-playing game (RPG).** A game in which players assume the role of an imaginary character.

**Root node.** The first node in a list to which all other nodes are connected.

**Sample.** A single measurement of a sound wave's amplitude.

**Sampling rate.** The frequency that a digital sound is recorded.

**Scan code.** The value sent by a keyboard that represents which key is pressed or released.

**Screen space.** Two-dimensional coordinates analogous to the screen's coordinates.

**Scripts.** A series of program instructions processed within a game engine. You use scripts to alter portions of a game without having to re-code the game engine.

**Secondary sound buffer.** A buffer that contains a sound wave.

**Segment.** A musical piece.

**Server.** The network application that serves as the central processing hub of the gaming world. Client applications connect to servers and begin communicating player actions back and forth. However, ultimately, the server handles the majority of the game-processing functionality.

**Service providers.** Network protocols.

**Session.** The time a game is in operation.

**Skills.** Much like attributes in the way they describe the abilities of a character. Skills can include anything from the ability to climb to how well a character can converse in tense situations.

**Skinned mesh.** A mesh that deforms to the shape of an underlying set of imaginary bones.

**Sky Box.** A texture-mapped 3-D cube that surrounds the viewer.

**Specular.** Color of highlights on a lit object.

**Spotlight.** A cone-shaped light that illuminates only objects within the cone.

**Sprite.** Free-moving blocks of pixel graphics, usually representing game characters and objects.

**Standard mesh.** *See Mesh.*

**States.** Not the states of our great country, but states of change or states of operation. At one moment, a program can be in a specific state, and in another moment, it can be switched to another state, changing the form of processing that a game follows. You can think of states as stoplights: A red-light state means that no cars can go; a green-light state means that cars can go.

**State-based processing (SBP).** The structure or flow of functions based on the currently set state.

**Status ailments.** Physical or mental conditions that increase or decrease a character's abilities and attributes.

**Streaming audio.** Large sound data cannot be stored effectively in memory. Playing large sounds involves playing small chunks of audio data in succession, giving the impression of continuous playback. The process of reading sound data in chunks is called streaming audio.

**Subset.** A set of polygons in a mesh, grouped by respective materials.

**Supporting characters.** Characters that support the protagonist of a story.

**Tech engine.** The engines that control the technical aspects of a game, such as graphics rendering, sound playing, and input processing.

**Template.** Predefined layouts of specific data. For example, a job application can be considered a template because it contains prewritten text with blanks that the applicant completes.

**Template hierarchy.** A structured list of templates.

**Template referencing.** A form of pointing to or referring to templates.

**Texture filtering.** Techniques used to alter the pixels of a texture-mapped polygon before being rendered.

**Texture group.** Polygons grouped by their respective textures.

**Texture map.** A bitmap image that is painted onto the surface of a polygon in order to increase the rendered polygon's visual appearance.

**Texture stage.** A step in the rendering pipeline that determines how a texture map is used when drawing polygons.

**Thread.** A single process of execution.

**Throttling mechanisms.** A mechanism that limits the flow of incoming or outgoing network data.

**Tile.** A block of pixel graphics used to piece together larger images.

**Transfer Control Protocol/Internet Protocol (TCP/IP).** A network transmission protocol used to transfer data over the Internet.

**Transformations.** Calculations used to modify coordinates.

**Transformed coordinates.** Coordinates that are analogous to the display.

**Translating.** The act of moving objects.

**Transparent blit.** Drawing operation that skips transparent pixels.

**Tree.** Not the big beautiful leafy kind, but a structure that contains nodes connected to other nodes in a branchlike manner. Think of a real tree—the trunk branches off to a tree limb, which branches off to a twig, which branches off to a leaf. All those points (the trunk, limb, twig, and leaf) are called nodes.

**Triangle fan.** A list of polygons created from a series of connected vertices around a central vertex.

**Triangle list.** A list of polygons created from groups of three vertices.

**Triangle strip.** A list of polygons created from a series of subsequently defined vertices.

**Trigger.** An object placed on a map that triggers the execution of a script when touched by the player.

**Unicode.** A 16-bit character capable of encoding all known characters.

**Untransformed coordinates.** 3-D coordinates.

**User Datagram Protocol (UDP).** A form of network transmission that does not track whether a client successfully receives network data.

**Vertex.** A single point in *n*-dimensional space. In 3-D terms, a vertex contains a trio of coordinates (X, Y, and Z) to define its spatial location.

**Vertex shader.** A series of directions that determines how vertices are processed and drawn.

**Vertex stream.** The conduit in which vertex data is sent from a data buffer to the renderer.

**View transformation.** Transformation that orients vertices around the viewing position.

**Viewing matrix.** A matrix that represents the view transformation.

**Viewpoint.** The eye-point of the viewer.

**Virtual Key Code.** A code used by Microsoft Windows that closely resembles a scan code.

**Weapon.** Items that can be used for attack (such as swords, daggers, sticks, and rocks).

**Wide characters.** *See Unicode.*

**Window.** A graphical rectangle belonging to an application. Used to display an application's output.

**Window message procedure.** An application's function that processes windows' messages.

**Workspace.** Much like a desk, but in virtual terms, the workspace manages all project-related materials (such as source code files, resources, and libraries) by grouping them into a list that can be freely navigated and altered to suit the project's needs.

**World space.** Three-dimensional coordinates oriented around the origin of a game's world.

**World transformation.** Converts from an object's local coordinates to world coordinates.

**World transformation matrix.** A matrix that represents the world transformation.

**Z-Buffer (or depth buffer).** An array of values that determines the depth (into the scene) of each pixel.

# APPENDIX E

# What's on the CD

Attached to the back cover of this book is a disc containing a spiral arrangement of approximately 650,000,000 bytes of data, commonly referred to as a CD. No installation is required to view the CD; therefore, only the files that you choose to copy or install will be transferred to your hard drive. You can run the CD on any operating system that can view graphical HTML pages; however, not all the programs can be installed on all operating systems.

If AutoRun is turned on, the HTML interface automatically loads into your default browser. If AutoRun is turned off, you can access the CD by following these steps:

1. Insert the CD into your computer's CD-ROM drive and close the tray.
2. Go to My Computer or Windows Explorer and double-click the CD-ROM drive.
3. Find and open the start_here.html file (this works with most HTML browsers). The Premier Press License Agreement will appear.
4. Take a moment to read the agreement. If you agree, click the I Agree button to accept the license and proceed to the user interface. If you do not agree to the terms of the license, click the I Disagree button. The CD will not load.

The opening screen of the Premier Press user interface contains navigation buttons and a content area. The navigation buttons appear on the left side of the browser window. You can navigate through the Premier Press user interface by clicking buttons. Each page loads accordingly, and the content displays on the right.

The following sections explain what the CD contains.

# DirectX 8.0 SDK

Because the title of this book is *Programming Role Playing Games with DirectX* and because you find frequent references to the DirectX SDK throughout the book, the full release of the DirectX 8.0 SDK is provided on the CD.

One of the best ways to round out your understanding of DirectX is to examine the sample programs and associated source code that Microsoft provides as part of the SDK. In particular, check out the Direct3D demo programs; they can teach you a lot about 3-D game programming.

Also included in the SDK is the DirectX online help. If you haven't used the DirectX API Help feature yet, you'll quickly learn that it is one of your best friends when it comes to developing 3-D graphics. Don't just use the index. Peruse the books under the Contents tab as well, because they contain valuable information on the architecture of features as a whole (as well as specific information about each component).

# GoldWave 4.23 Demo

GoldWave (by GoldWave Inc.) is a comprehensive digital audio editor. It contains the following features and more:

- Provides Multiple Document Interface for editing dozens of files in one session.
- Permits large file editing (up to 1GB in size).
- Has configurable RAM (fast) for hard disk (large) editing.
- Offers real-time graphs (amplitude, spectrum, bar, and spectrogram, X-Y, fire).
- Allows separate, resizable Device Controls window for accessing audio devices.
- Features real-time fast forward and rewind playback.
- Provides numerous effects (distortion, doppler, echo, filter, mechanize, offset, pan, volume shaping, invert, resample, equalizer, noise reduction, time warp, pitch, and more).
- Supports many file formats (WAV, MP3, OGG, AIFF, AU, VOX MAT, SND, VOC, raw binary data, and text data) and can convert to and from these formats.
- Has drag-and-drop cue points.
- Allows direct waveform editing with the mouse.

# MilkShape 3D 1.56 Demo

MilkShape 3D (by chUmbaLum sOft) is a low-polygon modeler, initially designed for Half-Life. During its development, many file formats were added. MilkShape 3D has all the basic operations—select, move, rotate, scale, extrude, turn edge, subdivide, and so on. MilkShape 3D also allows low-level editing with the vertex and face tool. Primitives such as spheres, boxes, and cylinders are also available. MilkShape 3D also has skeletal animation capabilities. This allows you to export and morph target animation like the ones in the Quake model formats or to export to skeletal animations like Half-Life or Genesis3d. MilkShape 3D currently supports 37 different file formats from 27 different games, engines, and programs.

# Paint Shop Pro Trial Version

On the CD, you will find a 30-day trial version of Paint Shop Pro (by Jasc Software, Inc.), one of the best tools available for image creation, editing, and retouching. Paint Shop Pro is a powerful paint program that can easily provide you with the essential tools you need to create textures and backdrops.

# Poser 4 Demo

Poser 4 (by Curious Labs, Incorporated) is a 3-D character animation and design tool for artists and animators. You can create images, movies, and posed 3-D figures from a diverse collection of fully articulated 3-D human and animal models. Libraries of pose settings, facial expressions, hand gestures, and swappable clothing are included. Posing and animating is fast and easy with Poser's unique interface. You can generate movies and 2D graphics from your posed models for content in Web, print, and video projects.

# trueSpace5 Demo

trueSpace (by Caligari Corporation) is widely used by 3-D artists and animators and has gained industry recognition for advanced capabilities such as hybrid radiosity rendering and direct manipulation of user interfaces. trueSpace5 provides features to satisfy the needs of two new markets: the design market and 3-D Web content creation.

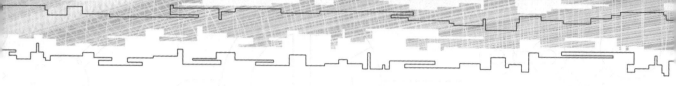

# Index

# M

# GAME DEVELOPMENT.
## IT'S SERIOUS BUSINESS.

"Game programming is without a doubt the most intellectually challenging field of Computer Science in the world. However, we would be fooling ourselves if we said that we are 'serious' people! Writing (and reading) a game programming book should be an exciting adventure for both the author and the reader."

—André LaMothe,
Series Editor

Premier
Press

Premier Press
www.premierpressbooks.com

PREMIER PRESS

GAME DEVELOPMENT

# Gamedev.net

## The most comprehensive game development resource

○ The latest news in game development
○ The most active forums and chatrooms anywhere, with
  insights and tips from experienced game developers
○ Links to thousands of additional  game development resources
○ Thorough book and product reviews
○ Over 1000 game development articles!
  Game design
  Graphics
  DirectX
  OpenGL
  AI
  Art
  Music
  Physics
  Source Code
  Sound
  Assembly
  And More!

# Gamedev.net

OpenGL is a registered trademark of Silicon Graphics, Inc.
Microsoft, DirectX are registered trademarks of Microsoft Corp. in the United States and/or other countries.

# TAKE YOUR GAME TO THE
# XTREME!

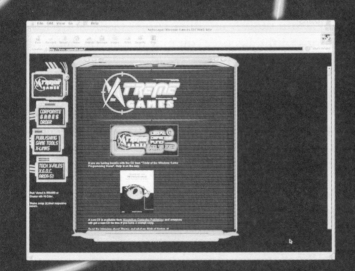

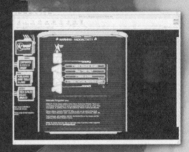

**Xtreme Games LLC** was founded to help small game developers around the world create and publish their games on the commercial market. Xtreme Games helps younger developers break into the field of game programming by insulating them from complex legal and business issues. Xtreme Games has hundreds of developers around the world, if you're interested in becoming one of them, then visit us at **www.xgames3d.com.**

# www.xgames3d.com

# License Agreement/Notice of Limited Warranty

By opening the sealed disc container in this book, you agree to the following terms and conditions. If, upon reading the following license agreement and notice of limited warranty, you cannot agree to the terms and conditions set forth, return the unused book with unopened disc to the place where you purchased it for a refund.

## License:

The enclosed software is copyrighted by the copyright holder(s) indicated on the software disc. You are licensed to copy the software onto a single computer for use by a single user and to a backup disc. You may not reproduce, make copies, or distribute copies or rent or lease the software in whole or in part, except with written permission of the copyright holder(s). You may transfer the enclosed disc only together with this license, and only if you destroy all other copies of the software and the transferee agrees to the terms of the license. You may not decompile, reverse assemble, or reverse engineer the software.

## Notice of Limited Warranty:

The enclosed disc is warranted by Premier Press, Inc. to be free of physical defects in materials and workmanship for a period of sixty (60) days from end user's purchase of the book/disc combination. During the sixty-day term of the limited warranty, Premier Press will provide a replacement disc upon the return of a defective disc.

## Limited Liability:

THE SOLE REMEDY FOR BREACH OF THIS LIMITED WARRANTY SHALL CONSIST ENTIRELY OF REPLACEMENT OF THE DEFECTIVE DISC. IN NO EVENT SHALL PREMIER PRESS OR THE AUTHORS BE LIABLE FOR ANY OTHER DAMAGES, INCLUDING LOSS OR CORRUPTION OF DATA, CHANGES IN THE FUNCTIONAL CHARACTERISTICS OF THE HARDWARE OR OPERATING SYSTEM, DELETERIOUS INTERACTION WITH OTHER SOFTWARE, OR ANY OTHER SPECIAL, INCIDENTAL, OR CONSEQUENTIAL DAMAGES THAT MAY ARISE, EVEN IF PREMIER AND/OR THE AUTHORS HAVE PREVIOUSLY BEEN NOTIFIED THAT THE POSSIBILITY OF SUCH DAMAGES EXISTS.

## Disclaimer of Warranties:

PREMIER AND THE AUTHORS SPECIFICALLY DISCLAIM ANY AND ALL OTHER WARRANTIES, EITHER EXPRESS OR IMPLIED, INCLUDING WARRANTIES OF MERCHANTABILITY, SUITABILITY TO A PARTICULAR TASK OR PURPOSE, OR FREEDOM FROM ERRORS. SOME STATES DO NOT ALLOW FOR EXCLUSION OF IMPLIED WARRANTIES OR LIMITATION OF INCIDENTAL OR CONSEQUENTIAL DAMAGES, SO THESE LIMITATIONS MIGHT NOT APPLY TO YOU.

## Other:

This Agreement is governed by the laws of the State of Indiana without regard to choice of law principles. The United Convention of Contracts for the International Sale of Goods is specifically disclaimed. This Agreement constitutes the entire agreement between you and Premier Press regarding use of the software.